Programming for Technology Students Using Visual Basic®

Peter Spasov
Sir Sandford Fleming College

Prentice Hall

Upper Saddle River, New Jersey   Columbus, Ohio

To my daughters,
Emilie, Hannah, and Anika

Library of Congress Cataloging-in-Publication Data

Spasov, Peter.
    Programming for technology students using Visual Basic / Peter
Spasov.
        p.   c.m.
    Includes index.
    ISBN 0-13-622044-4
    1. BASIC (Computer program language) 2. Microsoft Visual BASIC.
  I. Title.
  QA76.73.B3S654 1999
  005.2'768—sc21

                                                            98-2693
                                                               CIP

Executive Editor: Charles E. Stewart, Jr.
Assistant Editor: Kate Lisner
Production Editor: Alexandrina Benedicto Wolf
Cover photo: SuperStock Inc.
Cover Design Coordinator: Karrie M. Converse
Production Coordinator: Custom Editorial Productions, Inc.
Cover Designer: Raymond Hummons
Production Manager: Deidra M. Schwartz
Marketing Manager: Ben Leonard

This book was set in Times by Custom Editorial Productions, Inc., and was printed and bound by
Courier/Kendallville, Inc. The cover was printed by Phoenix Color Corp.

 © 1999 by Prentice-Hall, Inc.
Simon & Schuster/A Viacom Company
Upper Saddle River, New Jersey 07458

Microsoft Visual Basic, Microsoft Windows, Excel, Word for Windows, and MS-DOS are registered
trademarks of Microsoft Corp.

Printed in the United States of America

10 9 8 7 6 5 4 3 2

ISBN 0-13-622044-4

Prentice-Hall International (UK) Limited, *London*
Prentice-Hall of Australia Pty. Limited, *Sydney*
Prentice-Hall of Canada, Inc., *Toronto*
Prentice-Hall Hispanoamericana, S. A., *Mexico*
Prentice-Hall of India Private Limited, *New Delhi*
Prentice-Hall of Japan, Inc., *Tokyo*
Simon & Schuster Asia Pte. Ltd., *Singapore*
Editora Prentice-Hall do Brasil, Ltda., *Rio de Janeiro*

Preface

Several thousand years ago, Sappho saw some workers loading a ship at the dock. She asked one worker what he was doing. He replied, "I am carrying this crate to the boat." Sappho wasn't satisfied because she was looking for *the answer*. She asked another worker, and he replied, "We are preparing to undertake a voyage to discover new things." Sappho asked no more because she had found *the answer*. A computer program is a set of instructions to control the operation of a computer. It is important to understand the instructions; however, the aim is to write instructions to do something useful.

This is a *foundation* resource for learning computer programming. It so happens that we use the Visual Basic® language to do this. The book covers the fundamentals: program analysis, design, language elements, documentation, control structures, testing, algorithms, input/output processing, file processing, data structures, multimedia, object components, databases, and some under-the-hood insights about what makes a computer program tick. Acquiring all of these skills is necessary before one can undertake software development of the industrial-strength programs for which Visual Basic is typically used.

WHY USE THIS BOOK?

If you are already an accomplished programmer, this is not the book for you, but if you have never programmed before or have only rudimentary programming experience, read on. We can help you master the fundamentals required to create programs from scratch. This book emphasizes the problem-solving and programming concepts that are fundamental to all programming. Case studies for a small, fictitious manufacturing company provide context for programming in the real world. We introduce new material when it is needed in terms of solving a problem, so we can immediately use the knowledge for both business and technical applications as related to that small company, Cougar Canoe Company.

Since Visual Basic is rich with features, beginners may find it difficult to learn vital concepts using the off-the-shelf program. We start with a Visual Basic template (the "Introduction Template") to teach structured code. As you progress, we loosen the restrictions to *ease* you into using event-driven programming and visual interface design. By the end of Chapter 4, we discard the Introduction Template because you will then be in a good position to learn the advanced programming techniques that take full advantage of Visual Basic and third-party add-on resources.

WHAT YOU NEED TO KNOW

To begin this book, you must have a basic proficiency in Windows. We recommend Windows 95 or later versions. For details about the requirements, see the section Read Me Before Attempting the Hands-On Exercises (p. 1). These exercises assume that you can perform operations common to typical Windows applications. Ironically, after learning Visual Basic, you will have a better understanding of Windows itself.

BRIEF NOTE ABOUT VISUAL BASIC

Visual Basic is a powerful language that is used to develop a wide range of applications. It is virtually an industry-standard language. Business and industry use it for developing stand-alone programs, front ends to large-scale database systems, Internet interactivity (VB Script), office automation enhancements (such as Microsoft™ Office), and other types of software.

As this book was nearing completion, Microsoft released Version 5 of Visual Basic. Since this book is about fundamentals, the programs will run with both Visual Basic 4 and 5. (If you can sift through some implementation details, you can also use the book for Visual Basic 3). There are some differences between 4 and 5 in the way each uses the Visual Basic development system. When these differences occur, we explain how to perform operations using both versions. The other Version 5 improvements concern topics beyond the scope of this book. We do not duplicate resources that document the entire language. Instead, we prepare you to use the resources. The key is that you learn concepts, problem solving, and accompanying coding prior to encountering Visual Basic features such as designing the form and project management. Initially, we use a template version instead of off-the-shelf Visual Basic. A beginner can then master fundamental concepts prior to creating the Visual Basic form(s) and working with objects, properties, and events. The CD-ROM has files for 32-bit Visual Basic 4, which can also be used for Visual Basic 5. By performing a few additional operations, you also will be able to use the files for the 16-bit version of Visual Basic 4. Be sure to read the CD-ROM file README.TXT to find out about any updates.

PROGRAMMING FUNDAMENTALS

The fundamentals of programming require one to understand elements such as statements, variables, data types, and expressions. Programmers also need to understand a bigger picture. They must analyze, design, document, and test the program under development. We cover each of these key activities in program development. A case study approach with Cougar Canoe Company illustrates why certain program elements are used and explains why it is necessary to initially analyze the problem *away from the computer* prior to entering code *at the computer*. We provide sample problems with solutions, and then we pose additional problems. These become progressively more challenging as fewer hints are provided.

With off-the-shelf Visual Basic, there are abstract concepts such as events, objects, properties, and project files to understand before one can even begin to program in a Windows environment. To get started in the early chapters, we hide these concepts by employing the Introduction Template. You can then concentrate on the fundamentals without worrying about Windows environment considerations. At the end of Chapter 4, we introduce Windows event-driven programming concepts such as some objects, properties, events, and methods. Throughout the book we also cover Visual Basic's Help system and debugging tools. This way you can actually create programs; otherwise, you could be stuck with being able to code only by following paint-by-numbers style instructions.

BOOK ORGANIZATION

Each chapter has the following:

- Objectives to explain what you will learn.
- The scenario of an application requirement that illustrates why the content is covered.
- Topics to explain the content.
- Hands-on exercises (with questions) to provide practice with the content.
- Additional problem solving to check your mastery.

The topics typically include these:

- Examples.
- Sample problems with solutions.
- Documentation.
- Troubleshooting: Debugging and testing.
- Highlights to point out key points.

The appendices provide useful reference to topics and language elements. Appendix D can be a starting point for going beyond this book. The included CD-ROM contains the program files and supplemental information used in the exercises. It also contains answers to the questions and solutions to most problems. There is a simplified online help system that can be accessed using a web browser. The CD contains a working copy of Visual Basic 4. Be sure to check for possible updates posted at the web site for Prentice Hall.

INSTRUCTOR RESOURCES

The Instructor's Manual includes some additional questions with solutions as well as the solutions to the Additional Problem Solving exercises in each chapter.

THE CHAPTERS

Chapter 1 describes the relationship between the computer and programming languages. It introduces the programming requirements for Cougar Canoe Company, the case-study company. We cover language translation in relation to the operating environment and introduce our first program, the Hello World program. We progressively extend Hello while beginning discussions of syntax, documentation, and debugging.

Chapter 2 is a guide to solving problems without regard to the actual language, although the Introduction Template is used for concrete examples. The Hands-On Exercises include some interactive examples to graphically illustrate problem solving.

Chapter 3 explains elements that are typical to all languages. It again uses the Introduction Template to concentrate on fundamental elements. The Hands-On Exercises include the use of Help and Debug tools to monitor program execution.

Chapter 4 explains the concept of reusable modules (also known as *program partitioning*) and how they communicate with each other. The end of Chapter 4 introduces Windows-style event-driven programming.

Chapter 5 covers the fundamental decision-making structures used to change the flow of program execution. These are the variations of the If Then Else type statements, as well as the Select Case statement. The chapter includes the topics of input validation and error trapping, both of which are key components in a real-life program.

Chapter 6 explains the fundamental loop structures used to cause repetition of some program statements. These are the For Next, Do While/Until, and While/Until Do statements. The chapter also introduces the array data type since many typical loop applications involve the use of arrays. The Hands-On Exercise includes a mock program maintenance session.

Chapter 7 covers the topic of algorithms with a mix of business and technical examples.

Chapter 8 outlines the basics of file handling. We start with a simple viewer program and then examine how to handle data storage using files for sequential, random, and binary access. The program examples are a simple text editor and a prototype customer information program for storing records. The examples include fully functional standard Windows file dialogs.

Chapter 9 introduces the topic of data structures with some examples. We cover only some rudimentary structures, which are the stack, queue, and linked list. The culmination of this chapter with the earlier ones is a customer information program that stores customer records on disk and permits insertion and deletion of records.

Chapter 10 covers the use of graphics, animation, and multimedia. It includes the use of graphics files and the multimedia (MCI) control. This chapter includes a program that combines media elements to be a used as an elementary promotional marketing tool for a fictitious canoe company.

Chapter 11 covers the topic of ActiveX, OLE, and Automation. This topic covers the use of existing tools and applications in a Windows environment to add functionality to a Visual Basic program. The chapter includes a program that uses a word processor and spreadsheet program. Other programs control a web browser or replace it.

Chapter 12 is about database programming, probably the most common use for Visual Basic in the working world. Programs are front ends to access commercially available databases, such as Access, Paradox, and so on. We use the data control and Data Access Objects (DAO) as well as introduce remote data access, such as the use of Open Database Connectivity (ODBC).

HOW TO USE THIS BOOK

Generally, we present topics in a linear sequence. However, you can use embedded cross-referencing and the index to utilize sections out of order. If this book is being used for a conventional one-semester course, we recommend the following times for three- or four-hour weekly sessions. Spend two weeks for Chapter 1. Although the material can be easily covered in one week, it may be wise to use an extra week to familiarize students with the course, institution, and instructor and just basically ease into a new experience. There may be registration and facility logistics to work out. Generally, Chapters 2 to 4 require two weeks each since they provide thorough coverage of programming fundamentals. The remaining chapters can be covered in one week each because a thorough groundwork has already been provided.

An exception might be Chapter 7. In this case, you could omit certain exercises to suit a business or technology focus as suggested in the Hands-On Exercises. Depending on the institution, this may leave a few weeks for catching up. Chapter 9 can be omitted if you are not covering data structures. Depending on other considerations, some curricula may omit some of the later chapters. (Even if you have the opportunity to follow your own pace, we suggest that you try to maintain a schedule similar to that suggested here.) For an explanation of the typographic styles, refer to Appendix A. Also refer to the other appendices for addtitional references.

COMPUTER SCIENCE CURRICULUM

This book meets some of the curriculum requirements as specified by the ACM and the IEEE Computer Society. It covers PR: Introduction to a Programming Language, and it partially covers SE: Software Methodology and Engineering.

ACKNOWLEDGMENTS

The idea to write a book is oftentimes the result of a perceived need. Several years ago, Fleming College began to offer Visual Basic to students in technology courses. This experience showed me the need for a textbook covering programming fundamentals using Visual Basic. I want to acknowledge these former students and colleagues who pioneered early versions of the courses. Prentice Hall deserves much praise for getting this project off the ground. Charles Stewart provided strong support and immediately obtained editorial approval for the project. Kate Linsner expertly guided the project through the authoring phase. I thank the reviewers who made valuable suggestions concerning the manuscript: Susan Athey, Colorado State University; Merrill J. Gordon, Forsyth Technical College; David T. Lipp, Strayer College; Avram Malkin, Devry Institute of Technology; and Anthony J. Nowakowski, Buffalo State Community College. As a result of these reviews, I added the last three chapters, in addition to other modifications. Various production people did excellent work to put together the book and CD-ROM program disk. In particular, JaNoel Lowe, project editor at Custom Editorial Productions, Inc., did much to keep the book production on track and on time. I want to also acknowledge the very professional copy editing by Bobbie Dempsey. If any flaws remain, the fault is mine.

Of course, I thank my family, Renate, Emilie, and Hannah, for putting up with my focus on the book when we could have been enjoying family activities. It is with their patience, support, and understanding that I was able to complete this project. Thank you all.

Contents

Read Me Before Attempting the Hands-On Exercises

This section explains the requirements and logistics of performing the hands-on exercises. It also explains how to perform common tasks with the Microsoft Visual Basic® integrated development environment.

1. **Read each chapter first.** Each chapter ends with an exercise. The associated chapter contains information that will help you to understand why you are trying certain tasks. It also contains or provides hints to the answers.

2. **Set up Visual Basic.** If you do not have access to Visual Basic on your system, you will have to set it up.

3. **Develop a proficiency in Windows.** In order to do the exercises, you must know how to use Microsoft Windows® 95 or later. In particular, you will need to perform such typical Microsoft Windows® 95 or later operations as:

- Starting applications
- Opening files
- Saving files
- Selecting menu items and list items
- Selecting options
- Interacting with common dialog boxes
- Copy and paste operations
- Switching to other tasks

If you do not know how to perform most of these operations, spend time getting to know Windows, and return to this book after you have some familiarity with that operating system.

4. **Follow these steps to run Visual Basic.** To run Visual Basic in normal setups, follow these steps: First, click Start in the Taskbar and point the mouse to Programs. The list of Program items should appear. Second, point the mouse to the Visual Basic *group*

item, and then click the Visual Basic program item. Third, if you intend to use your own copy of Visual Basic, run the setup program as described in the package. If you are accessing Visual Basic from a network in a training facility, you may need to consult the staff at the facility for further instructions.

5. **Use the program disk.** The accompanying CD-ROM contains a directory named INTROP. This directory contains subdirectories CODE, ONLINE, and MEDIA. Copy directory INTROP with all of its subdirectories and files to your hard disk, and/or your reserved space on a server, or another place as directed by your instructor. From now on, we will refer to your copy of directory tree INTROP as the *program disk.*

The program disk for this book contains a directory named CODE. This directory will contain subdirectories for each chapter. These are named CH01 for Chapter 1, CH02 for Chapter 2, CH03 for Chapter 3, and so on. To start a chapter hands-on exercise, use the associated directory. Each directory will contain a text file containing the same questions posed in the exercise. You can use it for entering your answers.

Each chapter directory has a subdirectory named SOLN that contains solutions to the exercises. These are provided as a means to check your work and for code recovery in case your work is accidentally corrupted. Avoid copying code directly from a solution. By typing code manually from the book, you often gain more understanding of the code. You may become confused if you use Copy and Paste operations with the Windows clipboard; however, don't be shy about using Copy and Paste within your own program to avoid having to retype a lot of material.

Directory ONLINE contains a web site that acts like a simplified Help System. Use a browser to open file ONLINE\DEFAULT.HTM. Directory MEDIA contains the multimedia files used for Chapter 10. It is possible that the disk may contain additional resources so check the README file for the latest update.

6. **Adjust for two versions of Visual Basic 4.** Visual Basic 4 can be installed as a 32-bit version or a 16-bit version. If you are using the 32-bit version of Visual Basic 4, you don't need to do anything special to get started. The code files are in the format for the 32-bit version of Visual Basic 4. If you happen to be using the 16-bit version or working model, you can still use the CODE files with a bit of extra work. For details, refer to the file README.TXT in the CODE directory of the program disk. The CD-ROM also contains the Visual Basic Working Model. It is a scaled-down version of the 32-bit version of Visual Basic 4.

7. **Adjust for using Visual Basic 5.** Even though the files are in Visual Basic 4 (32-bit) format, you can use them with Visual Basic 5. If you intend to also use Visual Basic 4, you may wish to make a working copy of the files prior to running version 5. Then you will still be able to access the originals using version 4.

When you open a project, Visual Basic 5 may warn you that the project was saved in a previous version. Click **OK** and continue. Upon exiting Visual Basic or opening another project, Visual Basic 5 will ask if you want to save changes. The choice is yours.

8. **Complete the exercise tasks.** A chapter exercise will provide hands-on practice with program segments described in that chapter. In some cases you will work with additional program segments; other exercises will pose problems to be solved. These will become progressively more challenging, as fewer hints are provided.

9. **Answer questions.** The exercises in this book also pose questions for you to answer. Each directory contains a text file with the same questions, which you may answer using a text editor or word processor to modify the file. Some answers require diagrams, and you can use a drawing program or be creative in using ASCII art (making diagrams with keyboard symbols only).

To answer some of the questions, you may need information in addition to what is in the book. Some questions ask you to think creatively to find solutions. It may turn out that the answers you find on your own are revealed in future sections.

10. **If you need to suspend work, follow these guidelines.** There may be times when you are working on a program but must stop working before you complete the task. Before you exit an exercise, save your work. We suggest you save any modified Visual Basic form (and module) files first. To do this, select the file in the Project Window. Then select **Save Project** (not File) in the File Menu. Another method is to click the **Save** button on the Toolbar. When your work is saved, exit Visual Basic.

11. **Respond to prompts to save changes.** If you are prompted to save Project changes when you exit Visual Basic, click **Yes**. If you happen to be working with the Introduction Template in Chapters 1 to 4, you may find that you can only save the changes by specifying a new file name. This is necessary since the Introduction Template files were made as read-only files for your protection.

12. **Use the Introduction Template Project.** Chapters 1 to 4 use an Introduction Template to introduce program coding without having to deal with other features of Visual Basic. Each chapter directory contains its own read-only copy of the necessary files. When you open the Introduction Template using Visual Basic, you will need to do the following:

- Select item RUNME.BAS in the Project window (see Figure 1.10 in Chapter 1).

- Select **Save File As** (not Save Project As) from the File menu.

- Type in the new name and click **OK**.

- Select **Save Project As** (not Save File As) from the File menu.

- Type in the new name and click **OK**.

13. **Respond to references to Visual Basic directories and files.** On occasion, we will refer to files that are part of Visual Basic. Since each system is different, and you might even be using a network installation, we will state the file path with reference to the *main* Visual Basic directory. The start of the Visual Basic file hierarchy may be different for different systems, but its components are the same for all installations. For example, we may refer to a sample application that comes with all Visual Basic installations, such as the Calculator program. We would state that program CALC (file CALC.VBP) is in Visual Basic subdirectory SAMPLES\CALC. On a typical stand-alone system, the full path for the file might be

C:\PROGRAM FILES\MICROSOFT VISUAL BASIC\SAMPLES\CALC\CALC.VBP

On another system, it might be

X:\PUBLIC\PROGRAMMING\VB\SAMPLES\CALC\CALC.VBP

In the first case the main Visual Basic directory is C:\PROGRAM FILES\MICROSOFT VISUALBASIC. In the second case, the main Visual Basic directory is X:\PUBLIC\PRO-GRAMMING\VB. However, both use the same subpath relative to the start, which is SAMPLES\CALC\CALC.VBP.

Talking with Computers

This chapter describes the computer and its languages.

Once upon a time, a computer translated "The spirit is willing but the flesh is weak" into Russian. Then the computer translated it back into English. The result was "The vodka is strong but the meat is rotten." With programming, we always have to be careful what we tell the computer to do; the computer may do something totally unexpected.

After completing this chapter, you should be able to

- Explain what a program and a programmer do in terms of performing useful work.

- Create and modify a Hello World program.

- Describe basic language components such as translation, development system, and syntax.

- Describe the general process of procedural programming in terms of defining and coding a sequence of steps that includes documentation and debugging.

In This Chapter

Software developers write programs to solve application problems. In this section, we describe a scenario involving a fictitious company and introduce its programming requirements. To develop a program, we need a good understanding of the application.

The Cougar Canoe Company is a small-town company that builds canoes. Some models are standard; some are customized to meet customer specifications. Naturally, the prime activity of Cougar's employees is to assemble the canoes. For this to occur, people must plan ahead. Designers create assembly plans for the canoes and must plan the materials and tools for fabrication. Sales personnel or distributors need to find customers. Customer orders determine work scheduling. Since the economy will not work without money, various financial activities are also necessary. The company has to keep financial data such as money it needs to pay suppliers (accounts payable) and other expenses such as employee salaries. Revenues must also be tracked to determine whether any customers owe money (accounts receivable). Various sales activities take place to market the product and find customers. Some of these activities include production of sales literature and participation in various outdoor shows (see Figure 1.1).

Figure 1.1
The Activities of a Manufacturing Business

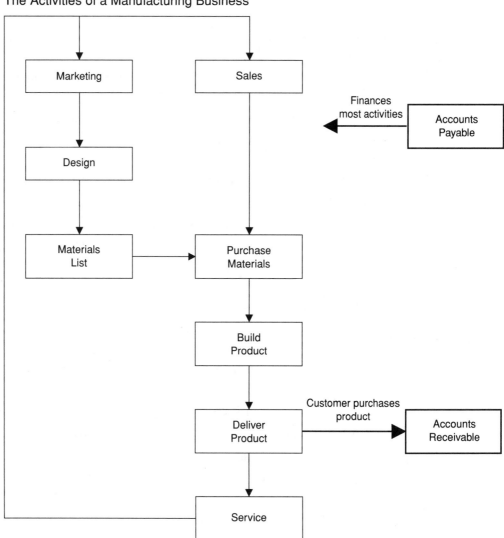

Let's consider one part of the business: To build canoes based on specific customer orders, it is necessary to order materials. Orders should take into account which materials are already in stock. The purchaser generates material orders that go to specific suppliers. Once the orders are placed, it is necessary to update financial information such as accounts payable.

Cougar's computer will be performing many tasks based on instructions such as business rules for entering material order information. These sets of instructions are computer programs (also known as *software*). The programmer must determine and write the required instructions for the computer to perform.

*A **program** is a set of detailed instructions that tells the computer how to perform a specified task.*

1.1   WHAT COMPUTERS DO

To give you a flavor for the purpose of programming, we list some common computer applications.

1.1.1   Office Applications

A desktop computer in an office typically has access to several programs. These are the types of programs with which most people are familiar:

- A word processing program permits a user to create a document.

- A spreadsheet program permits a user to create a financial statement such as for accounts receivable.

- A database program allows a user to cross-reference lists of materials and lists of possible suppliers.

- A computer-aided drawing (CAD) program gives a user the capability to design a product and to create technical drawings that can be used for manufacturing that product.

1.1.2   Real-Time Control

Many common devices have single-chip computers that are used for control.

- Typical automobiles have many single-chip computers.

- A programmable logic controller (PLC) manipulates the machinery and robots needed to assemble engines. Each robot also has a computer.

- A communications controller sends live audio and video over the Internet.

- A laser wand reads the universal product code (UPC) at the grocery-store checkout counter. Then it sends the data to another computer, which in turn updates inventory records. Notice that the latter computer is running an office application program.

A ***real-time program*** is defined as one that must produce a response within a specified (short) period of time. You can't afford to have a tardy braking system program. By contrast, a slow word processor may be annoying, but it is not life-threatening.

1.2   CAREERS IN PROGRAMMING

*The **programmer** creates the instructions that the computer uses to perform a given job.*

There are many different types of computer careers. Here we will concentrate on what is usually called the ***programmer/analyst*** (PA). The programmer is the person who creates programs. This sounds simple enough, but what kinds of activities are required to perform this job?

The Programmer Analyst (PA)   The PA performs a *systems analysis* of the program requirements, meaning that he or she attempts to understand and define the nature of the problem or to find an opportunity to do something better. It involves analyzing the objectives of the system, examining what is already in place, identifying requirements, and determining possible solutions.

Systems Analysis   In the true PA spirit, let's break down this term into *systems* and *analysis*. A system is a set of connected things or parts. The space shuttle and the human body are examples. Systems can consist of subsystems such as the thrusters for the space shuttle and the human body's nervous system. Cougar Canoe is a system with subsystems for parts inventory, manufacturing, accounting, and so on (see Figure 1.1).

To analyze something, one examines its detailed components and breaks it down into simpler components. To analyze the material order process for Cougar Canoe, one must determine how to identify the parts required, how to check the inventory, how to order parts, how to inform assembly people that parts are or are not available, and so on. We will not stress systems analysis much more, but note that it is a ***people*** function: The PA must communicate with all of the people involved in any system.

Programming Activity   The programming phase generally involves planning the program on a general level, writing the code, testing the code, and debugging (removing errors). (Chapter 2 describes these activities in more detail.) The programming and analysis functions are distinct, but programming cannot occur without prior analysis. The PA must also analyze the end result to determine if the program functions properly.

Categories   There are various categories of PAs. A company such as Cougar Canoe is not in the software business, but it does have information processing needs, so it needs in-house PAs to create or modify programs. Alternatively, Cougar Canoe could hire outside consultants to do the job.

A software company may produce general-purpose programs such as an accounting package or a mechanical stress analysis package. PAs are the prime workers for these types of companies, developing the software products marketed by the company.

An equipment manufacturer may produce computerized equipment such as video cameras, telecommunications switching equipment, and automobile braking systems. These systems need embedded controllers (specialized computers for control). PAs will be part of the design team that creates the control software. This industry typically refers to PAs as real-time software designers and programmers because the nature of programming is radically different from that of the other categories.

Last, a programmer might simply create programs for the fun of it, as a hobby. For the sake of brevity, in this book we will refer to the programmer/analyst, software designer, or similar personnel as the ***programmer***.

1.3   AN APPLICATION

We have seen that many of the activities going on at the Cougar Canoe Company can be computerized, meaning that they require programming solutions. Consider the following situation. The company wants to expand its sales to more stores (retailers). Its strategy is to produce multimedia promotional materials on disk. A marketing team and/or advertising consultant must determine and outline the components of the promotional presentation. Note that this preparation must be done before writing any computer programs. As a result of this planning, the team determines that one of the components of the presentation will be a message that says "Welcome to Cougar Canoe." Hence it is necessary to write a program to tell the computer to display the message.

Actually, it would be more practical to use a special program known as a ***multimedia authoring tool***. Authors use this tool to produce multimedia materials instead of writing a program (or programs) from scratch. However, this admittedly artificial example will provide context for the simplest program of all, the Hello World program. This is usually the first program that one learns.

1.4   THE HELLO WORLD PROGRAM

Consider the following Hello World program. When the user runs the program, it will display a message, "Welcome to Cougar Canoe." Unfortunately, a programmer cannot simply say the following:

```
Hello computer. Please display the message "Welcome to Cougar Canoe."
```

The computer will not understand this sentence. Instead, the programmer must use a set of special instructions that the computer can understand. This set of instructions is a computer program. The programmer could write (type in) the following program.

Example 1.1

```
Public Sub RunMe()

    PrintMsg "Welcome to Cougar Canoe"

End Sub
```

This is quite unlike a natural language such as English. The line `Public Sub RunMe()` starts the program and tells the computer that it will be receiving instructions. The line `PrintMsg "Welcome to Cougar Canoe"` actually displays the message (`PrintMsg` tells it to display the specified message). The line `End Sub` stops the program, telling it that it will not be receiving further instructions.

Later we will elaborate on this program, but for now, let's see how the computer behaves. When this program is run, a window appears (see Figure 1.2). When the user clicks on the button labeled **Run Me**, the message appears in the box labeled Program Output(s).

1.5   LANGUAGE TRANSLATION

As you can see, a computer performs tasks that are useful to us. We give the computer instructions in the form of a computer program for each job it is to perform. However,

Figure 1.2
A Hello World Program

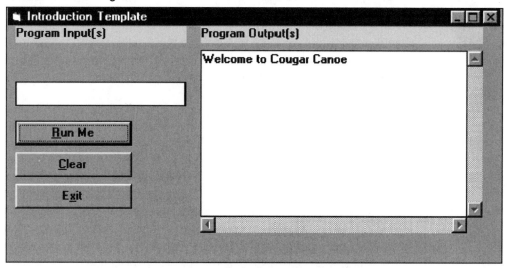

the computer understands only specifically coded numbers known as *machine code.* A human programmer writes a set of instructions in a language known as *source code,* which is closer to English. A translation process converts source code to machine code (see Figure 1.3).

1.5.1   Source Code and Machine Code

A special translation program coverts this instruction into machine language. The computer hardware works with *binary* data, which are simply on-and-off voltages represented as ones or zeros. Each one or zero is called a *bit* (binary digit). Binary data is organized into 8-bit groups known as *bytes* that represent such detailed instructions to the hardware as `Get a number from memory.`

Machine language is a sequence of bytes. Note that machine code looks quite ugly and unreadable. Part of the machine code for our sample program looks like the following sequence of ones and zeros. Although we may not understand it, computers can.

```
10001100 11011000 00110011 11011011 10001110 11010000 10001011 11100011
01010011 01010000 11101000 00001111 00000001 01010000 11001011 10110001
00100000 10111000 00000001 00000000 11010011 11011000 10000011 11111000
00000001 01110100 00001101 10111010 00011110 00000011 10110100 00001001
```

Figure 1.3
Translation

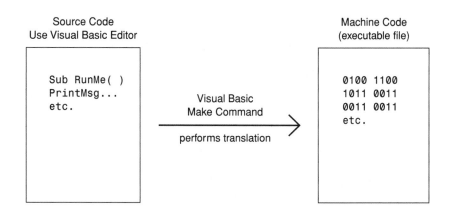

Following is a shorthand representation of the program.

```
8C D8 33 DB 8E D0 8B E3-53 50 B8 0F 01 50 CB B1
20 B8 01 00 D3 D8 83 F8-01 74 0D BA 1E 03 B4 09
```

Each two-character code represents a number written in the base 16 numbering system known as *hexadecimal*. This is a minor improvement, but is still cryptic to humans. You can see why it is desirable to write programs using source code. Take a look at the source code again.

Example 1.2

```
Public Sub RunMe()

    PrintMsg "Welcome to Cougar Canoe"

End Sub
```

This is not English or any other human language. However, the meaning here is more evident than in the machine code. The bulk of this book will cover the specifics of writing source code. For now, let's look at the big picture.

1.5.2   Languages and the Operating System Environment

*A **programming language** defines the rules for writing source code that can be translated into machine code.*

The computer runs a special prebuilt program known as an **operating system**. The operating system defines the overall computing environment. It manages all computer processing and memory as well as communication with such peripherals as the keyboard and monitor. Other programs, as well as users, interact with the computer and its peripherals using the operating system Windows is an example of an operating system. You may be using Microsoft Windows® 95, Microsoft Windows NT®, or Microsoft Windows 3.1® (or 3.11). (Technically, the latter is not an operating system since it requires the use of the Microsoft DOS® operating system.)

A programmer can use the Microsoft Visual Basic® language to create a program to run in Windows. Unfortunately, it is difficult to port (modify) this program so that it will run in a different operating system. A programming language defines the rules for writing programs. Although it is not a natural human language like English, it is much easier to use than machine language—the only language the computer really understands. Some of the commonly used languages are C++, COBOL, Java, and Visual Basic. Often, a programmer uses a language in an **integrated development environment** (IDE).[1] The IDE is essentially a special program used to create other programs. It is the software equivalent of a machine shop that is used to create other tools. Table 1.1 shows some of the tools.

Different languages use different terminology and tool organization. However, they all use these tools. You would expect Visual Basic to have these tools, and, in fact,

---

[1]*This is not the same IDE that refers to a hard disk interface.*

Table 1.1
Some Integrated Development Environment (IDE) Tools

Tool	Function
File facility	The standard features that permit you to load and save files; also used to manage a group of files that may be part of a single programming *project*.
Editor	Used for writing and modifying source code; some editors color-code the text to point out features of the syntax.
Debugger	Used for finding errors in the code and testing the operation of the program.
Make Facility	Translates source code into executable machine code (for some languages, this is known as a *compiler*).
Online help	Provides reference information to the programmer about the language and IDE, and also provides hints about probable causes of errors.

it does! The end-of-chapter exercise will familiarize you with the tools for Visual Basic. Note that Visual Basic is an IDE as well as a language, and the language is a drastic improvement over the older Basic language. It has many useful features that allow one to write programs that will run in Windows (see Figure 1.4). The IDE also permits one to draw typical components such as the window of a program (after all, there must be a reason for calling it *Visual* Basic). For reasons to be explained, we will initially concentrate on the nonvisual part. (Looking ahead, Figure 1.9 shows a typical screen for the Visual Basic IDE.)

Once you have made the source code into an executable file (with a .EXE extension), you can run the program as a *stand-alone* in Windows (without the Visual Basic IDE). To do this, you will need the following executable file:

App.EXE   The code that was made into an executable file

and a dynamic linked library (DLL) *interpreter* file:

VB40032.DLL   If the 32-bit version of Visual Basic 4 was used
VB40016.DLL   If the 16-bit version of Visual Basic 4 was used
MSVBVM50.DLL   If Visual Basic 5 was used

These are the minimum requirements for any program created using Visual Basic. Depending on other requirements, additional files may also be needed. The DLL file contains code for commonly performed tasks. When Windows runs a program, it checks to see if the required DLL file(s) are already loaded. If not, Windows will load them for the application to use. This is typical for any Windows application.

For Visual Basic programs, a DLL *run time interpreter* is necessary because the executable file isn't actually translated (compiled) completely into machine code. The executable file created by Visual Basic is in fact called *p-code* (packed code, sometimes called *pseudocode*), which is in a format that is almost executable. When the user runs the program, the run time interpreter goes into action. The interpreter translates p-code into machine code and executes it. This differs from programs created using compiled languages: A compiled program is one in which the source code is completely translated into machine code. No interpreter is required for further translation.

Figure 1.4
The Final Product

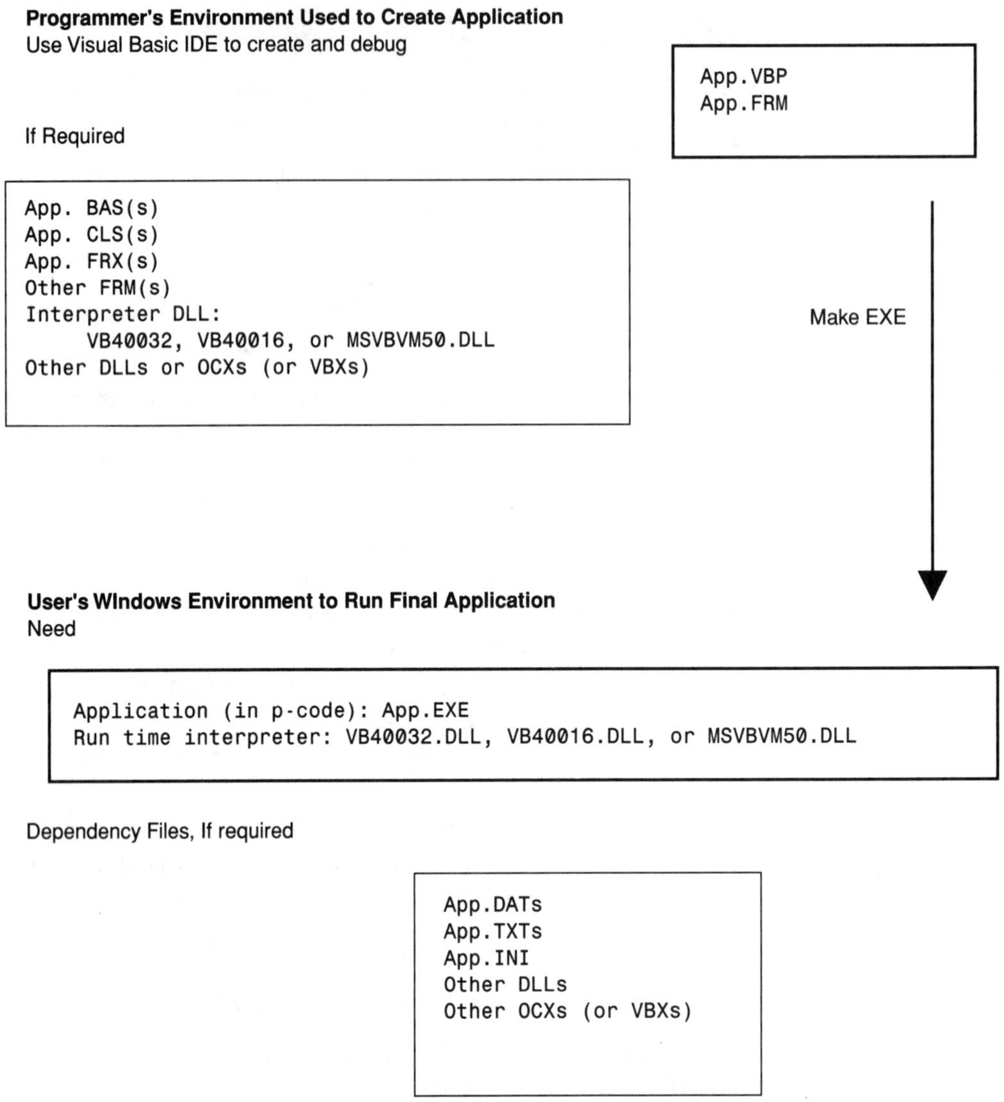

Programmer's Environment Used to Create Application
Use Visual Basic IDE to create and debug

If Required

```
App. BAS(s)
App. CLS(s)
App. FRX(s)
Other FRM(s)
Interpreter DLL:
    VB40032, VB40016, or MSVBVM50.DLL
Other DLLs or OCXs (or VBXs)
```

```
App.VBP
App.FRM
```

Make EXE

User's Windows Environment to Run Final Application
Need

```
Application (in p-code): App.EXE
Run time interpreter: VB40032.DLL, VB40016.DLL, or MSVBVM50.DLL
```

Dependency Files, If required

```
App.DATs
App.TXTs
App.INI
Other DLLs
Other OCXs (or VBXs)
```

App is any valid application file name (without extension).

For updated information, refer to your Visual Basic
documentation for dependency files.

Actually, we have simplified the situation since many realistic application programs make use of other Windows resources about which you may (or may not) have heard: ActiveX controls (.OCXs), formerly known as Object Linking and Embedding (OLE); OLE Control eXtensions; and Visual Basic eXtensions (VBXs) from earlier versions of Visual Basic. These are known as dependency files.

Normally, Visual Basic creates p-code and stores it in the executable (.EXE) file. The run time interpreter reads the p-code and translates it into instructions that the computer can understand. If you are using Visual Basic 5, you may choose to create **native code,** true machine code that the computer can run directly. Hence, Visual Basic 5 programs may be true compiled programs.

1.6   SYNTAX AND SYNTAX ERROR

Syntax defines strict grammar rules for a particular language and the correct spelling of certain words.

Programmers must follow strict syntax rules so that the source code will translate properly into machine code. Consider our initial program example.

Example 1.3

```
Public Sub RunMe()

    PrintMsg "Welcome to Cougar Canoe"

End Sub
```

The Visual Basic IDE will properly translate this code, but it will not be able to translate something like Example 1.4, which has broken some grammar (syntax) rules.

Example 1.4

```
Sub RunMe()

    ' WARNING! This will not work!
    PrintMessage Welcome to Cougar Canoe

End Sub
```

Visual Basic includes a syntax checking feature, which checks your code for the correct syntax and detects syntax errors, or violations of syntax rules. As you will see, there are other types of errors that can occur when programming, but syntax errors must be corrected first, or the computer will not translate source code into machine code.

Note that each programming language has its own syntax. You will be learning the syntax required for Visual Basic.

1.7   THE HELLO WORLD SYNTAX

To demonstrate the execution of each statement in the Hello World program, run the `CH01\HELLOSYN.EXE` program on the student disk.

```
Public Sub RunMe()
```

This statement defines the beginning of a block of code that Visual Basic recognizes. It must begin with the words `Public Sub` and end with parentheses (). The word `RunMe` is arbitrary, but note that it must be one word (no spaces are allowed in the middle). The word `Sub` refers to a block of code. The word `Public` means that the block of code is available elsewhere in the program.

```
PrintMsg "Welcome to Cougar Canoe"
```

The word `PrintMsg`[2] is a command that specifies an action to be performed. It tells the computer to print a message in the output box of the program window (see Figure 1.2). The message to be printed follows the command. It must be enclosed in double quotation marks (" ").

```
End Sub
```

This statement defines the end of a block of code. It must consist of exactly these words.

1.7.1   About the Syntax Errors

In our example about incorrect syntax, the line

```
PrintMessage Welcome to Cougar Canoe
```

created two syntax errors. First, `PrintMessage` is not recognized as a command. Second, the words `Welcome to Cougar Canoe` are not enclosed in quotation marks.

1.7.2   Learning Syntax

It may seem onerous to learn syntax. Initially, you will need to consult references often. These can be the reference section in this book, other manuals, and the online help in Visual Basic. However, as you write more and more programs, you will become more familiar with the syntax and you will not need to consult references as often.

1.8   PROCEDURAL PROGRAMMING USING VISUAL BASIC (VB)

Note that in Chapters 1, 2, 3, and much of 4, we will be using procedural programming. From the latter part of Chapter 4 until the end, we will be using event-driven programming. Visual Basic is designed to be used for something called *event-driven programming*, but we will first be using it for something called *procedural programming*. Thus, we need to talk a bit about the two types of programming.

1.8.1   Procedural Versus Event-Driven Programming

In procedural programming, we define a strict sequence of processing steps. A procedural program has a definite beginning when it runs; it obtains information from the user and displays it in a specific order; and then the program stops execution. There is a set sequence of processing steps. In contrast, an event-driven program can interact with the user in any order. There is no single start or stop to the order of the

---

[2]*This is recognized as a command when the beginner template is used. It is not an inherent command recognized by Visual Basic. Technically, it is a subprocedure created especially for this book. Its purpose is to ease the learning process. (Subprocedures will be explained in Chapter 4.)*

Figure 1.5
A Procedural Program Example

```
Welcome to the Cougar Canoe order system.

Enter the canoe model.
(User enters model)

Enter the length
(User enter the length)

Press Y if you are taxable, otherwise press N.
(User must press Y or N)

Please send a check for:  (price shown here)

Thank you for shopping at Cougar Canoe.
```

processing steps. Although event-driven programming is a more modern, user-friendly technique, procedural programming is better for beginning programmers. It is easier to learn since the programmer has more control over how the program will behave.

From the perspective of the user, who will actually be running the program, a procedural program is more restrictive. When a procedural program runs, it forces the user to interact with it in a fixed fashion. An event-driven program is flexible because it reacts to the user. Is it a good idea to learn event-driven programming? Yes, but a firm foundation of fundamentals is necessary before tackling the challenges of event-driven programming. (It is always a good idea to practice fundamental strokes in a quiet pool before swimming in rough waters!)

To get an idea of the differences between these types of programming, consider a simple program for calculating total price. The program disk contains a procedural example and an event-driven example for calculating total price. To run them now, refer to Section 1.8 in the Hands-On Exercises.

Figure 1.5 shows a possible sequence interaction between the user and the program for a typical procedural program.

The user runs the program and sees a prompt asking for the model. The user enters the model number and then sees a prompt for the length. He or she types in the length and then sees a prompt for the tax status. The user responds by typing Y for yes or N for no. The program responds by displaying the price. Note that the program determines what and when the user enters inputs and uses the inputs to calculate and display the result. Then the program stops. If the user wants to check another price, he or she has to run the program again and go through the same sequence of interactions.

An event-driven program may look like the one in Figure 1.6. The user can select model, length, and tax status whenever he or she wants. Then the user can click the **Find Price** button to see what the price is or is free to try other inputs and click **Find Price** again to compare prices. The program ends only when the user clicks the **Exit** button.

Event-driven programming appears to be the better choice, and rightfully so, but procedural programming is easier to create for beginners. It gives the programmer more control over how the program executes because he or she can define a strict sequence of processing steps. Event-driven programming offers more possibilities.

Figure 1.6
An Event-Driven Program Example

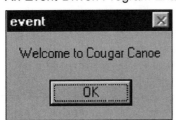 Message appears when program first runs.

User can select inputs in any order on the window.

The user can click on Find Price.

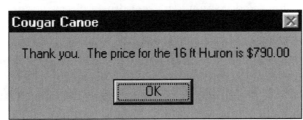

Program responds by showing the result based on the user's selection.

1.8.2   The Process

To *proceed* means to conduct a specific course of action. The process of procedural programming is to determine an orderly sequence of actions that are required from the beginning to the end of program execution and then write the source code using the correct syntax. Note that the process defines a sequence (or choice of possible sequences) to which the user must adhere.

The "total price" program

asks for the model number,
asks for the length,
asks if the item is taxable,
uses this information to calculate the price,
and displays the price,

in that order.

The following shows the basic idea of how to instruct the computer to perform the program operations in a procedural program. This is an informal illustration, meant only to give a flavor of what a program looks like. We will cover more details of writing formal program code in remaining chapters.

```
Start

    Input Model
    Input Length
    Input Tax Status
    Find Price using Model and Length
    If Taxable Then Total = Price + Tax
        Else (Otherwise) Total = Price
    Display Total


Stop
```

Note that there are instructions to input the information, process the information to determine a result, and then output the result(s). A program also performs logical decision-making operations. This program only adds the tax to the base price if the item is taxable.

To get a flavor of event-driven programming, consider the following, an informal version of the program. Again, note that this only provides a small taste of programming; the real work begins in the following chapters.

```
Start

    Define default Model, Length, Tax Status
    Find Price using Model and Length
    If Taxable Then Total = Price + Tax
        Else (Otherwise) Total = Price

User selects Model
    Find Price using Model and Length
    If Taxable Then Total = Price + Tax
        Else (Otherwise) Total = Price

User selects Length
    Find Price using Model and Length
    If Taxable Then Total = Price + Tax
        Else (Otherwise) Total = Price

User selects Tax Status
    Find Price using Model and Length
    If Taxable Then Total = Price + Tax
        Else (Otherwise) Total = Price

User clicks Find Price button
    Program displays Total

User clicks Exit button
    Program Stops
```

Note that the computer follows the instructions in a block only when the user tells it to do so. The exception is the Start block that runs when the program is initially launched. Most blocks happen to have the same instructions, in this case. For both procedural and event-driven programs, the programmer must determine the general sequence. Once the sequence is determined, the programmer will write the actual code using the language syntax. Chapter 2 elaborates on the process to create the sequence independent of the language syntax.

The process of event-driven programming is different. However, even with event-driven programming, it is necessary to use procedural programming techniques in parts of the program. With event-driven programming, the programmer uses an object-oriented programming (OOP) approach. (We will not say more about OOP at this time; we mention it now only in case you have heard about it.)

1.8.3   Why Visual Basic?

If it is a good idea to begin with procedural programming, why use an event-driven language such as Visual Basic? This is a good question. When you purchase Visual Basic off the shelf and study the documentation, you may be overwhelmed by the richness of its features. The claims about Visual Basic being easy to use are true if you take into account how complex certain Windows programming tasks would be without it.

Visual Basic has several advantages for beginners, one of which is that it is Windows based. By using a Windows-based programming environment, we can use an IDE with a consistent Windows look and feel, and we can access other Windows resources by task switching.

To take advantage of task switching, you will need to be proficient in Windows. You can then access Internet resources and online help, make notes, and do other things while working on a programming project. Also, the typical computer one buys these days already has Windows installed.

The main reason for using Visual Basic is Visual Basic itself! It is virtually an industry-standard language that often appears in programming-related job ads. It is an extremely powerful language that has been used to develop a wide range of stand-alone applications, such as financial analysis, multimedia presentations, and robotics. Many software consultants use it to develop front-ends to database systems. Recent developments include the use of Visual Basic for Applications as the programming language (macro[3]) for Microsoft ™ Office and several third-party applications. This is quite significant, since many enterprises are based on a Windows and Office computing environment. Of course, we can't forget the Internet. Information technology has become increasingly (Inter)network-centric, with a proliferation of web-based processing systems. One of the ways to add interactivity to web pages is to use Visual Basic Script. Since information technology is always changing, it remains to be seen whether new uses of Visual Basic develop and/or whether former uses are abandoned.

The introduction of Visual Basic in 1991 has spawned many imitators, and many software development products use a similar programming environment. Some, such as Visual C++, use the word *visual*. Others, such as Delphi, don't use this word. There is also a discipline known as *visual programming*.

The holy grail of software has been reusable software components. Visual Basic Extensions (VBXs) have come close to providing snap-together components that can be used in different programming projects. This includes those that use another language! The introduction of ActiveX (OCXs) components has improved reuse technology.

We have seen how great Visual Basic can be. By using Visual Basic to learn fundamentals, we position ourselves to master advanced software technology in the future.

---

[3]*A macro is like a mini-program: It defines a set of user actions to automate a task in an application program. For example, a macro in a word processor might be used to set up several headings in a certain way. The user can then set up headings in any document by using a single macro command.*

1.8.4   The Introduction Template

As mentioned, Visual Basic is so rich with features that it can be difficult for beginners to learn the discipline of programming. The Introduction Template eases the learning process by providing the essential features for learning programming fundamentals. By using the template, we can ignore the other features of the language. It is like a set of training wheels on a bicycle. Figure 1.7 shows the bare-bones Introduction Template.

A User's View

Let's look at the program from a user's perspective. The user first clicks the **Run Me** button. The space above the box is used for displaying prompting messages. A prompt guides the user for the type of input expected, and the user enters inputs in the Program Input(s) box. The Program Output(s) box shows the program results. Figure 1.8 shows one sequence of actions for the program to calculate total price.

Refer back to Figure 1.5. The program has generated the welcome message and obtained the canoe model from the user. It prompts the user to enter the canoe length (notice the prompt below Program Input(s) in Figure 1.8). The Program Output(s) box then provides some additional information about what inputs it expects.

The Programmer's View

Now let's consider how the programmer uses the template (see also Figure 9a or 9b). After opening the template file using Visual Basic, select the Main Module and click the **View Code** button. Begin typing or modifying the code. There are certain commands, such as `PrintMsg`, that are defined in the template. They are used for interacting with the input and output boxes. We will call these commands *template commands* and will say more about them later. The template commands are not native to Visual Basic. Instead, we use these commands for the rigorous procedural programming that is necessary for learning fundamentals.

After entering the code, run the program to see how it behaves.

Figure 1.7
The Introduction Template

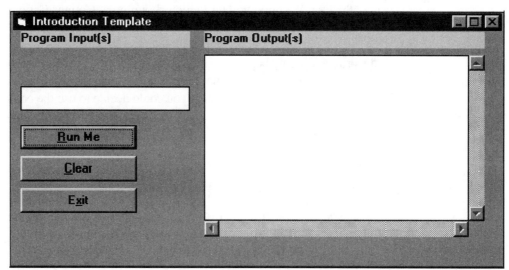

Figure 1.8
An Introduction Template Program

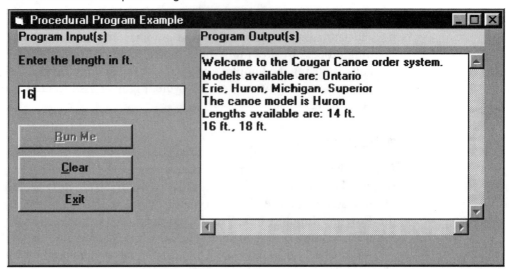

1.9   SAMPLE PROBLEM: EXTENDED HELLO WORLD

We have seen how to create a Hello World program (see Section 1.4). How can we extend the program to display something like the following?

```
We hope you will enjoy shopping at Cougar Canoe.
Please let us know what you think.
```

Try to find your own solution before looking at the solution below.

Solution

In this case, the requirement is quite specific. It is still helpful to rephrase or restate the requirement in such nonambiguous language as:
Display the line: We hope you will enjoy shopping at Cougar Canoe.
Display the line: Please let us know what you think.

Using the explanation of syntax already discussed (see Section 1.7), you might find that the program should begin with the line Sub RunMe(). Since the command PrintMsg was previously used to print a line, you could surmise that the same command could be used to print a different line. Similarly, you could decide to use the command again to print the second line. Again, by using the example in Section 1.7, you might deduce that the last line is End Sub. Example 1.5 shows the resulting code.

Example 1.5

```
Sub RunMe()

    PrintMsg "We hope you will enjoy shopping at Cougar Canoe."
    PrintMsg "Please let us know what you think."

End Sub
```

The explanation for the solution may seem too detailed. However, as we shall see, programming can quickly become complex. You will find it useful if you maintain a discipline of following rudimentary steps to solve more complex problems. Chapter 2 examines the discipline of program design.

1.10   DOCUMENTATION AND COMMENTS

There's only one thing worse than trying to continue from where you left off in a long programming project: It happens when you can't remember why you wrote the existing code in a certain way. Sometimes it is harder to fix up or modify a program written by somebody else. This is particularly true when there are no clues as to why certain code was used. So far we have only examined Hello World and some variations. Based on this, it would be difficult to understand why the situation about writing long programs or modifying someone else's program could be bad. For now, you will have to accept this on faith. Actually, most programming activity in business and industry involves modifying and/or correcting code written by other people.

The point is that good programmers always **document** their programs. Since you probably want to be a good programmer, you might as well develop the habit early, even if it may seem trivial at this point. It is necessary to explain the program so that others and/or you yourself can update the program in the future. To do this, we use **comments**. A comment is an explanation of code. To distinguish a comment from other code in Visual Basic, you begin the comment line with an apostrophe ('). Let's look at a commented version of Hello World, as shown in Example 1.6. This example uses the line continuation arrow described in Appendix A.

Example 1.6

```
Sub RunMe()

    ' This is a Hello World program
    ' Its purpose is to introduce a very simple example of a ➡
    program

    ' Demonstrate an example of using a command
    ' In this case, use the PrintMsg command to display a ➡
    message
    PrintMsg "Welcome to Cougar Canoe"

End Sub
```

Compare this with Example 1.3. Both programs do the identical task and in fact will be translated into identical machine code. The translator ignores comments. Comments are for people to read so that they can understand the nature and purpose of the program. Visual Basic ignores comments, as some other languages do. In Example 1.6, it may seem as if we are overdoing it, but the effort will pay off in the long run when programs become much more complex.

If you have not changed the Visual Basic environment options, Visual Basic color-codes comment text in green.

Exercise

Write comments to document the program of Example 1.5.

Solution

Of course, Example 1.7 shows only one possible solution. It follows a style consistent with that shown in Example 1.6.

Example 1.7

```
Sub RunMe()

    ' This is an extended Hello World program
    ' Its purpose is to check our ability to modify an existing ➡
    program

    ' Demonstrate that we can use the PrintMsg command twice
    ' to display two different lines of text
    PrintMsg "We hope you will enjoy shopping at Cougar Canoe."
    PrintMsg "Please let us know what you think."

End Sub
```

Later, we will elaborate more on standards and stylistic considerations.

1.11   TROUBLESHOOTING: DEBUGGING AND TESTING

An important part of program development is verifying whether a program does what it is supposed to do. If it does not, then you will have to determine what caused the problem and fix it. A Hello World program is fairly simple, so there is less likelihood of it not performing as expected. A syntax error (see Section 1.6) is possible. However, as we progress to creating more sophisticated programs, the likelihood of problems increases dramatically. Consider the program of Example 1.8.

Example 1.8

```
Sub RunMe()

    ' This program will welcome you to Cougar Canoe

    ' Okay, let's do it.
    PrintMsg "You are not welcome to Cougar Canoe"

End Sub
```

Is there anything wrong with this program? Visual Basic will run it without a squeak of a complaint, so this program must be correct. Wait a minute! It seems that the program is displaying a contradictory message. This is an example of a logical error. The program does not do what we *intended*. How could we have tested for this error? One method is to proofread the code. Another is to test run the program and see what happens. Another method is to release the code to the public and wait for a reaction, if any (beta testing). Proofreading is only useful for catching obvious errors. Test runs are required to detect subtle errors. Beta testing should occur only after you and/or your colleagues have tested to remove most errors. Did the documentation make it easier to spot the mistake?

Debugging is the process of looking for errors (bugs) and revising the program to remove the errors. A *program bug* is an error in the program. The purpose of the testing process is to look for bugs. Some bugs are not discovered until after a program has been shrinkwrapped and sold, and this is why software upgrades are common in the industry.

Types of error include

Syntax	Grammatical errors in coding that are detected by Visual Basic.
Logical	Unexpected program behavior that is not detectable by Visual Basic.
Runtime	Program performs an operation that causes program failure (crash).

Throughout the rest of this book, we will examine in more deatail how errors can be detected and corrected.

Exercise

Debug the program of Example 1.9 and write a corrected version. Explain what type of error(s) occurred.

Example 1.9

```
Sub RunMe()

    PintMsg "We hope you enjoy shopping at Cougar Canoe."
    PrintMsg Let us know what you think.

End Sub
```

Solution

Several syntax corrections are required. There is a spelling mistake in the command `PintMsg`, which should be spelled as `PrintMsg`. Also, the message for the second `PrintMsg` command should be enclosed in double quotation marks. Both are examples of syntax errors. Last, it is a good idea to document the program. Example 1.10 shows a corrected version.

Example 1.10

```
Sub RunMe()

    ' The program displays a welcome message
    ' It also demonstrates the correction of syntax errors
    ' for the program shown in Example 1.9

    ' Correct spelling. <PintMsg> should be <PrintMsg>
    PrintMsg "We hope you enjoy shopping at Cougar Canoe."
    ' Enclose the message in double quotation marks
    PrintMsg "Let us know what you think."

    ' And of course, don't forget to use comments
    ' to explain what the program is doing

End Sub
```

We will go through some of the debugging steps in more detail in the Hands-On Exercises at the end of the chapter.

Exercise

Debug the program of Example 1.11 and write a corrected version. Explain what type of error(s) occurred.

Example 1.11

```
Sub RunMe()

    PrintMsg "Explore the world under the sea"
    PrintMsg "using a Cougar Canoe."

End Sub
```

Solution

There is no complaint from Visual Basic when we run the program, but the displayed result seems odd. This is an example of a logic error. Example 1.12 shows one possible solution.

Example 1.12

```
Sub RunMe()

    PrintMsg "Explore the world under the sea"
    PrintMsg "using an aqualung."
    PrintMsg "Explore our wonderful lakes and rivers
    PrintMsg "using a Cougar canoe."

End Sub
```

SUMMARY

A computer program is a set of detailed instructions telling the computer how to perform a specified task. The task could be an office application or a real-time control application. The programmer creates the computer program that is used to perform a given job. To do this, she or he plans the program on a general level, writes the code, including comments for documentation, and debugs the program. The Hello World program is used to introduce the structure of a program to beginning programmers. Following is the basic layout for a Hello World program:

```
Sub RunMe()   ' Begins the program

    ' This is a template Hello World program
    ' It displays a message (or messages)

    ' Write comments to document purpose of program and its code

    ' Use <PrintMsg> command followed by statement to be displayed
    ' Each statement must be enclosed in double quotation marks
    ' as shown in following two lines
    PrintMsg "Welcome message here as required."
    PrintMsg "More lines of message if required."

End Sub        ' Ends the program.
```

By using correct syntax, the programmer writes the source code in a high-level language (Visual Basic in this case). Syntax defines the strict grammar rules for the language and the correct spelling of certain words. Visual Basic is also an integrated development system (IDE), which can be used to test the syntax. Then the programmer can use Visual Basic to translate the source code into machine code. Machine code can run without Visual Basic itself; however, certain files, such as VB40032.DLL or VB40016.DLL (depending on the version of Visual Basic), may be required.

In procedural programming, we define a strict, orderly sequence of processing steps that are required from beginning to end. We can then code this sequence using the Introduction Template. The Introduction Template provides essential features for learning programming without overwhelming the beginner with the rich but complex sophistication of the entire Visual Basic development system. The programmer also uses comments to document the program so that other programmers can understand the program. The programmer will need to debug the program to remove errors, such as errors in syntax.

The laboratory exercises and questions will give you hands-on practice required to get started with programming. For practical applications, programming is typically a complex activity. It will be important to use rudimentary steps when designing programs. Chapter 2 looks at the discipline of program design. The other chapters will add features that will be needed to make a typical practical program.

HANDS-ON EXERCISES

OVERVIEW

The activities will

- Check your understanding of a program.
- Familiarize you with some Visual Basic tools.
- Provide some programming experience with Hello World–style programs.

TO GET STARTED

1. Read the section "Read Me Before Attempting the Hands-On Exercises" if you have not already done so, particularly section 5 about copying directories.

   Note

   You will find the chapter files (such as CH01) in a subdirectory of the CODE directory on the program disk. (They may have been placed elsewhere by an instructor or system administrator, so if you can't find the files, check with your instructor.)

2. Run Windows.

3. Open the file CH01\EX01.TXT on your program disk and answer the questions. (The same questions are shown here so that you can still determine answers if you are not sitting in front of a computer.)

4. Run Visual Basic.

1.1   WHAT COMPUTERS DO

1. List the Windows programs that you already use with a reasonable degree of proficiency. Describe the behavior of one of the programs in terms of how you interact with it.

2. List some devices you regularly use that are controlled by single-chip computers. Describe what the computer does in terms of interacting with the device. It may help to imagine how the device could operate without the computer.

3. Consider a business, government, or nonprofit organization. Describe the kind of computer programs that would be used for its activities. Use Figure 1.1 as a guide to organizational activities.

1.2   CAREERS IN PROGRAMMING

4. Describe the difference between a programmer and a person who uses an existing application program.

5. Make a diagram similar to Figure 1.1 to overview the material order process.

6. Make a diagram similar to Figure 1.1 to describe programming activities.

1.3   AN APPLICATION

7. Is it realistic to write a single program, the purpose of which is to display a message? Explain. Would it be useful for a person to write such a program if he or she has never programmed before? Explain.

1.4   HANDS-ON EXERCISE: HELLO WORLD

Run the Stand-Alone Executable

Run the executable program HELLO.EXE. This program is in directory CH01 of your program disk. Click the **Run Me** button. You should see the message "Welcome to Cougar Canoe" in the Program Output(s) box. If necessary, refer to Figure 1.2.

This is an example of the final result. Note that HELLO.EXE is a binary executable that runs without Visual Basic. If you are unable to run this program, you may not have the correct DLL file in the correct directory (see Stand-Alone Execution in Section 1.5.2.)

Next, create the same program from scratch. Note that you can keep the stand-alone Hello World running while you work on other tasks.

Run Visual Basic

Your setup determines the method you use to run Visual Basic. If you are lucky enough to have a Windows desktop organized to quickly access Visual Basic, double-click the icon labeled **Microsoft Visual Basic**. If not, then you must use another method. Usually, you can click the **Start** button at the bottom left corner, select the Programs menu, and then select a Visual Basic item on that menu.

Figure 1.9a shows one example of the screen for the Visual Basic 4 Integrated Design Environment (IDE). Depending on your setup, your version of Visual Basic, and source code files, your screen may look slightly different. Figure 1.9b shows the IDE for Visual Basic 5.

Figure 1.9a
Visual Basic 4 Integrated Development Environment (with Introduction Template)

Title Bar—   Menu Bar—   Toolbar —   Project Window—

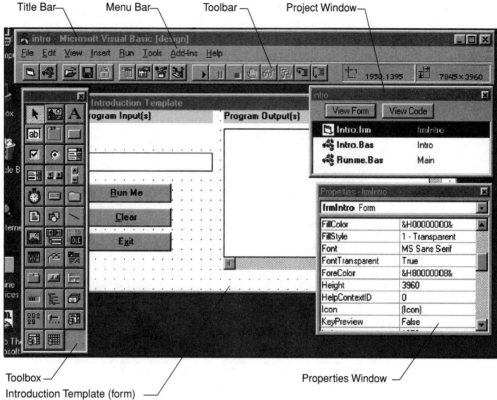

Toolbox—

Introduction Template (form) —

Properties Window —

Open the Introduction Template (see Section 1.8.4)

Visual Basic 4

When you first run Visual Basic, you will see a screen like that shown in Figure 1.9a, except that there will be no Introduction Template. Select **Open Project** from the File menu. This launches the Open Project dialog box.

Visual Basic 5

When you first run Visual Basic, you will see a dialog titled New Project. Click on the tab titled **Existing** to see the Open Project dialog box.

Select the appropriate drive and select directory **CH01** on the program disk. Select **INTRO** and click **OK**. (You will likely see the items listed in lowercase letters, but our convention is to use uppercase letters to specify specific files). Actually, you have opened file INTRO.VBP, since the default extension for a project file is .VBP.

Close the Properties Window, Form, and Toolbox, if applicable.

Reminder

The **Close** button of any window is the one labeled with an X on the upper right corner of the window.

If you happen to see a window titled Properties, click the **Close** button on its upper right corner.

Figure 1.9b
Visual Basic 5 Integrated Development Environment (with Introduction Template)

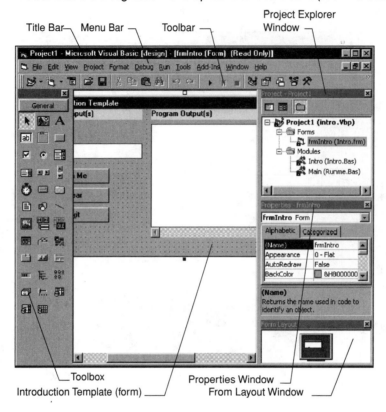

If the Project Window Is Not Visible   You may or may not see the Project window (see Figures 1.9a, 1.9b, or 1.10). If you do not see it, select **Project** or **Project Explorer** from the View menu. The Project window should be visible.

Viewing the Introduction Template

Visual Basic 4

If you see a window titled Introduction Template (see Figure 1.2), click on its **Close** button. The Introduction Template window should disappear. With Visual Basic 4, you do not need the Introduction Template to work with the code.

Visual Basic 5

The Project window has a button with a Folder icon named Toggle Folders. To see the name, move the mouse pointer to the button and wait for the pop-up balloon. Also refer to Figure 1.10b. If the Project window shows folders named Forms and Modules, click the **Toggle Folders** button to show the files only. This may make it easier to follow the rest of the instructions. The project files will be listed in a style similar to that shown in Figure 1.10a instead of 1.10b. You may prefer to work with a Windows Explorer-style file listing. In order to see a window titled Introduction Template (see Figure 1.2), click on the **plus** box (+) beside Project1 (intro.Vpd) inside the Project window (see Figure 1.9b). This will expand the items listed below it, and the box will change to a minus box (-). The Introduction Template window should appear. The Project window uses a Windows Explorer-style list. You will need the expanded list to work with program code.

If the Modules folder in the Project window is not open, click on the **plus** (+) box to open it. Then click on the item Main (Runme.Bas).

Remove the Toolbox   The Toolbox contains many buttons with different icons (see Figures 1.9a or 1.9b). If you do see it, click on its **Close** button. We won't be using these items until the latter part of Chapter 4.

The Project Window   At this point, your screen should look something like either Figure 1.9a or 1.9b. When you open a project file, you also open any associated files. In this case, you have also opened the *form* file `INTRO.FRM` and *module* files `INTRO.BAS` and `RUNME.BAS`.

The *form* (.FRM) and *module* (.BAS) files contain the source code, not the project file. We will explain about form, module, and project files in a future chapter.

Enter the Source Code (see Programmer's View in Section 1.8.4)

We recommend that you set up Visual Basic for Full Module view if it isn't already set up this way. To set up for Full Module view, do the following:

- Select **Options** from the Visual Basic Tools menu.
- You should see the Options dialog box.
- Click on the **Editor** tab.
- Select the check box for (Default to) Full Module View. This will turn on this item. If you checked it off, click it again to check it on.
- Click **OK**.

Visual Basic 5

For Full Module view, click the **Full Module** button. It is the second button at the bottom left corner of the Visual Basic Development System, as shown in Figure 1.10b.

Visual Basic 4

Select **RUNME.BAS** in the Project window and then click the **View Code** button in the Project window. You should see a window titled Main, as shown in Figure 1.10a. This is the Code window for the program file named RUNME.BAS. This is *very important.*

Visual Basic 5

Select **RUNME.BAS** in the Project window, and then click the **View Code** button in the Project window. You should see a window as shown in Figure 1.10b. This is the Code window for the program file named RUNME.BAS. This is *very important.*

The Code window should show the following:

```
Sub RunMe()

' Programmer writes code here

End Sub
```

Visual Basic automatically generates the first and last lines of a block of code. The comment line is included to remind us of where to type in the rest of the code. Change this code to the following:

```
Sub RunMe()
    PrintMsg "Welcome to Cougar Canoe"

End Sub
```

Figure 1.10a
Introduction Template Development Environment for Visual Basic 4 (showing Code Window without Properties Window, Toolbox, and Form).

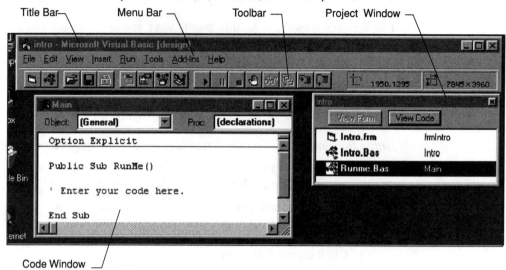

Save the Source Code

Saving a Module   Make sure that RUNME.BAS is highlighted in the Project window.

Visual Basic 4

Select **Save File As** from the File menu. Do not select Save Project As.

Visual Basic 5

Select **Save Runme.Bas As** from the File menu. Do not select Save Project As.

Figure 1.10b
Introduction Template Development Environment for Visual Basic 5 (showing Code Window without Properties Window, Toolbox, and Form).

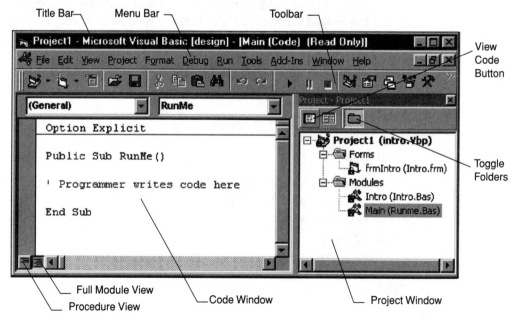

Note that you are saving a *module*, not a project. In the Save File As dialog box, specify your target drive and directory, if necessary. Type in the name **HELLO1** and click **OK**. Visual Basic will automatically append the appropriate file extension.

Saving a Project   Select **Save Project As** from the File menu. Do not select Save File As. Note that you are saving a *project*, not a module (or form). If you are prompted about changes to other files, ignore them. It is possible you may have accidentally modified them (or Visual Basic may think you have modified them).

If Visual Basic warns you that project INTRO is read-only, click **OK** and continue. The Introduction Template files were made read-only to prevent them from being modified. However, you can save read-write copies of the files by renaming them.

In the Save Project As dialog box, specify your target drive and directory, if necessary. Type in the name **HELLO1** and click **OK**. Visual Basic will automatically append the appropriate file extension.

The Project window for HELLO1 should show an item named HELLO1.BAS. Later we will discuss the project (.VBP), form (.FRM), and module (.BAS) files in more detail. For now, you will have to accept the process of saving two files as being necessary.

Warning

Visual Basic works with many different types of files. Leave out the file extension if you are in doubt about whether you are using a module, form, or project. Visual Basic will figure out the proper extension based on the context of your menu selection. A problem could occur when you specify an extension based on accidentally selecting the inappropriate Save item from the File menu. The result could be a catastrophic elimination of work previously done.

Test Run the Source Code

With Visual Basic you can check how the program will run before making (translating) it into machine code. Running your program is a two-step process. First, you need to run the Introduction Template. Select **Start** from the Visual Basic Run menu. This will run the Visual Basic program under test. In this case, it will run the Introduction Template. A window like that shown in Figure 1.2 should appear (with a blank program output).

Second, run your program within the Introduction Template. Click the **Run Me** button in the Introduction Template. This will run the program you wrote. The message appears in the box labeled Program Output(s). In the Introduction Template, click the **Clear** button to erase the outputs. Click the **Run Me** button again to run your program a second time.

If an error occurs, stop the Introduction Template and correct any typing mistakes in your code. To stop the Introduction Template, click the **Exit** button in the Introduction Template, or select **End** from the Visual Basic Run menu. The Introduction Window should disappear. You can now check your code and correct any mistakes. Save both the File and Project and try to run your program again.

Tip

When the Introduction Template is running, its task button appears in the Windows Taskbar at the bottom of the screen. Since Windows is a multitasking environment, the Introduction Template may disappear from view while it is running. This may happen if you intentionally or accidentally select another Windows task, such as clicking on the Visual Basic IDE itself. This will cover the Introduction Template. You can restore the Introduction Template to view by clicking its task button in the Windows Taskbar.

1.5   LANGUAGE TRANSLATION

1.5.1   Source Code and Machine Code

When you have determined that the program runs correctly in the Visual Basic environment, you can make an executable file. To do so, click the **Exit** button in the Introduction Template to stop the program.

Select **Make EXE File** (or **Make Hello1.exe**) from the File menu. The Make EXE File dialog box appear. Select the desired drive and directory. Click the **OK** button. You have just created an executable program named HELLO1.EXE.

Run the program as you would a Windows program, without using Visual Basic. It should operate as a stand-alone Windows program.[4] You can do this by task switching without shutting down Visual Basic itself.

To check that HELLO1.EXE is not a text file, view its contents using Windows Notepad. You see many strange characters because this file contains machine language code. If you are really interested in the gory machine language details, examine this file using the DOS or Windows DEBUG program. (You probably don't want to do this!)

1.5.2   Languages and the Operating System Environment

The Visual Basic Integrated Development Environment (IDE) works only with source code files. Try to open HELLO1.EXE using Visual Basic. The result will be an error message. Visual Basic works with source code, not machine code!

8. Refer to Table 1.1. Identify the tools you have used (probably three of them). Explain how to access the corresponding Visual Basic menu items.

9. Find the appropriate DLL file. State the full path name of the file in your system.

1.6   SYNTAX AND SYNTAX ERROR

Switch back to Visual Basic. Save *module* file HELLO1 (not the project) as **HELLO2**. Similarly, save the *project* (not the module file) as **HELLO2**. Allow Visual Basic to automatically add the extension. Click the **View Code** button in the Project window. Change your previous code to:

```
Sub RunMe()

    'Warning! This will not work!
    PrintMessage Welcome to Cougar Canoe

End Sub
```

Select **Start** from the Run menu to run the Introduction Template. Visual Basic will display the offending code and a message box indicating that there is a problem. Click **OK**. Visual Basic will highlight the line that contains the syntax error. Since there was a syntax error, you never had the opportunity to click the **Run Me** button.

You can also get more information. Try running the Introduction Template again, and then press the **F1** key. This launches the context-sensitive online help. Press **F1** whenever you encounter an error message. Visual Basic Help will display information related to the error. Since you have detected a problem, modify the code to the following:

---

[4]*Specific instructions will depend on your Windows version and setup.*

```
Sub RunMe()

    'Warning! This will not work!
    PrintMessage "Welcome to Cougar Canoe"

End Sub
```

Run the program. When you see the error message, press **F1**. Visual Basic Help should display the following:

```
Sub or Function not defined
```

The explanation may not make sense since the terminology is new. In this case, a command (keyword) is misspelled. Change the code to the following:

```
Sub RunMe()

    'This should work!
    PrintMsg "Welcome to Cougar Canoe"

End Sub
```

Run the program. It should operate as the first program did. Stop the program and save the module and project files if you wish.

1.7 MORE ABOUT THE HELLO WORLD SYNTAX

10. Explain the purpose of each line in the program you wrote in HELLO1.

11. Explain the two causes of syntax error in the program HELLO2.

1.8 PROCEDURAL PROGRAMMING USING VISUAL BASIC (VB)

Tip

A quick way to find the purpose of a button in the Visual Basic Toolbar, Project window, or other areas of the Visual Basic IDE is to move the mouse pointer to it and wait. Eventually, a pop-up help balloon will provide the name of the button.

Tip

A quick way to open a project is to click on the **Open Project** button (it looks like a folder) in the Visual Basic Toolbar. A quick way to start and end a program run is to click on the **Start** and **End** buttons, respectively, in the Visual Basic Toolbar.

The program PROCEED is an example of a procedural program, as shown in Figures 1.5 and 1.8. Open PROCEED and run the program. When prompted for the model, type in one of the five that are available, and press **Enter**. When prompted for the length, type in one of the three numbers, and press **Enter**. When prompted about Tax, press **Y** or **N** as stated. The program should show the canoe price. It will halt if an invalid input is entered.

Try various input combinations.

12. Was it necessary to enter inputs in a specified order? What order?

The program EVENT is an example of an event-driven program as shown in Figure 1.6. Open project EVENT and run the program. You should first see a welcome message, and then a window showing available selections will appear. Try various selections and click the **Find Price** button.

13. Was it necessary to select inputs in a specified order? Why or why not?

14. If possible, indicate what you think the processing steps are in the two programs. Are the steps more easily identified in one of the programs? If yes, explain why.

15. You probably found EVENT easier to use. Despite this, would it be a good idea to write a program such as PROCEED? Why?

One of the advantages of using Windows is task switching and the ability to copy and paste between applications. If you haven't already done so, open file EX01.TXT in directory CH01 using Notepad. Open project PROCEED and run the program using valid inputs of your choice.

You will copy the program outputs into the Windows clipboard. To do this, use the mouse to mark the text in the Program Outputs box. Press **Ctrl+C** to put the selected text in the clipboard. In the file EX01.TXT, click where indicated. You should see a flashing cursor. Press **Ctrl+V**. This places the clipboard contents at the cursor.

Note

To use a key combination such as CTRL+C, press **CTRL** first. Then press the second key (which here is C) and release it. Last, release the CTRL key.

If you have Internet access, use a web browser to find information about Visual Basic. You don't need to find details yet; just get a feel for how much information is available.

16. Although programs already exist for many business and technical activities, why might it be necessary to learn how to write code in a language such as Visual Basic?

1.9   SAMPLE PROBLEM: EXTENDED HELLO WORLD

Open project INTRO in directory CH01 on the program disk. Save *module* file RUNME as **HELLO3**. Save the *project* as **HELLO3**. Write program code to solve the sample problem. Test your solution.

1.10   DOCUMENTATION AND COMMENTS

Open project HELLO in directory CH01 of the program disk. Save *module* file RUNME as **HELLO4**. Save the *project* as **HELLO4**. Document the program as shown in Example 1.6. Then run the program.

17. Is there any difference between HELLO1 and HELLO4 in the way they run? Why?

18. What is the purpose for including comments?

Document the program of Exercise 1.5 and save the module and project files as HELLO5.

1.11   TROUBLESHOOTING: DEBUGGING AND TESTING

Open project INTRO in directory CH01 on the program disk. Save *module* file RUNME as **HELLO6**. Save the *project* as **HELLO6**.

Write program code as shown in Example 1.8. Save the project and run the program.

19. Does the program execute correctly? Explain why. Be sure to read the program documentation to determine whether the program actually does what it was intended to do.

Save the *module* file HELL06 as **HELL07**. Save the *project* as **HELL07**. Write program code as shown in Example 1.9. Save the project, and run the program. Note that you didn't even get the chance to click the **Run Me** button. Visual Basic displays a message box with the following message:

```
Sub or Function not defined
```

Before you click **OK**, press **F1**. Visual Basic Help will display a message. Don't worry if you don't understand the details yet. For now, just note that something was wrong.

Copy the first four lines of the Help message and paste it. To do this, drag the mouse (I-beam pointer) to highlight the lines in the Help window. Select **Copy** from the Edit menu in the Help window. Then Select the Notepad file **EX01.TXT** and click in the **paste area**. Select **Paste** from the Edit menu in the Notepad window. You should see the information you copied. Minimize Help and click **OK** in the message box.

20. According to the information presented by Help, where is the problem likely to be?

Correct the spelling of PintMsg so that it is now PrintMsg. Run the program again. Visual Basic highlights the next line and displays a message box with the message:

```
Syntax Error
```

Before you click **OK**, press **F1** to launch the Help message. Don't worry if you don't understand the details yet. For now, just note that something was wrong. Copy and paste the entire Help message. Minimize Help and click **OK** in the message box. Type in the quotation marks to correct the problem.

Tip

To tell the programmer that there is a syntax error, Visual Basic may highlight the offending code line in red.

21. What caused the error? How did Visual Basic Help assist you with finding the cause of the error?

Correct the error and run the program. Visual Basic will run the Introduction Template. Click **Run Me**, and the program should execute without error. Save the *module* file as **HELL08**. Save the *project* as **HELL08**.

Write program code as shown in Example 1.11. Save the project, and run the program. Assuming you haven't made any typographic errors, the program should contain only logic errors. If you encounter syntax errors, this is your opportunity to practice correcting them.

Correct the logic error. Use your imagination to come up with a different solution than that shown in Example 1.12.

ADDITIONAL PROBLEM SOLVING

Choose a business with which you are familiar, or research (or imagine) a business requirement. Describe the programming requirements for this business. Describe a possible requirement for a Hello World program. You may have to stretch reality a bit since the requirement could be mundane in real life. The program should display at least three lines of output. Write the Hello World program, document it, and run it. Debug the program if necessary. Demonstrate successful execution of the program.

CHAPTER 2

An Introduction to Problem Solving

This chapter is a guide to solving problems without regard to the actual language.

A long time ago in a tiny medieval kingdom, there lived a master sign painter. The painter's finest work was a picture of a red lion. One day, an innkeeper asked the painter to make a sign for her inn, The Green Unicorn. The painter created an elaborate red lion.

"Oh no," said the innkeeper, "I wanted a green unicorn."

"But I paint red lions really well" replied the sign painter.

This story tells us that it is important to know what a user wants and needs a program to do. A programmer designs a program for the user, not for herself or himself.

After completing this chapter, you should be able to

- Describe the characteristics of software deliverables and the design process.

- Create pseudocode given requirements and using recognized problem-solving steps.

- Create documentation that explains the purpose of the program instructions in relation to the program's purpose (primarily pseudocode for this chapter).

- Determine how to check for logical errors.

In This Chapter

The Cougar Canoe Company needs to determine a price for their product. Cougar asks us to develop a program to do this. This seems to be a simple task. Where do we begin? One could look at different strategies, as the sales team did when its members developed three options during a brainstorming session:

1. Buy all of the material, build, and then add up the costs and add a markup for profit.

2. Add up prices for the material, calculate labor, and add a markup for profit.

3. Use a competitor's price and reduce it.

Option 1 requires a large initial investment in inventory and commits the company to actually building without a firm sale (nobody will commit to buy without knowing the price). The idea of Option 3 is to gain market share; however, the competitor could be building a product of lesser quality. If Cougar's canoes are of a higher quality, it is likely that manufacturing costs will be higher. Option 2 seems the most reasonable. Having determined that Option 2 is a likely strategy, we can proceed, can't we?

Note that Option 2 has three component tasks:

1. Add up prices for the material.

2. Calculate labor.

3. Add markup to material and labor costs to achieve profit.

Would we write the program in components? If you were asked to *add* prices, what would you actually do? Will there be a **database** [1] containing material prices? How do you calculate labor? Adding is straightforward, but how do you determine a markup? You could use a simple rule of thumb or a sophisticated economic simulation. How will Cougar Canoe use the program? What data are required? Will there be special quantity discounts? Will the end result also be put in a database? The list of questions could go on and on.

We see that many things must be determined before we even begin programming! Remember that

- A computer program is a set of detailed instructions telling the computer how to perform a specified task.

- The programmer creates the instructions that the computer uses to perform a given job.

Our job is to determine and code a set of detailed instructions. This is a challenging task, especially for beginners who don't know what instructions exist (or what is available in a library of canned software). We *can* see that there is a problem-solving requirement—and we haven't even begun to look at the programming language. Problem solving is about structuring a solution to a nonambiguous task. It is the ability to pose a problem so that the machine will solve it for you.

2.1   THE SOFTWARE DELIVERABLES

When you purchase off-the-shelf software, you get a disk(s) with, or Internet access to, executable and associated files. There may be printed manuals and/or online documentation.

---

[1] *A database is an organized collection of information that permits one to pose questions (queries) such as "List all of the cities whose yearly rainfall exceeded 50 cm." Usually it is a collection of related tables, forms, and reports.*

Figure 2.1
Software Deliverables

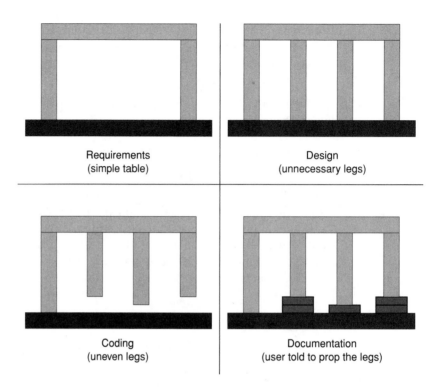

Requirements
(simple table)

Design
(unnecessary legs)

Coding
(uneven legs)

Documentation
(user told to prop the legs)

You might even get access to the vendor's help desk in case there are problems. This presumes that the off-the-shelf software is all you need, but in many business and industrial applications, this is not the case. Although off-the-shelf software components can be used, programming is often required to make them work together (also stated as "gluing them together").

When you *deliver* software—i.e., develop it for sale—you usually provide the user with four items, or deliverables, delivered sequentially. These are

- Requirements
- Design
- Coding
- User documentation

Before delivering software, you need to understand the problem the software is intended to solve. It doesn't make sense to paint a red lion for an inn called the Green Unicorn. Thus you start with a requirements phase, followed by a design phase, when you determine a list of instructions that will solve the problem. With a design in hand, you can move to a coding phase, when you encode the instructions into the correct syntax for a computer language. With a working program in hand, you or someone else must write instructions, or documentation, to guide people in using the program. Figure 2.1 shows an unfortunate consequence of many software projects. The system is overly complex for the actual requirements.

2.1.1   **Requirements**

Often, customers do not know what they require in a program. For example, managers at Cougar Canoe know that they want to calculate a canoe price based on material and labor costs. However, they have not determined how to obtain the information the program will use and how to display and store the prices. Hence, they may need to see prototypes with which to experiment. The customer can use the prototype to help finalize (specify) the exact requirements. (As you learn more about Visual Basic, you will see that it is ideal for building quick prototypes.)

To help a customer determine his or her needs, you need to perform a *systems analysis.* This means you have to identify and define problems in an *information system,* which is a collection of computing resources, business procedures/practices, people, and other resources that help an enterprise (such as Cougar Canoe) perform its functions. There are formal methods of performing systems analysis, but since systems analysis is a discipline of its own, we won't say much more. However, note that extensive systems analysis may be required to translate ambiguous problems into a reasonably clear set of requirements.

A program essentially has four requirements: input, process, output, and storage. To determine these requirements, you need to

- Identify inputs.

- Identify processing actions.

- Identify outputs that are immediately displayed.

- Identify which results of processing are to be stored.

Throughout most of this book, we will be working with programs with input, process, and output requirements. From Chapter 8 on, we will also consider storage requirements. The list above shows the requirements in more or less the order that the program executes them, but, in fact, the program designer is more likely to work through the list backward.

Consider Cougar Canoe's request. They want a program to calculate a canoe price, plain and simple. The output requirement is price. We can now work out how to do this, as will be shown later.

2.1.2   Design

Designing a program involves determining the nonambiguous steps to solve a problem based on the requirements. This is distinct from coding the steps in the correct syntax for a computer to translate and execute. Consider the requirement to convert temperature from Fahrenheit to Celsius: One of the design elements would be to state the conversion formula. Design is more or less independent of the programming language, but it is also the hardest part. You will see more about design later in this chapter.

2.1.3   Coding

In the coding phase we follow the steps (determined during design) into *statements* and *objects* using a programming language. You must write the statements in the correct syntax. For example, the formula for temperature conversion can only be written in a particular style. In some languages, such as Visual Basic, you can (or must) use objects. (An object is a collection of code and data.) For example, in Visual Basic you need to determine the object that will be used to display the result to the user. At this stage you can test for errors (see Section 1.11). After correcting the errors, you make (compile) the final result for distribution. Note that coding also includes program documentation and comments (see Section 1.10). Comments explain the relationship between the code and the design and requirements.

The rest of the chapters (excluding this one) will concentrate on coding. The discussion of objects begins in Chapter 4.

2.1.4   User Documentation

A program is a complex entity that interacts with the user and the computer (or network). The user sees only the final result. Hence, user documentation is important. It explains to the user how to use program features and probable causes of user error. The discipline (art or science) of creating user documentation involves determining topics, the layout of topics, a glossary, links between topics, examples, presentation style, multimedia elements, tutorial design, and other items. *User* documentation differs from *program* documentation (introduced in Section 1.10). User documentation is a specialty requiring a larger discussion outside the scope of this book; however, we will certainly elaborate on program documentation.

2.1.5   Case Study: A Conveyor Network

Prometheus Limited is a metals fabrication company that supplies Cougar Canoe with trim. The trim is used to line the upper edges of a canoe, providing structural strength. Cougar Canoe places an order for the appropriate trim when they schedule production of the corresponding model. Prometheus has a computerized warehouse with an extensive conveyor network. The network connects storage bins with loading bays for delivery trucks (see Figure 2.2). Prometheus needs a system that will bring the parts to a delivery truck.

Exercise

What are the *requirements* for a computer program to bring parts to a delivery truck once an order has been placed? Note that Figure 2.2 illustrates part of the conveyor network.

Solution

You may ask yourself: How would *I* bring the parts to a delivery truck? Then you might imagine yourself actually doing the task. You might come up with the following scenario:
   The following occurs when an order is placed:

1. The warehouse computer system will (among other things) locate the bin where the ordered parts are stored.

2. The system will locate an available loading bay for the delivery truck.

3. A truck driver will press the start button to initiate the transport of parts.

4. The system will configure switching gates so that the conveyor network will transport the parts from the bin to the loading bay.

5. A truck driver will press the stop button when all parts have been transported.

Figure 2.2
Conveyor Network Example

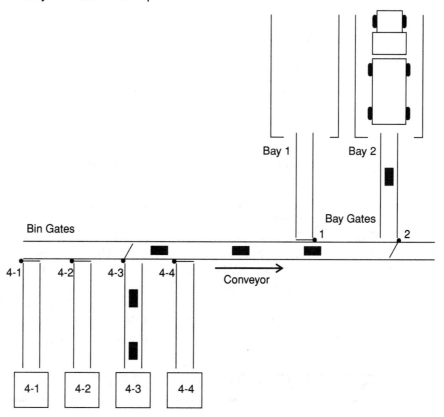

Bins: Trim Parts

Exercise

Refer to Figure 2.2 for this exercise. Design a program to bring the trim to the delivery truck. For now, do not consider the start and stop requirements. The trim is stored in Bin 4–3 and the truck is in Bay 2.

Solution

Refer back to the requirements, and note that you are *designing* a program for requirements 3, 4, and 5. The word *configure* is a bit vague: What does it mean? Gates can be open or closed, and the design determines which gates to open and which to close.

As an initial step, the design could consist of the following:

- Determine which gates to close and close them.

- Determine which gates to open and open them.

With a bit more detail, we could state these points in the program design:

- Close all gates.

- Open the bin gate for the bin containing the ordered parts.

- Open the gate for the bay where the delivery truck is located.

From this we could derive a very specific program that matches a specific delivery requirement:

- Close all gates.
- Open Bin 4–3 gate.
- Open Bay 2 gate.

In fact, this program is so specific that it will meet the requirements only if the desired part is in Bin 4–3 and the delivery truck happens to be in Bay 2.

Note
The design in the case study is independent of the programming language.

The exact code for opening and closing gates will depend on the physical implementation of the system as well as the programming language. This is an example of a real-time control system (see Section 1.1.2). Typically, it is easier to determine the requirements for controlling physical processes. These processes are governed by the laws of physics and not by the whims of human behavior. However, program coding and design may be more complex.

The solution also hints at some of the problem-solving steps. Note that it is possible to begin with general statements and then refine them into more specific statements. This is essentially the *stepwise refinement* technique.

2.2   PROBLEM-SOLVING STEPS

To identify the steps required to solve a problem, it is useful to examine the requirements in terms of computer operations. The basic computer operations are

- Input
- Process
- Output
- Store

To remember these operations, keep in mind the mnemonic IPOS, which means *i*nput, *p*rocessing, *o*utput, and *s*torage. To determine these operations, one often develops an *algorithm*. To develop a program to access the Internet in a Windows environment, you need to know how both Windows programs and the Internet behave. Similarly, to solve a programming problem, you need to have some idea of what the design solution will look like. Typically, the solution is an algorithm.

2.2.1   Algorithms

*An **algorithm** is a step-by-step sequence of instructions that describes how a computation will be performed.*

Before you can develop an algorithm, you need to know what an algorithm looks like. At this stage we will look at a simple algorithm, and in the following chapters, we will look at progressively more complex algorithms. (Chapter 7 specializes in algorithms.) The procedure for setting an alarm clock is one example of an algorithm:

1. Press the alarm button.

2. Toggle the Hour button *until* the desired hour setting is displayed.

3. Toggle the Minute button *until* the desired minute setting is displayed.

4. Release the alarm button.

5. Set the mode switch from normal to alarm.

(Even this example has some degree of ambiguity. What are the steps to implement *until*? Chapters 5 and 6 will show how to do just that.)

2.2.2   Types of Problems

Algorithmic Solutions

In the case study about Prometheus Limited, we looked at a problem with a definite solution. The solution prescribed a definite sequence of actions to move items from storage bins to loading bays using a conveyor network. The sequence of actions can be implemented with an algorithm.

Heuristic Solutions

Other problems may not have a definite solution. For example, how should Cougar Canoe increase its sales? Is it possible to develop computer programs to solve these kind of problems? The answer is "yes," but it will be more difficult to determine whether the best solution has been found. We cannot step back in time and replay different solutions in the exact historical circumstances. Basically, we have to determine the best algorithmic solution. Therefore, there is a need for procedures to design programs.

Unsolvable Problems?

Should the Internet be censored? This is a question of ethics, morality, and philosophy. Once a judgment is made, it may be conceivable to develop a program to filter content and prevent questionable content from being accessed by a web browser. To develop such a program, we need to develop an algorithm. In the process we will have to determine (or judge) whether there is such a thing as an unsolvable problem.

2.2.3   Software Life Cycle

Software development is a lengthy process with no guarantee of success. There are many cases of software projects going over budget (because they need more time than estimated), being late, containing many bugs, and not doing what they were expected to do. A spectacular example is the airport luggage handling system in one North American city that did everything but handle luggage.

Software is somewhat intangible. As demonstrated in the section about requirements, it is difficult to specify exactly what the software is supposed to do. However, it is necessary to specify requirements in advance (as much as possible) to begin the design. Therefore, it is necessary to have a process for developing programs.

The Phases

The software life cycle has six phases. Software developers should document each phase extensively. In this case, we examine the phases for developing a product information system for Cougar Canoe.

Concept Phase   Determine the needs and overall goals of the system. Cougar Canoe wishes to provide product information to retailers using floppy disk, CD-ROM, or the Internet. It seems that this would improve sales in the long run. Eventually the system may be expanded so that suppliers can improve the supply of components required by Cougar.

Requirements Phase   Determine the specific information that is required. Usually this is prepared by the client. During this phase we would determine the input, processing, output, and storage operations to be performed. Cougar Canoe identifies the specific information and general layout of information. For example, the user can select the canoe model to view from the main screen. It may include the ability to cross-reference facilities to view information by capability, such as the handling of whitewater conditions. This process would likely include market research of retailer needs.

Design Phase   A programmer or programming team converts the requirements to a detailed specification. The programmer designs screen layouts with appropriate buttons, tabs, drop-down lists, menus, and other items to *navigate* the product information system. He or she defines a database that contains product information, such as weight capacity. This database also contains links to multimedia files or file components to present some marketing information.

   The programmer designs structure charts and flow charts to describe the software components, further defining the operation of the components. For example, one module is executed when an associated button is clicked. This module takes information from the database to display the corresponding canoe description, graphic image, specifications, and other information. The programmer has defined the steps to do this in detail but has not actually written the code.

Coding Phase   Write the code using a specific programming language (or set of languages). In this case, the programmer will write the code using Visual Basic. He or she will use software components (perhaps an existing database) where possible. For example, items such as windows, buttons, tabs, and menus already exist. However, the programmer needs to write code that precisely specifies how to work with each component. In other cases, he or she needs to create the modules from the ground up or to create extended modules using existing modules. The programmer also needs to write code that specifies how the modules work together: This is *the glue that hold the blocks together*. It is possible that the programmer will write the code using a program such as Visual Basic Script (VBScript) to create interactive web pages for the Internet.

Testing Phase   Apply a formal set of explicit test cases to determine how well software operates. Note that prior implicit testing occurs during the programming phase. Initially the programmer uses experts inside Cougar Canoe to use the software in trial runs. In this *alpha* test stage, the experts complete survey forms to document the test results while using the software in a variety of predefined situations. The intent is to find problems that can be fixed prior to the subsequent phase. In the subsequent phase, it is released to some outside retailers to test the software in realistic working conditions. In this *beta* test stage, the volunteers provide feedback to the programmer about the software. If necessary (it usually is), the programmer modifies the software based on the test results.

Maintenance Phase   Distribute and install software and provide customer/client support. The programmer writes the user documentation and sets up the required disks. Alternatively, he or she may set up the files for Internet download. If the system was designed as a set of interactive pages, the required files are installed on the web server. In any case, Cougar should provide technical assistance when problems occur.

Life-Cycle Models

Two common process models for developing software are the Waterfall Model and the Incremental Prototyping Model. The Waterfall Model assumes a perfect world in which each phase can be completed in a systematic way in a linear sequence. The Incremental Prototyping Model is used when modifications are made during development. This often occurs because the exact needs may not be known until part of the program is already developed. Also, it may be necessary to experiment with different approaches before choosing an approach. For example, should the system use a telephone and implement speech recognition[2] when a user wants to find the price of a canoe? A stripped-down prototype can test feasibility before committing the entire project to this approach. It turns out that Visual Basic is ideal for incremental prototyping. Figures 2.3 and 2.4 illustrate both models.

In practice, we would normally use an Incremental Prototyping Model and try to *approximate* a Waterfall Model by being as exact as possible during the early phases. When detecting a fault after testing a part of the software system, one would normally go back and repeat the programming phase to modify the program code. For more severe problems, some design modification may be required. To modify the concepts, you would be forced to subsequently revise requirements and everything else down the line. The moral is to do your homework well in the concepts and requirements phases, thus reducing time-consuming (and expensive) modifications.

2.2.4   Structure Chart

A structure chart is one way of illustrating the components in a program.[3] These components are known as *modules*. Essentially it is a divide-and-conquer strategy. Divide the problem into smaller modules. Then further divide each module into smaller modules. Repeat this process until the modules are sufficiently simple to describe in terms of simple statements.

Recall our earlier scenario in which Cougar had to determine the cost of producing a canoe. For that task we identified three components:

1. Add up prices for the material.
2. Calculate labor.
3. Add markup to material and labor costs to achieve profit.

Figure 2.5 shows the relationships among three modules.

Let's now write a computer program. Recall that a computer program is a set of detailed instructions for the computer. In our scenario, many things must be determined before we can begin. Calculating labor (component 2) seems to be the easiest, so we will examine it further. We can divide the labor module into smaller modules, as illustrated in Figure 2.6. The mold requires significant cost to build, but it is reusable for building several canoes.

[2]*This is not far-fetched. Visual Basic can work with the telephone application programming interface (TAPI) and third-party voice recognition software modules.*
[3]*There are other mechanisms, such as data flow diagrams and Warnier-Orr notation.*

Figure 2.3
The Waterfall Model of
Software Development

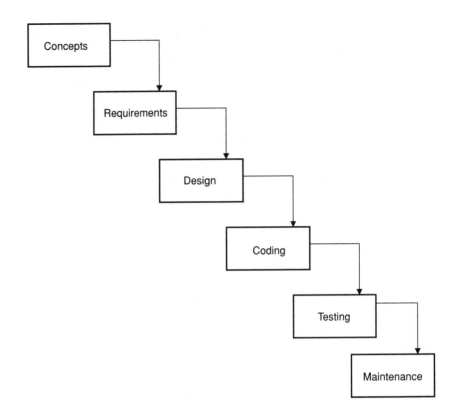

2.2.5   Flow Chart

Another development stage involves drawing a flow chart. It outlines detailed steps required for the sections already identified in the structure chart. Here we will introduce
flow charting and then see how to draw one for the labor module.

In general, a flow chart shows program operations and program sequence in a
graphical format. We can use flow charts for program modules that must execute in a sequence. The traditional flow chart uses standard symbols and was widely used when program design was primarily procedural (see Section 1.8.1). Figure 2.7 introduces the
common symbols that will be required for something such as a cost-of-labor calculation.
Figure 2.7 illustrates the following symbols:

- **Terminal**   The beginning or end of execution of a program module. It is also
  known as the *entry* or *exit point* because a module may use another module.

- **Flow Line**   Shows the sequence order from one part to the next.

- **Input/Output**   Shows the point from where data is brought into local
  memory from a physical device or external file.

- **Process**   Shows a point where data is modified. Typical processes are mathematical calculations or modification of text information (text processing).

- **Decision**   Shows a point where a decision must be made to determine the subsequent flow. It answers true or false to a question. Depending on the answer,
  program execution follows one of two possible flow-line paths.

A Flow Chart to Calculate Labor

The structure chart (Figure 2.6) maps each labor phase. After checking with Cougar
Canoe, we have found out that there are *rules of thumb* to provide estimates of how

Figure 2.4
The Incremental
Prototyping Model of
Software Development

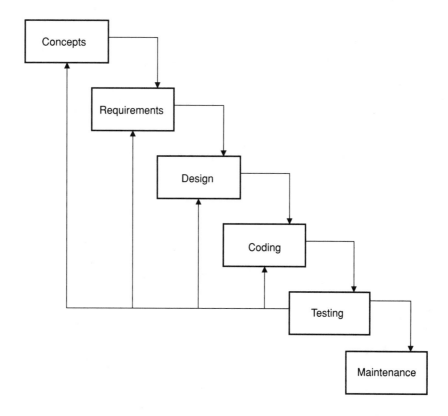

long each phase takes. The cost of labor then becomes the pay rate multiplied by the length of time. Perhaps the program won't be so hard after all. However, subsequent analysis reveals that the pay rate may well vary, depending on the phase and on whether it is a rush job requiring overtime. Hence we will make a flow chart (see Figure 2.8) to clarify the design. (In this case, we can simplify the situation by using total time for all work and assuming that craftspeople and clerical/administrative people work at the same rate.) The flow chart also illustrates the basic computer operations of obtaining inputs, processing (or calculating), generating outputs, and storing information (IPOS).

2.2.6   Pseudocode

To write the program code, you need to determine detailed steps. You can initially write pseudocode and then translate the pseudocode into the formal program code.

Figure 2.5
Structure Chart for
Determining Canoe Cost

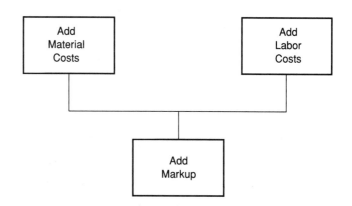

Figure 2.6
Structure Chart for Adding
Labor Costs

```
┌──────────┐      ┌──────────────┐      ┌──────────────┐
│ Clerical │      │Administrative│      │    Mold      │
│  Order   │      │  Overhead    │      │ Construction │
│ Process  │      │              │      │   Factor     │
└────┬─────┘      └──────┬───────┘      └──────┬───────┘
     └─────────────────┬─┴──────────────────────┘
                       │
              ┌────────┴────────┐
              │  Gather and     │
              │ Prepare Parts   │
              └────────┬────────┘
                       │
              ┌────────┴────────┐
              │   Build Hull    │
              └────────┬────────┘
                       │
              ┌────────┴────────┐
              │  Install Trim   │
              └────────┬────────┘
                       │
              ┌────────┴────────┐
              │  Apply Finish   │
              └─────────────────┘
```

***Pseudocode** is a set of nonambiguous step-by-step instructions that is similar to the instructions in a computer program.*

The difference between pseudocode and a computer program is that the pseudocode is written without concern for the syntax rules of the computer language. This permits the program developer to concentrate on logical problem-solving steps. To develop the pseudocode, it is useful to specify the basic computer operations of IPOS.

Pseudocode Example

Here is an example of a pseudocode that describes how to calculate labor costs based on the flow chart shown in Figure 2.8. We have also added a few comments (following single quotes [']) to assist with the explanation.

Example 2.1

```
Begin CalculateLabor ' Start the block of code for this calculation

    ' Get required inputs
    PayRate = Current Pay Rate from database
    TotalTime = Record of required time stored in database

    ' Adjust pay rate if overtime is required, a processing operation
    Is rush job? If yes
    Then PayRate = PayRate x OvertimeFactor

    ' Do actual calculation, another processing operation
    LaborCost = TotalTime x PayRate
```

Figure 2.7
A Generic Flow Chart

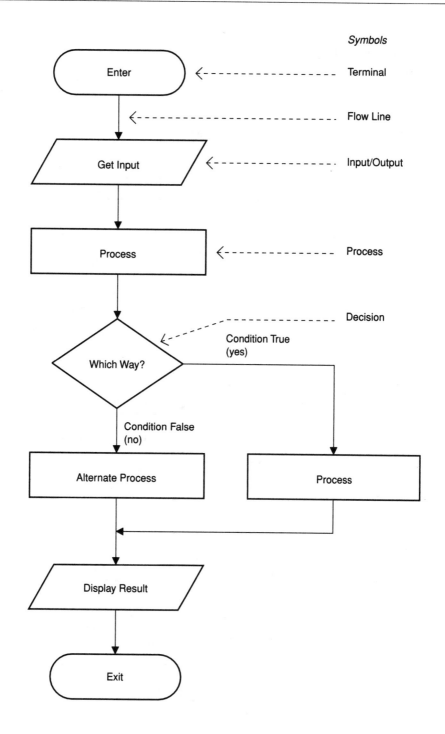

```
      ' Show result to the user, an output operation
      Output LaborCost
      ' Typically, also store result in a database for future use
      Store LaborCost
End CalculateLabor ' End the block of code for this calculation
```

This is a start. Remember that a pseudocode only shows steps. More detail is still needed.

Initially, the program will find information from a database to determine the rate of pay for the total time. These values will be stored in the *variables* PayRate and TotalTime. (For now, consider *variables* to be units of data that can be modified by a program.) The equals sign (=) indicates that a value will be stored. The program will

Figure 2.8
Flow Chart to Calculate
Labor Costs

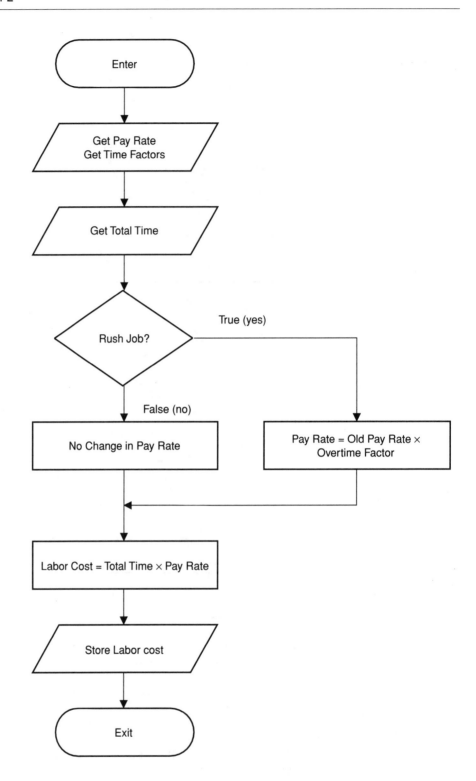

then find out if overtime work is required. If so, the pay rate will be adjusted by multiplying it by an overtime factor. Then it will multiply the time and pay rate values and store the result in a variable named `LaborCost`. Next, it will store this value for use by another module.

With pseudocode, the programmer can concentrate on the logical problem-solving steps. Then the programmer can translate the pseudocode into formal code during the coding phase.

2.2.7   Stepwise Refinement

First we outline a sequence of general steps, and then we need to determine the details. This process is called *stepwise refinement.* When you determine the steps required to solve a programming problem, it is sometimes necessary to break down a step into further detailed steps to translate the steps into program code. For example, how do we obtain inputs? How do we evaluate whether it is a rush job?

Stepwise Refinement Example

The use of a database is realistic. For now however, we will avoid database *queries* in order to avoid additional complexity.[4] To avoid additional complexity at this stage, we will display the labor cost instead of storing it.[5] Hence we will rewrite the pseudocode with more detail, as shown in Example 2.2.

Example 2.2

```
Begin CalculateLabor

    Prompt user "Enter current pay rate"
    Input PayRate
    Prompt user "Enter time required to build canoe"
    Input TotalTime
    Prompt user "Is this a rush job?"
    Input Answer
    If Answer is yes
        Then PayRate = PayRate x OvertimeFactor
    LaborCost = Time x PayRate
    Display LaborCost

End CalculateLabor
```

Here we have further specified how to obtain inputs and how to evaluate whether it is a rush job. GetInput is a module (a block of code) that determines what the user provided as input (keyboard entry). To evaluate whether a rush job is required, the program asks the user for a yes or no answer. If it is true that the answer is yes, the PayRate value will be adjusted.

> *Stepwise refinement is the process of breaking down the general steps in a design into finer detail until it is possible to rewrite the steps in terms of program statements with correct syntax. This is also known as* top-down development.

2.2.8   Coding Example: Calculate Labor Cost

In order to understand the solution, it is useful to have an actual working program with which to work (play). Example 2.3 shows one implementation of the final code.

---

[4]*A query is a way to retrieve information from the database. For example, you may want to ask (query) the database: Which customers have placed orders this month? What is the total amount of all orders placed by each customer?*
[5]*The additional complexities are topics such as parameter passing and scope of variables.*

For now, don't worry about understanding it in detail. Later chapters will fill in this information about coding syntax and language structure. The Exercises section will ask you to critique the program about improvements that should be made. If you wish, run this program now. (To do so, open project CH02\SOLN\LABCOST1 using Visual Basic.)

Example 2.3

```
Public Sub RunMe()

    ' Comments omitted on purpose! - except for this one ;-)

    Dim PayRate As Single, TotalTime As Single
    Dim Answer As String
    Dim LaborCost As Single

    PrintMsg "This is a prototype of a program to calculate"
    PrintMsg "the labor cost for building a canoe."

    InputNum "Enter current pay rate", PayRate
    InputNum "Enter time required to build canoe", TotalTime

    PrintMsg "Is this a rush job?"
    InputWords "Type Yes or No and press <Enter>", Answer
    If Answer = "Yes" Then PayRate = PayRate * 1.5

    LaborCost = TotalTime * PayRate

    PrintNum "The labor cost is ", LaborCost

End Sub
```

The big question is "Is there a resemblance between the program code of Example 2.3 and the pseudocode of Example 2.2?" Remember that the pseudocode shows logical steps without respecting the correct *syntax* (review Section 1.6 if necessary). The lines beginning with the word `Dim` in Example 2.3 are necessary for the program code. `PrintMsg`, `InputNum`, `InputWords`, and `PrintNum` are commands that Visual Basic understands when running the Introduction Template (see Section 1.8.4). You will become more familiar with the commands in Chapter 3. Also, Appendix B will give you an idea of what commands are available and what they do.

An Explanation of the Labor Cost Program

This section describes how this program works so that you can better see the relation between it and the pseudocode of Examples 2.1 and 2.2 and the flow chart of Figure 2.8. Following are segments of the code and an explanation of each.

```
Public Sub RunMe()
```

This statement starts the program. It is necessary syntax that tells the computer that instructions for it to execute are coming.

```
Dim PayRate As Single, TotalTime As Single
Dim Answer As String
Dim LaborCost As Single
```

Table 2.1
Sequence of Steps for Handling Inputs

Step	Display or Data Entered (or processed/stored)
Computer displays prompt to user	Enter current pay rate
User enters a number such as	5.00
Computer stores the number in `PayRate`	(5.00 stored in `PayRate`)
Computer displays prompt to user	Enter time required to build canoe
User enters a number, such as	40
Computer stores the number in `TotalTime`	(40 stored in `TotalTime`)

These statements tell the computer about the variables required in the program. The pseudocode of Example 2.2 does not describe this detail since **variable declarations** are necessary in formal code. (Chapter 3 covers the topic of variable declarations.)

```
PrintMsg "This is a prototype of a program to calculate"
PrintMsg "the labor cost for building a canoe."
```

These statements use the command `PrintMsg` to present information to the user. They inform the user as to what this program is about.

```
InputNum "Enter current pay rate", PayRate
InputNum "Enter time required to build canoe", TotalTime
```

These statements use the command `InputNum` to obtain numerical data from the user. Table 2.1 shows the sequence of steps using a plausible scenario of user inputs. `PayRate` and `TotalTime` refer to places in memory to store the data.

Note that the word *enter*s means "to type something in followed by pressing the Enter key." As you will see in the end-of-chapter exercise, the program is quite unforgiving. If the user enters something such as "5 dollars," the program will not work correctly. Only *numerical* data should be entered, because the instruction `InputNum` is very precise about requiring numerical input. `PayRate` and `TotalTime` are examples of **variables.** For now, consider variables to be storage locations in the computer memory.

```
PrintMsg "Is this a rush job?"
InputWords "Type Yes or No and press <Enter>", Answer
If Answer = "Yes" Then PayRate = PayRate * 1.5
```

These statements use the commands `PrintMsg` and `InputNum` to increase the pay rate factor by 50% if the user enters the word *Yes*. Table 2.2 shows the sequence of steps that continue the scenario from Table 2.1. Note that the asterisk (*) is the symbol used for multiplication.

Again the program is unforgiving. To specify Yes, it is necessary to enter the word *Yes* exactly as prompted. If the user enters *yes* instead of *Yes*, the program interprets the word *yes* to be different from the word *Yes,* and the pay rate will not be adjusted. We will later examine ways to keep the program from being so picky.

```
LaborCost = TotalTime * PayRate
```

Table 2.2
Sequence of Steps to Make a Decision

Step	Display or Data Entered (or processed/stored)
Computer displays message	Is this a rush job?
Computer displays prompt to user	Type Yes or No and press Enter
User enters a word, such as	Yes
Computer multiplies old value of `PayRate` by 1.5 and stores this result back into `PayRate` (since Answer **is** "Yes")	(Calculates 1.5×5.00 and stores the result of 7.50 back into `PayRate`)

This statement calculates the labor cost by multiplying the time by the pay rate. Then it stores the result into the variable `LaborCost`. Using the scenario presented so far, this means that 40 is multiplied by 7.50, and the result of 300 is stored in `LaborCost`.

```
PrintNum "The labor cost is ", LaborCost
```

This statement uses the `PrintNum` command to print out the result. Since the result is 300, it will print the following in the output text box of the Introduction Template.

```
The labor cost is 300
```

The `PrintNum` command has two parts. The first part is explanatory text, followed by the second part, which references the result to be printed.

```
End Sub
```

This statement ends the program. It is necessary syntax so that the computer knows that there are no more instructions for it to execute.

Closing Remarks

We have completed one example of problem solving—or have we? We have taken a problem requirements description, designed a solution, and then coded a solution. Yet there may be problems with the solution—we have not tested it yet. Before we look at debugging and testing, we will look at another sample, and then we will look at some documentation requirements.

2.2.9   Sample Problem: Calculate Material Cost

Let's try our hand at solving a similar problem: Determine the material cost of building a canoe. Recall that this is one of the three components identified by Cougar Canoe for determining canoe price.

If we know how to build a canoe, we should be able to state nonambiguous requirements. For the purpose of this exercise, we will list some materials to use for building a canoe, just in case you are not a master canoe builder. If you happen to be a master builder, please tolerate the liberties taken with this list. It is certainly missing some components and leaves out many specifics.

Fiberglass matting   Measured in square meters
Fiberglass resin   Measured in liters
Trim   Measured in meters

Let's restate the requirements: Determine the amount of material specified by "A List of Some Materials," and the cost of each. Then add the cost of each item and display the total to the user.

Pseudocode

To develop the pseudocode, we can look at some role models. Refer to Example 2.1 as one possible model. Example 2.4 is an adaptation of Example 2.1. Remember to use the basic computer operations of input, processing, output, and storage (IPOS) as a guide.

Example 2.4

```
Begin CalculateMaterial ' Start the block of code for this calculation

    ' Input data
    ' Need both amount and cost per unit amount

    AmountMatting = Required Amount from database
    UnitCostMatting = Required Cost from database

    AmountResin = Required Amount from database
    UnitCostResin = Required Cost from database

    AmountTrim = Required Amount from database
    UnitCostTrim = Required Cost from database

    ' Process data: Calculate Cost per item

    TotalMatting = AmountMatting x UnitCostMatting
    TotalResin = AmountResin x UnitCostResin
    TotalTrim = AmountTrim x UnitCostTrim

    ' Process data: Add item totals to make grand total

    CanoeMaterialCost = total of item costs

    ' Show result to user, an output operation
    Output CanoeMaterialCost

    ' No storage operation in this case.

End CalculateMaterial ' End the block for this calculation
```

Stepwise Refinement

The next process is stepwise refinement. Again, we will assume that the user will enter the required data instead of retrieving this information from a database. At this stage we should be more specific as to how the input, processing, and output operations are to be carried out.

Example 2.5

```
Begin CalculateMaterial
    Prompt user "Enter data for fiberglass matting"
    Prompt user "Enter required square meters"
```

```
        Input AmoutMatting
        Prompt user "Enter cost per square meter"
        Input UnitCostMatting

        Prompt user "Enter data for fiberglass resin"
        Prompt user "Enter required liters"
        Input AmountResin
        Prompt user "Enter cost per liter"
        Input UnitCostResin

        Prompt user "Enter data for trim"
        Prompt user "Enter required meters"
        Input AmountTrim
        Prompt user "Enter cost per meter"
        Input UnitCostTrim

        TotalMatting = AmountMatting x UnitCostMatting
        TotalResin = AmountResin x UnitCostResin
        TotalTrim = AmountTrim x UnitCostTrim
        CanoeMaterialCost = TotalMatting + TotalResin + TotalTrim

        Display CanoeMaterialCost

End CalculateMaterial
```

Coding

The pseudocode is reasonably well developed. Given some coding specifics, you should be able to create the code. Use Example 2.3 as a model for writing the necessary statements that begin with the word Dim. Note that there are eight *variables* (storage locations for data) in the pseudocode. Six variables are part of the input steps. Two variables are used in processing, one of which is displayed as output. Use Example 2.3 as a model for writing the statements beginning with the word PrintMsg or the word InputNum to perform the input steps. Similarly, use other statements in Example 2.3 to write the code for the processing and output steps. Don't forget the first line and last line of the program. (Try not to cheat by looking at the solution that follows!)

A Solution

If your code is similar to that of Example 2.6, congratulations. If not, compare your result with Example 2.6 to find out what you missed. It is possible that extra time and practice are necessary. This example also uses the line continuation arrow described in Appendix A.

Example 2.6

```
Public Sub RunMe()

    ' Comments omitted on purpose - except for this one ;-)

    Dim AmountMatting As Single, UnitCostMatting As Single
    Dim AmountResin As Single, UnitCostResin As Single
    Dim AmountTrim As Single, UnitCostTrim As Single
```

```
Dim TotalMatting As Single, TotalResin As Single, TotalTrim ➡
As Single
Dim CanoeMaterialCost As Single


PrintMsg "This is a prototype of a program to calculate"
PrintMsg "the material cost for building a canoe."
PrintMsg "   "

PrintMsg "Enter data for fiberglass matting"
InputNum "How many square meters of fiberglass matting?", ➡
AmountMatting
InputNum "What's the cost per square meter?", UnitCostMatting
PrintMsg "   "

PrintMsg "Enter data for fiberglass resin"
InputNum "How many liters of fiberglass resin?", AmountResin
InputNum "What's the cost per liter?", UnitCostResin
PrintMsg "   "

PrintMsg "Enter data for trim"
InputNum "How many meters of trim?", AmountTrim
InputNum "What's the cost per meter?", UnitCostTrim
PrintMsg "   "

TotalMatting = AmountMatting * UnitCostMatting
TotalResin = AmountResin * UnitCostResin
TotalTrim = AmountTrim * UnitCostTrim
CanoeMaterialCost = TotalMatting + TotalResin + TotalTrim

PrintNum "The material cost is ", CanoeMaterialCost
```

End Sub

You can run this program and it will work properly as long as you enter valid numbers. It is not forgiving with non-numeric inputs. You might speculate that something should be done about this. Indeed, we will eventually do something about it.

Is This Realistic?

This isn't a complex application. A more realistic program would automatically find the required materials when the user stated the canoe model. It would use the latest cost figures, and it might even offer bulk order discount prices. In addition, if the client accepted the canoe order, a sophisticated information system might automatically place and schedule the order.

2.3   DOCUMENTATION

During the development of pseudocode and the formal code, you may have a flash of insight and use a clever sequence of steps. Unless you have documented the code, you may not remember why you used those particular steps. Documentation explains the reason for writing the program in a certain way (see Section 1.10). Also, the documentation will explain your intent to others who need to modify your program. For example, your bank account program might check for a negative number when handling withdrawals. The reason for this may not be clear, but it is to prevent clever customers from increasing their balance by withdrawing negative amounts.

If you found earlier explanations of code sparse, it was because we wanted to demonstrate the usefulness of documentation. Here we will remedy the situation, and you may even find that your understanding of earlier program examples has improved as a result of the documentation.

2.3.1   Total Labor Cost Example

It would be useful to explain the rationale for the technique to calculate labor cost. We could rewrite the pseudocode of Example 2.2 as follows. Recall that Visual Basic comments begin with the single quote ('), and we will use this syntax for pseudocode as well.

Example 2.7

```
Begin CalculateLabor

    ' Given an hourly labor rate and number of hours required,
    ' find out the labor cost in dollars for building a certain canoe
    ' by multiplying the hourly labor rate by the number of
    ' hours required to build the canoe. Program displays
    ' total labor cost in dollars.

    ' Get hourly labor rate and number of hours required from user
    Prompt user "Enter current pay rate"
    Input PayRate
    Prompt user "Enter time required to build canoe"
    Input TotalTime

    ' If this is a rush job, then the hourly labor rate is adjusted
    ' by multiplying the hourly labor rate by an overtime factor.
    Prompt user "Is this a rush job?"
    Input Answer
    If Answer is yes
        Then PayRate = PayRate x OvertimeFactor

    ' Calculate the cost here
    LaborCost = Time x PayRate

    ' Show the cost to the user
    Display LaborCost

End CalculateLabor
```

The additional comments help to clarify the pseudocode. Admittedly, this may not have been necessary for this particular example. The value of documentation will become clearer when the programs become more complex, particularly when we consider that commercial programs typically have thousands of lines of code.

Some explanations followed Example 2.3; these were necessary to describe how to use Visual Basic. Much of the explanation about Visual Basic is not necessary for an experienced programmer. For example, it would not be necessary to explain the following.

```
Public Sub RunMe() ' Define the start of the program
```

However, it would be useful to summarize the program and then explain the steps. Generally, we can use parts of the pseudocode and some of the comments from pseudocode as comments in the formal code. We will have to use our judgment about whether or not to add additional explanations. Thus we could rewrite Example 2.3 as what is shown in Example 2.8.

Example 2.8

```
Public Sub RunMe()

    ' Written by Cody Wizard,
    ' Version History
    ' 12-20-96, initial version
    ' 12-21-96, added overtime feature
    ' 12-22-96, completed documentation

    ' Disclaimer, assumes user enters "legal" inputs!

    ' Given an hourly labor rate and number of hours required,
    ' find out the labor cost in dollars for building a certain canoe
    ' by multiplying the hourly labor rate by the number of
    ' hours required to build the canoe. Program displays
    ' total labor cost in dollars.

    Dim PayRate As Single    ' Hourly labor rate
    Dim TotalTime As Single  ' Number of hours required
    Dim Answer As String     ' Overtime required, "Yes" or "No"
    Dim LaborCost As Single  ' Total labor cost

    ' Tell user what this program will do
    PrintMsg "This is a prototype of a program to calculate"
    PrintMsg "the labor cost for building a canoe."

    ' Get hourly labor rate and number of hours required from user

    ' Prompt user "Enter current pay rate" and Input PayRate
    InputNum "Enter current pay rate", PayRate

    ' Prompt user "Enter time required to build canoe" and Input ➡
    TotalTime
    InputNum "Enter time required to build canoe", TotalTime

    ' Prompt user "Is this a rush job?" and Input Answer
    PrintMsg "Is this a rush job?"
    InputWords "Type Yes or No and press Enter", Answer

    ' If this is a rush job, then the hourly labor rate is adjusted
    ' by multiplying the hourly labor rate by an overtime factor.
    If Answer = "Yes" Then PayRate = PayRate * 1.5
```

```
    ' Calculate the cost here
    LaborCost = TotalTime * PayRate

    ' Show the cost to the user
    PrintNum "The labor cost is ", LaborCost

End Sub
```

Note

The DIM statements in Example 2.8 contain variables called PayRate, Total-Time, Answer, and LaborCost. Variables are named entities for storing values during program execution. Single and String are Visual Basic's way of referring to numerical and word (alphanumeric) values, respectively. (Chapter 3 will explain variables.)

Following are some further explanations of the code in Example 2.8.

Opening Comments

It is a standard practice to begin documentation with such information as that identifying the program creator(s) and the revision history. (No program is safe from revision!)

Disclaimer

Normally a program should be robust enough to handle anything a user may try to do. For now, to keep the example simple, we have ignored the possibility of user errors.

Explain Variables

Note that we did not comment directly about the lines beginning with the word Dim. A programmer would know that these tell the computer about the variables required in the program. However, note that the additional comments explain *what the variables will be used for*.

Tell the User About the Program

There are instructions that tell the user the purpose of the program. It is also important for the user (as well as the programmer) to know what to expect when running a program.

Get Inputs

Comments explain what input is obtained and how it is obtained.

Process Data

These types of comments explain the two processing phases. In the first phase, the program adjusts the hourly pay rate. In the second phase, the program calculates the final result, the total labor cost.

Display Output

Comments related to output display explain that results are being displayed to the user.

Store Data

In this case, we are not storing data in an off-line medium such as a disk.

Note

Documentation should explain the *purpose* of the instructions in relation to the *purpose* of the program. Comments should not normally rephrase instructions or explain *how* instructions work. However, it may be appropriate to comment on *how* an instruction works in a language tutorial situation (such as in this book) to assist a learner with understanding the programming language.

2.3.2   Total Material Cost Example

We will now add documentation to the pseudocode and code for the program to calculate the material cost for building a canoe (Examples 2.5 and 2.6).

Exercise

Revise the pseudocode of Example 2.5.

Solution

A revised pseudocode is shown in Example 2.9. Note that this is one possible solution that happens to follow a format similar to the preceding labor cost example.

Example 2.9

```
Begin CalculateMaterial

    ' Given required amounts of fiberglass matting, fiberglass resin,
    ' and trim, find out the material cost in dollars for ➡
      building a certain canoe
    ' by multiplying per-unit-cost of each item by the item amount
    ' Then add them up. Program displays total material
    ' cost in dollars. The following highlights steps

    ' Get number of square meters of and unit cost of fiberglass ➡
      matting
    Prompt user "Enter data for fiberglass matting"
    Prompt user "Enter required square meters"
    Input AmountMatting
    Prompt user "Enter cost per square meter"
    Input UnitCostMatting

    ' Get number of liters of and unit cost of fiberglass resin
    Prompt user "Enter data for fiberglass resin"
    Prompt user "Enter required liters"
    Input AmountResin
    Prompt user "Enter cost per liter"
    Input UnitCostResin

    ' Get number of meters of and unit cost of trim
    Prompt user "Enter data for trim"
```

```
        Prompt user "Enter required meters"
        Input AmountTrim
        Prompt user "Enter cost per meter"
        Input UnitCostTrim

        ' Calculate costs and grand total material cost
        TotalMatting = AmountMatting x UnitCostMatting
        TotalResin = AmountResin x UnitCostResin
        TotalTrim = AmountTrim x UnitCostTrim
        CanoeMaterialCost = TotalMatting + TotalResin + TotalTrim

        ' Output result
        Display CanoeMaterialCost

End CalculateMaterial
```

The comments that highlight steps explain why the pseudocode instructions are used.

Exercise

Improve the documentation of the code shown in Example 2.6.

Solution

Example 2.10 shows one possible solution following a format similar to that shown in Example 2.8.

Example 2.10

```
Public Sub RunMe()

    ' Written by Cody Wizard,
    ' Version History
    ' 12-27-96, initial version
    ' 12-28-96, added overtime feature
    ' 12-29-96, completed documentation

    ' Disclaimer, assumes user enters "legal" inputs!

    ' Given required amounts of fiberglass matting, fiberglass resin,
    ' and trim, find out the material cost in dollars for ➡
    building a certain canoe
    ' by multiplying per-unit-cost of each item by the item amount
    ' and then add them up. Program displays total material
    ' cost in dollars

    Dim AmountMatting As Single ' Square meters of fiberglass matting
    Dim UnitCostMatting As Single  ' Its cost per square meter
    Dim AmountResin As Single  ' Liters of fiberglass resin
    Dim UnitCostResin As Single ' Its cost per liter
    Dim AmountTrim As Single  ' Meters of trim
    Dim UnitCostTrim As Single ' Its cost per meter

    ' Subtotal costs of materials (i.e. unit cost x amount)
    Dim TotalMatting As Single, TotalResin As Single, TotalTrim ➡
    As Single
```

```
    ' Final material cost of canoe (sum of subtotal costs)
    Dim CanoeMaterialCost As Single

    ' Tell user what program will do
    PrintMsg "This is a prototype of a program to calculate"
    PrintMsg "the material cost for building a canoe."
    PrintMsg "   "  ' Simply adds a blank line for spacing

    ' Inform user that program will ask for fiberglass matting data
    PrintMsg "Enter data for fiberglass matting"
    ' Get number of square meters of and unit cost of ➥
    fiberglass matting
    ' Prompt user and input Amount Matting and Unit Cost Matting
    InputNum "How many square meters of fiberglass matting?", ➥
    AmountMatting
    InputNum "What's the cost per square meter?", UnitCostMatting
    PrintMsg "   "  ' Add blank line for spacing

    ' Inform user that program will ask for fiberglass resin data
    PrintMsg "Enter data for fiberglass resin"

    ' Get number of liters of and unit cost of fiberglass resin
    ' Prompt user and input Amount Resin and Unit Cost Resin
    InputNum "How many liters of fiberglass resin?", ➥
    AmountResin
    InputNum "What's the cost per liter?", UnitCostResin
    PrintMsg "   "

    ' Inform user that program will ask for trim data
    PrintMsg "Enter data for trim"

    ' Get number of meters of and unit cost of trim
    ' Prompt user and input Amount Trim and Unit Cost Trim
    InputNum "How many meters of trim?", AmountTrim
    InputNum "What's the cost per meter?", UnitCostTrim
    PrintMsg "   "

    ' Calculate subtotal costs of materials (i.e. unit cost x ➥
    amount)
    TotalMatting = AmountMatting * UnitCostMatting
    TotalResin = AmountResin * UnitCostResin
    TotalTrim = AmountTrim * UnitCostTrim

    ' Calculate final material cost of canoe (sum of subtotal ➥
    costs)
    CanoeMaterialCost = TotalMatting + TotalResin + TotalTrim

    ' Show the cost to the user
    PrintNum "The material cost is ", CanoeMaterialCost

End Sub
```

*The **comments** explain the purpose of the statements in the context of the problem being solved.*

2.4   TROUBLESHOOTING: DEBUGGING AND TESTING

In Section 1.11, we explained that it is important to verify whether a program does what it is supposed to do. We can't expect a program to read a user's mind, so we need to run tests to see if the program outputs are correct. Section 1.11 listed the three types of errors:

Syntax   Grammatical errors in coding that are detected by Visual Basic.

Logical   Unexpected program behavior that is not detectable by Visual Basic.

Runtime   Program performs an operation that causes program failure (crash).

We will have to make up tests to detect these errors and fix them when we find them. This is the debugging process.

2.4.1   Syntax Errors

We won't say much about these in this chapter since it concentrates on program logic instead of Visual Basic syntax (see Section 1.7). Apparently none of the program examples in this chapter had such errors. Otherwise, the programs would not have run in the first place.

2.4.2   Logical Errors

For Example 2.8 to calculate labor cost, we expect the program to output the correct final cost, given the appropriate inputs. The comments in the program are useful in posing test questions. The bottom line is: Does the program display total labor cost in dollars? Some procedural questions are:

- Does the program tell the user what this program will do?

- Does the program get all required inputs? (List each one explicitly.)

- Does the program adjust the hourly rate in the case of a rush job?

- Does the program leave the hourly rate alone in case it isn't a rush job?

- Does the program calculate the cost correctly?

- Does the program display the cost to the user?

- Does the program stop after displaying the cost?

If the answer to any of the above is no, the code will need to be revised. Additional questions include:

- Is it clear to the user as to what inputs are required?

- Is it clear to the user how to enter the inputs?

- Are there any typographical errors in the prompting and output display messages?

We can make up some test cases as shown in Table 2.3. In this case, we can independently calculate each result manually and compare it with the program output when identical inputs are used. As we will see, even this "relatively simple" program has warts and flaws (assuming we didn't intend to display currency symbols such as $).

Table 2.3
Some Test Cases for Calculating Labor Cost

Row	Input PayRate	Input TotalTime	Input Answer	Desired Output LaborCost	Program Output LaborCost
1	7.50	42.5	No	318.75	318.75
2	7.50	42.5	Yes	478.13	478.125
3	–9.50	5.25	No	*Negative pay not allowed*	–49.875
4	9.50	5.25	No	49.88	49.875
5	9.50	5.25	yes	74.81	49.875

Row 1

The program outputs the desired result.

Row 2

The program outputs the correct result, but there seems to be a rounding problem. Currency should be shown to two decimal points (most currencies work this way).

Row 3

The program returns a negative cost. The customer would certainly be pleased to be given money in order to purchase something!

Row 4

The program outputs the correct result, but there seems to be a rounding problem. Also, one might question whether the total time is realistic.

Row 5

The result is the same as that for Row 4. In fact, the program only uses the overtime factor if the user enters Answer spelled as capital Y, lowercase e, and lowercase s, with no spaces following the word.

Some of the errors, such as that shown in Row 2, are not severe. Others, such as the one in Row 3, would be very embarrassing. These are logical errors because in all cases the program still ran to completion. Obviously, to correct these errors, we have our work cut out for us. We can test the program of Example 2.10 for errors. The hands-on exercises will investigate these errors further.

2.4.3 Runtime Errors

Are there any errors that will cause the program to stop execution? Try entering non-numeric data when numeric data is expected. For example, if the user enters the word *dog* when prompted for the pay rate, the program will abort execution. This is because the command InputNum "Enter current pay rate", PayRate expects a numerical entry. Similarly, an input of *12.56a* would also cause a runtime error. On the other hand, if the user enters *123* when prompted for a Yes or No answer, the program interprets the answer as No. This is a logical error, not a runtime error, since the program continues execution.

Exercise

What kind of logic errors could we check in the program of Example 2.10?

Solution

Since this program is similar to the one for calculating labor cost, we could expect the errors to be similar. The bottom line is: Does the program display total material cost in dollars? Some procedural questions follow:

- Does the program tell the user what this program will do?
- Does the program get all required inputs? (List each one explicitly.)
- Does the program calculate the cost correctly?
- Does the program display the cost to the user?
- Does the program stop after displaying the cost?

Exercise

Suggest some guidelines for setting up test cases for this program.

Solution

Again, since this program is similar to that of Example 2.8, we could set up similar test inputs. These could be

- Enter all positive valid numbers.

  Is it likely that some outputs will show 3 or more decimal points?
- Enter some negative valid numbers.

  Will the program generate nonsense outputs?
- Enter some non-numeric inputs.

  Will there be a runtime error?

SUMMARY

To write a computer program to perform a given task, we need to rephrase a task in non-ambiguous language. Problem solving is about structuring the solution. It is the ability to pose a problem so that the machine will solve it for you. Since computers only do what you tell them to do, the true essence of programming is to tell the computer to do what you want it to do.

The software deliverables are the requirements, design, coding, and user documentation. This chapter concentrated on design. Coding (and more design) will be covered thoroughly in the rest of the book. User documentation is outside the scope of this book.

The first deliverable is the requirements. Here we state an understanding of the problem. To determine the requirements, we need to identify

- Inputs

- Processing actions

- Outputs that are immediately displayed

We did not discuss off-line data storage in this chapter.

To begin the problem-solving process, we need to determine an algorithm. An algorithm is a step-by-step sequence of instructions that describes how a computation is to be performed. Normally, we state an algorithm in terms of pseudocode or a diagram, such as a flow chart. A possible algorithm to determine canoe cost is

```
Calculate Cost
    Set Total to zero
    Add material cost to Total
    Add labor cost to Total
    Add overhead cost to Total ' such as percentage of marketing, ➡
    office expenses, etc.
End Calculate Cost
```

Generally, the software life cycle has six phases that can be followed using the waterfall or incremental prototyping model of development.

Concept Phase:	Determine the need and overall goals of the system.
Requirements Phase:	Determine the specific information that is required (input, processing, output, and storage to be performed).
Design Phase:	Converts the requirements to a detailed specification.
Coding Phase:	Write the code using a specific programming language (or a set of languages).
Testing Phase:	Apply a formal set of explicit test cases to determine how well the software operates.
Maintenance Phase:	Distribute and install the software. Provide customer/client support.

We can use structure charts and/or flow charts to illustrate the components of an algorithm (and program). The visual representation of the sequence of steps (actions) is useful in the design and programming phases.

Pseudocode is a set of nonambiguous step-by-step instructions that is similar to the instructions in a computer program. With pseudocode, the programmer can concentrate on the logical problem-solving steps, and can translate the pseudocode into formal code during the coding phase. Example 2.2 is an example of pseudocode, and Example 2.8 is an example of a Visual Basic implementation of this code.

Stepwise refinement is the process of breaking down a design's general steps into finer detail until it is possible to rewrite the steps in terms of program statements with correct syntax. This is also known as *top-down development.*

The Labor Cost Program of Example 2.3 is useful for illustrating the results of translating pseudocode into formal code using Visual Basic. The Labor Cost program has statements for distinct components. These are

- Start the program.

- Tell the computer about the variables required in the program.

- Present information to the user.

- Obtain numerical data from the user.

- Increase the pay rate factor by 50% if the user enters the word *Yes*.

- The program calculates the labor cost by multiplying the time by the pay rate.

- Print out the result.

- End the program.

Documentation explains why the program was written in a certain way. We usually find that our understanding of a program improves as a result of the documentation. We document the pseudocode or the program by writing comments, which help add clarity to the program code (or pseudocode). The comments summarize the program and explain the steps. We can organize comment blocks into the following types:

- Opening Comments

- Disclaimer

- Explain Variables

- Tell the User About the Program

- Get Inputs

- Process Data

- Display Outputs

- Store Data

There are three types of programming errors:

Syntax   Grammatical errors in coding that are detected by Visual Basic.
Logical   Program does something unexpected that is not detectable by Visual Basic.
Runtime   Program does an operation that causes program failure (crash).

The debugging process involves testing to detect errors and fixing those errors. In this chapter, we primarily focused on logic errors. To test the program, we check that it

- Does what it is supposed to do.

- Tells the user what its purpose is (what it will do).

- Gets all required inputs.

- Performs processing steps correctly.

- Stores data in off-line storage (when appropriate).

- Displays desired outputs to the user.

- Stops after outputs are displayed.

If any of the checks fail, we need to revise the program. In later chapters, we will use the Visual Basic debugging tools to examine program execution in detail to diagnose problems. Note that desired outputs are defined when we develop the requirements. Failure to correctly specify requirements will result in a program we may think is correct but that in fact does not do what it is supposed to do.

The exercises that follow will get you started with producing the software deliverables.

HANDS-ON EXERCISES

OVERVIEW

The activities will

- Check your understanding of what software is.
- Familiarize you with some problem-solving steps.
- Provide some experience with coding, documentation, and testing.

TO GET STARTED

1. Read the section "Read Me Before Attempting the Hands-On Exercises" if you have not already done so.
2. Run Windows.
3. Open the file CH02\EX02.TXT on the program disk and answer the questions. (The same questions are shown here so that you can still determine answers if you are not sitting in front of a computer.)
4. Run Visual Basic.

2.1 THE SOFTWARE DELIVERABLES

1. When you purchase software, you get a shrinkwrapped box containing manual(s) and disk(s). Explain where the deliverables are. Note that some of the requirements are inherently part of the package and may not be directly visible.

Figure 2.9
The Conveyor Demo Program

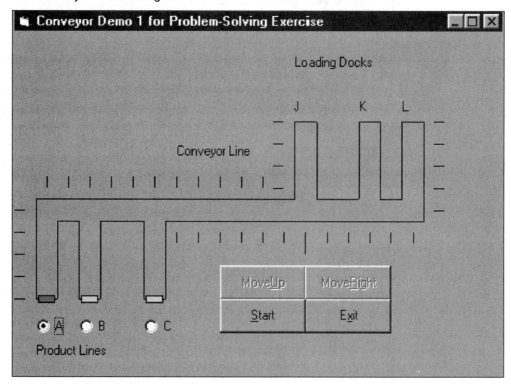

2. What is an information system?

3. What is the distinction between design and coding? Use an example, such as calcu-lating total distance given the distance between intermediate points.

Hands-On: Conveyor Network

Section 2.1.5 described a conveyor system. In this exercise you will run a program that simulates a similar system.

1. Run Windows if you haven't already done so.

2. Run Visual Basic if you haven't already done so.

3. Select **Open Project** from the File menu.

4. Select CONVEY1 from folder (directory) CH02 on the program disk. Click **OK**.

5. To run the program, select Start from the Run menu (or click the **Start** button in the Toolbar). You should see a window that looks like Figure 2.9.

   The objective is to move a product (A, B, or C) to one of the loading docks (J, K, or L) using combinations of the MoveUp and MoveRight commands. For practice, we will guide you in moving product C to dock J. Note that buttons MoveUp and MoveRight are dimmed. They are currently not accessible.

6. Select product line C. The Option button (white circle) corresponding to C should now have a dot in it.

7. Click the **Start** button. It toggles to a Stop button, and the MoveUp and MoveRight buttons will now be available. Click on the **MoveUp** and **MoveRight** buttons to move the package (highlighted in bright orange) along the conveyor lines to dock J. Use the following sequence:

   • Click **MoveUp** four times.

   • Click **MoveRight** seven times.

   • Click **MoveUp** four times.

8. To start over and move the next product, click the **Stop** button. Then select a new product and click **Start** to move it. If you click **Exit**, the simulation program will stop, and you will need to use the Visual Basic Start command to run it again. Ex-ample 2.11 shows the sequence for implementing a general statement to move product C to dock J.

Example 2.11

```
Move Product C to Dock J
     MoveUp
     MoveUp
     MoveUp
     MoveUp
     MoveRight
     MoveRight
     MoveRight
     MoveRight
     MoveRight
     MoveRight
     MoveRight
     MoveUp
     MoveUp
```

```
      MoveUp
      MoveUp
End Move Product C to Dock J
```

This mundane example illustrates the level of detail necessary to give step-by-step instructions to a computer. Now write a sequence of instructions (or program) to move product B to dock K. You should find that the required moves are: `MoveUp` 4 times, `MoveRight` 13 times, and then `MoveUp` 4 times. You can play more with this program or click **Exit** to move on to the next exercise.

2.2 PROBLEM-SOLVING STEPS

Conveyor Demonstration Program

4. The conveyor demonstration (`CONVEY1`) program illustrated three basic computer operations: input, process, and output. Explain how this program demonstrates these operations. What is the algorithm for this program?

Introduction to DELIV, the Delivery Robot

There are two interactive simulations to help you practice problem solving as well as documentation and debugging. In the first, a delivery robot named `DELIV` is used to pick up objects and move them elsewhere. To ask `DELIV` to move a part from one place to another, you can use a combination of six possible commands. The six commands are

```
MoveForward
MoveBack
MoveLeft
MoveRight
Pick
Place
```

`DELIV` only moves within a grid. Numbers indicate the row and letters indicate the column (like a street map). Each move command will move the robot to the next square (cell) in the grid. Figure 2.10 shows the simulation program `DELIVER1` after the robot has moved from the start position (cell 10C) to cell 8E. Note the commands used to move the robot.

The objective is to tell `DELIV` to move the item from one cell to another. For example, tell `DELIV` to deliver the item to cell 9H. Note that Figure 2.10 shows the item currently at cell 7G. `DELIVER1` will familiarize you with the robot since it shows the effects of each command immediately. Later you will use `DELIVER2`, which requires you to enter a program (the entire set of commands) in order to operate the robot. This more closely simulates the process of computer programming. `DELIVER2` will also expose you to logical and runtime errors.

Hands-On: Delivery Robot Version 1

In Visual Basic, stop program `CONVEYOR1` if you haven't already done so by clicking the **Exit** button on the Conveyor Demo. Open Project `DELIVER1` from folder `CH02` on the program disk.

To run the program, select Start from the Run menu (or click the Start button in the Toolbar). You should see a window that looks like Figure 2.10. For now, just examine the window.

In the terminology of Visual Basic, the program's window is known as its *form*. `DELIVER1` is a Visual Basic program that we happen to be using for the purpose of studying program development. The *form* for `DELIVER1` is the window with the grid,

Figure 2.10
Delivery 1 Program in Action

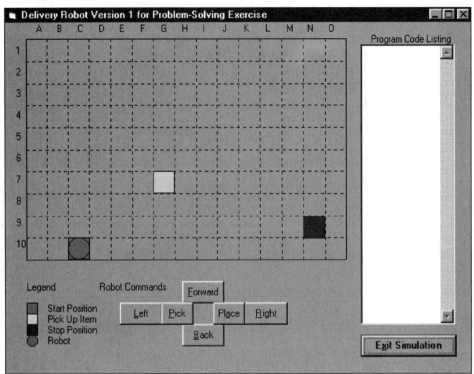

buttons, and so on. Now let's get to work instructing DELIV. The steps of this example will help you understand the robot commands and some of the problem-solving and program design steps. The requirement is as follows:

Deliver the item to cell 9H

Even this simplistic scenario requires that we think out a sequence of detailed commands in order to make DELIV to function the way we want it to. To analyze this system, answer the following questions.

5. What are the goals of the system?

6. What specific information is required? Write a detailed specification.

We can describe the design in terms of pseudocode. The pseudocode might look like that shown in Example 2.12.

Example 2.12
```
Move robot to item
Pick up item
Move robot to cell 9H
Place item
```

Note that the pseudocode reworded the requirements using words similar to the commands the robot understands. These are the words (verbs) *move*, *pick*, and *place*. Keep in mind that when writing a computer program in general, we will need to rewrite requirements in terms of words that translate easily into program instructions.

Since the robot is in cell 10C and the item is in cell 7G, we can refine the pseudocode as shown in Example 2.13:

Example 2.13

```
Move robot forward by three cells
Move robot right by four cells
Pick item
Move robot back by two cells
Move robot right by one cell
Place item
```

In the refinement, we specify how to use the words *move*, *pick*, and *place*. Thus we can directly translate these into the command sequence.

In the coding phase we write the code in our specific language. In this case, the language only has the six commands that can be understood by DELIV. These are Pick, Place, and the four variations of Move.

For simulation program DELIVER1, coding is accomplished by running this Visual Basic program and clicking in the robot commands. If you haven't done so already, select **Start** from the Run menu (or click the **Start** button in the Toolbar).

Click the **Forward** button to select the Forward command. The robot will move one cell forward. Try clicking on other **robot commands**. Note that the corresponding command will be displayed in the program listing box. Also, if you try to move the robot outside the grid, the simulation will beep and not complete the command. If you click **Pick** when the robot is not in position, the robot will still carry out the command, although it will have no effect on the item (a logical error, in a sense). Clicking **Place** when an item has not been picked up previously has a similar effect.

To start again, click **Exit Simulation** and run the simulation again (using the Visual Basic Start command).

Now it's your turn to figure out the code. Beginning with the robot in the start position, click the appropriate buttons in the appropriate order to implement the refined pseudocode. One possible program is shown in Example 2.14.

Example 2.14

```
MoveForward
MoveForward
MoveForward
MoveRight
MoveRight
MoveRight
MoveRight
Pick
MoveBack
MoveBack
MoveRight
Place
```

After clicking **Place**, click any movement button. You should see that the effect of Place is to leave the item in the cell.

More Practice?

Execute programs that do the following requirements:

- After leaving the item in cell 9H, move the robot back to the start position.

- Deliver the item (now in cell 9H) to cell 7F, and move the robot to the stop position.

Note that the requirements do not use the words *move, pick,* or *place.* Write the pseudocode by rewriting the requirements in terms of these three words. Write pseudocode, refine it, and test your code using the simulator. The solutions are stored in file CH02\SOLN\DELSOLN1.TXT, which you can view with any text editor. Note that the initial pseudocode for the second requirement might be similar to that of Example 2.14, with an additional statement about moving the robot to the stop position.

Hands-On: Delivery Robot Version 2

In Visual Basic, stop program DELIVER1 if you haven't already done so. Open Project DELIVER2 from folder CH02 on the program disk. To run the program, select **Start** from the Run menu (or click the **Start** button in the Toolbar). You should see a window with a grid, buttons, and other items (the program form) that looks similar to that of DELIVER1. Let's try to fulfill the same requirement as before:

Deliver the item to cell 9H.

Run the DELIVER2 program. Click on the **robot commands** as before to implement the program shown in Example 2.14. However, you will only see the commands listed in the Program Code Listing; you will not see the moves immediately. Instead, click the **Run Robot Program** button. The simulation will execute the commands in one-second intervals. Try it now. Click **Run Robot Program**.

Assuming you have entered the program correctly, the result should show both the robot and the item in cell 9H. If you didn't see this result, click **Clear Robot Program** and try again. If you already encountered a runtime error, restart the Visual Basic program DELIVER2.

This more closely mimics the way an actual computer program works. That is:

- Write (enter) the code first.
- Then run (execute) the program.
- See the results during execution.

Due the immediate response capability in simulation DELIVER1, if you accidentally gave an incorrect command, you could immediately apply a corrective command. With simulation DELIVER2, you will not see results until the program is run. Hence you have to make sure that all commands are entered in the correct sequence prior to running the program. Play more with this program, if you like. The following sections will give you practice with documentation, testing, and debugging using this robot simulation.

2.3 DOCUMENTATION

Using DELIVER2, let's develop a new program while documenting the progressive development stages. The requirement is

Deliver the item to cell 8F and return to the start position.

Determine how to move the robot from its start position to the item. Determine what to do once the robot has reached the item. Determine how to move the item to the new position. Determine what to do once the robot has reached the new position. Determine how to move the robot back to the start position. One possible pseudocode is shown in Example 2.15.

Example 2.15

```
Move robot to item
Pick up item
```

```
Move robot to cell 8F
Place item
Move robot to start position
```

In the documentation phase, indicate how the pseudocode steps relate to the requirements and analysis. One possibility is shown in Example 2.16.

Example 2.16

```
' Deliver the item to cell 8F and return to the start position

Move robot to item            ' Robot now ready to pick up item
Pick up item                  ' Necessary in order to transport item
Move robot to cell 8F         ' Brings item to desired position
Place item                    ' Leave item in desired position
Move robot to start position  ' Robot now completed task
```

Note that the comments explain *why* the pseudocode uses these specific steps. However, the first comment summarizes the task (describes the big picture).

Since the robot is in cell 10C and the item is in cell 8F, we can refine the pseudocode as shown in Example 2.17 (with accompanying comments):

Example 2.17

```
' Deliver the item to cell 8F and return to the start position

' Move robot to item
Move robot forward by three cells
Move robot right by four cells ' Now ready to pick up

Pick item                      ' Necessary in order to transport item

' Move robot to cell 8F
Move robot back by one cell
Move robot left by one cell    ' Now ready to place

Place item                     ' Leave in desired position

' Return robot to start position
Move robot left by three cells
Move robot back by two cells   ' Back in start position

' Task complete
```

Note the use of the words *move*, *pick*, and *place*. We should be able to translate these steps into the command sequence. Of course, other command sequences are also possible. The robot could have returned to the start position after placing the item:

```
Move robot back by one cell
Move robot left by three cells
Move robot back by one cell
```

As in a typical program, there are many possible detailed steps that will fulfill the same requirements. For this example, only one refinement phase was necessary. In general, for more complex requirements one would have to stepwise refine the pseudocode progressively in more detail during as many phases as are required, stopping when the pseudocode was detailed enough to convert the statements into formal code. Example 2.18 shows the program that implements the pseudocode of Example 2.17.

Example 2.18

```
MoveForward
MoveForward
MoveForward
MoveRight
MoveRight
MoveRight
MoveRight
Pick
MoveBack
MoveLeft
Place
MoveLeft
MoveLeft
MoveLeft
MoveBack
MoveBack
```

Click on the **robot commands** and run the robot program. After execution, the item should show as cell 8F and the robot should be back in the start position. Do *not* click Clear Robot Program so that the Program Code Listing remains visible.

It is one thing to read a solution, but it is even more useful to type in a solution yourself. This reinforces what you read. You will now document the code, and, as a bonus, you will learn two new Windows tricks if you don't know them already. If you clicked Clear Robot Program, you will have to click on the robot commands all over again. In this exercise, you will copy the Program Code Listing and paste it into a text document for further editing to add comments.

Highlight all of the text in the Program Code Listing as you would in any standard Windows editor. (Drag the mouse I-beam pointer over the text while holding down the left mouse button.) Copy this text into the Windows clipboard by pressing the **CTRL+C** keys (hold down **CTRL**, press **C**, release **C**, release **CTRL**).

Launch the Notepad editor (or your favorite word processor). Remember, you can launch anything using the Start button in the Windows Taskbar. With the editor window active (in technical terms, in focus), paste the document using **CTRL+V** or by selecting **Paste** from the Edit menu. Save the editor document in directory CH02 of the program disk as MYROB2.TXT. Edit the document to resemble Example 2.19 and save the document file when you are done.

Example 2.19

```
' Deliver the item to cell 8F and return to the start position

' Move robot to item
MoveForward      ' Move robot forward by three cells
MoveForward
MoveForward
MoveRight         ' Move robot right by four cells
MoveRight
MoveRight
MoveRight         ' Now ready to pick up

Pick              ' Pick item in order to transport it


' Move robot to cell 8F, which is back 1 and left 1
```

```
MoveBack
MoveLeft           ' Now ready to place

Place              ' Leave item in desired position

' Return robot to start position
MoveLeft           ' Move robot left by three cells
MoveLeft
MoveLeft
MoveBack           ' Move robot back by two cells
MoveBack           ' Back in start position
```

```
' Task complete
```

You could argue that simulation program DELIVER2 should have included a Copy button. However, we will ignore these user interface design issues for now.

2.4   TROUBLESHOOTING: DEBUGGING AND TESTING

We will continue working with DELIVER2 to demonstrate debugging and testing. Then we will return to the programs to calculate labor and material cost, which were mentioned earlier in this chapter.

Syntax errors are not possible in DELIVER2 because commands are entered by clicking buttons. However, there are plenty of possibilities for logical and runtime errors. Remember that a logical error occurs when the program still runs to completion but the result is not the desired result. Click **Clear Program**, if you haven't already done so. Click in the robot command sequence in Example 2.20 (without the comments) and click **Run Robot Program**.

Example 2.20

```
' Move item one cell to the right
' But whoa, this doesn't work

MoveForward
MoveForward
MoveRight
MoveRight
Pick
MoveRight
Place
```

Note the intention (requirement) of the program: It runs, but it doesn't do what we want it to do. Executing Pick when there is no item does not harm the program (or the robot), but it is ineffectual. Similarly, executing Place when the robot has not picked up the item does no harm, but also has no effect.

Runtime errors cause the program to crash. In this case, a robot crash causes the runtime error. An attempt to move the robot outside the grid makes it crash against the wall, and the robot program aborts execution.

If you haven't already done so, click **Clear Program**. Click in the robot command sequence in Example 2.21 (without the comments), and click **Run Robot Program**. For this example to work, the robot should be in cell 8F (as a result of running the program of Example 2.20).

Example 2.21

```
' Intend to return robot to start position
' by moving back and then left
' but....

MoveBack
MoveBack
MoveBack      ' ... accidentally moved too far back, kapow!
MoveLeft
MoveLeft
MoveLeft
```

The program aborts when attempting to execute the third MoveBack because of a collision with the bottom wall of the grid. The result is the same as clicking Exit Simulation. You have to relaunch the simulation from scratch by using the Visual Basic Run command.

Now develop a program that delivers the item one cell to the right and returns the robot back to the start position. In other words, you have to correct the previous logic and runtime errors. If necessary, peek at the solution in the text file CH02\SOLN\DELSOLN2.TXT using Notepad. Try other programs using DELIVER2 if you wish.

To debug and test the Calculate Labor Cost program, using Visual Basic, open project CH02\INTRO.

Visual Basic 5

Remember that the Project window has a button with a Folder icon named Toggle Folders. If the Project window shows folders Forms and Modules in the Explorer style, click the Toggle Folders button to show the files only. This may make it easier to follow the rest of the instructions.

In the Project window select the RUNME.BAS file. Make sure this file, not the files named INTRO, is highlighted. Then click **View Code.** Enter the first few lines of the program shown in Example 2.8. You may use different opening comments.

Visual Basic 4

From the File menu, Select **Save File As** (*not* Project As) and type LABCOST1 as the *file* name. From the File Menu, Select **Save Project As** (*not* File As) and type LABCOST1 as the *project* name.

Visual Basic 5

From the File menu, Select **Save Runme.Bas As** (*not* Project As) and type LAB-COST1 as the *file* name. From the File Menu, Select **Save Project As** (*not* Runme.Bas As) and type LABCOST1 as the *project* name.

Continue typing in the program while periodically backing up your work by Selecting **Save Project** from the File menu. Alternatively, you can click the **Save** button in the Visual Basic Toolbar.

To correct a syntax error, try running the program. If you made any typos that now cause syntax errors, Visual Basic will refuse to run the program. Correct the errors.

If you have no syntax errors, stop the program and make a few of your own to test out syntax error checking. For example, change one of the Dim statements to begin with the word Dom. Visual Basic will notice this immediately and will highlight the line in red. For now, ignore Visual Basic's warning.

Change one of the `PrintMsg` statements to use the command `PintMsg` instead. In this case, Visual Basic doesn't notice the error while editing the code.[9] Start the program (click the Toolbar **Start** button). Depending on how your Visual Basic options are set up, Visual Basic will flag the syntax errors now or later.[10] If no syntax errors are flagged, click the **Run Me** button. At this point, Visual Basic should flag the syntax errors. Visual Basic will refuse to continue execution until you correct these errors. Correct the syntax errors, and Visual Basic will execute the program.

Refer to Table 2.3 in Section 2.4.2. When Visual Basic has successfully started the Introduction Template, click the **Run Me** button, if you haven't done so already. Pay attention to the messages displayed in the Program Output(s) and to the prompts displayed by the Program Input(s). Type in your input; the program will wait at this point until you press the **Enter** key. Enter the data using Table 2.3, Row 1, and note the results.

Repeat the program for each test case row in Table 2.3. Note the logical errors that Section 2.4.2 describes, and note that the program will give a misleading result if you enter the word *yes* for overtime instead of *Yes*.

Note the crude formatting of the result and consider the following. Would it be useful to clarify the type of input (such as hours or dollars) required from the user? Should there be messages in the Program Output(s) box that echo back the inputs that the user has just entered?

Run the program again. When prompted for the current pay rate, type a long number that fills up the entire input box, such as **12345678901234567890123456**, and press **Enter**. The program simply hangs and will not proceed any further. But if you press **Back Space** twice to delete the last two digits and then press **Enter**, the program will continue, another logical error. You as the user are not aware that the program cannot handle input of more than 24 characters, although there is a visual cue of sorts when entering the twenty-fifth digit. This causes the previous digits to shift out of view.

To search for runtime errors, run the program again. When prompted for an input, press **Enter** without typing anything. This is known as a *null input* (nothing entered). You will see a runtime error message. For now, the explanation will be cryptic. After you click **OK** to respond to the error message, the program will abort. The program cannot handle someone pressing Enter without first typing something.

Run the program again. When prompted for pay rate, enter an amount such as **$12.50** (with the dollar sign and decimal point). The program will accept this. When prompted for the time required, enter an amount such as 45 hours. This will cause a runtime error. The command `InputNum` expects a numerical input. In Visual Basic, a valid currency input such as $12.50 is considered numerical, but something like "45 hours" is not numerical.

Run the program again. Enter valid input for the pay rate and time required. When prompted to type Yes or No, enter **0** (the digit zero) instead. This is a logical error of sorts. The program will simply interpret this as not Yes. The `InputWords` command will accept any combination of alphanumeric characters.

---

[9]*Dim is an inherent Visual Basic command (a keyword), whereas PrintMsg is specific to the Introduction Template; hence Visual Basic will only detect the error when attempting to compile the program.*
[10]*You have the option of telling Visual Basic to compile the entire code before execution or to compile only what is necessary when required. You can change this option by selecting Options from the Tools menu. If you are using Visual Basic 4, select the Advanced tab. If you are using Visual Basic 5, select the General tab. Select your compile options. Do not check Compile on Demand. By not compiling on demand, you force Visual Basic to check your entire program for syntax before it runs. The speed disadvantage is negligible for the relatively small programs we will be running.*

Run the program again. Enter very large numbers such as **9999999999999999999 99999** (24 nines) for both pay rate and time. Enter **Yes** when asked about overtime. You will encounter a runtime error that is an overflow. (Chapter 3 offers more information about overflows.)

Try some other data and see if you can find other situations to trigger errors. One of the programming skills we will be working on in the future is input validation and error trapping. It is the lack of both that increases the possibility of logic and runtime errors in this program. Click Exit on the Introduction Template to stop running the template.

To debug and test the Calculate Material Cost program, open project CH02\INTRO. In the Project Window select the RUNME.BAS file. Make sure that this file, not the files named INTRO, is highlighted.

Click **View Code**. Enter the first few lines of the program shown in Example 2.10. You may use different opening comments.

Visual Basic 4

Select **Save File As** (*not* Project As), and type **MATCOST1** as the file name.

Visual Basic 5

Select **Save Runme.Bas As** (*not* Project As), and type **MATCOST1** as the file name.

Select **Save Project As** (*not* File As) and type MATCOST1 as the project name.

Continue typing in the program. Periodically back up your work by Selecting **Save Project** from the File menu. Alternatively, click the **Save** button in the Visual Basic Toolbar.

To test the program, refer to the exercise in Section 2.4.3. Use the suggestions to set up your own test scenarios. Run the program with different inputs and observe the outputs.

7. If some inputs are negative numbers, does the program generate nonsense outputs? Explain.

8. When a non-numeric input is entered, does the program encounter a runtime error? Explain.

9. Speculate what you need to learn about programming in order to modify the program to avoid these errors.

ADDITIONAL PROBLEM SOLVING

Develop a program to calculate distance given a set of intermediate distances. Use a format similar to that for the programs in this chapter to calculate labor and material costs. Thus, you should be able to code a working program.

Hint

The code will use instructions such as PrintMsg, InputNum, InputWords, and PrintNum (see Examples 2.8 and 2.10). It will also perform addition (see Example 2.10).

Language Elements

This chapter introduces elements that are common to all programming languages.

If we are building a house, it is essential to understand the functionality of blocks, bricks, mortar, planks, and other items, and we need to know how to use a shovel, hammer, trowel, and other tools. This is even true when we work with prefabricated sections to build the house. Similarly, building a program requires extensive knowledge of the fundamental elements of a programming language, even when prefabricated components are available, as is the case with Visual Basic.

After completing this chapter, you should be able to

- Describe the three fundamental data types: Integer, Single, and String.

- Create statements that use variables and constants.

- Create statements that use operators.

- Identify and use keywords.

- Use debugging tools to examine program execution.

- Develop simple sequential programs.

In This Chapter

Cougar Canoe provides additional services to its customers that enhance customers' enjoyment of owning their canoes. Cougar Canoe supplies software that assists customers in planning trips. In this chapter we will consider simplistic prototypes of the components in the software. These include modules such as temperature and distance conversions. There is also a loan calculator that was originally intended for internal use by Cougar when it borrowed money. However, it can be adapted for use by customers who want to purchase on an installment plan. Often it is the little things that make the difference.

ABOUT THE ELEMENTS

A programming language such as Visual Basic has an organization and structure made up of fundamental elements. We need this understanding to piece the elements together in such a way to tell the computer how to solve a problem. With these elements we can build other elements (and add new elements) as we become more familiar with the language.

3.1   THE STATEMENT

*A **statement** is a line of actual (formal) code telling the computer what to do.*

A computer program consists of instructions that tell the computer what to do. Each complete instruction is a statement. In general, a program does several things using statements:

- Initialize
- Get Inputs
- Process Data (Do Computations)
- Display Outputs
- Store Data

Consider the program in that converts Fahrenheit to Celsius Example 3.1. Later you will see this example with detailed comments, but for now, examine its main components.

Example 3.1

```
Public Sub RunMe()

    ' Fahrenheit to Celsius Conversion Program

    ' Initialize
    Dim fFahr As Single, fCels As Single

    ' Get Inputs
    InputSng "Enter Temperature in Fahrenheit", fFahr

    ' Do Computations
    fCels = 5 / 9 * (fFahr - 32)

    ' Send Outputs
    PrintSng "Temperature in Celsius is ", fCels

End Sub
```

If you wish, execute this program now. To do so, open the project `CH03\FTOC01` on the student disk. This is an introductory program that lacks versatility. For example, it will crash if you enter letters or other non-numeric symbols. It will convert a temperature of -600°F without complaint (physically, it is impossible to achieve a temperature below absolute zero [-473°F]).

Some of the lines are comments (see Sections 1.10 and 2.3); these are the lines that begin with the single quote ('). The other lines are statements. Let's look at the components of the program.

```
Public Sub RunMe()
.
.
.
End Sub
```

The first and last lines begin and end a block of code (see Section 1.7).

```
' Fahrenheit to Celsius Conversion Program
```

The first comment shows the big picture and summarizes what the program does.

```
Dim fFahr As Single, fCels As Single
```

This statement performs initialization. In this case, it is a declaration. Since a computer program manipulates data in memory, it is necessary for it to do certain things (behind the scenes) to set up the memory resources. This needs to happen before a program executes code that performs actions visible to the user. `fFahr` and `fCels` are the program variables that contain values that can be modified by the program. We will explain more about declarations later.

```
InputSng "Enter Temperature in Fahrenheit", fFahr
```

This statement uses the command `InputSng` to obtain one input. It assigns the number that the user types in to the Fahrenheit variable `fFahr`. For example, if the user enters 212, variable `fFahr` will be assigned that value. It is similar to the command `InputNum` used in Chapter 2.

```
fCels = 5 / 9 * (fFahr - 32)
```

This statement performs a calculation. You may recognize the formula for converting Fahrenheit to Celsius, which involves division (/), multiplication (*), and subtraction (-). Note the use of the asterisk (*) instead of the familiar multiplication symbol (×).[1] The result of the calculation is stored in the Celsius variable `fCels`. If `fFahr` has the value of 212, then `fCels` will be assigned the value of 100.

```
PrintSng "Temperature in Celsius is ", fCels
```

This statement sends an output using the command `PrintSng`. The number it displays in the Program Outputs box is the value that was assigned to variable `fCels`. Here it will display the number 100. In general, we could have stored the answer in a file; however, we will leave the file accessing features of Visual Basic until Chapter 8. Command `PrintSng` is similar to the `PrintNum` command used in Chapter 2.

---

[1]*The multiplication symbol (×) is not an ASCII character. Since source code can be written using a normal text editor, we are restricted to using only ASCII.*

The Help Definition

The Visual Basic Help Glossary defines *statement* in this way:

A syntactically complete unit that expresses one kind of action, declaration, or definition. Normally a statement occupies a single line, although you can use a colon (:) to put more than one statement on a line. You can also use a line-continuation character to continue a single logical line onto a second physical line.

Following are sample statements. For now, ignore the ampersand (&).

```
PrintMsg "No one "      ' Normally occupy a single physical line
PrintMsg "can " : PrintMsg "have "    ' 2 statements on one line
' Next we have one statement on two lines
PrintMsg "a monopoly on a " _
& "good idea for long"
```

When these statements are executed, the following outputs are displayed:

```
No one
can
have
a monopoly on a good idea for long
```

The following sections will explain some actions, declarations, and definitions. Example 3.2 illustrates that although it is possible to combine several statements, it can make the code harder to read. Generally, we do not recommend combining statements.

Example 3.2

```
Public Sub RunMe()

    ' Fahrenheit to Celsius Conversion Program - using
    ' compacted statements

    Dim fFahr As Single, fCels As Single: InputSng "Enter ➡
    Temperature in Fahrenheit", fFahr
    fCels = 5 / 9 * (fFahr - 32): PrintSng "Temperature in ➡
    Celsius is ", fCels

End Sub
```

3.2   COMMENTS

As explained in Section 1.10, a comment is a programmer's explanation of code.

The computer ignores comments. The single quotation mark (') or the special word Rem is used to indicate that the line that follows the ' is a comment. Comments can also follow a statement on the same line.

Example 3.3

```
Sub RunMe()

    ' Fahrenheit to Celsius Conversion Program

    ' Comment on same line as statement
    Dim fFahr As Single, fCels As Single ' Initialize
```

```
' Comment using Rem word
Rem Get Inputs
InputSng "Enter Temperature in Fahrenheit", fFahr

' Comment using Rem word on same line as statement
' We must also use : to separate comment from statement
fCels = 5 / 9 * (fFahr - 32): Rem Do Computations

' Send Outputs
PrintSng "Temperature in Celsius is ", fCels

End Sub
```

If you view the code using Visual Basic, comments are easy to identify because Visual Basic color codes them in green.[2] A comment should explain the purpose of using certain executable statements in terms of the application for which the program is being used. The comments in the previous programs explain why certain statements are being used to convert Fahrenheit to Celsius—the application in this case.

3.3   CONSTANTS AND VARIABLES

3.3.1   Constants

*A **constant** is a reference to a value that remains fixed while the program is running.*

Often it is useful to use symbolic constants in place of values. You usually choose a symbolic name that identifies the purpose of the constant. For example, the value of pi (π) is a fixed number (approximately 3.141593), meaning that its value doesn't change.[3] Thus you could name the constant something such as PI.

Before you can use the constant, however, you must define it. In order to define a constant, you need to use the `Const` statement. The syntax is

Const *constantname* = *constantvalue*

For example, to define the value for pi (π), use a statement such as the following:

```
Const PI = 3.141593
```

According to Visual Basic rules, you could legally also use the following statement:

```
Const YoYo = 3.141593
```

Strange as it may seem, Visual Basic *will* accept the statement.

---

[2]*This is the default setting. You can change the color using the Environment Options/Editor Format. To do so, select **Options** in the Tools menu. With Visual Basic 4, select **Environment** in the **Options** menu. With Visual Basic 5, select the **Editor Format** tab. Select **Comment Text** and then select the desired color by clicking the **arrow** for color selection. Click the desired color and then click **OK**.*
[3]*For those who may need a bit of brushing up on geometry, pi (π) is the ratio of the circumference of a circle to its diameter. It is not possible to determine its exact value. Supercomputers have computed its value to thousands of decimal places, but the apparently random sequence continues forever.*

Const Statement Components

The `Const` statement has these parts:[4]

Const	Reserved word that begins the definition of a constant.
constantname	The name the programmer chooses for the constant.
=	Symbol (operator) used to assign a value (more about operators later).
constantvalue	The value the programmer assigns to the constant.

Here is a sample program that illustrates the use of a constant.

Example 3.4

```
Sub RunMe()

    ' Demonstrate use of a constant

    ' Define the constant
    Const PI = 3.141593

    ' Use constant in a statement
    PrintSng "The value of pi is approximately ", PI

End Sub
```

Example 3.4 illustrates the use of a constant. We will say more about the template command `PrintSng` later. For now, note that this statement prints a two-part message to the Output box. In the second part, it replaces the constant name with its actual value. Hence the result is

```
The value of pi is approximately 3.141593
```

You must define the constant *before* using it in a statement. For example, the following will not work:

Example 3.5

```
Sub RunMe()

    ' Demonstrate incorrect use of a constant

    ' Try to use constant in a statement
    PrintSng "The value of pi is approximately ", PI

    ' Define the constant after its use
    Const PI = 3.141593

End Sub
```

Points About Constants

Note the following points about constants. Refer also to Figures 3.1 and 3.2 in the next section to compare constants to variables (to be discussed).

---

[4]*For now, ignore the possibility of making a global constant.*

1. Constants can make your programs self-documenting and easy to modify. Unlike variables, constants can't be changed inadvertently while your program is running.

2. It is standard practice to name constants using all capitals. This emphasizes that it is fixed data.

3. In Visual Basic, you may need to set the appearance of a window using different colors, detect which mouse button was pressed, and other things. Code numbers are used to specify this information. For example, in some situations, 1 means that the left mouse button was pressed. In another situation, 255 means to turn something red. Neither of these meanings is obvious.

Typically, people don't want to memorize code numbers. Hence Visual Basic provides predefined constants such as `vbKeyLButton` and `vbRed`. It is not necessary for the programmer to define them since they are already defined and reserved for use by Visual Basic. Note that these constants use the prefix `vb` as their naming convention. The prefix indicates that it is a Visual Basic item.

3.3.2   Variables

*A **variable** is a unit of memory that can be altered during the execution of a program. Each variable is assigned a unique name.*

Visual Basic Help contains a more detailed definition. We have modified it slightly: A variable is a named storage location that contains data that can be modified by program statements during execution. The program statement refers to the variable by name. Figure 3.1 illustrates the use of a variable as well as a constant.

Figure 3.1
Constants and Variables
as Storage Blocks

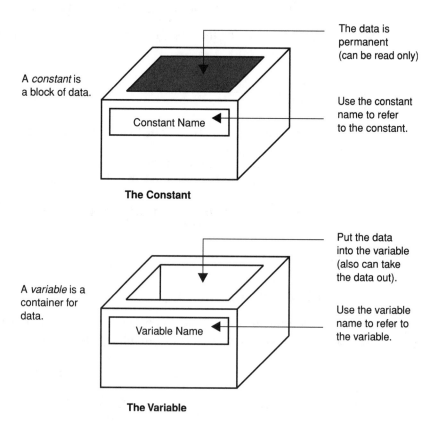

A *constant* is
a block of data.

The data is
permanent
(can be read only)

Constant Name

Use the constant
name to refer
to the constant.

The Constant

A *variable* is a
container for
data.

Put the data
into the variable
(also can take
the data out).

Variable Name

Use the variable
name to refer to
the variable.

The Variable

Variable Naming

1. The variable name is limited to 255 characters.

    jabberwockyinthedaysofyoreisentertainingbutmightnotbeagoodvariablename

    is a valid name, but is it a good name?

2. The name must begin with an alphabetic character.

    ~jabberwocky is not a valid name
    3jabberwockys is also not valid

3. The name cannot contain an embedded period.

    jabber.wocky is not a valid name

4. The name cannot be a reserved word (keyword).

    Const and End are not valid variable names since they are already used by Visual Basic. Hence, jabberwocky is a *valid* name, but fRadius is a *better* name if the variable represents the radius of a circle! (We will explain the reason for the *f* prefix shortly.)
    These rules also apply for naming constants, except that, by convention, constants are named in all capital letters.

Declarations

Before you can use the variable, you must ***declare*** it. When we enter a foreign country, we declare any plants or animals we might be bringing with us. Otherwise, the organisms could wreak havoc on the environment and the well-being of the inhabitants. Similarly, we should declare variables before using them in a program.

To declare a variable, you need to use the Dim statement. The statement to declare a variable is formally known as a ***variable declaration***. Similarly, to define a constant, we use a constant declaration. The syntax for a *simple* variable declaration is

```
Dim variablename As data type [, variablename As data type] . . .
```

This might be a good time to refer to the Syntax Conventions in Appendix A. Note that Dim and As are reserved words (also known as ***keywords***). The square brackets mean that we can declare more than one variable using the same declaration statement. Note that a comma separates variables in a Dim statement that's declaring more than one variable. Two examples follow:

```
Dim fRadius As Single ' Declare one variable
' Then declare three variables
Dim fRadius_1 As Single, fRadius_2 As Single, fRadius_3 As Single
```

Remember that we can include comments in any statement.

Section 3.4 covers data types, but until we look at more powerful features of Visual Basic, we will ignore other options for the declaration statement. When it is appropriate, we will cover other ways of declaring variables.[5] For now, examine the components of the elementary Dim statement used for declaring variables.

---

[5]*In particular, we will cover the topic of scope.*

Dim Statement Components

The elementary `Dim` statement has the following parts:

Dim	Reserved word that begins the declaration of a variable (or variables).
variablename	The name the programmer chooses for a variable.
As *data type*	Reserved word to indicate data type (Section 3.4 describes data types).

Example 3.6 includes a sample program that illustrates the use of variables.

Example 3.6

```
Sub RunMe()

    ' Demonstrate use of variables

    ' Calculate Area of a circle in sq. mm.
    ' given the radius entered by the user

    ' Declare fixed constant PI in circle
    Const PI = 3.141593

    ' Declare circle variables
    Dim fRadius As Single, fArea As Single

    ' Get user input to specify radius
    InputSng "Enter the radius in mm : ", fRadius

    ' Calculate the Area
    fArea = PI * fRadius * fRadius
    ' Show the area to the user
    PrintSng "When the radius is ", fRadius
    PrintSng "the area of the circle is ", fArea

End Sub
```

When calculating the area of a circle for any given radius (the variable), multiply it by itself and multiply it by the mathematical constant pi (π). The asterisk (*) is the multiplication operator. We will say more about the template procedure `InputSng` later; for now, note that it is used to obtain numerical data from the user. It also displays a message prompting the user for input. The following prompt will appear above the Input box:

```
Enter the radius in mm :
```

The user should type in a number and press **ENTER**. For example, if the number entered is 12.5, then the result shown in the output box would be

```
When the radius is 12.5
the area of the circle is 490.8739
```

Should You Declare? If So, When?

Customs officials typically expect you to declare any goods purchased in a foreign country before you return home. You might be able to save time and money by not declaring, but you will pay a stiff fine if you get caught. Visual Basic doesn't force you to declare variables. Whenever you use a new variable, Visual Basic will accept it. This is bad programming practice; it can lead to programming errors that may be difficult to track down. It also makes it harder for you or others to modify the program later. For this reason, the Introduction Template uses the Visual Basic option to force declarations. Each Visual Basic program contains a section called General Declarations. To force declarations, type the following in the General Declarations section:

```
Option Explicit
```

You can view the General Declarations section of the Introduction Template to find this statement. It states that all variables must be *explicitly* declared. Example 3.7 illustrates a problem that could occur if variables are not declared. What do you think it is?

Example 3.7

```
Sub RunMe()

    ' Demonstrate problem if variable
    ' declaration is not required

    ' Calculate Area of a circle in sq. mm.
    ' given the radius entered by the user

    ' Declare fixed constant PI in circle
    Const PI = 3.141593

    ' Declare circle variables
    Dim fRadius As Single, fArea As Single

    ' Get user input to specify radius
    InputSng "Enter the radius in mm : ", fRadius

    ' Calculate the Area
    fArea = PI * fRaduis * fRadius

    ' Show the area to the user
    PrintSng "When the radius is ", fRadius
    PrintSng "the area of the circle is ", fArea

End Sub
```

When you run the program, it will always calculate the area as zero. Why? Examine the code carefully. Did you find the cause? Note that one of the statements has a spelling mistake.

```
fArea = PI * fRaduis * fRadius
```

fRaduis and fRadius are interpreted as two different variables. Since the user entered data only for fRadius, Visual Basic assigned fRaduis the value of zero. Anything multiplied by zero is zero; hence, the area is zero.

If the Explicit Declaration option was used, Visual Basic would have warned you that fRaduis was not declared when it attempted to run the program. This situation is worse in long programs. If you don't specify explicit declarations, you will have a hard time finding where you accidentally used a new variable.

Initialization of Variables

Unless specified otherwise, numeric variables are automatically assigned a value of zero. Variables representing alphanumeric sequences (String variables) are initially assigned null, or no, value. As we shall see, we can assign variables to any legal value. This is what happened when the variable fRaduis was accidentally used in Example 3.7: Since we didn't assign a value, Visual Basic initialized it to zero.

Storage Allocation

Remember that the Dim statement is used to declare variables. It also has a second purpose: It allocates storage space. When a program is loaded for execution, it is loaded into random access memory (RAM) because this memory is quickly modifiable. Part of the memory is used for the machine code instructions; another part is used for variables. Figure 3.2 shows how variables (and constants) are used in memory.

The program refers to the location of the variable data by referring to the variable name. It reads the data and works with it using processor resources such as *registers* (a place in hardware where data is modified). Then the program can write results back into other (or the same) variables. Constants end up translated into fixed numbers in the program code. Variable references are like addresses specifying where in memory data is stored.

We can think of computer memory as a long street with houses. Each house has a number specifying its address. Different occupants can live in the houses, and sometimes new occupants move in to replace the original occupants. Like a house, a variable is location that can contain different occupants.

Remember that variables can be altered during the execution of a program. The Dim statement is crucial because it specifies how much of the memory is used and how the data is encoded. This is determined by the data type of the variable (discussed

Figure 3.2
Constants and Variables in
Program Memory

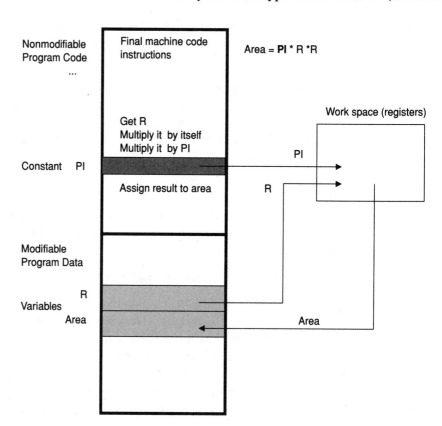

shortly). In a sense, using the `Dim` statement is like specifying how a house is built (how many rooms, etc.). Some houses can accommodate more occupants than others, and some houses have different facilities that permit different types of activities.

Points About Variables

Note the following points about variables:

1. Variables can make your programs more flexible because the user can enter data. Unlike constants or fixed data written in code, variables can change while your program is running.

2. Variable names primarily use lowercase letters, emphasizing that it is modifiable data.

Exercise

Let's say we wanted to write a program that will convert kilometers to miles (1.6 km per mile). What possible constants and variables would we use?

Solution

An analysis should show that we need to

- Input the number of kilometers.
- Multiply this number by a conversion factor.
- Display the result.

Hence, we need

- A variable representing the number of kilometers.
- A constant representing the conversion factor.
- A variable representing the result in miles.

We could name these as `fKilometers`, `KMTOMILES`, and `fMiles`, respectively.

3.4   DATA TYPES

3.4.1   The Big Picture

*A **variable** is a unit of memory that can be altered during execution of a program. Each variable is assigned a unique name. In other words, variables are chunks of data that the program can modify.*

The currency of global trade may be U.S. dollars, deutsch marks, or Japanese yen. We use some form of currency to purchase goods and services. In a sense, the currency of computer programs is data. One program module will provide data to another module and/or receive data from the same or another module. (Chapter 4 will elaborate on this process of data transfers between modules.) The point here is that programs use data. Programs use several data types—just as in international trade, for which several currency types are used. Ironically, declarations are required—again, as in international trade.

3.4.2   Common Visual Basic Data Types

Most programming languages support several *data types* (some use a different name for them). Visual Basic 4 supports eleven intrinsic data types, and we will cover the three main types: Integer, Single, and String.

The syntax for declaring these types is

Dim *integervariablename* **As Integer** [, *othervariablename* **As** *otherdata type*] . . .
Dim *singlevariablename* **As Single** [, *othervariablename* **As** *otherdata type*] . . .
Dim *stringvariablename* **As String** [, *othervariablename* **As** *otherdata type*] . . .

It is a good practice to indicate the data type when naming a variable. We will follow the *Hungarian Notation* that many programmers use. It is a technique used for identifying the data type by using a prefix when naming a variable. The prefixes are

n for Integer (*i* is reserved for *index*)
f for Single (the *f* refers to *floating point format*)
s for String (another reason for not using *s* for *single*)

For example, refer to the following:

```
' Declare variables
Dim nNumberOfCoins As Integer, fAmountOfMoney As Single
Dim sCurrencyName as String

' Assign appropriate values
sCurrencyName = "Nickel"
nNumberOfCoins = 24
fAmountOfMoney = 1.20 ' Amount in dollars for 24 nickels
```

Table 3.1 shows the characteristics of the three data types. String values are enclosed in quotation marks (").

Visual Basic uses the letter *E* to represent powers of ten for the Single data type; hence:

7.567E24 represents 7.567×10^{24}, which represents 10 multiplied by itself 24 times (a trillion trillion), multiplied by 7.567.
–9.00342E-12 represents -9.00342×10^{-12} which represents $-9.00342 \times 1/10^{12}$;
–9.00343 multiplied by the fraction 1 divided by 10 multiplied by itself 12 times.

Table 3.1
Common Visual Basic Data Types

Data Type	Description	Examples
Integer	Whole number between -32,768 and 32,767	12, 0, -45, -4579, and 4679
Single	Number from $\pm -3.403823 \times 10^{38}$ to $\pm 1.401298 \times 10^{-45}$	5.008, -0.00023, 7.567E24, and 9.00342E-12
String	Sequence of characters, enclosed in quotations, representing text information	"Charles Babbage", "R2D2", and "The world is round."

Let's look at a variation of the program of Example 3.6, which expects the radius to be entered as whole (integer) numbers.

Example 3.8

```
Public Sub RunMe()

    ' Demonstrate data types

    ' Calculate Area of a circle in sq. mm.
    ' given the radius entered by the user

    ' Declare fixed constant PI in circle
    Const PI = 3.141593

    ' Declare circle variables (and specify data types)
    Dim nRadius As Integer
    Dim fArea As Single
    Dim sMessage As String

    ' Get user input to specify radius
    InputInt "Enter the radius in mm : ", nRadius

    ' Calculate the Area
    fArea = PI * nRadius * nRadius

    ' Compose first message then echo back radius
    sMessage = "When the radius is "
    PrintInt sMessage, nRadius

    ' Compose second message and show the area to the user
    sMessage = "the area of the circle is "
    PrintSng sMessage, fArea

End Sub
```

There are several things to note in this program.

1. Variable declarations specify the data type.

2. Command `InputInt` accepts Integer type data from the user to assign it to variable `nRadius`.

3. The calculation for area is a Single data type because variable `fArea` was declared as `Single`.

4. Command `PrintInt` prints out Integer type data (stored in variable `nRadius`).

5. Command `PrintSng` prints out Single type data (stored in variable `fArea`).

6. Commands `PrintInt` and `PrintSng` use a string variable to specify the accompanying message.

7. Variable `sMessage` is used twice to specify two different messages.

When the user enters 10, the program output looks like this:

```
When the radius is 10
the area of the circle is 314.1593
```

The program will output the same result if the user enters 10.5. The `InputInt` command rounds 10.5 to the whole number 10. However, when the user enters 10.6, the output becomes

```
When the radius is 11
the area of the circle is 380.1328
```

The `InputInt` command rounds 10.6 to the whole number 11. (This is a good time to refer to the Introduction Template Command Summary in Appendix B.)

Visual Basic Help Hands-On Exercise

To get a little practice with what you've learned so far, launch Visual Basic Help by selecting **Contents** from the Visual Basic Help menu (or click the **Search** button if Visual Basic Help is already running). Click the **Index** tab, and then click in the first text box. Type **data types, summary**. Click **Summary** in the Index Entry box. Then click **Display**. Note the information about the data types. Don't worry if you do not understand all of the details, since you will need additional material to comprehend all of it.

3.4.3   The Details

In some cases it is useful to know what goes on "under the hood." Recall that the computer works with binary numbers. Sometimes the computer interprets binary numbers as coded instructions to tell it what to do (see Figure 1.3); at other times binary numbers are interpreted as data. This interpretation depends on the data type. The computer processor can select binary numbers in units of 8 bits, known as bytes. Each *byte* in memory has a unique address.

In the long street analogy discussed earlier, consider apartment buildings instead of houses. Each apartment is addressable. The resident in the apartment is a byte. Some buildings have only two apartments, some have four, and some are high-rises with numerous apartments.

The Integer Data Type

Integer data is stored as a 16-bit binary number. Since the computer accesses memory in bytes (8 bits), 2 bytes are required. The data is encoded using a *signed* binary system. Positive numbers start with a 0 bit, and negative numbers start with a 1 bit. There are 65,536 possible combinations of 16 bits (think of flipping 16 coins; there are only 65,536 possible combinations of heads or tails) (see Figure 3.3).

The Single Data Type

Single data is stored as a 32-bit number (4 bytes). The encoding is known as *floating point*, the binary equivalent of using scientific notation that is useful for representing numbers of any size (e.g., 1.208×10^{-7} is more convenient to write than 0.0000001208). In this system there is a sign bit to indicate positive or negative. The fraction section encodes a sum of fractions of 2, as shown in Figure 3.4. The exponent encodes what the fraction is multiplied by as a power of 2. This is a standardized coding scheme used by most computers.

The Single data type can be used to store numbers over a wider range than for Integer data.

Figure 3.3
The Integer Data Type

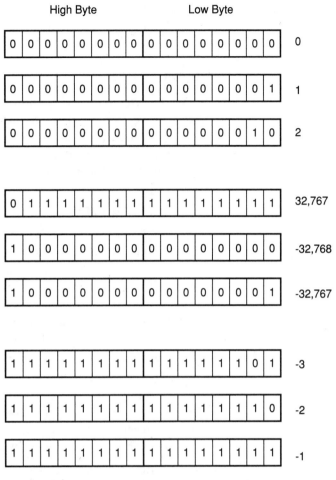

There are 65,536 possible combinations of ones and zeros
to represent numbers -32,768 to 32,767

Figure 3.4
The Single Data Type

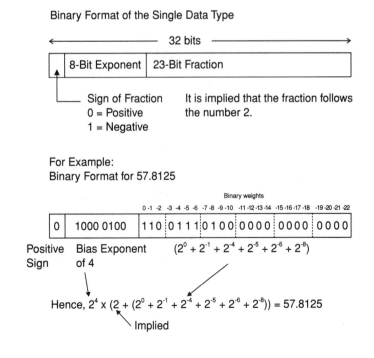

Exercise

Here is a challenge: Why would one use the Integer data type?

Solution

Consider the size and the way the information is encoded. Since the Integer type is smaller (requires fewer bytes), the program will be more memory efficient. The part about the information format is trickier: The binary format for the Single data type (see Figure 3.4) has three components. Therefore, the computer hardware has extra work to do to sort out the components during the behind-the-scenes processing.

The String Data Type

The ***ANSI Format for 16-bit Applications.***   The String data type is stored as a sequence of characters. In the ANSI (American National Standards Institute) system, each character is 1 byte. Table 3.2 shows the type of ANSI characters. ANSI codes 0 to 127 are identical to the ASCII (American Standard Code for Information Interchange) code (see Figure 3.5). Strings in general can be of variable length up to something less than 64 kilobytes (KB). A string can't be 64 KB long because some additional bytes are required for storage overhead. Note that 1 KB = 2^{10} = 1024.

Unicode Strings.   Visual Basic 5 and the 32-bit version of Visual Basic 4 stores strings as *Unicode.* Unicode requires 2 bytes to store each character. When using the ANSI code, only 256 (2^8 = 256) different characters are possible. With Unicode, 65,536 (2^{16} = 65,536) different characters are possible. A string encoded using Unicode can represent any character in any language on our planet. When the string only contains ANSI characters, the high byte in the 2-byte character is all zeros.

Fixed-Length Strings.   As we shall see in Chapters 8, 9, and 12, some data must be stored as fixed-length strings. These may improve program speed since overhead isn't required to determine the length of the string or to allocate or deallocate memory when the string length changes.

```
Dim sVariableName As String * length [, otherVariablename As ➡
otherdata type] . . .
```

Consider the program in Example 3.9.

Example 3.9

```
Sub RunMe()

    ' Demonstrate fixed-length string
```

Table 3.2
Character Types in the ANSI Code

ANSI Code	Types of Characters
0 to 31	Control characters representing nonprintable functions, such as carriage return or line feed
32 to 127	Printable alphanumeric characters or symbols, such as A, 3, and %
128 to 255	Printable special characters, such as some letters in international alphabets, accents, currency symbols, and fractions

Figure 3.5
The ANSI String
Data Type*

A String is a sequence of characters.

For example:

```
Dim sVar as String
sVar = "The tolerance is 15µm."
```

sVar is stored in memory as follows (1 byte per character in ANSI):

01010100	01101000	01100101	00100000	. . .
T	h	e	(space)	

00110001	00110101	00100000	10110101	01101101	00101110
1	5	(space)	µ	m	.(period)

Note "15" is made up of characters "1" and "5", not the number 15.

*Assignment statement for sVar is hypothetical since it uses non-ASCII µ.

```
' Declare fixed-length string
Dim sMessage As String * 20

sMessage = "Life is too short"
PrintMsg sMessage

sMessage = "to worry about every little thing."
PrintMsg sMessage    ' Truncated to 20 characters.

End Sub
```

In Example 3.9, the string is restricted to 20 characters. An ANSI string would be 20 bytes long. The equivalent Unicode string would be 40 bytes long; each pair is 1 byte of zeros followed by a byte with the ANSI code. When the program is run, the output will look like this:

```
Life is too short
to worry about every
```

Why didn't the program print the entire second line? Remember that the string was declared as 20 characters long. When sMessage is assigned to

```
"to worry about every little thing"
```

only the first 20 characters are stored in memory!

3.4.4   The Variant

Note

Beginners should *not* use the variant. In fact, the template commands will not accept variants.

Previously, we discussed the need to define the data type when declaring variables. Actually, the default data type in Visual Basic is the **variant.** A variant variable can contain any data type, and you do not need to worry about defining its type ahead of time.

This sounds good. In the hands of an experienced programmer, it can be a very powerful tool for necessary flexibility in complex programs. In the hands of a beginner, errors can occur since you depend on Visual Basic to interpret the data in the appropriate way. In fact, even professionals avoid it unless its use is necessary. Perhaps 1682 is a number (Single or Integer); perhaps it is part of a sentence (string) describing a year when Halley's comet was spotted. The variant is stored using more overhead than for the other data types in order to accommodate its changing nature. This makes programs that use variants less efficient, but there are certain situations with the advanced Visual Basic program when variants are necessary.

The program in Example 3.10 attempts to use variants. However, it will not run because the commands in the Introduction Template will not accept variants. If variants are to be discouraged, it wouldn't make sense to have commands that accept variants, would it? (Note that some languages such as Java and C++, do not use variants at all.) An end-of-chapter exercise will explore this example further.

Example 3.10

```
Sub RunMe()

    ' Demonstrate variant variables

    ' Try to calculate Area of a circle in sq. mm.
    ' given the radius entered by the user
    ' However, this program will not work!!!

    ' Declare fixed constant PI in circle
    Const PI = 3.141593

    ' Declare circle variables (and specify variant)
    ' Prefix vnt indicates variant
    Dim vntRadius As Variant
    Dim vntArea      ' Variant since data type not specified
    Dim vntMessage   ' ditto

    ' Get user input to specify radius
    ' Error here because InputInt expects integer data
    InputInt "Enter the radius in mm : ", vntRadius

    ' Calculate the Area
    vntArea = PI * vntRadius * vntRadius

    ' Compose first message then echo back radius
    ' Also error but we never get this far
    ' unless first error is corrected
    ' PrintInt expects string followed by integer
    vntMessage = "When the radius is "
    PrintInt vntMessage, vntRadius

    ' Compose second message and show the area to the user
    ' Ditto concerning errors
    vntMessage = "the area of the circle is "
    PrintSng vntMessage, vntArea

End Sub
```

3.4.5   Template Command Summary

Since we have covered data types, this is a good time to refer to information about the template commands:

1. `InputInt` prompt the user to input an Integer.

2. `InputSng` prompt the user to input a Single.

3. `InputStr` prompt the user to input a String.

4. `PrintMsg` prints a message.

5. `PrintInt` prints an explanation followed by an Integer value.

6. `PrintSng` prints an explanation followed by a Single value.

7. `PrintStr` prints an explanation followed by a String value.

For more details, refer to the Introduction Template Command Summary in Appendix B.

3.5   OPERATORS AND EXPRESSIONS

*An **operator** is a symbol that can cause a change in an expression such as an arithmetic operation. An **expression** is any part of a statement that evaluates to (expresses) one distinct value.*

Consider one of the statements in the program of Example 3.1.

```
fCels = 5 / 9 * (fFahr - 32)
```

This statement contains several operators and several expressions. To assist with the explanation, assume that variable `fFahr` has a value of 212. Table 3.3 will help you evaluate the statement.

There are several types of operators: arithmetic, string, comparison, and logical. This chapter will cover arithmetic and string operators. (The others are used for decision making, a topic covered in Chapter 5.)

Table 3.3
Evaluation of the statement: fCels = 5 / 9 * (fFahr - 32)

Expression	What happened
`(fFahr - 32)`	An expression that evaluates to 212 - 32 = 180 . The subtraction operator is the minus sign (-). The enclosing parentheses ( ) specify that this expression is evaluated first.
`5 / 9`	An expression that evaluates to approximately 0.5556. The division operator is the forward slash (/).
`5 / 9 * (fFahr - 32)`	An expression that evaluates to $0.5556 \times 180 = 100$. The multiplication operator is the asterisk (*).
`fCels = 5 / 9 * (fFahr - 32)`	An expression that *assigns* the value 100 to variable `fCels`. The assignment operator is the equals sign (=).

3.5.1   The Assignment Operator

The equals sign (=) is the ***assignment operator***. It *assigns* a value to a variable. The general syntax for a statement using the assignment operator is

```
[Let] variablename = expression(s)
```

For example, the following statement

```
fTax = 0.15 * fPrice
```

will assign variable `fTax` with the value of the expression `0.15 * fPrice`, which is 0.15 multiplied by the value stored in variable `fPrice`. The assignment operator does not mean "equals to." For example, the following statements are perfectly valid:

```
nCounter = 3                    ' Statement 1
nCounter = nCounter + 1         ' Statement 2
```

Mathematically, this is impossible if we interpret the operator to mean "equal to." In this case, `nCounter` is assigned to 3 in Statement 1. In Statement 2, `nCounter` is assigned to its previous value added to 1. Hence, in Statement 2, `nCounter` is assigned the value of 4. The key point is that a variable is being *assigned*.

Unfortunately, Visual Basic also uses the equals sign (=) to represent the equality relational operator (to be described in Chapter 5). The assignment operator (=) is *not* the same as equals to or equality. A variable name is always immediately to the left of the assignment operator. To avoid ambiguity, you may prefer to use the optional word `Let` to implicitly state that assignment is to be performed. Hence, you could have written the previous statements as

```
Let nCounter = 3                ' Statement 1
Let nCounter = nCounter + 1     ' Statement 2
```

3.5.2   Arithmetic Operators

Table 3.4 shows the arithmetic operators. The examples assumes single variables have been declared. Some operators may require additional explanation.

Exponentiation (^)

Exponentiation means to multiply a number by itself the number of times specified by an exponent. For example, `2^3` results in $2 \times 2 \times 2 = 8$. A negative exponent means a fraction of the result if the exponent were positive. For example, 2^-3 results in the fraction $^1/_8 = 0.125$.

Integer Division (\ )

Integer division involves rounding both numerators and denominators to whole numbers prior to division. The result of division is a whole number without the remainder. For example, 37.6 \ 5.2 would be rounded to 38 divided by 5. The result would be 7, and the remainder would not be shown.

Modulus (Mod)

The Modulus operator returns the remainder of division. For example, 37.7 Mod 5.2 would be the remainder of 38 divided by 5. Since 38 divided by 5 is $7^3/_5$, the remainder is 3.

Table 3.4
Arithmetic operators

Operator	Meaning	Example (f1 = 15.3 : f2 = 2.3)
^	Exponentiation	fAns = 2^-3 ' 0.125 is 1 divided by ' 2 multiplied by itself three times
-	Negation	fAns = -fAns ' -0.125 is negative of previous value
*	Multiplication	fAns = f1 * f2 '35.19 is 15.3 multiplied by 2.3
/	Floating Point Division	fAns = f1 / f2 ' 6.65217391304348 is 15.3 divided by 2.3
\	Integer Division	fAns = f1 \ f2 ' 7 since 15 divided by 2 is 7 with some remainder ' note 15.3 rounded to 15 and 2.3 rounded to 2
Mod	Modulus	fAns = f1 Mod f2 ' 1 is remainder of 15 \ 7
+	Addition	fAns = f1 + f2 ' 17.6 is 15.3 plus 2.3
-	Subtraction	fAns = f1 - f2 ' 13 is 15.3 subtract 2.3

Coin Change Application

The following shows how we can use the Modulus operator (Mod) in a simple example that converts pennies to the nearest number of dimes, a nickel if necessary, and the remainder (always less than five) in pennies. Example 3.11 shows the program (project CH03\COIN in the student disk).

Example 3.11

```
Public Sub RunMe()

    ' Coin Change Program
    ' Illustrates an application for the Integer Divide
    ' and Modulus (Mod) operators.
    ' E.g. 237 pennies becomes 23 dimes, 1 nickel
    ' with 2 pennies left over
    ' Written by Cody Wizard, Jan. 11, 1997

    ' Define constants and declare variables
    Const DIME = 10
    Const NICKEL = 5

    Dim nNumberOfPennies As Integer, nLeftOverPennies As ➡
    Integer
    Dim nNumberOfDimes As Integer, nNumberOfNickels As Integer

    ' Tell user briefly what this program is doing.
    PrintMsg "We convert pennies into dimes and nickels"
    PrintMsg " "

    ' Get number of pennies from user
    InputInt "Enter number of pennies ", nNumberOfPennies
    ' Echo back input to user
    PrintInt "Number of pennies is ", nNumberOfPennies
```

```
' Determine number of dimes
nNumberOfDimes = nNumberOfPennies \ DIME
nLeftOverPennies = nNumberOfPennies Mod DIME

' Determine number of nickels
' In this case, only possible answers are 0 or 1
nNumberOfNickels = nLeftOverPennies \ NICKEL
' Rest is left over as pennies
nLeftOverPennies = nLeftOverPennies Mod NICKEL

' Display outputs
PrintInt " Number of dimes is ", nNumberOfDimes
PrintInt " Number of nickels is ", nNumberOfNickels
PrintInt " Pennies left over is ", nLeftOverPennies

End Sub
```

Demonstration

To experiment with operators, run the demonstration program. Open project CH03\ OPDEMO1 on your student disk. In the hands-on exercises, you will work with the operators using the Visual Basic Debug window.

Order of Precedence

Table 3.4 also illustrates the order of *precedence*, which refers to the order in which operators are used in a statement. For example, exponentiation is performed before multiplication, which in turn is performed before addition. Multiplication and division (*, /) have the same precedence, and addition and subtraction (+, –) have the same precedence. Operators with the same precedence are executed from left to right. Consider the following statement.

```
fAns = 5 + 3 * 2 ^ 4 - 7 * -9 / 3
```

Visual Basic evaluates this as follows. The parentheses ( ) show intermediate results.

2 ^ 4 is evaluated to 16   ' ^ has highest precedence
–9 is negative nine   ' negation is next highest precedence
' Next evaluate * (multiplication) and / (division) in left-to-right order.
3 * (16) is evaluated to 48
7 * (–9) is evaluated to –63
(–63) /3 is evaluated to –21
' Next evaluate + (add) and – (subtract) in left-to-right order
5 + (48) is evaluated to 53
(53) – (–21) is evaluated to 74
fAns = (74) means that the value of 74 is assigned to variable fAns

Note that the assignment operator (=) has the lowest precedence, meaning it is always performed last.

Overriding the Order of Precedence

The parentheses ( ) can force some parts of an expression to be evaluated before others. Thus we can force addition operations to be performed before anything else. Consider the following:

```
fAns = ((5 + 3) * 2) ^ 4 - 7 * -9 / 3
```

This results in the following:

(5 + 3) evaluates to 8
((8) * 2) evaluates to 16
(16) ^ 4 evaluates to 65536
7 * –9 / 3 evaluates to –21
(65536) – (–21) evaluates to 65557
fAns = (65557) means that the value of 65557 is assigned to variable fAns.

3.5.3   A String Operator

The only string operator is *concatenation.* This strange-sounding word means "to combine two strings." Consider the code in Example 3.12.

Example 3.12

```
Public Sub RunMe()

    ' Demo the concatenation string operator.

    ' The string variables we will concatenate
    Dim sHead As String, sTail As String

    ' The string variable that will be the result of concatenation
    Dim sHeadTail As String

    ' Assign values to the strings we are going to join
    sHead = "In the beginning "
    sTail = " we can only look to the future."

    ' Now join them using the concatenation operator
    sHeadTail = sHead & sTail

    ' Show result
    PrintMsg sHeadTail

End Sub
```

Running this program will produce the following display:

```
In the beginning  we can only look to the future.
```

Concatenation has a lower precedence than any of the arithmetic operators mentioned earlier. Unfortunately (depending on your point of view), the plus operator (+) can also be used for concatenation if applied to strings. This may produce misleading results (logical errors) in certain situations, so we discourage the practice.

Use the & operator for concatenation to eliminate ambiguity and provide self-documenting code. Example 3.13 illustrates the distinction between concatenation and addition. It also shows how we can output the quotation mark itself. Note that we can also specify that the concatenation operation occurs when using the PrintMsg or PrintStr commands.

Example 3.13

```
Public Sub RunMe()

     ' Demonstrate string concatenation
     ' In this program we also show how to display
     ' the quotation mark itself.
     ' Also, the user is supposed to enter values
     ' that could be numeric.
     ' E.g. entering 123 and 456 will result in a
     ' string concatenation of 123456
     ' NOT in an arithmetic sum of 579 !
     ' But nothing stops a user from entering non-numeric
     ' data such as -> the medium is the message <-

     ' Written by Cody Wizard, Jan. 15, 1997

     Dim sQuote As String      'To display Quotation mark
     Dim sNum1 As String, sNum2 As String
     Dim sNum3 As String

     ' To display quotation marks, we need to
     ' use a string variable to represent the symbol
     ' This is because Visual Basic uses " ... " to
     ' delimit string values
     ' Quotation mark itself displayed by
     ' enclosing "" within "   "
     sQuote = """"

     ' Code should be reasonably self-documenting from here

     PrintMsg "  Echo back inputs without quotation marks"
     InputStr "Enter number 1", sNum1
     PrintStr "sNum1 = ", sNum1
     InputStr "Enter number 2", sNum2
     PrintStr "sNum2 = ", sNum2
     PrintMsg "" ' Prints out a null string to force new line

     PrintMsg "  Prove that plus (+) concatenates strings"
     PrintStr "sNum1 + sNum2 = ", sNum1 + sNum2
     PrintMsg "However, do note that string value shown "
     PrintMsg "without quotation marks."
     PrintMsg ""

     PrintMsg "  Echo back inputs with quotation marks to "
     PrintMsg "   emphasize they are strings"
     PrintStr "sNum1 = ", sQuote & sNum1 & sQuote
     PrintStr "sNum2 = ", sQuote & sNum2 & sQuote
     PrintMsg ""

     PrintMsg "  Show result of using concatenation "
     PrintMsg "   operator (&) and use quotation marks"
     ' Concatenate now
     sNum3 = sNum1 & sNum2
     PrintStr "sNum1 & sNum2 = ", sQuote & sNum3 & sQuote

End Sub
```

The program asks the user to enter two numbers. However, behind the scenes (to the user), the `InputStr` command is reading in string type data. Hence, if the user enters numbers **1234** and **5678**, the result will be 12345678. There is a logical error. The user is free to enter the words **cat** and **dog,** with the result being **catdog**.

Initial and Null String Values

Actually the initial value is *null*. If a string variable is not assigned to any value, Visual Basic automatically assigns it a null value. Null essentially means "nothing." In terms of memory storage, null means that the string variable has no characters (see Figure 3.5). The syntax for null is "" (two quotes with a no space between them). This is not the same as a *whitespace* character, which puts a space between visible characters. For example, if you entered `"Cougar"` & `"Canoe"`, the display would be `"CougarCanoe"`. This is the use of the null value. Entering `"Cougar"` &`" "` &`"Canoe"` would result in a display of `"Cougar Canoe"`. Note the use of the whitespace value. Example 3.14 also illustrates the difference.

Example 3.14

```
Public Sub RunMe()

    ' Demonstrate null strings

    Dim sNull As String, sIn1 As String, sIn2 As String
    Dim sIn1NullIn2 As String

    ' First show that strings are initially null.
    PrintMsg " String variables have default null value"
    PrintMsg " until they are reassigned."
    PrintStr " sIn1 value is : ", sIn1
    PrintStr " sIn2 value is : ", sIn2
    PrintMsg "" ' Blank line

    ' Now assign non-null values to strings
    PrintMsg "Next we will input values"
    PrintMsg "Please press <Enter> immediately after the word"
    InputStr "Enter any non-null value for sIn1", sIn1
    PrintStr " sIn1 value is : ", sIn1
    InputStr "Enter any non-null value for sIn2:", sIn2
    PrintStr " sIn2 value is : ", sIn2
    PrintMsg "" ' Blank line

    ' Explicitly assign null to show how to code it
    sNull = ""

    ' Concatenate with null to show effect of null
    sIn1NullIn2 = sIn1 & sNull & sIn2
    PrintStr "sIn1 & sNull & sIn2 is : ", sIn1NullIn2
    ' Concatenate with whitespace
    PrintStr " sIn1 & whitespace $ sIn2 is : ", sIn1 & " " & sIn2

End Sub
```

Note: String variables have a default value of null until they are assigned to something else. Is it possible to do more processing with strings? You bet you can, but you will have to use something other than operators. In Chapter 4 we will look at functions that can process strings by removing characters and other things.

3.6   KEYWORDS

Keywords *are words or symbols in a programming language that have reserved special meaning to a compiler or interpreter. You cannot use a keyword as a name. Table 3.5 shows the Visual Basic keywords that we have encountered so far. The keyword categories more or less resemble the task classification used in Visual Basic Help. In the hands-on exercises, we will explore the Help system further.*

For example, the following would be illegal:

```
' Try to declare End as a variable of type Single
Dim End as Single     ' Illegal since End is a keyword
```

Visual Basic highlights keywords in blue. If you insist, you can modify the Visual Basic editor options to highlight keywords in a foreground color other than blue.

Table 3.5
Common Keywords

Keyword	Meaning
Category: Operators	
=	Assignment operator. See Section 3.5.1. As we will see in Chapter 5, it can also mean equality.
^, *, /, \, Mod, +, -	Arithmetic operators. See Table 3.3 (Section 3.5.2).
&	Concatenation operator. See Section 3.5.3.
Category: Data Types	
Integer, Single, String, Variant	Data types. See Sections 3.4.2 and 3.4.4.
Category: Declarations	
Public Sub *procedurename* ()	Defines beginning of a procedure. See Note a.
End Sub	Defines end of a procedure. See Note a.
Dim, As	Used in declaration of variables. See Section 3.3.2.
Option Explicit	Statement that forces declaration of all variables.
Category: Miscellaneous	
Let	Used with = to clarify its use for assignment.
'	Indicates the beginning of a comment.

ᵃThe block of code that is bound by Public Sub and End Sub is known as a *procedure*. So far we have coded only one procedure whose name has always been RunMe.

Template Commands

Note that although commands such as `PrintMsg`, `PrintSng`, `InputSng`, and so on do have special meaning, they are not keywords in Visual Basic. They have been added to the set of Visual Basic commands by the person who wrote the Introduction Template program (`INTRO`).

3.7   SYNTAX ERRORS

Syntax errors are coding mistakes that prevent statements from being compiled. Section 1.6 introduced syntax errors. Now we can show more examples.

```
Sub RunMe()

    ' Demonstrate some syntax errors

    this first line is a syntax error because the single quote ➥
    is missing
    Dom nVar1 as Integer     ' Misspelling a keyword such as Dim
    Dim nVar2 as Integer     ' Okay
    PrintInt "nVar2 is: " nVar2    ' Missing comma before nVar2

End Sub
```

Syntax errors are easy to fix because the Visual Basic compiler will point them out to you and suggest ways to fix them. In some cases it will warn you when you try to enter the statement even as you are typing, so syntax error is almost not an issue with modern software development tools.

Errors of Style?

The following code will compile (no syntax errors) and run (no runtime errors). However, it breaks conventions practiced by many programmers.

```
Sub RunMe()

    ' This code violates some conventions

    Const bailofhay = 15
    Dim sVariable as Integer
    sVARIABLE = 2
    PrintInt "The output is ", bailofhay * sVARIABLE

End Sub
```

Exercise

What conventions have been broken?

Solution

The constant name is not in all capitals nor is the integer variable name prefixed by the lowercase *n*. The variable name mainly uses capitals, which implies that it is fixed in value instead of being variable.

3.8   TROUBLESHOOTING: RUNTIME ERRORS

Section 2.4 described runtime errors. Example 3.15 illustrates some of them. Later, in the Hands-On Exercises, you will use the Visual Basic debugging tools to step through the code. You will be able to correct an error and continue execution until you encounter the next error.

Example 3.15

```
Public Sub RunMe()

    ' Demonstrate some runtime errors
    ' We will use Visual Basic Debug to
    ' work past the errors.

    Dim fNumerator As Single, fDenominator As Single
    Dim fQuotient As Single
    Dim fSquare As Single, fSquareRoot As Single
    Dim nLarge As Integer

    ' Get the Numerator
    InputSng "Enter a numerator ", fNumerator
    PrintSng "The numerator is: ", fNumerator

    ' Assign Denominator to zero by default
    ' since we have simply not assigned it.

    ' Now try to divide
    fQuotient = fNumerator / fDenominator
    ' Use Debug Window to modify fDenominator
    ' so we can go past this point.

    PrintSng "The quotient is: ", fQuotient

    ' Let's see what happens when we try to
    ' find a square root of a negative number

    InputSng "Enter a positive number", fSquare

    ' First find square root of positive number
    fSquareRoot = fSquare ^ 0.5
    PrintSng "Square root of +ve: ", fSquareRoot

    ' Next try square root of negative number
    fSquare = -fSquare
    fSquareRoot = fSquare ^ 0.5
    PrintSng "Square root of -ve: ", fSquareRoot

    ' What happens if we enter a number outside the
    ' integer range -32768 to +32767
    InputInt "Enter a large number", nLarge

    ' An overflow error could occur if the result
    ' is outside the range

    nLarge = nLarge * nLarge
```

```
' What happens if we attempt to assign a
' numeric variable to an alphabetic string?

fSquare = "Square"
```

End Sub

The errors that occur are an attempt to

- Divide by zero.

- Find the square root of a negative number. (What, multiplied by itself, equals a negative number?)

- Enter a value outside the range of the data type.

- Perform an arithmetic calculation, the result of which is outside the range of the data type.

- Assign a different data type to a variable of another data type.

Visual Basic will (usually) automatically perform a data type conversion when possible. For example, if we enter a number such as 123.456 when the program is expecting an integer, Visual Basic will round the value to 123. As shown in Example 3.15, data type conversion is not always possible.

Exercise

What precautions should a programmer take to avoid the runtime errors encountered in Example 3.15?

Solution

Since we have yet to cover more about the language, it is not be possible to outline a specific solution here. However, speculation is still possible. A program could do the following:

- Check for a zero denominator before attempting division.

- Check for a negative number prior to attempting to find its square root.

- Perform input validation to ensure inputs are within range (and of the correct data type).

- Convert variables to a data type with a larger range.

- Check the data type of a variable prior to using it, if in doubt.

3.9   SAMPLE PROBLEMS

This section develops the requirements, design, code, and documentation for software. Recall the software life-cycle phases: concept, requirements, design, coding, testing, and maintenance. (At this stage, we will not yet consider the maintenance phase.)

3.9.1   Unit Conversions From Meters

Cougar Canoe provides a simple calculator for their customers to use when exploring the waterways with their canoes. It converts meters to feet and statute miles length information, and it converts meters to fathoms for water depth information.

Concept

Convert meters to feet, statute miles, and fathoms.

Requirements

- Input number of meters.
- Process by converting meters to feet, statute miles, and fathoms.
- Output feet, statute miles, and fathoms.
    Example: x meters is y feet
- Store Results is not applicable.

Wait a minute. How do we convert? At this point, we would refer to a published unit conversion table and find that

- 1 meter = 3.2808399 feet
- 1 meter = 0.000621377119 statute miles
- 1 meter = 0.54680665 fathoms

Design

Write pseudocode that looks something like that in Example 3.16.

Example 3.16
RunMe

```
' Get input
Meters = user input
Display info about Meters        ' we should also echo it back

' Process
Feet = 3.2808399 x Meters
Miles = 0.000621377119 x Meters
Fathoms = 0.54680665 x Meters

' Output
Display "For this number of meters,"
Display info about Feet
Display info about Miles
Display info about Fathoms
```

End RunMe

It seems evident from the processing steps that we will need to use variables of type Single. Some refinement is necessary when we consider how the `PrintMsg` and `PrintSng` operate. We need to compose the information that is used in each Print Type command. We can do this in the coding phase.

Coding

We can translate the pseudocode as follows.

Example 3.17

```
Public Sub RunMe()

    ' Convert meters to feet, miles, and fathoms

    ' Variables required
    Dim fMeters As Single, fFeet As Single
    Dim fMiles As Single, fFathoms As Single

    ' Tell user what program is about
    PrintMsg "This program converts meters to"
    PrintMsg "feet, miles, and fathoms"
    PrintMsg ""

    ' Get number of meters
    InputSng "Enter number of meters", fMeters
    PrintSng "The number of meters is ", fMeters

    ' Perform unit conversions
    fFeet = 3.2808399 * fMeters
    fMiles = 0.00062137119 * fMeters
    fFathoms = 0.54680665 * fMeters

    ' Display results
    PrintMsg "For this number of meters,"
    PrintSng " the number of feet is ", fFeet
    PrintSng " the number of miles is ", fMiles
    PrintSng " the number of fathoms is ", fFathoms

End Sub
```

When the user enters 5, the output will look like this:

```
This program converts meters to
feet, miles, and fathoms

The number of meters is 5
For this number of meters,
 the number of feet is 16.4042
 the number of miles is 3.106856E-03
 the number of fathoms is 2.734033
```

Although the output is not attractive, our present knowledge of programming does not permit us to use more flexible output formats, such as

```
5 meters = 16.4042 feet
```

(Don't worry, we will utilize more features of Visual Basic in the next chapter.) Note the output for fathoms. Visual Basic automatically displays scientific notation for numbers with many digits to the right of the decimal point.

Testing

Try different outputs. If a user enters **1e38**, the program will run successfully, but if the user enters **2e38**, there is a runtime error. Why? Remember what the range of the single data type is. When the program attempts to convert to feet, the range is exceeded; hence there is an overflow error. On the other hand, why would anyone expect to go such astronomical distances in a canoe?

3.9.2   A Simple Thank-You Form Letter

When a customer purchases a canoe, she or he receives a thank-you letter from the president of Cougar Canoe. For example, if Gord Elliot purchased a canoe, he would receive the following letter (deliberately simplified for the purposes of this exercise):

To *Gord Elliot*

Dear *Gord*

Thank you for purchasing one of our canoes.

Sincerely
Dawn Redbird, President

Concept

The overall goal is to write a standard thank-you letter addressed to a customer personally.

Requirements

Determine the specific information that is required. Look at the sample letter. The last three nonblank lines are the same. The first uses the customer's full name and the second uses the first name only.

- The required inputs are customer first name and last name.
- The required processing is to compose the letter.
- The required outputs are to display the letter.
- The required storage would be to save it to a file (but we will ignore this for now).

Design

Convert the requirements to a detailed specification of steps. We can state the design in terms of pseudocode by writing the steps to meet the requirements. Example 3.18 shows the sample pseudocode.

Example 3.18
RunMe

```
' Pseudocode for Simple Thank-You Form Letter

' Get inputs
Get first name
Get last name

' Process
Line 1 = "To" & first name & last name
Blank line
Line 2 = "Dear" & first name
```

```
        Blank line
        Rest of lines are constant as per sample letter

        ' Output
        Display Line 1, Blank, Line 2, Blank, Line 3 etc.

End RunMe
```

Certainly, we can refine the pseudocode to specify variables, their data type, and constants that could be used. The code that follows shows one possible solution.

Coding

Write the code using a specific language. Example 3.19 uses Visual Basic with the Introduction Template.

Example 3.19

```
Public Sub RunMe()

        ' A Simple Thank-You Form Letter
        ' Send standard thanks addressed personally
        ' to a customer.

        ' Written by Cody Wizard, Jan. 16, 1997

        ' Customer information
        Dim sFirstName As String, sLastName As String

        ' Customized lines
        Dim sLine1 As String, sLine2 As String

        ' Standard information
        Const LINE3 = "Thank you for purchasing one of our canoes."
        Const LINE4 = "Sincerely"
        Const LINE5 = "Dawn Redbird, President"

        ' Get customer information
        InputStr "Enter first name", sFirstName
        InputStr "Enter last name", sLastName

        ' Generate customized lines
        sLine1 = "To " & sFirstName & " " & sLastName
        sLine2 = "Dear " & sFirstName

        ' Output the letter
        PrintMsg sLine1 ' To so and so
        PrintMsg "" ' Blank line
        PrintMsg sLine2 ' Dear so and so
        PrintMsg "" ' Blank line
        PrintMsg LINE3  ' Thank you etc....
        PrintMsg "" ' Blank line
        PrintMsg LINE4  ' Sincerely
        PrintMsg LINE5  ' The President

End Sub
```

Testing

Run the program using different types of inputs. If you type in nonsense, the letter will look like nonsense.

3.9.3   Loan Balance

Cougar Canoe secured a long-term loan to expand its business. It now needs to determine its outstanding loan balance.

Concept

After borrowing money, the borrower pays it back in installments, usually monthly. Each payment includes an interest amount and a principal amount. The principal amount is what actually reduces the remaining balance. The following formula is used to determine the balance.

$$Balance = (1 + i)^n \times [MonthlyPayment \times \frac{((1 + i)^{-n} - 1)}{i} + AmountBorrowed]$$

where

n = number of payments made

i = monthly interest rate (as a decimal fraction)

Cougar Canoe's goal can be stated as: Calculate and display the loan balance using the formula above.

Requirements

We can determine the inputs, processing, and outputs as shown below. In this case, the interest rate is fixed, so it is not an input.

- Define fixed interest rate.
- Inputs are the amount borrowed, monthly payment installment, and number of payments made.
- Processing involves calculating the balance using the formula.
- The output is the balance.

Design

Example 3.20 shows a possible pseudocode for this problem. Interest rates are usually given as a yearly figure, so that figure must be divided by 12 to find the monthly interest rate.

Example 3.20
RunMe

```
' Pseudocode for Loan Calculation

Define monthly INTEREST as yearly rate / 12

Input AmountBorrowed
Input MonthlyPayment
```

```
      Input NumberOfPayments
      Balance = result of calculation of formula

      Display Balance

End RunMe
```

Before refining the code, it will be worthwhile to specify steps to use the formula, since it is relatively complex. We can break down the formula into groups of simpler calculations using Visual Basic operators. Remember that we can assign a variable to a modification of its previous value, and we can explicitly define the order of precedence using parentheses.

We can stepwise refine the calculation as follows:

```
' Initial step
Balance = (1 + INTEREST) ^ (-NumberOfPayments)
' Now modify Balance in steps
Balance = (Balance -1) / INTEREST
Balance = MonthlyPayment * Balance + AmountBorrowed
Balance = ((1 + INTEREST) ^ NumberOfPayments) * Balance
```

Coding

To write the code, we need to determine the data types. The number of payments is a whole positive number, so it should be specified as Integer. Since decimal values are involved, the rest will be specified as Single.

Example 3.21

```
Public Sub RunMe()

    ' Tell user the loan balance

    ' Yearly interest rate of 5%
    Const INTEREST = 0.05 / 12 '  Monthly interest rate

    Dim fAmountBorrowed As Single, fMonthlyPayment As Single
    Dim nNumberOfPayments As Integer
    Dim fBalance As Single

    ' Tell user what this program will do
    PrintMsg "Find out the balance remaining on the loan"

    ' Get required inputs
    InputSng "What amount did you borrow?", fAmountBorrowed
    PrintSng "Amount Borrowed is ", fAmountBorrowed
    InputSng "What is the monthly payment?", fMonthlyPayment
    PrintSng "Monthly Payment is ", fMonthlyPayment
    InputInt "How many payments?", nNumberOfPayments
    PrintInt "Number of payments is ", nNumberOfPayments

    ' Calculate Balance
    fBalance = (1 + INTEREST) ^ (-nNumberOfPayments)
    fBalance = (fBalance - 1) / INTEREST
    fBalance = fMonthlyPayment * fBalance + fAmountBorrowed
```

```
        fBalance = ((1 + INTEREST) ^ nNumberOfPayments) * fBalance

        ' Display balance remaining
        PrintSng "Remaining balance is ", fBalance
```

End Sub

Testing

Run the program and try different typical values, such as a monthly payment of 300 for a borrowed amount of 25,000. Try different numbers of payments, such as 1, 2, 3, and so on. The balance remaining should become successively smaller after each additional payment. Check that the amount paid off is less than the total amount. Remember that part of each payment is being used to pay off the interest instead of the principal. For example, does the following output seem reasonable?

```
Find out the balance remaining on the loan
Amount Borrowed is 25000
Monthly Payment is 300
Number of payments is 6
Remaining balance is 23812.69
```

The borrower has so far paid $300 \times 6 = 1800$.
The amount paid off is $25000 - 23812.69 = 1187.31$
The borrower has paid 612.69 in interest so far.

We can conclude that this output seems reasonable mathematically (if not financially). Of course, we can input some nonsense and expect that this particular program will bomb. Either it will output nonsense, or it will crash due to a runtime error. Our programs so far accept data on good faith. They do not validate the inputs.

SUMMARY

A programming language such as Visual Basic has an organization and structure of fundamental elements. It is crucial to understand the elements. Why? We need to piece the elements together in such a way to tell the computer how to solve a problem for us. The fundamental elements are

- Statements
- Comments
- Constants
- Variables
- Operators
- Expressions
- Keywords

With these, we can build up other elements and add new elements as we become more familiar with the language.

Let's review the definitions of these elements. First, a program is a sequence of statements. A statement, which is a line of actual (formal) code telling the computer what to do, contains other elements. Example 3.22, which is a slightly reworked version of Example 3.1, includes 12 statements. Count them.

Example 3.22

```
Sub RunMe()

    ' Fahrenheit to Celsius Conversion Program

    ' Initialize
    Const MULTIPLIER = 5 / 9
    Dim fFahr As Single, fCels As Single
    ' Get Inputs
    InputSng "Enter Temperature in Fahrenheit", fFahr

    ' Do Computations
    fCels = MULTIPLIER * (fFahr - 32)

    ' Send Outputs
    PrintSng "Temperature in Celsius is ", fCels

End Sub
```

A comment is a special type of statement. A comment should explain the purpose of using certain executable statements in terms of the application for which the program is being used. The comments in Example 3.22, which consists of a program that converts Fahrenheit to Celsius, explain why certain statements are being used for the conversion. The comments are the statements that begin with the single quote ('). Although the computer does not execute comments, they are crucial to the programmer.

A constant is a reference to a value that remains fixed while the program is running. In Example 3.22, we define a multiplier factor that is being used for temperature conversion.

```
Const MULTIPLIER = 5 / 9
```

Hence, when `MULTIPLIER` is subsequently used in another statement, the computer will know that it means five divided by nine. In more realistic (real-world) situations, we use constants to help us remember why certain fixed values are being used. For example, a typical Visual Basic program needs to change the color of text to red. It can do this by assigning a special variable to the value of 255. Which of the following statements shows the intent more clearly?

```
TextColor = 255 ' Not obvious that 255 means red
```

or

```
TextColor = vbRed     ' Meaning clearer
```

It turns out that we do not need to define this constant using the `Const` statement. Visual Basic inherently recognizes certain constants such as `vbRed`. The creators of Visual Basic used a naming convention that prefixes an inherent constant using `vb` and does not use all capitals. Our convention for our "roll-our-own" constants is to use all capitals. This is good because we can then tell the difference between the two types.

A variable is a unit of memory that can be altered during the execution of a program. Each variable is assigned a unique name. Example 3.22 shows variable declarations by using the `Dim` statement:

```
Dim fFahr As Single, fCels As Single
```

Variable names are limited to 255 characters. A variable's data type should be specified using the As keyword during declaration. By convention, we name variables using the following prefixes to identify each data type.

- The Integer prefix is *n*.

- The Single prefix is *f*.

- The String prefix is *s*.

A variable name should describe its intended purpose. For example, fBoxCar would not be a good substitute for fFahr in a temperature conversion program. By default, variables are initialized to zero for numeric or null for String data types, respectively. An example of assigning a value to a variable follows:

```
InputSng "Enter Temperature in Fahrenheit", fFahr
```

After the user presses **ENTER,** fFahr is assigned a value based on what the user typed. Hence the variable's value has been altered from zero to something else, assuming the user entered something other than zero.

Visual Basic has 11 data types. We have used only three of them so far. The following code shows the Integer, Single, and String data types in action.

```
' Declare variables
Dim nNumberOfCoins As Integer, fAmountOfMoney As Single
Dim sCurrencyName as String

' Assign appropriate values
sCurrencyName = "Nickel"
nNumberOfCoins = 24
fAmountOfMoney = 1.20 ' Amount in dollars for 24 nickels
```

Table 3.1 shows the characteristics of these three types. Figures 3.3, 3.4, and 3.5 show how these data types are stored in memory.

An operator is a symbol that can cause a change in an expression such as an arithmetic operation. An expression is any part of a statement that evaluates to (expresses) one distinct value. In Example 3.22, consider the statement

```
fCels = MULTIPLIER * (fFahr - 32)
```

Any part of this statement that evaluates to one value is an expression, and each of the following parts of the statement is an expression.

```
fFahr
MULITPLIER
(fFahr - 32)
MULTIPLIER * (fFahr - 32)
fCels
```

Let's say the user happened to enter –40 when prompted for the temperature in Fahrenheit. Then the expressions are evaluated as follows:

- fFahr evaluates to –40 (due to executing previous InputSng command).

- MULTIPLIER evaluates to 5/9 to approximately 0.5556 (due to Const statement).

- (fFahr –32) evaluates to –72. The minus operator (–) caused a change in this expression.

- `MULTIPLIER * (fFahr - 32)` evaluates to -40. The multiplication operator (`*`) caused a change in this expression.

- `fCels` evaluates to -40 due to assignment operation (when computer finishes execution of the statement). The assignment operator (`=`) caused a change in this expression.

We can organize operators into three types:

- Assignment (=)

- Arithmetic (See Table 3.4).

- Concatenation (&)

Table 3.4 shows the arithmetic operators in order of precedence. The order of precedence specifies which operations are executed before others. The concatenation operator joins strings together. For example, the expression `"A " & "stitch " & "in " & "time " & "saves " & "nine."` would evaluate to `"A stitch in time saves nine."`

Keywords are words or symbols in a programming language that have reserved special meaning to a compiler or interpreter. You cannot use a keyword as a name. Table 3.5 shows keywords we have encountered so far.

Syntax errors are coding mistakes that prevent statements from being compiled. They are statements that Visual Basic can't understand. For example, it couldn't understand

```
PriinnttSng sMessage fVariable
```

because the template command is misspelled and a comma is missing between the two variables. These are syntax errors.

A runtime error is an error that causes a program to prematurely stop execution. There are several possible sources for runtime error. To avoid their occurrence, a program could

- Check for a zero denominator before attempting division.

- Check for a negative number prior to attempting to find its square root.

- Perform input validation to ensure inputs are within range (and of the correct data type).

- Convert variables to a data type with a larger range.

- Check the data type of a variable prior to using it, if in doubt.

Chapter 4 will examine how to use these elements to organize programs into blocks of code. But moving on, though, practice with the language elements in the hands-on exercises.

HANDS-ON EXERCISES

OVERVIEW

The activities will

- Familiarize you with using operators, expressions, and statements.

- Familiarize you with using variables.

- Introduce you to using Visual Basic Help.

- Familiarize you with some debugging tools (breakpoints, single step, and watch expressions).

- Provide some experience with coding, documentation, and testing.

To Get Started

1. Read the section "Read Me Before Attempting the Exercises" if you have not already done so.

2. Run Windows.

3. Open the file CH03\EX03.TXT on the program disk and answer the questions. (The same questions are shown here so that you can still determine answers if you are not sitting in front of a computer.)

4. Run Visual Basic

3.1   THE STATEMENT

1. What is a statement? Give an example.

2. In general, for what does a typical computer program use statements?

Practice with the Fahrenheit to Celsius Program

In this exercise, you will create the program shown in Example 3.1. First, in Visual Basic, open project CH03\INTRO. In the Project Window, select the **RUNME.BAS** file. Make sure this file, not those named INTRO, is highlighted. Click **View Code**. Enter the first few lines of the program shown in Example 3.1.

Visual Basic 4

From the File menu, select **Save File As** (*not* Project As), and type **FTOC01** as the file name.

Visual Basic 5

From the File menu, select **Save Runme.Bas As** (*not* Project As), and type **FTOC01** as the file name.

From the File menu, select **Save Project As** (*not* File As), and type **FTOC01** as the project name.

Visual Basic 5

Select **Project Properties** from the Project menu. In the dialog box, type in a Project Name of **FTOC01** and click **OK**. The Visual Basic Title Bar should now state FTOC01 instead of PROJECT1.

Continue typing in the program while periodically backing up your work by selecting **Save Project** from the File menu. Alternatively, click the **Save** button in the Visual Basic Toolbar. Run the program several times using different inputs. If you encounter syntax errors, correct them and try again.

Using the Help Glossary: Definition of Statement

Now we can use Visual Basic Help to see the definition of a statement for ourselves.

Caution

When using Help, make sure that the topic title indicates a Visual Basic topic. If your version of Visual Basic includes other programs such as Crystal Reports, you may unintentionally view information about a program other than Visual Basic.

The Help system organization for Visual Basic 4 and Visual Basic 5 is quite different. In Visual Basic 4, the Help menu includes menu items for Contents and Books Online. The glossary and tutorial information is part of the Contents selection in the Help menu. In Visual Basic 5, the Help menu includes menu items for Microsoft Visual Basic Help Topics and Books Online. The glossary and tutorial information is part of the Books Online selection in the Help menu.

Visual Basic 4

Select **Contents** from the Help menu in Visual Basic. Then click the **Contents** tab in the Help Contents dialog box. Next, select **Visual Basic Help** and click **Open**. Select **Glossary** and click **Display**. A Visual Basic Help window will appear with the glossary.

Visual Basic 5

Select **Books Online** from the Help menu in Visual Basic. The Books Online application will run. Then select **Glossary** from the Help menu in the Books Online window. Alternatively, click the **Glossary** button in its Toolbar. You should see a window titled Books Online Glossary Help.

Click the S button and click **Statement** (scroll if necessary). You should see the same definition that is shown in this chapter.

Visual Basic 4

To capture the definition in the Windows clipboard, press the **CTRL+C** keys when you see the glossary definition. Click **anywhere** and the definition will disappear. For some reason, this trick only works if the item is selected directly from the Glossary. It is possible to indirectly select a glossary item when a link to it exists in another Help topic. However, the capture trick does not seem to work in this case.

Visual Basic 5

If you want to capture the definition in the Windows clipboard, drag the mouse pointer (hold down the left mouse button while doing this) to highlight the desired selection. Press the **CTRL+C** keys or select **Copy** from the Edit menu of the Books Online Glossary Help window. Note that this window may be set up to remain on top. If you prefer to change the setting, select **Keep Help on Top** from its Option menu. Then select **Not on Top**.

Debug Tools: Single Step the Program

These are the tools:

Breakpoint	Statement where execution will stop.
Step Over	Command that executes one statement.
Instant Watch	To view the value of a selected expression.

Visual Basic 4

Figure 3.6a shows the tools on the Visual Basic Toolbar.

Visual Basic 5

By default, you see only the Standard Toolbar as shown in the upper part of Figure 3.6b. To see other toolbars, such as the Debug toolbar, right-click on the **Standard Toolbar** (click on it with the right mouse button). Then select **Debug**

Figure 3.6a
Visual Basic 4 Toolbar

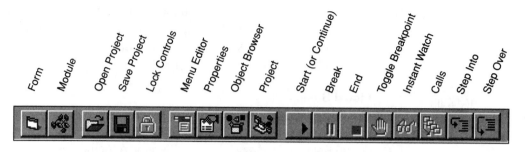

from the pop-up menu. The toolbars in the Visual Basic 5 integrated development environment (IDE) may be docked or floating. It is possible that the Debug toolbar will appear as a separate floating window outside the IDE. To dock it so that it is contained within the IDE, drag the window and place it just below the Standard Toolbar. You may have to attempt this several times, since docking can be quite tricky. You can also undock a toolbar by clicking on its docking handle (the two vertical lines on the left side) and then dragging the toolbar outside the IDE. The choice of using docked or floating toolbars is yours. Figure 3.6b shows the docked version.

Note that both the Standard and Debug toolbars have buttons for Start, Break, and End. You can use either set of buttons, since they do the same thing. We suggest that you add the Debug toolbar now so that you can use other buttons not available in the Standard Toolbar.

Figure 3.6b
Some Visual Basic 5 Toolbars

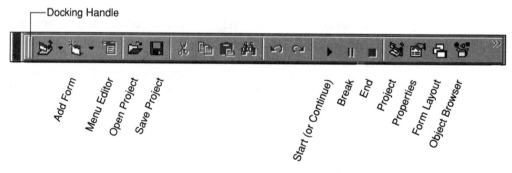

Standard Toolbar

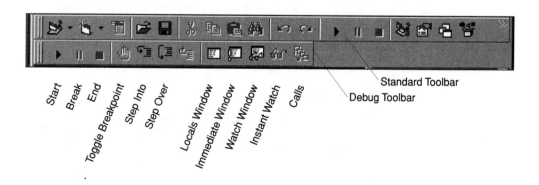

Refer to Figure 3.6a or 3.6b, depending on the version of Visual Basic you are using. If you look on your toolbar now, some buttons will be grayed. This means they are not available to you now. Click the **Exit** button to stop execution (if you haven't done so already). Note that the Toolbar **Start** button will be bold and the Break and End buttons will be grayed, as shown in Figure 3.6a or 3.6b.

Visual Basic Operating Modes

We should explain a bit about the Visual Basic modes. The modes are as follows:

Design   Edit program code.
Run   Compile code and execute.
Break   Suspend execution.

The Title Bar of Visual Basic should look like this:

```
ftoc01 - Microsoft Visual Basic [design]
```

Your project name will appear in place of `ftoc01`. The Toolbar Start button is available, and the Break and End buttons are not. After all, we can't suspend (Break) or end (End) execution if we haven't started it yet!

Click the Toolbar **Start** button. The Visual Basic Title Bar will change to look like this:

```
ftoc01 - Microsoft Visual Basic [run]
```

The Toolbar Start button will not be available. After all, we have already started! The Break and End buttons should now be available. Do not click the Run Me button in the Introduction Template, since we do not want to start execution of the Fahrenheit to Celsius code yet.

Click the Toolbar **Break** button. The Visual Basic Title Bar will change to look like this:

```
ftoc01 - Microsoft Visual Basic [break]
```

You may also see the Debug window. For now, click on its **Close** button (top right corner) to get it out of the way. The Toolbar Break button is not available because we have already suspended execution. The **Continue** (former Start) and **End** buttons are in context. Click these to continue or end execution, respectively. If you position the mouse pointer over the Continue (former Start) button, the pop-up balloon will display the word *Continue*. The button is in fact a Continue button, because Visual Basic has already started the Introduction Template. At this point, we can use tools for single stepping.

Set a Breakpoint

You should see the Code window for the Fahrenheit to Celsius program. If you don't, click **FTOC01.BAS** in the Project Window (see Figure 1.9a or 1.9b if you have forgotten what the Code window is). Then click **View Code**. Click anywhere in the following statement:

```
Public Sub RunMe()
```

Click the Toolbar **Toggle Breakpoint** button. The statement should now be highlighted in red.

Run to a Breakpoint

Click the Toolbar **Continue** button. Note that Visual Basic is now in the *run mode*. Click the **Run Me** button in the Introduction Template. The program will stop at the statement where we set the breakpoint. This statement will be highlighted in boldface type. Note that

Visual Basic is now in the *break mode*. The statement has not been executed yet, but it will be when we later single step. In fact, the Introduction Template is a Visual Basic program. It so happens that any code written by us will not execute until we click **Run Me**.

Single Step (Step Over)

Click the Toolbar **Step Over** button (or press **Shift+F8**). The program will stop at the following statement.

```
InputSng "Enter Temperature in Fahrenheit", fFahr
```

Visual Basic 4

A rectangular outline that surrounds this statement indicates the *current statement*.

Visual Basic 5

Visual Basic highlights this statement in yellow (assuming Option defaults for Execution Point Text have not been modified). This highlight indicates the *current statement*.

The current statement is the next statement to be executed. Although single step generally executes only one statement at a time, there are exceptions, and this is one of them. A definition to start a program and declarations are executed in one step. Also, comments are not executed. Figure 3.7 illustrates the general idea as to how the Code window should look (Figure 3.7 shows a different program).

Instant/Quick Watch—Initial Values

Double-click **the variable fFahr** in the statement to declare variables.

```
Dim fFahr As Single, fCels As Single
```

fFahr should be highlighted in blue. Click Toolbar **Instant/Quick Watch**. This launches an Instant/Quick Watch dialog. Note that the expression is fFahr, and its value is zero. This should make sense. Numeric variables are initialized to zero. Click **Cancel** in the Instant/Quick Watch dialog box.

Note

While Visual Basic 4 uses the term *Instant Watch*. Visual Basic 5 uses the term *Quick Watch*.

Repeat these steps for fCels. You should see that it also initialized to 0.

Tip

With **Visual Basic 5**, you can move the mouse (I-beam) pointer over a variable in the Code window during Break mode. Visual Basic will quickly display a pop-up balloon that shows the current value of the variable.

Single Step (Step Over) the InputSng Command

Click the Toolbar **Step Over** button (or press **SHIFT+F8**). You should see the Introduction Template window, which is waiting for you to enter the temperature value. If you don't see the window, you may have accidentally selected Step Into instead of Step Over. In that case, click **End** and start over again.

Enter some reasonable number (e.g., 45.6). Visual Basic will show the code again with the next statement highlighted as the current statement.

```
fCels = 5 / 9 * (fFahr - 32)
```

Double-click **fFahr** and look at its value using Instant Watch. Note that its value is what you happened to enter during execution of the InputSng command.

Check the **value for fCels** using Instant Watch. Note that its value is still zero. Why? The computer has stopped at this statement, but it hasn't executed it yet.

Incidentally, you can see the value of any expression. To select an expression, move the I-beam mouse pointer to the beginning. Hold down the left mouse button and drag the pointer over the end of the expression. It should be highlighted in blue. Click the Toolbar **Instant Watch** button. You should see the value of the expression. Try it now for the following expression.

```
(fFahr - 32) or fFahr - 32
```

You should see the value of fFahr minus 32 (e.g. 45.6 − 32 = 13.6).

You can tell if you haven't selected an expression because Visual Basic will complain when you select Instant Watch for something that isn't an expression. If you don't believe it, try to view the value of the following (one parenthesis missing).

```
fFahr - 32)
```

Tip

In the break mode, highlight an expression by dragging the mouse. Then move the I-beam mouse pointer over the expression. Visual Basic will quickly display a pop-up balloon that shows the current value of the expression. It is not necessary to click Quick Watch, unless you want additional information about the expression.

Check the value of the entire expression to the right of the assignment operator.

```
5 / 9 * (fFahr - 32)
```

The value should be the result of the formula (e.g., if fFahr is 45.6, the result is 7.555555), but remember that the result has not been assigned to fCels yet because the statement has not been executed.

Single Step (Step Over) the Computation Statement

Click the Toolbar **Step Over** button (or press **SHIFT+F8**). The PrintSng statement should be highlighted.

```
PrintSng "Temperature in Celsius is ", fCels
```

Check the **value of fCels** using Instant Watch. Variable fCels has been assigned a new value. The computation statement has been executed, and the result of the computation has been assigned to the variable.

Click the **Introduction Template window**. You may have to select the Introduction Template using the Windows Taskbar. Note that the Program Output(s) box is blank. This is because the PrintSng statement has not yet been executed.

Single Step (Step Over) the PrintSng Statement

Click the Toolbar **Step Over** button (or press **SHIFT+F8**). The program End statement should be highlighted.

```
End Sub
```

Click the **Introduction Template window**. Note that the Program Output(s) displays the result of the conversion. This is because the `PrintSng` statement has been executed.

Continue

Since all statements have been executed, click the Toolbar **Continue** button to repeat the process for new input values. If you click **Step Over** at the `End Sub` statement, you will in fact see code that is used to implement the Introduction Template. We don't want to concern ourselves with this code, so click **Continue**.

More Practice

Repeat the previous exercise several times until you feel comfortable with the procedure.

Remove the Breakpoint

To remove the breakpoint, view the code and click in the statement with the breakpoint. Then click the Toolbar Toggle Breakpoint, which will toggle the breakpoint off. The statement should no longer be highlighted in red.

Tip

With **Visual Basic 5**, you can toggle a breakpoint off by clicking the red dot beside it.

3.2   COMMENTS

3. What is a comment? Give an example of a *useful* comment.

4. What visual cue does Visual Basic provide to help you easily identify comments in the code?

5. What is the purpose of a comment?

3.3   CONSTANTS AND VARIABLES

6. What is a constant? Give an example. Then give an example of its use in a statement involving assignment.

7. What is a variable? Give an example. Then give an example of its use in a statement involving assignment.

The Area of Circle Program (Variable Demonstration)

Remember

To run an Introduction Template program, click the Visual Basic **Start** button in the Toolbar. Then click the **Run Me** button in the Introduction Template.

To find the area of a circle, open project INTRO in directory CH03. Select the **RUNME.BAS** file in the Project window and select **Save File As** from the File menu to save the *file* as VARDEMO1. Select **Save Project As** from the File menu to save the *project* as VARDEMO1.

Type in the code shown in Example 3.6, saving the project periodically. Now run the program to make sure it works. Correct errors if necessary, and then stop the program and put a breakpoint at the first line.

```
Public Sub RunMe()
```

Run the program. Single step (Step Over) to see how the statements operate. Use Instant Watch to check the value of expressions during execution. In particular, check the value of variables in each statement. Make sure you check the Introduction Template Program Output(s) box before and after stepping over (executing) each PrintSng command.

Note the following:

- fRadius is initialized to zero.
- The value of PI is 3.141593.
- After the InputSng command is executed, the value of fRadius is whatever you entered.
- Prior to executing the area calculation (fArea = PI * fRadius * fRadius), fArea has a value of zero.
- After executing the area calculation, fArea has been assigned the calculation result.
- The PrintSng commands display the results in the Program Output(s) box.

Hazards of Not Declaring

Stop the program and remove the breakpoint. Modify the program to include the typographical error mentioned in Example 3.7:

```
fArea = PI * fRaduis * fRadius
```

Your program should still include the Option Explicit statement. Run the program. Visual Basic will warn you that fRaduis is not defined. This is useful information since it might be hard to detect the misspelling visually.

Now comment out the Option Explicit statement as follows:

```
' Comment out the Option Explicit statement
' Option Explicit
```

Run the program again. This time you will not see the warning, but it will always display the area as zero. Now we can see how a clever programmer might be able to find the cause of the error (assuming he or she never thought about Option Explicit).

Put a breakpoint on the first statement. Run the program. Step over the instructions. When you reach the following calculation statement,

```
fArea = PI * fRaduis * fRadius
```

use Instant/Quick Watch to examine the value of each expression.

You should find that fRadius has the value you entered, but that fRaduis has the value of zero. Our clever programmer will likely puzzle over this, since both are supposed to have the same value. At this point, she is likely to notice the spelling error, and perhaps wonder why she didn't use Option Explicit in the first place. Remove the breakpoint.

3.4 DATA TYPES

Learning About Data Types Using Visual Basic Help

Visual Basic has a rich help system. It is useful to gain skills in navigating through this system. At this point, we will explore it tentatively, since you would have to be an experienced programmer to understand all of it.

Visual Basic 4

Launch Visual Basic Help by selecting **Contents** from the Visual Basic Help menu (or click the **Search** button if Visual Basic Help is already running). Click the **Index** tab, and then click in the **first text box**. Type **data types, summary**. Click **Summary** in the Index Entry box, and then click the **Display** button.

Visual Basic 5

Launch Visual Basic Help by selecting **Microsoft Visual Basic Help Topics** from the Help menu (or click the **Help Topics** button if Visual Basic Help is already running). Click the **Index** tab. Click in **the first text box**. Type **data types**. Click **Data Types** in the Index Entry box, and then click the **Display** button. This displays the Topics Found dialog. Select **Data Type Summary** from the list and click **Display**.

Note the information about the data types. You should see a table displaying the data type summary. Don't worry if you do not understand all the details; you will need additional material to comprehend all of it.

What is a data type? Note the underlined (green dotted line) Help topic. When you place the mouse pointer on a Help topic, the mouse pointer changes to a hand. Click on **the Help topic**. You should see the glossary definition about data type; that is, you would have found the same thing by using the Glossary. Answer the question again, using your own words and examples.

8. What is a data type?

For now, we will only consider the Integer, Single, and String data types.

About the Integer Data Type

When showing information on a specific topic, Help often provides a link to related topics. Note the underlined topic, **See Also**, and then click on it. Click on **Integer Data Type** (and click **Display** if necessary). For now, note only the first and last sentences.

Highlight **the first sentence**. Select **Copy** from the Edit menu (or press **CTRL+C**). Switch to your text file EX03.TXT. Paste the sentence in the indicated spot. Repeat the process for the last sentence.

Demonstrating an Overflow Error.   To demonstrate an overflow error, open Project CH03\INTRO. Then save the RUNME file as DEMO1 in folder CH03; save the project as DEMO1 in folder CH03. Type in the following code (first and last line already pretyped):

```
Public Sub RunMe()

    Dim nIntegerMax As Integer

    nIntegerMax = 32765

    nIntegerMax = nIntegerMax + 1
    nIntegerMax = nIntegerMax + 1
    nIntegerMax = nIntegerMax + 1

End Sub
```

To monitor how an overflow can occur, put a breakpoint on the first statement, `Public Sub RunMe()`. Run the program, which should stop at the breakpoint.

Click **Step Over** (avoid Step Into for now) for each instruction, noting the value of *nIntegerMax* using Instant Watch each time. Figures 3.7a and 3.7b show the Code window after the breakpoint has been stepped over. The program is about to execute `nIntegerMax = 32765` (the current statement).

Figure 3.7a
The Visual Basic 4 Code Window During a Debugging Session

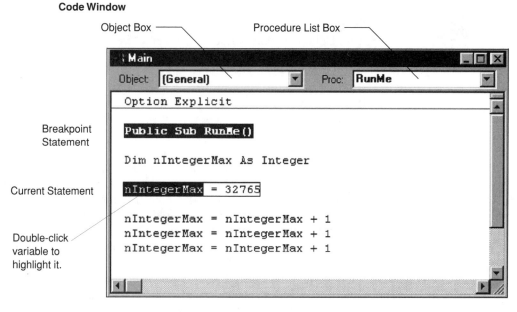

Figure 3.7b
The Visual Basic 5 Code Window During a Debugging Session

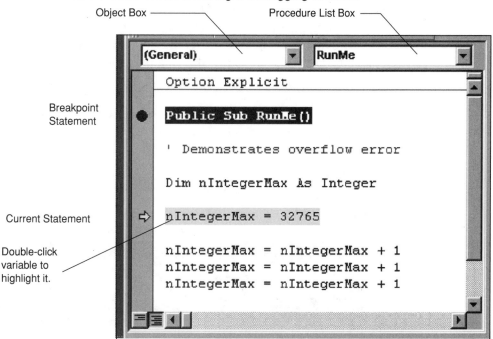

Note the effect of the assignment operator (=). The first one assigns `nIntegerMax` from the default value of 0 to 32,765. The second one assigns `nIntegerMax` to its former value (32,765), plus 1 to 32,766. The process continues, but at the last assignment statement you can see an *overflow error*. We have attempted to go past the range.

Added Watch Expressions. In situations when you want to monitor an expression often, it may be more convenient to convert the Instant/Quick Watch to an Added Watch.

When you click **Instant/Quick Watch**, click the **Add** button on its dialog. The watch expression now shows up in the Debug window.

Visual Basic 4

If the Debug window is not visible, select **Debug** window from the View menu. You can switch back and forth between the Code window and the Debug window to see the *watch expression* while single stepping. You may find it convenient to re-size and move the two windows to view both simultaneously. This is done by performing standard Windows positioning and sizing operations. Figure 3.8a shows the Debug window.

Visual Basic 5

To view both the Code and Debug windows within the IDE at the same time, resize both windows and the panes of the Debug window. To resize the windows with the Visual Basic IDE, move the mouse pointer to a window border. The pointer will change to a double-arrow pointer. Hold down the left mouse button and move the pointer to shift the position of the border. You may have to fiddle with the different windows until you get the sizes you want. Figure 3.8b shows the Debug window.

The Debug window shows an expression, its value, and its *context* (availability). The Visual Basic 5 Debug window also shows the data type. Remember that anything that evaluates to a distinct value is an expression. Hence, a variable name is an expression since it is assigned a value. In this case, *context* means that expression nIntegerMax is part of a block of code named RunMe that belongs to the Main module. (We will say more about *context* in Chapter 4).

Figures 3.8a and 3.8b show the Debug window that corresponds to the Code window shown in Figures 3.7a and 3.7b. The Debug window shows the initialized value of nIntegerMax. After stepping over the following statement,

```
nIntegerMax = 32765
```

the Debug Window will show the new value as a result of executing the assignment in the statement. Once you are finished using an added watch expression, you can remove it.

Figure 3.8a
The Added Watch Expression in the Visual Basic 4 Debug Window

Debug Window

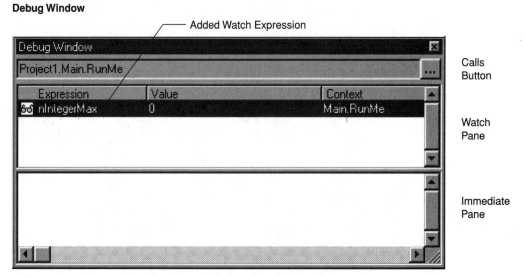

Figure 3.8b
The Added Watch Expression in the Visual Basic 5 Debug Window

Debug Window

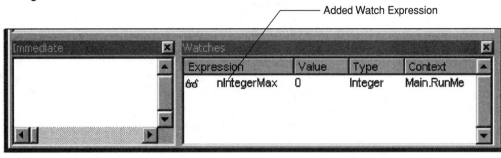

Immediate Pane   Watch Pane

Visual Basic 4

To remove a watch expression, select **Edit Watch** from the Tools menu, and then click **Remove**.

Visual Basic 5

To remove a watch expression, select **Edit Watch** from the Debug menu, and then click **Remove**.

Alternatively, right-click the expression in the Debug window and click **Delete Watch**.

Creating an Underflow Demo. To create an underflow demo program, edit the overflow program to become the following:

```
Public Sub RunMe()

    Dim nIntegerMin As Integer

    nIntegerMin = -32766

    nIntegerMin = nIntegerMin - 1
    nIntegerMin = nIntegerMin - 1
    nIntegerMin = nIntegerMin - 1

End Sub
```

You can actually do this without much typing since Visual Basic has a standard Replace menu item. Double-click **nIntegerMax** to highlight it. Select **Replace** from the Edit menu. You should see the Replace dialog box with your highlighted item in the Find What box. Type in **nIntegerMin** in the Replace With box. Click the **Replace** button repeatedly until all desired items are replaced.

Repeat the process to replace + (the addition operator) with – (the subtraction operator). Manually change the third statement to nIntegerMin = –32766. Remove the watch expression.

Underflow Demo. Run the program and repeat the steps you performed in the Overflow Demo. Note that when the program tries to subtract 1 from -32768, Visual Basic flags the error as overflow. It doesn't distinguish between overflow and underflow. It flags the error as overflow whenever the program tries to exceed the range of the data type.

Creating a Rounding Demo.   To create a rounding demo, change the program to the following:

```
Public Sub RunMe()

    Dim nInteger As Integer

    nIntegerNum = 15

    nIntegerNum = nIntegerNum / 2
    nIntegerNum = nIntegerNum / 2
    nIntegerNum = nIntegerNum / 2

End Sub
```

Single step the program and note that 15/2 (7.5) is rounded up to 8. Change the program to initialize `nIntegerNum` to 17. Add it as a watch expression. Then single step the program and note that 17/2 (8.5) is rounded down to 8.

Try other divisors and other initial values. Note that Visual Basic will round a result to the nearest whole number. If the result is halfway between two whole numbers, Visual Basic will round it to the nearest even number. Remove the watch expression.

About the Single Data Type

Use Help to find information about the Single data type. For now, note only the first sentence. Highlight it. Select **Copy** from the Edit menu (or press **CTRL+C**). Switch to your text file `EX03.TXT`. Paste the sentence in the indicated spot. Figure 3.4 illustrates the IEEE 32-bit floating point number format. Change the DEMO program to the following:

```
Public Sub RunMe()

    Dim fSingleNum As Single

    fSingleNum = -32.567

    fSingleNum = fSingleNum ^ 3
    fSingleNum = fSingleNum ^ 7
    fSingleNum = fSingleNum ^ 11

End Sub
```

Add a breakpoint to the first line and run the program. Add `fSingleNum` as a watch expression. Monitor the value while single stepping. Note the use of exponential notation. An overflow will occur during execution of the last computation. Remove the watch expression.

About the String Type

To investigate the characteristics of the String data type, change the DEMO program to the following:

```
Public Sub RunMe()

    Dim sStringText As String

    sStringText = "Hello Cougar Canoe "
    sStringText = sStringText & sStringText

End Sub
```

Add a breakpoint to the first line and run the program. Add sStringText as a watch expression. Monitor the value while single stepping. Note that its initial value is a *null string* ("").

The initial assignment statement gives the variable a value of "Hello Cougar Canoe." The second assignment statement concatenates a copy of this string to itself. To view the entire value, stretch the Debug window horizontally. Then stretch the Value field (the mouse pointer will change to a double arrow). To do this, move the mouse pointer to the border separating Value and Context in the Title Bar of the Watch pane (see Figure 3.8). It should turn into a double arrow. Hold down the **left mouse button and drag the border** to the desired position.

Continue single stepping. Click **Start** when done and repeat the exercise if you wish. Click **End** to stop execution. Remove the watch expression and close the project.

A Data Type Demonstration Program (Optional)

There is a program that you can use to investigate how different data types are stored in memory. To use it, open Project DATATYPE.

Note

This program includes a constant named DATAFILE that may have to be modified. Modify the constant value in the code to suit your system. For example, if you don't have a C drive, you will have to change

```
Const DATAFILE = "C:\DATATYPE.DAT"
```

to

```
Const DATAFILE = "A:\DATATYPE.DAT"
```

if you are using A drive.

Moving on, click the Toolbar **Start** button to run the program. Note that you can enter data in the Value box and select a desired **Conversion Option**. Then click **Convert**. The Hex box shows how the data is stored in memory using hexadecimal (base 16) digits. The scrollable box on the right shows binary equivalents of the hex digits. Figure 3.9 shows a possible display.

If you type in **30891** in the Value box, select **Integer**, and click **Convert**, the Hex box will show 78AB. Using the scrollable box, you would find that Hex 7 is Binary 0111, Hex 8 is Binary 1000, and so on to work out the binary equivalent of 0111 1000 1010 1011. Try converting the Single value 57.8125. You should see a Hex result of 42 67 40 00. This corresponds to binary 0100 0010 0110 0111 0100 0000 0000 0000. Compare this binary sequence to that shown in Figure 3.4. They should match. Refer to Figure 3.5. Select the **String** option and type in the sentence **The tolerance is 15 μm**. (In order to type the Greek mu (μ), hold down the **ALT** key and use the Numeric keypad to type in **0181**.) After clicking **Convert**, you should see a long sequence of Hex numbers. Use the scrollable list to convert them to binary code, and compare your binary equivalents to those shown in Figure 3.5. They should match. Experiment with other conversions, such as verifying the binary equivalents for the Integers shown in Figure 3.3.

3.5   OPERATORS AND EXPRESSIONS

Use Visual Basic Help to find the order of precedence for the operators we have covered so far. Describe the steps you took to find the information in Help.

Figure 3.9
Data Type Demonstration Program

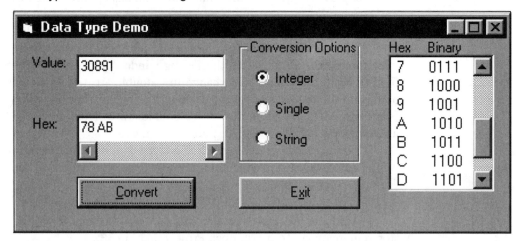

Integer 30891 is stored in memory as the 16-bit number
Hex 78 AB; which in binary is 0111 1000 1010 1011.

Coin Change Demo

To run the coin change demo, open `Project CH03\COIN`. Run the program and try different input values for the number of pennies, such as **347**. Add a breakpoint at the first statement. Single step the program. Add and monitor expressions. Repeat the process for different values, and then remove the watch expressions and the breakpoint.

The Concatenation Demo

To run the concatenation demo, open Project `INTRO`. Use **Save File** `RUNME` as `CONCAT` in folder `CH03`, and then use **Save Project As** to save `CONCAT` in folder `CH03`. Type in the code shown in Example 3.13. Add a breakpoint at the first statement. Single step the program, and add and monitor expressions. Repeat the process for different numerical and non-numerical inputs. Remove the watch expressions and the breakpoint.

The Null Demo

To run the null demo, open Project `INTRO`. Use **Save File** to save `RUNME` as `NULLDEMO` in folder `CH03`, and use **Save Project As** to save `NULLDEMO` in folder `CH03`. Type in the code shown in Example 3.14. Add a breakpoint at the first statement. Single step the program, and add and monitor expressions. Repeat the process for different inputs. Remove the watch expressions and the breakpoint.

3.6 KEYWORDS

You will use Help to find out about keywords.

Visual Basic 4

Explore using online Help by selecting **Contents** from the Help menu in Visual Basic. Click the **Contents** tab in Help Topics: Visual Basic Help. Open the **Visual**

Basic Help topic (the Book icon). This shows additional subtopics. Select **Glossary** and display it. Click the **K** button. Select the **glossary item for keyword** to view the definition.

Clicking anywhere causes the glossary window to disappear. However, you can capture the text onto the clipboard as follows: Before clicking, press **CTRL+C**, the magic Copy command. In the your text document, press **CTRL+V** to paste it. Again, select **keyword**. Press **CTRL+C** and paste the definition in the appropriate area of your file EX03.TXT. Click **See Also** to return to the main Visual Basic Help window. Then click **Keywords by Task**. This launches the Keywords by Task window. Note that there are many categories. For now, you will only need to examine a few of them.

Scroll down if necessary and select **Operators**. You will see the arithmetic operators. Click any of these to see further information about a selected operator. Ignore the comparison and logic operators for now. This part of Help categorizes the *concatenation* operator as *arithmetic*. Nobody has yet created documentation that is perfectly consistent. However, the Visual Basic Help Operator Summary window classifies the *concatenation* operator separately from the *arithmetic* operators.

To return to the main Help window, click the **Back** button or click the **See Also** item. Then you can again view Keywords by Task. If you have been exploring new topics, you may have to experiment to return back to the Keywords by Category window. The effort you make in exploring Help now will eventually pay off later when you need to find information to solve a problem.

At this point you are hopefully viewing the Keywords by Task window. Select the **Variables and Constants** category. You will see some of the keywords we have already discussed. Select and view information about some of the keywords we have already discussed, such as Let, Const, and Dim.

Visual Basic 5

To view online Help, select **Books Online** from the Visual Basic Help menu. Click the **Glossary** button on its toolbar, and then click **K**. Select the Glossary item for keyword to view the definition. Highlight the definition, press **CTRL+C** to copy it onto the clipboard, and paste the definition in the appropriate area of your file EX03.TXT.

Select Microsoft Visual Basic Help Topics from the Visual Basic Help menu. Click the **Index** tab if necessary. Type in **operator** and select **operators** from the list. Click **Display**. This shows the Topics Found dialog box. Scroll the list and select **Operator Summary**. Click **Display**.

In the Operator Summary Help topic window, select **Concatenation Operators**. This will show two selections. Select **& Operator** and **Read the Information in This Topic**. Click the **Back** button, select the **+ Operator,** and read this information. You should note that + is normally used for arithmetic addition but can also serve to concatenate strings. (We recommend that you use only & for concatenation to avoid ambiguity.) Click **Back** to return to the Operator Summary topic. Select **Arithmetic Operators**, and view information about these operators.

Now let's try to find other keywords. If you are still viewing a help topic, click **Help Topics**. Otherwise you will have to select **Help** from the Help menu again. Click the **Index** tab if necessary. Type the word **keyword**. You will see an indented list of subcategory words listed below item keywords. At this stage, we are mainly familiar with the data types, operators, and variables and constants items. Select the **data types** item and click **Display**. Select topics about intrinsic data types, and view information about the Integer, Single, and String data types.

Click **Help Topics**, type the Index word *keywords*, and select the category item Variables and Constants. Click **Display**. Select and view information about some of the keywords we have already discussed, such as Let, Const, and Dim.

3.7   SYNTAX ERRORS

We will just do a bit of work with syntax here. Find the Visual Basic Help Glossary items for syntax, syntax checking, and syntax error. Paste the definitions in the appropriate area of your file EX03.TXT.

Open Project INTRO. Use **Save File As** to save RUNME as CH03\SYNTAX, and use **Save Project As** to save project INTRO as CH03\SYNTAX. Find out how your syntax checking is set up. Select **Options** from the Tools menu in Visual Basic.

Visual Basic 4

Click the **Environment** tab.

Visual Basic 5

Click the **Edit** tab.

Note some settings in the dialog box. Make sure that both Require Variable Declaration and Auto Syntax Check are checked on.

Try to enter a statement like the following:

```
dim nIntegerNum as integer, dim fSingleNum as single
```

Visual Basic should respond with a warning. Keyword dim is typed in twice in the same statement. Remove the extra dim, so that you are entering something like

```
Dim nIntegerNum As Integer, fSingleNum as single
```

Visual Basic converts lowercase letters to uppercase where appropriate. Hence you should have something like the following:

```
Dim nIntegerNum As Integer,  fSingleNum As Single
```

Keywords are highlighted in blue. To check out context-sensitive help, click a keyword such as Dim, and press **F1**. Visual Basic launches Help to display the topic about Dim.

3.8   TROUBLESHOOTING: RUNTIME ERRORS

For this exercise on runtime errors, open Project INTRO. Use **Save File As** to save RUNME as CH03\RUNERR1, and then use **Save Project As** to save INTRO as CH03\RUNERR1. Type in the code shown in Example 3.15. In this exercise we will use Debug tools to work past several runtime errors.

Run the program. When prompted for a numerator, enter a valid number such as –45.6. Visual Basic will display the runtime error dialog. Click the **Debug** button. You should see the Code window with the following statement highlighted:

```
fQuotient = fNumerator / fDenominator
```

Notice that Visual Basic is in the break mode.

Examine the values of the variables in this statement using Instant/Quick Watch. Note that the value of fDenominator is zero (0). Next, highlight the expression fNumerator/fDenominator and examine it using Instant Watch. This division by zero is the cause of the runtime error. Normally, a programmer would either check to find out why the denominator is zero and/or add code to perform an alternative operation if the denominator is zero. However, the programmer may wish to check execution of the rest of the code. It would be useful to intervene and modify the variable to something else so that it is possible to continue execution past this statement. One way to modify a value while in the break mode is to change it using the Debug window.

Visual Basic 5

The Debugger will show that the value of the quotient is -1.#INF if the numerator was negative and 1.#INF if the numerator was positive. These are special floating point numbers reserved for negative and positive infinity, respectively. Mathematically, a number divided by zero is impossibly large; hence it is infinite.

Stop the program if it is not already in the design mode. Set a breakpoint at the division statement.

```
fQuotient = fNumerator / fDenominator
```

Run the program and enter a nonzero number. The program will halt at the breakpoint (now in break mode). Click in the Immediate pane of the Debug window (see Figures 3.8a and 3.8b to identify the immediate pane). Type in something like

```
fDenominator = 5
```

and press ENTER. You have intervened to change the value. Click the Code window. Highlight the expression fNumerator / fDenominator and examine it using Instant/Quick Watch. Now it has a defined value, depending on what you entered as the numerator.

Reminder

The variable at the left of an assignment statement still has its earlier value until the statement executes. This value will be zero (or null) if the variable has never been used before.

Click the **Continue** button in the Toolbar. The program continues with its execution and prompts you for a positive number. Enter something like **55.40**. You will encounter another runtime error. Click the **Debug** button, and you should see the Code window with the following statement highlighted:

```
fSquareRoot = fSquare ^ 0.5
```

Use Instant/Quick Watch to check the values of expressions fSquare and fSquare ^ 0.5, respectively. Raising something to the exponent of 0.5 is the same as taking its square root. The cause of the error is that fSquare has a negative value. Use the Debug window to change its value back to positive. For example, type in something like the following:

```
fSquare = 55.40
```

and press ENTER. You have intervened to change the value. Click the **Code** window. Highlight the expression fSquare ^ 0.5 and examine it using Instant Watch. Now it has a defined value, depending on what you entered as the square.

Click the **Continue** button in the Toolbar. The program continues with its execution and prompts you for a large number. Enter something like **600** (but smaller than 32767). You will encounter another runtime error. Click the **Debug** button. You should see the Code window with the following statement highlighted:

```
nLarge = nLarge * nLarge
```

Use Instant Watch to check the values of expressions `nLarge` and `nLarge` `*` `nLarge`, respectively. The multiplication will result in a number that is outside the range of the Integer data type. Use the Debug window to change `nLarge` to something smaller, such as 60. Examine the expressions again using Instant Watch. Both expressions should now have defined values.

Click the **Continue** button in the Toolbar. The program will encounter another error. Click the **Debug** button. The code window will highlight the following statement:

```
fSquare = "Square"
```

Using Instant Watch, note that `Square` is a defined string value. The variable `fSquare` has its former value. However, an attempt to assign a string to a Single data type variable will cause an error. At this point we can stop program execution.

If you wish, run through this exercise again. Note that if you press **F1** when the error is encountered, Visual Basic will display a Help topic about the error. Try this if you wish.

3.9   SAMPLE PROBLEMS

Unit Conversions From Meters

Use **Open Project** to open `INTRO`. Then select **Save File As** to save the RUNME file as `CH03\METERTO1`. Use **Save Project As** to save INTRO as `CH03\METERTO1`. Type in the code shown in Example 3.17. Run and test the program. Modify the program so that it will input kilometers instead of meters.

A Simple Thank-You Letter

Use **Open Project** to open INTRO. Use **Save File As** to save the RUNME file as `CH03\THANKU1`. Use **Save Project As** to save INTRO as `CH03\THANKYU1`. Type in the code shown in Example 3.19. Run and test the program. Modify the program so that the thank-you letter will also mention the canoe model. In Chapter 1 both the PROCEED and EVENT programs listed available canoe models as Ontario, Erie, Michigan, Huron, and Superior. It is not necessary to check that a proper model was entered when this program prompts for the canoe model.

Loan Balance

Click on **Open Project** to open INTRO. Use **Save File As** to save RUNME as `CH03\LOAN1`. Use **Save Project As** to save INTRO As `CH03\LOAN1`. Type in the code shown in Example 3.21. Run and test the program.

Mystery Program: Troubleshoot and Improve Documentation

Click on **Open Project** to open MYSTERY (in directory `CH03`). Use **Save File As** to save MYSTERY as NETPAY, and the use **Save Project As** to save MYSTERY as NETPAY. Notice the poor programming style. Your task is to improve the program and correct the logic error(s). The program is supposed to calculate yearly net pay after deducting pension plan contributions and income tax from the gross pay. Enjoy.

Following is the output based on gross pay of $45,000, a pension deduction of 5%, and an income tax rate of 20%. This user will certainly be shocked to find that his net pay is negative. (A government might not complain, though.)

```
Gross pay is 45000
% deduction for pension plan is 5
% deduction for income tax is 20

Net Pay is -1080000
```

Use Debug Tools to troubleshoot the program. Rewrite the code using suggested naming conventions. Also, you might improve the program output. Don't peek now, but you can find a possible solution in the program disk as CH03\SOLN\NETPAY.

Programmers often have to revise programs originally written by others. Perhaps this exercise gives the flavor of how difficult this is, particularly if the program to be modified was poorly written. Sometimes the program you have to modify is one you wrote many months (or years) earlier, so do yourself a favor and use good documentation and style.

ADDITIONAL PROBLEM SOLVING

Develop a program that converts Celsius to Fahrenheit.

CHAPTER 4

Programming Blocks

This chapter introduces the functional blocks of code that make up every program.

A manufacturer uses molds to make plastic toys. The manufacturer wouldn't try to custom-mold each toy, so the mold is reusable for different production runs. Even with a fixed mold, it is possible to use plastics of different colors so that toys are not identical. Similarly, a program uses sections of reusable code when it performs similar procedures. It uses data to specify exactly what the section of code produces.

After completing this chapter, you should be able to

- Design a program based on partitioning it into functional units.

- Create and use simple subprocedures, functions, and event procedures.

- Write statements that call procedures using arguments.

- Explain the difference between local and global variables.

- Describe the principles of event-driven programming using the terms *object, form, control, property, event,* and *event procedure*.

In This Chapter

In Chapter 2 Cougar Canoe determined the three components necessary to determine the price of a canoe:

1. Add up prices for the material.

2. Calculate labor.

3. Add markup to material and labor cost to achieve profit.

Would we write the program in components? What if we also wanted to determine the final bill after delivering the canoe to a customer?

4.1   PARTITIONING MODULES

*A **module** is a set of step-by-step statements that tell the computer how to do a subtask.*

To execute a task, we typically need to carry out subtasks, such as taking steps (a subtask) in order to walk (a task).

The components for determining canoe price is one example of a task that requires subtasks. We can partition the task of finding canoe price into modules (blocks of code) that do the following:

- Add material prices, (The `Material` Module).
- Calculate labor (The `Labor` Module).
- Add markup to material and labor costs (The `Markup` Module).

Another scenario involves a bank. The bank's program calculates monthly earnings. The program is organized into modules that handle different subtasks required to perform the main task of calculating earnings. These modules to calculate earnings from

- Loan interest charged to each client (The `Loan` Module).
- Service charges to each account holder (The `Service` Module).
- Interest gains from investments (The `Investment` Module).

Each program module is reusable. The same `Loan` Module is executed when finding earnings for any client. The `Service` and `Investment` modules are similarly reusable for each account and investment, respectively.

Exercise

Describe modules for the following task. Create the bill that Cougar Canoe would send to a customer after shipping the canoe.

Solution

- Determine canoe price (The `CanoePrice` Module).
- Determine delivery cost (The `DeliveryCost` Module).
- Determine taxes (The `Tax` Module).
- Add canoe price, delivery cost, and taxes (The `AddItems` Module).

Note that the `CanoePrice` Module is itself made of three modules: Material, Labor, and Markup.

4.1.1   Structure Charts

After organizing a task into subtasks, we can present the program structure pictorially using structure charts (see Section 2.2.4). The blocks in the structure chart illustrate the hierarchy of tasks. Figure 4.1 shows one for the final bill task described in the exercise.

The main module is `FinalBill`. It uses modules `CanoePrice`, `DeliveryCost`, `Tax`, and `AddItems`. `CanoePrice` in turn uses Material, Labor, and Markup. It is possible that `DeliveryCost` and other modules may need to be broken down further into finer-detail modules.

4.1.2   Procedures

Procedures are modules, blocks of statements that completely execute a task or a subtask. Visual Basic Help defines a procedure as "a named sequence of statements executed as a unit." Look at any program, such as the one in Example 4.1 or one with a bit more capability (Example 4.2).

Figure 4.1
Structure Chart for Determining Final Bill

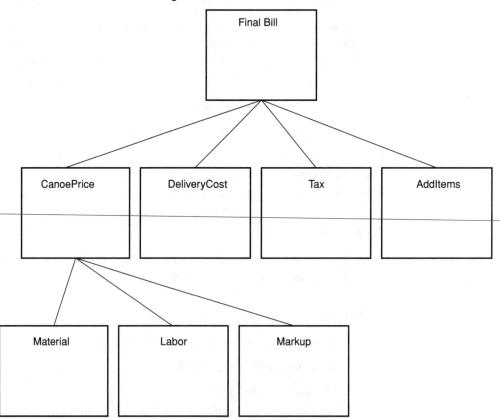

Example 4.1

```
Public Sub RunMe()

    ' Programmer writes code here
    PrintMsg "Welcome to Cougar Canoe"

End Sub
```

Example 4.2

```
Public Sub RunMe()

    ' Fahrenheit to Celsius Conversion Program

    ' Initialize
    Dim fFahr As Single, fCels As Single

    ' Get Inputs
    InputSng "Enter Temperature in Fahrenheit", fFahr

    ' Do Computations
    fCels = 5 / 9 * (fFahr - 32)

    ' Send Outputs
    PrintSng "Temperature in Celsius is ", fCels

End Sub
```

We have been using a procedure all along. It is named RunMe. In principle, we could have named it something else, such as WalkYou; however, the Introduction Template works only if there is at least one procedure named RunMe. We can always add new procedures, though, and the main procedure RunMe can simply use the new procedures, as in Example 4.3.

Example 4.3

```
Public Sub RunMe()

    ' This procedure must always exist in the
    ' Introduction Template

    ' Call (invoke, execute, launch) the WalkYou procedure
    WalkYou

End Sub

Public Sub WalkYou()

    ' A new procedure
    PrintMsg "Welcome to Cougar Canoe"

End Sub
```

Here we see two procedures, RunMe and WalkYou.

To define a procedure, we must begin and end the procedure declaration. To begin a (sub) procedure declaration, the syntax is

Public Sub *name*( )

where *name* is the name for the procedure.[1] You cannot use keywords such as End to name a keyword.

For example

```
Public Sub RunMe()
```

is a valid statement to begin a procedure declaration. To end a procedure declaration, simply use the statement

```
End Sub
```

Any statements that follow it do not belong to the procedure. Every statement must belong to a procedure, with a few exceptions such as `Option Explicit`. For simplicity, we have omitted some variations in the syntax.

When you click the **Run Me** button in the Introduction Template, the procedure RunMe will execute. Remember that Visual Basic must be in the Run Mode, unless you are working with an executable version (one that has been made into an EXE file). When procedure RunMe executes the statement WalkYou, this causes the procedure WalkYou to execute. In programming parlance, RunMe *calls* the WalkYou procedure. After the *called* procedure, WalkYou, has executed, the calling procedure, RunMe, continues execution. To illustrate this, consider the next program. After WalkYou has been called the first time, the RunMe procedure calls it a second time and yet a third time (see Example 4.4).

Example 4.4

```
Public Sub RunMe()

    ' This procedure must always exist in the
    ' Introduction Template

    ' Call the WalkYou procedure
    WalkYou
    ' Call it again
    WalkYou
    ' And call it again
    WalkYou

End Sub


Public Sub WalkYou()

    ' This procedure called by another procedure
    PrintMsg "Welcome to Cougar Canoe"

End Sub
```

[1]*The keyword* Public *is optional. However, if you omit it, the keyword* Public *is implied since this is the default. It is a good idea to include it, since this will point out that the procedure is public instead of private. At this point, the distinction is not important, but it will be.*

The output from this code will look like this:

```
Welcome to Cougar Canoe
Welcome to Cougar Canoe
Welcome to Cougar Canoe
```

In a real-world situation, programmers create procedures that contain many statements. Our simple examples merely used one-line statements. Procedures are useful because they permit us to reuse code in the same program. They also help with the design, since the steps identified in the stepwise refinement process can directly translate to procedures.

Exercise

Write a program that converts Fahrenheit to Celsius four times.

Solution

Here is a simple example of code reuse: Example 4.5 reuses the code from Example 4.2.

Example 4.5

```
Public Sub RunMe()

    ' Convert Fahrenheit to Celsisus Four Times
    FahrToCels
    FahrToCels
    FahrToCels
    FahrToCels

End Sub

Public Sub FahrToCels()

    ' Fahrenheit to Celsius Conversion Procedure

    ' Initialize
    Dim fFahr As Single, fCels As Single

    ' Get Inputs
    InputSng "Enter Temperature in Fahrenheit", fFahr

    ' Do Computations
    fCels = 5 / 9 * (fFahr - 32)

    ' Send Outputs
    PrintSng "Temperature in Celsius is ", fCels

End Sub
```

4.1.3   Partitioning Into Basic Operations

Recall that a computer program generally performs the following operations:

- Input
- Process

- Output

- Store

When an operation requires many statements, it is useful to define a procedure for the operation. Hence, we could partition a program into procedures for the Input, Process, Output, and Store operations.

4.2   ARGUMENTS AND PARAMETERS

Consider the task of calculating the final bill (see Figure 4.1). One of the subtasks is to determine the delivery cost. Would the cost be the same for a canoe delivered next door as for one delivered halfway around the world? The `DeliveryCost` procedure needs additional information, such as distance and mode of transportation. Let's consider only one mode of transportation for now. Procedure `FinalBill` needs to specify the distance when calling `DeliveryCost`. The result of executing `DeliveryCost` will vary depending on the distance.

That's not all. Procedure `AddItems` needs such additional information as the canoe cost, the delivery cost, and the tax in order to calculate a result. In fact, the information it requires are the results from procedures `CanoePrice`, `DeliveryCost`, and `Tax`. Similarly, `CanoePrice` needs information from procedures `Material`, `Labor`, and `Markup`.

A programming language needs a mechanism for providing information to a procedure so that it can complete its subtask. It also needs a way for the procedure to give the result back to the calling procedure that needs it. Well, what do we need? Check out the subheading. We need arguments and parameters.

*An **argument** is a constant, variable, or expression passed to a procedure.*

*A **parameter** is a variable name by which an argument passed to a procedure is known within the procedure. This variable receives the argument passed into the procedure. Its scope ends when the procedure ends.*

So, what does this all mean? (Don't worry about scope for now.) Procedure `DeliveryCost` needs information about distance; hence distance is a parameter. Look at the declaration carefully. Note that a parameter is a variable. Let's say that costs based on distance depend only on the nearest kilometer. Then we could use the Integer data type for distance. There is no danger of overflow as long as we stay on the planet and don't go in circles! Hence we shall name this parameter `nDistance`. So what is the argument?

If Cougar Canoe needed to deliver a canoe 500 kilometers away, the argument would be the expression 500 (a value in this case). If Cougar Canoe needed to deliver a canoe based on the value stored in variable nDistanceToVancouver, the argument would be the variable nDistanceToVancouver. If Cougar needed to deliver to Lillooet via Vancouver, the argument could be the following expression: `nDistanceTo-Vancouver + nDistanceBetweenVancouverAndLillooet`.

The parameter specifies the generic type of information as defined in the procedure declaration. The argument specifies the actual information used when the procedure is called. ***Passing*** refers to the process of transferring information from the calling procedure to the called procedure using arguments. It can also refer to the process in which the called procedure sends a result back to the calling procedure. In sports or games, one player typically passes an object (such as a hockey puck) to another player. Example 4.6 illustrates the calling process with passing, and Figure 4.2 provides a pictorial illustration.

Example 4.6

```
Public Sub RunMe()

    ' Convert Fahrenheit to Celsisus

    ' Declare variable for actual temperature to convert
    Dim fActualTemp As Single

    ' Tell user what this program does
    PrintMsg "Program converts Fahrenheit to Celsius"
    PrintMsg ""
    ' Get Input
    InputSng "Enter Temperature in Fahrenheit", fActualTemp
    PrintSng " Temperature in Fahrenheit is: ", fActualTemp

    ' fActualTemp represents temperature in Fahrenheit

    ' Perform conversion by passing argument fActualTemp
    ' when calling procedure FahrToCels
    FahrToCels fActualTemp

    ' Now fActualTemp represents temperature in Celsius

    ' Display result
    PrintSng "  Temperature in Celsius is: ", fActualTemp

End Sub


Public Sub FahrToCels(fTemperature As Single)

    ' Fahrenheit to Celsius Conversion Procedure
    ' It uses the parameter fTemperature

    ' Do Computation
    fTemperature = 5 / 9 * (fTemperature - 32)
    ' When procedure exits, it returns fTemperature

End Sub
```

Note that we can provide some degree of self-documentation when using procedures. By naming procedures and arguments appropriately, we can tell at a glance what a program does without having to examine the code for the procedures being called.

During program execution:

- A calling procedure passes arguments to the called procedure for it to use.

- The called procedure assigns the arguments to its input parameters.

- The called procedure executes.

Figure 4.2
The Calling Process for a Temperature Conversion Example

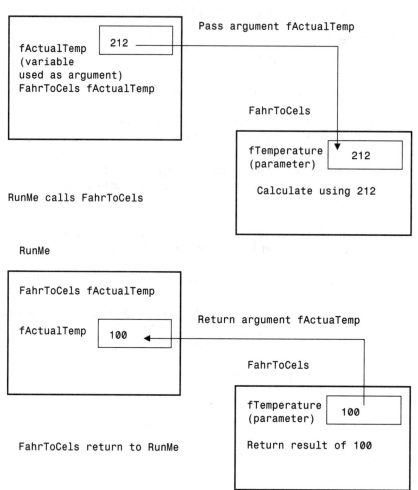

- The called procedure assigns the execution results to output parameters.
- The called procedure assigns output parameters to arguments.
- The called procedure passes arguments to the calling procedure for it to use.

In this case:

- RunMe calls FahrToCels and passes argument fActualTemp to it.
- FahrToCels assigns fTemperature to the value of fActualTemp.
- FahrToCels executes; this modifies the value of fTemperature.
- FahrToCels assigns fActualTemp to the value of fTemperature.
- FahrToCels returns execution control to RunMe.
- RunMe continues execution.

The syntax to begin a (sub) procedure declaration is

Public Sub *name*[(*arglist*)]

where *name* is the name for the procedure, and *arglist* is a list of variables (if any) representing arguments that are passed to the function when it is called. Multiple variables are separated by commas.

Exercise

Write the following program: Given a starting temperature in Fahrenheit, it outputs three temperatures in increments of 10 Fahrenheit degrees and outputs their equivalent temperatures in Celsius.

Solution

Example 4.7 shows the solution for this exercise.

Example 4.7

```
Public Sub RunMe()

    ' Display three temperatures in Fahrenheit in
    ' increments of ten degrees and also
    ' display their Celsius equivalents

    ' Declare variable for actual temperature to convert
    Dim fActualTemp As Single
    ' Declare holding variable for original Fahrenheit input
    Dim fFahr As Single

    ' Tell user what this program does
    PrintMsg "Program displays three temperatures in F and C"
    PrintMsg ""

    ' Get Input
    InputSng "Enter Start Temperature in Fahrenheit", fFahr
    PrintSng "  1st Temperature in Fahrenheit is: ", fFahr

    ' Calculate first conversion
    fActualTemp = fFahr
    FahrToCels fActualTemp

    ' Display first result
    PrintSng "  1st Temperature in Celsius is: ", fActualTemp

    ' Calculate and display next two temperatures
    fActualTemp = fFahr + 10
    PrintSng "  2nd Temperature in Fahrenheit is: ", ➡
    fActualTemp
    FahrToCels fActualTemp
    PrintSng "  2nd Temperature in Celsius is: ", fActualTemp

    fActualTemp = fFahr + 20
    PrintSng "  3rd Temperature in Fahrenheit is: ", ➡
    fActualTemp
    FahrToCels fActualTemp
    PrintSng "  3rd Temperature in Celsius is: ", fActualTemp

End Sub
```

```
Public Sub FahrToCels(fTemperature As Single)

    ' Fahrenheit to Celsius Conversion Procedure
    ' It uses the parameter fTemperature

    ' Do Computation
    fTemperature = 5 / 9 * (fTemperature - 32)

    ' When procedure exits, it returns fTemperature

End Sub
```

4.3   LOCAL AND GLOBAL (PUBLIC) VARIABLES

4.3.1   Local Variables

A *local* variable is declared inside the declaration of a procedure using the keyword Dim. It is only visible to that procedure, meaning its *scope* is local. The scope of a variable refers to when a variable may be accessed during execution of a program. Consider Example 4.8.

Example 4.8

```
Option Explicit

Public Sub RunMe()

    ' Simple Local Variable Demo
    ' It attempts to use variables
    ' that are out of scope.
    ' Syntax errors generated

    nLocalDee = 1    ' Not valid
    nLocalDum = 3    ' Not valid
    TweedleDee   ' Call procedure
    TweedleDum   ' Call procedure
    TweedleDee   ' Call this one again

End Sub

Public Sub TweedleDee()

    Dim nLocalDee As Integer
    nLocalDee = 5    ' Valid
    nLocalDum = 7    ' Not valid

End Sub

Public Sub TweedleDum()

    Dim nLocalDum As Integer
    nLocalDum = 9    ' Valid
    nLocalDee = 13   ' Not valid

End Sub
```

Only procedure `TweedleDee` may use variable `nLocalDee`; only procedure `TweedleDum` may use variable `nLocalDee`.

Hence, the scope of `nLocalDee` is local to procedure `TweedleDee`. The scope of `nLocalDum` is local to procedure `TweedleDum`. Note that local variables are visible only to the procedure in which they are declared.

In Exercise 3, we used the Debug tools to single step. If we attempt to access `nLocalDum` while stepping through the code for procedure `TweedleDee`, Visual Basic would complain that `nLocalDum` is out of context. Only `nLocalDee` is in context when `TweedleDee` is executing. The context (or scope) for `nLocalDum` is procedure `TweedleDum`. The context of a variable defines which procedures may access it. In other words, it is the same as the scope.

4.3.2   Global Variables

A *global* variable is declared in the General Declarations area using the keyword `Public`. It is visible to all procedures, meaning its scope is global. The General Declarations area also contains the procedure declarations. Figure 4.3 shows the Visual Basic Code window. Note that we can select the General Declarations area or any procedure from the Proc: drop-down list.

The syntax for a global declaration is

Public *variablename* **As** *data type* [**,** *variablename* **As** *data type*] . . .

Figure 4.3
Visual Basic Code Window Showing General Declarations Area and Procedures

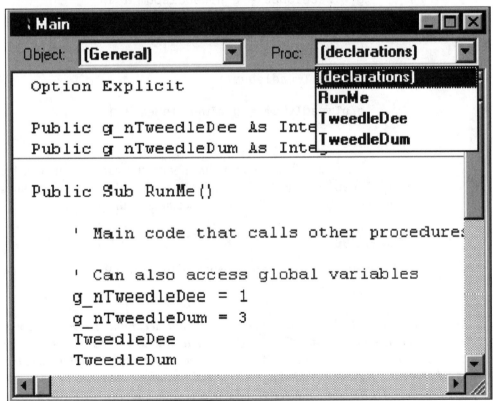

The declaration uses the keyword `Public` instead of `Dim`.[2] The word `Public` as a keyword is helpful. It implies that the variables are publicly available to all procedures in the program. By convention, we use an additional prefix of g underscore (g_) to remind us that the variable is global. Example 4.9 illustrates the declaration and use of global variables.

Example 4.9

```
Option Explicit

Public g_nTweedleDee as Integer    ' Global variables
Public g_nTweedleDum as Integer
'

Public Sub RunMe()

    ' Main code that calls other procedures
    ' Can also access global variables
    g_nTweedleDee = 1
    g_nTweedleDum = 3
    TweedleDee
    TweedleDum
    g_nTweedleDee = g_nTweedleDum + 6

End Sub


Public Sub TweedleDee()

    g_nTweedleDee = g_nTweedleDum + 1

End Sub


Public Sub TweedleDum()

    g_nTweedleDum = g_nTweedleDee + 1

End Sub
```

Note that all procedures can modify the variables at will; hence the scopes of g_nTweedleDee and g_nTweedleDum are global to all procedures. This means that global variables are visible to all procedures in the program.

Exercise

What are the values of the variables in Exercise 4.9 after the program executes?

---

[2]*Actually we could use the keyword* Dim *and all would seem fine. However, we would have created a module-level variable instead of global one. The distinction is that module-level variables are only known to procedures in the module. When using the Introduction Template, this is module* Main *(File* RUNME.BAS *or a renamed version of it). A global variable would also be known to any procedure in any other modules and forms such as the* Intro *module and form (*INTRO.BAS *and* INTRO.FRM*).*

Solution

g_nTweedleDee has the value of 11 and g_nTweedleDum has the value of 5. This is a trick question: The global variables retain their value after procedure RunMe has executed. However, if you ended the Visual Basic program (e.g., clicked Exit), the variables would be *empty*. The Introduction Template is a metaprogram of sorts. It launches (calls) the procedure RunMe, which in turn may call other procedures we have coded.

4.3.3 A Business Account Application

Like most businesses, Cougar Canoe tracks their accounts receivable and accounts payable. An accounts receivable system keeps track of the amount of money owed to the company. Typically, these are outstanding bills charged to customers. An accounts payable system keeps track of money owed to suppliers and creditors. It also keeps track of money that the company must pay its employees. The program of Example 4.10 demonstrates the concept of updating these accounts. It also illustrates a sample situation in which local and global variables could be used.

Procedure RunMe (as is usual in the Introduction Template) is the main program. It initializes the accounts using global variables, and then it directs the operation of the other procedures to do the actual work of updating the accounts. Finally, it outputs the status of the accounts.

Procedure BillCustomer updates the global variable for accounts receivable. It also updates customer-specific information that isn't (and shouldn't be) visible to other procedures. In this case it uses a local variable to represent what the customer owes, which is personal and private information.

Procedure PayRoll updates the global variable for accounts payable. It also updates employee-specific information that isn't (and shouldn't be) visible to other procedures. In this case it uses a local variable to represent an employee's pension contribution, which is personal and private information. Note that all procedures must have access to the accounts. Hence the program uses global variables to represent them. Study Example 4.10 carefully.

Example 4.10

```
Option Explicit

    ' Declare Global (public) variables
    Public g_fAccountReceivable As Single
    Public g_fAccountPayable As Single
    '


Public Sub RunMe()

    ' Update accounts receivable and payable
    ' It adds customer billings to accounts receivable
    ' and adds employee wages to accounts payable

    ' Program demonstrates scope of variables
    ' Procedures BillCustomer and PayRoll can
    ' modify both accounts receivable and payable since they
    ' are global (accessible to all procedures)
```

```
    ' Procedures BillCustomer and PayRoll also
    ' use local variables which are not visible to any
    ' other procedure

    ' Start off with opening balance
    InputSng "Opening Accounts Receivable?", ➡
    g_fAccountReceivable
    PrintSng "Opening Accounts Receivable is ", ➡
    g_fAccountReceivable
    InputSng "Opening Accounts Payable?", g_fAccountPayable
    PrintSng "Opening Accounts Payable is ", g_fAccountPayable
    PrintMsg ""

    ' Update accounts receivable
    BillCustomer "Moe", 635
    BillCustomer "Larry", 955
    BillCustomer "Curly", 525

    ' Update accounts payable
    PayRoll "Susan", 1200
    PayRoll "Alvin", 1045

    ' Show account updates
    PrintMsg ""
    PrintSng "Updated Accounts Receivable is ", ➡
    g_fAccountReceivable
    PrintSng "Updated Accounts Payable is ", g_fAccountPayable

End Sub


Public Sub BillCustomer(sCustomer As String, fAmount As Single)

    ' Updates the accounts receivable and customer's account
    ' Input parameters:
    '    sCustomer = customer's name
    '    fAmount = amount billed to customer
    ' Output parameters: <none>
    ' Modifies global variable g_fAccountReceivable

    ' Declare local variable
    Dim fCustomerOwes As Single

    ' Update Accounts Receivable
    g_fAccountReceivable = g_fAccountReceivable + fAmount

    ' Input and update customer information.
    ' This is fake since we would normally get information
    ' from a database and store updates back to database
    PrintMsg ""
    PrintStr "The customer is ", sCustomer
    InputSng "Enter customer's outstanding account", ➡
    fCustomerOwes
```

```
        PrintSng "Customer's previous account was ", fCustomerOwes
        fCustomerOwes = fCustomerOwes + fAmount
        PrintSng "Customer billed an additional ", fAmount
        PrintSng "Customer now owes ", fCustomerOwes

End Sub


Public Sub PayRoll(sEmployee As String, fWage As Single)

    ' Updates the accounts payable
    ' and handles employee pension contribution
    ' Input parameters:
    '    sEmployee = employee's name
    '    fWage = net pay
    ' Output parameters: <none>
    ' Modifies global variable g_fAccountPayable

    ' Declare local variable
    Dim fPensionContribution As Single

    ' Update Accounts Payable
    g_fAccountPayable = g_fAccountPayable + fWage

    ' Input and update employee information.
    ' This is fake since we would normally get information
    ' from a database and store updates back to database
    PrintMsg ""
    PrintStr "The employee is ", sEmployee
    InputSng "Enter % contribution to pension", ➥
    fPensionContribution
    PrintSng "Employee wage before deduction is ", fWage
    PrintSng "% Pension contribution is ", fPensionContribution
    'Convert to decimal
    fPensionContribution = fPensionContribution / 100
    fPensionContribution = fPensionContribution * fWage
    fWage = fWage - fPensionContribution
    PrintSng "Wage after deduction is ", fWage
    PrintSng "Pension contribution is ", fPensionContribution

End Sub
```

Exercise

For the program of Example 4.10, what are the characteristics of the opening comments in the procedures called by RunMe? Why would this information be important?

Solution

The opening comments in both BillCustomer and PayRoll summarize what the procedure does, describe input parameters, describe output parameters (none in this case), and state which global variables are modified. This type of information would be important to a programmer who is or will be using the procedure in her or his program. It tells the programmer the expected result, what kind of input data is required, and how the results will be returned. It is also useful to be aware of potential side effects, since other parts of the program will also be using the global variables. Note that other parts of the program will not be directly affected by modifications to the local variables.

4.3.4   A Little Bit Under the Hood

On the surface, we covered most of what you need to know about local and global variables. However, there is a bit of programming wisdom you should know.

Rule of Thumb

Use local variables when possible. Pass arguments when it is necessary to share information between procedures. Remember, though, that sometimes it is desirable to use global variables.

Generally, the exception occurs in situations in which we cannot predict when any procedure needs to use information that must be shared. In principle, we could rewrite Example 4.10 so that each procedure uses its own local copy of the accounts. Procedures BillCustomer and PayRoll could use additional parameters representing accounts receivable and accounts payable, respectively. They could receive the initial account data as an argument and return back an update by passing the updated argument back to RunMe. Hence it *seems* that we did not need global variables. (In fact, you will rewrite the program in the hands-on exercises.) The rule of thumb is particularly true in procedural programming, which we are presently doing.

Distributed Processing Scenario

What if this is only the beginning of the development of a major tracking system? The system runs continuously, and various activities could trigger updates at any time. An order to purchase fiberglass matting and other supplies could automatically trigger an update to accounts payable. A confirmed delivery could trigger an update to accounts receivable. All of these activities need to update universal account information. By passing arguments instead of using global variables, it would be necessary to have one central main program that keeps track of the final totals. All transactions would have to go through this centralized system of control.[3] By using global information, processing can be *distributed*, and any transaction can be done independently. This is similar to event-driven programming. We will become more involved with this as we start to use Visual Basic for event-driven programming instead of procedural programming.

As you may guess, we have tremendously simplified the situation. In fact, we would want the account information accessible only to those procedures that need the information. It shouldn't be possible to create deviant procedures that wreak havoc on this critical data. This is the realm of access modifiers used in true object-oriented programming, which we will not cover here.

---

[3]*A transaction is a recording of an event involved with conducting business. A customer order is an example of a transaction.*

Storage in Memory

The key difference between global and local variables lies in the way they are stored in memory. Global variables are stored in a fixed address, while local variables may end up being stored in different addresses every time the associated procedure is called. Think about going to a hockey or baseball game or the ballet. Some people have reserved seats. Every time they attend the event, they always sit in their reserved seat (usually with the best view). Other people need to sit in the first available seat they can find, usually a different seat for each event.

Addresses in computer memory are like seats in a stadium, arena, or theater. Each seat is a byte in memory. We can address each seat by row letter and number designation, starting with Row A Number 1 and so on up to Row Z (or AE or whatever) Number 100 (or whatever). Integer data type variables are couples; they require two seats (2 bytes). Single data type variables make up a typical family; they require four seats (4 bytes). String data type variables are groups; they require a seat (byte) for each character.

Local variables are stored in a section of memory known as the *stack*. According to Visual Basic Help, a stack is a fixed amount of memory used by Visual Basic to preserve local variables and arguments during procedure calls. To help understand what a stack is, consider a card game. After the dealer distributes the cards, the players (procedures) take turns placing cards on the deck. The stack is like the deck of cards. Each player places cards on the deck in turn. The cards represent the player's local variables. As each player takes his or her turn, more cards are placed on the deck. As each procedure is called, more local variables are placed on the deck. In this particular game, players take (pull) their cards from the deck in reverse order. When a called procedure returns to the calling procedure, its local variables are pulled from the stack. Hence this area of memory in stack is now available for new local variables when the returned to procedure calls yet another procedure. Figure 4.4 illustrates the stack for the program of Example 4.11. The stack must also store necessary overhead information, such as arguments (if used) and housekeeping information that is necessary for the processor to find the appropriate machine code instructions.

Example 4.11

```
Option Explicit
Public g_nBuck As Integer
'

Public Sub RunMe()

    ' Demonstrate nested calls and scope of variables
    ' can also 'sort of' see stack
    Dim nRunMe As Integer
    g_nBuck = g_nBuck + 1
    nRunMe = nRunMe + 2
    PassBuck

End Sub


Public Sub PassBuck()

    Dim nPassBuck As Integer
    g_nBuck = g_nBuck + 1
```

```
        nPassBuck = nPassBuck + 4
        PassBuckAgain    ' A nested call

End Sub


Public Sub PassBuckAgain()

        Dim nPassBuckAgain As Integer
        g_nBuck = g_nBuck + 1
        nPassBuckAgain = nPassBuckAgain + 8
        ' To demonstrate recursive calls
        ' and eventual stack overflow (in this case)
        ' remove the single quote that follows ...
        ' PassBuck

End Sub
```

If we remove the single quote from the statement ' PassBuck, procedure PassBuckAgain will call PassBuck, which in turn will call PassBuckAgain,

Figure 4.4
Local and Global Variables
in Memory

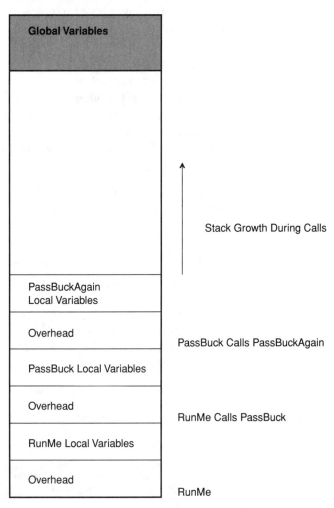

which will call `PassBuck` again, and so it continues until something really bad happen, such as running out of memory. During each recursive call, the computer puts (pushes) a new set of local variables onto the stack. The stack eventually grows so large that it can no longer fit in memory. The result is *stack overflow*, generating the stack overflow runtime error. If this program is compiled and executed as a stand-alone program, the error will occur, and we must terminate the program. Fortunately, the Windows operating system polices the use of memory by all programs; hence, an attempt by this application to steal more memory is trapped, and memory used by other applications is protected.

A recursive call occurs when a procedure eventually gets called again before it has completed execution an earlier time. Should you use recursive calls? The answer is yes, provided there is a mechanism to stop the recursion. (Chapter 5 covers decision logic, which is used to provide such a mechanism.)

Reentrant Procedures

Recursive calls are one example of reentrant procedures. In a nonprocedural programming situation, it is possible for the execution of a procedure to be interrupted. The computer then executes another procedure, but it is possible that this new procedure may call the original procedure that was interrupted! This scenario could occur in a real-time control or event-driven program.

Consider a real-time control program to control a robot. The program uses procedure `DriveMotor` to drive any of its motors. `DriveMotor` may be executing to control the gripper motor. During this time an external crash alarm signal triggers an interruption. The program suspends execution of `DriveMotor`. It launches the `PreventCrash` procedure. Procedure `PreventCrash` calls (reenters) procedure `DriveMotor` to drive the arm motor. Think about what would happen if procedure `DriveMotor` used global variables instead of local variables. After `PreventCrash` completed its task, procedure `DriveMotor` would resume processing to control the gripper motor. However, the global variables would have been corrupted. `DriveMotor` has already modified them when controlling the arm motor. With local variables, each instance of `DriveMotor` would be using its own variables. Wouldn't you prefer to use your own toothbrush instead of sharing?

Review Scope of Variables

The scope of variables defines the visibility of a variable. For example, a variable declared as `Public` is visible to all procedures in the program. Variables declared in procedures are visible only within the procedure and lose their value between calls (unless they are declared `Static`). (We will consider Static variables in Chapter 6.)

4.4 PROGRAMMER-DEFINED SUB PROCEDURES AND FUNCTIONS

We have been using *sub* procedures already. Consider a statement from the Fahrenheit to Celsius conversion program of Example 4.6.

```
FahrToCels fActualTemp
```

Prior to the call, variable `fActualTemp` is an argument whose value is the temperature in Fahrenheit. After the call is complete, argument `fActualTemp` is returned and has a value of the equivalent temperature in Celsius. Specifically, `FahrToCels` is an example of a sub procedure (or subroutine). Now consider a statement like the following:

```
fCels = Celsius(fFahr)
```

Does this statement look more intuitive? It should imply that `fCels` is assigned the Celsius equivalent of a temperature in Fahrenheit. Do you remember using functions in your high school math classes? You may have used such typical math functions as:

$$y = f(x), y = \sin(\Theta), y = \cos(\Theta), \text{etc.}$$

A program *function* is a special type of procedure, a block of code (procedure) that always returns one value. A function returns the value inherently because we assign a variable to the function's name when the function is called. Consider the program of Example 4.12.

Example 4.12

```
Option Explicit

Public Sub RunMe()


    ' Demonstrate a function

    Dim fFahr As Single, fCels As Single
    Dim fTwiceCels As Single, fCelsOfTwiceFahr As Single

    InputSng "Enter Temperature in Fahrenheit", fFahr
    PrintSng "Fahrenheit temperature is ", fFahr

    ' Use (call) the function
    fCels = Celsius(fFahr)
    fTwiceCels = 2 * Celsius(fFahr)
    fCelsOfTwiceFahr = Celsius(2 * fFahr)

    ' Display results
    PrintSng "Celsius temperature is ", fCels
    PrintSng "Twice Celsius temperature is ", fTwiceCels
    PrintSng "Celsius of twice Fahrenheit is ", ➡
    fCelsOfTwiceFahr

End Sub


Public Function Celsius(fFahrenheit As Single) As Single

    ' Function declaration
    ' Function returns Celsius equivalent of
    ' Fahrenheit temperature specified by
    ' parameter fFahrenheit

    ' Do Computation
    Celsius = 5 / 9 * (fFahrenheit - 32)
```

```
' When function exits, it returns Celsius

End Function
```

Let's examine a variation of this program.

Example 4.13

```
Option Explicit

Public Sub RunMe()
    ' Note that calling a function results in returning a ➥
    single value,
    ' hence a function call can be used as an expression

    Dim fFahr As Single

    InputSng "Enter Temperature in Fahrenheit", fFahr
    PrintSng "Fahrenheit temperature is ", fFahr

    ' Display results by passing arguments to PrintSng
    ' which are expressions containing the function call
    PrintSng "Celsius temperature is ", Celsius(fFahr)
    PrintSng "Twice Celsius temperature is ", 2 * ➥
    Celsius(fFahr)
    PrintSng "Celsius of twice Fahrenheit is ", Celsius(2 * fFahr)

End Sub


' Function Celsius is same as before
Public Function Celsius(fFahrenheit As Single) As Single

    ' Function declaration
    ' Function returns Celsius equivalent of
    ' Fahrenheit temperature specified by
    ' parameter fFahrenheit

    ' Do Computation
    Celsius = 5 / 9 * (fFahrenheit - 32)

    ' When function exits, it returns Celsius

End Function
```

There are some things to note in these examples: Check the function declaration. It starts with the keyword Function and ends with keyword As, followed by a data type. When a function finishes executing, it returns as an expression.

A sub procedure declaration (see Example 4.11 or earlier) uses the Sub keyword and does not end with a data type assignment.[4] A sub procedure does not return a value directly. It may only return value(s) indirectly by passing arguments.

---

[4]*Languages such as C, C++, or Java use only functions. Instead of using sub procedures, the function is declared to be of type void. Void means that it doesn't return any value directly.*

To define a function, we must begin and end the function declaration. The syntax for beginning a function declaration is

Public Function *name*[(*arglist*)] **As** *datatype*

where *name* is the name for the procedure.[5] You cannot use keywords such as End to name a function. *arglist* is a list of variables (if any) representing arguments that are passed to the function when it is called. Multiple variables are separated by commas. For example:

```
Public Function GiveMeFive() As Integer

Public Function Average(fNum1 As Single, fNum2 As Single) As
Integer
```

are valid statements to begin a function declaration. To end a function declaration, simply use the statement

End Function

Any statements that follow it do not belong to the declared function. Every statement must belong to a procedure (sub or function), with a few exceptions, such as Option Explicit. (There are a few other variations, which, for simplicity's sake, we will not mention.)

Box Volume Demonstration

Example 4.14 illustrates the use of both sub and function procedures. We use sub procedures when we do not expect a result. InputInt (declared in the Introduction Template) is an exception. Note that both sub and function procedures can use multiple parameters. When calling procedures, the arguments may have the same name as the parameters used in the declaration (e.g., BoxVolume), or they can be different. Also note that a function can return a data type that is different than the data types used for its parameters/arguments (e.g., GetDimension).

The procedures are documented, and the comments explain what input arguments are expected. They explain what is returned, either arguments returned for sub procedures or what the function returns. Each sub or function procedure also includes an introductory description of what the procedure does. There are additional comments throughout the program to explain the purpose of using certain statements in order to accomplish the program's objective (see Example 4.14).

Example 4.14

```
Option Explicit

Public Sub RunMe()

     ' Box Volume Program
     ' Written by Cody Wizard, Jan. 24, 1997
```

---

[5]*The keyword* Public *is optional. However, if you omit it, the keyword* Public *is implied, since this is the default. It is a good idea to include it, since this will point out that the procedure is public instead of private.*

```
        ' Sub RunMe requires no arguments

        ' Demo use of both functions and sub procedures
        ' We will calculate the volume of a box

        ' Use function GetDimension to obtain each of
        ' the box's dimensions
        ' Use sub EchoDimension to echo back entered dimension
        ' Use function BoxVolume to calculate box volume
        ' Use template command PrintInt to output volume

        ' Box Dimensions
        Dim nLength As Integer, nWidth As Integer
        Dim nHeight As Integer, nBoxVolume As Integer

        ' Get box dimensions from user
        nLength = GetDimension("Length")
        EchoDimension "length", nLength
        nWidth = GetDimension("Width")
        EchoDimension "width", nWidth
        nHeight = GetDimension("Height")
        EchoDimension "height", nHeight

        ' Determine box volume
        nBoxVolume = BoxVolume(nLength, nWidth, nHeight)

        ' Display box volume to user
        PrintInt "Box volume is ", nBoxVolume

End Sub


Public Function GetDimension(sPrompt As String) As Integer

    ' Input:
    '    sPrompt specifies the prompt message displayed
    '    above input box
    ' Function returns the integer of what the user enters
    ' in the Input Box of the Introduction Template
    ' Function causes runtime error if user enters
    ' non-numeric data or a number outside integer range

    Dim nInteger As Integer
    sPrompt = "Input " & sPrompt
    InputInt sPrompt, nInteger
    GetDimension = nInteger

End Function


Public Sub EchoDimension(sName As String, nInteger As Integer)

    ' Inputs:
    '    sName is the dimension category, e.g., length
```

```
'    nInteger is the dimension value
' Outputs:  <none>
' Procedure composes an echo-back message and prints
' it to the Output Box of the Introduction Template
' This reminds the user as to what was entered
' Procedure causes runtime error if it is passed
' arguments that don't match the parameter data types

   sName = "Box " & sName & " is "
   PrintInt sName, nInteger

End Sub


Public Function BoxVolume(nLength As Integer, nWidth As ➡
Integer, nHeight As Integer) As Integer

   ' Inputs:
   '    nLength, nWidth, and nHeight are box dimensions
   ' Function multiplies them to return the volume
   ' Function causes runtime error if it is passed
   ' arguments that don't match the parameter data types

   BoxVolume = nLength * nWidth * nHeight

End Function
```

We Have Used Procedures All Along

The template commands such as `PrintMsg`, `InputInt`, and others are, in fact, sub procedures. These procedures are declared in the Intro module (file INTRO.BAS). This is the reason why they are not highlighted in blue, as are the keywords in code examined using Visual Basic. The template commands are not intrinsic to the Visual Basic language; they are add-ons to the standard language. In conjunction with other parts of the Introduction Template, their purpose is to provide a simple means to develop simple procedural programs. The next section discusses functions that are intrinsic to the Visual Basic language.

4.5   LIBRARY FUNCTIONS

*A **library function** is a keyword. It is an inherent function that has already been defined in Visual Basic. The programmer does not need to code the function declaration.*

Visual Basic includes a rich set of functions that we can use to perform more complex tasks. We do not need to declare them and write the code to implement them. There are mathematical, data conversion, time and date, formatting, string manipulation, and other functions. These functions are also keywords.

Let's say we needed to find the number of characters in a string. We could use the `Len` and `LenB` functions in statements that look like the following:

```
nNumberOfCharacters = Len(sStringVariable)
nNumberOfBytes = LenB(sStringVariable)
```

If the value of `sStringVariable` is *"hello"* then `nNumberOfCharacters` is assigned a value of 5, and `nNumberOfBytes` is assigned a value of 10 (with the 32-bit version of Visual Basic). Function `Len` returns the number of characters in the string specified by its argument. `LenB` returns the number of bytes required to store the string. The 32-bit version of Visual Basic uses Unicode, which requires 2 bytes per character.

Since library functions are keywords, we cannot use them to name our own variables, constants, or procedures. Note that Visual Basic does not highlight all library functions in blue; however, you can click on **any library function** and press **F1** to see context-sensitive help about the function.

4.5.1 How to Find Library Function Information

To see the steps, run Visual Basic now, or wait until you get to the Hands-On Exercises at the end of this chapter. The starting point is the main Visual Basic Help window. To view this window, select Contents from the Help menu. Click the **Contents** tab. If the **Visual Basic Topics** book icon is closed, double-click to open it. Then double-click the **Contents** topic. The main Help window will show the following links, among other items.

- Functions
- Programming Language Summary
- Keywords by Task

The topic link to Functions shows every library function alphabetically. The Programming Language Summary includes functions in its alphabetical listing. The third master topic link we will describe is Keywords by Task. Once you select this topic, there are keyword categories such as string manipulation, financial, and other task categories. This is useful if you do not know whether the function you need exists. You can check an appropriate category to see if there is a function that does the job you want.

A Scenario

Let's say you were working on a program involving finances. In this program you want to calculate the net present value of an investment based on a series of periodic cash flows (payments and receipts) and a discount rate. This sounds difficult. Well, maybe it isn't. First, click on `Keywords by Task`. It seems reasonable to click `Financial`, since you are trying to determine something financial. In the Financial Keyword Summary, you will see a reference to Calculate Present Value. It seems reasonable to click on the link NPV. This launches the Help topic for the NPV function to calculate net present value. This could be your ticket to greater productivity.

Another method is to use trial and error. You can type in a word in the code window. Click on **the word** and press **F1**. If it is a library function, Help will display information about it.

As in the previous example, let's say you are interested in finding a net present value. You try possible keywords, and perhaps you eventually type in NPV. After you press ENTER, Visual Basic automatically capitalizes the letters. This is a good indication that NPV might be a keyword. Click on the word **NPV** and press **F1** to launch the Help topic. Note that in Visual Basic, library functions are also known as Visual Basic functions.

4.5.2   Finding the Sine of an Angle

The following program illustrates the use of the mathematical function to find the sine of an angle by using a library function.

Example 4.15

```
Public Sub RunMe()
    ' Demonstrate library function to find sine

    ' Pi is a mathematical constant equal to approximately ➡
    3.1415926535897932.
    Const PI = 3.14159265358979
    ' Angle and sine
    Dim fAngle As Single, fSine As Single

    ' Get angle in degrees
    InputSng "Enter Angle in degrees", fAngle
    PrintSng "The angle in degrees is ", fAngle

    ' Convert degrees to radians
    fAngle = fAngle * PI / 180

    ' Find sine
    fSine = Sin(fAngle)

    ' Display result
    PrintSng "The sine is ", fSine

End Sub
```

Note that function `Sin` expects an argument representing the angle in radians. (Visual Basic Help is useful in case you have forgotten what you learned in Geometry 101. The Help topic for `Sin` reminds us how to convert degrees into radians.)

4.5.3   Data Conversion Functions

Often it is necessary to convert data from one data type to another. A typical scenario is to compose a string from expressions. Each expression could be a different data type. Any output to the Introduction Template Output box ultimately must be a string. Behind the scenes, template commands such as `PrintInt` and `PrintSng` convert the numeric arguments into strings to display them in the box. Let's say we want the sine program of Example 4.15 to display an output like the following when the user enters 45.

```
Sine of 45° is 0.7071068.
```

To do this, we could use the program in Example 4.16.

Example 4.16

```
Public Sub RunMe()

    ' Demonstrate data conversion to improve format
    ' of program outputs

    ' Pi is a mathematical constant
    Const PI = 3.14159265358979 ' Approximate value
```

```
        Const DEG = 176 ' ANSI code for degree symbol

        ' Angle and sine
        Dim fAngle As Single, fSine As Single

        ' Ultimately we must use strings to compose
        ' a more sophisticated display message
        Dim sMsg As String

        Dim sDEG    ' Pseudo constant for degree character
        sDEG = Chr(DEG) ' Chr function converts ANSI code to ➡
        character

        ' Get angle in degrees
        InputSng "Enter Angle in degrees", fAngle

        ' Find sine, note that argument is
        ' an expression that evaluates to radians
        fSine = Sin(fAngle * PI / 180)

        ' Compose message for program output
        sMsg = "Sine of " & CStr(fAngle) & sDEG
        sMsg = sMsg & " is " & CStr(fSine) & "."

        ' Display our output
        PrintMsg sMsg

End Sub
```

The American National Standard Institute (ANSI) defines a code number for each text character. These are printable characters such as A, #, and 7, and for ***control*** characters (these have an effect on the text) such as a carriage return and tab. Since any ANSI code is normally stored as a byte (8 bits) in memory, the code numbers range from 0 to 255. The characters one sees on a standard English U.S. keyboard have codes between 32 (the space character) to 126 (the ~ character). Codes 128 to 255 are used for some fractions and for some characters and symbols used in some languages other than English. They are not available by pressing keys on a standard keyboard. Codes 0 to 31 are used for control characters such as tab and backspace, which are also on the keyboard.[6] For example, we cannot type in the symbol for degree (°). Using Help, we can find that its ANSI code is 176. The statement

```
sDEG = Chr(DEG) ' Chr function converts ANSI code to character
```

generates the character for the degree symbol. Library function Chr returns the character associated with the ANSI code as the argument. Since DEG has a value of 176, the function returns the degree character.

The following statements compose the message:

```
' Compose message for program output
sMsg = "Sine of " & CStr(fAngle) & sDEG
sMsg = sMsg & " is " & CStr(fSine) & "."
```

---

[6]*Not all control characters have equivalent keyboard keys. For example, formfeed does not have a keyboard equivalent.*

Library function CStr (Convert to String) returns a string representation of its argument. Incidentally, template commands InputInt and InputSng use functions CInt and CSng to convert strings to Integer and Single data types, respectively. What the user types into the Input box is a string; hence, any input representing numerical information must be converted. We can improve the format of the numeric output. With the program of Example 4.16, if the user entered 0.3455679, we would see

```
Sine of 0.3455679° is 6.031261E-03.
```

Perhaps we would prefer an output that displays all numbers with four decimal points, and a leading zero if the number is less than one. Then the output would look like this:

```
Sine of 0.3456° is 0.0060.
```

To do this, we can modify the program to use the Format function:

```
' Compose message for program output
sMsg = "Sine of " & Format(fAngle, "0.0000") & sDEG
sMsg = sMsg & " is " & Format(fSine, "0.0000") & "."

' Display our output
PrintMsg sMsg
```

The Format function is an extremely flexible function that can be used to display numbers in a specified style, including currency, time, and date styles. A simplified description of its syntax is

Format(*expression*[,*format*])

The *expression* parameter will accept any valid expression to convert to a string. The *format* parameter is optional. If it isn't used, no special style will be applied to the string version of the expression. If it is used, it will accept a string argument specifying a style. Help describes the possible arguments for a variety of styles. For example, when used as the argument for PrintMsg,

```
PrintMsg Format(Date, "m/d/yy")
```

this will display the following if the system date is January 24, 1997:

```
1/24/97
```

Date, another library function, returns the system date currently recognized by your computer. In our sine program example, the argument passed to parameter *format* (when calling function Format) is "0.0000". This means that the string representing the number should have at least one digit before the decimal point and should have four-digit precision after the decimal point. To discover the wealth of possible format styles and to discover interesting functions such as Date, explore the Visual Basic Help system.

4.6   EVENT PROCEDURES

4.6.1   Introducing Event-Driven Programming

Section 1.8 discussed the difference between procedural and event-driven programming. Consider the difference between the Chapter 1 programs PROCEED and EVENT (Figures 1.5 and 1.6). As with typical procedural programs, PROCEED decided when and what the user should enter. It displayed a result after collecting the inputs in its prescribed order. For example, if you, the user, entered the model number and later decided you would like to change it, it was too late. Your only choice at that point would be to run the program again. With the EVENT program, you could select (instead of typing in) inputs in any order you wished. You could also change your mind about any selection before you clicked the button to find the price.

In contrast, an event-driven program responds to the user, who decides in what order the program will execute procedures. In event-driven programming, an *event* is an action, such as clicking the mouse or pressing a key, that is recognized by a Windows program. An *event procedure* is a procedure that is automatically called when an associated event occurs.

This differs from functions and sub procedures, which have to be called in a program statement. For example, clicking the **Find Price** button in the EVENT program causes the execution of an event procedure to calculate and display the price. In fact, when a user selects the model number, length, or tax status, other event procedures execute. They are invisible to the user, but behind the scenes they set up data required for the price calculation.

Normally a user triggers an event that causes an event procedure to execute. However, we can also write code in an event procedure that triggers another event. The Windows system itself can trigger certain events (such as the passage of time). With all of these activities going on, it is even more crucial that programs be well designed prior to coding. You cannot predict the order in which event procedures will execute; however, the event procedures themselves are often procedural in nature. Also, event procedures can call functions and subprocedures (see Figure 4.5).

When the EVENT program runs, it initializes data and displays a standard Windows-style message box with an OK button. At this point, nothing else can occur until the user acknowledges the box by clicking **OK** (or pressing **Enter**). At this point, the user can do anything in any order. In fact, since default data has already been assigned, he or she may even click **Find Price** immediately. This will launch a standard Windows-style message that requires that the user click **OK**. We will now begin to develop programs similar to this one.

4.6.2   The Welcome to Cougar Canoe Program

First, consider a simple Hello World program. Figure 4.6 shows this program in action after the user has clicked the **Hello** button. The object names will make more sense after we examine the code. For now, Figure 4.6 will give us a tour of the screen buttons used by this program.

Clicking **Goodbye** causes the text box to display the message: Thank you for visiting. Clicking **Clear** causes the text box to become blank; clicking **Exit** terminates the program. This is a fully functional Windows program, so the user can resize the window at will or use the standard minimize, maximize, and exit buttons at the upper right corner of the window.

The following program shows the only code statements that were necessary. You can see why this language is called *Visual* Basic: There was no need to add code for standard Windows functionality. In the hands-on exercises at the end of this chapter, you will see how easy it is to create the visual part of the program using simple point-and-click (with some typing) techniques. Now let's see how the program ties in with the visual part.

Figure 4.5
Informal Event Chart for
the EVENT Program

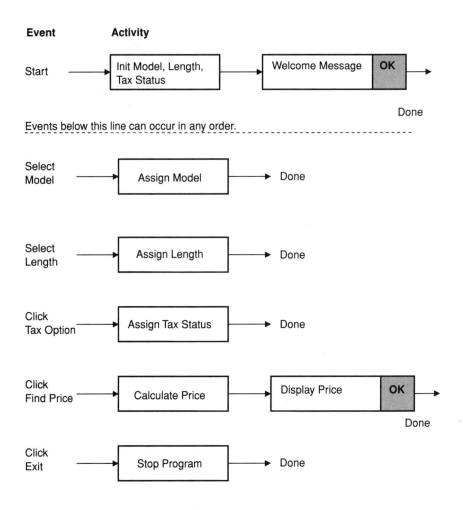

Example 4.17

```
Option Explicit

Private Sub cmdHello_Click()

    ' Executes to display Welcome message when user clicks the ➡
    Hello button
    txtWelcome.Text = "Welcome to Cougar Canoe"

End Sub


Private Sub cmdGoodbye_Click()

    ' Executes to display Goodbye message when user clicks the ➡
    Goodbye button
    txtWelcome.Text = "Thank you for visiting"

End Sub


Private Sub cmdClear_Click()
```

Figure 4.6
The WELCOME Program
(including object names)

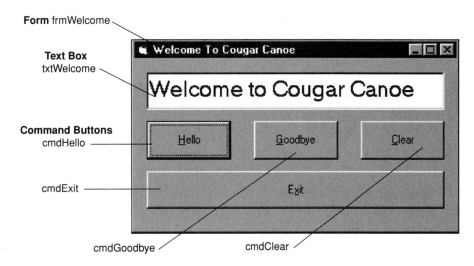

```
      ' Executes to clear message when user clicks the Clear button
      txtWelcome.Text = " "

End Sub


Private Sub cmdExit_Click()

      ' Executes to exit program when user clicks button Exit
      End

End Sub
```

It may be intuitive to see how the program works generally: When the user clicks on a button, the corresponding event procedure executes. For example, clicking on the button named cmdHello (see Figure 4.6) causes procedure cmdHello_Click to execute. Clicking the button named cmdExit causes the program to execute the End statement, which in turn causes the program to terminate.

The keywords Private Sub begin the declaration of an event procedure. It is possible to declare an event procedure using the keywords Public Sub, but Visual Basic assigns Private Sub by default. The distinction becomes important for large programs that use multiple windows. Let's say we write a program with several windows (forms). Each window has its own code. The keyword Private ensures that code associated with other windows cannot accidentally call the procedure that belongs to another window.

4.6.3   Developing an Event-Driven Visual Basic Program

There are two phases to creating an event-driven Windows program using Visual Basic (as opposed to using the Introduction Template), both of which are done after designing the program:

Phase 1   Create the visual layout (the easy part, but perhaps more fun than Phase 2).
Phase 2   Code the statements (the hard part, but perhaps more important than Phase 1).

The Visual Components

The visual components are known as *objects*. Each Visual Basic program must have at least one form object. The form is the part that looks like a window. Form objects contain control objects, and there are several types of control objects: The TextBox and CommandButton are two examples of types. We use controls to receive user input, display output, and trigger event procedures.

*An **object** is a combination of code and data that can be treated as a unit. Examples are the form object and various control objects.*

*A **form object** is a window or dialog box. Forms are containers for controls.*

When we were using the Introduction Template, we were using a program with a prebuilt form. We have seen dialog boxes used in the EVENT program. The initial welcome message is a dialog box, and the program displayed the canoe price using a dialog box. In both cases, the user had to click the OK button in the dialog box in order to proceed.

*A **control object** is an object, contained by a form, that is used to receive user input, display output, and trigger other activities (event procedures).*

The CommandButton and TextBox control objects are used in the WELCOME program. The CommandButton is for user input, and a user must click it to carry out a command. The TextBox can be used for both input and output. In the WELCOME program, it displays an output. In the Introduction Template, the boxes for Program Input(s) and Program Output(s) are text boxes. Control objects may have event procedures associated with them. By default, Visual Basic declares event procedures using the keyword Private instead of Public. The keyword Private indicates that event procedures associated with controls in other forms cannot access it (subtlety we need not worry about at this stage).

4.6.4   Properties

*A **property** is an attribute of an object.*

Every object has several properties. A property is a characteristic of an object, a special type of variable associated with an object. This is similar to object characteristics in the physical world: For example, each table will have properties that can be used to distinguish it from other tables. These properties are height, width, length, material, weight, color, present location, and others. We can say that the value of the properties of each table are different. Visual Basic form and control objects have properties associated with them. Each object has a Name property.

*The **Name** property identifies a form or control object.*

Let's consider some object properties in the WELCOME program (see Table 4.1).

When we design a program, we can specify the property settings during the visual layout phase. We can also write code that will modify the values when the program runs. Table 4.2 illustrates some different values.

Note that Text and Caption properties are strings. In the visual design mode, we can enter these values without quotation marks. However, if assigning property values in code, the quotation marks must be used (see Example 4.17). We can use the Caption property to assign an *access key* to a control. An *access key* is a key pressed while holding down the ALT key that allows the user to carry out a command instead of using the mouse. For example, pressing ALT+H will have the same effect as clicking the Hello button (see Figure 4.6). The user will see the H underlined (Hello). Typical Windows programs use ALT+X to exit. To assign an access key, we must include an ampersand (&) in the caption immediately preceding the character we want to designate as an access key. The character will be underlined.

Assigning Property Settings

We can assign most property values during the visual layout phase (design time) by typing the settings in the Properties window. Using the Properties Window is similar to writing information in a table such as Table 4.2. The other way to assign property settings

Table 4.1
Description of Some Object Properties

Property Keyword	What It Defines
Name (applies to all objects)	Identifies the form or control object. String data type.
Caption (applies to CommandButton, Form, and others) (does not apply to TextBox and others)	Determines the text displayed in or next to a control. String data type.
Text (applies to TextBox and others) (does not apply to Form and CommandButton)	Also known as an edit control. It displays text that can be modified by the user and/or code. String data type.
Top (applies to all objects)	For a form, it defines its vertical position on the screen. For control objects, it is their vertical position with respect to the top edge of the form. Integer data type.
Left (applies to all objects)	For a form, it defines its horizontal position on the screen. For control objects, it is their horizontal position with respect to the left edge of the form. Integer data type.
Height (applies to all objects)	The vertical size of an object. Integer data type.
Width (applies to all objects)	The horizontal size of an object. Integer data type.

Table 4.2
Some Property Settings in the WELCOME Program

Object Keyword	Property Keyword	Setting
Form	Name	frmWelcome
	Caption	Welcome To Cougar Canoe
	Height	3090
	Left	2040
	Top	1355
	Width	5400
TextBox	Name	txtWelcome
	Text	(modified by code)
	Height	600
	Left	195
	Top	195
	Width	4890
CommandButton	Name	cmdHello
	Caption	&Hello
	Height	600
	Left	195
	Top	975
	Width	1380
CommandButton	Name	cmdGoodbye
	Caption	&Goodbye
	Height	600
	Left	1950
	Top	975
	Width	1380
CommandButton	Name	cmdClear
	Caption	&Clear
	Height	600
	Left	3705
	Top	975
	Width	1380
CommandButton	Name	cmdExit
	Caption	E&xit
	Height	600
	Left	195
	Top	1755
	Width	4890

is to use statements in code, which will set the properties at runtime. Consider the statement in event procedure `cmdHello_Click`:

```
txtWelcome.Text = "Welcome to Cougar Canoe"
```

It states: Assign the string expression "Welcome to Cougar Canoe" to the Text property of the TextBox object named (whose Name property is) txtWelcome. This is a long sentence; Visual Basic is much more concise.

To set form or control properties at runtime (with the exception of the Name property), place a reference to the property on the left side of an assignment statement. The syntax is

NameOfObject.PropertyKeyword = expression that specifies setting

To reference any property, state the object name and a dot followed by the property keyword. For example, to change the caption of a command button named cmd-StartStop,

```
cmdStartStop.Caption = "&Stop"
```

Examine Example 4.17 again. Clicking a command button (other than cmdExit) will cause a change to what the user will see in the text box.

4.6.5   Controls and Control Prefixes

Notice the naming conventions for the object names. Table 4.3 shows the object name prefixes used by most Visual Basic programmers. A prefix convention improves the readability of code. For example, consider a procedure named BeginTransaction_Click. It would be useful to know whether this procedure occurs when the user clicks on a command button, a menu item, or inside a picture.

Table 4.3 shows about half of the controls that are available in the Professional Edition of Visual Basic. Of course, we've only familiarized ourselves with a few of them up to this point. If you need yet more controls, you can buy add-ons from third-party software suppliers. Very few people (if any) know all the words in their native language; similarly, very few programmers know all the keywords and objects in Visual Basic. We will further develop our Visual Basic vocabulary so that we can be reasonably fluent programmers.

4.6.6   Events

*An **event** is an action recognized by an object, such as clicking the mouse or pressing a key, and for which you can write code to respond. Events can occur as a result of a user action or program code, or they can be triggered by the system.*

The Click Event

The Click event occurs when the user presses and then releases a mouse button over an object. It can also occur when the value of a control is changed. Many objects (but not all of them) recognize the Click event. The form, command button, and text box objects recognize the Click event. One example of a Click event is a user moving the mouse pointer over a command button and pressing and releasing the button. Pressing the access key combination for the command button also causes the Click event. If there is a Click event procedure associated with the object, Visual Basic will execute it. In the WELCOME program, clicking on a command button will launch the associated Click event procedure. However, clicking on the text box or on the form

Table 4.3
Some Objects Including Naming Prefixes

Prefix Convention	Object Keyword	Purpose
cbo	Combobox	User can enter information in text or select from a list.
chk	CheckBox	User can make yes or no type selection.
cmd	CommandButton	User can activate a process.
dat	Data Control	Select and display specified information from a database.
dir	DirListBox (Directory List)	Display directories and paths to permit user to select a file.
drv	DriveListBox	Display disk drives to permit user to select a file
fil	FileListBox	Display list of files to permit user to select a file or group of files.
fra	Frame	To group controls together. See Option Button.
grd	Grid	Display data in a series of rows and columns.
hsb	HScrollBar (Horizontal Scroll Bar)	User can adjust a quantity (similar to sliding tuner of a radio).
img	Image	Displays a graphic.
lbl	Label	Display text information to user (user can't modify it).
lin	Line	Displays a line.
lst	ListBox	Displays a list of items from which the user can select one or more.
mci	Multimedia	Control playback and recording of audio and video.
mnu	Menu	User selects activity using a standard Windows-style menu.
ole	OLE Container	Permits access to objects and links to other applications that support Object Linking and Embedding (OLE).
opt	OptionButton (also known as a radio button)	User can make one selection from a group of selections. Other selections are automatically turned off. Usually grouped within a frame (See Frame control).
pic	PictureBox	Display a graphic from a bitmap, icon, or metafile.
shp	Shape	Display rectangle, square, oval, circle, rounded rectangle, or rounded square.
txt	TextBox	User can enter text information.
tmr	Timer	Execute code at regular intervals.
vsb	VScrollBar (Vertical Scroll Bar)	User can adjust a quantity (similar to sliding volume control of an amplifier).

(outside a control) will do nothing. This is because the program does not have an event procedure associated with these objects. We could modify the program to add Click event procedures for the form and text box.

Event Procedure Declaration Syntax

The Event declaration starts with the keywords `Private Sub`. This is followed by the control object name (such as `cmdHello`) followed by an underscore (_) and the event keyword (such as `Click`). To end a declaration, use the statement `End Sub`. (The program listings in this section show examples.) The Visual Basic development environment will automatically generate the opening and closing declaration statements if you double-click a control object when in the design mode.

The Load Event

The Load event occurs when a form is loaded. When the user runs a program, at least one form (the startup form) receives the load event. Some Visual Basic programs use more than one form. Typically, a Load event procedure initializes settings and global variables required by the program. The program illustrated in Figure 4.7 illustrates a load event procedure.

4.6.7   The Simple Calculator Program

When a user runs the simple calculator program, he or she can type numbers in the text boxes and click the corresponding command button to display the result of an arithmetic operation (see Figure 4.7). The code for the program is shown in Example 4.18. Visual Basic lists the event procedures in alphabetic order. Remember that event procedures can execute in any order, depending on what the user does. Procedure `Form_Load` is an exception: It executes when the program starts. Once an event procedure completes executing, the program will wait for the next event before executing further procedures.

Figure 4.7
The SIMCALC Program (including object names)

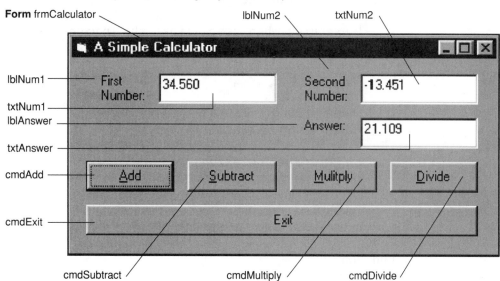

Example 4.18

```
Option Explicit

Private Sub Form_Load()

    ' Executes when program first starts
    ' Initialize numbers in case user tries to
    ' perform calculations prior to entering inputs
    txtNum1.Text = "0"
    txtNum2.Text = "1"
    txtAnswer.Text = ""
    ' Prevent user from typing in Answer
    txtAnswer.Locked = True

End Sub


Private Sub cmdAdd_Click()

    ' Executes when user clicks button Add
    Dim fNum1 As Single, fNum2 As Single
    Dim fAnswer As Single

    ' Get inputs
    fNum1 = CSng(txtNum1.Text)
    fNum2 = CSng(txtNum2.Text)

    ' Perform calculation
    fAnswer = fNum1 + fNum2

    ' Display answer
    txtAnswer.Text = CStr(fAnswer)

End Sub


Private Sub cmdDivide_Click()

    ' Executes when user clicks the Divide button
    Dim fNum1 As Single, fNum2 As Single
    Dim fAnswer As Single

    ' Get inputs
    fNum1 = CSng(txtNum1.Text)
    fNum2 = CSng(txtNum2.Text)

    ' Perform calculation
    fAnswer = fNum1 / fNum2

    ' Display answer
    txtAnswer.Text = CStr(fAnswer)

End Sub
```

```
Private Sub cmdMultiply_Click()

    ' Executes when user clicks the Multiply button
    Dim fNum1 As Single, fNum2 As Single
    Dim fAnswer As Single

    ' Get inputs
    fNum1 = CSng(txtNum1.Text)
    fNum2 = CSng(txtNum2.Text)

    ' Perform calculation
    fAnswer = fNum1 * fNum2

    ' Display answer
    txtAnswer.Text = CStr(fAnswer)

End Sub


Private Sub cmdSubtract_Click()

    ' Executes when user clicks the Subtract button
    Dim fNum1 As Single, fNum2 As Single
    Dim fAnswer As Single

    ' Get inputs
    fNum1 = CSng(txtNum1.Text)
    fNum2 = CSng(txtNum2.Text)

    ' Perform calculation
    fAnswer = fNum1 - fNum2

    ' Display answer
    txtAnswer.Text = CStr(fAnswer)

End Sub


Private Sub cmdExit_Click()

    End     ' Exit the program

End Sub
```

The Load event procedure (Form_Load) performs some useful initialization. The Text properties for the input numbers (operands) are initialized to valid numerical values in case the user clicks a command button prior to typing in numbers. Assigning the Locked property to True forces the answer text box (TextBox txtAnswer) to reject any user attempt to modify its contents by typing inside the box. By default, a user can type inside a text box (which actually modifies its Text setting). When the user types in a text box (txtNum1 or txtNum2), the program will automatically set the corresponding Text property to the user's input. For example, in Figure 4.7, the user typed in **34.560** and **-13.451**, hence `txtNum1.Text` is set to `"34.560"` and `txtNum2.Text` is set to `"-13.451"`. (Since the Text property is a string data type, we show its setting enclosed in quotation marks.)

If the user clicks the **Add** (CommandButton `cmdAdd`) button, the `cmdAdd_Click` event procedure will execute. The procedure will declare some local variables as type Single and assign the variables to what is in the text boxes. Library function `CSng` is the Convert to Single function; hence, the String value of the Text properties will be converted. The procedure will perform the addition. Using the Convert to String function (`CStr`), it will set the Text property of TextBox `txtAnswer` to a string representing the numerical answer. Remember that we can perform only arithmetic operations on numerical data types (such as Single and Integer), and that the Text property stores a String data type.

Note that the syntax for the Load event procedure uses the `Form` keyword (instead of the object name) followed by an underscore and the event keyword. We will work with this program in the hands-on exercises.

User Interface Design of a Form

There are a few recommended guidelines for setting the layout and appearance of a form:

- Align controls for symmetry.
- Use consistent fonts for text information.
- Have a descriptive title.
- End labels associated with text boxes with a colon.
- Provide some separation between controls, such as command buttons.

4.6.8   An Event-Driven Version of the Labor Cost Program

Section 2.3.1 described a procedural program to calculate the labor cost for building a canoe. Figure 4.8 shows one possible event-driven implementation of this program. The *E* in the program name LABCOSTE stands for "event-driven."

The user can enter inputs in any order prior to clicking the Canoe Cost button. The program also uses a check box (labeled Rush job?), which the user can click on or off. The user can modify any input at will. (Contrast this flexibility with the rigorous sequence of statements illustrated in the flow chart of Figure 2.8.) Example 4.19 shows the code for LABCOSTE.

Example 4.19

```
Option Explicit
     ' Given an hourly labor rate and number of hours required,
     ' find out the labor cost in dollars for building a certain canoe
     ' by multiplying the hourly labor rate by the number of
     ' hours required to build the canoe. Program displays
     ' total labor cost in dollars. The following highlights steps

Private Sub Form_Load()
```

Figure 4.8
The LABCOSTE Program

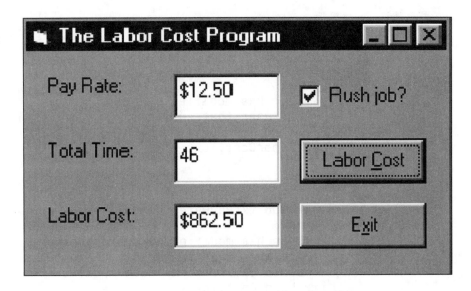

```
' Initialize data when program starts
txtLaborCost.Locked = True ' Prevent user from modifying
' Set up some default values in case user tries to
' determine cost before inputting data
txtPayRate.Text = "$12.50"
txtTotalTime.Text = "45"

' Update total cost based on default values
cmdLaborCost_Click  ' Can also call event procedure in code

End Sub


Private Sub cmdLaborCost_Click()

    ' User clicks button to calculate cost based
    ' on inputs typed in text boxes
    Dim fPayRate As Single    ' Hourly labor rate
    Dim fTotalTime As Single ' Number of hours required
    Dim fLaborCost As Single    ' Total labor cost

    ' Get hourly labor rate and number of hours required from user
    fPayRate = CSng(txtPayRate.Text)
    fTotalTime = CSng(txtTotalTime.Text)

    ' Adjust by overtime factor if this is a rush job
    If chkOvertime.Value = 1 Then fPayRate = fPayRate * 1.5

    ' Calculate the cost here
    fLaborCost = fTotalTime * fPayRate

    ' Show the cost to the user
    txtLaborCost.Enabled = True      ' Enable the box
    txtLaborCost.Text = Format(fLaborCost, "Currency")
```

```
End Sub


Private Sub chkOvertime_Click()

     ' User has modified overtime setting
     ' Cue user that answer may no longer be valid
     ' since the overtime setting has been modified
     txtLaborCost.Text = ""

End Sub

Private Sub txtPayRate_Change()

     ' User has modified pay rate input
     ' Cue user that answer may no longer be valid
     ' since pay rate has been modified
     txtLaborCost.Text = ""

End Sub


Private Sub txtTotalTime_Change()
     ' User has modified the total time input
     ' Cue user that answer may no longer be valid
     ' since total time has been modified
     txtLaborCost.Text = ""

End Sub


Private Sub cmdExit_Click()

     End     ' User exits program

End Sub
```

Compare the code with that shown in Example 2.8. The text boxes are appropriately named `txtPayRate`, `txtTotalTime`, and `txtLaborCost`. The command buttons are named `cmdLaborCost` and `cmdExit`. The check box is named `chkOvertime`. Procedure `Form_Load` shows that it is also possible to call event procedures by using statements in code. It calls `cmdLaborCost_Click` to calculate and display the result based on the initial values. Both `txtPayRate_Change` and `txt-TotalTime_Change` execute when the respective control receives the change event. It occurs when the user modifies the contents of these text boxes. To cue the user that the result displayed in the box labeled Labor Cost may not be valid, the procedures cause the contents of this box to disappear.

In procedure `cmdLaborCost_Click`, we have a sneak preview of decision logic (to be covered in Chapter 5). The procedure multiplies `fPayRate` by `1.5` if the user clicks on it in the check box. The Value property of a check box control is set to 1 if a user clicks on it to check it on. If the user clicks on it again to "uncheck" the check box, the Value is set to 0. This happens whether an event procedure is or is not associated with the check box. The If statement causes `fPayRate` to be multiplied by 1.5 *only* when the value of check box control `chkOvertime` is set to 1.

The Change Event

The change event indicates that the contents of a control have changed. Both the TextBox and Label controls can receive this event. The Form, CommandButton, and CheckBox cannot. It can occur when a user changes the text in a TextBox control, or if the Text property has been modified as the result of executing code. It can also occur if the Caption property of a Label has been modified as the result of executing code.

Cue the User

Since the user can modify inputs at will, it would be useful to clear the result when this occurs. Otherwise, the user may not realize that the result does not correspond to the inputs. Hence the purpose of procedures `txtPayRate_Change`, `txtTotalTime Change`, and `chkOvertime_Click` is to clear the result. We could have used these procedures to calculate a new result, thus eliminating the need for the Labor Cost button.

4.6.9   Some Technical Talk About Object-Oriented Programming

In more technical terms, a property is a data member that describes the attributes of an object class. Properties are in fact variables that are associated with the object. For example, all objects of the command button class (control CommandButton) have data members defining their Caption property. A specific named object is called *an instance of the corresponding object class*. A *class* is a template for defining the appearance and behavior of an object. For example, CommandButton is a class. This class defines what command button objects can do and what they cannot do (events to which they can respond). It defines how command buttons can appear and how they cannot appear (properties). The Caption property is a data member of the CommandButton class, and `cmd-Hello` is an instance of the CommandButton class (its Name property is `cmdHello`).

SUMMARY

This chapter is about writing programs in modules known as procedures. A module is a set of step-by-step statements that tell the computer *how* to do a subtask. Procedures are modules, blocks of statements that completely execute a task or a subtask. Visual Basic Help defines a procedure as a named sequence of statements executed as a unit. It is useful to partition a program into modules (procedures) that perform each of its fundamental operations of input, processing, output, and storage.

An argument is a constant, variable, or expression passed to a procedure; a paremeter is a variable name by which an argument passed to a procedure is known within the procedure. This variable receives the argument passed into the procedure. Its scope ends when the procedure ends.

The *scope* of a variable refers to when a variable may be accessed during execution of a program. Local variables are visible only to the procedure in which they are declared; global variables are visible to all procedures in the program.

Rule of Thumb

Use local variables when possible. Pass arguments when it is necessary to share information between procedures, but know that sometimes it is desirable to use global variables.

PROGRAMMER-DEFINED SUB PROCEDURES AND FUNCTIONS

A function is a block of code (procedure) that always *returns a value*. A sub procedure does not return a value directly. It may only return value(s) indirectly by passing arguments.

Visual Basic includes a rich set of already-set-up functions that we can use to perform more complex tasks. We do not need to declare them and write the code to implement them. These functions, called *library functions,* include mathematical, data conversion, time and date, formatting, string manipulation, and other functions. These functions are also keywords. Their use saves the programmer time, since the programmer does not need to develop them but simply uses them.

An event is an action recognized by an object, such as clicking the mouse or pressing a key, and for which you can write code to respond. Events can occur as a result of a user action or program code, or they can be triggered by the system.

An object is a combination of code and data that can be treated as a unit. Examples are the form object and various control objects. A form object is a window or dialog box. Forms are containers for controls. A control object is an object contained by a form that is used to receive user input, display output, and trigger other activities (event procedures). When an object receives an event, a Visual Basic program will automatically execute a procedure known as an *event procedure* if one was coded for that particular object-and-event combination.

A property is an attribute of an object. The Name property identifies a form or control object.

REUSABLE COMPONENTS

If there exists a library of software components, ready to be assembled to do anything you need, why do we need programmers? Recent history has shown that the introduction of new technologies spurs new demands for services. We will need people who can assemble the components.

Since the introduction of Visual Basic in 1991, there has been a growth of reusable components. Programmers created modules known as Visual Basic Extensions (VBXs); these were usually created with the C++ language. Reusability has been further extended with ActiveX components (OCXs). A typical module already possesses sophisticated functionality. In principle, one can build programs by simply assembling components like you would with children's interlocking blocks. However, these off-the-shelf components are not enough. A customer will always demand extra functionality, and the programmer still has to create solutions to real-world problems. You, like the architect who designs a building with standard (and sometimes custom) parts, just have to solve them differently.

HANDS-ON EXERCISES

OVERVIEW

The activities will

- Enable you to create reusable modules (sub procedures and functions).
- Enable you to create programs that use existing modules (library functions).
- Familiarize you with more debugging tools (Step Into, Step Over, Calls buttons).
- Familiarize you with some objects and properties.
- Familiarize you with event-driven programming.

To Get Started

Note

This section assumes that you have already set up the Debug toolbar and worked with Watch expressions, Breakpoints, Single Step operations, and the Debug window, as covered in the Chapter 3 Hands-On-Exercises.

1. Read the section "Read Me Before Attempting the Hands-On Exercises" if you have not already done so.
2. Run Windows.
3. Open the file CH04\EX04.TXT on your student disk and answer the questions. (The same questions are shown here so that you can still determine answers if you are not sitting in front of a computer.)
4. Run Visual Basic.

4.1   PARTITIONING MODULES

The scenario in Chapter 1 briefly described the material order process. Make a structure chart similar to that in Figure 4.1 for an online material ordering system. Use your imagination to fill in details.

   1. Define procedure and procedure call. Give an example of each.

The Initial Procedure Demonstration

To run the Initial Procedure demonstration program, open project INTRO in directory CH04, and select the RUNME.BAS file in the Project window.

Visual Basic 4

Select **Save File As** from the File menu and type **WALKU1** to name the *file.* Then click **Save**.

Visual Basic 5

Select **Save Runme.Bas As** from the File menu and type **WALKU1** to name the *file.* Then click **Save**.

   Select **Save Project As** from the File menu and type in **WALKU1** to name the *project.* Then click **Save**.

Full Module View

In Visual Basic, there are two options for viewing procedures in the code window. They are

  • Full Module View: Shows all procedures as a single scrollable listing.

  • Not Full Module View: Shows only one procedure at a time.

To make your choice, select **Options** in the Tools menu, and click the **Editor** tab. Click on the **Full Module View** check box to select or remove the choice.

Visual Basic 5

You can also quickly switch between Full Module and Procedure view by clicking their respective buttons at the bottom left corner of the Code window (see Figure 1.10b).

The instructions in this exercise assume that you have selected Full Module View. Later, you can choose the other option if you prefer.

Enter and Run the Program

Type in the code shown in Example 4.4. Save the project periodically. Run the program to make sure it works, and correct errors if necessary.

The Initial Fahrenheit-to-Celsius Demonstration

To work with the Fahrenheit-to-Celsius demonstration program, open project INTRO in directory CH04. Then select the RUNME.BAS file in the Project window.

Visual Basic 4

Select **Save File As** from the File menu and type **FTOCP1** to name the *file*. Then click **Save**.

Visual Basic 5

Select **Save Runme.Bas** from the File menu and type **FTOCP1** to name the *file*. Then click **Save**.

Select **Save Project As** from the File menu and type in **FTOCP1** to name the *project*. Then click **Save**.

Type in the code shown in Example 4.5. Save the project periodically. Run the program to make sure it works, and correct errors if necessary.

Initial Problem Solving

Write a program that converts Celsius to Fahrenheit three times. It should use a procedure to perform the actual work of conversion. Use reasonable descriptive names for the procedure and the variables. Run the program to make sure it works, and correct errors if necessary.

4.2   ARGUMENTS AND PARAMETERS

2. Describe the difference between arguments and parameters, and explain the passing process. Use examples if necessary.

Troubleshooting: Investigate Procedure Calls Using Debug Tools

To view a demonstration program for debug tools, open project INTRO. Save the RUNME file as **FTOCP2**, and save the project as **FTOCP2**. (Alternatively, you could modify the FTOC1 program instead of starting all over. To do this, save file FTOC1.BAS as **FTOC2** and save project FTOC1 as **FTOC2**.)

Type in the code shown in Example 4.6 (or modify existing code, if applicable), and save the project periodically. Run the program to make sure it works.

Reminder

To run an Introduction Template program, click the **Visual Basic Start** button in the Toolbar. Then click the **Run Me** button in the Introduction Template.

Correct errors if necessary. Stop the program, and place a breakpoint at the line

```
Public Sub RunMe()
```

Run the program. It should halt at the breakpoint; you are now in the Break Mode. Single step through the program by using the **Step Over** Toolbar button, not the Step Into button. Stop stepping when you reach the following procedure call:

```
FahrToCels fActualTemp
```

Examine the argument `fActualTemp` before and after the statement is executed. Remember that a rectangular outline indicates the current statement (the next statement to be executed). Remember too that you can use the **Instant Watch** Toolbar button. Note that the argument before the call has the Fahrenheit value you entered, but after the call, the argument has the Celsius value. Click the **Continue** Toolbar button (or select **Continue** from the Run menu) if you accidentally stepped past the statement.

```
End Sub
```

Stepping Into Procedures

By using step *over*, we execute a call to a procedure and then move on to the statement that follows the call. We did not step through the code of the procedure (in this case `FahrTo-Cels`) itself. With the Step Into Toolbar button, we can execute each statement in the called procedure line by line. We have to be careful though: Introduction commands such as `PrintMsg` and `InputSng` are also procedures. If you use Step Into instead of Step Over, you will in fact execute each statement in the Introduction command line by line. This does no harm to program execution, but it will probably make the exercise more awkward.

Remove the breakpoint from the following statement:

```
Public Sub RunMe()
```

Add a breakpoint to the following line:

```
FahrToCels fActualTemp
```

Run the program. When it stops at the breakpoint, examine the argument `fActualTemp` using Instant Watch. Click the **Step Into** Toolbar button, *not* Step Over. Visual Basic should be ready to execute the first statement of the procedure.

```
Public Sub FahrToCels(fTemperature As Single)
```

Examine the parameter `fTemperature` using Instant/Quick Watch. (Note that Visual Basic 4 uses the term ***Instant Watch*** and Visual Basic 5 uses the term ***Quick Watch***.) The value of `fTemperature` should be the same as the value of `fActualTemp`. Note that you can still examine `fActualTemp` even if it is not in the current statement.

At this point, you should use Step Over. This will get you in the habit of using Step Into only when you explicitly want to step into a called procedure. Use it when the current statement is the one that calls the procedure. This permits you to execute each statement in the called procedure line by line. Otherwise use Step Over, and the current statement will become the one after the call. Single step twice so that the current statement is

```
End Sub
```

Examine the value of parameter `fTemperature`; it should have the Celsius value. Step over again. The current statement should be

```
PrintSng "  Temperature in Celsius is: ", fActualTemp
```

Note that the program execution has returned back to procedure `RunMe` from `FahrToCels`. This statement is the one that follows the procedure call. Examine the variable fActualTemp; it should be the Celsius value. Remember that fActualTemp is the argument returned by procedure FahrToCels. At this point, click the **Continue** button. Repeat this exercise using different input values.

Use *Step Over* when you are interested only in the *result* of executing a procedure call. Use *Step Into* when you are interested in interested *how* the called procedure implements the result.

Problem Solving

Write the following program: Given a starting temperature in Celsius, the program will output three temperatures in increments of ten Celsius degrees and output their equivalent temperatures in Fahrenheit. Document the program thoroughly. Use the Debug tools to monitor how arguments are passed during execution of the program.

4.3   LOCAL AND GLOBAL (PUBLIC) VARIABLES

3. Describe the difference between local and global variables. Explain the difference in terms of how to declare them and when they are accessible during program execution.
4. Explain what is meant by *scope* of variables.
5. Why would a global variable also be known as *public*?

The Local Variables Demonstration Program

To view the local variables demonstration program, open project INTRO. Save the RUNME file as LOCAL1. Save the project as LOCAL1.

Type in the code shown in Example 4.8. Save the project periodically. Proofread the code to ensure it is the same as shown in Example 4.8, and run the program.

6. What happens when the program of Example 4.8 is run? Explain the results.

Visual Basic displays the message Variable not defined. It also highlights the variable in the statement

```
nLocalDee = 1   ' Not valid
```

Note that Visual Basic is still in design mode, so it won't even compile the program. Click **OK**. Do not modify the code yet. Try to run it again. When you see the message box, press **F1** instead of clicking OK. Context-sensitive Help launches to present information about undeclared variables. Study this information.

Visual Basic 5

Instead of pressing **F1**, you can click the **Help** button in the warning message.

You may well ask yourself, "But didn't I declare the variables?" Your inner conscience might reply, "Well, yes you did, but you did not declare them in procedure RunMe." Switch back to Task Visual Basic from task Help and click **OK** in the warning message, if you haven't already done so. Edit the statement to put a single quote in front of it. The statement becomes

```
'nLocalDee = 1   ' Not valid
```

It is now valid, since the computer will ignore comments.

Tip

Sometimes it useful to comment out code during program development. You can test the effects of different statements without having to retype them. Put a single quote in front of the statement you want to temporarily remove. To include the statement again, delete the single quote.

Run the program again. It will halt at the next invalid statement:

```
nLocalDum = 3    ' Not valid
```

Again, the problem is that nLocalDum was not declared in procedure RunMe. Comment out the statement. Repeat the process until the program runs (no syntax errors). You should have commented out four statements in total. It is not possible to use nLocalDum in procedure TweedleDee because it is declared in procedure TweedleDum. Similarly, nLocalDee can't be used in procedure TweedleDum.

Stop the program. Set a breakpoint at each of the three Public Sub statements. In the declaration for nLocalDee, add a watch expression for the local variable:

```
Dim nLocalDee As Integer
```

To do this, click in the variable **nLocalDee**.

Visual Basic 4
Select **Add Watch** from the Tools menu, and click **OK**.

Visual Basic 5
Select **Add Watch** from the Debug menu, and click **OK**.

Similarly, in the declaration for nLocalDum, add a watch expression for the local variable. We prefer to add watch expressions by selecting the variables in the declaration statements. This will do a better job of illustrating scope when we step through program execution in break mode.

Click on the Debug window. Note that both variables are *out of context*. In other words, they are *out of scope*, because the variables do not currently exist in memory. The program only creates them when the associated procedure executes (is called). You will see this as you step through the program. Also, note the Context field in the Debug window. The context for nLocalDee is Main.TweedleDee, meaning that the variable is local to procedure TweedleDee, which in turn is part of the *main* program.

Run the program. When the program halts at the breakpoint in procedure RunMe, examine the Debug window.

Visual Basic 5
If the Watch pane is not visible, click the **Watch Window** button in the Debug toolbar. Then size this window and others in order to see all of the watch information.

Both variables are still out of context because the procedures have not been called yet. Click **Continue**. Execution should halt at the next breakpoint. The current statement (surrounded by a rectangular outline) should now be

```
Public Sub TweedleDee()
```

Look at the Debug window. Variable `nLocalDee` now has an initialized value of 0, but variable `nlocalDum` remains out of context. Single step two statements and check the value of `nLocalDee`; it should be 5. Click **Continue**. The current statement should now be

```
Public Sub TweedleDum()
```

Check the Debug window. Variable `nLocalDum` now has an initialized value of 0. Variable `nlocalDee` is now out of context. Single step two statements and check the value of `nLocalDum`; it should be 9.

Click **Continue**. The current statement should be in procedure `TweedleDee`. Examine the Debug window. Note that variable `nLocalDee` has been reinitialized to 0. Single step the procedure, and you should see the same results as you did the first time. This shows that local variables disappear after the procedure exits. If the program calls the same procedure again, new copies of the local variables will be made.

Now click the **Continue** button. Click **End** to stop program execution. If you like, modify the code to use different integer constants and repeat the exercise.

The Global Variables Demonstration Program

To run the global variables demonstration program, open project `INTRO`. Save the `RUNME` file as `GLOBAL1`. Save the project as `GLOBAL1`.

Type in the code shown in Example 4.9. Save the project periodically. Run the program to make sure it works (at least check that it has no syntax or runtime errors), and correct errors if necessary. In the General Declarations section of the program, add watch expressions for the global variables:

```
Public g_nTweedleDee As Integer  ' Global variables
Public g_nTweedleDum As Integer
```

Visual Basic 4

Click **on each variable**, and select **Add Watch** from the Tools menu. Then click **OK**.

Visual Basic 5

Click on each variable, and select **Add Watch** from the Debug menu. Then click **OK**. With Visual Basic 5 you can quickly add a watch: Right-click a variable and select **Add Watch** from the pop-up menu.

We prefer to add watch expressions by selecting the variables in the declaration statements. This will do a better job of illustrating scope when we step through program execution in break mode.

Click on the **Debug** window. Note that both variables are empty, because we haven't run the program yet. The context for both is `Main`, because they were declared in the General Declarations area. They are global; hence they belong to the main program.[7] Set a breakpoint at

```
Public Sub RunMe()
```

---

[7]*We are fibbing a bit to avoid explaining Visual Basic modules and forms. The Introduction Template uses three files. The RUNME.BAS file is a Visual Basic module, so it must have a name. The author named it* `Main`. *When* `RUNME.BAS` *is saved as a new file, the name will be retained unless you change it.*

Run the program. When the program halts at the breakpoint, examine the Debug window. Both variables have been initialized to zero. Step over the statements until the current statement is

```
TweedleDee
```

Examine the Debug window. Both variables have been assigned new values. Click **Step Into** to begin single stepping inside the `TweedleDee` procedure. Single step inside the procedure. Check the Debug window to monitor changes to the variables. Repeat the process for the `TweedleDum` procedure. In particular, single step the following statement:

```
g_nTweedleDee = g_nTweedleDum + 6
```

Examine the Debug window. `g_nTweedleDee` should have a value of 11 and `g_nTweedleDum` should have a value of 5. Now click the **Continue** button, and then stop the program. If you like, modify the code to use different integer constants and repeat the exercise.

The Business Account Application

To use the business account application, open project `INTRO`. Save the `RUNME` file as `ACCOUNT1`. Save the project as `ACCOUNT1`. Type in the code shown in Example 4.10. Save the project periodically. Run the program to make sure it works, and correct errors if necessary.

Add watch expressions for each variable by selecting each in their respective declaration statement. Set breakpoints at appropriate statements. Run the program and single step the statements. Monitor the status of the variables in the Debug window. If you wish, add watch expressions for the procedure parameters. If necessary, use the mouse to drag the split bar between the Watch pane and the Immediate pane of the Debug window (see Figure 3.7). This will permit you to view more watch expressions without having to use the scroll bar beside the Watch pane.

While single stepping a procedure such as `BillCustomer`, click the **Calls** button in the Debug window (it has three dots). This will launch the Call dialog box, which shows a list of all active procedure calls. An active procedure call is one that was started but hasn't yet completed execution. In this case, note that `BillCustomer` has been called by `RunMe`, which in turn has been called by `cmdRunMe_Click`.

The Calls dialog box shows the active calls in the order of the most recent call on top (like the stack mentioned in Section 4.3.4). If you have read Section 4.6, you may recognize `cmdRunMe_Click` as being an event procedure. When we run the Introduction Template, it is necessary to click the **Run Me** button to call the `RunMe` procedure.

A Bit Under the Hood

To run the stack demonstration program (see Section 4.3.4), open project `INTRO`. Save the `RUNME` file as **NEST1**. Save the project as **NEST1**. Type in the code shown in Example 4.11, and save the project periodically. Run the program to make sure it works, and correct errors if necessary.

Set a breakpoint in each of the `RunMe`, `PassBuck`, and `PassBuckAgain` procedures. Add watch expressions for each variable by selecting each in their respective declaration statement. Run the program. Execution will halt at the first breakpoint in `RunMe`. Note that variables `nPassBuck` and `nPassBuckAgain` are out of context. Click the **Calls** button. Note that procedure `cmdRunMe_Click` called `RunMe`.

Click the Toolbar **Continue** button. Execution will halt in PassBuck. Note that when PassBuck is called, nRunMe remains in context. This is because procedure RunMe is still active; it hasn't finished executing. To verify this, click the **Calls** button. The Calls dialog will show that PassBuck is now on top of the stack (see Figure 4.4). Click the **Continue** button. Execution will halt in PassBuckAgain, and all variables will be in context. Click the **Calls** button. The Calls dialog will show that PassBuckAgain is now on top of the stack (see Figure 4.4). Note that Figure 4.4 ignores procedure cmdRunMe_Click.

Click **Step Over** until the current statement is in the PassBuck procedure. Examine the Debug window and click the **Calls** button. Note that nPassBuckAgain is out of context. The Calls dialog shows that PassBuckAgain has been pulled off the stack.

Click **Step Over** once. The current statement will be in the RunMe procedure. Similarly, note that nPassBuck is out of context and PassBuck has been pulled off the stack.

Click **Step Over** once. The current statement will be in the cmdRunMe_Click procedure. Only the global variable is in context. Note that RunMe has also been pulled off the stack.

Recursive Calls

Stop program execution. Remove the quote from the following statement in procedure PassBuckAgain:

```
' PassBuck
```

Make sure you are still using breakpoints. Run the program. When execution halts at a breakpoint, click **Continue** to proceed. Repeat this approximately 20 times, and then examine the Debug window. Click the **Calls** button. You should see a long list of successive calls from top to bottom. The bottom of the stack will show that cmdRunMe_Click called RunMe, which called PassBuck. At this point PassBuck called PassBuckAgain, which in turn called PassBuck (recursive call), which in turn called PassBuckAgain, and so on until the top of the stack. Also note that global variable g_nBuck has increased in value. The local variables have not increased in value. Each time a procedure is called (even in a recursive call), it creates new copies of its local variables.

Stack Overflow

You will now deliberately create a stack overflow runtime error. Remove all of the breakpoints, and click **Continue**. Visual Basic will display the runtime error message. Click the **Debug** button. In the Debug window, note the value of global variable g_nBuck. This will give you some idea of how large the stack grew. Click the **Calls** button in the Debug window, and note that the stack has grown very large. The overflow occurred because there is no more room in memory for the stack to grow. Don't worry; Visual Basic itself and any other running applications (if any) still have enough memory. Only NEST1 has run out of memory.

4.4 PROGRAMMER-DEFINED SUB PROCEDURES AND FUNCTIONS

7. What is a function? Does it return one value?

A Program With a Function That Converts Fahrenheit to Celsius

To run this program, open project INTRO. Save file RUNME as **FTOCP5**, and save the project as FTOCP5. Type in the code shown in Example 4.13, saving the project periodically. Run the program to make sure it works, and correct errors if necessary. Set a breakpoint at the statement

```
PrintSng "Celsius temperature is ", Celsius(fFahr)
```

Run the program. When it halts at the breakpoint, examine the argument `fFahr` using Instant Watch. It should include the value you entered earlier. Click **Step Into**. The current statement should be

```
Public Function Celsius(fFahrenheit As Single) As Single
```

Examine the parameter `fFahrenheit` using Instant Watch. It should be the same as the argument you viewed earlier. Click **Step Over**. The current statement should be

```
Celsius = 5 / 9 * (fFahrenheit - 32)
```

Examine the function name `Celsius` (in this statement) using Instant Watch. It should still have a value of zero, because the statement has not been executed yet. Click **Step Over**, and examine the function name again. It should now have the equivalent value in Celsius. This is because the statement has been executed. Click **Step Over**. The current statement should be

```
PrintSng "Twice Celsius temperature is ", 2 * Celsius(fFahr)
```

Examine parameter `fFahr` using Instant Watch. Note that it has the same value as before. Examine expression `Celsius(fFahr)`. Note that it has a value that is the Celsius equivalent of the Fahrenheit temperature. Stop here and ponder: `Celsius(fFahr)` is an expression. It evaluates to a value. Also examine the expression `2 * Celsius(fFahr)`. This also evaluates to a value. This is because a function call returns a value.

Click **Step Into**. Note that function `Celsius` is called again. Continue single stepping and monitor expressions.

8. In the previous program, a call to function `Celsius` was used as an argument when calling the command `PrintSng` (a sub procedure). Why can we use a function call as an argument to a template command?

The Box Volume Program

To run this program, open project INTRO. Save file RUNME as **BOXVOL1**. Save the project as **BOXVOL1**. Type in the code shown in Example 4.14, and save the project periodically. Run the program to make sure it works, correcting errors if necessary. Set a breakpoint at the statement

```
Public Sub RunMe()
```

Remind yourself about the difference between Step Over and Step Into. In this exercise, use Step Into only when the current statement is one that calls function `GetDimension`, sub procedure `EchoDimensio`, or function `BoxVolume`. Now single step the program while monitoring variables, arguments, and parameters using watch expressions. Check to see if you can designate `EchoDimension` as a watch expression (you can't). Repeat the exercise using different input values.

4.5   LIBRARY FUNCTIONS

9. What is a library function?

Help For Visual Basic Functions

Visual Basic 4

Run Visual Basic Help. Click the **Contents** tab and open (double-click) the **Visual Basic Help** book icon. Display the **Contents** topic. You should see the main Visual Basic Help window. There is a master topic link to Functions, which shows every library function alphabetically. Click **the link to Functions**. You will see a long list of available functions. Click the **S** button and click on **the topic for Sin**.

Visual Basic 5

Run Visual Basic Help. Click the **Contents** tab and open (double-click) the **Language Reference** book icon. This lists several other book icons that list language features by category. Open (double-click) the **Functions** book icon. This shows alphabetic book icons. Open (double-click) the **S** book icon and click on **the topic for Sin**.

You will see a description about the Sin function. Notice that there is a link to related topics (indicated by the broken green underline) labeled See Also and a link labeled Example (indicated by the solid green underline). Click on **the Example** and study it. Click **See Also** to check the list of related topics.

Visual Basic 4

Click the **Contents** button, and display Contents Topic. Click the link to **Programming Language Summary**. Click the **S** button. Scroll through the list to find topic **Sin**, and click on it. This is another way to find information if you are not sure whether the keyword is a function. This list is much longer because it includes many items in addition to functions.

Visual Basic 5

Click **Help Topics** in the Help window, and click the **Index** tab. Type in **keyword** and select subitem **math** of item keywords. Click **Display** and select the link to **Sin**. This is another way to find the same information.

Note that you can also find a specific keyword directly by using the Help Index. To do this, type in the keyword you are looking for, such as **Sin**. (This technique is not useful if you don't know the keyword ahead of time.) Next, you will try to find out what functions are available for string manipulation. At this point, you don't know the keywords, so you will need to use another technique to find this information.

Visual Basic 4

Click the **Contents** button and display Contents Topic. Click the link to **Keywords by Task**. This might be useful if you didn't have any idea whether a function existed or what it might be called. Let's say you wanted to print out a long sequence of dots. Scroll through the list of keyword task categories. One category is String Manipulation. Since a long sequence of dots is a string, this is a good candidate for further investigation. Click the **String Manipulation** list item.

Visual Basic 5

Click **Help Topics** and click the **Index** tab. Type in **keyword**. This might be useful, since it lists categories by task. Let's say you want to print out a long sequence of dots. Scroll through the list of keyword task categories. One category is String Manipulation. Since a long sequence of dots is a string, this is a good candidate for further investigation. Select subitem **string manipulation** of item key‐words. Click **Display**.

You will see a summary of tasks. Read them. Note that one of them states "Create string of repeating character." This sounds like just what we need. There is a choice of two keywords associated with this action. Keyword String seems to be a more likely candidate. If you are wrong, you can always try again. Click **String**. You will see a description of this function. For example, if you want to create the string of ten dots ("..........."), you could use something like this:

```
sDots = String(10, ".")
PrintMsg sDots
```

The Sine Math Function Program

To open the sine math program, open project INTRO. Save the RUNME file as **MATH1**, and save the project as **MATH1**. Type in the code shown in Example 4.15, saving the project periodically. Run the program to make sure it works. Correct errors if necessary. Set a breakpoint at the statement

```
Public Sub RunMe()
```

Run the program. When it halts at the breakpoint, step over statements until the current statement is

```
fAngle = fAngle * PI / 180
```

Use Instant Watch to view expressions fAngle and fAngle * PI / 180. Note that the purpose of this instruction is to convert degrees into radians, since this is what the Sin function expects as an argument. Failure to perform the conversion will give misleading results when the Sin function is used. Click **Step Over**. The current statement should be

```
fSine = Sin(fAngle)
```

Check the value of expressions fAngle and Sin(fAngle). Again, note that a function call is an expression (it has a value). Next, you will attempt to step into the function to monitor the execution of function Sin. Click **Step Into**, *not* Step Over. What happened? The current statement is

```
PrintSng "The sine is ", fSine
```

We didn't see any code inside function Sin. Now click **Step Into** to step into the code for PrintSng. The current statement is now

```
Sub PrintSng(Msg As String, var As Single)
```

Note that the Title Bar of the Code window is now Intro instead of Main. The code for sub procedure PrintSng resides in the file INTRO.BAS. Click **Continue** to complete execution of the program. If you want to see your code again, select **MATH1.BAS** in the Project window before clicking **View Code**.

Library Functions Are in Machine Code

Why can we step into a command such as PrintSng but not into a library function? Remember from Chapter 1 that we create source code. In order to execute the program we create, Visual Basic must initially compile it into an executable format (machine code).[8] The sub procedures and functions that the programmer creates are also in source code format. Library functions are different. They are already available as machine code modules. When Visual Basic compiles a statement that uses a library function, it replaces the call with a call referencing a machine code module. The source code for a library function simply isn't available. In fact, it is likely that the original codes for library functions were created in C++, compiled, and then linked into the Visual Basic package.

The Program Using a Data Conversion Function

To open this program, open project INTRO. Save the RUNME file as MATH2, and save the project as MATH2. Type in the code shown in Example 4.16, saving the project periodically. Run the program to make sure it works, and correct errors if necessary.

Single step the program. Note how the Chr and CStr functions operate. Modify the program to use the Format function as described in Section 4.5.3. Run the program and note the difference in the displayed output. Use Help to find out more about the Format function. Try different format arguments to experiment with different output styles.

4.6   EVENT PROCEDURES

10. In terms of its relationship with a user, what is a key feature of event-driven programs?
11. When is an event procedure called?

The WELCOME Program

In this section, you will build the WELCOME program described in Section 4.6.2, so you might want to review Section 4.6.2 before continuing. Figure 4.6 shows the final result (during execution). We will give detailed step-by-step instructions for creating this program. Then you can use the same general procedures to build other event-driven programs. If you are still running Visual Basic with the Introduction Template, exit Visual Basic; you should start from scratch. This will be the first time we will be using Visual Basic the way it was intended to be used.

Setting Up the Visual Basic Development Environment   Up to this point, we have been working with Visual Basic so we could work with the Introduction Template (refer to Figures 1.10a and 1.10b; your screen might have looked similar to them, depending on your version of Visual Basic). Now run Visual Basic without opening an existing project.

Visual Basic 5

You will see a New Project dialog box. Click the **New** tab and click on the icon for **Standard EXE**; then click **Open**.

When you are working with a new project, you will see a rectangular window with the title Form1, similar to that shown in Figure 4.9. In fact, this is the form object. If you don't see it, select **Form1** in the Project window. Click **View Form** (for Visual Basic 4) or **View Object** (for Visual Basic 5) in the Project window.

With normal event-driven programming, you will also need to see the Toolbox and the Properties window (see Figures 1.9a and 1.9b). If you don't see them (your screen

---

[8] *We have simplified again. Visual Basic compiles the source code into p-code (packed code), which it then interprets to translate the p-code into machine code during execution.*

Figure 4.9
The Default Form Object

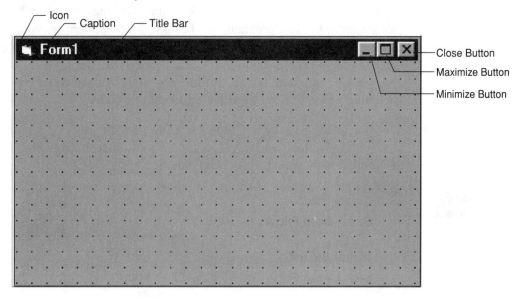

will look something like Figures 1.10a and 1.10b), you must select them from the View menu. To view the Toolbox, select **Toolbox** from the View menu. To view the **Properties** window, select Properties (or Properties Window) from the View menu.

Your screen should look something like Figures 1.9a and 1.9b, except that form Form1 will be shown instead of Introduction Template. The Project window will be titled Project1, and it will show only one item, Form1. In Visual Basic, each program is a project. You can always reposition and resize the windows within the Visual Basic Integrated Development Environment (IDE) to suit your screen and personal taste.

About Projects.   A *project* is a set of modules (and forms). In Visual Basic, a project file has the .VBP extension.

The *project file* is like a packing list describing items, not the items themselves. For example, if you ordered a kit from Cougar Canoe, they would send you a huge crate containing all the materials required for assembling your canoe. It would also contain a list describing all the materials contained in the crate. Like a packing list, the project file lists all the other files in the project.

The Introduction Template is in fact a project. This project (the INTRO project) contains modules INTRO.FRM, INTRO.BAS, and RUNME.BAS (see Figures 1.9a and 1.9b). To reinforce this fact, open file INTRO.VBP using Notepad. There will be some strange information, but you will see references to the three files. For safety reasons, close Notepad immediately (do not modify INTRO.VBP). The default project name is Project1. Our current project has only one form named Form1. The default form is Form1.

About Forms.   A *form* is a window or a dialog box that defines the visual appearance of the window. It also contains the code (event procedures) associated with the window. Although you haven't done anything with this form, it already has built-in functionality. You can compile the project and run it as a normal Windows file if you want, and you haven't even done any development! It is not worthwhile compiling it, but you can run it within the Visual Basic IDE.

Click the **Run** button in the Toolbar. The program will run, and you see a window with the title Form1. Click on the **Form1** icon (see Figure 4.9). You will see the Control menu, which is fully functional. Click on the **Minimize** button in the upper right corner (see Figure 4.9). The program will become a button item on your Windows Taskbar. Click on the taskbar button **Form1**. The program will be restored. Resize the window. Click on the **Maximize** button, and then click on the **Close** button. We admit that this is a very boring program, but the thrilling part is that fundamental Windows functionality is built in without having to write a single line of code.

Save the Form.   Our general *procedure* (no pun intended) for saving programs will be to save the files first, and then save the project. After that, clicking the **Save** button on the Toolbar will save whatever needs saving.

Visual Basic 4

Select **Save File As** from the File menu.

Visual Basic 5

Select **Save Form1 As** from the File menu.

Do *not* select Save Project or Save Project As. Save file FORM1 as WELCOME. Visual Basic will automatically assign the .FRM extension; thus, the full name will be WELCOME.FRM.

Save the Project.   Select **Save Project As** from the File menu. Do *not* select Save File or Save File As. Save project PROJECT1 as WELCOME. Visual Basic will automatically assign the .VBP extension so the full name will be WELCOME.VBP.

Tip

It is best not to type in the file extensions. Let Visual Basic assign the appropriate extension depending on your menu selection. There are enough people who have selected Save Project As and given the project name a form (.FRM) extension, accidentally wiping out a form on which they have worked long and hard.

Remember that there is phase to create the visual layout and a phase to code program statements. Visual layout comes next.

Setting Some Properties.

Visual Basic 4

If you haven't clicked **View Form** on the Project window, do so now. The Properties window should look something like Figure 4.10a.

Visual Basic 5

If you haven't clicked **View Object** on the Project window, do so now. The Properties window should look something like Figure 4.10b. Note that the Properties window has an Alphabetic and a Categorized tab. You can choose which one you want, but we will be using the Alphabetic selection for the rest of this book. Also, unlike Visual Basic 4, the Name property will appear at the top of the list in parentheses.

Figure 4.10a
The Visual Basic 4 Properties Window

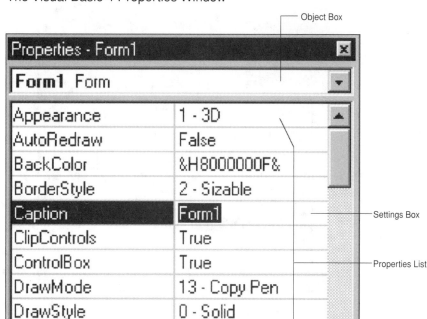

You can use the Properties window to change property settings in the design mode. In this case, there is only one object, the form object named Form1.

Changing the Caption Property.   Click (or double-click) in the **Settings** box for the Caption property (See Figures 4.10a and 4.10b). Type **Welcome to Cougar Canoe** in the Settings box. You should see that the form now has the caption Welcome to Cougar Canoe.

Changing the Name Property.   Use the scroll bar in the Properties window to locate the Name property. It is currently set to Form1. Click (or double-click) in the **Settings** box for the Name property. Type **frmWelcome** in the Settings box. Note that the title of the Properties window and the name in the Object box have changed to refer to a Form object named frmWelcome.

This is all you will do with the form for now. Next you will populate the form with the controls as shown in Figure 4.6; then you can resize the form so that the control objects will fit nicely.

Adding Controls and Setting Their Properties.   You place controls on a form by using the Toolbox (see Figures 4.11a and 4.11b). You will start by adding the Exit button. In this section we will guide you with the steps to add (draw) a control and modify its properties, including size and position. You can then use the same steps for other controls.

Your Toolbox may look different than ours; depending on your setup and your version of Visual Basic, there may be fewer or more buttons. In later chapters we will show you how to add and remove controls. A typical Visual Basic project uses only a subset of all the available controls. Figures 4.11a and 4.11b show the controls that we will use in this book.

Figure 4.10b
The Visual Basic 5
Properties Window

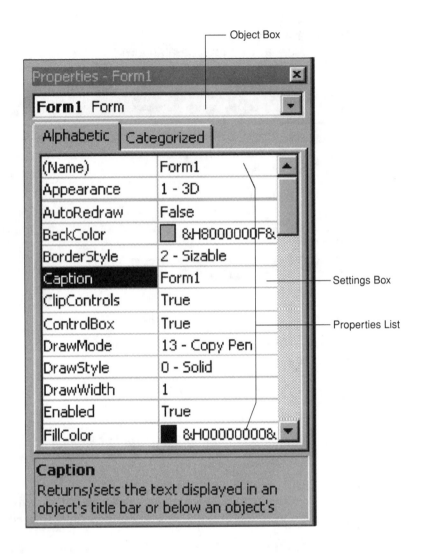

Adding the Exit button.   Double-click the command button in the Toolbox. Visual Basic will place the command button on the form. It will be surrounded by sizing handles, which you can use to size the control to the desired size (see Figure 4.12).

Modifing Some Properties of the Button.   If you click in the form outside the button, the sizing handles will disappear from the button. Click on the button again; the sizing handles should reappear. The sizing handles indicate which control you have currently selected. Note that the Object box (see Figures 4.10a and b) of the Properties window has changed. The Object box indicates that the properties window currently shows the properties of the command button instead of the form.

   Now you will change some properties of the button. First, click on it to make sure it is the selected object. The Object box in the Properties window should indicate that the object is the command button. The button will have sizing handles. Click (or double-click) in the **Settings** box for the Name property (see Figures 4.10a and 4.10b). Type cmdExit in the Settings box.

Visual Basic 5

The Properties window will label the Name property in parentheses as the first property when using the Alphabetic property listing.

Figure 4.11a
The Visual Basic 4 Toolbox
(Only controls used in this
book are labeled)

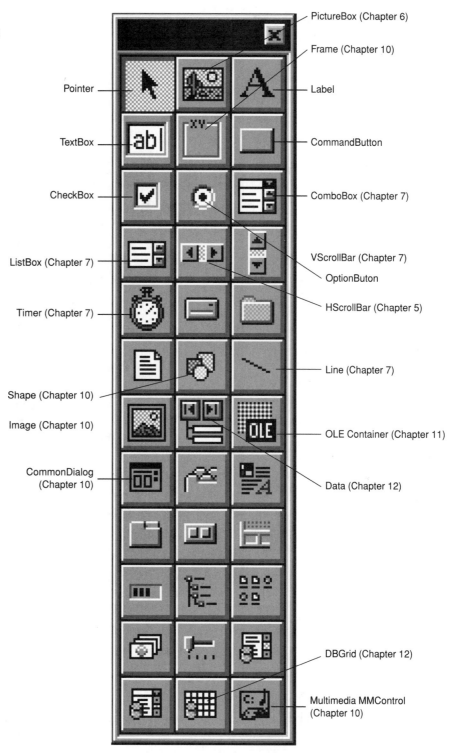

Pointer

TextBox

CheckBox

ListBox (Chapter 7)

Timer (Chapter 7)

Shape (Chapter 10)

Image (Chapter 10)

CommonDialog
(Chapter 10)

PictureBox (Chapter 6)

Frame (Chapter 10)

Label

CommandButton

ComboBox (Chapter 7)

VScrollBar (Chapter 7)

OptionButton

HScrollBar (Chapter 5)

Line (Chapter 7)

OLE Container (Chapter 11)

Data (Chapter 12)

DBGrid (Chapter 12)

Multimedia MMControl
(Chapter 10)

Click (or double-click) in the **Settings** box for the Caption property. Type **E&xit**
in the Settings box; the *x* will be underscored. The ampersand specifies the access key,
which in this case is **Alt+X**.

Modifying the Size and Position of the Button Using the Mouse.   To drag an object with
a mouse, click on it with the left button, hold down the left button, and move the object

Figure 4.11b
The Visual Basic 5 Toolbox (Only controls used in this book are labeled)

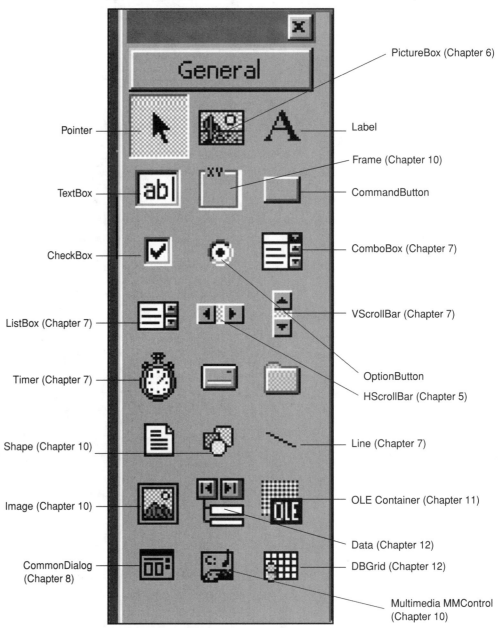

until it is in the desired position. Now click on the button and drag it to the desired position using the mouse.

To resize a control, select it. The sizing handles will appear. Move the mouse pointer over a sizing handle of the control. The pointer will change to a double arrow. This indicates that the mouse is in sizing mode. By selecting a left or right handle, you can size the control horizontally. By selecting an upper or lower handle, you can size the control vertically. By selecting a corner edge handle, you can size the control in both dimensions. Hold down the left mouse button and move the pointer until you have achieved the desired size; release the button.

Figure 4.12
The Form After the Placement of the Command Button

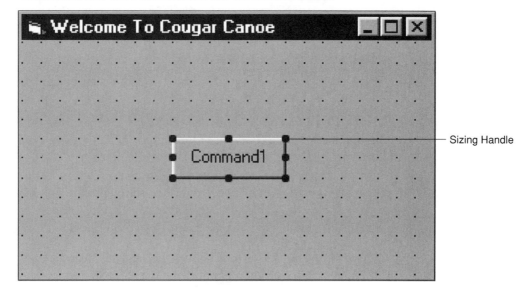

Click the button. Check the Properties window (make sure the Object box indicates that the button is selected). Make sure the button has sizing handles. Experiment with moving and resizing the button. Note that resizing modifies the settings of the Height and Width properties. Note that modifying the position changes the settings of the Left and Top properties.

Sizing and Positioning the Form.

Visual Basic 4

You can similarly size the Form. First select it. No sizing handles will appear, but you can move the pointer to an edge and the pointer will change to a double arrow. To position it on the screen, move the mouse pointer to its Title Bar. Hold down the left mouse button and drag the Form to the desired position. When you run the program, the Form will appear in the position to which you dragged it.

Visual Basic 5

Click on the **Form** (do not click on any of its controls). The Form will appear with sizing handles. You can size the Form by dragging a sizing handle to a desired position. Visual Basic 5 uses the Form Layout window (see Figure 1.9b) to show where the Form will appear when the user first runs the program. If the **Form Layout** window is not visible, select this item from the View menu. To set the default position of the Form, move the mouse pointer to the Form icon in the Form Layout window. Hold down the left mouse button and drag the Form to the desired position.

Tip

With simple programs in Visual Basic 5, the default Form position selected by Visual Basic is usually fine. Hence, you may prefer to close the Form Layout window (click on its **Close** button) to leave more room for the other Visual Basic windows.

Refer to Figures 4.13 or 4.6 and resize the form by moving and sizing the command button so that is appears similar to the Exit button shown in Figure 4.13. Figure 4.13 shows the work in progress, but there is still more to do. Click the **Save** button on the Toolbar to back up the work in progress.

Tip

How do you delete a control? Simply select the **control** and press **Delete**.

Adding the Hello, Goodbye, and Clear Buttons.   Refer to Figure 4.6 to add the other buttons and modify their property settings. Remember that you have to select the object before you can modify its properties. Change the property settings so that one button has a Name property of cmdHello and a Caption property of &Hello, another button has a Name property of cmdGoodbye and a Caption property of &Goodbye, and a third button has a Name property of cmdClear and a Caption property of &Clear. Position and size the buttons so they to appear similar to those shown in Figure 4.6.

Adding the TextBox.   Refer to Figures 4.11a and 4.11b and double-click the TextBox control. A text box with the default name Text1 will be placed on the form. Set its Name property to txtWelcome.

You will now change its Font property. Click on the **Settings** box for the Font property. A **button with three dots** will appear; click on it. Visual Basic will present you with the Font dialog box. Select a **larger size**, such as **18**. If you wish, select **a different font and font style**, and click **OK**. Notice a difference in the appearance of the text displayed in the box.

Change the setting of the Text property to be nothing (null, blank). Thus, when the user runs the program, nothing will appear in the text box. Otherwise the user will see something like Text1 in the box when she runs the program. Resize and position

Figure 4.13
Work in Progress for the WELCOME Program

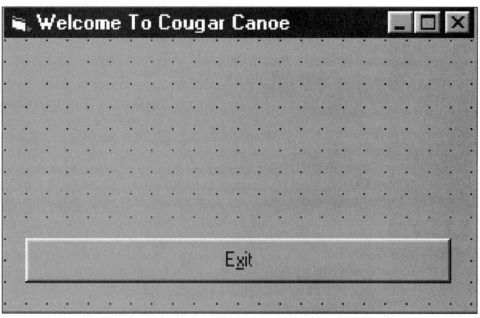

the text box so it appears similar to that shown in Figure 4.6, except that the box will be blank.

Now save the project to back up your work.

Tip

If you are unsure which Toolbox button to use for a control, move the mouse pointer over a Toolbox button and wait a while. A yellow balloon will pop up to identify the control.

Tip

Do the following to find online help about a control. Place it on the form or select an existing control. Make sure it is selected. Press **F1** to launch context-sensitive help. The Help topic will explain the control. If you don't want the control, simply delete it.

Entering the Code.   Run the program. You should see a window with all components. Click **the buttons**. Nothing will happen because you have not entered any code yet. Note that while the program is running, you can click in the text box and type inside it. The text style will be the same as the Font property setting. To stop execution, click the **WELCOME Close** button (top right-hand corner), or click the **Visual Basic Stop** button in the Toolbar. Visual Basic should be in the design mode.

The easiest way to add code is to double-click a control. Let's start by adding the code for the Exit button. Double-click the **cmdExit** button. You should see the familiar Code window. Visual Basic has already entered the start and end statements of the procedure for you. Alternatively, you could click the **View Code** button on the Project Window and select the control from the Object box (see Figures 3.7a and 3.7b). Simply type the keyword **End** between the two statements. The event procedure will look like

```
Private Sub cmdExit_Click()
    End
End Sub
```

To find out what the keyword **End** means, click on it and press **F1**. Visual Basic will display the Help topic about this keyword. (End is used to terminate execution, as one would suspect.)

Run the program. Click the **Exit** button and the program will terminate. Run the program again. Press **Alt+X**, and the program will terminate. So far so good; you have successfully created your first event procedure.

Refer to Example 4.17 (Section 4.6.2). Double-click each button and enter the code for its event procedure. Save the project.

Running the Program.   Click the **Visual Basic Start** button. Click **Hello**, and the message "Welcome to Cougar Canoe" will appear. Click **Goodbye**, and the message "Thank you for visiting" will appear. Click **Clear**, and the message will disappear. Click **Exit** to stop the program.

An event procedure executes in response to your action of clicking a button. If you wish, run the program again ,and click on the buttons in a different order. Try the various access keys, such as ALT+H, ALT+G, and ALT+C. Put in breakpoints just to confirm that the event procedures are really executing in response to the mouse clicks or access keys.

Running the Program With Focus. During execution, in a Windows program *focus* refers to the control that can receive keyboard commands. Run the program, and do not touch the mouse. Observe. Either the text box has a flashing cursor, or one of the buttons has a bolder border. This will depend on the order in which you placed the objects during the visual layout phase. Press the **TAB** key. If you previously had a flashing cursor, it will disappear and one of the buttons will have a bold outline. If you previously had a button with a bold outline, another button will have a bold outline or the text box will have a flashing cursor.

Press **TAB** a few times and observe the effects. Press **TAB** until the Hello button is highlighted (as shown in Figure 4.6). It now has the focus. Press **ENTER**. The Hello message should appear. Since the Hello button has the focus, it is able to receive input from the keyboard.

Press **TAB** until the Goodbye button has the focus. Press **ENTER**. The thank you message should appear. Press **TAB** until the Clear button has the focus. Press **TAB** until the cursor in the text box is flashing. You should be able to type in the box. The tab order for ordering when each control has the focus is initially determined by the order in which you placed the controls on the form.

To improve the user interface, set the `Locked` property of the text box to `True`. This prevents the user from editing the contents of the box. Set the `TabStop` property of the text box to `False`. This prevents the text box from receiving the focus by using the TAB key. The user can still click in the box with the mouse. To modify the tab order, change the TabIndex settings of the command buttons You can modify them so that the Hello button has the initial focus, and pressing Tab moves the focus from left to right, top to bottom.

Building Future Forms. We provided detailed instructions for creating the `WELCOME` program because it is the first program in which you had to build the form visually and write event procedure code. It is the first program that required you to use Visual Basic as it comes off the shelf. In the future, we will only provide a diagram illustrating the completed form. Sometimes we will include a table listing objects with the applicable property settings. In other cases we will give a brief description of the objects, since the exact placement and size of controls is usually not important.

Table 4.2 in Section 4.6.2 is an example of such a table. You can modify the `WELCOME` program to have the same Left, Top, Height, and Width settings as shown in the table. Then your program will look exactly like that shown in Figure 4.6. Save the project one last time. Let's get started with the remaining programs.

The SIMCALC Program

Section 4.6.7 describes the calculator program. You might want to review this section now before continuing. To start, select **New Project** from the File menu.

Visual Basic 4

Select **Save File As** from the File menu.

Visual Basic 5

Select **Save Form1 As** from the File menu.

Save the `FORM1` file as `SIMCALC`. Select **Save Project As** from the File menu, and save *project* `PROJECT1` as `SIMCALC`. Depending on your computing environment and what you had been doing previously, you may have to set up a few things.

Visual Basic 4

If the Project Window isn't visible, select **Project** from the View menu. If the form isn't visible, select **Form** from the View menu (or click **View Form** on the Project window).

Visual Basic 5

If the Project Explorer window isn't visible, select **Project Explorer** from the View menu. If the Form isn't visible, select **Object** from the View menu (or click **View Form** on the Project Explorer window).

Similarly, select other items from the View menu if necessary. Build the form so that it appears similar to that shown in Figure 4.7. Note that you will also be using the Label control (see Figures 4.1a and 4.1b or use the pop-up balloon on the Toolbox). Labels, like command buttons, show visible text as the Caption property. Set the Caption property of Label lblNum1 as First Number:. Similarly, set the Captions of the other labels. You can either set the Text properties of the text boxes as blanks or make them the same as the Name setting. The latter may be useful, since it will cue you as to which text box you are working with. Note that the Form_Load event described in Section 4.6.3 will initialize the Text property settings when the program is run. Save the project to back up your work.

Enter the code as shown in Example 4.18. When you double-click the **Form** in the design mode, the Code window will appear with the first and last lines of the Form_Load event procedure. It is very important that the code uses the exact object names as you set for the Name properties when building the form.

Run the program. You should be able to type in numbers in the text boxes and perform calculations by clicking on buttons. If you try to divide by zero or use non-numeric inputs, a runtime error will occur.

Next you will examine execution in some detail. Set breakpoints for the first lines of procedures Form_Load, cmdAdd_Click, and cmdSubtract_Click. Set watch expressions for txtAnswer.Text as follows: Highlight the expression anywhere in any statement where it appears. The Edit Watch dialog box has two list boxes for context. In the Procedure list box, select (All Procedures). Similarly add watch expressions for txtNum1.Text and txtNum2.Text while ensuring that (All Procedures) is selected as the Procedure context in all cases. The Module Context should remain set as frm-Calculator for all watch expressions.

Run the program. It should immediately halt at the breakpoint in the Form_Load procedure. Note that the form is not visible. It will not become visible until the Form_Load has completed execution. Use Step Over to single step. Monitor the watch expressions in the Debug window. When you single step past the last statement in Form_Load, the form will appear. Do not click any buttons yet.

Type **some numbers** in the text boxes for the first and second numbers. The text properties have not changed yet. Click the **Add** button. The program will halt at the breakpoint, with Visual Basic in the break mode. The text properties will change (observe the Debug Window). It is very important that you notice that the Text property settings are strings, not a numeric data type. Single step the cmdAdd_Click procedure. Use instant watch expressions to observe that function CSng returns a numeric value (i.e., its value is not enclosed in quotation marks). Stop single stepping when the current statement is

```
txtAnswer.Text = CStr(fAnswer)
```

Click on the **form**. Note that text box txtAnswer does not show the result of addition. Click **Step Over** and click the **form** again. Now the form will show the result of addition. The result of executing the previous statement is to assign the Text property of txtAnswer to the setting of the answer (after it has been converted to a string by function CStr). Single step and Visual Basic will again be in the run mode, and the single step buttons are grayed (not in context).

Change the **input values**. Click the **Subtract** button and repeat the single step exercise you did previously. Note when the Text property settings change. Also note the effect of using library functions CSng and CStr; they both perform data type conversions.

The LABCOSTE Program

Section 4.6.8 describes the event-driven version of the labor cost program. You might want to review this section now before continuing. To start, select **New Project** from the File menu.

Select **Save File As** from the File menu. Save the FORM1 file as LABCOSTE, and select **Save Project As** from the File menu. Save *project* PROJECT1 as LABCOSTE.

Build the form so that it appears similar to that shown in Figure 4.8. Name the text boxes appropriately as txtPayRate, txtTotalTime, and txtLaborCost. Name the command buttons appropriately as cmdLaborCost and cmdExit. Name the label controls as lblPayRate, lblTotalTime, and lblLaborCost.

You will be using a new control. Double-click the **CheckBox** button on the toolbox to add it to the form. Position it, and name it as chkOvertime. Set its Caption to Rush Job?, and set its Value property to 0 Unchecked. To set its Value property, click in the **Settings** box for the Value property of the check box control. A **Property button** will appear. Click on it and select **0 - Unchecked** from the list. Some properties, such as the Value property of a check box, have only a few possible settings.

Note

When clicking the Settings box in the Properties window, you will sometimes see a Properties button, depending on the property. If the button has a down arrow caption, it means that there are only a few possible settings. Double-click in the settings box to toggle through the possible settings, or select the setting from the pop-up list when clicking the properties button.

Save a backup copy of the project. Enter the code as shown in Example 4.19. When you double-click on a text box object in design mode, the Code window will automatically show the first and last lines of the Change event procedure. Save the project. Run the program and experiment with different input values. Put in breakpoints at the beginning of various event procedures. Run the program and single step statements and monitor watch expressions. You may find it convenient to reposition the Code window and Form object in break mode so that you can view both at the same time. Otherwise click each to view them alternatively. In particular, note the value of watch expression chkOvertime.Value when the user (in this case you) has checked it off and when the user has checked it on. By now you should have some familiarity with elementary event-driven programs.

Tip

To see all of the objects by Name, click on the **Object box button** in the Properties window (see Figures 4.10a and 4.10b). If you don't remember the visual location of an object, you can select it by **Name** from the Object box in the Properties window.

Help About the Toolbox and Controls

Visual Basic 4

To find out more information about the Toolbox, select **Contents** in the Help menu. Click the **Contents** tab. Open the **Visual Basic** book icon and select **Development Environment** (after Glossary). Scroll through the list and select **Toolbox**.

Visual Basic 5

To find out more information about the Toolbox, select **Microsoft Visual Basic Help Topics** in the Help menu. Click the **Index** tab. Select topic **Toolbox, standard controls**, and click **Display**.

The Help topic window shows information about standard controls only. Check the See Also link and investigate information about controls we have already used. When you view information about any standard control, Help provides links to the Properties, Methods, and Events that the object supports. (Ignore Methods for now.) For example, if you view Help information about the CommandButton control, you will see that it has a long list of Properties, but the Text property is not on this list. The Events list shows Click, DragDrop, and others. A Command button does not receive a Load or Change event.

For practice, view the topics about Properties and Events. You might not understand much of it at this stage; you won't yet have all the background knowledge required to understand it. Your ability to understand the explanations in the Help system will improve as you practice creating Visual Basic programs. However, for navigational practice, view some topics and note that you can use the Back button to return to a previous topic.

You can find out the same sort of information about events using the Code window. If necessary, refer to Figures 3.7a and 3.7b. The Object box (top left box) lists objects by Name. If you select a Command button from the Object box, the Procedure box (top right box) will show the corresponding event. Click the **arrow button** in the Procedure box. You will see a list of events that the object receives. You could write event procedures for each of these when necessary.

Visual Basic assigns a default event for each object. For Form, it is Load; for CommandButton, it is Click; and for TextBox, it is Change. Double-clicking the object in design mode automatically generates the declaration template (start and end) of an event procedure for its default event. If you accidentally triggered the creation of a declaration template you don't want, no harm is done, but you might want to delete it to remove unnecessary clutter in the Code window.

4.7 SAMPLE PROBLEMS

After you have tried to solve the problems, refer to the solutions in subdirectory CH04\SOLN. It is possible that your solutions may be better.

Improve the SIMCALC Program

Improve SIMCALC so that the result will go blank whenever the user types in any of the input boxes. Refer to the LABCOSTE program for an idea of how to do this.

Improve the Style and Documentation for an Information Gathering Prototype

Cougar Canoe is prototyping a system for gathering customer information. The system will eventually send customer profiles to various representatives in various regions. It will use the area code of the customer's telephone number to do this. Their contract programmer developed a prototype to split a telephone number into its area code and local number. Note that this is only a first step. The prototype is designed for the North American market, where telephone numbers are defined as a three-digit area code followed by a seven-digit local number.

Figure 4.14 shows the prototype in action. The user entered the full telephone number of **800 555 1212**. The area code is 800 and 555-1212 is the local number. Your task is to improve the programming style and naming conventions for objects and variables. At this stage it is not necessary to add code to add robustness to the program. For example, if the user enters the area code in parentheses, as in **(800) 555-1212**, the output will be misleading. Example 4.20 shows the code listing, and Figure 4.14 illustrates the output. You can create the program from scratch or open Project GATHER01 and modify it.

Example 4.20

```
Option Explicit

' — - IMPROVE THIS PROGRAM — -
'
' Improve naming conventions
' Add comments to explain code better
' Improve indentation and statement spacing
' Program is supposed to accept a full
' North American telephone number, including area
' code, and display the area code and local
' telephone number in separate boxes

Private Sub Command1_Click()
Dim Pony As String
Dim Dog As String, Cat As String
Pony = Text1.Text
Dog = Left(Pony, 3)
Cat = Right(Pony, 8)
Text2.Text = Dog
```

Figure 4.14
A Poor Excuse for Gathering Telephone Number Data

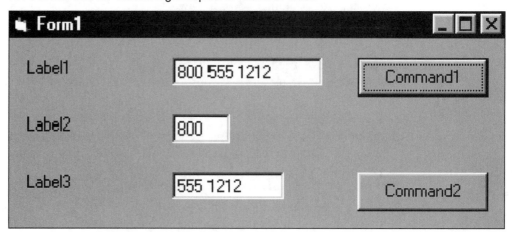

```
Text3.Text = Cat
End Sub


Private Sub Command2_Click()
End
End Sub

Private Sub Form_Load()
Text2.Locked = True
Text3.Locked = True
Text2.Text = ""
Text3.Text = ""
Text1.Text = ""
End Sub

Private Sub Text1_Change()
Text2.Text = ""
Text3.Text = ""
End Sub
```

Remember that you can use Help to find out about such functions as Left and Right.

A Word About Maintenance

This exercise simulates program maintenance. Perhaps your eventual task is to add solidity to handle incorrect inputs and also take into account telephone numbers outside North America. Often one has to modify programs written by others. Our example is an artificial case, and the program is so small that you would be better off creating a new program. However, there is a lot of legacy code in business, with thousands of statements. Here it does not make sense to start from scratch.

ADDITIONAL PROBLEM SOLVING

Create a version of the business account application program described in Section 4.3.3 that uses parameter passing instead of global variables.

Modify the Labor Cost program in such a way that the Labor Cost button is no longer required. The program will automatically calculate a new result whenever the user modifies an input. Note that you may have to set valid text properties in design mode instead of using the Form_Load procedure.

Create an event-driven version of the business account application described in Section 4.3.3 (Example 4.10).

CHAPTER 5

Decision Logic

This chapter introduces code that can compare data in order to select alternative actions.

Decisions, decisions—there are always decisions. Commercial programs work in complex environments: You use a web search engine to find information. The search engine program compares stored data with your search criteria and decides whether to include the data as a search result. With decision-making capability, a program may also avoid conditions that cause runtime errors.

After completing this chapter, you should be able to

- Design a program based on using selection and sequence code units.

- Create and use the `If Then` statement and its variations.

- Create and use the `Select Case` statement and its variations.

- Use comparison and logic operators to write Boolean expressions.

- Write programs that use input validation and error trapping.

- Use three new controls: the check box, option button, and scroll bar.

In This Chapter

Cougar Canoe wants a program that will allow customers to register their canoe purchase. The system will permit Cougar Canoe to contact customers about new accessory products and seminars about canoeing. Cougar's representatives can follow up on product problems and repairs, or simply check to find out how much customers enjoy a product. This is no small task.

In this chapter we begin by looking at the fundamental decision-making structures used to change the flow of program execution. Once we are familiar with three structures, we can examine two key components, *input validation* and *error trapping*. Out there in the real world, programs must employ these two components.

5.1 THE FUNDAMENTAL CONTROL STRUCTURES

The three fundamental control structures are

- Sequence
- Selection
- Repetition

5.1.1 The Sequence Structure

Up to now, we have only covered the sequence structure. In a procedure, the program executes each statement, one after the other, in a linear sequence. With procedural programs, including the Introduction Template, once a program starts, it calls sub procedures and/or functions in a set sequence. In event-driven programs, event procedures are called in an unpredictable order (with a few exceptions such as Form_Load). However, once the event-procedure starts, it continues executing each statement, one after the other, until the procedure exits.

5.1.2 The Selection Structure

Note

The selection structure involves evaluating a condition to determine if it is True or False. Then the program makes a choice as to what action to take.

The selection structure is the focus of this chapter. We have seen hints about this structure earlier, particularly with the Labor Cost program, which evaluates a condition to determine if it is True or False and subsequently makes a choice as to what action to take. For example, the Labor Cost program (Example 2.8 in Section 2.3.1) includes the following statement with comments:

```
' If this is a rush job, then the hourly labor rate is adjusted
' by multiplying the hourly labor rate by an overtime factor
If Answer = "Yes" Then PayRate = PayRate * 1.5
```

The variable `PayRate` (of type Single) is multiplied by 1.5 ***if and only if*** the variable `Answer` has a value of `"Yes"` (a String). Otherwise, the value of `PayRate` remains unchanged. Hence, if `PayRate` has a value of 6.70 and the Answer variable has a value of `"Yes"`, `PayRate` will have a value of 10.05 after the statement executes. Figure 2.8 shows the flow chart of the program, and shows the selection structure embedded within the sequence structure. The diamond represents the evaluation of a condition; the flow away from the diamond shows the two alternative actions.

5.1.3   The Repetition Structure

The repetition structure is discussed in depth in Chapter 6. It is a set of statements that are executed repeatedly ***while*** a specified condition is true.

5.2   SELECTION STATEMENTS

Visual Basic includes a number of selection statements. These are

- `If Then`
- `If Then Else`
- `If Then ElseIf Else`
- `Select Case`
- `Choose`
- `Switch`
- `If`

Typically, these are multiline statements, meaning they may contain multiple lines, so it is necessary to include keywords that indicate the end of the statement. For example, the If-type statements end with the keywords `End If`, as shown in the following example:

```
If nNum = 1 Then
    sDigit = "1"
Else
    sDigit = "Not 1"
End If
```

The exception occurs when the entire statement can fit on one line, such as the following statement in the Labor Cost program:

```
If Answer = "Yes" Then PayRate = PayRate * 1.5
```

The `Select Case` statement ends with the keywords `End Select`, as in the following example:

```
Select Case nNum
    Case 0
        sDigit = "0"
    Case 1
        sDigit = "1"
```

```
        Case 2
            sDigit = "2"
        Case Else
            sDigit = "Not 0, 1 or 2"
End Select
```

In Visual Basic terminology, a selection structure is still a called statement even if it contains distinct stand-alone statements within the structure itself. In other languages this type of structure with multiple statements within a statement may be called a compound statement.

5.3   THE IF THEN STATEMENT

5.3.1   The Equality Comparison Operator (=) and the Assignment Operator (=)

Recall our initial sample:

```
If Answer = "Yes" Then PayRate = PayRate * 1.5
```

Ponder the use of the equals sign (=) in this sample. In the first instance, the equals sign is an equality comparison operator, meaning it is used to compare two expressions. In this case, it checks whether the value of Answer is the same as the string constant "Yes". The result of the comparison is True or False. In the second instance, the equals sign is the *assignment* operator. In this case, PayRate is assigned the value of its previous value multiplied by 1.5.

Note

When the equals sign (=) is part of the comparison part of an If-type statement, it is an equality comparison operator. Otherwise, it is an assignment operator.

To avoid ambiguity, use the Let Keyword when using the equals sign as an assignment operator. So far, I have never seen a real-life Visual Basic program that actually used the Let keyword.

5.3.2   Some Other Samples

Here are two more samples:

```
If nNumber <> 0 Then nAnswer = nOtherNumber / nNumber

If nAge > 17 Then
    sMessage = "Since you are " & CStr(nAge)
    sMessage = sMessage & " years old, please vote."
    txtMessage.Text = sMessage
End If
```

Note that the first If Then statement fits on one line, hence it does not require the words End If. The second If Then statement consists of several (sub) statements. It

requires the words End If to indicate the end of the structure. The following pseudocode
will explain how this code segment executes when a program is run:

```
If Number is not equal to zero, Then okay to divide
(otherwise Number unchanged)

If Age is greater than 17, Then
    Compose message to tell user that they should vote
    Display message in text box
(otherwise, no change to message or text box)
```

These samples also introduce some other comparison operators. These are not the equal
to (<>) and the greater than (>) operators.

Exercise

For what application would the following or a similar statement be useful?

```
If nNumber <> 0 Then nAnswer = nOtherNumber / nNumber
```

Solution

Use it to avoid a divide-by-zero runtime error.

> *Note*
>
> The If Then statement has two parts: conditional expression and conditional
> statements. The syntax is
>
> **If** *condition expression* **Then** *conditional statement*
>
> or
>
> **If** *condition expression* **Then**
>   *conditional statement(s)*
> **End If**

The If Then statement executes the conditional statement(s) only if the value of
the condition expression is True.

5.4   THE IF THEN ELSE STATEMENT

With the If Then statement, if the condition being evaluated is True, then an action
will be taken. Otherwise, no action will be taken. With the If Then Else statement,
an alternative action is taken if the condition is False. Consider the following sample:

```
nAge = CInt(txtAge.Text)

If nAge >= 18 Then
    sMessage = "Since you are " & CStr(nAge)
    sMessage = sMessage & " years old, please vote"
    txtMessage.Text = sMessage
Else
    sMessage = "Sorry, you cannot vote."
    txtMessage.Text = sMessage

End If
```

The pseudocode could be

```
Get Age

If Age is greater than or equal to 18, Then
    Compose message to tell user that they should vote
    Display message in text box
Else (otherwise)
    Compose message to tell user that they cannot vote
    Display message in text box
```

This sample uses the greater than or equal to (>=) comparison operator. Note that library function CInt performs conversion to return a value of type Integer. Also, CStr performs conversion to return a value of type String.

Exercise

What do you think would happen if the user in the previous sample entered 17.6?

Solution

The result is

```
"Since you are 18 years old, please vote. "
```

The input is rounded to the nearest integer. Since 17.6 is rounded to 18, the condition is True. We could overcome this deficiency by adding extra logic or by using the Single data type.

5.4.1   Use Indentation

It is a good idea to indent (tab) statements that perform an action within a selection statement. The following is legal syntax but is considered poor programming style. Ask yourself whether it is easy to read.

```
' Legal but poor style
nAge = CInt(txtAge.Text)
If nAge >= 18 Then
sMessage = "Since you are " & CStr(nAge)
sMessage = sMessage & " years old.  Please vote"
txtMessage.Text = sMessage
Else
sMessage = "Sorry, you cannot vote."
txtMessage.Text = sMessage
End If
```

5.4.2   Improve the Customer Information System, Version 2

Part of Cougar Canoe's system is to assign customers to local representatives based on the area code of the customer telephone number. The customer enters her or his full telephone number, including area code (This is the North American system) in a format such as **345 112 4523** or **(345) 112 4523**. Hence, it is necessary for a program to detect whether the customer used parentheses and then later remove them to store area codes in a consistent format without parentheses. The program of Example 5.1 shows a possible implementation. We made comment lines short to minimize horizontal scrolling inside the Code window.

Example 5.1

```
Option Explicit

' Split a telephone number into its area code
' and local number. Some people put the
' area code in parentheses.
' This version assumes user enters
' telephone number as
' (xxx) xxx xxxx -or- xxx xxx xxxx


Private Sub Form_Load()

    ' Initialize operation of program.
    txtAreaCode.Locked = True    ' Prevent user from editing
    txtLocalTel.Locked = True
    txtAreaCode.Text = ""    ' Initially blank boxes
    txtLocalTel.Text = ""
    txtGetTel.Text = ""

End Sub

Private Sub cmdEnter_Click()

    ' Do the main work of splitting the telephone
    ' number into the area code and local components

    Dim sFullTel As String
    Dim sAreaCode As String, sLocalTel As String
    Dim nLength As Integer ' Length of full tel string

    sFullTel = txtGetTel.Text    ' Get user input
    nLength = Len(sFullTel) ' Find number of characters

    ' If parentheses used, strip them off the area code
    If (InStr(sFullTel, "(") = 1) Then
        ' First "(" found, hence strip off first "("
        sAreaCode = Right(sFullTel, nLength - 1)
        ' Strip off last ")" and whatever follows
        sAreaCode = Left(sAreaCode, 3)
    Else
        ' No parentheses used, hence we only need
        ' the first three digits
        sAreaCode = Left(sFullTel, 3)
    End If

    ' Local number is last 8 characters of number
```

```
        ' Note it assumes one character is a space
        sLocalTel = Right(sFullTel, 8)
        ' Display area code and local number
        txtAreaCode.Text = sAreaCode
        txtLocalTel.Text = sLocalTel

End Sub

Private Sub txtGetTel_Change()

        ' Cue user that result may be invalid due
        ' to possible modification of this input
        txtAreaCode = ""
        txtLocalTel = ""

End Sub


Private Sub cmdExit_Click()
    End ' End the program
End Sub
```

The program shows some ***string manipulation*** functions you may not be aware of. Function Len returns the length of the complete telephone string. Function InStr returns the position of the first occurrence of the second argument within the string specified by the first argument. In other words, the comparison operation is true only if "(" is the first character in the full telephone number. Function Right returns a specified number of characters from the right side of the string; the number is specified by the second argument. Argument nLength -1 specifies all of the characters except the first one in order to remove the first parentheses. Function Left returns the specified number of characters from the left of the string. In this case, it returns the three leftmost characters. At this point, you should be able to work out the rest of the code details. For more information about the functions, refer to Visual Basic Help. The program still lacks solidity. The user can enter data with leading spaces or other variations. Figure 5.7 in the Hands-On Exercises shows the appearance of the program.

Note

The If Then Else statement has two parts: conditional expression and conditional statements. The syntax is

If *condition expression* **Then**
    conditional statement(s) associated with True condition
Else
    conditional statement(s) associated with False condition
End If

The If Then Else statement executes the conditional statement(s) associated with the True condition, only if the value of the condition expression is True; otherwise, it executes the statement(s) associated with the False condition.

5.5   THE IF THEN ELSEIF ELSE STATEMENT

With the `If Then ElseIf Else` statement we can evaluate alternative conditions when an initial condition is false. Generally we use a process of elimination logic with this statement. Consider the following logical reasoning:

- If the temperature is at or below zero Celsius, then we know that water freezes.

- Otherwise, check if the temperature is at or above 100 degrees Celsius; if it is, then water boils.

- Otherwise (through elimination of the previous two conditions), water must be liquid.

The following statement can be used to express this:

```
If CSng(txtTemperature.Text) <= 0 Then
    txtWater.Text = "Frozen"
ElseIf CSng(txtTemperature.Text) >= 100 Then
    txtWater.Text = "Boiling"
Else
    txtWater.Text = "Liquid"
End If
```

Flow charts can be useful for illustrating the flow of execution within a decision structure. Figure 5.1 illustrates a flow chart for this statement.

Figure 5.1
Flow Chart Illustrating
the If Then ElseIf Else
Statement

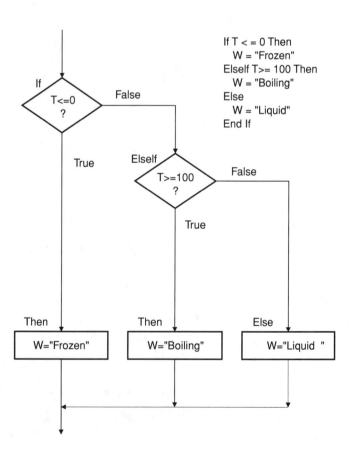

5.5.1   Improve the Customer Information System, Version 3

We can improve our program from Example 5.1 so that it will handle a larger variety of inputs to obtain useful results. Example 5.2 shows the changes to the `cmdEnter_Click` procedure.

Example 5.2

```
Private Sub cmdEnter_Click()

    ' Do the main work of splitting the telephone
    ' number into the area code and local components

    Dim sFullTel As String
    Dim sAreaCode As String, sLocalTel As String
    Dim nLength As Integer ' Length of full tel string

    ' Trim off leading and trailing spaces first
    sFullTel = Trim(txtGetTel.Text)
    nLength = Len(sFullTel)

    ' If "( " [( followed by space] used, strip them off the
    ' area code
    If (InStr(sFullTel, "( ") = 1) Then
        ' First "( " found, hence strip off first "( "
        sAreaCode = Right(sFullTel, nLength - 2)
        ' Strip off last ")" and whatever follows
        sAreaCode = Left(sAreaCode, 3)
    ' If "(" used, strip them off the area code
    ElseIf (InStr(sFullTel, "(") = 1) Then
        ' First "(" found, hence strip off first "( "
        sAreaCode = Right(sFullTel, nLength - 1)
        ' Strip off last ")" and whatever follows
        sAreaCode = Left(sAreaCode, 3)
    Else
        ' No parentheses used, hence we only need
        ' the first three digits
        sAreaCode = Left(sFullTel, 3)
    End If

    ' Local number is last eight characters of number
    ' Note it assumes one character is a space
    sLocalTel = Right(sFullTel, 8)
    ' Display area code and local number
    txtAreaCode.Text = sAreaCode
    txtLocalTel.Text = sLocalTel


End Sub
```

The `Trim` function removes any spaces that are in front of or behind the user input. The procedure initially checks for the occurrence of a left parenthesis followed by a space, and if it finds this condition, it deletes the parenthesis. Otherwise, it checks for the occurrence of a left parenthesis (followed by numerical characters; if it finds this condition, it deletes the parenthesis. Otherwise it assumes the user simply did not use parentheses. However, the program still makes many presumptions by assuming a cooperative customer.

> **Note**
>
> The `If Then ElseIf Else` statement has two parts: a conditional expression and conditional statements. The syntax is
>
> `If` *condition expression* `Then`
>
>> *conditional statement(s) associated with True condition*
>
> `ElseIf` *alternate condition expression* `Then`
>
>> *conditional statement(s) associated with alternate True condition*
>
> `[ additional ElseIf blocks if used ]`
>
> `Else`
>
>> *conditional statement(s) associated with False condition*
>
> `End If`
>
> The `If Then Else` statement executes the conditional statement(s) associated with the `True` condition only if the value of the condition expression is `True`; otherwise, it executes the statement(s) associated with a `False` condition.

5.6   COMPARISON OPERATORS

*A **comparison operator** is one or two symbols (characters) that indicate a relationship between two or more expressions. The relationship can be* `True` *or* `False`.

5.6.1   Presenting the Operators

Table 5.1 illustrates comparison operators. The result of a comparison operation returns one of two values: `True` or `False`.

It is possible to compare numerical expressions or string expressions. For numerical comparisons note that (1 / 2 <> 0.5) is `False` because 1 divided by 2 is exactly 0.5. On the other hand, the square root of 2 is approximately 1.41421, but it isn't *exactly* that, so (Sqr(2) = 1.41421) evaluates to `False`. String comparisons are more or less based on an alphabetical sort. Words that appear later in an alphabetically sorted list have higher values. Since the word *Cougar* would appear before *cougar*, it has a lower value. Similarly, *Cat* has a lower value than *Dog*.

5.6.2   The Boolean Data Type

The If-type statements evaluate a condition to determine an action. The condition is a Boolean data type that may be `True` or `False`. Consider the following event procedure that uses a Boolean data type.

Table 5.1
Comparison Operators

| Symbol | Description | Expression Examples That Are | |
		True	False
<	Less than	-7.8<4.5	4.5<-7.8
<=	Less than or equal to	0.67<=0.68	0.68<=0.67
>	Greater than	"cougar">"Cougar"	"Cougar">"cougar"
>=	Greater than or equal to	"Dog">="Cat"	"Cat">="Dog"
<>	Not equal	1.000.<>1	1/2<>0.5
=	Equal	Sqr(2)*Sqr(2)=2	Sqr(2)=1.41421

Example 5.3

```
Private Sub cmdBoolean_Click()

    Dim bResult As Boolean

    ' User types in boxes txtEx1 and txtEx2
    bResult = (txtEx1.Text = txtEx2.Text)
    ' Result appears in box txtBoolean
    txtBoolean.Text = CStr(bResult)

End Sub
```

If the user types **Cougar** in both input text boxes and clicks the button, the Boolean result text box will in fact show the word True. If the user types in different words in each of the input text boxes, the displayed result will in fact show the word False. True and False are Visual Basic keywords. The result of a comparison evaluates to what is called a ***Boolean*** data type. The term comes from the name of George Boole, who developed symbolic logic during the 1850s. Boolean data type is not the Integer, Single, or String data type and can have only one of two values: True or False. When other numeric data types are converted to Boolean values, 0 becomes False while all other values become True. When Boolean values are converted to other data types, False becomes 0 while True becomes –1.

5.7 Logic Expressions

George Boole's symbolic logic used logical operators. Logical operators can prove to be very useful. Consider a bank. A bank typically operates under a complex set of business rules such as the following:

- A withdrawal is allowed if the amount is less than the balance and if it is less than the daily limit, or

- The amount may exceed the daily limit if prior arrangements were made (provided that the amount is still less than the balance), or

- The amount may exceed the balance by a specified credit limit if the account is a special credit account.

Phew, this is quite a mouthful. It would help to express these rules in pseudocode.

Example 5.4

```
If
    (Withdrawal < Balance) And (Withdrawal < Daily Limit)
        Or
    (Withdrawal < Balance) And (Exceed Daily Permission = True)
        Or
    ((Balance - Withdrawal) > (- Limit)) And (Special = True)
Then
    Withdrawal Allowed
```

The words And and Or are examples of Boolean operators. We can use Boolean operators to compare two expressions to evaluate the combination as True or False. Table 5.2 illustrates the Boolean operators.

If we investigate logical operators using Help, we would find that there are two other operators: Eqv and Imp. Use Eqv to perform a logical equivalence on two expressions as illustrated in the following code segment:

```
Dim bResult As Boolean
bResult = 10 > 8 Eqv 8 > 6  ' Result True because both are True
bResult = 8 > 10 Eqv 6 > 8  ' Result True because both are False
bResult = 10 > 8 Eqv 6 > 8  ' Result False because both are different
```

Table 5.2
Boolean Operators

Operator Keyword	Description	Examples That Are	
		True	**False**
And	Evaluates to True only if *both* expressions evaluate to True	nA > nB And nC > nD nC < nD And nB > nC	nA < nB And nC > nD nD > nB And nD < nC
Or	Evaluates to True if *either* or both expressions evaluate to True	nA < nB Or nC > nD nA > nB Or nC > nD	nA < nB Or nC < nD nD > nB Or nD > nC
Not	Evaluates to True only if the expression is False	Not(nA < nB) Not(nC > nB)	Not(nA > nB) Not(nC < nB)
Xor	Evaluates to True if *only one* of the expressions evaluates to True. It is the Exclusive Or operator.	nA > nB Xor nD > nC nA < nB Xor nD < nC	nA < nB Xor nD > nC nA > nB Xor nC > nC
' Sample assignments: nA = 10: nB = 8: nC = 6: nD = 4			

The `Eqv` operator returns `True` if both logical expressions are the same, but it returns `False` if they are different.[1] Use `Imp` to perform a logical implication on two expressions. The result is `False` only if the first expression is `True` but the second expression is `False`. Other conditions will imply `True`. The following illustrates this:

```
Dim bResult As Boolean
bResult = 10 > 8 Imp 8 > 6  ' Result True because True implies True
bResult = 8 > 10 Imp 6 > 8  ' Result True because False may imply Anything
bResult = 10 > 8 Imp 6 > 8  ' Result False because True does not imply False
bResult = 8 > 10 Imp 8 > 10 ' Result True because False may imply Anything
```

For more information, refer to Help.

5.7.1   Order of Precedence

Recall the order of precedence discussed in Section 3.5.2. Each operation in an expression is performed in a predetermined order that is known as *the order of precedence*. Unless overridden by parentheses, the computer performs arithmetic operations first (see Table 3.4), in left-to-right order. Next, it performs comparison operations in left-to-right order. Finally, it performs logical operations. Table 5.3 shows the complete order of precedence: the highest to lowest order as top to bottom from left to right, with one exception—all comparison operators have equal precedence. That is, the computer performs each comparison in left-to-right order. Remember that the parentheses can override the precedence order.

The assignment operator (=) has the lowest precedence. For more information, refer to the Visual Help topic Operator Precedence.

Table 5.3
Operator Precedence

Arithmetic	Comparison	Logical
Exponentiation (^)	Equality (=)	Not
Negation (-)	Inequality (<>)	And
Multiplication and division (*,/)	Less than (<)	Or
Integer division (\)	Greater than (>)	Xor
Modulo arithmetic (Mod)	Less than or Equal to (<=)	Eqv
Addition and subtraction (+,-)	Greater than or Equal to (>=)	Imp
String concatenation (&)	Like Is	

[1]*The Imp operator also performs a bitwise comparison of identically positioned bits in two numeric expressions and sets the corresponding bit to 1 if they are the same. For example, 10 Eqv –2 returns a result of 11 because decimal 10 is binary 0000000000001010, and decimal –2 is binary 1111111111111110. The identical bits are highlighted in bold. Hence, the result is binary 0000000000001011, which turns out to be decimal 11.*

Exercise

What value is assigned to bFlag? Explain why.

```
Dim bFlag As Boolean
bFlag = 5 * 6 > 30 And 2 - 7 < 18 * 2
```

Solution

False. The computer evaluates the statement as follows:

```
bFlag = 30 > 30 And -5 < 36
bFlag = False And True
bFlag = False
```

5.7.2   Improve the Customer Information System, Version 4

We can improve our program of Example 5.2 so that it will handle a larger variety of inputs and obtain useful results.

Example 5.5

```
Private Sub cmdEnter_Click()

' Split a telephone number into its area code
' and local number.  Some people put the
' area code in parentheses.
' This version assumes user enters
' telephone number with area code as
' ( xxx ) -or- (xxx) -or- xxx
' and local number as xxx xxxx -or- xxxxxxx
' If local part is not numerical then display "Invalid"
Dim sFullTel As String
Dim sAreaCode As String, sLocalTel As String
Dim nLength As Integer ' Length of full tel string
Dim bValidFlag As Boolean    ' Flag whether local number is valid


' Trim off leading and trailing spaces first
sFullTel = Trim(txtGetTel.Text)
nLength = Len(sFullTel)

' Local number is last seven characters if no spaces
' (it represents a valid number) ...
If IsNumeric(Right(sFullTel, 7)) Then
    sLocalTel = Right(sFullTel, 7)
    bValidFlag = True
Else
    sLocalTel = Right(sFullTel, 8)
End If

' ... or 8 characters if fourth character is a space
' and rest are valid numbers
If (InStr(sLocalTel, " ") = 4) And _
    IsNumeric(Left(sLocalTel, 3)) And _
    IsNumeric(Right(sLocalTel, 4)) Then bValidFlag = True

' If "( " used, strip them off the area code
```

```
' as long as local number is valid
If ((InStr(sFullTel, "( ") = 1) And bValidFlag) Then
    ' First "( " found, hence strip off first "( "
    sAreaCode = Right(sFullTel, nLength - 2)
    ' Strip off last ")" and whatever follows
    sAreaCode = Left(sAreaCode, 3)
' If "(" used, strip them off the area code
' as long as local number is valid
ElseIf ((InStr(sFullTel, "(") = 1) And bValidFlag) Then
    ' First "(" found, hence strip off first "( "
    sAreaCode = Right(sFullTel, nLength - 1)
    ' Strip off last ")" and whatever follows
    sAreaCode = Left(sAreaCode, 3)
' If local number invalid then tell user so
ElseIf Not (bValidFlag) Then
    sAreaCode = ""   'Redundant but helps to make it explicit
    sLocalTel = "Invalid"
Else
    ' Otherwise assumes number must be okay
    ' No parentheses used, hence we only need
    ' the first three digits
    sAreaCode = Left(sFullTel, 3)
End If

' Display area code and local number
txtAreaCode.Text = sAreaCode
txtLocalTel.Text = sLocalTel

End Sub
```

The IsNumeric function is very useful. It accepts a string argument and returns a Boolean result. If the argument represents a valid number, the function returns True; otherwise, it returns False. For example, IsNumeric("-5.06") would return True despite the space following digit 6, and IsNumeric("456 7897") would return False because of the space between digits 6 and 7. The first time we use IsNumeric, it tells us whether the user entered the local portion of the telephone number with spaces. The second use of IsNumeric tells us whether the first character is a digit in an eight-character string.

Of course, the program's main purpose is to illustrate the use of Boolean operators. It uses the And operator extensively. Consider the following statement (with comments):

```
' ... or 8 characters if fourth character is a space
' and rest are valid numbers
If (InStr(sLocalTel, " ") = 4) And _
    IsNumeric(Left(sLocalTel, 3)) And _
    IsNumeric(Right(sLocalTel, 4)) Then bValidFlag = True
```

The program has already determined that the local portion of the full telephone number should be eight characters. Three conditions must be met before the string data can be considered to represent a valid local number: The first condition is that the fourth character is a space. The second condition is that the first three characters represent a number. The third condition is that the last four characters can represent a number. Study the example to see how the And operator is used in other statements. The program only processes the area code if the local number portion is legal. The Boolean variable bValidFlag is used to indicate whether the local number is valid.

Exercise

Does the program of Example 5.4 have any logical errors?

Solution

You bet it does! For example, if the user enters 679 345 67.5, the program will display the local number as 345 67.5. Note that `IsNumeric("67.5")` returns `True` because 67.5 is a valid number. However, it is not a valid telephone number!

There are other errors. Perhaps it is necessary to scrap development and start from scratch! (We will do this later.)

5.7.3   Using the Or Operator

Example 5.6 illustrates the use of the `Or` operator, and Figure 5.2 illustrates the program in action.

If the user clicks any check box to check it on and subsequently clicks Run, the display will show Stop. Only when none of the check boxes is checked off and the user clicks Run will the display show Go. Note that the program modifies the Caption setting of a Label to use as a display.

Example 5.6

```
Option Explicit

Private Sub chkStop1_Click()
```

Figure 5.2
A Simple Demonstration of the Or Operator

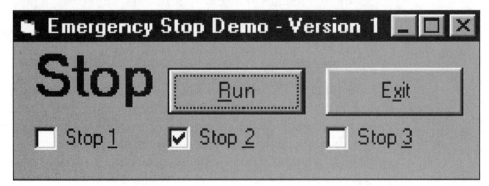

Any combination of active Stop
checks will trigger a stop action.

```
       ' Cue user that input modified
       lblStopGo.Caption = ""
End Sub

Private Sub chkStop2_Click()
       ' Cue user that input modified
       lblStopGo.Caption = ""
End Sub

Private Sub chkStop3_Click()
       ' Cue user that input modified
       lblStopGo.Caption = ""
End Sub

Private Sub cmdExit_Click()
       End
End Sub

Private Sub cmdRun_Click()
       ' Or operator demo
       ' Any Stop action will display Stop
       If chkStop1.Value = 1 Or chkStop2.Value = 1 Or ➡
       chkStop3.Value = 1 Then
           lblStopGo.Caption = "Stop"
       Else
           lblStopGo.Caption = "Go"
       End If
End Sub
```

The check box Value setting becomes 1 when the user clicks it to check it off. A subsequent click will check if off to set the Value property to 0. Clicking on a check box also causes the display to go blank so that the user knows it is necessary to click Run to get an update.

5.7.4 A Robot Control Example

Behind the scenes, Boolean operators work with data on the bit level. A bit can be a 1 or a 0. A byte consists of 8 bits. The Boolean operators actually work with each bit in the expressions. A bit value of 1 is True and a bit value of 0 is False. Refer to Table 5.2 to confirm the following logic operations.

```
        11010100        11010100
And     01100010   Or   01100010
        01000000        11110110
```

An And operation results in 1 if, and only if, *each* of the bits being operated on is a 1. An Or operation results in 1 if *any* of the two bits being operated on is a 1.

Binary numbers can be converted into decimal integers. Each bit from right to left represents an increasing power of two, starting with 2^0. Note that $2^0 = 1$, $2^1 = 2$, $2^2 = 4$, and so. For example, 10010011 represents 147, since the binary number represents 128+16+2+1.

You can also use the Windows calculator to see how numbers are represented in binary. Run the calculator and select **Scientific** from the View menu. Click the **Dec** option button. Type in a decimal integer, and click the **Bin** option button. The calculator will display the binary equivalent.

Figure 5.3
Robot Control Scenario

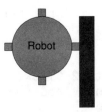

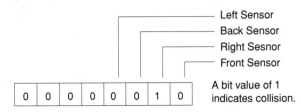

Robot sensor detects collision with wall on the right.
The robot should move left when collision on the right is detected.

Binary representation of sensor status

Programs involved in controlling real-time systems such as robots typically perform Boolean processing. Consider a robot with sensor switches used to detect whether the robot collides with an object. Figure 5.3 illustrates the situation.

Example 5.7 shows pseudocode for collision avoidance. `btSensor` represents the 8-bit data read from the sensors.

Example 5.7

```
' Pseudo code for robot collision avoidance
' Constants define binary representation of sensor data
FRONT = 1      ' Binary 0000 0001
RIGHT = 2      ' Binary 0000 0010
BACK = 4       ' Binary 0000 0100
LEFT = 8       ' Binary 0000 1000

If btSensor And FRONT = FRONT Then Move Back
If btSensor And RIGHT = RIGHT Then Move Left
If btSensor And BACK = BACK Then Move Front
If btSensor And LEFT = LEFT Then Move Right
```

5.8   NESTED IF THEN TYPE STATEMENTS

It is possible to write an `If Then`-type statement inside the body of another, a condition called *nesting*. The following shows three levels of nesting:

```
If nNum1 = 1 Then
    nNum = nNum + 1
    If nNum2 = 2 Then
        nNum = nNum + 1
        If nNum3 = 3 Then
            nNum = nNum + 1
        Else
            nNum = nNum + 2
        End If
```

```
Else
     nNum = nNum + 5
End If
Else
     nNum = nNum + 10
End If
```

The execution of a nested If-type statement depends on the condition of the statement it is nested inside. For example, our nested example is equivalent to coding the following:

```
If (nNum1 = 1) And (nNum2 = 2) And (nNum3 = 3) Then nNum = nNum + 3
If (nNum1 = 1) And (nNum2 = 2) And (nNum3 <> 3) Then nNum = nNum + 4
If (nNum1 = 1) And (nNum2 <> 2) Then nNum = nNum + 5
If (nNum1 <> 1) Then nNum = nNum + 10
```

The level of nesting depends on your computer memory resources.

5.8.1   Improve the Customer Information System, Version 5

Example 5.8 illustrates an application of nested If Then–type statements. We again improved the solidity, but this program, which includes some tricky nested logic, is still problematic. For example, it will accept an input such as (?@#) 234 6678. Thus we need to go back and design the program properly.

Example 5.8

```
Private Sub cmdEnter_Click()

' Split a telephone number into its area code
' and local number.  Some people put the
' area code in parentheses.
' This version assumes user enters
' telephone number with area code as
' ( xxx ) -or- (xxx) -or- xxx
' and local number as xxx xxxx -or- xxxxxxx
' If area code or local is not numerical then display "Invalid"

    Dim sFullTel As String
    Dim sAreaCode As String, sLocalTel As String
    Dim nLength As Integer ' Length of full tel string
    Dim bValidFlag As Boolean   ' Flag whether local number is valid

    ' Trim off leading and trailing spaces first
    sFullTel = Trim(txtGetTel.Text)
    nLength = Len(sFullTel)

    ' Process string only if first char is ( or first three ➡
    char is a number
    If (InStr(sFullTel, "(") = 1) Or (IsNumeric(Left(sFullTel, ➡
    3))) Then

        ' Local number is last seven characters if no spaces
        ' (it represents a valid number) ...
        If IsNumeric(Right(sFullTel, 7)) Then
            sLocalTel = Right(sFullTel, 7)
            bValidFlag = True
```

```
    Else
        sLocalTel = Right(sFullTel, 8)
    End If

    ' ... or 8 characters if fourth character is a space
    ' and rest are valid numbers
    If (InStr(sLocalTel, " ") = 4) And _
        IsNumeric(Left(sLocalTel, 3)) And _
        IsNumeric(Right(sLocalTel, 4)) Then bValidFlag = True

    ' If "( " used, strip them off the area code
    ' as long as local number is valid
    If ((InStr(sFullTel, "( ") = 1) And bValidFlag) Then
        ' First "( " found, hence strip off first "( "
        sAreaCode = Right(sFullTel, nLength - 2)
        ' Strip off last ")" and whatever follows
        sAreaCode = Left(sAreaCode, 3)
        ' If "(" used, strip them off the area code
        ' as long as local number is valid
    ElseIf ((InStr(sFullTel, "(") = 1) And bValidFlag) Then
        ' First "(" found, hence strip off first "( "
        sAreaCode = Right(sFullTel, nLength - 1)
        ' Strip off last ")" and whatever follows
        sAreaCode = Left(sAreaCode, 3)
        ' If local number invalid then tell user so
    ElseIf Not (bValidFlag) Then
        sAreaCode = ""   'Redundant but helps to make it explicit
        sLocalTel = "Invalid"
    Else
        ' Otherwise assumes number must be okay
        ' No parenthesis used, hence we only need
        ' the first three digits
        sAreaCode = Left(sFullTel, 3)
    End If
    ' Display area code and local number
    txtAreaCode.Text = sAreaCode
    txtLocalTel.Text = sLocalTel

Else

    ' Area code must be invalid
    txtAreaCode.Text = ""
    txtLocalTel.Text = "Invalid"

End If

End Sub
```

The program only processes the local number portion if it determines that the area code portion starts with an opening parenthesis [( ] or a number. Three If-type structures follow each other within the Then part of the first If statement. One of these has two ElseIf words. Note that an ElseIf condition is checked only if the Then condition is False. The second ElseIf condition is checked only if the first ElseIf is evaluated as False. The Else statements are executed only if the immediately preceding ElseIf condition is evaluated as False.

More clearly, if a Then condition is True, the statements within its block are executed up until an ElseIf, Else, or End If keyword pair is found. If a Then condition is False, each ElseIf condition (if any) is evaluated in turn. The statements within an ElseIf block are executed up until another ElseIf, Else, or End If keyword pair is found. If all previous conditions are False, then the statements within the Else block are executed. Imagine this program rewritten without indentations and comments. Would it be even harder to understand?

5.9   THE SELECT CASE STATEMENT

Part of Cougar Canoe's customer service system requires matching customers to their corresponding service representative. For example, each area code calling area has its own service representative. The list might look like this:

Customers whose area code is	have a service representative in
416	Toronto
905	Oakville
705	Peterborough
519	London
303	Denver
504	New Orleans

and so on. Figure 5.4 shows the program during execution. The user types in the area code and clicks the **Find** button. The program then displays the representative's location.

In principle we could write a program that uses an If Then ElseIf Else statement with a very long sequence of ElseIf blocks. Example 5.9 shows another solution.

Example 5.9

```
Private Sub cmdFindRep_Click()

    ' Find the representative based on area code
    ' Note that some typical input variations of five
    ' or fewer characters are captured.
    Select Case txtAreaCode.Text

    Case "416", "(416)", "416 ", " 416 ", "416   "
        txtRep.Text = "Toronto"
```

Figure 5.4
Program Using Select Code to Find a Customer Service Representative

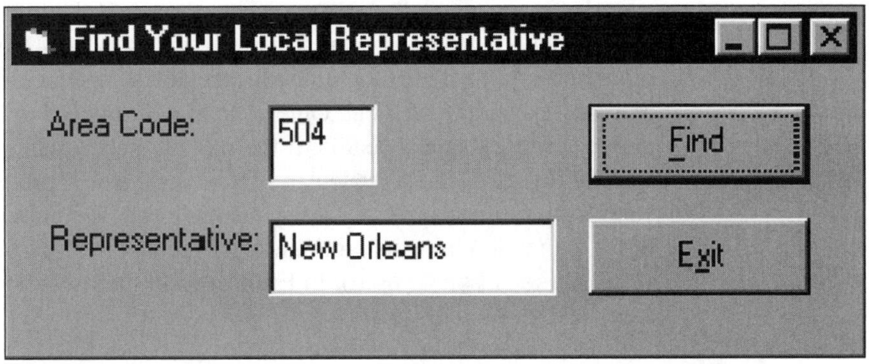

```
        Case "905", "(905)", "905 ", " 905 ", "905   "
            txtRep.Text = "Oakville"
        Case "705", "(705)", "705 ", " 705 ", "705   "
            txtRep.Text = "Peterborough"
        Case "519", "(519)", "519 ", " 519 ", "519   "
            txtRep.Text = "London"
        Case "303", "(303)", "319 ", " 319 ", "319  "
            txtRep.Text = "Denver"
        Case "504", "(504)", "504 ", " 504 ", "504   "
            txtRep.Text = "New Orleans"
        Case Else
            txtRep.Text = "See Head Office"
        End Select

End Sub
```

The Select Case statement selects a group of the statements to execute, depending on the value of the expression that is being tested (in this case, txt Area-Code.Text). The statement has three mandatory parts (the Select Case statement is in fact a compound, or meta, statement since it contains statements within it). The first part to begin this compound statement is

Select Case *expressionbeingtested*

The expression being tested is typically a variable. The statement will test to see if the variable value matches any of the specified values. In Example 5.9, we need to determine whether the user input **(txtAreaCode.Text)** matches any of the specified area codes. The second part is a list of statement blocks with the following format:

Case *expressionlist(n)*
    statement block(n)

The Else-type statement block is optional. Its format is

Case Else
    statement block for else condition

The expression list is exactly that: a list of expressions. If the expression being tested matches any of the expressions in the list, the program executes the corresponding statement block up until the next Case word or the words End Select, if there are no following Case lines. Execution then proceeds past the line End Select. If the expression being tested does not match any of the expressions in the list, the program proceeds to the next Case word or the End Select line, whichever comes first. The expression list can also include ranges as well as multiple expressions, as will be shown in Example 5.10.

In Example 5.9, the program checks to see if the user input (txtAreaCode.Text) matches any of the items in the following list: "416", "(416)", "416 ", " 416 ", "416". If the input matches, then the program will execute the statement txtRep.Text = "Toronto" and exit out of the statement. Otherwise, it will proceed to check the next list, the one with the variations of area code 905. If there is a match, it will set the output to "Oakville" and exit the Select Case statement. Otherwise. it will proceed to the next list to check for variations of area code 705. This sequential process continues. If it finds no matches in any of the expression lists, the program will execute the block of statements associated with the words Case Else (if used). In Example 5.9, the user should see the Head Office if their area code is not in the lists.

The third and last part of the `Select Case` compound statement is the following substatement:

```
End Select
```

It marks the end of the `Select Case` compound statement. Execution proceeds with the statements that follow this line. Example 5.10 shows how `Select Case` can be used to determine if the number matches specified ranges.

Example 5.10

```
Private Sub cmdRange_Click()

    ' Demonstrate Select Case to determine whether number
    ' belongs to the specified ranges
    Dim nNumber As Integer
    nNumber = CInt(txtNumber.Text)  ' Get user choice

    Select Case nNumber  ' Evaluate Number

    Case 1 To 10 ' Number between 1 and 10.
        txtRange.Text = "Between 1 and 10"

    Case 11, 12, 13    ' Number between 11 and 13.
        txtRange.Text = "Between 11 and 13"

    Case 14 To 17, 21 To 30
        txtRange.Text = "Between 14 and 17 or 21 and 30"

    Case Else   ' Other values.
        txtRange.Text = "Not between 1 and 17 or 21 and 30"

    End Select


End Sub
```

We can also specify ranges and multiple expressions to specify matching criteria. Note that Example 5.9 uses the keyword To for specifying a range. Commas (,) separate list items and ranges. The following example

```
Case "Bangkok", "London" To "Rome", "Tokyo"
```

would check whether the string being tested was Bangkok, Tokyo, or anything that falls between London and Rome in alphabetical order (more or less, since the ordering is done strictly by ASCII code). For more information about the `Select Case` Statement, refer to Visual Basic Help.

Exercise

Modify Example 5.9 so that the program checks for all possible input variations. (**Hint:** Think about preprocessing the data before using something like the `Select Case` statement. Preprocessing is an operation to modify input data so that it is easier to work with. In this case, we can remove unnecessary spaces.

Solution

Let's think about it. There would be many possible variations of entering area codes. Do we really want to list each one? Is there any way to make the number of combinations smaller? We used functions like LTrim (Left Trim) and RTrim (Right Trim) earlier for removing spaces. Check out the listing in Example 5.11.

Example 5.11

```
Option Explicit

Private Sub Form_Load()

    ' Blank out displays
    txtAreaCode.Text = ""
    txtRep.Text = ""
    ' Prevent user from typing in more than 5 characters
    txtAreaCode.MaxLength = 5
    ' Prevent user from typing in Representative box
    txtRep.Locked = True

End Sub

Private Sub cmdFindRep_Click()
    ' Find the representative based on area code
    ' Note that all typical input variations of five
    ' or fewer characters are captured

    Dim sAreaCode As String
    sAreaCode = txtAreaCode.Text      ' Get input

    ' Preprocess data
    sAreaCode = LTrim(sAreaCode)      ' Strip off leading spaces
    sAreaCode = RTrim(sAreaCode)      ' Strip off trailing spaces
    ' Could also use Trim to strip off both at same time

    ' Possible to do further preprocessing to remove
    ' parentheses if desired
    ' However if we reject any inputs with one parenthesis,
    ' we have only two possibilities when the user is
    ' restricted to a maximum of five characters.
    ' Note that:  txtAreaCode.MaxLength = 5

    Select Case sAreaCode
        ' Reject any inputs with only one parenthesis!
    Case "416", "(416)"
        txtRep.Text = "Toronto"
    Case "905", "(905)"
        txtRep.Text = "Oakville"
    Case "705", "(705)"
        txtRep.Text = "Peterborough"
    Case "519", "(519)"
        txtRep.Text = "London"
    Case "303", "(303)"
        txtRep.Text = "Denver"
```

```
        Case "504", "(504)"
            txtRep.Text = "New Orleans"
        Case Else
            txtRep.Text = "See Head Office"
        End Select

End Sub

Private Sub txtAreaCode_Change()
    ' Cue user that data modified
    txtRep.Text = ""
End Sub
```

Another Solution

Visual Basic properties offer useful features. We could insist that only digits be entered by setting the MaxLength property of the text box to 3. Thus the user could only enter three-digit numbers as valid input. Other alternatives would be to present a list of options from which the user can select. (We will use lists in future chapters.)

5.10 OTHER SELECTION FUNCTIONS

The If Then and its variations and the Select Case statements are the most common selection structures. We will cover the other types very briefly, and you can investigate them further using Visual Basic Help if they show promise for solving your application programming problems.

5.10.1 Choose Function

The Choose function selects and returns a value from a list of arguments. If nIndex had a value of 3 in the following example,

```
sGetModel =  Choose(nIndex, "Ontario", "Erie", ➡
"Michigan","Huron", "Superior")
```

sGetModel would be assigned "Michigan" since it is the third item in the list of canoe models offered by Cougar Canoe.

5.10.2 Switch Function

The Switch function evaluates a list of expression pairs. It returns the second expression associated with the first expression in the list of pairs if it is the first one that is True. Consider an example about finding the currency conversion factor:

```
fFactor = Switch(sCurrency = "$ Can", 1.33, sCurrency = "DM", 1.6, ➡
sCurrency_
 = "$ Au", 1.4, sCurrency = "Pounds", 0.73)
```

If the variable sCurrency has a value of "$ Au" for Australian dollars, then the Switch function will return a value of 1.4 because it was associated with the expression sCurrency = "$ Au".

5.10.3   IIf Function

The IIf function returns one of two parts, depending on the evaluation of an expression. It returns the first part if the expression is True; otherwise, it returns the second part. The following example is used to flag whether one is taxable:

```
sTaxStatus = IIf(fIncome > 5000, "Taxable", "Not Taxable")
```

The function returns the string "Taxable" if the value of fIncome is greater than 5,000; otherwise, it returns "Not Taxable".

5.11   INPUT VALIDATION

In a perfect world, the user would always enter inputs that are acceptable. However, since the world isn't perfect, a program should ensure that inputs make sense for the operation to be carried out. For example, in the calculator program of Example 4.18 (see Section 4.6.7), how can we ensure that the user enters numbers instead of alphabetic characters, or simply enters nothing at all? If the user enters something that is not numeric, the program should provide some kind of alternative action. In this case, the alternative action could be to simply discard the input and refuse to continue with the operation until the input is valid. Consider the following alternative to one of the event procedures in the simple calculator program.

Example 5.12
```
Private Sub cmdAdd_Click()

    Dim fNum1 As Single, fNum2 As Single
    Dim fAnswer As Single

    If IsNumeric(txtNum1.Text) And IsNumeric(txtNum2.Text) Then
        ' Get inputs
        fNum1 = CSng(txtNum1.Text)
        fNum2 = CSng(txtNum2.Text)

        ' Perform calculation
        fAnswer = fNum1 + fNum2

        ' Display answer
        txtAnswer.Text = CStr(fAnswer)
    Else
        ' Reject addition operation
        txtNum1.Text = ""
        txtNum2.Text = ""
        txtAnswer.Text = "Invalid number(s)"
    End If

End Sub
```

The IsNumeric Function

The library function IsNumeric is very useful: It returns True if the argument can be recognized to represent a number; otherwise, the function returns False. Failure to include such input validation could result in runtime errors. An attempt to convert a string to a Single data type would generate an error if the string did not represent something convertible to a number. However, this solution requires rewriting a lot of code for the other command button click procedures. We can create and use a function (named `ValidNumbers` in this case) to minimize the rewrite.

Example 5.13

```
Function ValidNumbers() As Boolean

' Returns True if both inputs are valid numbers
' Returns False if any input is not a number,
' and informs user that inputs invalid

' In this case use this function to demonstrate input validation
' for the simple calculator program
    If IsNumeric(txtNum1.Text) And IsNumeric(txtNum2.Text) Then
        ' If both inputs are numbers then okay ...
        ValidNumbers = True
    Else
        ' ... otherwise reject operation
        txtNum1.Text = ""    ' Tell user that input(s) invalid
        txtNum2.Text = ""
        txtAnswer.Text = "Invalid number(s)"
        ' Tell calling procedure that operation should not proceed
        ValidNumbers = False
    End If

End Function


Private Sub cmdAdd_Click()

    Dim fNum1 As Single, fNum2 As Single
    Dim fAnswer As Single

    ' Perform addition only if both inputs okay
    If ValidNumbers Then
        ' Get inputs
        fNum1 = CSng(txtNum1.Text)
        fNum2 = CSng(txtNum2.Text)

        ' Perform calculation
        fAnswer = fNum1 + fNum2

        ' Display answer
        txtAnswer.Text = CStr(fAnswer)
    End If


End Sub
```

We can similarly modify the other command button event procedures. In this case, input validation prevented us from experiencing potential runtime errors. (There is still another potential runtime error, which we will deal with later.) Input validation is also required to prevent *logical errors.* Is it reasonable to permit negative withdrawals from a bank account? Do you remember the labor cost program? Refer to Figure 4.8 and Example 4.19 in Section 4.6.8. The program will run without complaint if the user enters zero or a negative number for any of the inputs! Hence, it would make sense to rewrite the program to reject negative number inputs. Example 5.14 shows the major procedures in the rewritten program. We have also used our variable naming convention.

Example 5.14

```
Option Explicit

    ' Given an hourly labor rate and number of hours required,
    ' find out the labor cost in dollars for building a certain ➡
    canoe
    ' by multiplying the hourly labor rate by the number of
    ' hours required to build the canoe.  Program displays
    ' total labor cost in dollars.  The following highlights steps

    ' Form_Load sets up default values
    ' txtPayRate_Change erases labor cost result
    ' txtTotalTime_Change erases labor cost result
    ' cmdCanoeCost updates labor cost result

Sub MsgInvalid(sIn1 As String, sIn2 As String, sMsg As String)

    ' Indicate to user that inputs sIn1 and sIn2 invalid with
    ' message specified in sMsg sent to box sOut
    txtPayRate.Text = ""
    txtTotalTime.Text = ""
    txtLaborCost.Text = sMsg

End Sub


Function ValidNumbers(sIn1 As String, sIn2 As String) As ➡
Boolean

    ' Returns True if both inputs sIn1 and sIn2 are valid ➡
    numbers
    ' Returns False if any input is not a number

    If IsNumeric(sIn1) And IsNumeric(sIn2) Then
        ' If both inputs are numbers then okay ...
        ValidNumbers = True
    Else
        ' ... otherwise reject  operation
        ' Tell calling procedure that operation should not ➡
        proceed
        ValidNumbers = False
    End If
```

```
End Function


Private Sub cmdLaborCost_Click()

    ' Calculate labor cost based in hourly rate, hours and ➡
    whether it is overtime
    Dim fPayRate As Single   ' Hourly labor rate
    Dim fTotalTime As Single ' Number of hours required
    Dim fLaborCost As Single    ' Total labor cost

    ' Get hourly labor rate and number of hours required from user

    If ValidNumbers(txtPayRate.Text, txtTotalTime.Text) Then

        ' Proceed if operands are valid numbers or tell user ➡
        they are not numbers
        fPayRate = CSng(txtPayRate.Text)
        fTotalTime = CSng(txtTotalTime.Text)
        ' Proceed if both values are positive
        If fPayRate > 0 And fTotalTime > 0 Then
            ' Adjust by overtime factor is this is a rush job
            If chkOvertime.Value = 1 Then fPayRate = fPayRate * 1.5
            ' Calculate the cost here
            fLaborCost = fTotalTime * fPayRate
            ' Show the cost to the user
            txtLaborCost.Text = Format(fLaborCost, "Currency")
        Else    ' Otherwise tell user that numbers negative
            MsgInvalid txtPayRate.Text, txtTotalTime.Text, ➡
            "Negative number(s)"
        End If   ' End +ve check

    Else
        ' Tell user that inputs were non-numeric
        MsgInvalid txtPayRate.Text, txtTotalTime.Text, "Non- ➡
        numeric input(s)"

    End If   ' End ValidNumbers check

End Sub
```

Note that we made function ValidNumbers more flexible so that it could be used in more programs that use two input boxes to gather data. Example 5.14 also uses a sub procedure (MsgInvalid) to tell the user that inputs are invalid for whatever reason. Does this program still have logical errors? Well, for one thing, it will accept an input for total time that is expressed as currency! It is a judgment call as to whether any positive inputs are valid, but it would seem that a pay rate of $0.01 is unrealistic.

Exercise

How can we modify the labor cost program to accept any pay rate from $5.00 to $50.00 per hour and to accept any total time from 25 to 75 hours?

Solution

Modify two lines (statements).

```
If fPayRate > 0 And fTotalTime > 0 Then
```

becomes

```
If (fPayRate >= 5 And fPayRate <=50)  And (fTotalTime >= 25 And ➡
fTotalTime <= 75) Then
```

and

```
MsgInvalid txtPayRate.Text, txtTotalTime.Text,"Negative number(s)"
```

becomes something like

```
MsgInvalid txtPayRate.Text, txtTotalTime.Text,"Input(s) out of range"
```

A more extensive redesign is possible using Visual Basic controls such as scroll bars. If you want to look ahead, check Figure 5.10 in the Hands-On section. The user cannot type in the boxes. Instead, the user must change the scroll bar settings. You will be building this program.

5.12   TROUBLESHOOTING: ERROR TRAPPING

We used input validation to avoid both runtime and logical errors. Unfortunately, there are some nasty situations that can bring program execution to its knees. A runtime error can occur while the program is running as a stand-alone executable or within the Visual Basic Integrated Development Environment (IDE). We have already implemented some error trapping. One approach is to check for information returned by each function after it is called. For example, the `IsNumeric` function will return `True` only if the string is convertible to a number. The simple calculator program (Example 5.13) only performs the arithmetic operation if the call to function `ValidNumbers` returns the value `True`. One approach for handling errors is to prevent them from happening. For example, to prevent a divide-by-zero error we can modify the `cmdDivide_Click` procedure in the simple calculator (see Example 5.15).

Example 5.15

```
Private Sub cmdDivide_Click()

    Dim fNum1 As Single, fNum2 As Single
    Dim fAnswer As Single

    ' Perform addition only if both inputs okay
    If ValidNumbers Then
        ' Get inputs
        fNum1 = CSng(txtNum1.Text)
        fNum2 = CSng(txtNum2.Text)

        If fNum2 <> 0 Then
            ' Okay to divide
            fAnswer = fNum1 / fNum2
            ' Display answer
            txtAnswer.Text = CStr(fAnswer)
```

```
        Else
            ' Not okay to divide
            txtAnswer.Text = "Can't divide by 0"
        End If
    End If

End Sub
```

Fantastic. This prevents the program from trying to divide by zero. However, other "what if" scenarios can still occur. What if one tried to divide 5E22 by 3E-20? This would cause an overflow error. No error would occur if the same inputs were used for addition, subtraction, and multiplication. We can't realistically prevent every possible error from occurring and have a useful program at the same time. What we can do, though, is *trap* errors.

5.12.1   Error Handler Routines

Error trapping *is the process of intercepting errors.*

If an error occurs without error trapping, the program will simply terminate. If we can intercept the error, we can provide some alternate action or at the very least provide more information to the user before the program terminates. Consider the normal process of driving a car. You cannot predict when you might encounter slippery road conditions. This is an exception to normal driving conditions. The car might suddenly slide out of control. You need to be able to handle the car in the event it slides. Similarly, you have to set up a program to handle unanticipated exceptions. Example 5.16 illustrates a technique for handling errors.

Example 5.16

```
Private Sub cmdDivide_Click()

    Dim fNum1 As Single, fNum2 As Single
    Dim fAnswer As Single
    On Error GoTo ErrorHandler  ' Set up error handling

    ' Get inputs
    fNum1 = CSng(txtNum1.Text)
    fNum2 = CSng(txtNum2.Text)
    fAnswer = fNum1 / fNum2
    ' Display answer
    txtAnswer.Text = CStr(fAnswer)

    Exit Sub

ErrorHandler:
    txtNum1.Text = "1"  ' Reset inputs to safe defaults
    txtNum2.Text = "1"
    Select Case Err.Number  ' Determine cause of error
    Case 6   ' Overflow
            txtAnswer.Text = "Overflow.  Try different numbers."
    Case 7   ' Out of memory
            txtAnswer.Text = "Out of memory. Close some ➥
            applications."
```

```
      Case 11 ' Division by zero
            txtAnswer.Text = "Attempt to divide by zero."
      Case 13 ' Type mismatch
            txtAnswer.Text = "Type mismatch.  Enter numbers."
      Case 28 ' Out of stack space
            txtAnswer.Text = "Out of stack space.  Restart ➥
            program."
      Case Else   ' Other errors
            txtAnswer.Text = "Unexpected error.  I am as ➥
            surprised as you are."
      End Select

End Sub
```

The statement

On Error GoTo *LineLabel*

sets up error handling. It tells the computer what to do if *any* error should occur. Without this instruction, the computer simply would not know what to do and would give up executing the program. The LineLabel is any user-defined label (in this case, ErrorHandler is our label). The key point is that it tells the computer to proceed with execution as usual—unless an error occurs. In that case it should stop whatever it is doing and go immediately to the labeled block of code. If you don't use an On Error statement, any runtime error that occurs will be fatal; that is, an error message will appear and execution will stop.

The statement

```
Exit Sub
```

tells the computer to exit the procedure and return to the point from where it was called. Without the statement, program execution would proceed with the statements in ErrorHandler block. Note that if there was no error, program execution would only reach the Exit Sub statement. Note that ErrorHandler is not a procedure that is called by other code; instead, it can be triggered any time an exception occurs. Figure 5.5 illustrates the process.

The ErrorHandler block uses a Visual Basic object known as the Err object in addition to the form and control objects already mentioned. The Err object contains information about runtime errors. One of its properties is the Number property. When the program runs and an error occurs, it sets the Number property of the Err object to the code corresponding to the cause of the error. Each error has a corresponding code number, which you will see illustrated in Example 5.16. For a complete list, refer to Visual Basic Help (see Figure B.1 in Appendix B).

At topic Trappable Errors, click **Miscellaneous Messages**. Example 5.17 shows that we can use error trapping to handle errors in called subprocedures (or functions). Event procedure cmdDivide_Click calls Divide1, which calls Divide2, which calls Divide3. We admit this is an artificial example, but a real-life program (with thousands of lines of code) would often have procedures calling other procedures, which in turn would call other procedures. If an error occurs while executing Divide3, it will not be able to handle the error. Hence, it will return control to the calling procedure, Divide2. Since it can't handle the error, control will pass to Divide1, and then to cmdDivide_Click, where the error will finally be handled. However, this situation

Figure 5.5
Error Exception Handling

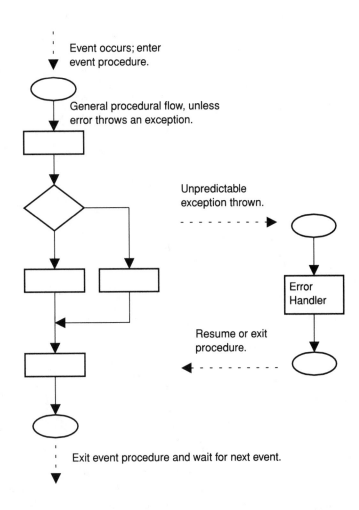

Event occurs; enter
event procedure.

General procedural flow, unless
error throws an exception.

Unpredictable
exception thrown.

Error
Handler

Resume or exit
procedure.

Exit event procedure and wait for next event.

does illustrate one problem: An error could have occurred in any of the called procedures. In general, unless *each* procedure has error trapping, we don't really know where the error occurred in a complex program with nested calls.

Example 5.17

```
Private Sub cmdDivide_Click()

On Error GoTo ErrorHandler  ' Set up error handling

    Divide1 ' Call procedure to divide
    Exit Sub

ErrorHandler:
    txtNum1.Text = "1"  ' Reset inputs to safe defaults
    txtNum2.Text = "1"
    Select Case Err.Number  ' Determine cause of error
        Case 6  ' Overflow
            txtAnswer.Text = "Overflow.  Try different ➡
            numbers."
        Case 7  ' Out of memory
            txtAnswer.Text = "Out of memory. Close some ➡
            applications."
```

```
              Case 11 ' Division by zero
                  txtAnswer.Text = "Attempt to divide by zero."
              Case 13 ' Type mismatch
                  txtAnswer.Text = "Type mismatch.  Enter numbers."
              Case 28 ' Out of stack space
                  txtAnswer.Text = "Out of stack space.  Restart program."
              Case Else   ' Other errors
                  txtAnswer.Text = "Unexpected error.  I am as surprised ➡
                  as you are."
          End Select

    End Sub


    Sub Divide1()
        Dim fLocal1 As Single   ' Arbitrary local variable
        Divide2 ' Call nested procedure to divide
        fLocal1 = fLocal1 + 2   ' Arbitrary operation
    End Sub


    Sub Divide2()
        Dim fLocal2 As Single   ' Arbitrary local variable
        Divide3 ' Call nested procedure to divide
        fLocal2 = fLocal2 + 4   ' Arbitrary operation
    End Sub

    Sub Divide3()

        Dim fNum1 As Single, fNum2 As Single
        Dim fAnswer As Single

        ' Get inputs
        fNum1 = CSng(txtNum1.Text)
        fNum2 = CSng(txtNum2.Text)
        fAnswer = fNum1 / fNum2
        ' Display answer
        txtAnswer.Text = CStr(fAnswer)


    End Sub
```

5.12.2   Inline Error Trapping

An alternative way is to use inline error trapping. With inline error trapping, we check for possible errors immediately after the statements that might cause the error. Example 5.18 shows the use of inline error trapping.

Example 5.18

```
Private Sub cmdDivide_Click()

    ' Inline error trapping demo
```

```
    Dim fNum1 As Single, fNum2 As Single
    Dim fAnswer As Single
    On Error Resume Next   ' Set up error handling

    ' Get inputs, if error occurs reset them to safe values
    fNum1 = CSng(txtNum1.Text)
    fNum2 = CSng(txtNum2.Text)

    fAnswer = fNum1 / fNum2
    If Err.Number = 0 Then  ' Error code number of 0 means no error
        txtAnswer.Text = CStr(fAnswer)  ' Display division
    Else    ' ... Otherwise handle error
        txtNum1.Text = "1"  ' Set inputs to safe values
        txtNum2.Text = "1"
        ' Display error information
        txtAnswer.Text = CStr(CVErr(Err.Number)) & " " & ➡
        Err.Description
    End If

End Sub
```

The following statement tells the computer what to do if an error occurs:

On Error Resume Next

In this case, the computer should abort execution of the current statement and continue with the next one. For example, if the user attempted to divide by zero, the output would be

```
Error 11 Division by zero
```

Since an error occurred, the computer automatically set the Number property of the Err object to the applicable code (which, in the case of divide by zero, is 11). The function CVErr returned the error number message (in this case Error 11). However, since CVErr returned a Variant data type, we convert it to a string using CStr. The Description property of the Err object is a String describing the source of the error (Division by zero).

A side effect can be misleading messages: One error may cause another error, but Err.Number is always set to the most recent error. If the user entered non-numeric data for text box txtNum2, the computer would not execute the statement

```
fNum2 = CSng(txtNum2.Text)
```

Instead, it would set Err.Number to 13 (for type mismatch). Hence, fNum2 would remain at the initial value of zero. Then, when the computer executed the statement

```
fAnswer = fNum1 / fNum2
```

a division by zero error would occur. This would set Err.Number to 11. The program would tell the user about the division by zero error. The user may not realize that the error was caused by entering non-numeric data.

It is a good idea to check Err.Number after any section of code that might generate an error. If you don't, an error may occur earlier in the code and, if a subsequent operation happens to clear Err.Number, your code wouldn't be able to take into account the earlier error. Any procedure call could reset the Err.Number to zero if it executes correctly. On-line help advises that to retain values for later use, you should assign the values of Err properties (such as the Number property) to variables before calling another procedure.

5.13   APPLICATION: PARSING INPUT TEXT

As promised, we will redesign version 5 of the customer information system (Example 5.8). *Parsing* means to break down data into its component parts. Example 5.19 shows a possible solution as pseudocode: the algorithm for parsing the input in general terms.

Example 5.19

```
' Pseudocode to accept telephone number as (xxx) xxx xxxx
' or xxx xxxxxxx or
' some other variations and return an area code and local
' telephone number

Get FullTel
Trim off leading and trailing spaces

Strip off first "(" if applicable
Trim off leading spaces

AreaCode = first three characters of FullTel
LocalTel = remaining characters of FullTel
Trim leading and trailing spaces
If AreaCode not a 3-digit number then reject input

Strip off first ")" from LocalTel if applicable
Trim leading spaces

Split LocalTel to remove center spaces if used
' e.g., local # in xxx xxxx format

Rejoin LocalTel
If LocalTel not a seven-digit number then reject input

Display Outputs
```

Figure 5.6 shows the program during execution. This user entered a five-digit number, such as 34567, in the box labeled Complete Telephone Number. After she clicked Enter, the input text box cleared and a previously hidden label and text box revealed themselves to show the error code and error description, respectively. Upon the user's entering valid data and clicking Enter, the area code and local telephone number appeared in their respective boxes. The error label and text box disappeared from view. Example 5.20 shows the complete code for the Customer Information System to date.

Example 5.20

```
Option Explicit

' Split a telephone number into its area code
' and local number.  Some people put the
' area code in parentheses
' This version assumes user enters
' telephone number with area code as
' ( xxx ) -or- (xxx) -or- xxx
' and local number as xxx xxxx -or- xxxxxxx

Private Sub Form_Load()
    ' Initialize the Customer Information Prototype
```

Figure 5.6
Prototype of Customer Information System in Action

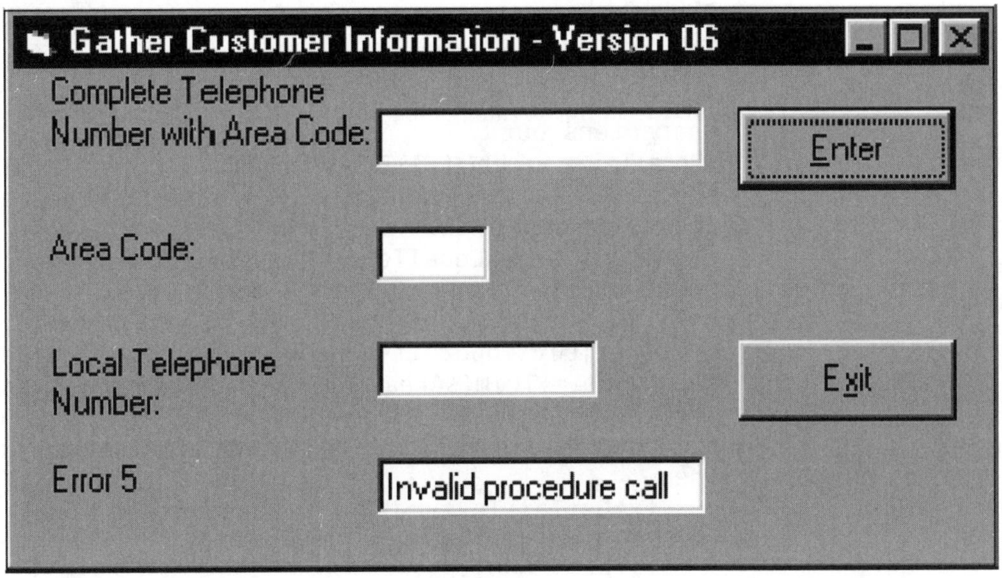

The user recently attempted to enter a five-digit number.
This triggered a runtime error that the program trapped.

```
        txtAreaCode.Locked = True    ' Prevent user from modifying
        txtLocalTel.Locked = True
        txtAreaCode.Text = ""    ' Clear displays
        txtLocalTel.Text = ""
        txtGetTel.Text = ""
        txtErrorMsg.Text = ""    ' Initially hide error message
        txtErrorMsg.Locked = True
        lblErrorCode.Caption = ""
        txtErrorMsg.Visible = False
End Sub


Private Sub cmdEnter_Click()
    ' Do the main work in the program
    Dim sFullTel As String
    Dim sAreaCode As String, sLocalTel As String
    Dim nLength As Integer ' Length of full tel string
    Dim bValidFlag As Boolean    ' Flag whether local number is valid
    ' Temporary variables for string handling two segments of local number
    Dim sPreLocal  As String, sPostLocal As String

    On Error Resume Next    ' Trap errors

    ' Trim off leading and trailing spaces first
    sFullTel = Trim(txtGetTel.Text)
    nLength = Len(sFullTel)

    ' If first character is "(" then strip it off
    If Left(sFullTel, 1) = "(" Then
        sFullTel = Right(sFullTel, nLength - 1) ' Removes first character
```

```
            sFullTel = LTrim(sFullTel)  ' Remove leading spaces if applicable
            nLength = Len(sFullTel) ' Update length
    End If

    ' Break input into potential area code and local number
    sAreaCode = Left(sFullTel, 3)    ' Area code is first three ➡
    characters but ...
    sLocalTel = Right(sFullTel, nLength - 3)    ' Local number is rest
    sLocalTel = Trim(sLocalTel) ' Remove leading and trailing ➡
    spaces if applicable
    nLength = Len(sLocalTel)     ' Now have length for local ➡
    portion only

    ' ... reject input if area code is not a three-digit number
    sAreaCode = Trim(sAreaCode)      ' Trim off spaces to check ➡
    for three digits
    If (Len(sAreaCode) <> 3) Or (IsNumeric(sAreaCode) = False) ➡
    Then
            txtGetTel.Text = "" ' Cue user that input must be ➡
            reentered
            txtAreaCode.Text = ""
            Exit Sub    ' ... and try again
    Else
            txtAreaCode.Text = sAreaCode      ' Area code okay
    End If

    ' Strip off ")" if it exists
    ' ( in this case, we don't care whether matching "(" ➡
    previously found)
    If Left(sLocalTel, 1) = ")" Then
            sLocalTel = Right(sLocalTel, nLength - 1) ' Removes ➡
            first character
            sLocalTel = LTrim(sLocalTel)  ' Remove leading spaces ➡
            if applicable
            nLength = Len(sLocalTel) ' Update length
    End If

    ' Temporarily split up local number to check for spaces in ➡
    between
    sPreLocal = Left(sLocalTel, 3)
    sPostLocal = Right(sLocalTel, nLength - 3)
    ' Trim off spaces and check whether correct number of digits
    sPreLocal = Trim(sPreLocal)
    sPostLocal = Trim(sPostLocal)
    ' Rejoin and check whether it is a seven-digit number
    sLocalTel = sPreLocal & sPostLocal

    ' Accept input if local telephone number is a seven-digit number
    If Len(sLocalTel) = 7 And IsNumeric(sLocalTel) Then
            txtLocalTel.Text = sPreLocal & " " & sPostLocal
            ' Note that we keep sLocalTel as a seven-character string
            ' in case we build on this program and need to
            ' convert it to a number
    Else
            ' ... otherwise reject the input
```

```
            txtGetTel.Text = "" ' Cue user that input must be ➡
            reentered
            txtLocalTel.Text = ""
        End If


        ' Error handling
        If Err.Number <> 0 Then
            ' Display error message
            lblErrorCode.Caption = CStr(CVErr(Err.Number))
            txtErrorMsg.Visible = True
            txtErrorMsg.Text = Err.Description
        Else
            ' ... otherwise remove previous error message
            txtErrorMsg.Text = ""
            txtErrorMsg.Visible = False
            lblErrorCode.Caption = ""
        End If

End Sub


Private Sub txtGetTel_Change()
    ' Cue user that result may be invalid due
    ' to possible modification of this input
    txtAreaCode.Text = ""
    txtLocalTel.Text = ""
End Sub


Private Sub cmdExit_Click()
    End ' End program
End Sub
```

Figure 5.6 shows an invalid procedure call error. This can occur during execution of cmdEnter_Click for inputs such as 12345. This is because in this example sAreaCode is assigned the first three characters (in this case 123) and nLength is assigned to the remaining number of characters (in this case 2). The function call Right(sLocalTel, nLength - 3) is invalid because it cannot handle a negative argument ($2 - 3 = -1$). Part of the code in procedure cmdEnter_Click also checks whether the area code portion of the input is a three-digit number. If the potential sAreaCode fails the test, the procedure exits using the statement Exit Sub. Thus there are two possible exit points from this procedure. Some purists insist that all procedures should have one entry point and one exit point. This makes sense if we want to design our programs to use only the three control structures mentioned at the beginning of the chapter: sequence, selection, and repetition.

Example 5.21 shows an alternate version of cmdEnter_Click that has only one exit point. It uses a flag variable. A *flag variable* is a true/false (or on/off) status indicator. Initially, the procedure sets the flag at True, but if any invalid conditions are found, the procedure clears the flag (sets it at False). Finally, when it comes time to update the display, the procedure checks the flag to see if it is okay to show the result.

Example 5.21

```
Private Sub cmdEnter_Click()
' Version 7 uses a flag to determine whether inputs valid

    Dim bOKFlag As Boolean
```

```
Dim sFullTel As String
Dim sAreaCode As String, sLocalTel As String
Dim nLength As Integer ' Length of full tel string
Dim bValidFlag As Boolean   ' Flag whether local number is valid
' Temporary variables for string handling two segments of ➥
local number
Dim sPreLocal  As String, sPostLocal As String

On Error Resume Next    ' Trap errors

bOKFlag = True  ' Assume OK for now and turn off if not okay

' Trim off leading and trailing spaces first
sFullTel = Trim(txtGetTel.Text)
nLength = Len(sFullTel)

' If first character is "(" then strip it off
If Left(sFullTel, 1) = "(" Then
    sFullTel = Right(sFullTel, nLength - 1) ' Removes first character
    sFullTel = LTrim(sFullTel)  ' Remove leading spaces if applicable
    nLength = Len(sFullTel) ' Update length
End If

' Break input into potential area code and local number
sAreaCode = Left(sFullTel, 3)    ' Area code is first three ➥
characters but ...
sLocalTel = Right(sFullTel, nLength - 3)    ' Local number is rest
sLocalTel = Trim(sLocalTel) ' Remove leading and trailing ➥
spaces if applicable
nLength = Len(sLocalTel)     ' Now have length for local ➥
portion only

' ... reject input if area code is not a three-digit number
sAreaCode = Trim(sAreaCode)      ' Trim off spaces to check ➥
for three digits
If (Len(sAreaCode) <> 3) Or (IsNumeric(sAreaCode) = False) Then
    bOKFlag = False    ' ... and flag that result not okay
End If

' Strip off ")" if it exists
' ( in this case, we don't care whether matching "(" ➥
previously found)
If Left(sLocalTel, 1) = ")" Then
    sLocalTel = Right(sLocalTel, nLength - 1) ' Removes ➥
    first character
    sLocalTel = LTrim(sLocalTel)  ' Remove leading spaces ➥
    if applicable
    nLength = Len(sLocalTel) ' Update length
End If

' Temporarily split up local number to check for spaces in between
sPreLocal = Left(sLocalTel, 3)
sPostLocal = Right(sLocalTel, nLength - 3)
' Trim off spaces and check whether correct number of digits
sPreLocal = Trim(sPreLocal)
sPostLocal = Trim(sPostLocal)
' Rejoin and check whether it is a seven-digit number
sLocalTel = sPreLocal & sPostLocal
```

```
' Reject input if local telephone number is not a seven-digit number
If (Len(sLocalTel) <> 7) Or (Not IsNumeric(sLocalTel)) Then
    bOKFlag = False
End If

' If inputs okay then display result
If bOKFlag Then
    txtAreaCode.Text = sAreaCode
    txtLocalTel.Text = sPreLocal & " " & sPostLocal
    ' Note that we keep sLocalTel as a seven-character string
    ' in case we build on this program and need to
    ' convert it to a number
Else
    ' ... otherwise cue user that inputs must be reentered
    txtGetTel.Text = ""
    txtAreaCode.Text = ""
End If

' Error handling
If Err.Number <> 0 Then
    ' Display error message
    lblErrorCode.Caption = CStr(CVErr(Err.Number))
    txtErrorMsg.Visible = True
    txtErrorMsg.Text = Err.Description
Else
    ' ... otherwise remove previous error message
    txtErrorMsg.Text = ""
    txtErrorMsg.Visible = False
    lblErrorCode.Caption = ""
End If

End Sub
```

SUMMARY

The sequence structure is a sequential linear progression of statements. The selection structure evaluates a condition to determine if it is true or false; then the program makes a choice as to what action to take. The repetition structure is a set of statements that are executed repeatedly while a specified condition is true. The focus of this chapter is the selection structure.

Visual Basic has a number of selection statements:

- `If Then`
- `If Then Else`
- `If Then ElseIf Else`
- `Select Case`
- `Choose`
- `Switch`
- `IIf`

These statements use comparison and logical operators to evaluate a condition. When the equals sign (=) is part of the comparison part of an If-type statement, it is an equality comparison operator; otherwise, it is an assignment operator.

The syntax of an `If Then` statement is

If condition **Then** *statement*

or

If *condition* **Then**
    statement sequence
End If

Example
```
' Only divide if denominator is not zero
If fDenominator <> 0 Then fResult = fNumerator / fDenominator
```

The syntax of an `If Then Else` statement is

If *condition* **Then**
    statement sequence
Else
    statement sequence
End If

A comparison operator is one or two symbols (characters) that indicate a relationship between two or more expressions. The relationship can be `True` or `False`. Table 5.1 shows the comparison operators that result in expressions being evaluated as `True` or `False`.

The Boolean data type has only two values, `True` or `False`. When other numeric data types are converted to Boolean values, 0 becomes `False`; all other values become `True`. When Boolean values are converted to other data types, `False` becomes 0; `True` becomes -1.[2]

Table 5.2 shows the Boolean operators. Boolean operators use Boolean values to return a Boolean result.

A nested `If Then` statement is one in which an `If Then`–type statement is inside the body of another `IfThen`–type statement.

The Select Case statement selects a group of statements to execute, depending on the value of the expression being tested.

The other selection functions are

- `Choose`
- `Switch`
- `IIf`

Refer to Section 5.10 or Visual Basic Help for more information on these functions.

To validate user input, use decision logic to force the user to enter valid data.

---

[2]*The Boolean data type is stored as a 16-bit integer in memory. False is all zeros, 0000 0000 0000 0000, and True is all ones, 1111 1111 1111 1111. Those who know digital logic will recognize these values as being complements of each other and that all 1s represents decimal −1 when using 2s complement binary.*

To enable error trapping, use one of the `On Error` statement variations. This will provide some alternate action, or at the very least it will provide more information to the user before the program terminates due to a runtime error. Error Trapping is a means of catching errors during execution and to handle them in a more graceful fashion than simply letting the program terminate.

The `Err` object has useful properties such as the error code number (`Err.Number`) and a descriptive phrase to explain a bit about the source of the error (`Err.Description`). Function `CVErr` returns the most recent error code as a variant in the format Error *error-code* where *errorcode* is an integer. This is a variant, so you may need to convert it.

HANDS-ON EXERCISES

OVERVIEW

The activities will

- Enable you to use `If Then`–type statements and `Select Case` statements.
- Enable you to create programs that use comparison and logic operators.
- Enable you to create programs that perform input validation and error trapping.
- Familiarize you with the option button, check box, and scroll bar controls.
- Familiarize you with alternatives to text box–style inputs.

To Get Started

1. Read the section Read Me Before Attempting the Hands-On Exercises if you have not already done so.

2. Run Windows.

3. Open the file `CH05\EX05.TXT` on your student disk and answer the questions. (The same questions are shown here so that you can still determine answers when you are not sitting in front of a computer.)

4. Run Visual Basic.

Note

To save a Form: Select **Save File/Form1** As from the File menu. If you are using Visual Basic 4, the menu item will be Save File As; if you are using Visual Basic 5, the menu item will be Save Form1 As.

5.1   ABOUT THE FUNDAMENTAL CONTROL STRUCTURES

1. Describe the difference between the sequence structure and the selection structure.

2. In the Hands-On exercises for Chapter 2, you wrote a program for the delivery robot DELIV. Invent a new command (or set of commands) for DELIV that can be used to determine whether to pick up the object (as a selection structure). Describe the command(s). Write a program to deliver the item to cell 9H using the command(s).

5.2   SELECTION STATEMENTS

3. Using Visual Basic Help, find all the different selection statements that can be used in the language. Remember to check the title bar of any Help screens to make sure you are not looking at information from third-party add-ons, such as Crystal Reports. List the selection statements and briefly describe them.

4. Describe the steps used to find the information for each statement type.

5.3   THE IF THEN STATEMENT

In Exercise 4.6, you ran the LABCOSTE program (see Example 4.19). Open *project* CH04\LABCOSTE again. Set a breakpoint at

```
Private Sub cmdLaborCost_Click()
```

Run the program. When the program halts at the breakpoint, single step it. Do this for two scenarios: The check box is checked off, and the check box is checked on. Note the following statements in particular.

```
' Adjust by overtime factor if this is a rush job
If chkOvertime.Value = 1 Then PayRate = PayRate * 1.5

' Calculate the cost here
LaborCost = TotalTime * PayRate
```

When chkOvertime.Value is 0, and the current statement is

```
If chkOvertime.Value = 1 Then
```

note that expression chkOvertime.Value = 1 has a value of False. When you single step, the current statement becomes LaborCost = TotalTime * PayRate, and the statement PayRate = PayRate * 1.5 *is not* executed (since the condition was false).

However, when chkOvertime.Value is 1, and the current statement is

```
If chkOvertime.Value = 1 Then
```

note that expression chkOvertime.Value = 1 has a value of True. When you single step, the current statement becomes PayRate = PayRate * 1.5, and the statement PayRate = PayRate * 1.5 *is* executed (since the condition was True). Note that the If Then statement executes the conditional statement only if the value of the condition expression is True.

5.4   THE IF THEN ELSE STATEMENT

Improve the Customer Information System, Version 2

Select **New Project** from the File menu. Then select **Save File/Form1 As** from the File menu. Save *file* FORM1 as **GATHER02** in directory CH05. Select **Save Project As** from the File menu, and then save *project* PROJECT1 as **GATHER02** in directory CH05.

Create a form that looks like Figure 5.7. The form Name property should be frmGather2. Name the label boxes as **lblGetTel, lblAreaCode**, and **lblLocalTel** from top to bottom. Similarly, name the text boxes as **txtGetTel, txtAreaCode**, and **txtLocalTel**. Name the command buttons as **cmdEnter** and **cmdExit**. Set the other properties so that the form looks like Figure 5.7.

Enter the program code as shown in Example 5.1. Run the program. It should handle both inputs using parentheses and those without, although the program is still far from foolproof. Pause the program. Set a breakpoint at the statement

```
Private Sub cmdEnter_Click()
```

Continue execution, type in a different telephone number, and click **ENTER**. The program will halt at the breakpoint. Single step the program for conditions when you, the user, enter the telephone number with a leading parenthesis and without. Monitor expressions using Instant/Quick Watch. Particularly note the value of the expressions in the condition expression of the `If Then Else` statement. The program will *always* execute the `If` *condition expression* part of the statement. If the first character is a left parenthesis, then expression `(InStr(sFullTel, "(") = 1` is True. Note that you will single step the statements associated with `Then` and skip the `Else` part. If the first character is not a left parenthesis (such as a digit), the expression `(InStr(sFullTel, "(") = 1` is False. Note that the next single step will skip the `Then` part to execute the `Else` part of the statement.

5.5   THE IF THEN ELSEIF ELSE STATEMENT

Improve the Customer Information System, Version 3

Save *file* GATHER02 as **GATHER03** in directory **CH05**. Select **Save Project As** from the File menu. Save *project* GATHER02 as **GATHER03** in directory **CH05**. Modify the procedure `cmdEnter_Click` as shown in Example 5.2. Change the Name of the form to **frmGather03** and change the version part of its Caption to **Version 03**.

Run the program. It should handle both inputs using parentheses and those without, although the program is still far from foolproof. Set a breakpoint at the statement

```
Private Sub cmdEnter_Click()
```

Single step the program. Try inputs such as

```
( 123 ) 456 7890
(123) 456 7890
123 456 7890
```

Figure 5.7
Program GATHER02 in Design Mode

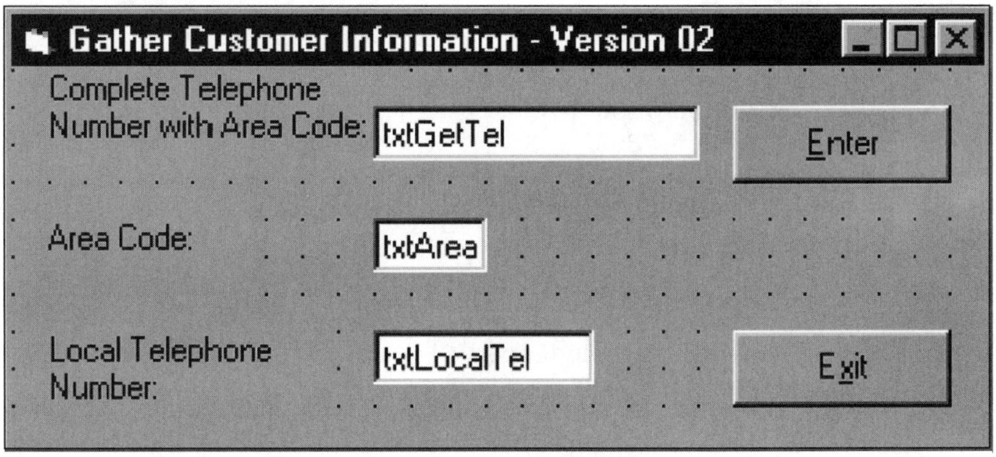

Note that the program executes the `Then`, `ElseIf`, and `Else` parts of the `If Then ElseIf Else` statement, respectively. In all three cases, it should display 123 as the area code and 456 7890 as the local number.

5.6   COMPARISON OPERATORS

Find information about the comparison operators using Visual Basic Help. Remember to check the title bar of any Help screens to make sure you are not looking at information from third-party add-ons, such as Crystal Reports.

5.7   LOGIC EXPRESSIONS

Using Visual Basic Help, find information about the logic expressions and operators. Remember to check the title bar of any Help screens to make sure you are not looking at information from third-party add-ons, such as Crystal Reports.

To help you understand how the operators work, we included a simple demonstration program. To begin, open *project* `LOGIC01`. Run the program. You should see something similar to Figure 5.8. Click any option buttons and check boxes to see the change in the result. You should be able to verify for yourself that

- `AND` returns `True` if and only if both expressions are `True`.

- `OR` returns `True` if any of the expressions are `True`.

- `XOR` returns `True` if only one of the expressions is `True`.

- `NOT` returns the opposite of the expression. It requires one expression.

Note how option buttons behave differently than check boxes. Only one option is permitted. Selecting an option automatically turns off other options. A check box can be checked on or off independent of the other check boxes. Study the code to see how the program works.

Improve the Customer Information System, Version 4

Open *project* GATHER03. Save *file* GATHER03 as **GATHER04** in directory CH05. Select **Save Project As** from the File menu. Save *project* GATHER03 as **GATHER04** in directory CH05. Modify the procedure `cmdEnter_Click` as shown in Example 5.5. Change the Name of the form to **frmGather04**, and change the version part of its Caption to state **Version 04**. Run the program to see if it handles a larger variety of inputs. For example, try

```
123 456 7890
123 4cf 7890
```

The program should display the message

```
Invalid
```

for the second input. Set a breakpoint at

```
Private Sub cmdEnter_Click()
```

Single step the program for different input conditions. In particular, monitor the Boolean variable `bValidFlag` and the expressions involving logic and comparison operators.

Figure 5.8
The LOGIC01 Program in Action

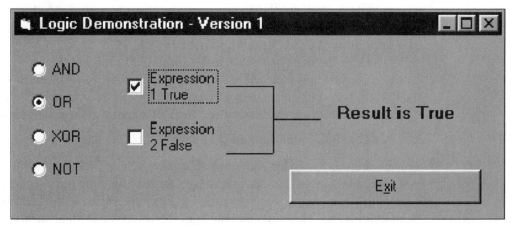

Or Demonstration for Emergency Stop Simulation

Start a new project and save the form file and project as EMERGEN1. Refer to Figure 5.2 and Example 5.6. Name the form frmEmergen1 and populate it with the controls as shown in Figure 5.2. Refer to Example 5.6 to set the Name property of each control. Modify the settings of the other properties as required. Note that you can set the Font property of a label to increase its size.

Enter the **code shown in Example 5.6**. Run the program. If any Stop check box is checked, clicking **Run** will cause the Stop message to appear. The Go message will appear only if none of the Stop check boxes is checked. Single step the cmdRun_Click procedure to investigate how the Or operator works.

5.8   NESTED IF THEN–TYPE STATEMENTS

Improve the Customer Information System, Version 5

Open *project* GATHER04. Save *file* GATHER04 as GATHER05 in directory CH05. Select **Save Project As** from the File menu. Save *project* GATHER04 as GATHER05 in directory CH05. Modify the procedure cmdEnter_Click as shown in Example 5.8. Change the Name of the form to **frmGather05**, and change the version part of its Caption to state **Version 05**.

Run the program. Note that it rejects more inputs than version 4. This is because we have added more logical constraints. However, there are glitches. For example, an input with an extra space in the local portion, such as 364 123 567, is accepted (the local number has six digits instead of the required seven). Logically, it should be rejected. Set a breakpoint at the line

```
Private Sub cmdEnter_Click()
```

Run the program and single step for a variety of inputs. Note the execution flow through the nested If Then structure.

5.9   THE SELECT CASE STATEMENT

Select **New Project** from the File menu. Select **Save File/Form1 As** from the File menu. Save *file* FORM1 as **AREA02** in directory CH05. Select **Save Project As** from the File menu. Save *project* PROJECT1 as **AREA02** in directory CH05.

Create a form that looks like Figure 5.4. Refer also to Example 5.11. Name the form **frmArea02** and populate it with the controls as shown in Figure 5.4. Refer to Example 5.11 to set the Name property of each control. Modify the settings of the other properties as required. Name the form as **frmArea02**, and set its Caption to **Find Your Local Representative-V2**.

Enter the **code as shown in Example 5.11**, and run the program. It should show the corresponding representative when numbers such as **416, 905, 705, 519, 303,** and **504**, or their equivalents with parentheses, are entered. Otherwise, the program will inform the user to see the head office. Set a breakpoint at the statement

```
Private Sub cmdFindRep_Click()
```

Run the program and enter an input, such as **705**. When execution stops at the breakpoint, single step the program. Note that the program executes each of the preceding `Case` expressions to evaluate whether the value of `sAreaCode` belongs to a list of expressions. This will continue until it reaches the sub statements

```
Case "705", "(705)"
    txtRep.Text = "Peterborough"
```

Since the value of `sAreaCode` is one of the expressions in the list (`"705"`, `"(705)"`), the program executes `txtRep.Text = "Peterborough"` and skips the following `Case` expression lists to execute the line `End Select`. Repeat this exercise with different inputs.

Using Visual Basic Controls to Your Advantage

With Visual Basic, we can use visual solutions to reduce the need for code in some circumstances. You will do this with the Area Code program. To begin, save *file* AREA02 as **AREA03** in directory CH05. Select **Save Project As** from the File menu. Save *project* AREA02 as **AREA03** in directory CH05.

Change the code of the `Form_Load` procedure so that it will set the MaxLength property of TextBox `txtArea` to 3 (i.e, `txtArea.MaxLength = 3`). Run the program. Note that it is not possible to enter more than three characters; this eliminates the need to preprocess the input and to check for parentheses.

Challenge   Simplify the code of Example 5.11.

Solution   You could have something like Example 5.22. Try this program for yourself.

Example 5.22

```
Option Explicit

' Find customer representative based on area code

Private Sub Form_Load()
    ' Blank out displays
    txtAreaCode.Text = ""
    txtRep.Text = ""
    ' Prevent user from typing in more than 3 characters
    txtAreaCode.MaxLength = 3
    ' Prevent user from typing in Representative box
    txtRep.Locked = True
End Sub

Private Sub cmdFindRep_Click()
```

```
' Find the representative based on area code
' Note that only three characters accepted

Dim sAreaCode As String
sAreaCode = txtAreaCode.Text ' Get input

Select Case sAreaCode
Case "416"
    txtRep.Text = "Toronto"
Case "905"
    txtRep.Text = "Oakville"
Case "705"
    txtRep.Text = "Peterborough"
Case "519"
    txtRep.Text = "London"
Case "303"
    txtRep.Text = "Denver"
Case "504"
    txtRep.Text = "New Orleans"
Case Else
    txtRep.Text = "See Head Office"
End Select

End Sub

Private Sub txtAreaCode_Change()
    ' Cue user that data modified
    txtRep.Text = ""
    End Sub

Private Sub cmdExit_Click()
    End
End Sub
```

Using Option Buttons

The AREA03 program is quite solid. The user has to enter a valid input to see a valid response. However, it would be better to make life easier for the user. One approach is to present a list of selections from which the user can select. This is what you will do with the AREA04 program.

On of the Visual Basic controls is the option button (Toolbox item OptionButton). We can group option buttons together, but it is only possible for the user to select one option. Selecting any option automatically turns off any other option button that was on. In this case, we only need one group of options; hence, it is not necessary to use yet another new object, the Frame control. (If you are curious about creating option button groups using the Frame control, refer to Visual Basic Help.) Now let's begin by working on the new version of the area code program. Figure 5.9 shows how AREA04 looks when running. Example 5.23 shows its code.

Example 5.23

```
Option Explicit
    ' Find customer representative based on area code

    Private Sub Form_Load()
```

```
            txtRep.Text = ""
            ' Prevent user from typing in Representative box
            txtRep.Locked = True
        End Sub

        Private Sub opt303_Click()
            Dim sAreaCode As String
            sAreaCode = "303"    ' Find representative once
            FindRep sAreaCode            ' selection made
        End Sub

        Private Sub opt416_Click()
            Dim sAreaCode As String
            sAreaCode = "416"    ' Find representative once
            FindRep sAreaCode            ' selection made
        End Sub

        Private Sub opt504_Click()
            Dim sAreaCode As String
            sAreaCode = "504"    ' Find representative once
            FindRep sAreaCode            ' selection made
        End Sub

        Private Sub opt519_Click()
            Dim sAreaCode As String
            sAreaCode = "519"    ' Find representative once
            FindRep sAreaCode            ' selection made
        End Sub

        Private Sub opt705_Click()
            Dim sAreaCode As String
            sAreaCode = "705"    ' Find representative once
            FindRep sAreaCode            ' selection made
        End Sub
```

Figure 5.9
The AREA04 Program to Find Customer Service Representative

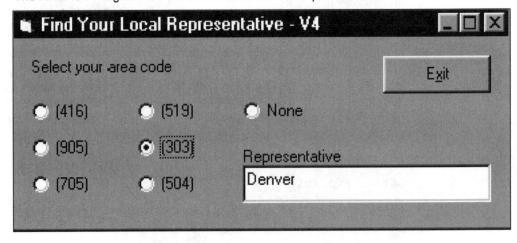

```
Private Sub opt905_Click()
    Dim sAreaCode As String
    sAreaCode = "905"    ' Find  representative once
    FindRep sAreaCode              ' selection made
End Sub

Private Sub optNone_Click()
    Dim sAreaCode As String
    sAreaCode = "None"    ' Not on list
    FindRep sAreaCode
End Sub

Sub FindRep(sAreaCode As String)

' Find the representative based on area code
Select Case sAreaCode
    Case "416"
        txtRep.Text = "Toronto"
    Case "905"
        txtRep.Text = "Oakville"
    Case "705"
        txtRep.Text = "Peterborough"
    Case "519"
        txtRep.Text = "London"
    Case "303"
        txtRep.Text = "Denver"
    Case "504"
        txtRep.Text = "New Orleans"
    Case Else
        txtRep.Text = "See Head Office"
    End Select

End Sub

Private Sub cmdExit_Click()
    End
End Sub
```

To begin creating the AREA04 program, select New Project from the File menu. Select Save File/Form1 As from the File menu. Save *file* FORM1 as **AREA04** in directory CH05. Select **Save Project As** from the File menu. Save *project* PROJECT1 as **AREA04** in directory CH05.

Create a form that looks like Figure 5.9. Refer also to Example 5.23. Name the form **frmArea04** and populate it with the controls as shown in Figure 5.9. Refer to Example 5.23 to set the Name property of each control. Modify the settings of the other properties as required. Name the form **frmArea04** and set its Caption to **Find Your Local Representative - V4**.

Enter the **code as shown in Example 5.23**, and run the program. It should show the corresponding representative when an option button is clicked. A more appropriate technique would be to use a list box when the selection is larger; however, we will leave the use of this control until later chapters.

5.10   OTHER SELECTION FUNCTIONS

5. Use Visual Basic Help to find information about the functions Choose, Switch, and IIf. Why are they called *functions* instead of *statements*?

5.11   INPUT VALIDATION

The Labor Cost program should reject negative inputs. Here we will rewrite the Labor Cost program of Chapter 4 to use input validation before proceeding with calculations.

The Labor Cost Program, Version 2

Open *project* LABCOSTE from directory CH04. Save *file* LABCOSTE as **LABCOST2** in directory CH05. Select **Save Project As** from the File menu. Save *project* LABCOSTE as **LABCOST2** in directory CH05. Modify the code as shown in Example 5.14. Change the Name of the form to **frmLabcost2**, and change the caption to include -**V2** (to indicate version 2).

Run the program. If you enter a negative number, the program should display a message about negative numbers. If you enter a non-numeric input, the program will display another message. If necessary, set a breakpoint and use single stepping to investigate how this is done.

The Labor Cost Program, Version 3

Refer to Figure 5.10. The user simply clicks on the scroll bar arrows or drags the scroll box to change the pay rate or the total time. The user is restricted to using only those values permitted by the scroll bars. Thus, we can eliminate a coding for input validation. As an added bonus, the user doesn't need to click any cost button; updates to the price occur instantaneously as soon as the user modifies any scroll bar setting or clicks the check box.

Save *file* LABCOST2 as **LABCOST3** in directory CH05. Select **Save Project As** from the File menu. Save *project* LABCOST2 as **LABCOST3** in directory CH05. Modify the code as shown in Example 5.14. Change the Name of the form to **frmLabcost3**, and change the version part of the Caption to - **V3**.

You can resize the existing form to accommodate the scroll bars. Position the text boxes and labels and remove the Labor Cost button. You should be able to identify the horizontal scroll bar (Toolbox item HScrollBar) control in the Tool Box. Remember, you can position the cursor over a Toolbox button and wait for the yellow pop-up balloon to

Figure 5.10
Using Scroll Bars to
Restrict User Input

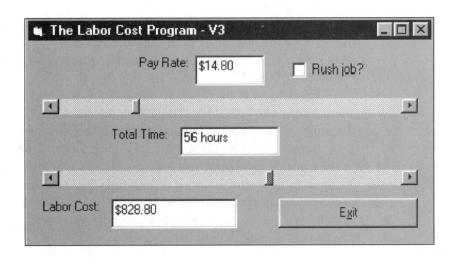

identify the control for you. Add the two horizontal scroll bars. Set some of the properties of the upper scroll bar as follows:

```
Name    hsbPayRate
Min     500
Max     5000
Value   2750
```

For the lower scroll bar, set some of its properties as follows:

```
Name    hsbTotalTime
Min     25
Max     75
Value   50
```

Note that the Value property determines the position of the scroll box between the left (Min) and right (Max) of the scroll bar. When you are done, your form should look something like Figure 5.10, except that it will be in design mode. Now enter the code shown in Example 5.24.

Example 5.24

```
Option Explicit

    ' Labor Cost Program - Version 3 , Using Scroll Bars
    ' Given an hourly labor rate and number of hours required,
    ' find out the labor cost in dollars for building a certain canoe
    ' by multiplying the hourly labor rate by the number of
    ' hours required to build the canoe.  Program displays
    ' total labor cost in dollars.  The following highlights steps.

    ' Form_Load sets up default values
    ' hsbPayRate and hsbTotalTime and chkOvertime event procedures
    ' call the LaborCost general procedure to calculate and
    ' display updated cost figure


Private Sub Form_Load()

    txtLaborCost.Locked = True ' Prevent user from editing
    txtPayRate.Locked = True
    txtTotalTime = True

    ' Set up initial values based on default scroll bar settings
    txtPayRate.Text = Format(CSng(hsbPayRate.Value / 100), ➡
    "Currency")
    ' Note that scroll bar is scaled to be 100 times
    ' the pay rate.  By dividing by 100 we get pay rate to ➡
    nearest penny
    txtTotalTime.Text = CStr(hsbTotalTime.Value) & " hours"
    ' Time to nearest hour
    ' Time is always to the nearest hour

    ' Update total cost based on default values
    LaborCost
```

```
End Sub

Private Sub chkOvertime_Click()
    LaborCost   ' Update cost
End Sub

Private Sub hsbPayRate_Change()
    ' Update text display for hourly pay rate to nearest pennies
    txtPayRate.Text = Format(CSng(hsbPayRate.Value / 100), "Currency")
    LaborCost   ' and update cost change
End Sub

Private Sub hsbPayRate_Scroll()
    ' Update text display for hourly pay rate to nearest pennies
    txtPayRate.Text = Format(CSng(hsbPayRate.Value / 100), "Currency")
    LaborCost   ' and update cost change
End Sub

Private Sub hsbTotalTime_Change()
    ' Update text display for time to nearest hour
    txtTotalTime.Text = CStr(hsbTotalTime.Value) & " hours"
    LaborCost   ' and update cost change
End Sub

Private Sub hsbTotalTime_Scroll()
    ' Update text display for time to nearest hour
    txtTotalTime.Text = CStr(hsbTotalTime.Value) & " hours"
    LaborCost   ' and update cost change
End Sub

Private Sub cmdExit_Click()
    End ' End Program
End Sub

Sub LaborCost()

    ' Do the main work to update labor cost and display it
    Dim PayRate As Single    ' Hourly labor rate
    Dim TotalTime As Single ' Number of hours required
    Dim LaborCost As Single    ' Total labor cost

    ' Proceed since operands must be valid numbers since they were
    ' entered using scroll bars
    PayRate = CSng(hsbPayRate.Value / 100)  ' PayRate to nearest pennies
    TotalTime = CSng(hsbTotalTime.Value)    ' Time to nearest hours
    If chkOvertime.Value = 1 Then PayRate = PayRate * 1.5
    ' Calculate the cost here
    LaborCost = TotalTime * PayRate
    ' Show the cost to the user
    txtLaborCost.Text = Format(LaborCost, "Currency")

End Sub
```

When you double-click a **horizontal scroll bar**, the code window will show the start and end statements for its Change event procedure. We also want the same code in a scroll bar's Scroll event procedure. To define the start and end statements, select the desired scroll bar object from the Object box in the Code window (see Figures 3.7a and 3.7b). Then select the **Scroll** event from the Procedure box (labeled Proc:). The Scroll event occurs whenever the user drags the scroll box. The Change event occurs when the user clicks on the scroll bar arrows or has just finished dragging the scroll box. (The program aesthetics are better if the program behaves the same way in response to both events. For more information, refer to Visual Basic Help.)

Run the program. It should immediately display the result when you modify a scroll bar setting or click the check box. When the user interacts with a scroll bar to change the position of the scroll box, the Value property of the scroll bar will change. The Min and Max properties determine the minimum and maximum possible values. Thus the program restricts the range of variable `PayRate` to $5.00 to $50.00 (Min of 500 to Max of 5000). Note that the program uses a scaled value. The pay rate scroll bar represents the pay rate multiplied by 100. The total time range is 25 hours to 75 hours (Min of 25 to Max of 75). Note that most event procedures call sub procedure `LaborCost` to update the result. In fact, `LaborCost` is just a modification of `cmdLaborCost_Click` in an earlier version of the program.

5.12   TROUBLESHOOTING: ERROR TRAPPING

We will jump ahead to immediately try version 4 of the calculator. (If you prefer, you may start from Example 5.15 for version 3.) Refer to Example 5.18 for version 4 of the calculator. Figure 4.7 will remind you what it should look like.

To begin, open *project* SIMCALC from directory CH04. Save *file* SIMCALC as **SIMCAL4** in directory CH05. Select **Save Project As** from the File menu. Save *project* SIMCALC as **SIMCALC4** in directory CH05. Change the Name of the form to **frmCalculator4**, and change Caption to include **-V4** (to indicate version 4). Modify the code for the `cmdDivide_Click` procedure to conform to Example 5.18. Similarly, modify the `cmdAdd_Click`, `cmdSubtract_Click`, and `cmdMultiply_Click` procedures to use error trapping.

Run the program, trying different inputs. For example, enter **0** as the second number and click **Divide**. The display should look like this:

```
Error 11 Division by zero
```

Enter **5e78** as the first number and **6** as the second number, and click **any arithmetic button**. The display should look like this:

```
Error 6 Overflow
```

Enter **non-numeric** data in any box, and click **any arithmetic button**. The display should be

```
Error 13 Type mismatch
```

The program will recover and run. If you wish, examine the operation of error trapping in detail using breakpoints and single stepping.

5.13   APPLICATION: PARSING INPUT TEXT

In this section, you will write a program for the customer information system that will parse the text data. To do so, open *project* GATHER05. Save *file* GATHER05 as **GATHER06** in directory CH05. Select **Save Project As** from the File menu. Save *project* GATHER05 as **GATHER06** in directory CH05. Change the Name of the form to **frmGather06**, and change the version part of its Caption to state V06. You will need to resize the form to accommodate an extra label and box. (For a reminder of what the program will look like, see Figure 5.6.) Set the Name of the additional label to **lblErrorCode**, and set its Caption to **Error Code**. Set the Name of the additional text box to **txtErrorMessage**.

Modify the code for procedure cmdEnter_Click as shown in Example 5.21. For the rest of the code, use Example 5.20. Note that the Form_Load procedure initially makes the additional label and text box invisible to the user. Run the program, trying different inputs for full telephone numbers. Try nonsense inputs to check whether the program will reject the input. Enter null or a small number, and you should see an error message, which will cause the additional label and text box to become visible. They remain visible until a valid input is processed to turn it off again.

Set a breakpoint and single step the cmdEnter_Click procedure to see how it parses the data for different input formats.

ADDITIONAL PROBLEM SOLVING

In Section 4.3.3 we looked at a business account application. Develop an event-driven version of the program listed in Example 4.10. It should also include input validation to reject unreasonable inputs such as pension contributions greater than 100%. Include error trapping where appropriate.

CHAPTER 6

Repetition (Arrays and Loops)

This chapter introduces data and code execution that can repeat itself.

Repetition is a characteristic of many programs. For example, you want to search for information on the World Wide Web using a search engine. The search engine is a program that repeatedly examines stored data to find out the addresses of web pages that meet your criteria.

After completing this chapter, you should be able to

- Design a program that uses arrays for data storage and performs repetitive operations upon those arays.

- Design a program based on using Repetition, Selection, and Sequence code units.

- Write programs that load controls at runtime.

- Use the For Next, Do...Loop and While...Wend statements.

- Write programs that perform numerical calculations, such as factorials and numerical integration.

In This Chapter

The new front-end system we've been building will permit Cougar Canoe to contact customers about new accessory products and information seminars about canoeing. Cougar's representatives can follow up with product problems and repairs, or the system can simply be used to find out how much customers enjoy the product. Cougar's system will need to able to select each unit of customer information and work with it in a consistent manner. There is repetition here: The program processes customer data the same way for each customer. The data format is similar for each customer. We continue the process of building the information system.

> An **array** is a replication of data. The name of the array can be used to refer to different data elements in the array.

The customer information system can use arrays to represent lists of canoe models, prices, addresses, and so on.[1]

> The **repetition structure** is a set of statements that are executed repeatedly while a specified condition is true.

The customer information system can use a Repetition structure to generate an invitation notice for each customer from a list of customers.

6.1   ARRAYS

6.1.1   Introducing the Array for a Price Information Application

We introduce arrays in this chapter because repetition statements (loops) typically use them. Hence we will talk about arrays first.

What Is an Array?

Picture yourself in an elevator. There are buttons indicating each floor, such as 1, 2, 3, 4, and so on. The elevator only travels to floors; it doesn't travel to cities, rivers, or other places. We can think of each floor as being a variable that specifies a destination for the elevator. One way to identify these variables would be the following:

```
Floor n
↑
Floor 4
Floor 3
Floor 2
Floor 1
```

Floor n represents the top floor, where n is the number of the top floor, such as 54 for a 54-story building. In elevators we do not normally find buttons where each button is labeled with the word *Floor,* as follows:

```
Floor n
↑
```

---

[1]*It actually makes more sense to use a data structure that is more flexible than an array, but we want to start off with simpler solutions and then subsequently use more sophisticated techniques.*

```
Floor 4
Floor 3
Floor 2
Floor 1
```

Instead, we would more likely see buttons like the following:

```
Floor:
n
↑
4
3
2
1
```

We know that each button represents a floor, and the number tells us which floor. In programming terms, this is in fact an *array*. The *array* is a collection of floors that is named Floor. Each individual floor is an *element* of the array. A number known as an *array index* identifies each element. Let's say we wanted to represent the floors of a 54-story building in Visual Basic. We could write code something like the following:

```
Dim bFloor(1 To 54) As Boolean  ' Declare array with 54 elements

bFloor(4) = True    ' Assign value to element 4
bFloor(3) = False   ' Assign value to element 5
```

In this case, the array is bFloor. It has 54 elements. The declaration statement includes the number of elements by stating the element range in parentheses. To identify an element, we need to use the array name with its index in parentheses. To specify the fourth floor, we use an index of 4 in parentheses to identify the fourth element. Similarly, an index of 3 identifies the third element. Arrays can be of any data type, but in this case we used Boolean. If an array element is True, the elevator will stop at the floor indicated by that element. If an array element is False, the elevator will not stop at the floor. In other words, pushing the button will make the element True.

In our analogy, an elevator can use the Floor array. The Floor array can only contain floor elements. It cannot contain city or river elements. Therefore, an array is a collection of sequentially indexed elements of the *same type*. Note that each element in an array has a unique numerical subscript that identifies it. To identify an element, state its numerical index. Note also that changing an element does not affect other elements.

Cougar Canoe Uses an Array

The price information system for Cougar Canoe can make use of arrays. For example, we can use arrays to store price information for the various canoe models. Table 6.1 shows the pricing information.

We could store each price as a single data type variable, as follows:

```
fOntario14 = 460: fOntario16 = 525: fOntario18 = 636
fErie14 = 590: fErie16 = 675: fErie18 = 760 ' Etc ...
```

However, it would be more convenient to use the same variable name or some kind of common reference such as in Table 6.1. Then if we want to find a price, we only need to know the model's row and the length's column.

We could set up an array containing the price of all 14-foot canoes as Single. The following declares this array.

Table 6.1
Canoe Prices Based on
Model and Length

	14 feet	16 feet	18 feet
Ontario	$460	$525	$635
Erie	$590	$675	$760
Huron	$689	$790	$870
Michigan	$955	$1130	$1380
Superior	$1120	$1400	$1650

```
Dim fPrice14ft(1 To 5) As Single
```

Now we can access each element using an index. In this case the index represents the canoe model. Index 1 references the Ontario model, index 2 references the Erie model, and so on. To access an array element, we need to specify its index. The following code segment assigns prices:

```
' Assign prices for 14-ft canoes
fPrice14ft(1) = 460 ' Index 1 refers to Ontario model
fPrice14ft(2) = 590 ' Index 2 refers to Erie model
fPrice14ft(3) = 689 ' Index 3 refers to Huron model
fPrice14ft(4) = 955 ' Index 4 refers to Michigan model
fPrice14ft(5) = 1120 ' Index 5 refers to Superior model
```

Here we have used a one-dimensional array named fPrice14ft. An array is a collection of variables (or meta variables), and each collection (item) is of the same data type. Each element in the collection has a unique identifier known as *an index* or *subscript*. To access any element of array, we need to state its subscript in parentheses. Figure 6.1 illustrates the one-dimensional array in addition to the others we will cover soon.

We have defined an array for 14-foot canoes. Similarly, we can use arrays to store the price for 16-foot and 18-foot canoes. An alternative is to use a two-dimensional array to represent something like Table 6.1 with rows and columns. A row subscript represents the canoe model as before. An additional column subscript would represent canoe length. Now we can declare a two-dimensional array to contain price information.

```
' Declare 2D array for Canoe Price
' as model name by canoe length
' Row subscript: Ontario, Erie, Huron, Michigan, Superior
' Column subscript: 14 ft, 16 ft, 18 ft
Dim fPrice(1 To 5, 1 To 3) As Single
```

In this case, the first, or row subscript, represents model as before. The second, or column subscript, represents the canoe length. Column subscript 1 references 14-foot lengths, column subscript 2 references 16-foot lengths, and column subscript 3 references 18-foot lengths. To access each element (price information) in a two-dimensional array, we need to specify both subscripts. The following code segment assigns prices:

```
' Assign prices for 14-ft canoes
fPrice(1, 1) = 460 ' Ontario
fPrice(2, 1) = 590 ' Erie
fPrice(3, 1) = 689 ' Huron
fPrice(4, 1) = 955 ' Michigan
fPrice(5, 1) = 1120 ' Superior
```

```
' Assign prices for 16-ft canoes
fPrice(1, 2) = 525 ' Ontario
fPrice(2, 2) = 675 ' Erie
fPrice(3, 2) = 790 ' Huron
fPrice(4, 2) = 1130 ' Michigan
fPrice(5, 2) = 1400 ' Superior

' Assign prices for 18-ft canoes
fPrice(1, 3) = 635 ' Ontario
fPrice(2, 3) = 760 ' Erie
fPrice(3, 3) = 870 ' Huron
fPrice(4, 3) = 1380 ' Michigan
fPrice(5, 3) = 1650 ' Superior
```

Arrays can be multidimensional. If Cougar Canoe also offers the choice of fiberglass or Kevlar, a third subscript representing canoe material could be used. For the third dimension, subscript 1 could represent fiberglass and subscript 2 could represent Kevlar. The following code segment shows a declaration and three sample assignments:

```
Dim fPrice(1 To 5, 1 To 3, 1 To 2) As Single

fPrice(2, 3, 1) = 760 ' Erie, 18 ft., fiberglass
fPrice(4, 1, 2) = 2130 ' Michigan, 14 ft., Kevlar
fPrice(4, 3, 2) = 2690 ' Michigan, 18 ft., Kevlar
```

Figure 6.1 illustrates the organization structure of one-, two-, and three-dimensional arrays.

Exercise

How can we use constants to make a program for price information more self-documenting?

Solution

We could write code that looks like the following. Note that a constant name must begin with a letter.

```
Const ONTARIO = 1
Const L14FT = 1

Dim fPrice(1 To 5, 1 To 3) As Single

fPrice(ONTARIO, L14FT) = 460  ' Canoe model and length is evident
```

6.1.2   Declaration Syntax

Now we will revisit the syntax for the Dim statement. In general it is

Dim *varname*[([*subscripts*])][**As** *type*][, *varname*[([*subscripts*])]] ➡
[**As** *type*]] . . .

The square brackets indicate optional components of the statement. If we are declaring (non-array) variables instead of array variables, we do not state the subscripts. However, if we declare an array, it is necessary to enclose the subscripts in parentheses. An array can be multidimensional. In fact, Visual Basic permits a maximum of 60 dimensions; however, memory space may impose tighter restrictions.

Figure 6.1
Array Examples for Price
Information Data

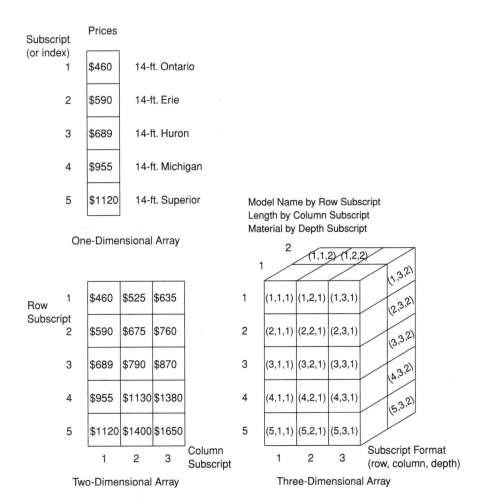

The subscript syntax is

[*lower* **To**] *upper* [,[*lower* **To**] *upper*] . . .

Note that the lower subscript is optional. If it is not used, the default is zero, unless it is overridden by the **Option Base** statement. Subscripts should be integers. If you insist on using Single data type values, they will be rounded to the nearest Integer (or Long data type). The upper boundary is limited to $2^{31} - 1$, which is the maximum of the Long data type. The Long data type is similar to the Integer data type, except that it uses 4 bytes instead of 2 for storage. Here are some sample declarations and their use:

```
Dim sName(3, 2) As String, nQuantity As Integer, fFactor(-4 To 6) ➡
As Single

sName(0, 2) = "WhoAmI"
nQuantity = 6
fFactor(-2) = 8.9


' Following are illegal, the first causes a runtime error
' The others cause syntax errors
sName(4, 2) = "TryMe" ' First subscript is out of range
nQunatity(1) = 5     ' It is not an array
fFactor(-1, 3) = -8.9   ' It is not a 2D array
```

In practice, the memory available will limit the number of dimensions and the subscript range of each. For example, a declaration of

```
Dim fRidiculous(1 To 128, 1 To 2000000000) as Single
```

would attempt to reserve 1,024 gigabytes ($128 \times 2 \times 10^9 \times 4$ bytes) of memory! The default lower bound is zero. We can set the default to another value using the `Option Base` statement in the general declarations area. For example:

```
Option Explicit
Option Base 1

Private Sub cmdTest_Click()
    Dim sName(3, 2) As String    ' Same as Dim sName(1 To 3, 1 To 2) ➡
    As String

End Sub
```

Use the `Dim` statement to declare variables and arrays. In other words, it dimensions the modifiable memory locations.

6.1.3   Two Problem-Solving Exercises

Exercise 1

A ticket agency sells tickets for concerts. Write a program that records the names of those who reserved tickets and the number of tickets they reserved. Our initial task is to determine how to represent ticket reservations.

Solution

Since tickets may correspond to specific seats in a concert hall, theater, or auditorium, we could use an array index (or indices) to represent the seat identity. Since people are reserving the tickets, we would associate their name with the seat identity; hence the array data type would be String. For a simple sequential seat-numbering system for something such as seat 1 to seat 1000, we could use the following declaration:

```
Dim sTicketHolder(1 To 1000) As String
```

The system could record reservations with code like this:

```
sTicketHolder(1) = "Rebecca Williams"   ' First reservation
sTicketHolder(2) = "Brad Williams"  ' Second reservation
     ' Similarly for other names
sTicketHolder(125) = "Petra Mok"    ' 125th reservation
```

A more sophisticated seat-numbering system might identify seats using a row-and-seat (column) numbering scheme. Hence the declaration for a theater with 50 rows of 20 seats each could look like this:

```
Dim sTicketHolder(1 To 50, 1 To 20) As String    ' 50 rows of 20 ➡
seats each
```

This system could use the following code to record reservations:

```
sTicketHolder(1, 10) = "Rebecca Williams"   ' Front row center
sTicketHolder(1, 11) = "Brad Williams"   ' Next to front row center
     ' Similarly for other names
sTicketHolder(8, 5) = "Petra Mok"      ' Row 8 Seat 5
```

For a large stadium, seats may also be categorized into wings. We could use a third-dimension index to identify a wing. For a stadium with North, South, East and West wings, a declaration and associated constant definitions could be

```
Dim sTicketHolder(1 To 50, 1 To 20, 1 To 4) As String
     ' 50 rows of 20 seats each in each of 4 wings
Const NORTH = 1
Const SOUTH = 2
Const EAST = 3
Const WEST = 4
```

The system could record reservations with:

```
sTicketHolder(1, 10, NORTH) = "Rebecca Williams"   ' Front row ➡
center in North wing
sTicketHolder(1, 11, NORTH) = "Brad Williams"  ' Next to front ➡
row center in North wing
     ' Similarly for other names
sTicketHolder(8, 5, WEST) = "Petra Mok"   ' Row 8 Seat 5 in West wing
```

Exercise 2

A lumber company sells boards in standard thicknesses, widths, and lengths. Standard thickness and width are stated in inches nominally (they are not exact). Lengths are stated in feet. Some examples are 1×3, 2×4, 2×6, 4×4, and other thickness $\times$ width types in lengths of 8 feet, 10 feet, 12 feet, and others.

Write a program that will keep track of how many boards are in stock for each type. Our initial task is to determine how to represent the quantities in stock.

Solution

Since we are dealing with quantities, the Integer (or Long) data type would seem appropriate in a three-dimensional array. The first subscript could represent thickness in nominal inches. The second could represent width in nominal inches. The third could represent length in feet. Hence we could have the following type of declaration:

```
Dim nInStock(1 To 16, 1 To 16, 1 To 24) As Integer
```

The system could update the stock during any sales transaction with:

```
' Sample sale of ten 8-ft 2 x 4 studs reduces stock by ten
nInStock(2, 4, 8) = nInStock(2, 4, 8) - 10
```

This will be an inefficient solution because certain lengths, such as 5 and 13 feet, are very rare. Also, there are no standard sizes such as 5×15 boards. Instead, we might use a two-dimensional array for some common sizes:

```
Const SIZE1x2 = 1: Const SIZE2x2 = 2: Const SIZE2x3 = 3
Const SIZE2x4 = 4: Const SIZE3x4 = 5: Const SIZE4x4 = 6
Const LEN8 = 1: Const LEN10 = 2: Const LEN12 = 3: Const LEN16 = 4
```

```
Dim nInStock(1 To 6, 1 To 4) As Integer

' Sample sale of ten 8-ft 2 x 4 studs reduces stock by ten
nInStock(SIZE2x4, LEN8) = nInStock(SIZE2x4, LEN8) - 10
```

6.1.4   Control Arrays

A *control array* is a group of controls that share the same Name, type, and event procedures. For example, we could have a simple calculator that uses four command buttons with
the same Name property. However, each will have a different Index property. The Index
property for each must be unique, similar to the subscript used for a one-dimensional
array variable.

Referring to Figure 4.7, we can modify the program in such a way that the buttons
for addition, subtraction, multiplication, and division become cmdCalculate(0),
cmdCalculate(1), cmdCalculate(2), and cmdCalculate(3), respectively.

All command buttons, except cmdExit, have their Name property set to
cmdCalculate. However, each uses a unique setting for its Index property. Example 6.1
shows the code for the newly revised calculator.

Example 6.1

```
Option Explicit

Private Sub Form_Load()

    ' Initialize numbers in case user tries to
    ' perform calculations prior to entering inputs
    txtNum1.Text = "0"
    txtNum2.Text = "1"
    txtAnswer.Text = ""
    ' Prevent user from typing in Answer
    txtAnswer.Locked = True

End Sub

Private Sub cmdCalculate_Click(Index As Integer)

    ' Control array demo for simple calculator
    ' Depending on Index argument, we perform
    ' addition if Index = 0
    ' subtraction if Index = 1
    ' Multiplication if Index = 2
    ' Division if Index = 3

    Dim fNum1 As Single, fNum2 As Single
    Dim fAnswer As Single
    On Error Resume Next   ' Set up error handling

    ' Get inputs, if error occurs reset them to safe values
    fNum1 = CSng(txtNum1.Text)
    fNum2 = CSng(txtNum2.Text)

    Select Case Index
    Case 0
```

```
            fAnswer = fNum1 + fNum2
        Case 1
            fAnswer = fNum1 - fNum2
        Case 2
            fAnswer = fNum1 * fNum2
        Case 3
            fAnswer = fNum1 / fNum2
        Case Else
            fAnswer = 0
        End Select

        If Err.Number = 0 Then   ' Error code number of 0 means ➥
        no error
            txtAnswer.Text = CStr(fAnswer)   ' Display division
        Else     ' ... Otherwise handle error
            txtNum1.Text = "1"   ' Set inputs to safe values
            txtNum2.Text = "1"
            ' Display error information
            txtAnswer.Text = CStr(CVErr(Err.Number)) & " " & ➥
            Err.Description
        End If

End Sub


Private Sub txtNum1_Change()
    ' Cue user that answer no longer valid
    txtAnswer.Text = ""
End Sub
Private Sub txtNum2_Change()
    ' Cue user that answer no longer valid
    txtAnswer.Text = ""
End Sub

Private Sub cmdExit_Click()
    End
End Sub
```

When the user clicks on one of the command buttons named cmdCalculate, the Index property is set corresponding to the actual button clicked. In the event procedure cmdCalculate_Click(Index As Integer), the program performs the calculation depending on the setting of Index passed to it. For example, if the user clicked on the divide button, Index would be set to 3, and division would be performed as specified in the Select Case statement. Note that control arrays permit code reuse. Without the control array, we would either have to duplicate much of the code for each button or use general procedure calls. (In the Hands-On Exercises at the end of this chapter, we will see how to create control arrays.)

As we can see, arrays can be quite useful for representing information; however, arrays are even more useful when used in loops (or repetition structures).

6.2   REPETITION STATEMENTS

Chapter 5 gave an overview of the three fundamental control structures that can be used to develop any program:

- Sequence
- Selection
- Repetition

The Repetition structure is a set of statements that is executed repeatedly *while* a specified condition is True. It can also work in reverse, executing repeatedly *until* a condition is True. Generally, there are two categories of repetition statements:

- Those that execute a preset number of times (such as the For Next and For Each Next statements).

- Those that execute an undetermined number of times (such as the Do...Loop and While...Wend statements).

6.3   THE FOR NEXT STATEMENT

The For Next statement is useful to perform an operation a specific (predetermined) number of times. Let's look at an example.

6.3.1   A Yearly Sales Total Application

Let's say we wanted to total Cougar Canoe's monthly sales to obtain a yearly total. The monthly sales are stored in an array with subscript 1 representing January, and so on. Example 6.2 shows the part of the code that calculates the total; Figure 6.2 shows the program in action.

Example 6.2

```
Private Sub cmdYearlyTotal_Click()

    ' When user clicks button Yearly Total,
    ' add all the monthly sales figures and
    ' display the total to txtYearlySales

    Dim nCounter As Integer, fYearlySales As Single
    Dim fMonthlySales(1 To 12) As Single     ' 1D array of ➡
    monthly sales

    On Error Resume Next

    fYearlySales = 0     ' Explicit initialization of total to zero

    ' Add the monthly totals ...
    For nCounter = 1 To 12 Step 1
        fMonthlySales(nCounter) = ➡
        CSng(txtMonthlySales(nCounter).Text)      ' Get monthly sales
```

```
        fYearlySales = fYearlySales + fMonthlySales(nCounter) ➡
            ' Add it to yearly total
    Next nCounter

    ' ... to get the yearly total which we can now display

    If Err.Number = 0 Then   ' Error code number of 0 means no error
    txtYearlySales.Text = Format(fYearlySales, "currency")
    Else     ' ... Otherwise handle error
        ' Display error information
        txtYearlySales.Text = CStr(CVErr(Err.Number)) & " " & ➡
        Err.Description
    End If

End Sub
```

Here we are using a control array consisting of txtMonthlySales(1) to txtMonthlySales(12) to represent string inputs January to December. The user should type in the monthly sales in each respective box before clicking the button. If the user forgets one input or more, a type mismatch error occurs due to the error trapping (see Section 5.12).

The heart of the program is the For Next loop (For Next statement):

```
' Add the monthly totals ...
For nCounter = 1 To 12 Step 1
    fMonthlySales(nCounter) = ➡
    CSng(txtMonthlySales(nCounter).Text)   ' Get monthly sales
     fYearlySales = fYearlySales + fMonthlySales(nCounter) ➡
    'Add it to yearly total
Next nCounter
```

The initial statement

```
For nCounter = 1 To 12 Step 1
```

specifies that the statements enclosed between lines For and Next are to be repeated. The first repetition starts with nCounter assigned to a value of 1. The keyword Step specifies that 1 is added to nCounter during each repetition cycle. The keyword To specifies that the last repetition cycle occurs when nCounter has increased (incremented) to the value of 12. Variable nCounter is what is known as a *loop counter*. It keeps track of the repetitions.

The statements

```
fMonthlySales(nCounter) = CSng(txtMonthlySales(nCounter).Text)    ' ➡
Get monthly sales
fYearlySales = fYearlySales + fMonthlySales(nCounter)  ' Add it ➡
to yearly total
```

are repeated (executed) 12 times. Each repetition in a loop structure is known as an *iteration*. During each iteration a different element of the array fMonthlySales is assigned to the monthly input. The monthly input is the Text setting of the corresponding element in control array txtMonthlySales converted to Single. In the second statement, fYearlySales is assigned to its previous value plus the monthly sales. Table 6.2 illustrates the result of each iteration. Later, in the Hands-On Exercises at the back of this chapter, you can single step the program to witness similar behavior when you enter your own values.

Figure 6.2
The Yearly Sales Program
in Action

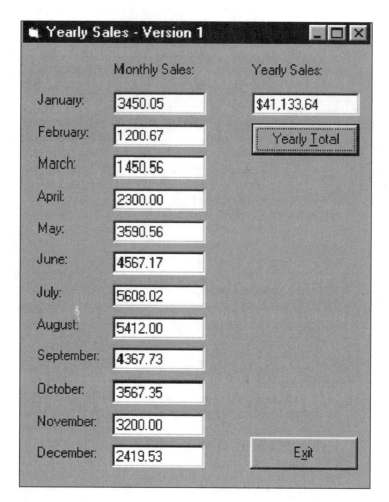

The statement

```
Next nCounter
```

specifies that any statements following it are not part of the repetition cycle. The computer will automatically increment (increase) variable nCounter and go back to repeat execution of the statements that are between lines For and Next.

Review Problem

Why does a type mismatch error occur if the user forgets to enter an input?

Solution

Consider this statement:

```
fMonthlySales(nCounter) = CSng(txtMonthlySales(nCounter).Text) ➥
' Get monthly sales
```

Let's say the user didn't enter anything for the month of August. Then txtMonthlySales(8).Text would have a value of Null (it is a String). The CSng function would attempt to convert value Null to Single. Since Null can't be converted to a Single value, there will be a type mismatch error.

Table 6.2
Iteration Results During Execution of the Program in Figure 6.2

Month	nCounter	fMonthlySales (nCounter)	fYearlySales
(initial index)			0
January	1	3450.05	0 + 3450.05 = 3450.05
February	2	1200.67	3450.05 + 1200.67 = 4650.72
March	3	1450.56	4650.72 + 1450.56 = 6101.28
April	4	2300.00	6101.28 + 2300.00 = 8401.28
May	5	3590.56	8401.28 + 3590.56 = 11991.84
June	6	4567.17	11991.84 + 4567.17 = 16559.01
July	7	5608.02	16559.01 + 5608.02 = 22167.03
August	8	5412.00	22167.03 + 5412.00 = 27579.03
September	9	4367.73	27579.03 + 4367.73 = 31946.76
October	10	3567.35	31946.76 + 3567.35 = 35514.11
November	11	3200.00	35514.11 + 3200 = 38714.11
December	12	2419.53	38714.11 + 2419.53 = 41133.64

6.3.2   General Characteristics and Syntax

Figure 6.3 illustrates the general looping operation of the For Next statement. The syntax is[2]

```
For counter = start To end [Step stepsize]
    [loop statements]
Next [counter]
```

The sequence of execution is as follows:

1. Upon beginning the statement, *counter* is assigned the value of *start.*

2. If *stepsize* is positive, loop processing will continue if *counter* is less than or equal to *end.* Otherwise, execution will continue with the statement following the Next statement.

3. If *stepsize* is negative, loop processing will continue if *counter* is greater than or equal to *end.* Otherwise, execution will continue with the statement following the Next statement.

---

[2]*We omitted the Exit For option to keep this syntax simple and clean.*

4. Once the loop starts and all *loop statements* have executed, *stepsize* will be added to *counter*.

5. At this point, either the statements in the loop will execute again (based on the same test that caused the loop to execute initially), or the loop will be exited and execution will continue with the statement following the Next statement.

6. If Step isn't used, the default value of one will be used for *stepsize*.

Example 6.3

```
' Some For Next demos

' 5 + 7 + 9 + 11 + 13 = 45
For nCounter = 5 To 13 Step 2
     nSum = nSum + nCounter
Next nCounter
nSum = 0      ' Reset to zero


' 15 + 10 + 5 + 0 + (-5) = 25
For nCounter = 15 To -5 Step -5
     nSum = nSum + nCounter
Next nCounter
nCounter = 0     ' Reset to zero


' No iterations since nCounter > end value
```

Figure 6.3
Flow Chart of For Next
Statement

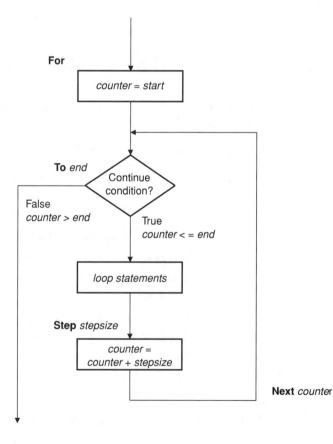

```
For nCounter = 20 To 10 Step 1
    nSum = nSum + nCounter
Next nCounter
```

6.3.3   A Factorial Calculation

Another application for the For Next loop is for calculating factorials. A *factorial* of an integer is the integer multiplied by the next smaller integer, which in turn is multiplied by the next smaller integer, and so on until the program reaches 1. The symbol for a factorial operation is the exclamation mark (!). The mathematical definition is

$$n! = 1 \times 2 \times 3 \times 4 \times \ldots \times n, \text{ when } n > 0$$
$$0! = 1$$

For example, the factorial of 5 is: $5! = 1 \times 2 \times 3 \times 4 \times 5 = 120$. It may seem odd to have a function such as a factorial, but if you are interested in betting odds (a pun, get it?), you may find the factorial useful. Consider that the equation for the number of combinations of n items taken r number of times at a time is

$$\frac{n!}{(n-r)!r!}$$

This could be useful to work out the probability of being dealt a certain hand in cards. For example, if a deck of cards has 54 (n) cards, and you wanted to pick five (r) cards, the number of combinations is 3,162,510. The probability of getting a specific hand of five (such as Ace, King, Queen, Jack, and Ten, all in hearts) is 1 out of 3,162,510. (Perhaps Cougar Canoe needs to determine the risks of offering a draw for a free canoe in order to lure new customers!)

It might be useful to include a factorial button in our simple calculator. After all, even the Windows calculator includes the factorial function when you select the scientific mode. Example 6.4 shows the code for version 6 of the simple calculator. The form is similar to earlier versions, except that an extra element has been added to control array cmdCalculate: Element cmdCalculate(4) has a Caption property of &Factorial.

Example 6.4

```
Option Explicit

    ' Version 6 of the Simple Calculator Program
    ' Now it includes a Factorial function

Private Sub Form_Load()
    ' Initialize numbers in case user tries to
    ' perform calculations prior to entering inputs
    txtNum1.Text = "0"
    txtNum2.Text = "1"
    txtAnswer.Text = ""
    ' Prevent user from typing in Answer
    txtAnswer.Locked = True

End Sub
```

```
Private Sub cmdCalculate_Click(Index As Integer)
    ' Control array demo for simple calculator
    ' Depending on Index argument, we perform
    ' Addition if Index = 0
    ' Subtraction if Index = 1
    ' Multiplication if Index = 2
    ' Division if Index = 3
    ' Factorial if Index = 4

    Dim fNum1 As Single, fNum2 As Single
    Dim fAnswer As Single
    On Error Resume Next  ' Set up error handling

    ' Get inputs, if error occurs reset them to safe values
    fNum1 = CSng(txtNum1.Text)
    fNum2 = CSng(txtNum2.Text)

If Err.Number <> 0 Then
        HandleError
        Exit Sub
    End If

    Select Case Index
    Case 0
        fAnswer = fNum1 + fNum2
    Case 1
        fAnswer = fNum1 - fNum2
    Case 2
        fAnswer = fNum1 * fNum2
    Case 3
        fAnswer = fNum1 / fNum2
    Case 4
        fAnswer = Factorial(CInt(fNum1)) ' Find the factorial
    Case Else
        fAnswer = 0
    End Select

    If Err.Number <> 0 Then
        HandleError
    Else
        txtAnswer.Text = CStr(fAnswer) ' Display division
    End If

End Sub


Function Factorial(nNum As Integer) As Single
    ' Returns nNum! or zero and throws error code of 17 if nNum < 0
    Dim nCounter As Integer, fFactorial As Single

    fFactorial = 1  ' initial value
    On Error Resume Next
    If nNum = 0 Then ' 0!=1
        Factorial = 1
```

```
        ElseIf nNum < 0 Then ' Negative factorial forbidden
            Factorial = 0    ' Return 0 and
            Error 17    ' Generate error "Can't perform requested operation"
        Else
            ' n! = 1x2x3x4x...xn
            For nCounter = 1 To nNum Step 1
                fFactorial = fFactorial * nCounter
            Next nCounter
            Factorial = fFactorial  ' Return result
        End If

End Function


Sub HandleError()
    ' Otherwise handle error
    txtNum1.Text = "1"  ' Set inputs to safe values
    txtNum2.Text = "1"
    ' Display error information
    txtAnswer.Text = CStr(CVErr(Err.Number)) & " " & Err.Description
End Sub


Private Sub txtNum1_Change()
    ' Cue user that answer no longer valid
    txtAnswer.Text = ""
End Sub

Private Sub txtNum2_Change()
    ' Cue user that answer no longer valid
    txtAnswer.Text = ""
End Sub

Private Sub cmdExit_Click()
    End
End Sub
```

The heart of the factorial operation is in the For Next loop contained within function Factorial:

```
' n! = 1x2x3x4x...xn
For nCounter = 1 To nNum Step 1
    fFactorial = fFactorial * nCounter
Next nCounter
Factorial = fFactorial  ' Return result
```

Note that this loop does calculate a factorial. The statement after the loop returns the factorial result to the procedure that called function Factorial.

6.3.4   Creating Controls During Runtime

Another useful feature of control arrays and repetition statements is their use in adding other controls on the fly. For example, suppose Cougar Canoe wants the sales total to date for the first quarter only (January to April). The program could provide an option

Figure 6.4
The Yearly Sales Program
in Design Mode

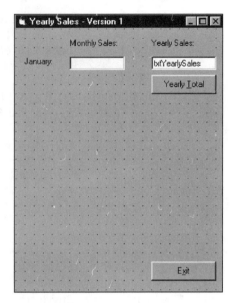

that displays the required window (form object), which will contain the inputs (the text box and associated label objects) as specified by the option. We won't get sophisticated here, but we will demonstrate a technique for adding controls on the fly.

Refer to Figure 6.2 and then check out Figure 6.4. In design mode, the form contains control array elements `lblMonthlySales(1)` and `txtMonthlySales(1)`, which correspond to the sales input for January. However, it doesn't contain the others. In order to load controls during runtime, it is necessary that they belong to a control array and that at least one element is contained in the form. Example 6.5 shows the `Form_Load` event procedure for the Yearly Sales program. The `Format` function finds the month corresponding to the number of days

Example 6.5

```
Private Sub Form_Load()

    ' Initialize Yearly Sales Program
    ' Set up YearlySales controls
    ' And dynamically create the Monthly input controls

    Dim nCounter As Integer, nPosition As Integer
    Dim nDays As Integer, sMonth As String

    txtYearlySales.Locked = True    ' Prevent user edit
    txtYearlySales.Text = "" ' Clear the total

    ' Populate the form with monthly labels and text boxes
    ' based on exiting label and text box for January
    For nCounter = 2 To 12 Step 1
        Load lblMonthlySales(nCounter)  ' Create new label object
        nPosition = lblMonthlySales(nCounter - 1).Top + 400 ➥
        ' Position it 400 twips down³
```

---

³*Chapter 10 will describe positioning units such as twips.*

```
            lblMonthlySales(nCounter).Top = nPosition
            nDays = (nCounter * 33) - 33 ' Rough total of days ➡
            since beginning of year
            sMonth = Format(nDays, "mmmm")  ' Find month ➡
            corresponding to number of days
            lblMonthlySales(nCounter).Caption = sMonth & ":" ' Set ➡
            caption to month
            lblMonthlySales(nCounter).Visible = True     ' Make the label visible
            Load txtMonthlySales(nCounter)   ' Create new text box object
            txtMonthlySales(nCounter).Top = nPosition    ' Position it
            txtMonthlySales(nCounter).Visible = True      ' Make the ➡
            text box visible
        Next nCounter

End Sub
```

The magic of adding a control is accomplished by the Load statement. If you look up Load in Visual Basic Help, it offers a choice of contexts: The keyword Load can be an event, as in the Form_Load event procedure. It can also be a statement instructing the computer to load (add) an object. The Load statement instructs the computer to add an element to an *existing* control array. There can also be a corresponding Unload statement to remove an element from an existing control array.

6.4   THE DO...LOOP STATEMENT

The Do...Loop statement is useful for performing an operation an undetermined number of times. There are four variations:

- Do While Loop
- Do Until Loop
- While Do Loop
- Until Do Loop

Let's look at a few applications.

6.4.1   A Find Function for the Yearly Sales Program

Let's say we want to be able to quickly find the months in which sales exceed a certain amount. Version 2 of the Yearly Sales Total program prototypes this functionality. The user can click a button to find the first month in which monthly sales met or exceeded a $4,000 target.

To find a month, we need statements to check each month. This is a repetitive operation; however, it is only necessary to repeat this action until we find a month that meets the criteria. Thus the number of iterations (repetitions) is not predictable. We may find that the first month meets the criteria, or perhaps none has (meaning all 12 iterations were done for nothing). Example 6.6 shows the part of the code that finds the month, and Figure 6.5 shows the program in action.

Figure 6.5
The Yearly Sales Program
With Find Function

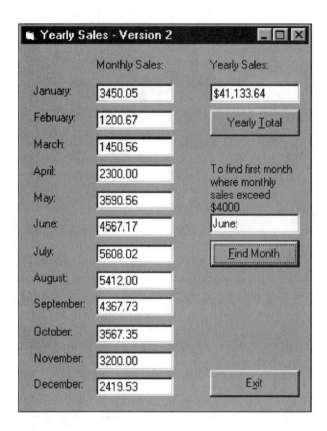

Example 6.6

```
Private Sub cmdFind_Click()
    ' Find first month where monthly sales
    ' exceed $4000
    ' Demonstrates Do While Loop
    On Error Resume Next

    Dim nIndex As Integer, bFound As Boolean

    bFound = False   ' Assume not found initially
    txtFound.Text = ""   ' Clear result initially
    nIndex = 1   ' Initialize index to refer to first month

    ' Keep looking for the monthly sales >= 4000 until
    ' it is found or until we have searched all 12 months
    Do While (nIndex <= 12) And Not bFound
        If CSng(txtMonthlySales(nIndex).Text) >= 4000 Then
            ' Display the found month and ...
            txtFound.Text = lblMonthlySales(nIndex).Caption
            bFound = True    ' ... flag it was found
        End If
        nIndex = nIndex + 1 ' Refer to next month
    Loop

    ' Display error if found
    If Err.Number <> 0 Then
        txtFound.Text = CStr(CVErr(Err.Number)) & " " & ➥
        Err.Description
    End If
```

End Sub

The button used to find the month is named cmdFind. The loop that performs the actual search is

```
nIndex = 1  ' Initialize index to refer to first month

' Keep looking for the monthly sales >= 4000 until
' it is found or until we have searched all 12 months
Do While (nIndex <= 12) And Not bFound
    If CSng(txtMonthlySales(nIndex).Text) >= 4000 Then
        ' Display the found month and ...
        txtFound.Text = lblMonthlySales(nIndex).Caption
        bFound = True   ' ... flag it was found
    End If
    nIndex = nIndex + 1 ' Refer to next month
Loop
```

The first statement (actually outside the loop) initializes the counter. The counter is necessary for keeping track of the iterations (repetitions). The loop condition is (nIndex <= 12) And Not bFound. As long as this condition is True, the statements between lines beginning with Do While and Loop are repeated. These statements will repeat until nIndex has exceeded 12, meaning that all 12 months have been checked, or if bFound is True, meaning that a month with sales exceeding \$4,000 has been found. An If Then statement, nested inside the loop, is used to set the flag (bFound) if a suitable month is found. Table 6.3 illustrates the results of each iteration for the inputs shown in Figure 6.5.

6.4.2 General Characteristics and Syntax of the Do {While | Until} Loop Statement

Figure 6.6 illustrates the general looping operation of the Do While Loop statement and Do Until Loop statement. The syntax is[4]

```
Do {While | Until} condition
    [statements]
Loop
```

Table 6.3
Iteration Results During Execution of the Program in Figure 6.5

Month	nIndex	fMonthlySales(nIndex)	(nIndex <= 12) And Not bFound
January	1	3450.05	True And Not False = True
February	2	1200.67	True and Not False = True
March	3	1450.56	True and Not False = True
April	4	2300.00	True and Not False = True
May	5	3590.56	True and Not False = True
June	6	4567.17	True and Not True = True And False = False
			Therefore exit the loop.

[4]We omitted the Exit Do option to keep the syntax simple and clean.

A common typographic convention for syntax is to indicate a choice between items by enclosing them in braces. A vertical bar separates the items from which to choose. In this case, the statement can be either a Do While Loop:

```
Do While condition
    [statements]
Loop
```

or a Do Until Loop:

```
Do Until condition
    [statements]
Loop
```

The sequence of execution for each type of loop is as follows: The Do While Loop repeats a block of statements *while* a condition is True (until the condition is False). The Do Until Loop repeats a block of statements *until* a condition becomes True (while the condition is False). The following uses a Do Until Loop for the same purpose as the Do While Loop in Example 6.6.

```
nIndex = 1  ' Initialize to refer to first month

' Keep looking for the monthly sales >= 4000 until
' it is found or until we have searched all 12 months
Do Until (nIndex > 12) Or bFound
    If CSng(txtMonthlySales(nIndex).Text) >= 4000 Then
        ' Display the found month and ...
        txtFound.Text = lblMonthlySales(nIndex).Caption
        bFound = True   ' ... flag it was found
    End If
    nIndex = nIndex + 1
Loop
```

Exercise

How can we find the last month in which monthly sales exceeded $4,000?

Solution

Use a countdown strategy as follows:

```
nIndex = 12  ' Initialize to refer to last month
' Keep looking for the monthly sales >= 4000 until
' it is found or until we have searched all 12 months
Do While (nIndex >= 1) And Not bFound
    If CSng(txtMonthlySales(nIndex).Text) >= 4000 Then
        ' Display the found month and ...
        txtFound.Text = lblMonthlySales(nIndex).Caption
        bFound = True   ' ... flag it was found
    End If
    nIndex = nIndex - 1
Loop
```

6.4.3   Mathematical Expansions

Have you ever wondered how Visual Basic and other languages could provide marvelous functions such as sine and cosine? It turns out that we can compute the sine (or cosine) of an angle with formulas that use only the arithmetic operations of addition,

Figure 6.6
Flow Chart of Do {While | Until} Loop Statement

The Do While Loop and Do Until Loop operate in opposite ways.

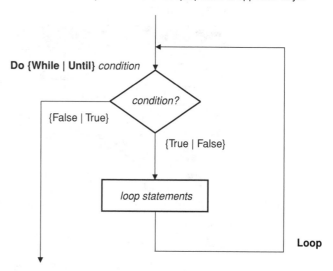

Do {While | Until} *condition*

condition?

{False | True}

{True | False}

loop statements

Loop

subtraction, multiplication, and division. These formulas are known as ***Taylor expansions***. To understand how this works, we would have to have some expertise in calculus. Instead, we simply accept the technique at face value. For example, the Taylor expansion formula for the sine of angle *x* is:

$$\sin(x) = \frac{x}{1!} - \frac{x^3}{3!} + \frac{x^5}{5!} - \frac{x^7}{7!} + \ldots$$

This formula is valid for any *x*. Note that the expansion continues forever; however, each term becomes successively smaller and successively less significant. We just need to determine how precise we want the calculation to be. For example, if *x* is 0.5 radians, the expansion using four terms would be

$$\sin(0.5) \approx 0.5 - 0.0208333 + 2.604 \times 10^{-4} - 1.55 \times 10^{-6} \approx 0.47942550$$

This is close to the result of 0.47942554 using a calculator or the Visual Basic sine function. It also looks like a former acquaintance, the factorial, has reappeared. This gives us an opportunity to reuse some code. Figure 6.7 shows a program that shows the result of using the Taylor expansion for sine; Example 6.7 shows the program code.

Example 6.7

```
Option Explicit

' THE SINE EXPANSION PROGRAM
' (general declarations) area
' This program demonstrates the use of a loop for
' calculating a Taylor expansion to calculate
' the sine.  It also displays the result of the Sine
' function so the user can view the difference
' between the two.  The user can select the accuracy
' of the expansion calculation by selecting an option.

' Sine expansion formula for x:
' Sine x = x - x^3/3! + x^5/5! - x^7/7! + ...
```

Figure 6.7
The Expansion Program in Action

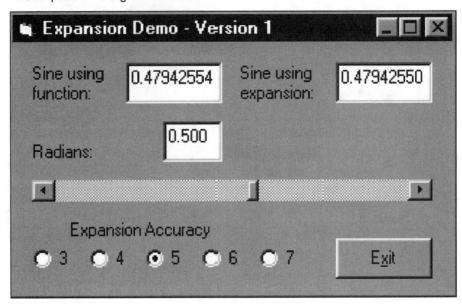

```
' Global Variable used for tolerance in expansion
' Expansion calculation ends when the difference
' between the most recent term and second most
' recent term is less than the tolerance
Dim m_fTol As Single      ' Tolerance is 10^(-optTol.Index)

Private Sub Form_Load()
    ' Need to initialize fTol
    optTol_Click(3)       ' This also calls hsbArgument_Change
End Sub

Private Sub hsbArgument_Change()
    ' Updates the results.  Any other event procedure
    ' will call this one when updates are required.
    ' Reads radian setting from scroll bar
    ' and calls functions to calculate sine
    ' using expansion and VB function Sin
    ' and displays the results

    Dim fRadian As Single
    Dim fSine As Single

    On Error Resume Next

    ' Get radian inputs, note scaling of Value setting
    fRadian = CSng(hsbArgument.Value) / 1000
    txtArgument.Text = Format(fRadian, "0.000")
    ' Find sine using expansion
    fSine = SineExpansion(fRadian)
    ' Show sine found using expansion
    txtExpansion.Text = Format(fSine, "0.00000000")
```

```vb
    ' Show sine found using function
    txtFunction.Text = Format(Sin(fRadian), "0.00000000")

    If Err.Number <> 0 Then HandleError

End Sub


Function SineExpansion(fX As Single)
    ' Returns the sine of fX based on using the Taylor expansion.
    ' See comments in (general declarations)

    Dim fSine As Single ' The sine in progress
    Dim fPreviousSine As Single ' Sine from previous iteration
    Dim nCount As Integer    ' +/- factor to determine whether ➡
    to + or -
    Dim nTerm As Integer      ' Term factor for exponent and ➡
    factorial argument

    On Error Resume Next

    fSine = fX   ' First expansion term
    nCount = 1  ' First time in loop
    nTerm = 3 ' Term exponent for first time in loop
    Do
        fPreviousSine = fSine     ' Get previous expansion term
        fSine = fSine + ((-1) ^ nCount) * (fX ^ nTerm / ➡
        Factorial(nTerm))
        nCount = nCount + 1 ' Update +/- factor
        nTerm = nTerm + 2    ' Update term factor
    Loop Until (Abs(fSine - fPreviousSine) < m_fTol)
    SineExpansion = fSine    ' Return value

    If Err.Number <> 0 Then HandleError

End Function


Function Factorial(nNum As Integer) As Single
    ' Returns nNum! or zero and throws error code of 17 if nNum < 0
    Dim nCounter As Integer, fFactorial As Single
    On Error Resume Next

    fFactorial = 1   ' initial value
    If nNum = 0 Then
        Factorial = 1
    ElseIf nNum < 0 Then
        Factorial = 0    ' Return 0 and
        Error 17      ' Generate error "Can't perform requested ➡
        operation"
    Else
        For nCounter = 1 To nNum Step 1
            fFactorial = fFactorial * nCounter
```

```
          Next nCounter
          Factorial = fFactorial
      End If

End Function


Private Sub hsbArgument_Scroll()
    ' Mirror scroll bar Change event procedure
    hsbArgument_Change
End Sub


Private Sub optTol_Click(Index As Integer)
    ' Cause update due to accuracy change
    m_fTol = 10 ^ -Index    ' Modifies accuracy
    hsbArgument_Change  ' Do the calculation change
End Sub


Sub HandleError()
        ' Display error message in message box
        MsgBox Err.Description, , CStr(CVErr(Err.Number))
End Sub


Private Sub cmdExit_Click()
    End
End Sub
```

One thing to note is that function `Factorial` is exactly the same as that used in Example 6.4. Code reuse is always a plus. The program's main work is to calculate the Taylor expansion, which is done in the following code segment in function `SineExpansion`. The segment includes a `Do Loop Until` Loop statement.

```
fSine = fX   ' First expansion term
nCount = 1   ' First time in loop
nTerm = 3 ' Term exponent for first time in loop
Do
    fPreviousSine = fSine    ' Get previous expansion term
    fSine = fSine + ((-1) ^ nCount) * (fX ^ nTerm / ➥
    Factorial(nTerm))
    nCount = nCount + 1 ' Update +/- factor
    nTerm = nTerm + 2   ' Update term factor
Loop Until (Abs(fSine - fPreviousSine) < m_fTol)
SineExpansion = fSine    ' Return value
```

The first three statements perform necessary initialization before entering the loop. The next line `Do` begins the loop. The computer then executes the line

```
fPreviousSine = fSine    ' Get previous sine
```

It has already entered the loop. This is a key point. There was no prior condition checking to decide whether or not to enter the loop; the decision is made at the end of the loop in the line

```
Loop Until (Abs(fSine - fPreviousSine) < m_fTol)
```

Note the expansion term in the Taylor expansion for sine in the line

```
fSine = fSine + ((-1) ^ nCount) * (fX ^ nTerm / ➡
Factorial(nTerm))
```

nTerm represents term factors 3, 5, 7, and so on that were shown in the formula. The radian x is represented by variable fX.

6.4.4 General Characteristics and Syntax of the Do Loop {While | Until} Statement

Figure 6.8 illustrates the general looping operation of the Do Loop While statement and Do Loop Until statement. The difference is that condition checking is done after the loop is entered instead of before. Hence there is always at least one iteration of a Do Loop While or Do Loop Until statement. The syntax is[5]

Do
    [*statements*]
Loop {While ¦ Until} *condition*

A common typographic convention for syntax is to indicate a choice between items by enclosing them in braces. A vertical bar separates the items from which to choose. In this case, the statement can be either a Do Loop While:

Do
    [*statements*]
Loop While *condition*

or it can be a Do Loop Until:

Do
    [*statements*]
Loop Until *condition*

The sequence of execution for each type of loop is as follows: For both types of loops, the block of statements is executed (at least the first time). The Do Loop While repeats a block of statements *while* a condition is True (until the condition is False); the Do Loop Until repeats a block of statements *until* a condition becomes True (while the condition is False).

A Word About Numerical Accuracy

Many nonlinear functions, such as trigonometric functions, logarithms, and exponential functions, are used for engineering, scientific, simulation, graphical processing, audio processing, economic system modeling, and other purposes. Computers use fixed precision as determined by the number of bits in Single data type numbers. It is possible to be more precise by using the Double data type with 64 bits, but it is still a limit. Taylor expansions based on an infinite series of arithmetic operations can generate the values for nonlinear functions; thus it is impossible to be 100% accurate. We can't expand until infinity, and we can't use an infinite number of bits to store data! There is a possibility of

---

[5]*We omitted the Exit Do option to keep the syntax simple and clean.*

Figure 6.8
Flow Chart of Do Loop
{While | Until} Statement

The Do Loop While and Do Until operate in opposite ways.

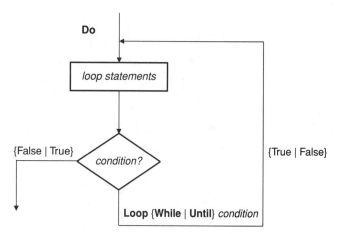

significant errors when dealing with numbers close to the limits of the data type range. Consider that the distance from the Earth to the Sun is approximately 1.496×10^{11} meters. With a 23-bit fraction ($2^{-23} = 1.192092895508 \times 10^{-7}$), we could only express this distance roughly to the nearest 10 kilometers.

After ten years and seven billion dollars, the European Space Agency produced the Ariane 5 for launching satellites into orbit. Less than 40 seconds after its maiden launch, the rocket crashed into the mangrove swamps of French Guiana. A guidance system computer tried to convert the sideways velocity from a 64-bit format into a 16-bit format. The number was too big, and an overflow resulted.

A Word About Math Processing Units

Modern microprocessors typically include processing units that perform floating point math in hardware. This can include nonlinear functions. Behind the scenes, a language's library function could be a machine code module that works directly with the math processing hardware unit. This greatly speeds execution since there is no need to write code in a higher-level language to implement the function. However, the limitations about accuracy still hold true. The processing units can only use a finite number of bits and can only repeat iterations for a Taylor expansion calculation a finite number of times.

6.5   THE WHILE...WEND STATEMENT

The While...Wend statement executes a series of statements as long as a given condition is True. The syntax is

```
While condition
     [statements]
Wend
```

6.5.1   An Enter Number Program

Example 6.8 illustrates a use of the While...Wend statement in procedure SetNumber.

Example 6.8

```
Option Explicit
' Program to demonstrate While...Wend statement
' It finds the digits in data typed in by the user
' and displays them.
' The user types in box txtEnterNumber.  When the user
' presses <Enter>, procedure SetNumber is called to
' do the processing work and display the result of
' only digits in box txtNumber.

Private Sub txtEnterNumber_KeyPress(KeyAscii As Integer)

    ' Called when user presses a standard key on the keyboard
    ' But it only does something if the key pressed is the Enter key
    If KeyAscii = vbKeyReturn Then
        KeyAscii = 0      ' Gets rid of annoying beep
        SetNumber    ' Process entry to collect digits only
    End If

End Sub


Sub SetNumber()

    ' Strip off all nondigit keys from user entry
    ' to convert it to a number
    ' Called from txtEnterNumber_KeyPress when user presses Enter

    Dim sEntry As String      ' Original user entry
    Dim sNumber As String     ' User entry with only digits
    Dim nNext As Integer, sKey As String * 1
    ' Note sKey is declared as string with only one character

    sEntry = txtEnterNumber.Text      ' String entered by user
    nNext = 1    ' Point to first character
    ' This loop will check for digits until all characters are ➡
    searched
    While nNext <= Len(sEntry)
        sKey = Mid(sEntry, nNext, 1)
        ' Append key to number if key is a digit
        If (sKey >= "0" And sKey <= "9") Then sNumber = sNumber & sKey
        ' Point to next character in entered string
        nNext = nNext + 1
    Wend

    txtNumber.Text = sNumber      ' Display number to user

End Sub


Private Sub cmdExit_Click()
    End
EndSub
```

Note that this example uses the `While...Wend` statement to increment a counter variable (`nNext`) that points to the characters in the string entered by the user. The statements in the loop are executed as long as the condition (`nNext <= Len(sEntry)`) evaluates to `True`, meaning that there are still more characters to check. As you can see, the `Do... Loop` statement provides a more structured and flexible way to perform looping.

6.5.2   The KeyPress Event

Wouldn't it be easier to simply press ENTER after typing in a text box? Moving the mouse to click an ENTER button (or pressing TAB to move the focus to the button) is extra effort for the user. The KeyPress event procedure is a way of making life easier for the user, and doing just that is a programmer's job.

A text box can recognize the KeyPress event. It occurs whenever a user presses a standard ASCII (American Standard Code for Information Interchange) key on the keyboard while the text box has the focus (while it receives keystrokes). ASCII keys are the keys found on the standard keyboard sold in the United States. It includes alphanumeric keys, punctuation marks, and controls such as ENTER, TAB, and BACK SPACE. It does not include nonstandard keys such as function keys (e.g., F1), arrow keys, and numeric keypad keys. As discussed earlier, each ASCII key has a corresponding code that is its ASCII code. For example, the ENTER key has an ASCII code of 13 (0D in hexadecimal[6]).

In Example 6.8, when the user presses an ASCII key, the program passes the `KeyAscii` argument to the event procedure. It is an Integer that represents the key's ASCII code. `vbKeyReturn` is one of the constants predefined in Visual Basic; its value is the ASCII code for the ENTER (also known as RETURN) key.

6.6   AN ENGINEERING APPLICATION

Cougar Canoe needs to perform some design calculations. First, it will be necessary to find the volume of components. To find the volume a program can add the cross-sectional areas over the length of the component. This is known as *integration*. In this section we will develop a prototype program to find the area under a curve. Later, we could extend the prototype to find the cross-sectional area, and then to find the volume.

6.6.1   Understanding the Problem

To develop this program, we need a solid understanding of calculating area. Figure 6.9 illustrates a technique for finding the area under a curve. Each point on the curve has a coordinate defined by its relative position along the X-axes and Y-axes. The area can be approximated by adding the area of a rectangle and triangle for each segment of the

[6]*If you view Help topic Key Code Constants, you will see the values expressed in hexadecimal. The key codes are not the same for all ASCII codes, but they are typically the same for common ASCII controls.*

curve. Any two points can define a segment, but the closer together they are, the closer the approximation is to the actual area. Once the areas of all segments are determined, the total area is the sum of all area segments. The area of segment *n* (where *n* could be any point such as *i* or *j*) is

```
rectangle(n) width × rectangle(n) height + ½ × triangle(n)
height × triangle(n) width
```

where

- rectangle(*n*) width and triangle(*n*) width is $X(n+1) - X(n)$

- rectangle(*n*) height is minimum of $Y(n)$ and $Y(n+1)$

- triangle(*n*) height is absolute value of $Y(n+1) - Y(n)$

6.6.2 Developing the Algorithm

Expressing the problem in the form of an equation makes it easier to develop the pseudocode. The pseudocode could look like Example 6.9.

Example 6.9

```
Collect all points X(n)
Collect all points Y(n)

Initialize total area = 0

For all points n, starting with n=2      ' find area for each ➡
segment and add to total area
    width = X(n) - X(n-1)      ' same for both rectangle and triangle
    rectangle height = min of Y(n), Y(n-1)
    triangle height = abs(Y(n)-Y(n-1))
    area(n) = width × rectangle height + ½ (width × triangle height)
```

Figure 6.9
Finding the Area Under a Curve

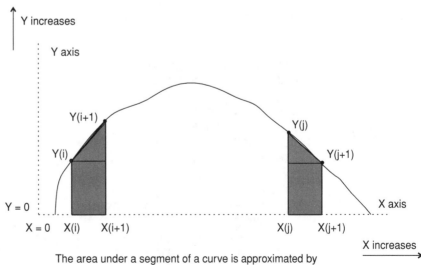

The area under a segment of a curve is approximated by adding the areas of the corresponding rectangle and triangle.

Then add the areas of all segments.

```
        total area = total area + area(n)
until all n points done
Display total area
```

It seems that this program is a natural for using the repetition structure (loop) and arrays. By adding small areas to make up a total area, we are in fact performing *numerical integration*.

6.6.3   Troubleshooting: The Prototype Program

You can continue development by clarifying how points will be collected. We have already developed a prototype of the program, which demonstrates a few more Visual Basic features that can add a more graphical look and feel to a program. Our prototype is a crude forerunner of a computer-aided design (CAD) tool since the user can actually draw the curve using the program. Figure 6.10 shows the program in operation. The user clicks the Start Curve button to begin drawing the curve. Then the user clicks in the area defined by the axes. The program draws a curve by connecting each of the acceptable clicked points with a line. When the curve is drawn, the user can click Calculate Area.

Example 6.10 shows the code. Before we say much more about it, note that there are a few deliberate bugs (logical errors). These errors were left in for troubleshooting practice in the Hands-On Exercises. Therefore, Figure 6.10 shows the program after *you* have debugged it.

Example 6.10

```
Option Explicit
    ' This program is supposed to calculate the area
    ' under a curve, but.....
    ' There are a few errors (for the reader to debug)
    ' Also documentation needs improving


    Dim m_nCount As Integer
    Dim m_fY(200) As Single
    Dim m_fX(100) As Single


Private Sub cmdArea_Click()
    Dim fVar1 As Single
    Dim fVar2 As Single
    Dim fVar3 As Single
    Dim fVar4 As Single
    Dim fVar5 As Single
    Dim nVar6 As Integer

    fVar1 = 0
    For nVar6 = 1 To m_nCount
        fVar2 = 0
        fVar3 = m_fX(nVar6) - m_fX(nVar6 - 1)
        If m_fY(nVar6) > m_fY(nVar6 - 1) Then
            fVar4 = m_fY(nVar6 - 1)
        Else
            fVar4 = m_fY(nVar6)
```

Figure 6.10
The Area Calculation Program in Action

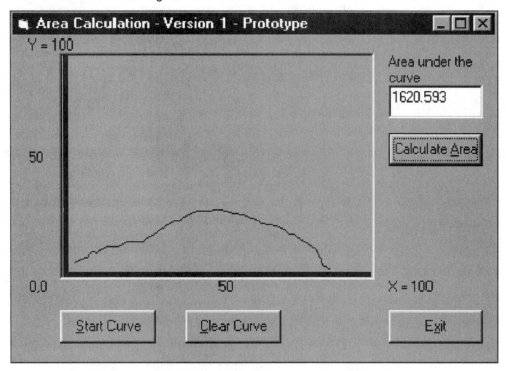

```
        End If
        fVar5 = Abs(m_fY(nVar6) - m_fY(nVar6 - 1))
        fVar2 = fVar3 * fVar4 + (1 / 2) * fVar3 * fVar5
        fVar1 = fVar1 + fVar2
    Next nVar6

    txtArea.Text = CStr(fVar1)

End Sub

Private Sub cmdClear_Click()
    picGraph.Cls
End Sub

Private Sub cmdExit_Click()
    End
End Sub

Private Sub cmdStartCurve_Click()

    picGraph.DrawWidth = 4
    picGraph.Line (0, 100)-(0, 0)    ' Draw vertical axis
    picGraph.Line (0, 0)-(100, 0)    ' Draw horizontal axis
    picGraph.DrawWidth = 1

End Sub
```

```
Private Sub Form_Load()
    picGraph.ScaleMode = 0  ' Set custom scale
    picGraph.Scale (-1, 101)-(101, -1)
    picGraph.AutoRedraw = True  ' Repaint graphics if ever another ➥
    window covers this one, or we have minimized it

    m_nCount = 0

End Sub


Private Sub picGraph_MouseDown(Button As Integer, Shift As ➥
Integer, X As Single, Y As Single)

    ' Using MouseDown event to record user mouse clicks on
    ' the picture box and to display curve connecting click points

        If m_nCount < 0 Then
            MsgBox "Error in Application"
            End ' Terminate program if this happens
        ElseIf m_nCount = 0 Then
            m_fY(0) = Y
            m_fX(0) = X
        Else
            If X >= m_fX(m_nCount - 1) Then
                m_fY(m_nCount) = Y
                m_fX(m_nCount) = X
                picGraph.Line (m_fX(m_nCount - 1), m_fY(m_nCount - 1))- ➥
                (m_fX(m_nCount), m_fY(m_nCount))
        Else
Beep

        End If

    End If

End Sub
```

We won't say much about the program since we will work with it extensively later, but we'll mention a few points for now. As promised, it does use a repetition statement (For Next in procedure cmdArea_Click). It also uses arrays, as evidenced in the general declarations and the use of the arrays in cmdArea_Click, cmdStartCurve_Click, and picGraph_MouseDown. Essentially, when the user clicks Start Curve, subsequent clicking in picture box picGraph is supposed to assign elements of arrays m_fX and m_fY with the coordinates of the points where the user clicked. It is supposed to also draw a line between each new point and the previous one. Procedure cmdArea will use the information stored in arrays m_fX and m_fY to calculate the area, as illustrated in the pseudocode of Example 6.9. The prefix m_ indicates that these are module-level variables accessible to any procedure in the form module. Earlier we used global variables with the g_ prefix. The difference is that global variables are accessible to the code in all forms and modules (.BAS files). Module variables are accessible only to the code in the form or module in which they are declared.

6.6.4   The Picture Box Control

The Find Area program introduces the picture box control. The picture box (named `picGraph`) is used for displaying graphics. Here we have used it for graphing a curve with its corresponding axes. The desired coordinate system for the graph is from 0 to 100 for both the X- and Y-axes. The normal Windows coordinate system starts with the origin at the top left corner. In normal graphs, the origin usually starts at the bottom left corner. We can set up the coordinate system by modifying the ScaleMode property of the picture box and applying the `Scale` method. We could use some statements like these:

```
picGraph.ScaleMode = 0  ' Set custom scale
picGraph.Scale (-1, 101)-(101, -1)
```

Actually, this makes the coordinate system –1 to 101 for both axes. It turns out that we need room for the axes themselves. The ScaleMode property defines the unit of measurement for coordinates of an object. This property only applies to objects that support graphics, such as the form object and picture box control object.

Picture Box Methods

A *method* is a procedure that acts on an object. Most objects support some methods. With the picture box you can use the `Cls` method, `Line` method, `Scale` method, and others. The `Scale` method defines the coordinate system of the object. The `Cls` method clears graphics and text generated at runtime from a form object or picture box object. In procedure `cmdClear_Click()`, we used the method as follows:

```
picGraph.Cls
```

The code in `cmdStartCurve_Click()` illustrates the `Line` method:

```
Private Sub cmdStartCurve_Click()
    picGraph.DrawWidth = 4
    picGraph.Line (0, 100)-(0, 0)     ' Draw vertical axis
    picGraph.Line (0, 0)-(100, 0)     ' Draw horizontal axis
    picGraph.DrawWidth = 1
End Sub
```

The DrawWidth property defines the width of any lines drawn on the picture box. Since we want the axes to be fairly wide, we set them to 4. The `Line` method uses two arguments separated by the minus sign to indicate the start point and end point of the line. Then the DrawWidth property is set to 1. Subsequent clicking in the picture box should draw the lines for the curve, except that the lines will be thinner.

Syntax for Using Methods

The syntax for methods uses the object name followed by dot (.) followed by *method*, as follows:

object_name.method_name [*arguments if any*]

For example, to draw a circle on `picGraph` at point 25,25 with a radius of 10, you would apply the `Circle` method to the object named `picGraph`:

```
picGraph.Circle (25,25), 10
```

The MouseDown Event

Example 6.10 also uses an event procedure for MouseDown. Only particular objects such as the picture box will receive and recognize a MouseDown event. It happens when the user presses any mouse button. When the event occurs, the event procedure receives four arguments. `Button` is an Integer code that specifies which mouse button was pressed. `Shift` specifies which, if any, of the SHIFT, CTRL, or ALT keys were pressed. The X and Y parameters indicate the X, (horizontal) and Y, (vertical) coordinates of the mouse pointer when the event occurred. In Example 6.10, procedure `picGraph_MouseDown` made use of the X and Y parameters only.

SUMMARY

Arrays are a collection of variables (elements) with the same name and same data type. Each element is referenced by a unique subscript (or group of subscripts) enclosed in parentheses. It is possible to have control arrays. Each element has the same name but is referenced by a unique index.

The declaration for an array is

Dim *varname*[([*subscripts*])][**As** *type*][, *varname*[([*subscripts*])][**As** *type*]] . . .

The subscript syntax (if used) is

[*lower* **To**] *upper* [,[*lower* **To**] *upper*] . . .

Note that the lower subscript is optional. If it is not used, the default is zero unless overridden by the `Option Base` statement. Subscripts should be integers.

The Repetition structure is a set of statements that are executed repeatedly *while* a specified condition is true. It can also work in reverse; execute repeatedly *until* a condition is true. Generally there are two categories of Repetition statements.

- Those that execute a preset number of times (such as the `For Next` and `For Each Next` statements).

- Those that execute an undetermined number of times (such as the `Do...Loop` and `While...Wend` statements).

The syntax of the `For Next` statement is

For *counter* = *start* **To** *end* [**Step** *stepsize*]
    [*loop statements*]
Next [*counter*]

There are four variations of the `Do...Loop` statement. The syntax of one, the Do While Loop, is

Do While *condition*
    [*statements*]
Loop

The syntax for the `Do Until Loop` statement is

Do Until *condition*
    [*statements*]

Loop

The syntax for the Do Loop While statement is

```
Do
    [statements]
Loop While condition
```

The syntax for the Do Loop Until statement is

```
Do
    [statements]
Loop Until condition
```

The syntax of the While...Wend statement is

```
While condition
    [statements]
Wend
```

With arrays and Repetition statements, we can create more versatile programs.

HANDS-ON EXERCISES

OVERVIEW

The activities will

- Enable you to use arrays
- Enable you to use the For Next, Do While/Until Loop, Do Loop While/ Until and While...Wend statements.
- Enable you to create programs that create controls during runtime.
- Enable you to create programs that perform repetitive operations.
- Familiarize you with program maintenance by debugging an existing program to remove logical errors.

To Get Started

1. Read the section Read Me Before Attempting the Hands-On Exercises if you have not already done so.
2. Run Windows.
3. Open the file CH06\EX06.TXT on your student disk and answer the questions. (The same questions are shown here so that you can still determine answers when you are not sitting in front of a computer.)
4. Run Visual Basic.

6.1 ARRAYS

1. What is an array? In particular, what is the common characteristic of each element in any array? How is each element identified?
2. Make up an example of involving the use of a one-dimensional array. Make up an example for a two-dimensional array. Make one up for multidimensional arrays.

3. For the following code segment, how many elements are in each of the arrays?

```
Const MAXROW = 50
Const MAXNUMBER = 60
Const REGULAR = 21
Const TAKEN = True
Const AVAILABLE = False

Dim bSeat(MAXROW, MAXNUMBER) As Boolean
Dim sClient(1 To MAXROW, 1 To MAXNUMBER) As String
Dim fRegularPrice(REGULAR To MAXROW, 1 To MAXNUMBER) As Single
Dim fSpecialPrice(1 To REGULAR, 1 To MAXNUMBER) As Single
```

4. The previous code segment represents information about the floor seats in a theater. The theatre has a balcony with 15 rows that are each 20 seats wide. All seats have the same price. Write the declarations for arrays representing balcony seat information. Invent your own names, but remember to use the appropriate prefix convention.

5. Write statements to indicate that

- Seat number 7 in Row 4 is taken.

- Seat number 5 in Row 10 is available.

- Seat number 23 in Row 35 costs $17.50.

Improve the Simple Calculator, Version 5

To work with this exercise, open *project* SIMCALC4 in directory CH05. Save *file* SIMCALC4 as SIMCALC5 in directory CH06. Select **Save Project As** from the File menu. Save *project* SIMCALC4 as SIMCALC5 in directory CH06. Change the Name of the form to frmCalculator5, and change the version part of its Caption to state Version 05.

Create a Control Array   You will be changing the command buttons for arithmetic into a control array. Click on **one of the buttons such as cmdAdd**. Change its Name property setting to **cmdCalculate**. Note that the Index property is *no entry*; this is because it is not yet a control array. Change the Index property setting to **0**. Now change the Name settings of cmdSubtract, cmdMultiply, and cmdDivide to **cmdCalculate**. Note that their Index properties are automatically set to 1, 2, and 3, in that order. If not, then set the Index properties manually so that

- Caption &Add corresponds to Index 0.

- Caption &Subtract corresponds to Index 1.

- Caption &Multiply corresponds to Index 2.

- Caption &Divide corresponds to Index 3.

Your Properties window should now look something like Figure 6.11.

Reuse and Then Discard Old Event Procedures   Since you have renamed the controls, their corresponding event procedures will now be collected as general procedures. The new control array elements do not have code yet. You can confirm this by double-clicking **a button such as the Add button**. You will be viewing the Code window. Note that cmdCalculate_Click(Index As Integer) has no code (yet). If you select the **(General)** item in the Object box, note that the former event procedures will now be collected as general procedures. Your Code window should look something like Figure 6.12. If necessary, resize the immediate pane of the Debug window (see Figure 3.7) so you can view all Watch expressions.

Figure 6.11
The Properties Window Showing a Control Array

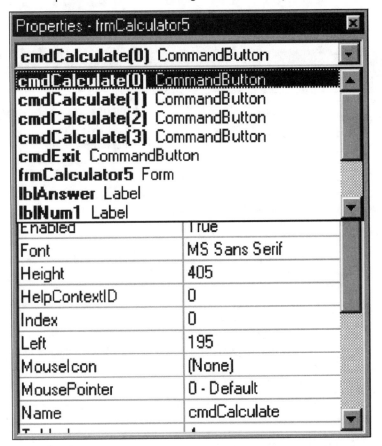

Click on the Object Box button to show control array elements and other controls.

Each control array element has the same Name setting, but the Index settings will differ.

Note that the event procedure for `cmdCalculate_Click` as shown in Example 6.1 is very similar to any of the former event procedures. You can copy and paste any of the former click event procedures as the code for `cmdCalculate_Click`. Then edit the code so that it looks like the following segment from Example 6.1.

```
Private Sub cmdCalculate_Click(Index As Integer)

    ' Control array demo for simple calculator
    ' Depending on Index argument, we perform
    ' Addition if Index = 0
    ' Subtraction if Index = 1
    ' Multiplication if Index = 2
    ' Division if Index = 3

    Dim fNum1 As Single, fNum2 As Single
    Dim fAnswer As Single
    On Error Resume Next  ' Set up error handling

    ' Get inputs, if error occurs reset them to safe values
    fNum1 = CSng(txtNum1.Text)
    fNum2 = CSng(txtNum2.Text)

    Select Case Index
```

Figure 6.12
Code Window Showing Former Event Procedures Are Now General Procedures

Since former object cmdAdd now has a new name, its event procedure
is collected as a general procedure.

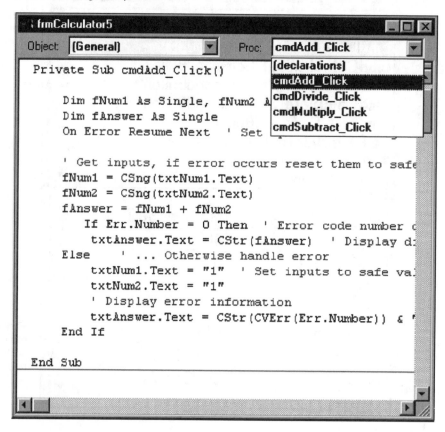

```
    Case 0
        fAnswer = fNum1 + fNum2
    Case 1
        fAnswer = fNum1 - fNum2
    Case 2
        fAnswer = fNum1 * fNum2
    Case 3
        fAnswer = fNum1 / fNum2
    Case Else
        fAnswer = 0
    End Select


    If Err.Number = 0 Then   ' Error code number of 0 means no error
        txtAnswer.Text = CStr(fAnswer)   ' Display division
    Else     ' ... Otherwise handle error
        txtNum1.Text = "1"   ' Set inputs to safe values
        txtNum2.Text = "1"
        ' Display error information
        txtAnswer.Text = CStr(CVErr(Err.Number)) & " " & Err.Description
    End If

End Sub
```

After you have entered the code of cmdCalculate_Click, double-click **each of the buttons with this name**. Note that each shows the same code. You can remove the former event procedures, such as cmdAdd_Click. Highlight each in its entirety by dragging **the mouse I-beam pointer from the Sub statement to the End Sub statement**. Press the DELETE key. Repeat this deletion process for general procedures cmd-Subtract_Click, cmdMultiply_Click, and cmdDivide_Click.

Running the Program   Run the program. Make sure it still works in the same way as the former calculator program. Put a breakpoint at the line

```
Private Sub cmdCalculate_Click(Index As Integer)
```

Run the program and enter **some input numbers**. Click **any of the arithmetic operator buttons**. When execution breaks, check the value of Index. Single step the program and note how the Select Case statement determines which operation to perform. Click the **Run** button to continue execution. Repeat the single-stepping process for each of the other arithmetic operator buttons.

6.2   REPETITION STATEMENTS

Using Visual Basic Help, find all the different repetition statements that can be used in the language. Remember to check the title bar of any Help screens to make sure you are not looking at information from third-party add-ons, such as Crystal Reports.

6. Describe the steps used to find the information for each statement type.

6.3   THE FOR NEXT STATEMENT

The Yearly Sales Program, Version 1

Select **New Project** from the File menu. Select **Save File As** from the File menu. Save *file* FORM1 as YRSALES1 in directory CH06. Select **Save Project As** from the File menu. Save *project* PROJECT1 as YRSALES1 in directory CH06.

Modify the form in such a way that it looks like Figure 6.4. The form Name property should be frmYearlySales1. Refer to Example 6.2 to see how to name the controls. For example, the Yearly Total button should be named **cmdYearlyTotal**. The text box for the yearly sales should be named **txtYearlySales**. The text box for January is an element of a control array; name it **txtMonthlySales** and set its Index property to **1**. Refer to the listing in Example 6.5 for information on how to name other controls. Name the label object corresponding to Caption January as **lblMonthlySales**. Set the Index property to **1**. Name the Exit button **cmdExit**.

Type in the code shown in Examples 6.2 and 6.5. Also, enter the following code for the remaining event procedures and the Option Base statement:

Example 6.11

```
Option Explicit
Option Base 1


' For Sub cmdYearlyTotal_Click(), see Example 6.2
' For Sub Form_Load(), see Example 6.5


Private Sub txtMonthlySales_Change(Index As Integer)
    txtYearlySales.Text = ""     ' Cue user that input changed
End Sub
```

```
Private Sub cmdExit_Click()
    End
End Sub
```

Run the Program   Save the project and run the program. The form should look something like Figure 6.2 without the number entries. Enter **some numbers for each of the months** (perhaps the same as those shown in Figure 6.2). Click the **Yearly Total** button. The Yearly Sales box should show the sum of all of the months.

The Infinite Loop

If your program hangs during execution and does not respond to any user actions, it may be stuck in a loop. This is a logical error since the computer is repeating the statements in the loop. Due to a flaw (the logical error), the condition for remaining in the loop stays forever True. (This is great for true love, but not so good for program execution!) If your program hangs during execution, press **CTRL+BREAK** to force Visual Basic to stop executing the program.

Single Step the For Next Loop   Set a breakpoint at the beginning of the procedure cmdYearlyTotal_Click. Add Watch expressions for fMonthlySales, fMonthly Sales (nCounter), and nCounter. Run the program. Enter legal numerical values for each of the months, and click **Yearly Total**. Single step the program until you reach the statement

```
For nCounter = 1 To 12 Step 1
```

Single step three more times. The current statement should be

```
Next nCounter
```

Visual Basic 5

If the Watch window is not visible, select it by clicking the **Watch Window** button on the Debug toolbar, or select **Watch Window** from the View menu.

Look at the Debug window. It should look something like Figures 6.13a and 3.13b, depending on the numeric input you entered. You may need to resize the Watch pane fields by dragging the Expression, Value, Type (for VB5), and Context heading borders.

Single step. The value for nCounter should change to 2. Position and resize the Code and Debug windows so you can see both at once. Continue single stepping and note how the repetition progresses by incrementing nCounter and assigning each new array element with the appropriate Text setting from the associated text box. The repetition stops once nCounter has reached 13 and then excutes the statements following the loop. Note also that the Debug window shows that the subscript is out of range. Why? Think about it. The array was declared for a subscript range of 1 to 12 only. This is not a problem since we are no longer using the subscript; however, we do need to heed its value if we want to use the array again. Add a Watch expression for fYearlySales. Single step the program and note how its value is incremented similarly to that shown in Table 6.2. Of course, your values will differ if you entered different inputs.

Visual Basic 5

If you have a Watch expression for an array declaration, you can toggle between an expanded or collapsed view by clicking on the **+ or - box** (see Figure 6.13b). When expanded, you can see the value of all elements. To see other Watch expressions, you may prefer to collapse the view of the array.

Subscript Out of Range Error   Enter the following code temporarily after the For Next statement.

```
' Generate a subscript out of range error
' Add a phantom 13th month to yearly total
fYearlySales = fYearlySales + fMonthlySales(nCounter)
```

Run the program. Enter **valid values** and click **Yearly Total**. Single step the program again, but note what happens when you try to execute the new statement you just added. Since fMonthlySales(13) was not included in the range in the declaration, the runtime error will occur. The program nicely traps the error and displays the error information. Remove the offending lines and check that this runtime error no longer occurs when you run the program. Save the project. We will return to this program later to investigate control creation during runtime.

Add a Factorial Function to the Simple Calculator, Version 6

To start this exercise, open *project* SIMCALC5 in directory CH06. Save *file* SIMCALC5 as SIMCALC6 in directory CH06. Select **Save Project As** from the File menu. Save *project* SIMCALC5 as SIMCALC6 in directory CH06. Change the Name of the form to frmCalculator6, and change the version part of its Caption to state **Version 06**.

Resize the Exit button to leave room for a new button under the Add button. Place a new command button under the Add button. Resize it so it is the same size as the Add button. Name the button as **cmdCalculate** and set its Index property to **4**. Change its Caption to **&Factorial**.

Figure 6.13a
Visual Basic 4 Debug Window Showing the First Iteration of the Loop in Example 6.2

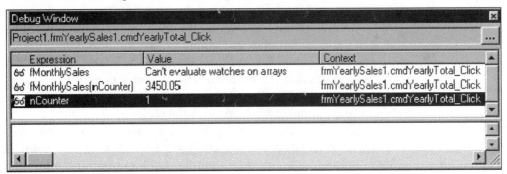

Note that *fMonthlySales* cannot be evaluated since it refers to a collection of elements in the array. However, *fMonthlySales (nCounter)* can be evaluated since it is an element.

Figure 6.13b
Visual Basic 5 Debug Window Showing the First Iteration of the Loop in Example 6.2

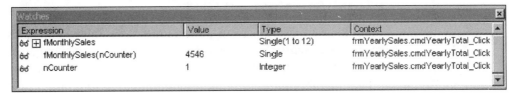

Note that *fMonthlySales* can be expanded since it refers to a collection of elements in the array. However, *fMonthlySales(nCounter)* can be evaluated as only one item since it is an element.

Modify the code of the program so that it is the same as Example 6.4. Save the project and run the program. Do not click the **Factorial** button yet. Make sure that the former arithmetic operations still operate. Enter a small number such as **4** as the first number, and click **Factorial**. The result should be 24 since $1 \times 2 \times 3 \times 4 = 24$. Enter **5** as the first number, and click **Factorial**. The result should be 120, since $24 \times 5 = 120$. Try other numbers. Note how the program handles negative numbers, zero, and numbers that are too large. You may note how rapidly the factorial grows as you try larger numbers. If you wish, compare the results with those for the Windows Calculator. Make sure to select **Scientific View** if you use the Windows Calculator.

Set a breakpoint at the beginning of function Factorial. Set Watch expressions for nCounter, nNum, and fFactorial. Single step the program and note how the For Next loop statement executes.

Creating Controls During Runtime

Open *project* YRSALES1 in directory CH06. Set a breakpoint at the beginning of Form_Load. Run the program and single step through the procedure. You won't be able to see the form since it isn't loaded yet; however, you may be interested in monitoring how the Format function returns the name of the month depending on the number of days. Once you have stepped through the procedure, click the **Run** button on the Visual Basic Toolbar. Experiment more with the program, if you like.

6.4   THE DO...LOOP STATEMENT

Add a Find Function to the Yearly Sales Program, Version 2

Open *project* YRSALES1 in directory CH06. Save *file* YRSALES1 as **YRSALES2** in directory CH06. Select **Save Project As** from the File menu. Save *project* YRSALES1 as **YRSALES2** in directory CH06. Change the Name of the form to **frmYearlySale2**, and change the version part of its Caption to state **Version 2**.

Refer to Figure 6.5 and Example 6.6. Add a label, text box, and command button control for the find month functionality. Use Example 6.6 as a guide for setting the Name properties. Use Figure 6.5 as a guide for setting the Caption properties of the label and the command button. Save the project.

Add the code shown in Example 6.6. Save the project, and run the program. Enter **values such as those shown in Figure 6.5**. Click **Yearly Total** and then click **Find Month**. The result should be the total sales and the first month with sales exceeding $4,000. Click the **Break** button to put Visual Basic in break mode. Set a breakpoint at the first statement in procedure cmdFind_Click. Add Watch expressions for

```
bFound
lblMonthlySales(nIndex).Caption
nIndex
txtMonthlySales(nIndex).Text
```

Click the Toolbar **Continue** button. Enter some different numbers for monthly sales, and click **Find Month**. When the program stops at the breakpoint, resize and position the Code and Debug windows so you can both view at once. If necessary, resize the Immediate pane and/or Watch pane of the Debug window (see Figures 3.8a and 3.8b) so you can view all Watch expressions. Single-step the program and monitor the execution of the Do While loop statement. Note that the loop will continue until sales exceeding $4,000 (bFound set True) is found, or until all 12 months have been searched (nIndex > 12).

Repeat this single-stepping exercise for input scenarios when at least one month has sales exceeding $4,000 or none of the months has sales exceeding $4,000. Depending on your inputs, you should see an execution scenario similar to Table 6.3 if June is the first month with sales exceeding $4,000. Stop program execution.

Mathematical Expansion to Find the Sine, Version 1

Select **New Project** from the File menu. Select **Save File As** from the File menu. Save *file* FORM1 as **EXPANS1** in directory CH06. Select **Save Project As** from the File menu. Save *project* PROJECT1 as **EXPANS1** in directory CH06. Name the form as **frmExpans1**. Set its Caption to **Expansion Demo - Version 1**.

Refer to Figure 6.7 and Example 6.7. You will be using a new control, the horizontal scroll bar. The corresponding Toolbox button should be intuitive, but in case it isn't, move the mouse pointer over the buttons and wait for the pop-up balloon to appear. Move the pointer until you find the button, for which the balloon will say HscrollBar. Set the properties of the HScrollBar control as follows:

Name	hsbArgument
LargeChange	40
Max	4000
Min	-4000
Value	0

In Example 6.7, note that the option buttons (another new control) are elements of a control array. Add an option button (control object OptionButton). Name it as **optTol**, set its Index to **3**, and set its Caption to **3**. Add the other option buttons using the same Name and similarly set their Index and Caption properties as **4**, **5**, **6**, and **7**. Set one Value property of one of these option buttons as **True**. If you try to set another option button Value to **True**, the former one will become **False**. Only one option button (in a group of buttons) can have a True value.

Now modify the rest of the form so that it resembles Figure 6.7. Also use Example 6.7 as a guide to setting the other properties, if necessary. Save the project.

Enter the code shown in Example 6.7. To enter the code for hsbArgument_Scroll, double-click **hsbArgument**. The Procedure box of the Code window will show the default event of Change. Click on the **Procedure** box, scroll if necessary, and select **Scroll**. Enter all of the code as shown in Example 6.7. Save the project.

Run the program. With the mouse, drag the scroll box, or click on the scroll bar arrows, or click on the scroll bar outside the scroll bar. All of these actions should cause the scroll box to move left or right, depending on which side you clicked or the direction you are dragging the scroll box. The displays in the text box should change correspondingly. If you want, use a calculator to confirm that the correct sine value is shown. Remember to use radians if you choose to cross-check with a calculator.

Click on an **option button that is currently not selected**. The one that was formerly selected is no longer selected. Instead, the one you clicked on is selected. When you select a higher accuracy, the expansion result should be closer to the function result. In some cases, you may not see any difference.

Single Stepping the Program

Set a breakpoint in the procedure hsbArgument_Scroll (not Change). Run the program. The program shouldn't halt until you **drag** the scroll box. This verifies that the

Scroll event only occurs when the user drags the scroll box. Click the **Step Into** button. Continue to single step with the **Step Into** button until the current statement is part of Function SineExpansion. At this point use the **Step Over** button to avoid single stepping the called function Factorial (unless you want to step through it), but don't single step quite yet. First, add Watch expressions for the following:

```
fSine
fPreviousSine
nCount
nTerm
Abs(fSine - fPreviousSine)
m_fTol
```

Resize and position the Code and Debug windows so you can view both at once. If necessary, resize the Immediate pane and/or Watch pane of the Debug window so you can view all Watch expressions. Single step (using Step Over) and note carefully the progress through the Do Loop code. Once you have single stepped past the loop, click **Continue** (or press **F5**). Repeat this exercise for other scroll bar values.

Hint

If your (Debug) toolbar is not visible, you can use F8 for Step Into and SHIFT+F8 for Step Over.

A Bit About the Scroll Bar   Stop the program. In Design mode, select the **scroll bar**. Click **LargeChange** in the Properties window. Press **F1** for context-sensitive help, and read the information about the LargeChange property. Click **See Also** and choose **Max, Min Properties**. Read the information, and read the information about the Value property.

A Bit About Option Buttons and Check Boxes   Use Help to find out more about the option button and check box controls. Note that the OptionButton control has a Value property, the setting of which can be Boolean True or False. Only one option button may have a True value. When the user clicks an option button, its Value is set to True; the others are automatically set to False. It is possible to group option buttons using the Frame control. For example, one group could select tolerance, another group could select font size, and another could select text color. Note that the check box has a Value property the setting of which can be Integer 0, 1, or 2 for unchecked, checked, and grayed, respectively. Any check box may have any of these values. When the user clicks a check box, the Value property toggles between 0 and 1. To set the Value to 2, it is necessary to use program code. Check box controls are used to display multiple choices from which the user can select several choices, such as the Environment options in Visual Basic itself.

6.5   THE WHILE...WEND STATEMENT

An Enter Number Program

Select **New Project** from the File menu. Select **Save File/Form1 As** from the File menu. Save *file* FORM1 as **ENTNUM1** in directory CH06. Select **Save Project As** from the File menu. Save *project* PROJECT1 as **ENTNUM1** in directory CH06. Name the form as **frmEnterNumber1**. Set its Caption to **Enter Number - Version 1**.

Figure 6.14
The Enter Number Program

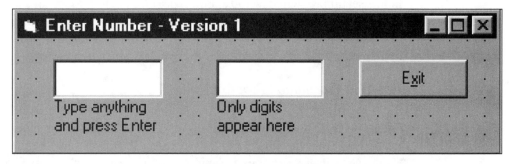

Refer to Figure 6.14 and Example 6.8. Add the controls, and then size and position them to resemble Figure 6.14. The left and right text boxes are `txtEnterNumber` and `txtNumber`, respectively. Set the Locked property of txtNumber to `True`. To enter the code for `txtEnterNumber_KeyPress`, double-click **txtEnterNumber**. The Procedure box of the Code window will show the default event of Change. Click on the **Procedure** box, scroll if necessary, and select KeyPress. Note that Visual Basic automatically creates the first and last lines of the procedure, including the parameter `KeyAscii` as Integer. At this stage, you may delete the lines for procedure `txtEnterNumber_Change`, since you will not be writing any code for this procedure. Now you can proceed to enter all of the code shown in Example 6.8. Save the project.

Run the program. Type something like **2 for 1 Special** and press **ENTER**. The second box should show 21. The program will only show the digits you entered. You don't need to click anything; just press **ENTER**. This is more convenient way of data entry for a user.

Set a breakpoint in the `txtEnterNumber_KeyPress` procedure. Run the program. Whenever you press a key in the box, program execution will break. Examine the value of `KeyAscii`. Note that its value is an integer corresponding to the ASCII code of the key you pressed. To confirm this, use Help to find the ASCII code (Character Set 0–127). Continue execution and repeat this for several more keystrokes. Stop execution and remove the breakpoint. Set up Watch expressions for the following (select Add Watch instead of using Instant/Quick Watch):

```
nNext
sNumber
Len(sEntry)
KeyAscii
```

Also set up a Watch expression for `KeyAscii = vbKeyReturn`, except that when you see the Edit Watch dialog box, select Watch Type option **Break When Value is True**. The other Watch expressions used the default Watch Type option of Watch Expression.

Run the program. Type in **alphabetic and numeric characters**, and press **ENTER**. Visual Basic will enter Break mode because the expression `KeyAscii = vbKeyReturn` is now `True`. Position the Code and Debug windows so that you can see both. Single step (Step Into) the program and monitor the progress of execution through the `While...Wend` loop. When the loop has completed executing, click **Continue** to put Visual Basic in Run Mode. Repeat the exercise with other inputs. When you are done, stop execution. Note that because the program changes `KeyAscii` to 0 when you press **ENTER**, the Text property of the text box does not include the ENTER character. ASCII 0 is the null character.

6.6   AN ENGINEERING APPLICATION

In this section we will develop a prototype program to find the area under a curve. Much of the design has already been done; what remains is to improve the documentation and to fix the bugs. You probably will develop a better appreciation of thorough documentation after trying to fix the logical errors, otherwise known as **bugs**.

The Area Calculation Program

Build the Initial Program   Select **New Project** from the File menu. Select **Save File/ Form1 As** from the File menu. Save *file* FORM1 as **AREA1** in directory CH06. Select **Save Project As** from the File menu. Save *project* PROJECT1 as **AREA1** in directory CH06. Name the form as **frmaArea1**. Set its Caption to **Area Calculation - Version 1 - Prototype**.

Refer to Figure 6.10 and Example 6.10. You might prefer to add other controls before the picture box. If you double-click a Toolbox button, Visual Basic will place the control in the middle of the form. This can be awkward if the picture box is already there. An alternative is to single-click the Toolbox button and draw the control exactly where you want it. You can do this by moving the cross-hair pointer to the desired top left position for the control on the form. Then press down the mouse button and drag to the desired bottom right control and release the mouse button. My personal preference is to double-click. If I need to add more controls, I would temporarily resize the picture box to be small so that it is out of the way. Later I can resize it to the final desired size.

To add a picture box (Toolbox button PictureBox), look at the corresponding Toolbox button, which has an icon that looks like desert scenery. If you are not sure, move the mouse pointer over the buttons and wait for the pop-up balloon to appear. Move the pointer until you find the button where the balloon says PictureBox. Double-click it and a rectangle appears on the form. Now you can set its properties. In this case, you only need to position it (Left and Top properties), size it (Width and Height properties), and set its Name to pic-Graph. The final form should look like Figure 6.10 without the graphics inside the picture box and with no text in the text box.

Enter the code shown in Example 6.10. Note that the default event for the picture box is Click. Hence you will have to use the Procedure box in the Code window to select the MouseDown event. Section 6.6 in the main part of this chapter explained why the MouseDown event is being used instead of the Click event. The coordinate information X and Y is passed to a MouseDown event procedure but not to a Click procedure. Save the project.

Run the program and click **the buttons** and click **inside the picture box**. Note that the program is partially operational. Clicking **Start Curve** will show the axes in the picture box. Clicking **inside the picture box** will do nothing. Clicking **Calculate Area** will show a result of zero. Clicking **Clear Curve** will remove the axes. Clicking **Exit** will stop execution. If by some miracle it is fully operational (you can draw a curve and calculate its area), you lucked out by managing to accidentally type in the corrections! (In that case, if you are always so lucky, you might not need to learn programming.) Another possibility is that you will encounter runtime errors or that it does not behave as described; this means you made a typographic error. Check your code carefully to find the errors, correct them, and try again. It is enough that you have to find the intentional errors; you don't really want to look for the unintentional ones!

Note

If you really get stuck you can work with the prewritten program that is saved in CH06\SOLN as project AREA1HLP.

Troubleshooting: Let the Debugging Begin Previously, we have used the debugging tools to monitor program execution for instructional purposes. Now we will use them for their intended purpose—to track down causes for program error. The program is supposed to permit the user to click in the picture box to connect a line between each point and the previously clicked point. At this stage, you should review the pseudocode and the explanations in Section 6.6 of the main part of the chapter. Where would one begin to look? Something is supposed to happen when the user clicks in the picture box, isn't it? Would it make sense to set a breakpoint in picGraph_MouseDown? Okay let's try it. Set the breakpoint in picGraph_MouseDown.

Run the program. Click **Start Curve**. It apparently works. Click inside the **picture box**, and single step through the procedure. Now say to yourself, "Wouldn't it be nice if there were more comments?" Thank your lucky stars that the original code writer didn't use strange variable names such as *Moe*, *Larry*, and *Curly*. You might want to click **Continue** and try again several times. You will notice something peculiar: Every time that picGraph_MouseDown executes, it always executes the statements

```
ElseIf nCount = 0 Then
    fY(0) = Y
    fX(0) = X
```

inside the If Then block statement. Presumably, this should not be the case. The array elements are a clue. Their subscripts are zero. Does this mean that this block of code should only execute when the user clicks in the picture box for the first time? Maybe this would be a good time to add in some comments to explain this assumption.

These statements are executed if nCount is zero. You can confirm this by checking the value of nCount during single stepping. The question is: What should cause nCount to be different and why? The variable name provides a hint, but what exactly is it supposed to count? You can look for other occurrences of nCount. To do this, highlight it and select Find from the Edit menu in Visual Basic. When you see the **Find** dialog box, make sure that the Search option **Current Module** is selected. Click the **Find Next** button several times until you find all the uses of the variable in the code.

Procedure cmdArea_Click uses the same variable, but we haven't used this procedure yet. To make sure, click the **Calls** button in the Debug window (see Figure 3.7) when the current statement is one inside picGraph_MouseDown. You should note that only picGraph_MouseDown was called. You should have found that variable nCount is declared in the General Declarations; hence it is a module-level variable. It is also used in Form_Load, where it is initialized to zero.

Aha, the variable is module level. We should really name it as m_nCount to make this more apparent. Stop the program and select **Replace** from the Edit menu. When you see the Replace dialog box, fill in the information as shown in Figure 6.15. Then click **Replace** repeatedly until you have replaced all occurrences of nCount. Using Replace All is risky unless you are absolutely certain there will be no undesirable side effects.

Investigate the code in cmdArea_Click. Variable m_nCount is used only to set the upper limit for the loop. As we have seen, m_nCount is always zero. It seems that m_nCount is being used to count the number of points that are clicked into the picture box by the user to define the points on the curve (to be drawn). Perhaps this would be a good time to add comments to explain this. Look at the pseudocode in Example 6.9. The

Figure 6.15
The Replace Dialog Box in Visual Basic

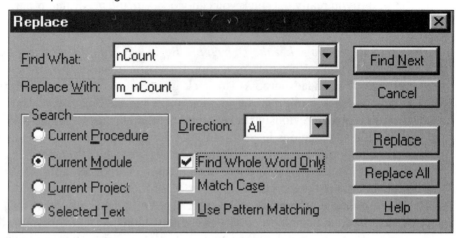

purpose of picGraph_MouseDown would seem to be to collect the points on the graph. Perhaps this would be a good time to add comments to explain this.

Now we seem to have an understanding of the cause of the problem and a bit better understanding of the program. Would it be reasonable for every click (Mouse-Down event) inside the picture box to increment m_nCount? Note that the Else part of the If Then block in picGraph_MouseDown uses the Line method. It would make sense that we increment m_nCount inside this procedure whenever a new X, Y point is being recorded. Add statements to increment the count. Hence the event procedure for picGraph_MouseDown will look like the following. The comments you added may be different. The bold type indicates the modifications.

```
Private Sub picGraph_MouseDown(Button As Integer, Shift As Integer, ➡
X As Single, Y As Single)

' Using MouseDown event to record user mouse clicks on
' the picture box and to display curve connecting click points

    If m_nCount < 0 Then     ' Negative count should not be possible
        MsgBox "Error in Application"
        End ' Terminate program if this happens
    ElseIf m_nCount = 0 Then      ' This is the first click in ➡
    the picture box
        fY(0) = Y    ' Hence we can record the first X,Y point
        fX(0) = X
        m_nCount = m_nCount + 1 ' Add new X,Y point to the collection
    Else     ' Connect this X,Y point to the previous X,Y point
        If X >= fX(m_nCount - 1) Then
            fY(m_nCount) = Y     ' Record the point
            fX(m_nCount) = X
            ' ... and draw a line from it to previous point
            picGraph.Line (fX(m_nCount - 1), fY(m_nCount - 1))- ➡
            (fX(m_nCount), fY(m_nCount))
            m_nCount = m_nCount + 1 ' Add new X,Y point to the collection
        Else
            Beep
```

```
        End If

    End If

End Sub
```

Remove the breakpoint and try running the program. Click **Start Curve**, and then click in the picture box a few times. You should see some lines being drawn. This looks good—perhaps the program works. Click **more in the picture box**. If you click to the left of the most recently clicked point, you will hear a beep and no line will be drawn. Click **again**. It is only possible to draw a line from left to right. Continue clicking **in the box** until the curve reaches the far right (necessary for finding the next bug). Click **Calculate Area**. An area will be calculated. So far, so good. Click **Clear Curve.** The line and axes are removed.

Now click **Start Curve** again. The axes will appear; however, when you click **inside the picture box**, the program will only beep and no line will be drawn. Click **Break** to put Visual Basic in break mode. This is a good time to experiment to improve our understanding of the MouseDown event. Set a breakpoint at the beginning of the procedure. Run the program. Click **Start Curve**, and then click in the picture box. When the program breaks, examine the X and Y arguments of `picGraph_MouseDown`. Click **Continue** and repeat the exercise. You should note that X increases from left to right to correspond with the horizontal scale. Similarly, Y increases from bottom to top, as shown on the vertical scale.

Repeat the exercise; this time, examine the sequence carefully. Single step through the procedure. Click **Continue** and click **again in the picture box**. Repeat the process. Notice that the `Else` part always executes in the following `If Then` statement.

```
If X >= fX(m_nCount - 1) Then
    fY(m_nCount) = Y     ' Record the point
    fX(m_nCount) = X
    ' ... and draw a line from it to previous point
    picGraph.Line (fX(m_nCount - 1), fY(m_nCount - 1))- ➡
    (fX(m_nCount), fY(m_nCount))
    m_nCount = m_nCount + 1 ' Add new X,Y point to the collection
Else
    Beep
End If
```

The condition X >= fX(m_nCount - 1) is apparently always `False`. Let's examine why. The next time your program breaks in the procedure, examine the value of m_nCount. Notice that it is 100 or close to 100 (assuming you drew the first curve close to the right edge). Is this what we want? It is certainly what we told the computer to do, but not what we really wanted. There is a logical flaw in the program design. The program is trying to draw a curve from where it left off last time!

Think. How can we start every new curve from the beginning? One way would be to reset the counter m_nCount to zero when we start a new curve. Add a statement to clear the count in `cmdClear_Click` as follows.

```
Private Sub cmdClear_Click()
    picGraph.Cls
    m_nCount = 0      ' Clear the count to start a new curve
End Sub
```

Run the program. It appears to work, but if you don't bother to click **Start Curve**, you will find that you can still draw the curve. Is this a problem? It may not be a problem, but it doesn't exactly display the behavior a user might expect. It would also make the code cleaner if clicking Start Curve would also clear the area result. This can be easily accomplished by the following modification.

```
Private Sub cmdStartCurve_Click()

    picGraph.DrawWidth = 4
    picGraph.Line (0, 100)-(0, 0)    ' Draw vertical axis
    picGraph.Line (0, 0)-(100, 0)    ' Draw horizontal axis
    picGraph.DrawWidth = 1
    txtArea.Text = "" ' Cue the user that area no longer valid

End Sub
```

It appears that the program does what is expected. Congratulations. You have just debugged the program. There are still more improvements that can be made, such as only allowing the curve to be drawn when the user clicks Start Curve.

Improve the documentation of this program now that you have a better understanding of it. If you want to view one possible solution, examine project AREAS1 in directory CH06\SOLN. You might also want to use Debug tools to investigate how the loops in the program operate to collect curve points and calculate and sum all area segments to obtain a total area under the curve.

ADDITIONAL PROBLEM SOLVING

Develop a prototype program to set a new password. If the user types an input that contains at least one digit, the input becomes the new password. If the input does not contain at least one digit, the attempted password setting is rejected. Note that you may find the PasswordChar and MaxLength properties for a text box useful. By the way, the password should contain at least four characters. You may also wish to restrict the password to a maximum length.

CHAPTER 7

Algorithms

This chapter introduces you to instructing a computer to do what you want it to do.

There is a legend that describes a temple in Hanoi in which Buddhist monks are moving a stack of 64 golden rings. Each ring is a different diameter, and all are stacked in such a way that a smaller ring rests on top of a larger ring. The monks move a ring from one peg to another according to a precise set of rules. There are three pegs, and the monks can only place a smaller ring on top of another. Also, they can move only one ring each day. According to the legend, when the monks have moved all the rings to make a new stack on another peg, the world will end!

These monks have in fact followed an algorithm. They followed certain prescribed steps to move all of the rings from one peg to another.

After completing this chapter, you should be able to

- Modify algorithms that are commonly used for a variety of applications.

- Write programs that use other types of data.

- Write programs that use list boxes and combo boxes.

- Write programs that use additional features of Visual Basic.

In This Chapter

Cougar Canoe needs to maintain customer information; thus it needs a program that can search a list of customers to find and/or update the information. One of their suppliers, Coyote Electronics, is designing a new product. They are excited by the potential popularity of a portable geographic positioning system. Their software will need to perform such design calculations as determining circuit values. Software for both companies will have to use carefully crafted step-by-step sequences for problems that include finding a customer in a list and calculating a voltage in a circuit with several components. In fact, you *could* solve these problems without a computer—but you still need to know the sequences. However, because the sequences often involve extensive repetition, it would be impractical to solve the problems without the fast processing operations provided by a computer.

ABOUT THIS CHAPTER

In this chapter we will briefly review algorithms, and then dive into some programming examples. For each example, we will describe the general principles of the algorithm the program illustrates. For the details, we will rely primarily on the comments in the program code. Different programs will also illustrate some new feature about Visual Basic that is useful and describe the general principles of the feature. (For more details, you can always use Visual Basic Help. Since Visual Basic is very rich in its capabilities, we hope that you have gained sufficient confidence with Visual Basic Help to explore the system and apply thorough detective work to discover other useful features. Appendix D also shows additional resources for tips and hints.) The programs and algorithms covered are

- **Alarm Clock:** This program illustrates a logic sequencing algorithm and state transitions. It also features useful functions for handling time and date data. We introduce the Timer control for handling events that are triggered by the passage of time.

- **Amortization Schedule:** This program generates a table illustrating payments one makes for a typical loan, such as a mortgage. The program illustrates a procedural calculation. It uses the Currency data type, which is useful for typical financial applications.

- **The Method of Least Squares:** This is another procedural calculation for a technical application like those used in science or engineering. It determines the straight line equation that best fits a collection of data measurements. The program also illustrates the `PSet` method for plotting points and more uses for the `Line` method.

- **The Generate Random Data Program:** Sometimes it is useful to generate test data that is random in nature. Random data would also be useful for developing games. This section describes the use of the random function `Rnd` and the list box control (Toolbox item ListBox), since both of these will be useful in some of the programs that are developed later in the chapter. With list box, items can be easily added (for view) or removed. It is also possible to highlight selected items that are listed in a list box control.

- **The Sequential Search Program:** This program determines whether and where a user-specified item can be found in a list of items. The algorithm would also be useful for office automation programs in which one would select Find from an Edit menu to determine where a word or phrase could be found in a document. The algorithm illustrates a repetitive trial-and-error process that either reveals the whereabouts of the item or indicates the absence of the item. This section also shows how to use variable-sized arrays when size requirements are not known. Last, it shows more uses for the list box control by highlighting an item listed in the control.

- **Binary Search:** The binary search algorithm uses fewer trial-and-error attempts to determine whether and where a user-specified item can be found in a list. However, the items in the list must arranged in order of smallest to largest or largest to smallest. This type of algorithm could be used in applications such as spell checking or finding the telephone number in an electronic telephone book.

- **Successive Approximation:** Successive approximation is used for technical calculations when it is not possible to simply plug numbers into a formula. However, it is possible to test whether an answer is correct. This algorithm is a process for guessing and testing the answer. It improves the guess until the answer is found. We use an electronic circuit modeling program to illustrate the algorithm. We introduce the combo box control (Toolbox item ComboBox). We can use the combo box to offer a choice of selections from which the user can choose. This section also illustrates the use of the Debug object for monitoring program execution.

- **The Selection Exchange Algorithm:** This is one of two algorithms we cover that will sort a list of items and reorder them from smallest to largest. The algorithm also illustrates a repetitive process. In this section, we use the string comparison function, `StrComp`, to compare items based on alphabetical instead of numerical order. This type of algorithm would be useful in a program that generates a list of clients for a business.

- **Bubble Sort:** This is the second of two algorithms that will sort a list of items. It shows another way to perform the same task.

7.1   WHAT IS AN ALGORITHM?

7.1.1   Overview

After analyzing a programming requirement, the programmer must develop a general solution. The general solution is the algorithm. We can write an algorithm in terms of pseudocode, a structure chart, a flow chart, or combinations of these problem-solving steps. (Section 2.2 discussed these steps; you may wish to review Section 2.2 now before proceeding.)

Remember that an algorithm is a step-by-step sequence to solve a problem in a fixed period of time. It describes *how* a computation is to be performed. As humans we are already familiar with algorithms. Many of us follow algorithm steps every day. Here are some examples:

- Preparing a meal

- Following traffic regulations when driving a car or riding a bike

- Playing a game

We don't think of the sequences involved as algorithms because we are already so familiar with the activity that we don't need to think about the steps. If you are a touch typist or an accomplished musician, you don't need to think about where the keys (strings, holes, or whatever) are. For those of us who are not accomplished in these fields, we would need to think explicitly about what key to press next. Preparing a meal is an algorithm because there are definite steps for obtaining the ingredients, processing the ingredients, and serving the ingredient mix (lost your appetite?). We wouldn't normally think about meal preparation in these terms. Despite how we think about it, though, the algorithm steps are definitely part of the process of meal preparation.

7.1.2   How to Develop an Algorithm

In Chapter 2 we looked at problem-solving steps. Sometimes a design simply falls into place after the requirements have been rigorously defined. A design *might* fall into place because of our own rich memory of experiences; often it is a matter of creative insight and making use of your own knowledge base or repertoire of similar algorithms. It is beyond the scope of this book to discuss creative problem solving, conceptual block busting, and other psychological aspects about how we think. However, we can add to the knowledge base of algorithm ideas. This chapter will give examples of some common algorithms. You will have to find your own creative method to adapt them for your own purposes. The following chapters will also illustrate some special-purpose algorithms to add to your personal collection of ideas.

7.2   AN ALARM CLOCK

Section 2.2.1 looked at an algorithm for a digital alarm clock. It showed the following algorithm to describe the steps for setting an alarm clock.

```
Press Alarm button
Toggle Hour button until desired hour setting is displayed
Toggle Minute button until desired minute setting is displayed
Release Alarm button
Set mode switch from normal to alarm
```

The algorithm describes the sequence for a typical alarm clock found in on average home. We will now show how to write a program that behaves similarly. For a real alarm clock, simply plug it in and follow the algorithm. If only programming were that simple.[1] As a guide for programming, this algorithm still displays some degree of ambiguity. Note that we should be able to implement the logic for *until* since we know about program statements for decision logic and repetition.

     The Alarm Clock program illustrates sequence logic. It also illustrates some neat Visual Basic features to handle time and date information. To visualize the system, we can design the visual layout. Figure 7.1 shows the layout for the program in design mode. The form more or less mimics a real digital alarm clock. The item that looks like an old-fashioned stopwatch is the Visual Basic *Timer control*. The Timer icon disappears in run mode, but it is very much alive, as we will see.

Figure 7.1
The Alarm Clock Program in Design Mode

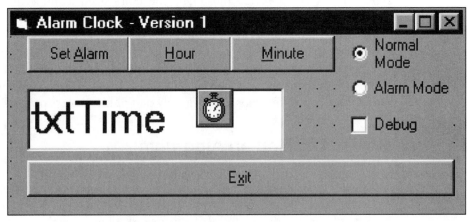

---

[1]*Maybe this is why professional Visual Basic programmers earn anywhere from $50,000 to $83,000. This is the salary range according to the February 1997 issue of* Visual Basic Programmer's Journal (VBPJ).

Now look at the earlier pseudocode. Can we use it? In a real alarm clock we can use one finger to hold down the Set Alarm button while pressing (toggling) the Hour and Minute buttons. Option buttons mimic a slider switch for setting the operating mode. With the form as shown, we are more or less limited to clicking with the mouse or pressing the corresponding access key. Hence we will have to modify the use of the Set Alarm button.

7.2.1   A Bit About State Transitions

Look at the keyboard of a typical computer. If you press the **CAPS LOCK** key, pressing **any alphabetic key** will generate capital letters. Pressing **it again** will turn off the feature. Thus the alphabetic keys behave differently, depending on their state (mode) of operation. Similarly, pressing the **NUM LOCK** key will permit the numeric keypad to generate numbers or cursor movements. Thus the keypad keys behave differently, depending on their state.

> A **state** is a description of a system that specifies how the system will behave depending on the order in which certain inputs occur. The crucial point is that a state of a system is dependent on the previous inputs (or input history).

In general, a system can have several states. Consider a traffic light system (see Table 7.1). Note that the traffic light, depending on its state, will behave differently for identical inputs. Each input causes a transition from one state to the next. The system proceeds from one state to the next (downward). When it reaches the final state, it returns to the first state and starts over again. State transitions are a useful way for describing systems. In our case, we can define two states for the Set Alarm button to mimic: holding it down and not holding it down. The state transition description can be fairly simple, as shown in Table 7.2.

Table 7.1
State Transition Example for Traffic Light Control

State: Lights Turned On	Input: Elapsed Time (Before Going to Next State)
East-West Green North-South Red	1 minute
East-West Yellow North-South Red	5 seconds
East-West Red North-South Red	3 seconds
East-West Red North-South Green	1 minute
East-West Red North-South Yellow	5 seconds
East-West Red North-South Red	3 seconds

Table 7.2
State Transitions for the
Set Alarm Button Action

State of the Alarm Clock System	Input: To Cause Transition to Next State
Permit and display alarm setting.	Click
Show actual time. Do not permit alarm setting changes.	Click

When the user clicks the button, the system just switches between the two states. For convenience, we will label the states as the On State and Off State, respectively. We can use an event procedure to recognize the click event applied to the button. In pseudocode we can express this as follows:

```
SetAlarmButton_Click

    If On State Then
        Processing to generate On State outputs
        State = Off State
    Else (If Off State Then)
        Processing to generate On state outputs
        State = On State
    End If
```

However, we need a mechanism for expressing the state as well as initializing it. One way is to use a Boolean flag variable that can be toggled `True` or `False`. Another way, as we will see in the final code, is to modify and use the Caption of the button. This is useful because the user will also see a visible indication of the state. *Never* forget the user!

7.2.2   The Timer Control

A Timer control can execute code at regular intervals by causing a Timer event. The Timer control, invisible to the user, is useful for background processing. In this case, we can cause the time display to change at one-second intervals. The Timer control only recognizes the Timer event. This event occurs when a preset interval for a Timer control has elapsed. The corresponding Timer event procedure tells a Visual Basic program what to do after each Timer control interval has elapsed. The interval's frequency is stored in the control's Interval property, which specifies the length of time in milliseconds. The Timer control's Enabled property specifies whether the control will respond to a Timer event. Whenever the Timer control's Enabled property is set to `True` and the Interval property is greater than zero, the Timer event waits for the period specified in the Interval property. If the Enabled property is `False`, the control ignores the Timer event. To trigger a Timer event every second, set the Enabled property to `True` and set the Interval property to 1000 (1,000 milliseconds).

7.2.3   The Date Data Type and Related Functions

The Date data type is used for expressing the date and time in year, month, day, hour, minute, and second. Consider the following code segment, which displays the time one hour ahead of the actual time in a message box. For example, if we ran the code segment at 12:06:05 PM, the message box would display 01:06:05 PM.

```
Dim dtTime As Date    ' Declare a date variable
dtTime = Time    ' Use Time function to get current system time
dtTime = dtTime + "01:00:00" ' Add one hour
MsgBox Format(dtTime, "hh:mm:ss AM/PM")
```

The prefix dt indicates that the variable is a date (and time) data type. The d prefix by itself indicates a Double data type (which we will use later in the chapter). We can perform arithmetic operations to add hours, minutes, and/or seconds by using the familiar hh:mm:ss format to express hours, minutes, and seconds. The Format function, among its other uses, recognizes certain date and time formats. (To find out more about Format, use Help to view information about the Format function.)

7.2.4   The Pseudocode

We can look at our general algorithm. Consider

- The visual appearance (see Figure 7.1)
- State transitions
- The Timer control
- The Date data type and related functions

The algorithm in pseudocode can look like Example 7.1.

Example 7.1

```
Form_Load   ' Initialize settings
    Call Timer_Timer to display initial time
    Alarm Setting = arbitrary valid value
    SetAlarm.Caption = "Release Alarm" and ...
        Call SetAlarm to set On State for alarm setting control

Timer_Timer    ' Timer event every second
    Time Display = Time        ' Display system time
    If Alarm Mode option True then call CheckAlarm

CheckAlarm
    If Time = Alarm Setting then Beep

SetAlarm_Click
    If Caption = "Set Alarm" (On State) Then
        Caption = "Release Alarm" 'State = Off State
        Disable Timer
        Time Display = Alarm Setting
        Enable Hour and Minute buttons
    Else If Caption = "Release Alarm" (Off State) Then
        Caption = "Set Alarm" 'State = On State
        Enable Timer
        Disable Hour and Minute buttons

Hour_Click
    If On State Then
        Alarm Setting = Alarm Setting + 1 hour
        Time Display = Alarm Setting
```

```
Minute_Click
    If On State Then
        Alarm Setting = Alarm Setting + 1 minute
        Time Display = Alarm Setting

Exit_Click
    End
```

Some of the logic is redundant. For example, SetAlarm_Click will only enable the Hour and Minute buttons for the On State; hence the Hour and Minute click procedures will be called only if the system is in the On State. The If Then statements in the Hour and Minute procedures are also redundant, but redundant code is useful for making the logic clearer to the programmer and to make revising or enhancing the program easier.

7.2.5   The Code for the Alarm Program

Now we will skip several stages of stepwise refinement to show one implementation in Example 7.2. The comments explain the principle of operation. (For more details about certain Visual Basic functions, refer to the online Help system.)

Example 7.2

```
' Alarm Clock Program - Version 1
' Program displays time and generates alarm beeps if set up
' Also illustrates use of VB features for using
' live data and time information based on
' computer system settings
' To set up alarm:
'    Click (Press) Alarm button
'    Click (Toggle) Hour button until desired hour setting is displayed
'    Click (Toggle) Minute button until desired minute setting is displayed
'    Click (Release) Alarm button
'    Set mode switch from normal to alarm

' Debug time feature for testing the clock
' Can remove it from production version of program
' Programmer can choose Debug feature using a check box
' It permits manual changes of time to be something other
' than the real system time
' Since this alarm clock is based on system settings,
' there is no time setting like in an off-the-shelf clock

Option Explicit

Const MSGTITLE = "Alarm Clock"   ' Title for error message box if used

' m_dtAlarmSetting defines the setting for an alarm
' Procedure CheckAlarm uses m_dtAlarmSetting to compare with actual time
' Procedure cmdSetAlarm_Click uses m_dtAlarmSetting for ➡
displaying the alarm setting to user
' Procedures cmdHour_Click and cmdMinute_Click modify the setting
Dim m_dtAlarmSetting As Date '
```

```
'
Private Sub Form_Load()
    ' Set up initial conditions for alarm clock program

    Dim sToday As String    ' Used for displaying date in Title Bar
    tmrTime_Timer    ' Display initial time

    ' Set up Caption to display date
    ' (There is no mechanism in this program to roll over
    ' the date if the program runs from one day to the next)
    sToday = Date
    frmAlarmClock1.Caption = "Alarm Clock  " & sToday & "  - V1"

    m_dtAlarmSetting = "07:00:00 AM"  ' Set up default alarm setting

    ' Set up initial settings for alarm mode control
    cmdSetAlarm.Caption = "Release &Alarm"  ' Need to be in On State
    cmdSetAlarm_Click    ' ... since this call will put it in Off State

    End Sub

Private Sub tmrTime_Timer()
    ' Generates the time display update every second
    ' (tmrTime.Interval = 1000 for 1000 ms)

    ' Static keyword means that this procedure will use the
    ' previous value from last call instead of re-initializing
    Static dtDebugTime As Date    ' For debugging and development only

    ' Under normal operation Debug choice is 0 (not selected)
    ' When selected, programmer can modify the time independent
    ' of actual system time to test program operation.
    ' Can modify debug time as follows.
    ' Select Debug choice, Break program, and put
    ' breakpoint in declaration statement tmrTime_Timer.
    ' Continue execution.  When break occurs, use
    ' the Debug window to assign dtDebugTime to any
    ' legal value, e.g. dtDebugTime = "1:34:00 PM"
    ' Then remove breakpoint and continue execution.
    ' From this point, alarm clock will use your fake debug time
    ' until you de-select the Debug choice.

    If chkDebug.Value = 0 Then  ' Using acutal system time
        txtTime.Text = Format(Time$, "hh:mm:ss AM/PM")
    ElseIf chkDebug.Value = 1 Then  ' ... or using debug time
        dtDebugTime = dtDebugTime + "00:00:01"
        txtTime.Text = dtDebugTime
    Else    ' In theory, we should never see chkDebug with a ➡
    value of 2
        MsgBox "We've got a problem"
        End
    End If
```

```
    ' If we are in alarm mode, generate alarm if
    ' the time is the same as the alarm setting
    If optAlarmMode.Value = True Then
        CheckAlarm
    ElseIf optNormalMode.Value = True Then
        ' No need to check alarm
    Else
        ' If neither is true something is seriously wrong
        MsgBox "We've got a problem here"
        End
    End If

End Sub


Sub CheckAlarm()
    ' Called by tmrTime_Timer every second if we
    ' are in the alarm mode.
    ' Checks if actual hour: minute same as alarm setting

    Dim bAlarm As Boolean    ' Flag to indicate alarm condition
    Dim sAlarmSetting As String ' Used for extracting hh: mm ➡
    portion of alarm setting
    Dim sTime As String ' Used for extracting hh:mm portion of actual time

    On Error Resume Next

    ' Get time from text box which can be real or debug time
    ' Note that we only need time to nearest minute
    sAlarmSetting = Format(m_dtAlarmSetting, "hh:mm AM/PM")
    sTime = Format(txtTime.Text, "hh:mm AM/PM")
    ' Set alarm flag if actual hh:mm = setting hh:mm
    If sTime = sAlarmSetting Then bAlarm = True

    If bAlarm Then Beep

    If Err.Number <> 0 Then ' Error handling if necessary
        MsgBox CStr(CVErr(Err.Number)) & " " & Err.Description, , MSGTITLE
    End If

End Sub


Private Sub cmdSetAlarm_Click()
    ' Mimics the functionality of holding down the Alarm button
    ' in order to change alarm time settings
    ' Hence the button represents two "states"
    ' On State:  In Alarm Setting Mode,
    ' Caption "Release &Alarm" cues user how to enter Off State
    ' Hour and Minute buttons available to user
    ' Off State: In Actual Time Display Mode,
    ' Caption "Set &Alarm" cues user how to enter On State
    ' Hour and Minute buttons now out of context (not available)
```

```
    ' Use button Caption to keep track of which state we are in

On Error Resume Next

If cmdSetAlarm.Caption = "Set &Alarm" Then
    cmdSetAlarm.Caption = "Release &Alarm"
    ' Disable Timer to prevent it from display actual time
    tmrTime.Enabled = False
    txtTime.Text = Format(m_dtAlarmSetting, "hh:mm AM/PM")
    cmdHour.Enabled = True
    cmdMinute.Enabled = True
ElseIf cmdSetAlarm.Caption = "Release &Alarm" Then
    cmdSetAlarm.Caption = "Set &Alarm"
    ' Enable Timer
    tmrTime.Enabled = True
    tmrTime_Timer    ' Update display right away
    cmdHour.Enabled = False
    cmdMinute.Enabled = False
Else    ' In theory, should never happen since nothing else ➥
"should" modify Caption
    MsgBox "We've got a problem"
End If

    ' The Else part just adds a bit of extra robustness to the code
    If Err.Number <> 0 Then ' Error handling if necessary
        MsgBox CStr(CVErr(Err.Number)) & " " & Err.Description, , MSGTITLE
End If

End Sub


Private Sub cmdHour_Click()
    ' Increment Hour alarm setting if Set Alarm clicked on
    ' (See cmdSetAlarm_Click)
    If cmdSetAlarm.Caption = "Release &Alarm" Then
        ' Add hour to setting
        m_dtAlarmSetting = m_dtAlarmSetting + "01:00:00"
        ' Show setting to user
        txtTime.Text = Format(m_dtAlarmSetting, "hh:mm AM/PM")
    End If

End Sub


Private Sub cmdMinute_Click()
    ' Increment Minute alarm setting if Set Alarm clicked on
    ' (See cmdSetAlarm_Click)
    ' Note that 59 + 1 resets Minute to 0 and causes Hour to increment
    If cmdSetAlarm.Caption = "Release &Alarm" Then
        ' Add minute to setting
        m_dtAlarmSetting = m_dtAlarmSetting + "00:01:00"
        ' Show setting to user
        txtTime.Text = Format(m_dtAlarmSetting, "hh:mm AM/PM")
    End If
```

```
End Sub


Private Sub cmdExit_Click()
    End
End Sub
```

The ability to use the actual system time is useful, but this makes program testing awkward. The issue of being able to test a program is very real. We would like to try the program for different time settings without having to wait or modify the system settings. The Debug feature allows this. We can remove the feature before compiling the program to make an executable file.

The MsgBox Function

The `MsgBox` function can have four arguments: The first argument is the message that appears in the body of the box; the second argument can specify buttons that appear in the body of the box (we omit the argument, so the default OK button appears in the message box); and the third argument specifies the text that appears in the Title Bar of the Message box. We don't need the fourth argument, which can be used to specify a help file to provide context-sensitive help. Recall that a function returns a value. In this case we are using the `MsgBox` function without using the value it returns.

7.3   AMORTIZATION SCHEDULE

An amortization schedule would interest anyone who had to or is still paying a mortgage or any other kind of loan. Perhaps Cougar Canoe needs to borrow a modest amount to assist with cash flow. The amount borrowed is the principal, and interest on the principal is charged at a yearly rate. Payments are usually due monthly: Each monthly payment pays off the accumulated interest; any portion remaining reduces the principal.

Figure 7.2 shows the program and an amortization table. The program shows the schedule of payments and illustrates the Currency data type and formatting features of Visual Basic. Each month's payment includes an interest portion that is the interest on the unpaid balance. For example, 10 percent of $2,000 divided by 12 (for monthly interest) is $16.67. The remainder of the monthly payment is the amortized amount. For example, $300 − $16.67 = $283.33. This amount goes to repay the loan by reducing the balance. In this case, $2,000.00 − $283.33 = $1,716.67. The payments continue until the remaining balance is less than or equal to the monthly payment. Monthly interest is charged on this amount. In this case, the monthly interest on $264.19 is $2.20 (see row No. 007 in Figure 7.2). The final payment is $264.19 + $2.20 = $266.39. The program also calculates the total interest. In this case, it will cost Cougar Canoe $66.39 to borrow $2,000.

7.3.1   The Pseudocode

Calculation of an amortization schedule requires

- Calculating interest and amortized portions of a monthly payment.

- Reducing the principal.

- Repeating the above until the last payment (balance < monthly payment).

Figure 7.2
The Amortization Program

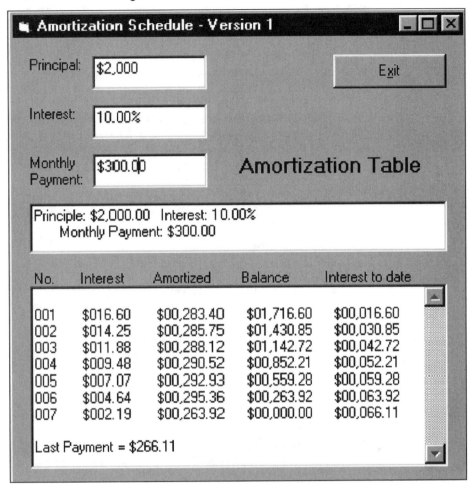

- Calculating the interest portion of the last payment.
- Determining when the last payment occurs.

Some basic input handling features also need to be determined. It would be convenient for the user to simply press **ENTER** in any of the Principal, Interest, or Monthly Payment boxes and see the change in the amortization table. Input validation should ensure that no sneaky person will try to make negative monthly payments in order to make money! Another possibility is that the monthly payments are too low to reduce the principal. One possible pseudocode is shown in Example 7.3.

Example 7.3

```
Form_Load
    Initialize default Principal, Interest Rate, Monthly Payment
    Generate Column Headings for Amortization Table
    Call AmortizationTable to generate default table

AmortizationTable
    ' This is the heart and soul of the program
    Get inputs Principal, Interest Rate, Monthly Payment
    Interest = Interest Rate / 100 / 12 ' monthly rate as a fraction
```

```
            Count = 0 ' Count is month number
            Accumulated Interest = 0
            Monthly Interest = Interest * Principal' First month's interest

            If Principal < 0 Or Interest Rate < 0 Or Monthly Payment < 0 Then
                Shame on tricky user
            Else If Monthly Interest < Monthly Payment Then ' Okay to proceed
                While Principal >= Monthly Payment
                    Count = Count + 1
                    Monthly Interest = Interest * Principal
                    Amortized Amount = Monthly Payment - Monthly Interest
                    Principal = Principal - Amortized Amount
                    Accumulated Interest = Accumulated Interest + Monthly ➡
                    Interest
                    Display Count, Monthly Interest, Amortized Amount, ...
                        Principal, Accumulated Interest
                Loop
                Count = Count + 1
                Monthly Interest = Interest * Principal
                Principal = 0
                Display Count, Monthly Interest, Amortized Amount, ...
                    Principal, Accumulated Interest

        Else    ' Monthly payments too low
            Warning, warning! The payments are too low, do you want ➡
            to go broke?

    Principal_, Interest Rate_, Monthly Payment_KeyPress
            When ENTER pressed, call AmortizationTable

    Principal_, Interest Rate_, Monthly Payment_Change
            Clear the results to cue user that input change ➡
            invalidates last result

    Exit_Click
            End
```

7.3.2   The Currency Data Type

The Currency data type is useful for calculations involving money and for fixed-point calculations in which accuracy is particularly important. The CCur function converts an expression to a currency. In fact, you can use your own local currency. Use the Windows control panel to select your locale setting. This will set up the appropriate thousands separators and other currency options. The Format function also recognizes Currency as a predefined format style. Consider the following segment of code. When the user clicks on the form, the Print method will display the output on the form.

```
Private Sub Form_Click()
    Dim cMoney As Currency
    Dim fMoney As Single

    fMoney = 12.345678 * 100 / 12
    cMoney = CCur(fMoney)
    fMoney = fMoney + fMoney
```

```
        cMoney = cMoney + cMoney
        Print cMoney, fMoney    ' Prints 205.7614 205.7613
        Print Format(cMoney, "Currency"), Format(fMoney, ➡
        "Currency")      ' Prints $205.76 $205.76
End Sub
```

7.3.3   The Code for the Amortization Program

We now skip several stages of stepwise refinement to show one implementation in Example 7.4. The comments explain the operation. You might want to investigate the use of the Space function for setting the spacing of the outputs. (For more details about certain Visual Basic functions, refer to the online Help system.)

Example 7.4

```
' Amortization Program
' Generates an amortization table given a loan, yearly interest rate, and
' monthly payment.  The table shows the reduction in the principal (balance),
' the monthly interest component, principal paid component, and ➡
the accumulated
' interest for each month until the loan is paid off
' User inputs the data.  Upon pressing ENTER in any of the input boxes,
' the program calls Sub AmortizationTable to generate the table

Option Explicit
Const MSGTITLE = "Amortization Schedule"      ' used for Message Box
Const LF = 10    ' Line feed
Const CR = 13    ' Carriage Return
Private Sub Form_Load()
    Dim sColHead As String

    ' Initialize some default values
    txtPrincipal.Text = "$2,000"
    txtInterest.Text = "10.00%"
    txtPayment.Text = "$250.00"
    txtAmortization.Text = ""
    txtAmortization.Locked = True
    txtAmortHead.Locked = True

    ' Column headings for amortization table
    sColHead = " No." & Space(7) & "Interest" & Space(8) & ➡
    "Amortized" & Space(8) & "Balance"
    sColHead = sColHead & Space(10) & "Interest to date"
    lblAmortHead.Caption = sColHead

    AmortizationTable   ' Generate default amortization schedule
End Sub


Sub AmortizationTable()
    ' Does the main work for this program.  It generates the amortization
    ' table.  Called by Form_Load and any time the user presses ENTER
    ' (a KeyPress event when KeyAscii is the ENTER key code)
```

```
Dim fPrincipal As Single  ' Initial principal
Dim fInterest As Single, sInterest As String   ' Interest rate
Dim cPayment As Currency   ' Monthly Payment
Dim sTitle1 As String, sTitle2 As String   ' User for ➡
summary information
Dim sAmortization As String  ' Buffer to store table output ➡
in progress
' When procedure near completion we assign txtAmortization.Text ➡
to sAmortization
Dim nCount As Integer   ' Number of payments
Dim cMonthlyInt As Currency ' Monthly interest
Dim cAccumulatedInt As Currency ' Accumulated interest
Dim cAmortized As Currency  ' Monthly Amortized Amount
Dim sCRLF As String ' Carriage return and line feed
Dim sMonthly As String ' To hold string for monthly status

sCRLF = Chr(CR) & Chr(LF)   ' New line for next monthly ➡
payment display

' Generate the Amortization Table
On Error Resume Next

fPrincipal = CCur(txtPrincipal.Text)
' Parse % from interest
sInterest = Trim(txtInterest.Text)
If Right(sInterest, 1) = "%" Then
    sInterest = Left(sInterest, Len(sInterest) - 1)
End If
fInterest = CSng(sInterest) ' Now have numerical interest
cPayment = CCur(txtPayment.Text)

' Convert % interest to decimal
fInterest = fInterest / 100

' Generate summary information for user
sTitle1 = "Principal: " & Format(fPrincipal, "Currency")
sTitle1 = sTitle1 & "   Interest: " & Format(fInterest, "Percent")
sTitle2 = "      Monthly Payment: " & Format(cPayment, "Currency")

txtAmortHead.Text = sTitle1 & sCRLF & sTitle2 & sCRLF

' Convert interest to monthly rate
fInterest = fInterest / 12

' Some explicit initialization even though VB defaults ➡
numeric variables to zero
nCount = 0
cMonthlyInt = 0
cAccumulatedInt = 0

' Need to account for monthly payments too low to reduce principal
' and if user tries to trick us by using negative inputs
```

```
        cMonthlyInt = CCur(fInterest * fPrincipal)
        If fPrincipal < 0 Or fInterest < 0 Or cPayment < 0 Then
            txtAmortization.Text = "No no, negative inputs are not allowed!"
        ElseIf cMonthlyInt < cPayment Then
            ' Okay to calculate amortization
            ' ... otherwise balance will increase instead of paid off

            Do While fPrincipal >= cPayment
                nCount = nCount + 1
                cMonthlyInt = fInterest * fPrincipal
                cAccumulatedInt = cAccumulatedInt + cMonthlyInt
                cAmortized = cPayment - cMonthlyInt
                fPrincipal = fPrincipal - cAmortized
                sMonthly = Format(nCount, "000") & Space(7) & Format ➡
                (cMonthlyInt, "$000.00")
                sMonthly = sMonthly & Space(7) & Format(cAmortized, ➡
                "$00,000.00")
                sMonthly = sMonthly & Space(6) & Format(fPrincipal, ➡
                "$00,000.00")
                sMonthly = sMonthly & Space(6) & ➡
                Format(cAccumulatedInt, "$00,000.00")
                sAmortization = sAmortization & sCRLF & sMonthly

            Loop      ' Done one iteration for monthly status

            nCount = nCount + 1 ' Count last payment
            cMonthlyInt = fInterest * fPrincipal ' Interest on last payment
            'cAccumulatedInt = cAccumulatedInt + cMonthlyInt    ➡
            Accumulate interest last time
            cAmortized = fPrincipal ' Amortized amount = last balance
            fPrincipal = 0   ' Balance is now zero, loan paid off

            sMonthly = Format(nCount, "000") & Space(7) & ➡
            Format(cMonthlyInt, "$000.00")
            sMonthly = sMonthly & Space(7) & Format(cAmortized, ➡
            "$00,000.00")
            sMonthly = sMonthly & Space(6) & Format(fPrincipal,➡
            "$00,000.00")
            sMonthly = sMonthly & Space(6) & ➡
            Format(cAccumulatedInt, "$00,000.00")

            sAmortization = sAmortization & sCRLF & sMonthly

            ' Add last payment
            sAmortization = sAmortization & sCRLF & sCRLF & "Last ➡
            Payment = " & Format(cAmortized +_ cMonthlyInt, "currency")
            txtAmortization.Text = sAmortization

        Else      ' Situation when monthly payment too low

            sAmortization = sAmortization & sCRLF & "First month's ➡
            interest is " & Format(cMonthlyInt,_ "currency")
            txtAmortization.Text = sAmortization
        End If
```

```vb
        If Err.Number <> 0 Then ' Error handling if necessary
            MsgBox CStr(CVErr(Err.Number)) & " " & Err.Description, ➥
            , MSGTITLE
            txtAmortization.Text = ""    ' Clear amortization table ➥
            since it is not valid
        End If

    End Sub


    Private Sub txtPrincipal_KeyPress(KeyAscii As Integer)
        If KeyAscii = vbKeyReturn Then
            KeyAscii = 0
            AmortizationTable
        End If
    End Sub


    Private Sub txtInterest_KeyPress(KeyAscii As Integer)
        If KeyAscii = vbKeyReturn Then
            KeyAscii = 0
            AmortizationTable
        End If
    End Sub


    Private Sub txtPayment_KeyPress(KeyAscii As Integer)
        If KeyAscii = vbKeyReturn Then
            KeyAscii = 0
            AmortizationTable
        End If
    End Sub


    Private Sub txtPrincipal_Change()
        txtAmortization.Text = ""    ' Cue user that input changed
        txtAmortHead.Text = ""
    End Sub


    Private Sub txtInterest_Change()
        txtAmortization.Text = ""    ' Cue user that input changed
        txtAmortHead.Text = ""
    End Sub


    Private Sub txtPayment_Change()
        txtAmortization.Text = ""    ' Cue user that input changed
        txtAmortHead.Text = ""
    End Sub


    Private Sub cmdExit_Click()
        End
    End Sub
```

7.4   The Method of Least Squares

The Coyote Electronics Company needs to determine some component values. They have experimentally plotted the relationship between input and output signals, and the points seem to fit a straight line. A component value could be determined by finding the slope of the straight line that best fits the plotted points. Even with non-linear electronic circuits, a straight line can model a portion of a component's behavior, a signal gain and signal bias. Figure 7.3 illustrates the Least Squares Line Fitting program and the best straight line to fit the points.

The program shown in Figure 7.3 looks suspiciously like the Area Calculation Program from Figure 6.10. In fact, we will use some of the same principles for this program. The equation for each point on a straight line is

$$y = mx + b$$

where y represents the point's vertical coordinate, m represents the slope or gain (the ratio of vertical travel to horizontal travel), x represents the point's horizontal coordinate, and b represents an offset or bias. When we need to fit a straight line, we have the points with the X and Y coordinates. The problem is to find the slope m and offset b that best fit the straight line. The general algorithm is

Set N as the total number of points
Set SumXY as the sum of the xy products for each point (i.e., $x_1y_1 + x_2y_2 + ... + x_Ny_N$)
Set SumY as the sum of the y coordinates (i.e., $y_1 + y_2 + y_3 + ... + y_N$)
Set SumX as the sum of the x coordinates (i.e., $x_1 + x_2 + x_3 + ... + x_N$)
Set SumX^2 as the sum of the square of the x coordinates (i.e., $x_1^2 + x_2^2 + ... + x_N^2$)

Figure 7.3
The Least Squares Program Line Fitting Program

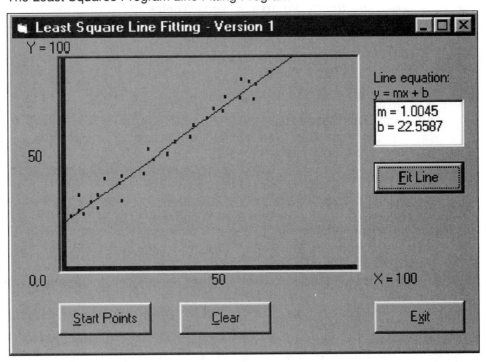

To determine the slope, use the following equations:

```
Denominator =   N SumX² - SumX SumY
m = (N SumXy - SumX SumY) / Denominator
b = (SumX² SumY - (SumX)²) / Denominator
```

7.4.1   The Pseudocode

We have the basic equations for determining the slope m and offset b. An initial pseudocode could be

```
Obtain X, Y points
Calculate and display m, b
Plot y = mx + b
```

Example 7.5 shows a refinement of this pseudocode. The form and some procedures may be similar to the Area Calculation program (see Section 6.6).

Example 7.5

```
Form_Load
    Initialize Picture Box properties
    Flag Start Points = False
    N = 0      ' Point Count

StartPoints_Click
    Draw axis
    Flag Start Points = True

Graph_MouseDown
    ' Record the points
    If Start Points = True Then
        N = N + 1
        Y(N) = Y position
        X(N) = X position
        Plot Point


FitLine_Click
    ' Actually use method of least squares here
    For Counter = 1 to N
        SumXY = SumXY + X(Counter) * Y(Counter)
        SumY = SumY + Y(Counter)
        SumX = SumX + X(Counter)
        SumX2 = SumX2 + X(Counter)^2
    Next Counter
    Denominator = N * SumX2 - (SumX)^2
    m = (N * SumXY - SumX * SumY) / Denominator
    b = (SumX2 * SumY - SumX * SumXY) / Denominator

    Plot y = mx + b    ' Will work out details later

Clear_Click
```

```
        Clear picture box
        N = 0
        Flag Start Points = False

    Exit_Click
        End
```

7.4.2   The Visual Basic PSet and Line Methods

The pseudocode does not describe how to plot the points or the straight line. It turns out that this is really easy with a picture box. The `PSet` method draws a point on an object such as a picture box. The following statement is used in procedure `picGraph_Mouse-Down` to draw a point at the point where the user clicked. Remember that the Mouse-Down event passes the mouse pointer coordinates as X and Y.

```
picGraph.PSet (X, Y)     ' Plots the point
```

The `Line` method will draw a line on an object such as a picture box. All you need to specify are the *X, Y* coordinates of the end points. For example, in the Area Calculation program in Section 6.6, we drew the axis as follows:

```
picGraph.Line (0, 100)-(0, 0)    ' Draw vertical axis
picGraph.Line (0, 0)-(100, 0)    ' Draw horizontal axis
```

We can draw the straight line once we have the slope (*m*) and offset (*b*). Since the equation is $y = mx + b$, all we need to do is to substitute some values:

$$\text{When } x = 0, y = b$$
$$\text{When } x = 100, y = 100m + b$$

Thus we can use the `Line` method with the two points. We can also draw the line with a different color. To specify a color, we can use the `QBColor` function as the optional third argument for the `Line` method:

```
picGraph.Line (fStartX, fStartY)-(fEndX, fEndY), QBColor(4)
```

The argument of 4 for `QBColor` specifies the color red. Use VB Help to find out how to set other colors with `QBColor`.

7.4.3   The Code for the Least Squares Program

We now skip several stages of stepwise refinement to show one implementation in Example 7.6.

Example 7.6
```
' Least Squares Program to fit "best" straight line for a set of points
' It finds the slope (m) and offset (b) given experimental points
' The straight line equation is y = mx + b
' User clicks Start Plot to begin recording experimental points
' User clicks in graph area (picGraph) to record each point
' (Actually we use the MouseDown event, not the Click event)
' User clicks Fit Line, and the program lauches cmdFitLine_Click
```

```
' to do the main work.  It determines m and b and plots the ➥
straight line.
' User can subsequently click Clear to start again.

Option Explicit

Dim m_nCount As Integer ' Keeps track of number of points
Dim m_fY(200) As Single ' Y coordinate of all points
Dim m_fX(200) As Single ' X coordinate of all points
' Flag whether in mode to click in points on graph
Dim m_bStartFlag As Boolean
Const LF = 10    ' Line feed
Const CR = 13    ' Carriage Return

' For version 2, could add display showing point coordinates
' using Mouse_Move event

Const MSGTITLE = " Least Squares Line Fit"

Private Sub Form_Load()
    ' Set up initial conditions upon launch of program
    picGraph.ScaleMode = 0  ' Set custom scale
    picGraph.Scale (-1, 101)-(101, -1)
    picGraph.AutoRedraw = True  ' Repaint graphics if ever another window
    ' covers this one, or we have minimized it
    ' This is redundant but it is good to explicitly state initialization
    m_nCount = 0

    ' Prevent user from plotting before clicking Start Plot
    m_bStartFlag = False

End Sub

Private Sub cmdStartPoints_Click()
    ' When user clicks this button, we display the axis
    ' and permit the user to plot a new set of points

    On Error Resume Next

    picGraph.DrawWidth = 4
    picGraph.Line (0, 100)-(0, 0)     ' Draw vertical axis
    picGraph.Line (0, 0)-(100, 0)   ' Draw horizontal axis
    picGraph.DrawWidth = 2  ' Make dots reasonably prominent

    ' Flag that it is okay to click in points
    m_bStartFlag = True

    If Err.Number <> 0 Then ' Error handling if necessary
        MsgBox CStr(CVErr(Err.Number)) & " " & Err.Description, ➥
        , MSGTITLE
        txtLine.Text = ""    ' Clear result since it is not valid
    End If

End Sub
```

```
Private Sub picGraph_MouseDown(Button As Integer, Shift As ➡
Integer, X As Single, Y As Single)
        ' Using MouseDown event to record user mouse clicks on
        ' the picture box and to display points to be fitted by straight line

        On Error Resume Next    ' In case user goes hog-wild and ➡
        clicks forever

        If m_bStartFlag Then  ' Flag to permit point plotting only ➡
        when user clicked Start Plot
            If m_nCount < 0 Then
                MsgBox "Error.  Negative count occurred", , MSGTITLE
                End ' Terminate program if this happens, shouldn't ➡
                have negative count!
            Else
                ' Record point and draw point using X, Y
                m_nCount = m_nCount + 1   ' Increment count for ➡
                next click by user
                m_fY(m_nCount) = Y ' Record Y coordinate
                m_fX(m_nCount) = X ' Record X coordinate
                picGraph.PSet (X, Y)    ' Plots the point
            End If
        End If  ' End of m_bStartFlag check

        If Err.Number <> 0 Then ' Error handling if necessary
            MsgBox CStr(CVErr(Err.Number)) & " " & Err.Description, ➡
            , MSGTITLE
            txtLine.Text = ""   ' Clear line text since it is not valid
        End If

End Sub


Private Sub cmdFitLine_Click()
        ' Procedure that does the main work to fit a straight line
        ' using the method of least squares
        ' Line equation is y = mx + b ; [fy = fm * fx + fb]
        ' Hence this procedure finds line paramters m and b given ➡
        set of x, y points
        ' and subsequently plots the line

        ' Line equation variables (lowercase convention for mathematical ➡
        variables)
        Dim fy As Single, fm As Single, fx As Single, fb As Single

        Dim fStartX As Single, fStartY As Single    ' Start point ➡
        for final line plot
        Dim fEndX As Single, fEndY As Single    ' End point for ➡
        final line plot

        ' Intermediate variables used in least squares technique
        '  m_nCount is the total number of points
        Dim nCount As Integer   ' Local counter used to calculate the following
        Dim fSumXY As Single    ' Sum of all X * Y products for each point
```

```vb
        Dim fSumY As Single ' Sum of all the Ys
        Dim fSumX As Single ' Sum of all the Xs
        Dim fSumX2 As Single    ' Sum of all the X^2s
        Dim fTemp As Single ' Temporary scratchpad for a bit of optimization

        Dim sCRLF As String ' Carriage return and line feed

        On Error Resume Next

        sCRLF = Chr(CR) & Chr(LF)   ' New line for text to display ➡
        m, b line parameters

        ' Okay, let's get to work ...
        ' Find values of intermediate variables
            ' (local variable initial values are zero)
        For nCount = 1 To m_nCount Step 1
            fSumXY = fSumXY + m_fX(nCount) * m_fY(nCount)
            fSumY = fSumY + m_fY(nCount)
            fSumX = fSumX + m_fX(nCount)
            fSumX2 = fSumX2 + m_fX(nCount) ^ 2
        Next nCount

        ' Find the slope m and the offset b
        fTemp = m_nCount * fSumX2 - fSumX ^ 2    ' Divisor is same for both
        fm = (m_nCount * fSumXY - fSumX * fSumY) / fTemp
        fb = (fSumX2 * fSumY - fSumX * fSumXY) / fTemp

        ' Found the line parameters, now display it
        txtLine.Text = "m = " & Format(fm, "##0.####") & sCRLF
        txtLine.Text = txtLine.Text & "b = " & Format(fb, "##0.####")

        ' Determine start and end point of line in order to plot it
        fStartX = 0
        fStartY = fb
        fEndX = 100
        fEndY = fm * fEndX + fb
        ' Now plot the final line
        picGraph.DrawWidth = 1  ' Can also set style if desired
        picGraph.Line (fStartX, fStartY)-(fEndX, fEndY), QBColor(4)

        ' Prevent user from adding more points until Start Points clicked.
        m_bStartFlag = False    ' Prevent further points added

        If Err.Number <> 0 Then ' Error handling if necessary
            MsgBox CStr(CVErr(Err.Number)) & " " & Err.Description, ➡
            , MSGTITLE
            txtLine.Text = ""   ' Clear result since it is not valid
        End If

End Sub


Private Sub cmdClear_Click()
        ' Clear the plot
```

```
        picGraph.Cls
        picGraph.DrawWidth = 1  ' Let other procedures modify width ➡
        of graphics
        ' Must reset points
        m_nCount = 0  ' Cleared count but old points still remain
        m_bStartFlag = False
        txtLine.Text = ""    ' Clear Area to cue user

End Sub


Private Sub cmdExit_Click()
    End
End Sub
```

7.5   THE GENERATE RANDOM DATA PROGRAM

The Generate Random Data program is actually a necessary measure to develop another program. Cougar Canoe needs to be able to locate a customer from a list of customers. In order to develop a program to accomplish that, we need to have a customer list with which to test the program. One way to create the test data is to be able to generate a list. It would be best to use a list with random alphabetic sequences which could then mimic a typical list of names, cities, or any other information. We will develop a random data generator, which we can then build upon for use in developing the other programs. Figure 7.4 shows the program in action; we admit that it doesn't seem too exciting. Use the scroll bar to select the number of items. The user clicks Seed New List to generate a new list of characters. We could adapt the principle to create interesting games of chance, such as Roll the Dice and Blackjack. Perhaps Cougar Canoe could use the program as a basis for creating an online lottery system to entice customers. In the case of Figure 7.4, the user clicked one of the list items to select it.

This sounds fine, but how do we generate a random character? Good, you figured it out: Use Visual Basic Help to see if there is a way to generate a random character. After some resourceful detective work, we would find information about the Rnd function.

7.5.1   The Random Function: Rnd

To illustrate this function and the related Randomize function, we will use a simple program that simulates rolling one die. The program is a bare-bones form. Simply click on the form. A message box will show a value between 1 and 6. Click **OK** and click **the form** again. Another value between 1 and 6 will appear. Repeat the process.

Example 7.7

```
Private Sub Form_Load()
    'Initialize the random-number generator with a
    ' seed based on the system timer
    Randomize
End Sub
```

Figure 7.4
Program to Generate
Random Characters

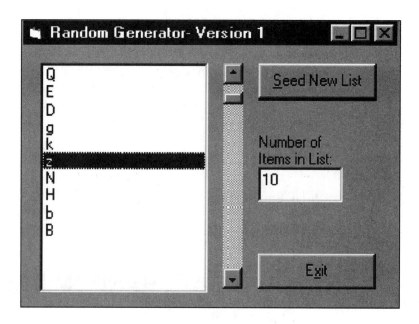

```
Private Sub Form_Click()
    ' Generate random value between 1 and 6
    MsgBox Int((6 * Rnd) + 1)
End Sub
```

Before calling Rnd, the program uses the Randomize statement (without an argument) to initialize the random-number generator with a seed based on the system timer. A *seed* is an initial value used to generate pseudo-random numbers. For example, the Randomize statement creates a seed number used by the Rnd function to create unique pseudo-random number sequences. The Rnd function returns a value less than 1 but greater than or equal to 0. The first call to Rnd will generate a number based on the seed generated by Randomize. Each successive call to the Rnd function uses the previous number as a seed for the next number in the sequence.

To understand why a seed is necessary for generating a random sequence, let's look at how the Rnd function operates. For example, begin with any four-digit number (the seed) and square it. The middle four digits will be a pseudo-random number. Square this four-digit number and extract the four middle digits from the result. Square this four-digit number. Repeat the process to generate more four-digit numbers. The sequence will appear random in that the sequence follows no apparent predictable order. (We don't know whether this is the exact method used by Visual Basic's Rnd function, but it would be similar.) It scales the generated number to something between 0 and 1, such as dividing the four-digit result by 10,000. To generate a sequence in other integer ranges, use the following formula:

Int((*upperbound* - *lowerbound* + **1) * Rnd** + *lowerbound***)**

where *upperbound* is the highest number in the range, and *lowerbound* is the lowest number in the range.

In this case, we use the Randomize and Rnd functions without arguments. It is possible to use arguments to repeat a random sequence. Visual Basic Help explains the details.

7.5.2 The Pseudocode

Example 7.8 shows a possible pseudocode. We have rocketed past several phases of program development.

Example 7.8
```
ItemCount_Change/Scroll
    Item Count text = ItemCount value

Seed_Click
    'Clean up former list if applicable
    ' Generate new list
    Do While List Count < ItemCount value
        Random Integer = Rnd scaled between ASCII code for "A" to "z"
            ' note some codes in range are for [ \ ¦ ^ _ `
        If Random Integer is a letter Then
            Character = Chr(Random Integer)
            List Count = List Count + 1
            List(List Count) = Character
        End If
    Loop
```

We still need to determine some details, such as how to clean up a new list and how to handle the list itself. This is where we introduce another useful Visual Basic control, the list box.

7.5.3 The List Box Control

A list box control displays a list of items from which the user can select one or more. The selected item appears highlighted. If the number of items exceeds the number that can be displayed, a scroll bar is automatically added to the list box control. The list box contains a string array in which each element is a list item. The Project window in Visual Basic behaves like a list box (see Figure 1.9 or 1.10). We do not need the highlighting feature for this program. However, highlighting will prove useful when we need to search for an item in the list. If the item is found, the program will highlight it in the list. (Remember that the reason for developing a random generator program is to provide test data for a search program.)

Like any typical control, the list box supports various properties, events, and methods. In this case we are interested in the ListCount property and the AddItem and RemoveItem methods. ListCount returns the number of items in the list. To add or delete items in a list box control, use the AddItem or RemoveItem methods. Consider the following code segment:

```
lstItem.AddItem "Bert"    ' Item 0
lstItem.AddItem "Barny"   ' Item 1
lstItem.AddItem "Ernie"   ' Item 2
lstItem.RemoveItem 1      ' Remove Barny and Ernie becomes Item 1
MsgBox lstItem.ListCount   ' Should see two items: Bert, Ernie
```

The message box will display the number 2. To use the AddItem method, specify a string that will be added. To use the RemoveItem method, specify an integer that identifies the item number. This is actually the ListIndex property. The first item in the list is ListIndex 0, and the value of the ListCount property is always one more than the largest ListIndex value. We can imagine that more sophisticated operations are possible, such as inserting and removing selected list items, but we will leave these operations until later.

7.5.4   The Code for the Random Generator Program

Example 7.9 shows the code for this program. Note that `vsbItemCount` refers to the vertical scroll bar control shown Figure 7.4. A vertical scroll bar reacts to events in the same way as a horizontal scroll bar.

Example 7.9

```
' Random Generator Program
' Generates sequence of random characters.  The sequence
' length is set by the user within a limit of 1 to 200
' (Min to Max settings of vsbItemCount)
' Uses the Rnd function seeded by the System Time
' Displays sequence of characters in a list box (lstItem).

Option Explicit
Const MSGTITLE = "Random Generator"

Private Sub Form_Load()
    ' Initialize appearance based on default scroll bar setting
    vsbItemCount_Change
End Sub

Private Sub vsbItemCount_Change()
    ' Set number of items in list and show user
    txtItemCount.Text = CStr(vsbItemCount.Value)
End Sub

Private Sub vsbItemCount_Scroll()
    vsbItemCount_Change
End Sub

Private Sub cmdSeed_Click()
    ' Does the work to remove earlier list (if applicable)
    ' then generates and displays new list of random characters

    Dim nCount As Integer    ' Keep track of characters in list
    Dim nChar As Integer     ' Character ASCII code to be ➡
    randomly generated

    On Error Resume Next

    ' Clean up old list after first time, note ListCount is 0 ➡
    first time
    For nCount = 1 To lstItem.ListCount
        lstItem.RemoveItem 0
    Next nCount

    Randomize    ' Seed random generator based on system time

    nCount = 0
    Do While nCount < vsbItemCount.Value
        nChar = Int((122 - 65 + 1) * Rnd + 65)  ' Generate ➡
        random character
        If nChar < 91 Or nChar > 96 Then      ' Only add letters
```

```
                    lstItem.AddItem Chr(nChar)
                    nCount = nCount + 1
            End If
        Loop

        If Err.Number <> 0 Then ' Error handling if necessary
            MsgBox CStr(CVErr(Err.Number)) & " " & Err.Description, ➡
            , MSGTITLE
            'txtLine.Text = ""    ' Clear result since it is not valid
        End If

End Sub


Private Sub cmdExit_Click()
    End
End Sub
```

The ASCII codes for letters *A* to *z* range from 65 to 122. However, we also need to eliminate characters with ASCII codes 92 to 95 (characters [, \, |, ^, _, and `). List items are added and removed during runtime. In fact, it is only possible to add and remove list box items using program code. Now we can use the coding technique in this program to test our next program.

7.6   THE SEQUENTIAL SEARCH PROGRAM

Recall that Cougar Canoe needs a program that can search a list of customers to find and/or update the information. Here we will look at the basic sequential search algorithm, which illustrates a brute-force technique. (Later we will look at more elegant and sophisticated techniques.) Figure 7.5 shows the program in action. The user selected 43 items and clicked Seed New List to generate the test sequence. In this case, the random generator is more sophisticated. The sequence consists of multicharacter strings, although none seem to match a word in any known human language. The user types in the character sequence and presses **ENTER** or clicks **Find**. If the character sequence is not in the list, the program displays a message box stating that the item is not in the list. In this case, the item is in the list, so the program highlights the item.

7.6.1   The Algorithm

This technique uses a crude process:

```
Get item for which to look
Start at beginning of the list
Compare list item with item for which to look
If they are the same, then mark the spot
Otherwise, repeat the process with the next item in the list
Continue until the item is found or we have reached the end of the list
Tell the user where the item is (if found) or that it was not found
```

The algorithm is known as sequential search because items are checked in a linear sequential order from start to finish.

Figure 7.5
Sequential Search Program

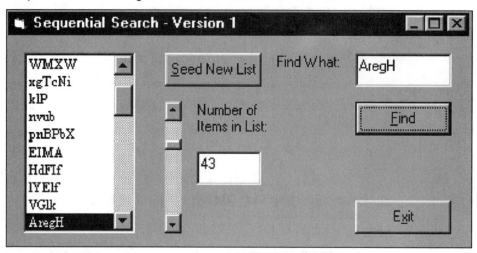

7.6.2   The Pseudocode

Actually, we have already stated a first-level pseudocode when describing the algorithm. Now we need to be more specific in describing the algorithm. Find Item is what the user types in for the search.

Example 7.10

```
Find_Click
    List Count = first item index
    Repeat While Find Item <> List(List Count) And List Count ➡
    <= Number Of Items
        List Count = List Count + 1
    End Loop
    If List Count > Number Of Items Then
        Item not found
    Else
        Found item is List(List Count)
    End If
```

For the sake of brevity, we will omit other necessary pseudocode for the program, such as the generation of random character sequences. Instead, we will show them in the final code.

7.6.3   Static and ReDim

The program will also illustrate two keywords. We used `Static` earlier in the Alarm program of Example 7.2. We use it if we want a local variable to retain its previous value when the procedure is called again. `ReDim` is useful for resizing arrays. The program will use an array of strings. The list length is limited by the maximum value the user can scroll. However, when we declare an array, Visual Basic will reserve a specific amount of memory: If we don't use all of the array elements, the memory space is wasted. In our small program, this isn't a big deal, but it will be problem if we need to scale up the program to handle a much larger data set. For the sake of preserving memory, we would like to use only the memory that is needed. To dynamically size an array, we declare it as usual but do not specify the size. However, the ReDim statement must be used to specify a size prior to accessing any array element. The program code, to follow, will illustrate the use of ReDim for variable-sized arrays.

7.6.4 The Selected Property

The Selected property returns or sets the selection status of an item in a file list box or list box control. This property is an array of Boolean values with the same number of items as the List property. The property setting is only available during runtime. Normally, a program uses the Selected property to find out what a user has selected from a list box. In this case, we will do the reverse. The program will set the Selected property of an item (if found) to True. This will highlight the item (see Figure 7.5). It will reveal where the found item is located to the user.

7.6.5 The Code for the Sequential Search Program

Here is the final code. Check out how the random character sequences are generated.

Example 7.11

```
' Sequential Search Program
' Find element in a list of elements if it exists

' User clicks Seed New List to generate a randomly
' created list for demonstration purposes
' User can enter search criteria and program
' will show where on list item is or display
' message that item not found

' Note it may be useful to set Font property of lstItem
' to something with serifs such as Times Roman
' With sans serif fonts it may be difficult to
' tell lowercase L from capital I and other similarities

Option Explicit
' Need flag to prevent cmdSeed_Click from attempting
' to clean up a nonexistent list (first time it is invoked)
' and to prevent cmdFind to look for items when cmdSeed_Click
' has not been invoked yet.  The first cmdSeed_Click call
' will set the flag True.
Dim m_bStartOnce As Boolean

Const MSGTITLE = "Sequential Search"

Private Sub Form_Load()
    vsbItemCount_Change
End Sub
```

```vb
Private Sub vsbItemCount_Change()
    txtItemCount.Text = CStr(vsbItemCount.Value)
End Sub

Private Sub vsbItemCount_Scroll()
    vsbItemCount_Change
End Sub


Private Sub cmdSeed_Click()
    Dim nCount As Integer
    Dim sChar As String * 1 ' Character to be randomly generated
    Dim nChar  As Integer    ' Character ASCII code to be randomly ➥
generated
    Dim sItem As String ' Next list item to be randomly generated, a ➥
pseudoword
    ' Number of list items can vary but we need to keep track of how
    ' many items there were the last time the list was seeded
    Static nItemCount As Integer      ' Static keyword to ➥
preserve values between calls
    ' Static bStartOnce As Boolean
    Dim sItems() As String     ' Dynamically sized array
    ReDim sItems(vsbItemCount.Value) ' Size it

    On Error Resume Next

    ' Clean up old list except for one item after first time
    If m_bStartOnce = True Then
        For nCount = 1 To nItemCount
            lstItem.RemoveItem 0
        Next nCount
    End If

    Randomize    ' Seed random generator based on system time

    nCount = 0  ' Initialize to start loop
    Do While nCount < vsbItemCount.Value
        lstItem.AddItem nCount
        sItem = BuildWord()
        lstItem.List(nCount) = sItem
        sItems(nCount) = sItem   ' Add to word list we will search
        nCount = nCount + 1
    Loop

    nItemCount = nCount ' Record number of items for next call ➥
to this procedure
    ' Print lstItem.ListCount
    ' Flag that we have completed procedure at least once
    m_bStartOnce = True

    If Err.Number <> 0 Then ' Error handling if necessary
        MsgBox CStr(CVErr(Err.Number)) & " " & Err.Description, ➥
        , MSGTITLE
    End If
```

```
End Sub


Function BuildWord() As String
    ' Return a randomly generated set of alphabetic characters
    ' Perhaps the name BuildWord is inappropriate because
    ' it is improbable that result will be a word defined in the
    ' dictionary

    Dim nCharCount As Integer, nChar As Integer
    Dim sWord As String

    nCharCount = 1
    Do While nCharCount <= WordLength
        nChar = Int((122 - 65 + 1) * Rnd + 65)   ' Generate ➡
        random character
        If nChar < 91 Or nChar > 96 Then      ' Only add letters
            sWord = sWord & Chr(nChar)
            nCharCount = nCharCount + 1
        End If
    Loop

    BuildWord = sWord

End Function



Function WordLength() As Integer
    ' Return a random length for random "word" to be generated
    WordLength = Int((8 - 3 + 1) * Rnd + 3)
End Function


Private Sub txtFind_KeyPress(KeyAscii As Integer)
    ' Performs sequential search to find first item if user ➡
    presses ENTER
    If KeyAscii = vbKeyReturn Then
        KeyAscii = 0
        cmdFind_Click
    End If
End Sub

Private Sub cmdFind_Click()
    ' Performs sequential search to find first item if user ➡
    clicks this button
    Dim nCount As Integer

    On Error Resume Next

    If m_bStartOnce = True Then
        While txtFind.Text <> lstItem.List(nCount) And ➡
        nCount <= lstItem.ListCount
            nCount = nCount + 1
        Wend
        If nCount > lstItem.ListCount Then
```

```
                     ' Message box using Exclamation Icon
                     MsgBox "Search text is not found", ➥
                     vbExclamation, MSGTITLE
                Else
                     lstItem.Selected(nCount) = True
                End If
           End If

           If Err.Number <> 0 Then ' Error handling if necessary
                MsgBox CStr(CVErr(Err.Number)) & " " & ➥
                Err.Description, , MSGTITLE
           End If

     End Sub


     Private Sub cmdExit_Click()
           End
     End Sub
```

7.7   BINARY SEARCH

The sequential search algorithm is necessary for something like a word processor application. The user will sometimes need to find occurrences of specific words or phrases in
a long document. A typical word processor will have a Find menu item. The program
will have to search the document text sequentially. Consider how we would look up a
word in a dictionary or find someone's telephone number in a telephone book: We
would make use of the alphabetic order. Typical information systems store data in either
an alphabetic or a numerical order. If the data is stored in a sorted order, we can use a
more efficient search technique. The binary search program will work with a random
list that is also sorted. The program looks similar to the Sequential Search program
shown in Figure 7.5. In fact, the user wouldn't notice the difference unless he or she
reads the Title Bar and notices that the list items are ordered alphabetically, or if the user
has very long lists, since this program works much more quickly.

7.7.1   The Binary Search Algorithm

The binary search algorithm makes use of the fact that items are listed in a sequential
order from smallest to largest or vice versa. This technique uses the following process
(assuming order from smallest to largest):

```
Get item for which to look
Start at middle of the list
Compare list item with item for which to look
If they are the same then mark the spot
If item to look for is larger, then discard lower half of list ➥
and repeat process for upper half
If item to look for is smaller, then discard upper half of list ➥
and repeat process for lower half
Continue until the item is found or we have reached the end of the list
Tell the user where the item is or that it was not found
```

The key is that we do not need to check every item. Figure 7.6 illustrates the technique for a list of nine items that could represent telephone area code numbers. In the first iteration, the item halfway down the list is compared to the item being looked for (in this case, 604). Since the number 514 is found, the item (if it exists) must be in the higher half, because 604 is larger than 519. In the second iteration, item 7 is checked since it is at the midpoint. The higher index number is arbitrarily used as the midpoint if there is an even number of items to check. It doesn't matter, as long as we are consistent throughout the entire process. Since the number 709 is found, the item (if it exists) must be in the lower half of the remaining list portion (604 is smaller than 709). In the third iteration, item 6 is checked since it is at the midpoint (again arbitrarily assigned as the higher number with an even number of items). Since number 702 is found, the process repeats to look again in the lower half of the remaining portion (609 is smaller than 702). However, the remaining portion is now reduced to one item. If the item exists, it is found. Failure to find the item once the list portion is reduced to one means that the item is not in the list.

7.7.2   The Pseudocode

Example 7.12 shows the pseudocode for the algorithm.

Example 7.12

```
Find_Click
    Lower Bound = 0
    Upper Bound = List Count
    Search Done = False
    Found = False

Do Until (Search Done = True) Or (Found = True)
    Current = (Upper Bound - Lower Bound) /2
    If Item = List(Current) Then ' Found item
        Found = True
    Else If Item > List(Current) Then ' Look in upper half next
        Lower Bound = Current + 1
    Else
        Upper Bound = Current - 1 ' Look in lower half next
    End If
    If Lower Bound > Upper Bound Then
        Search Done = True   ' List has been searched
    End If
Loop
```

7.7.3   The Code for the Binary Search Program

Example 7.13 shows the code for procedure cmdFind_Click and function BuildWord. The rest of the program, except for one line in cmdSeed_Click, is the same as the sequential search program shown in Example 7.11. The modification to BuildWord is necessary in order to generate the random list in alphabetic order. Procedure cmdSeed_Click calls the function with the statement

```
sItem = BuildWord(nCount + 65) ' Used in binary search program
```

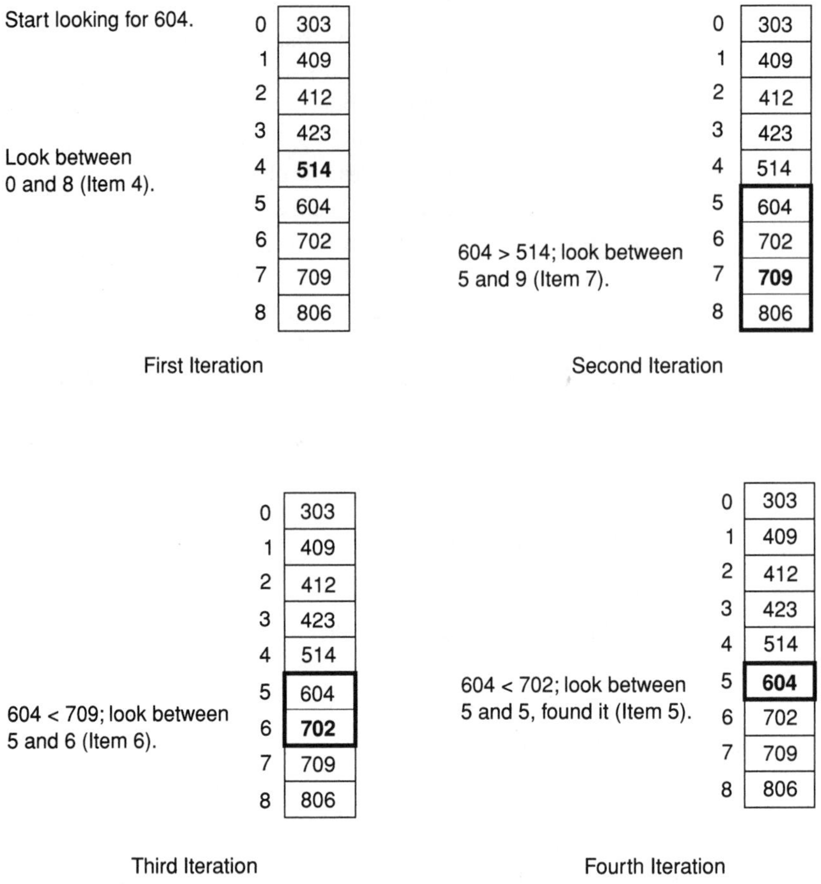

Figure 7.6
Binary Search Example

Start looking for 604.

First Iteration		Second Iteration	
0	303	0	303
1	409	1	409
2	412	2	412
3	423	3	423
4	**514**	4	514
5	604	5	604
6	702	6	702
7	709	7	**709**
8	806	8	806

Look between 0 and 8 (Item 4).

604 > 514; look between 5 and 9 (Item 7).

First Iteration

Second Iteration

Third Iteration		Fourth Iteration	
0	303	0	303
1	409	1	409
2	412	2	412
3	423	3	423
4	514	4	514
5	604	5	**604**
6	**702**	6	702
7	709	7	709
8	806	8	806

604 < 709; look between 5 and 6 (Item 6).

604 < 702; look between 5 and 5, found it (Item 5).

Third Iteration

Fourth Iteration

instead of

```
sItem = BuildWord() ' ... was used in sequential search program
```

In this program, the first character of each item is sequential and unique. The rest of the characters are random. Since nCount + 64 must correspond to an ASCII code, it was necessary to limit the maximum list size to 51 (vsbItemCount.Max = 51).

Example 7.13

```
Private Sub cmdFind_Click()
    ' Performs binary search to find item
    Dim nLB As Integer, nUB As Integer  ' Lower and Upper bound
    ' lstItem.ListCount is Number of elements in list
    Dim nCurrent As Integer ' Pointer to current position
    ' txtFind.Text is search value
    Dim bFlag As Boolean     ' Indicate whether list searched
    Dim bFound As Boolean    ' Indicate whether item found or not
    Dim nIteration   ' Iteration Counter to illustrate number of attempts

    On Error Resume Next

    If m_bStartOnce = True Then ' Search only if list exists

        nLB = 0 ' Initial lower bound at beginning of list
        nUB = lstItem.ListCount ' Initial upper bound at end of list
```

```
            bFlag = False    ' Haven't completed search (haven't even begun!)
            bFound = False    ' Search item not found yet (if ever)
            ' Continue search until item is found or entire list searched
            Do Until (bFlag = True) Or (bFound = True)
                nIteration = nIteration + 1 ' Counting iterations for illustration
                nCurrent = Int((nLB + nUB) / 2) ' find midpoint between bounds
                If lstItem.List(nCurrent) = txtFind.Text Then
                    bFound = True     ' Means item found and we can exit loop
                ElseIf txtFind.Text > lstItem.List(nCurrent) Then
                    nLB = nCurrent + 1  ' Means item could be in upper ➥
                    half of list section
                Else
                    nUB = nCurrent - 1  ' Means item could be in lower ➥
                    half of list section
                End If

                If nLB > nUB Then bFlag = True   ' List has been searched

        Loop

        If bFound = False Then
            ' Message box using Exclamation Icon
            MsgBox "Search text is not found", vbExclamation, MSGTITLE
        Else
            lstItem.Selected(nCurrent) = True
        End If

        ' Display number of iterations
        txtIteration.Text = CStr(nIteration)
    End If

    If Err.Number <> 0 Then ' Error handling if necessary
        MsgBox CStr(CVErr(Err.Number)) & " " & Err.Description, , ➥
        MSGTITLE
        End If

End Sub


Function BuildWord(nStartChar As Integer) As String
    ' Return a generated set of alphabetic characters
    ' starting with the ASCII code specified by nStartChar
    ' Perhaps the name BuildWord is inappropriate because
    ' the result will not be a word defined in the dictionary

    Dim nChar As Integer
    Dim sWord As String

    For nChar = 0 To WordLength - 1 ' Length is random
        sWord = sWord & Chr(nChar + nStartChar)
    Next nChar

    BuildWord = sWord

End Function
```

We have also added another enhancement. Text box `txtIteration` shows the user how many times the loop was repeated. This shows that relatively few iterations are required. The maximum number of iterations for a list of 51 items is 6. Consider that $51/2 = 26$, $26/2 = 13$, $13/2 = 7$, $7/2 = 4$, $4/2 = 2$, and $2/1 = 1$. Each iteration cuts the search space by two. The algorithm is named a *binary search* due to this halving sequence. Use the binary search algorithm to search for an item in a sorted list. Later in this chapter, we will look at algorithms to perform sorting to create a sorted list from an unsorted one.

7.8   SUCCESSIVE APPROXIMATION ALGORITHM

The successive approximation algorithm can be used to solve some complex math equations. In principle it is similar to a binary search. However, iterations can continue for a long time, since it is in effect hunting for an answer that is *close enough* to satisfying an equation. Since computers are good at handling complex mathematics, this section will demonstrate some mathematical modeling capabilities. For some, the math in this section may be complex or even completely new. Not everyone has to understand the details of mathematics or electronics; the background explanation in this section should be sufficient to guide you through this application of math and electronics.

7.8.1   The Diode Circuit Application

*An electronic circuit uses the flow of electrons to do work. The fundamental characteristics of a circuit are voltage, current, and resistance. **Voltage** refers to the force applied to electrons, such as that supplied by a battery. **Current** refers to the amount of electron flow. **Resistance** is a characteristic that limits current given an applied voltage. By definition, resistance = voltage ÷ current.*

Remember Coyote Electronics? They are designing a portable geographic positioning system. It so happens that Cougar Canoe is interested in selling it in their retail outlets. During the circuit design phase, it is necessary to model the behavior of a circuit using a program. Typically, an electronic circuit uses nonlinear components—outputs are not proportional to inputs. In this section, we will model a circuit with one nonlinear component. The program will calculate circuit voltage and current values (see Figure 7.7). This program will illustrate one specific technical application; however, there are many applications involving nonlinear equations, such as economic forecasting and models of ecological systems.

The form shows a schematic diagram of the circuit being modeled. The triangular symbol with a line is a diode.[2] The symbol at the top is a resistor. The two parallel lines symbol at the left is the voltage supply, and the bottom left symbol represents the ground. The user inputs the source voltage, a resistor value, and a tolerance (which we will explain in a moment). The program calculates the voltage at the connection between the resistor and the diode. It also calculates the current through both components. Current is shown in

---

[2] *The symbol for a diode is normally filled in. Although Visual Basic does have polygon controls that can be filled in, the triangle isn't available. An alternative is to use an image, but we kept it simple by constructing the symbol using line objects.*

milliamperes (mA), and the resistor value is shown in ohms. If you have electronics experience, you are probably aware that the voltage at the diode should be approximately 0.7 volts. (After working with the program, you will appreciate the reason why this approximation is used.) Now, let's look at the equations that model the circuit:

$$I_D = I_S(e^{\frac{V_D}{nV_T}} - 1)$$

$$I_R = \frac{V_{Source} - V_D}{R}$$

I_D represents the current through the diode.
I_R represents the current though the resistor.
V_D represents the voltage at the junction between the diode and the resistor.
The resistor value (resistance) is R.
Diode constants are $nV_T = 25.7$ millivolts and $I_S = 0.1$ pico-amperes.
In this circuit the same current must flow through the resistor and the diode. Hence the program needs to solve the following equation:

$$I_R = I_D \quad \text{or} \quad I_R - I_D = 0$$

The e in the first equation above represents the exponential function that happens to describe many natural phenomena. If you are unfamiliar with it, just note that it is nonlinear. For example, $e^{0.5} = 1.6487212707$, $e^1 = 2.718281828459$, $e^2 = 7.389056098931$, and $e^3 = 20.08553692319$. You can see how rapidly the function grows for small increases of the exponent.

7.8.2   The Algorithm

Imagine we are on a wilderness canoe trip, and we need to determine distance using a triangulation technique. Let's say that nobody brought a calculator or laptop computer.

Figure 7.7
Diode Circuit Program

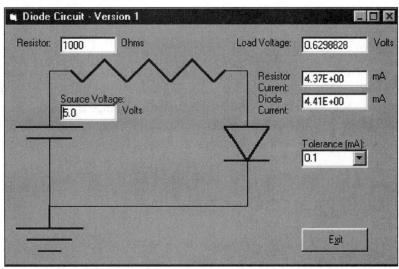

To do a manual calculation of distance using triangulation, we need to find the square root of a number. Let's say we need to find the square root of 60: We must solve for x in the following equation:

$$x^2 = 60 \quad \text{or} \quad x^2 - 60 = 0$$

How could we do it? We would have to use a trial-and-error guessing procedure. The process could go something like this:

Guess between 0 and 60 that x = 60 ÷ 2 = 30
Try: $30^2 = 900$
This is much too large; x must be less than 30.
Guess between 0 and 30 that $x = 30 \div 2 = 15$
Try: $15^2 = 225$
This is still too large; x must be less than 15.
Guess between 0 and 15 that $x = 15 \div 2 = 7.5$
Try: $7.5^2 = 56.25$
This is too small; x must be larger than 7.5.
Guess between 7.5 and 15 that $x = (15 + 7.5) \div 2 = 11.25$.
Try: $11.25^2 = 126.26$
This is too large; x must be less than 11.25.
Guess between 7.5 and 11.25 that $x = (11.25 + 7.5) \div 2 = 9.375$
Try: $9.375^2 = 87.89$
This is too large; x must be less than 9.375.
Guess between 7.5 and 9.375 that $x = (9.375 + 7.5) \div 2 = 8.4375$
Try: $8.4375^2 = 71.19$
We continue the process until we feel we are close enough (when guess^2 = 60).

The general nonlinear equation is: $f(x) - y = 0$. We can describe an algorithm for solving x when given y as follows:

```
Max = y
Min = 0
    x = (Max + Min) / 2
    Evaluate f(x)
    If f(x) > y then Max = x
    If f(x) < y then Min = x
Repeat Try Until f(x) is close enough to y
```

This is similar to the binary search, except that the binary search is crisp: The item is found, or it is determined that the item is not in the list. The successive approximation search does use a strategy of dividing the search range by 2, but it is not as cut-and-dried as the binary search. With successive approximation applications, the program may repeat iterations for a long time, depending on how close the approximation must be.

7.8.3   The Pseudocode

Example 7.14 shows the pseudocode for the main part of the program that implements the algorithm.

Example 7.14

```
FindVdiode
    If Vsource >= 0 And Resistor > 0 then     ' Use only valid ➡
    positive values
        Tol is the tolerance entered by user
        Vsource is the source voltage entered by user
        Resistor is the resistor value entered by user
        Max = Vsource  ' Initial search limits
        Min = 0
        Do
            Guess = (Max + Min) /2
            Ir = (Vsource - Guess) / Resistor     ' Guess ➡
            resistor current
            Id = Is * (Exp(Vd/nVt) - 1)     ' Guess diode current
            Error = Ir - Id
            If Error <= -Tol Then Max = Guess
            If Error >= Tol Then Min = Guess
        Loop Until Absolute Value of Error < Tol
        Vd = Guess
        Display Id, Ir, Vd
    Else If Vsource > 0 and Resistor = 0 Then
        Warn user about short circuit     ' Would burn out fuse
    Else (negative inputs)
        Warn user that this model does not handle negative values
    End If
```

The program will use the combo box control to permit the user to select a tolerance from a list of tolerances. It will also use the Debug object for illustrating some problematic aspects of numerical accuracy. Hence we will explain both objects before showing the final code.

The Double Data Type

Due to the numeric precision required, we use Double-type variables. The Double data type is a double-precision floating-point value stored as a 64-bit (8-byte) floating-point number. The range is $-1.79769313486232 \times 10^{308}$ to $-4.94065645841247 \times 10^{-324}$ for negative values and from $4.94065645841247 \times 10^{-324}$ to $1.79769313486232 \times 10^{308}$ for positive values.

7.8.4   The ComboBox

A combo box control combines the features of a text box control and a list box control. Users can enter information in the text box portion, or select an item from the list box portion, of the control. In our case, users will only select a tolerance. Figure 7.7 shows the combo box for selecting Tolerance in milliamperes (mA). In Figure 7.7, note that the difference between resistor current and diode current is less than the tolerance. Figure 7.8 shows the combo box after the user has clicked the arrow and made another selection.

The combo box recognizes the Click event. We will use this event procedure to call FindVdiode. Thus when the user clicks on the arrow and selects one of the items from the list, the program will recalculate the results. We will make use of the List and ListIndex properties. The ListIndex property returns or sets the index of the currently selected item in the control. It is an integer. The List property returns or sets the items to which the ListIndex refers. It is a String.

Let's try to make sense of this by using an example: Let's say the combo box control is named cboTol. Furthermore, let's say that the combo box is set up to show the eight selections shown in Figure 7.8. There is also a ninth selection that will become visible when the user scrolls down the list. The ListIndex and List properties in this example are as follows:

ListIndex	List (String Quotations Not Shown)
0	0.1
1	0.01
2	0.001
3	0.0001
4	0.00001
5	0.000001
6	0.0000001
7	1E-08 (Visual Basic formats number in scientific notation.)
8	1E-09 (Visual Basic formats number in scientific notation.)

The program will use a variable of type Double named dTol, which we can assign as follows:

```
' Get Tolerance from user selection in combo box
dTol = CDbl(cboTol.List(cboTol.ListIndex)) * 10 ^ -3
```

Let's say that the user selected the fourth item, as shown in Figure 7.8. When the user makes the selection, the program automatically assigns cboTol.ListIndex to 3 (fourth item when counting from 0). Hence the expression cboTol.List (cboTol.ListIndex) evaluates to cboTol.List(3). The setting of the List property is a string. In this case, it is the fourth string (0.0001), which is the item referred to by subscript (or index) 3. The CDbl function converts this string to the equivalent number as a Double. The factor 10^-3 converts mA to Amperes.

Figure 7.8
Using the ComboBox
Control

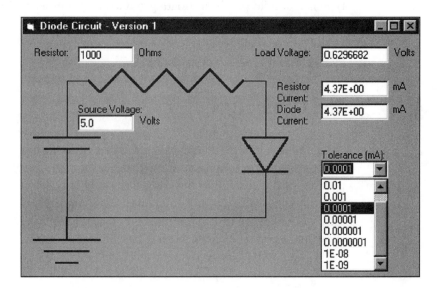

7.8.5   Troubleshooting: The Debug Object

The Debug object sends output to the Debug window at runtime. It has no properties or events, and it only supports the Print method. For example, we could display the results of interim execution with something like this:

```
Debug.Print "nCount, nFactorial"
nFactorial = 1
For nCount = 1 To 7 ' 7!
    nFactorial = nFactorial * nCount
    Debug.Print nCount, nFactorial
Next nCount
```

When executed, the following appears in the immediate pane of the Debug window:

```
nCount, nFactorial
1               1
2               2
3               6
4               24
5               120
6               720
7               5040
```

This might be useful when developing and debugging a program. The programmer can see how program execution progresses, but the debug statements would be removed prior to the final compilation.

7.8.6   The Code for the Diode Circuit Program

Finally, this is how this program is implemented:

Example 7.15

```
' Diode Circuit Program
' Demonstrates Trial and Error Search Technique
' to find solution to a nonlinear equation

' In this case, try to solve for V when
' (Vs - V)/R = Is * (exp(V/nVt) - 1)
' given the other parameters
' This models a simple circuit with a resistor and a diode
' In practice, electronic designers would assume
' the voltage across diode is 0.7 volts.
' This program shows a more accurate value

Private Sub Form_Load()
    txtVs.Text = "5.0"      ' Initial default inputs
    txtR.Text = "1000"

    Dim nIndex As Integer
    ' Tolerance selections in mA
    For nIndex = 0 To 8 Step 1
        cboTol.AddItem CStr(CSng(10 ^ -(nIndex + 1)))
    Next nIndex
```

```
                    cboTol.ListIndex = 0      ' Default tolerance
                    FindVdiode      ' Find and display results using initial ➡
                    defaults

                End Sub

                ' Procedure FindVdiode has comments to explain the technique

                ' User types in Vs, R and selects a calculation tolerance
                ' Program calls FindViode in response to these input changes
                ' and displays result of voltage (V) and
                ' current through the diode (Id) and the resistor (Ir)
                ' Currents should be the same but we can only get close
                ' to being the same

                Option  Explicit

                ' Message title when message box displays runtime error
                ' if one should occur
                Const MSGTITLE = "Diode Circuit"


                Sub FindVdiode()
                    ' This procedure does the main work to solve
                    ' for V (voltage across diode) for the equation
                    ' (Vs - V)/R = Is * (exp(V/nVt) - 1)
                    ' Search for V using a repeated trial-and-error process
                    ' Initally guess V as halfway between Vs (max limit) and 0 ➡
                    (min limit)
                    ' Try Ir = (Vs - V) / R ; current through resistor
                    ' Try Id = Is * (exp(V/nVt) - 1) ; current through diode
                    ' If Ir is equal to Id then we guessed V correctly
                    ' If Ir < Id then we guessed too low and V must be higher ➡
                    than guess
                    '     Set max limit as old guess
                    ' If Ir > Id then we guessed too high and V must be lower ➡
                    than guess
                    '     Set min limit as old guess
                    ' Make a new guess as halfway between max limit and min limit
                    ' Repeat the guessing process until Ir is approximately equal to Ir
                    ' It is not possible to get an exact match due to numerical
                    ' precision limits

                    Dim dVs As Double, dR As Double ' Source voltage and ➡
                    resistor value
                    Dim dTol As Double  ' Tolerance that specifies how close ➡
                    the match needs to be
                    Dim dMax As Double, dMin As Double ' Max and Min limits for the search
                    Dim dV As Single     ' Voltage across the diode
                    Dim dIr As Double, dId As Double     ' Current through ➡
                    resistor and diode
                    Dim dGuess As Double     ' The guess for V that will be updated
                    Dim dError As Double     ' The difference between Ir and Id ➡
                    to determine
                                             ' when match is close enough
```

```
On Error Resume Next

' Get voltage source and resistor values
' from user entries in text boxes
dVs = CDbl(txtVs.Text)
dR = CDbl(txtR.Text)

' Get Tolerance from user selection in combo box
dTol = CDbl(cboTol.List(cboTol.ListIndex)) * 10 ^ -3

' Debug --- Remove from final version
'Debug.Print "Diode Circuit Test ", Time

' Now the fun begins.
' Look for V using a trial and error search
' to find V when Ir and Id are equal
' or ¦Ir - Id¦ < Tol

If dVs >= 0 And dR > 0 Then ' Okay to use search algorithm
            ' User values are physically possible
    ' Initialize search limits
    dMax = dVs
    dMin = 0
    Do
    ' Debug --- Remove from final version
    'Debug.Print "Max and Min"
        'Debug.Print dMax, dMin

        dGuess = (dMax + dMin) / 2  ' Guess halfway between limits
        dIr = (dVs - dGuess) / dR   ' Resistor current ➡
        based on guess
        dId = 0.0000000000001 * (Exp(dGuess / 0.0257) - 1)  ➡
        ' Diode current based on guess
        dError = dIr - dId  ' Find out how close we are to ➡
        true voltage
        If dError < -dTol Then dMax = dGuess     ' Guess too ➡
        high, look next in lower half
        If dError > dTol Then dMin = dGuess ' Guess too ➡
        low, look next in upper half

        ' Debug --- Remove from final version
        'Debug.Print "Ir and Id"
        'Debug.Print dIr, dId
    Loop Until Abs(dError) < dTol  ' Keep looking until we ➡
    are close enough

    dV = dGuess ' Got the final voltage
    txtV.Text = CStr(dV)     ' Display voltage
    txtId.Text = Format(dId * 1000, "Scientific") ' ➡
    Display diode current in mA
    txtIr.Text = Format(dIr * 1000, "Scientific") ' ➡
    Display resistor current in mA
```

```
            ElseIf dVs = 0 And dR >= 0 Then   ' Dead circuit
                txtV.Text = 0    ' Display all outputs as zero
                txtId.Text = 0
                txtIr.Text = 0

            ElseIf dVs > 0 And dR = 0 Then   ' Short-circuit condition
                MsgBox "Oops, short circuit, we just blew up the diode"
                CueUser ' Clear outputs

            Else     ' Shame on user for trying negative values
                MsgBox "Negative Vs or R not allowed"
                CueUser ' Clear outputs
            End If

            If Err.Number <> 0 Then ' Error handling if necessary
                MsgBox CStr(CVErr(Err.Number)) & " " & ➡
                Err.Description, vbCritical, MSGTITLE
                CueUser ' Clear outputs if applicable
            End If
        End Sub

    Private Sub cboTol_Click()
        ' Generate new result when user selects tolerance
        FindVdiode
    End Sub


    Private Sub txtR_Change()
        ' Blank out results when modifies resistor input
        CueUser
    End Sub

    Private Sub txtR_KeyPress(KeyAscii As Integer)
        ' Generate new result when user presses ENTER at Resistor
        If KeyAscii = vbKeyReturn Then
            KeyAscii = 0
            FindVdiode
        End If
    End Sub

    Private Sub txtVs_Change()
        ' Blank out results when modifies voltage source input
        CueUser
    End Sub

    Private Sub txtVs_KeyPress(KeyAscii As Integer)
        ' Generate new result when user presses ENTER at Voltage ➡
        Source
    If KeyAscii = vbKeyReturn Then
        KeyAscii = 0
        FindVdiode
    End If

End Sub
```

```
Sub CueUser()
    ' Cue user by blanking out answers
    ' if any input data is changed
    txtV.Text = ""
    txtId.Text = ""
    txtIr.Text = ""
End Sub


Private Sub cmdExit_Click()
    End
End Sub
```

The following shows an example of interim outputs displayed in the Debug window when the single quotes are removed from the Debug.Print statements. Note how the Max and Min values get progressively closer together. Also note that although the initial difference between If and Id is very high, they do converge as they get closer together.

```
Diode Circuit Test              8:13:45 PM
Max and Min
    5               0
Ir and Id
    0.0025          1.76418827842463E+29
Max and Min
    2.5             0
Ir and Id
    0.00375         132822749.498143
Max and Min
    1.25            0
Ir and Id
    0.004375        3.64448555341976E-03
Max and Min
    1.25            0.625
Ir and Id
    0.0040625       695.751817622317
Max and Min
    0.9375          0.625
Ir and Id
    0.00421875      1.59237478256827
Max and Min
    0.78125         0.625
Ir and Id
    0.004296875     7.61799638411857E-02
Max and Min
    0.703125        0.625
Ir and Id
    0.0043359375                    1.66624361269261E-02
Max and Min
    0.6640625       0.625
Ir and Id
    0.00435546875                   7.79268937850303E-03
Max and Min
    0.64453125      0.625
```

```
Ir and Id
    0.004365234375              5.3291972999993E-03
Max and Min
    0.634765625    0.625
Ir and Id
    0.0043701171875             4.40706053636515E-03
```

A nonzero tolerance is necessary. We can try to use a zero tolerance by modifying the loop condition as follows:

```
Loop Until dError = 0
```

The result is that the loop will go on forever. Eventually, the smallest possible error will be found, but due to fixed precision, it will not be zero. There is no data type that is stored using an infinite number of bits. (The Hands-On Exercises in this chapter are the best place to investigate this further.)

7.8.7   Improve the Numerical Accuracy

The diode circuit program of Example 7.15 usually works like a charm. However, if we try small source voltage values such as 0.1 volts, the differences between the two currents are significant unless the user notices and tries smaller tolerances. For example, with the following inputs,

Source Voltage = 0.1 Volts
Resistor = 1000 Ohms
Tolerance = 0.1 mA

the outputs are

Load Voltage = 0.05 Volts
Resistor Current = 5.00E-02 mA
Diode Current = 6.00E-10 mA

The difference between the two currents is significant. The problem is that the current values are even smaller than the tolerance. If we make the tolerance too small for larger currents, however, the error of current difference may never get small enough to stop the loop. It is possible to predict the magnitude of the current based on the inputs. Another solution is to modify the tolerance if the resulting currents are larger than the tolerance. Repeat the process until the tolerance is smaller than the current. All we need to do is to modify the code for general procedure FindVdiode. Example 7.16 shows this modification.

Example 7.16

```
Sub FindVdiode()
    ' See Example 7.15.  This version modifies the tolerance
    ' when currents get smaller than the tolerance
    Dim dVs As Double, dR As Double
    Dim dTol As Double
    Dim dMax As Double, dMin As Double
    Dim dV As Single
    Dim dIr As Double, dId As Double
    Dim dError As Double, dGuess As Double
    Dim nCount As Integer
```

```
On Error Resume Next

' Get voltage source and resistor values
' from user entries in text boxes
dVs = CDbl(txtVs.Text)
dR = CDbl(txtR.Text)

' Get Tolerance from user selection in combo box
dTol = cboTol.List(cboTol.ListIndex) * 10 ^ -3

' Now the fun begins.
' Look for V using a trial-and-error search
' to find V when Ir and Id are equal
' or ¦Ir - Id¦ < Tol

If dVs >= 0 And dR > 0 Then ' Okay to use search algorithm
    ' Initialize search limits
    dMax = dVs
    dMin = 0

    dTol = dTol * 10    ' Compensate for first time in loop
    ' If necessary adjust tolerance in case currents very low
    Do
        dTol = dTol / 10  ' Reduce tolerance every time ➡
        through the outer loop
        Do
            ' Guess halfway between limits
            dGuess = (dMax = dMin) / 2
            ' Resistor current based on guess
            dIr = (dVs - dGuess) / dR
            ' Diode current based on guess
            dId = 0.0000000000001 * (Exp(dGuess / 0.0257) - 1)
            ' Find out how close we are to true voltage
            dError = dIr - dId
            ' Guess too high, look next in lower half
            If dError < -dTol Then dMax = dGuess
            ' Guess too low, look next in upper half
            If dError > dTol Then dMin = dGuess
        ' Keep looking until we are close enough
        Loop Until Abs(dError) < dTolare close enough
    Loop Until dTol < dIr And dTol < dIr  ' Repeat outer loop ➡
    until tolerance small enough

    dV = dGuess ' Got the final voltage
    txtV.Text = CStr(dV)     ' Display voltage
    txtId.Text = Format(dId * 1000, "Scientific") ' Display ➡
    diode current in mA
    txtIr.Text = Format(dIr * 1000, "Scientific") ' Display ➡
    resistor current in mA
    ' Illustrate use of Debug window
    Debug.Print "Ir, Id"
    Debug.Print dIr, dId
    Debug.Print "Ir - Ir, Error"
    Debug.Print dIr - dId, dError   ' Debug purpose
    Debug.Print "Tol ", dTol
```

```
            ElseIf dVs = 0 And dR >= 0 Then  ' Dead circuit
                txtV.Text = 0    ' Display all outputs as zero
                txtId.Text = 0
                txtIr.Text = 0

            ElseIf dVs > 0 And dR = 0 Then  ' Short-circuit condition
                MsgBox "Oops, short circuit, we just blew up the diode"
                CueUser

            Else    ' Shame on user for trying negative values
                MsgBox "Negative Vs or R not allowed"
                CueUser
            End If

            If Err.Number <> 0 Then ' Error handling if necessary
                MsgBox CStr(CVErr(Err.Number)) & " " & Err.Description, ➡
                vbCritical, MSGTITLE
                CueUser ' Clear outputs if applicable
            End If

        End Sub
```

Now when we use the following inputs:

Source Voltage = 0.1 Volts
Resistor = 1000 Ohms
Start Tolerance = 0.1 mA

The outputs are the following:

Load Voltage = 0.05 Volts
Resistor Current = 1.56E-02 mA
Diode Current = 1.53E-02 mA

7.9   SELECTION EXCHANGE SORT

7.9.1   A Brief Word About Sorting

Sorting *is the process of putting the data in alphabetical or numerical order based on the value of the data.*

Cougar Canoe needs to maintain customer information, so the company needs a program that can search a list of customers to find and/or update the information. We have already seen how efficient the binary search program is (Example 7.13). Now we need to develop a program that can sort lists. In practice, sorting could occur dynamically when customers are added or deleted from a list that is stored in a file on disk. We will work with file handling and list modification operations in the next two chapters, but for now, we will consider how to generate a sorted list. Two sorting algorithms we will describe are the selection exchange sort and the bubble sort. Both sorting techniques work by comparing two items at a time. If those items are out of order, they are switched. If they are not out of order, they are left alone. The two algorithms differ in the sequence of comparing and switching (when applicable).

7.9.2   The Selection Exchange Sort Algorithm

The basic principle of the selection exchange sort is to start at the beginning of the list. Scan the rest of the list to look for the smallest item. When it is found, exchange it with the first item—unless it is already the smallest item. Then start from the second item in the list and scan the remainder of the list to select the second smallest item. When it is found, exchange the pair—unless the second item is already the second smallest item. Then start from the third item in the list and scan the rest of the list to select the third smallest item. When found, exchange the pair—unless the third item is already the third smallest item. Continue this sequence until the last pair is reached, and switch the pair if necessary. This sort technique is best illustrated by using the diagram shown in Figure 7.9. It shows the following sequence:

1. Start pass at item 0. Scan the list and find that item 5 is the smallest item. Exchange them.

2. Start pass at item 1. Scan the list to find if any item is smaller than it. None are found, so leave it alone.

3. Start pass at item 2. Scan the rest of list to find if any item is smaller than it. None are found, so leave it alone.

4. Start pass at item 3. Scan the rest of the list to find if any item is smaller than it. None are found, so leave it alone.

5. Start pass at item 4. Scan the rest of the list to find if any item is smaller than it. None are found, so leave it alone.

6. Start pass at item 5. Scan the rest of the list and find that item 7 is the smallest item remaining. Exchange them.

7. Start pass at item 6. Scan the rest of the list to find if any item is smaller than it. None are found, so leave it alone.

8. Start pass at item 7 (the last pair). Scan the next item. Since it is smaller, exchange the pair.

7.9.3   The Pseudocode

Example 7.16 shows the pseudocode for the algorithm.

Example 7.17

```
Sort_Click
    MinIndex = PassIndex
    For PassIndex = 0 To ListCount - 2
        For ScanIndex = PassIndex To ListCount - 1
            If Item(MinIndex) > Item(ScanIndex) Then
                MinIndex = PassIndex
            End If
        Next ScanIndex
        If PassIndex < MinIndex Then
            Exchange Item(PassIndex), Item(MinIndex)
        End If
    Next PassIndex
```

Figure 7.9
Selection Exchange
Sort Example

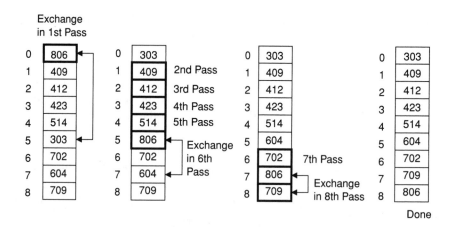

We could refine the code to detail how to exchange as follows:

```
' Exchange Item(PassIndex), Item(MinIndex)
Exchange = Item(PassIndex)
Item(PassIndex) = Item(MinIndex)
Item(MinIndex) = Exchange
```

7.9.4   The String Comparison Function StrComp

It is possible to compare strings using the standard comparison operators >, <, and so on, but these comparisons are based on the binary values of the strings. Remember that characters are stored in computer memory using their binary ANSI codes (see Figure 3.5). The comparison operators would use these binary values to perform numerical comparisons. However, the numerical order of ANSI codes does not always correspond to conventional alphabetical order. For example, letter *Z* would be smaller than letter *b* because its ANSI code is smaller. Do not despair, though: The Microsoft Visual Basic development team had people like us in mind when they included the string comparison function. We can use it for textual comparison (alphabetical ordering) instead of binary comparison (numerical ordering). The function StrComp returns a value indicating the result of a string comparison. The syntax for *textual* comparison is

StrComp(*string argument 1, string argument 2,* **1)**

To specify a binary comparison, change the third argument to 0 or omit it. It returns

−1	*if string argument* 1 is less than *string argument 2*
0	*if string argument* 1 is equal to *string argument 2*
1	*if string argument* 1 is greater than *string argument 2*
Null	if any string argument is Null

For example, the following statement will assign nScan to nMin if the string lstItem.List(nMin) is greater than lstItem.List(nScan).

```
If StrComp(lstItem.List(nMin), lstItem.List(nScan), 1) = 1 Then
    nMin = nScan ' Compared item is the new minimum
End If
```

Another option is to use the Option Compare statement at the module level to declare the default comparison method to use when string data is compared. Option Compare Text results in string comparisons based on a case-insensitive text sort order determined by your system's locale. The locale setting on your computer determines how to handle information based on language- and country-specific conventions. (For more information, refer to Visual Basic Help.)

7.9.5   The Code for the Selection Exchange Sort Program

Figure 7.10 shows the program during execution. The user seeded the list with 50 items and clicked Sort. During the sorting process, the Status box displays "Sorting In Progress." After the alphabetical sort is complete, the Status box displays "Sorted." Note that it required 1,225 iterations of the inner loop (see Example 7.17) to complete the sort.

Example 7.18 shows the code for procedure cmdSort_Click and the opening comments in the General Declarations section. The other procedures are identical to those in the Sequential Search program shown in Example 7.11.

Example 7.18

```
' Selection Exchange Sort Program
' Sorts list to re-order elements from smallest to largest

' Basic algorithm is to make a pass to find smallest
' value.  Smallest value is assigned to top of list section
' Repeat pass for remainder of list without the minimum.
' Each pass will generate the next smallest value
' that is assigned to the top of that section.
' Passes continue until there are only two left in a section.
' These are exchanged if necessary and sort is complete.

' User clicks Seed New List to generate a randomly
' created list for demonstration purposes.
' User clicks Sort and list is sorted
```

Figure 7.10
Selection Exchange Program

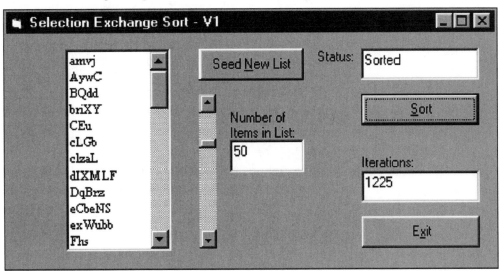

```vb
' Sort time depends on number of items and computer speed, e.g.,
' for a 166 MHz system and 200 items, it may take 5 seconds to sort
' if the DoEvents in the loop is commented out
' If Debug statements used, execution time increases significantly

Private Sub cmdSort_Click()
    ' Perform main work to rearrange list items in
    ' alphabetical order using the
    ' Selection Exchange Sort algoritm

    ' lstItem.ListCount is number of elements in list
    Dim sMin As String   ' Minimum
    Dim nPass As Integer    ' Item pointer
    Dim nScan    ' Pointer to another item to compare with
    Dim nMin As Integer ' Pointer to current minimum item
    Dim sExchange As String ' Use to make the exchange
    Dim nIteration   ' Keep track of number of iterations for info only
    On Error Resume Next

    cmdSeed.Enabled = False ' Disable button for duration of sort

    ' Show status in status box in case loop takes a long time
    txtStatus.Text = "Sorting In Progress"
    txtIteration.Text = ""
    DoEvents     ' Show Text property change while this ➡
    procedure in progress

    ' Debug ---- Remove from final version
    'Debug.Print "Selection Exchange Test  ", Time

    ' Pass through the list and exchange items when
    ' necessary until sorting complete
    For nPass = 0 To lstItem.ListCount - 2 Step 1

        nMin = nPass     ' Initially assume first item in section ➡
        is the minimum
        ' Find smallest item in section

        ' Debug ---- Remove from final version
        'Debug.Print "Pass ", nPass

        For nScan = nPass + 1 To lstItem.ListCount - 1 Step 1
            'Textual comparison to check if lstItem.List(nMin) ➡
            > lstItem.List(nScan)
            If StrComp(lstItem.List(nMin), lstItem.List(nScan), ➡
            1) = 1 Then
                nMin = nScan ' Compared item is the new minimum
            End If
            ' Debug ---- Remove from final version
            'Debug.Print "Scan index"
            'Debug.Print nScan
            nIteration = nIteration + 1
        Next nScan

        If nPass < nMin Then    ' Found a smaller value
```

```
                    ' Debug ---- Remove from final version
                    'Debug.Print "Exchange top of pass item and ➡
                    remaining minimum"
                    'Debug.Print lstItem.List(nPass), lstItem.List(nMin)

                    ' ... then exchange item with current minimum
                    sExchange = lstItem.List(nPass)
                    lstItem.List(nPass) = lstItem.List(nMin)
                    lstItem.List(nMin) = sExchange
              End If
              DoEvents    ' Permit user to abort sort
                        ' and see sorting process
                        ' but at the expense of slowing execution
        Next nPass

        txtStatus.Text = "Sorted"
        txtIteration.Text = CStr(nIteration)
        cmdSeed.Enabled = True   ' Enable new sort

        If Err.Number <> 0 Then ' Error handling if necessary
            MsgBox CStr(CVErr(Err.Number)) & " " & Err.Description, ➡
            , MSGTITLE
         End If

End Sub

                    ' See Example 7.11 for Form_Load, ➡
                    vsbItemCount_Change/Scroll,
                    ' WordLength, BuildWord, cmdSeed_Click, cmdExit
```

To investigate how the program operates in detail, remove the single quotes from the Debug.Print statements, but be warned that this will significantly increase execution time since it takes additional time to print the information. Here is a sample output in the Debug window when the original list was seeded with six items. Note how each exchange is for a sequentially higher item.

```
Selection Exchange Test        8:10:20 AM
Pass              0
Scan index
    1
Scan index
    2
Scan index
    3
Scan index
    4
Scan index
    5
Exchange top of pass item and remaining minimum
lmuZVc          aJXXMK
Pass              1
Scan index
    2
Scan index
    3
```

```
Scan index
    4
Scan index
    5
Exchange top of pass item and remaining minimum
lmuZVc          ClxSqR
Pass            2
Scan index
    3
Scan index
    4
Scan index
    5
Pass            3
Scan index
    4
Scan index
    5
Pass            4
Scan index
    5
Exchange top of pass item and remaining minimum
SXaAK           QtMgYZ
```

Note that the Seed button is disabled while the sort algorithm is executing. This prevents the user from corrupting the seed value while the list is being sorted. Once the sort is completed, the user is free to click Seed to generate a new start list.

7.9.6   DoEvents

Note that `cmdSort_Click` procedure (Example 7.18) uses the `DoEvents` statement near the beginning. The `DoEvents` function yields execution so that the operating system can process other events. In this case, we use it so that text box `txtStatus` will show the message "Sorting In Progress" *during* execution of this event procedure. Otherwise the text changes become visible only *after* the event procedure has executed. By this time it is too late, since the sorting is complete. It is generally good practice to inform the user of lengthy processing; otherwise, the user has no idea that the program is functioning normally. He or she may believe that the program is hung and will use the "Vulcan nerve pinch" (CTRL+ALT+DEL) to terminate program execution.

7.10   BUBBLE SORT

Figure 7.11 illustrates the basic principle of a bubble sort. Starting at the beginning of the list, compare the first item with the next item. If the first item is larger, exchange them. Continue with the next item and compare this pair. Perform an exchange if necessary. Continue this process until the last pair. Now the largest item is at the bottom of the list. Return to the top of the list and repeat the process (pass) all over, omitting the bottom item, which is already in the correct position. Continually repeat the process (pass) until exchanges are no longer required. This means that the list is sorted. In Figure 7.11 we can see why this is called a *bubble* sort. The smaller elements move upward by one position during each pass. This resembles something bubbling to the surface.

7.10.1   The Algorithm and Pseudocode

Example 7.19 shows the algorithm for the bubble sort. The flag is set to True so that at least one pass through the list will be made. The outer loop will continue as long as the flag is True, since this indicates that the data is not in order. In the inner loop, the flag is cleared to False. This says that the elements are in order until an exchange of pair elements is made. If an exchange is required, the flag will set to True to indicate that further passes may be necessary. After each scan pass (the inner loop exits), the bottom element of that section is in order, hence it is not included in the next pass of pair checking. Once a scan pass (inner loop) executes without requiring an exchange (Flag Exchange remains False), the list is considered to be sorted. The outer loop will cease iterations.

Example 7.19

```
Sort_Click
    Flag Exchange = True      ' Assume exchange required
    PairCount = ListCount - 1

    ' Outer loop to repeat passes through the list
    While Flag Exchange = True
        Flag Exchange = False ' Assume data in order unless ➡
        exchange made

        ' This is the scan loop, the largest remaining element falls
        'to the bottom of pass section
        For ScanIndex = 1 To PairCount
            If Item(ScanIndex) > Item(ScanIndex + 1) Then
                Exchange Item(ScanIndex), Item(ScanIndex + 1)
                Flag Exchange = True    ' An exchange was required
            End If
        Next ScanIndex

        PairCount = PairCount - 1 ' Reduce pass section size
            ' since last element in position

    Wend
```

Figure 7.11
Bubble Sort Example

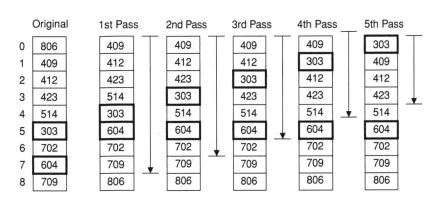

Done after sixth pass because no exchanges were necessary; hence, sorted.

7.10.2   The Code for the Bubble Sort Program

Example 7.20 shows the code for procedure cmdSort_Click and the opening comments in the General Declarations section. The other procedures are identical to those in the Sequential Search program shown in Example 7.11. During execution, it would look similar to the Selection Exchange program shown in Figure 7.10, except that the title would be different.

Example 7.20

```
' Bubble Sort Program
' Sorts list to re-order elements from smallest to largest
' Basic algorithm is to examine each (overlapping) pair from
' the beginning to end of the list.  The smallest element
' of each pair is assigned to the beginning of the pair.
' Repeat this process until it no longer exchanges
' the position in any pair.
' In effect, the smaller values "bubble" from the bottom
' to the top of the list.

' User clicks Seed New List to generate a randomly
' created list for demonstration purposes
' User clicks Sort and list is sorted

' Sort time depends on number of items and computer speed, e.g,
' for a 166 MHz system and 200 items it may take 12 seconds to sort
' if the DoEvents in the loop is commented out

Private Sub cmdSort_Click()
    ' Perform main work to rearrange items in
    ' alphabetical order using a Bubble Sort Algorithm

    ' lstItem.ListCount is number of elements in list
    Dim nScanIndex   ' Pointer to another item to compare with
    Dim sExchange As String ' Use to make the exchange
    Dim nIteration   ' Keep track of number of iterations for info only
    Dim bFlagExchange As Boolean
    Dim nPairCount As Integer

    On Error Resume Next

    cmdSeed.Enabled = False ' Disable button for duration of sort

    ' Show status in status box in case loop takes a long time
    txtStatus.Text = "Sorting In Progress"
    txtIteration.Text = ""
    DoEvents     ' Show Text property change while this ➡
    procedure in progress

    ' Debug --- Remove from final version
    ' Debug.Print "Bubble Sort Text ", Time

    bFlagExchange = True
    nPairCount = lstItem.ListCount - 2   ' Number of pairs to check
```

```
        ' Outer loop to repeat passes through the list
        ' Countinue scan passes until exchanges no longer required
    While bFlagExchange = True

        bFlagExchange = False    ' Reset flag for next pass

        ' Debug --- Remove from final version
        'Debug.Print "Pair count ", nPairCount

        ' This is the scan loop, the largest remaining element ➡
        falls to the bottom of pass section
    For nScanIndex = 0 To nPairCount Step 1
            ' Textual comparison, is Item(nScanIndex) > ➡
            Item(nScanIdex+1) ?
        If StrComp(lstItem.List(nScanIndex), ➡
        lstItem.List(nScanIndex + 1), 1) = 1 Then
                ' Exchange items if first element in pair is larger
                ' Debug --- Remove from final version
                'Debug.Print " Pair exchange required"
                'Debug.Print lstItem.List(nScanIndex), ➡
                lstItem.List(nScanIndex + 1)
                sExchange = lstItem.List(nScanIndex)
                lstItem.List(nScanIndex) = lstItem.List(nScanIndex + 1)
                lstItem.List(nScanIndex + 1) = sExchange
                bFlagExchange = True    ' Set flag if exchange required
        End If
        nIteration = nIteration + 1 ' For curiosity, check ➡
        iteration rate
        DoEvents    ' Permit user to abort sort
                ' and see sorting process
                ' but at the expense of slowing execution
    Next nScanIndex
        nPairCount = nPairCount - 1 ' Reduce pass section size ➡
        since last element in position

    Wend

    txtStatus.Text = "Sorted"
    txtIteration.Text = CStr(nIteration)
    cmdSeed.Enabled = True   ' Enable new sort

    If Err.Number <> 0 Then ' Error handling if necessary
        MsgBox CStr(CVErr(Err.Number)) & " " & Err.Description, ➡
        , MSGTITLE
    End If
End Sub

        ' See Example 7.11 for Form_Load, ➡
        vsbItemCount_Change/Scroll,
        ' WordLength, BuildWord, cmdSeed_Click, cmdExit
```

To investigate how the program operates in detail, remove the single quotes from the `Debug.Print` statements, but be warned that this will significantly increase execution time since it takes additional time to print the information.

SUMMARY

To solve a programming problem you need to have some idea of what the design solution looks like. Typically the solution is an algorithm. An algorithm is a step-by-step sequence to solve a problem in a fixed period of time. It describes *how* a computation is to be performed. To be able to modify algorithms for your own purposes, it is useful to be familiar with a variety of existing algorithms. Then you will be able to pick and choose features and components from the different algorithms to build your own. You will likely need to check other resources, such as other chapters in this book, other books about programming, and the additional resources shown in Appendix D. For a review of the algorithms described in this chapter, the best place to look is the beginning of this chapter.

HANDS-ON EXERCISES

OVERVIEW

The activities will

- Enable you to use various algorithms, such as those for logic sequencing, standard financial calculations, standard scientific procedures, searching for data, and sorting data.

- Enable you to use some additional features of Visual Basic.

To Get Started

1. Read the section Read Me Before Attempting the Hands-On Exercises if you have not already done so.

2. Run Windows.

3. Open the file CH07\EX07.TXT on your student disk and answer the questions. (The same questions are shown here so that you can still determine answers when you are not sitting in front of a computer.)

4. Run Visual Basic.

7.1   WHAT IS AN ALGORITHM?

1. Explain what an algorithm is.

2. List the three ways that an algorithm can be written.

3. Describe a common activity you do as an algorithmic activity.

4. Operating systems need to be able to run several programs (processes) at the same time. The operating system is a program that implements several algorithms. One of these algorithms is a solution to something called the *Dining Philosophers Problem*. Research to find out about the algorithm. Some sources of informatin are technical books about operating systems and the World Wide Web. Describe the algorithm.

ABOUT FURTHER EXERCISES

You might not have the interest or time to examine every program described in this chapter. If your inclination is toward information-system business-type applications, you could work on the following programs:

7.3   Amortization Table
7.5   Generate Random Data (necessary for programs that follow)
7.6   The Sequential Search Program
7.7   Binary Search
7.9   Selection Exchange Sort
7.10 Bubble Sort

If your inclination is toward technical engineering–type applications, you could work on the following programs:

7.2   An Alarm Clock (involves state transitions normally used in real-time control)
7.4   The Method of Least Squares
7.5   Generate Random Data (necessary for sort programs that follow)
7.8   Successive Approximation
7.9   Selection Exchange Sort
7.10 Bubble Sort

7.2   AN ALARM CLOCK

To run this program, select **New Project** from the File menu. Select **Save File/Form1 As** from the File menu. Save *file* FORM1 as **ALARM1** in directory CH07. Select **Save Project As** from the File menu. Save *project* PROJECT1 as **ALARM1** in directory CH07.

Modify the form so that it looks like Figure 7.1. You can find the Timer control in the Toolbox. It doesn't matter where you place the Timer control, since it is not visible when the program runs. The form Name property should be frmAlarm-Clock1. Refer to Example 7.2 to see how to name the controls. Following are some property setting suggestions:

TextBox	Name	txtTime
	Font	MS Sans Serif (Style = Regular, Size = 24)
	Locked	True
Timer	Name	tmrTime
	Enabled	True
	Interval	1000

Save the project. Type in the **code shown in Example 7.2,** and save the project.

Run the program. Click **Set Alarm.** Then click **Hour** and **Minute** as required to set the alarm time to a few minutes past the present time. Click **Release Alarm.** Click **Alarm Mode,** and wait. The alarm should beep every second when the time equals the alarm time. Click **Normal Mode** to turn off the alarm. Click the **Debug** check box. The program should show a different time (unless you happen to start the program at exactly 12:00 PM).

Note the comments in trmTime_Timer about the debug time. Modify the debug time and modify the alarm settings. Test the alarm action for different debug times. When you are done, stop execution.

7.3   AMORTIZATION SCHEDULE

To run this program, select **New Project** from the File menu. Select **Save File/ Form1** As from the File menu. Save *file* FORM1 as **AMORT1** in directory CH07. Select **Save Project As** from the File menu. Save *project* PROJECT1 as **AMORT1** in directory CH07.

Modify the form so that it looks like Figure 7.2. The form Name property should be frmAmortization1. Refer to Example 7.4 to see how to name the controls. Following are some property setting suggestions (from top to bottom):

TextBox	Name	txtPrincipal
	Locked	False
TextBox	Name	txtInterest
	Locked	False
TextBox	Name	txtPayment
	Locked	False
TextBox	Name	txtAmortHead
	Locked	True
	MultiLine	True
TextBox	Name	txtAmortization
	Locked	True
	MultiLine	True
	ScrollBars	2 - Vertical

Save the project. Type in the **code shown in Example 7.4**, and save the project.

Run the program. Type in **different inputs** and press ENTER. You should see a new amortization schedule. Set a breakpoint in procedure AmortizationTable, and run the program. Single step to investigate how the program executes. Remove the breakpoint, and stop execution.

7.4   THE METHOD OF LEAST SQUARES

To run this program, open *project* AREA1 in directory CH06. Save *file* AREA1 as **LEASTSQ1** in directory CH07. Select **Save Project As** from the File menu. Save *project* AREA1 as **LEASTSQ1** in directory CH07. Change the Name of the form to frmLeastSquares1 and change the version part of its Caption to state Least Square Line Fitting-Version.

Modify the form so that it looks like Figure 7.3. Name button Fit Line as cmdFit-Line. Name button Start Points as cmdStartPoints. Name the text box as txtLine. Modify its size and change its MultiLine property to True. Save the project.

Type in the **code shown in Example 7.6**. Note that leftover event procedures from the original project (AREA1) can now be found as general procedures. You can cut and paste some of this code to reduce typing. Delete the code you don't need. Save the project.

Run the program. Click **Start Points**. Click in the **picture box**. A point should appear where you clicked. Click in some more points, and then click **Fit Line**. The program should show the straight line that best fits the points. It should also display the line equation parameters in the text box. Click **Clear** to start over again. Set a breakpoint in procedure cmdFitLine_Click, and run the program. Single step to investigate how the program executes. Remove the breakpoint, and stop execution.

7.5   THE GENERATE RANDOM DATA PROGRAM

To run this program, select **New Project** from the File menu. Select **Save File/Form1 As** from the File menu. Save *file* FORM1 as **RANDOM1** in directory CH07. Select **Save Project As** from the File menu. Save *project* PROJECT1 as **RANDOM1** in directory CH07.

Modify the form so that it looks like Figure 7.4 (except that Figure 7.4 shows the program in run mode—you will not see any entries or the scroll bar in the list box during design mode). Note that the large box is a list box control, not a text box control. You should be able to locate the list box control in the Toolbox by using the pop-up Help balloons. Double-click the button to place the control on the form. Add the other controls. Name the form **frmRandom1**. Refer to Example 7.9 to see how to name the controls. Following are some property setting suggestions:

ListBox	Name	lstItem
VScrollBar	Name	vsbItemCount
	Max	200
	Min	1
	Value	50
TextBox	Name	txtItemCount
	Locked	True
CommandButton	Name	cmdSeed
CommandButton	Name	cmdExit

Save the project. Type in the **code shown in Example 7.9,** and save the project. The good news is that you will able to modify this program to create many of the other programs in this chapter.

Run the program. Use the scroll bar to select the number of items. Click **Seed New List**. You should see a list of letters. Depending on what you selected with the scroll bar, you should see a second scroll bar appear with a list box. Click **Seed New List**. You should see different data appear. Every time you click **Seed New List,** a new random sequence should appear.

Set a breakpoint in procedure cmdSeed_Click. Run the program and monitor how the procedure executes by single stepping. Stop execution.

The Object Browser

Here we will give you a quick introduction to another development tool. For now, you might find it a useful way to check which event procedures you have since you may not have created procedures for some objects and may have created several procedures for different events for other objects. The object browser is normally used for advanced object-oriented programming, but you might find it useful. The object browser will list all of the event procedures, controls, and properties associated with the form. (We will return to the Object Browser in Chapter 11 to examine it in more detail.)

To use the object browser, stop execution so that Visual Basic is in the design mode. Select **Object Browser** from the View menu. Alternatively, click the **Object Browser** button in the Toolbar.

Visual Basic 4

You should see the Object Browser dialog box. Make sure that the Libraries/Projects box is selected for Project1. The Classes/Modules box should list your form by name. Select the **form name in the Classes box**. Then you can scroll the

Methods/Properties box to see all of the procedures. If you are interested in seeing the code of a procedure, select **the procedure**, such as vsbItemCount_Change. Once selected, click the **Show** button. This will also close the Object Browser dialog box. If you haven't used the Show button, you can finish using the Object Browser by clicking the **Close** button.

Visual Basic 5

You should see the Object Browser window. The top list box may display <All Libraries>. Select Project1 in the top list box. The Classes box should list your form by name. Select the **form name in the Classes box**. Then you can scroll the Members box to see all of the procedures. If you are interested in seeing the code of a procedure, right-click **the procedure** (such as vsbItemCount_Change), and select **View Definition** from the pop-up menu. You will now be viewing the Code window at the selected procedure. The Object Browser is a selectable window. Note that you can switch back and forth between the Object Browser window and Form windows by selecting them from the Window menu, or by clicking their respective buttons. For example, click the **Object Browser** button on the Toolbar, and you will see the Object Browser window. Click the **View Code** on the Project Explorer. You should now see the Code window.

7.6   THE SEQUENTIAL SEARCH PROGRAM

To run this program, open *project* RANDOM1 in directory CH07, if it isn't already open. Save *file* RANDOM1 as **SEARCH1** in directory CH07. Select **Save Project As** from the File menu. Save *project* RANDOM1 as **SEARCH1** in directory CH07. Change the Name of the form to **frmSearch1,** and change its Caption to state **Sequential Search-Version 1**.

Modify the form to look like Figure 7.5 (except that Figure 7.5 shows the program in run mode—you will not see any entries or the scroll bar in the list box during design mode). Name the new button **cmdFind**. Name the new text box txtFind, and save the project.

Refer to Example 7.11 and modify the existing code so that it is the same as Example 7.11. Save the project.

Run the program. Use the scroll bar to select the number of items. Click **Seed New List**. You should see a list of letter sequences (pseudo words). Depending on what you selected with the scroll bar, you should see a second scroll bar appear with a list box. Click **Seed New List**. You should see different data appear. Note the list contents. To test the Find feature, type **something that you know for sure is in list** in the Find What box. Press **ENTER** or click **Find**. Note that it must be exact, with the same use of uppercase and lowercase letters. The program should highlight the item in the list. Try to find something that is not in the list. The program should display a dialog box informing you that the item is not in the list. If you happen to press **ENTER** without entering anything, you will see an error message.

Set a breakpoint in procedure cmdFind_Click. Run the program, and monitor how the procedure executes by single stepping. Stop execution.

7.7   THE BINARY SEARCH PROGRAM

To run this program, open *project* SEARCH1 in directory CH07, if it isn't already open. Save *file* SEARCH1 as **SEARCH2** in directory CH07. Select **Save Project As** from the File menu. Save *project* SEARCH1 as **SEARCH2** in directory CH07. Change the Name of the form to **frmSearch2**, and change its Caption to state **Binary Search-Version 2**. Save the project.

Add a text box named **txtIteration** and a label named **lblIteration**. Size and position both above the Exit button (cmdExit). Set lblIteration.Caption to **Iterations** and set txtIteration.Text as **nothing** (blank). Refer to Example 7.13, and modify the code for procedure cmdFind_Click and function BuildWorld as shown. Also find the following statement in cmdSeed_Click:

```
sItem = BuildWord()
```

Modify it to the following:

```
sItem = BuildWord(nCount + 65) ' Used in binary search program
```

Save the project. Run the program and experiment with it the same way you did for the Sequential Search program.

7.8 SUCCESSIVE APPROXIMATION: THE DIODE CIRCUIT PROGRAM

To run this program, select **New Project** from the File menu. Select **Save File/Form1 As** from the File menu. Save *file* FORM1 as **DIODE1** in directory CH07. Select **Save Project As** from the File menu. Save *project* PROJECT1 as **DIODE1** in directory CH07.

Modify the form so that it looks like Figure 7.7. The form Name property should be **frmDiode1**. Refer to Example 7.15 to see how to name the controls. For aesthetic appeal, you can also draw the circuit. You can draw a line by double-clicking the **Line** control button in the Toolbox. A line with sizing handles (dots on each end) will appear. Click on a **sizing handle** and drag **the end of the line to the desired position**. Drag **the other end to another position**. Add more **line controls**, and size and position them to draw a circuit (see Figure 7.7). To change the width of a line, change the setting of its BorderWidth property. To add a combo box, double-click the **ComboBox** control button in the Toolbox. Following are some property setting suggestions (from left to right, top to bottom):

TextBox	Name	txtVs
TextBox	Name	txtR
TextBox	Name	txtV
	Locked	True
TextBox	Name	txtIr
	Locked	True
TextBox	Name	txtId
	Locked	True
ComboBox	Name	cboTol
CommandButton	Name	cmdExit

Save the project. Enter the **code shown in Example 7.15**, and save the project. Run the program. You should see load voltage, resistor, and diode current values. Click on the **arrow in the combo box**. Choose **another tolerance selection**. You should see a change in output. Enter **different values for the source voltage and the resistor**. Some sample results appear in the following table, so you can check whether you entered the code correctly.

Notice the last two rows, which show the sensitivity of the exponential function. The load voltage result hasn't changed much, but the currents have.

Remove the single quotes from the Debug.Print statements. Run the program and check the result displayed in the Debug window. Experiment with the program and stop execution.

Source Voltage	Resistor	Tolerance	Load Voltage	Resistor Current	Diode Current
3.0	120	0.001	0.6680145	1.94E+01	1.94E+01
12.0	100	0.001	0.713228	1.13E+02	1.13E+02
0.3	100	0.01	0.2994141	5.86E-03	1.15E-05
0.3	100	1E-08	0.2999988	1.17E-05	1.17E-05

The More Accurate Version

Save the *file* and save the *project* as DIODE2. Modify the code for procedure FindVdiode as shown in Example 7.16. Save the project. Run the program. Check that it gives more accurate results for small input source voltages. For fun, try to find the source voltage that will cause overflow error.

7.9   SELECTION EXCHANGE SORT

Open *project* SEARCH1 in directory CH07, if it isn't already open. The Sort program will be a modification of the Sequential Search program. (Do not use the Binary Search program.) Save *file* SEARCH1 as **SORT1** in directory CH07. Select **Save Project As** from the File menu. Save *project* SEARCH1 as **SORT1** in directory CH07. Change the Name of the form to **frmSort1** and change its Caption to **Selection Exchange Sort-V1**. Save the project.

Change the Name setting of text box txtFind to **txtStatus**. Change the Name setting of command button cmdFind to **cmdStatus**. Note that event procedure cmdFind_Click is now archived as a general procedure. You may choose to copy and paste code segments as required instead of writing new code from scratch. Modify other parts of the form so that the final result resembles Figure 7.10 (except that Figure 7.10 shows the program in run mode—you will not see any entries or the scroll bar in the list box during design mode). Make sure you add the text box (txtIteration) and label to show iteration information.

Type **the code for procedure cmdSort_Click and the opening comments** in the General Declarations section as shown in Example 7.18. You might be able to copy segments from general procedure cmdFind_Click to minimize typing. When you are done, delete the old procedure cmdFind_Click. Save the project.

Run the program. Use the scroll bar to select **the number of items**. Click **Seed New List**. The list box shows items in a random order. Click **Sort**. You may have to wait to see the results. During this time, the status box will show the message, "Sorting In Progress." Eventually it should show "Sorted." Check the contents of the list box. Note that all items are arranged top to bottom from smallest to largest in textual order. Repeat the process for different amounts of items. Stop execution.

To investigate how the program operates in detail, remove the single quotes from the Debug.Print statements, but be warned that this will significantly increase execution time since it takes additional time to print the information. Run the program. Check the results in the Debug window. If you wish, also set a breakpoint and investigate loop iterations in more detail by single stepping. Stop execution and remove all breakpoints.

7.10   BUBBLE SORT

Open *project* SORT1 in directory CH07, if it isn't already open. Save *file* SORT1 as **SORT2** in directory CH07. Select **Save Project As** from the File menu. Save *project* SORT1 as **SØRT2** in directory CH07. Change the Name of the form to frmSort2 and change its Caption to Bubble Sort-V2. Save the project.

Type the **code for procedure cmdSort_Click and the opening comments** in the General Declarations section as shown in Example 7.20. Save the project. Investigate the operation of this program the same way you investigated the Selection Exchange Sort program (SORT1).

ADDITIONAL PROBLEM SOLVING

Choose one or two of the following problems.

1. Modify the Alarm Clock program so that clicking the Minutes button from 59 to 00 does not cause the hour alarm setting to increase. You might want to check out the DatePart function and related functions using Visual Basic Help.

2. Develop a program that generates an earnings schedule for a guaranteed investment certificate. It should also show the date for each month. You can modify the Amortization Schedule program for this purpose.

3. Develop a program that determines what monthly payment will pay off a loan within a fixed period of time. Every 12 months there is an insurance charge that is 2% of the remaining principal. The inputs are the loan principal, interest rate, and desired number of payments. Use an algorithm similar to a search or a successive approximation algorithm.

CHAPTER **8**

File Handling

This chapter introduces you to storage operations.

Humans have seemingly always had the desire to preserve records of their activities and pass them from generation to generation. As evidence, we can visit the cave in Altamira, Spain, to see the ancient images drawn on the cave's ceiling, which, as far as we know, were probably made sometime between B.C. 14,000 and 9500. In present times we need to preserve information created by computer programs, which store information in a file on a disk. We can then subsequently retrieve the information from the file.

After completing this chapter, you should be able to

- Write programs that can view files.

- Write programs that can modify files.

- Write programs that use the common dialog control.

- Write programs that use menu controls.

- Customize message boxes.

- Write programs that facilitate keyboard use.

In This Chapter

Cougar Canoe requires a system that permits them to enter information about their customers. This information should be stored permanently and be retrievable at any time. Thus the program will permit an employee to type and/or select information about each customer and store it to a file. It will also permit an employee to view any of the file information that has been stored. In other words, Cougar Canoe will need a program that can handle files.

ABOUT THIS CHAPTER

To warm up, we will start off with a simple viewer program that permits you to look at the contents of a file in text format. It will introduce the fundamental file operation of reading the contents of a file. Then we will look at Visual Basic's file controls and the file types that Visual Basic can handle. The next program we will examine is a simple text editor to demonstrate the basic techniques for saving information to a file. The last program will be the initial prototype of a customer information system. It will permit the user to read and write customer records that are recorded in a file in an organized manner.

8.1   A SIMPLE TEXT FILE VIEWER

There are programs that can create fancy word processing, presentation, and/or graphics documents. It takes months of work to create these commercial programs. Sometimes the vendors offer free stripped-down versions that permit anyone to look at the document contents but not modify (edit) them: The Microsoft Word and PowerPoint viewers are two prime examples. It is also possible to build a viewer that can look at any reasonably sized text file. Figure 8.1 shows the program in operation.

In Figure 8.1, the user has selected the File menu, and the program shows the contents of the `Welcome.txt` file, which is stored in directory `pstemp` in drive C:. The program also shows some additional information about the file (partially hidden behind the File menu items). This is an educational demo intended to teach file handling, so we can't do anything yet to edit the file. That will come later. The demo does include some professional features such as a File menu and a caption that shows the file name.

Example 8.1 shows the complete code listing. Don't worry about understanding all of it yet; we will be explaining segments of it in due time. At this point, we are only showing just how little code is required to obtain this degree of functionality. Procedure `mnuOpen_Click` does the main work; the comments give you a general idea of how it operates. We will cover the details in the next section.

Example 8.1

```
' The Simple Viewer Program
' It is the first file handling demo
' Program demonstrates Sequential File Access
' User can select Open menu item and view file contents

Option Explicit

Const MSGTITLE = "Viewer Demo"   ' Message box title
```

Figure 8.1
The Simple Viewer Program

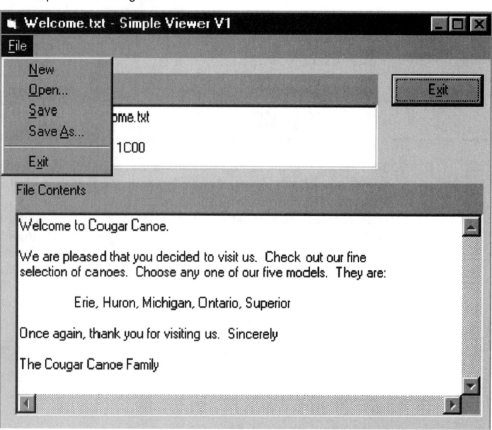

```
Private Sub cmdExit_Click()
    Close    ' Close all opened files
    End
End Sub

Private Sub mnuExit_Click()
    cmdExit_Click
End Sub

Private Sub mnuNew_Click()
    MsgBox "This feature not available yet", , MSGTITLE
End Sub

Private Sub mnuOpen_Click()
    ' When user selects Open from the File menu, this event ➡
    procedure runs
    ' It displays a standard Windows-style Open File dialog box ➡
    with most
    ' of the functionality already built in
    ' To do this, use the CommonDialog object with the ShowOpen ➡
    method

    Dim sCRLF As String * 2 ' To generate new line in multiline ➡
    text boxes
```

```
        Dim sFilter As String    ' Shows File Type information
        Dim sNextLine As String  ' Line read in from file
        Dim sBuffer As String    ' Buffer that stores contents of file
        Dim nFileNum As Integer  ' File number to handle file access

        On Error Resume Next

        sCRLF = Chr(13) & Chr(10)

        ' Specify File Dialog Filter format
        ' This is the list the user sees for combo box "Files of Type:"
        ' Filter syntax is: object.Filter [= description1 ¦filter1 ➡
        ¦description2 ¦filter2...]
        ' [description] describes the type of file
        ' [filter] specifies the filename extension
        sFilter = "Text (*.txt)¦*.txt¦Pictures(*.bmp;*.ico)¦*.bmp;*.ico"
        sFilter = sFilter & "¦Data (*.dat)¦*.dat¦All Files (*.*)¦*.*"

        ' Set some properties for the "File Open Dialog"
        dlgFile.Flags = cdlOFNFileMustExist ' Only permit existing ➡
        files to be opened
        dlgFile.Filter = sFilter     ' Define "Files of Type:" list
        dlgFile.DefaultExt = ".txt" ' Default file extension
        dlgFile.FilterIndex = 1 ' By default, show only files with ➡
        default extension
        ' In design mode, CancelError set True

        ' This is where the action starts.  Launch the File Open ➡
        dialog now!
        dlgFile.ShowOpen      ' Display the File Open dialog

        If Err.Number = cdlCancel Then  ' User clicked Cancel
            MsgBox "Operation cancelled", , MSGTITLE
            lblFileContent.Caption = "File Contents"
            Exit Sub
        End If

        txtFileInfo.Text = dlgFile.filename ' Show selected file ➡
        with full path information
        txtFileInfo.Text = txtFileInfo.Text & sCRLF & dlgFile.FileTitle ➡
        ' Show file name portion only
        ' Show Flag info.  See VB Help Topic Flags Property (File Dialog)
        txtFileInfo.Text = txtFileInfo.Text & sCRLF & "File Dialog ➡
        Flag = " & Hex(dlgFile.Flags)

        nFileNum = FreeFile     ' Get next available file number
        ' Enable I/O to file for sequential input access
        ' Cue user that file opening in progress
        lblFileContent.Caption = "Opening file ...."
        DoEvents

        Open dlgFile.filename For Input As #nFileNum
```

```
            ' Trap file open errors if they occur
            If Err.Number <> 0 Then
                MsgBox CStr(CVErr(Err.Number)) & " " & Err.Description, ➡
                , MSGTITLE
                lblFileContent.Caption = "File Contents"
                Exit Sub
            Else
                ' Read in file data into buffer one line at a time
                ' until we reach the end of the file.
                Do While Not EOF(nFileNum) ' Loop until end of file.
                    Line Input #nFileNum, sNextLine   ' Get one line
                    sBuffer = sBuffer & sNextLine & sCRLF  ' and add it ➡
                    to buffer
                Loop

                ' Display contents of file using the buffer
                txtFileContent.Text = sBuffer

                ' Close the file since it has been loaded
                Close nFileNum

                ' Cue user that file has been loaded if no errors ➡
                detected during loading
                If Err.Number = 0 Then
                    frmViewer1.Caption = dlgFile.FileTitle & " - Simple ➡
                    Viewer V1"
                End If
                lblFileContent.Caption = "File Contents"

            End If

            If Err.Number <> 0 Then        ' Error Handling if necessary
                MsgBox CStr(CVErr(Err.Number)) & " " & Err.Description, ➡
                , MSGTITLE
            End If

        End Sub

        Private Sub mnuSave_Click()
            MsgBox "This feature not available yet", , MSGTITLE
        End Sub

        Private Sub mnuSaveAs_Click()
            MsgBox "This feature not available yet", , MSGTITLE
        End Sub
```

8.2   THE COMMON DIALOG CONTROL

Note

A dialog box will appear when the program requires additional information from
the user or must provide additional information to the user.

8.2.1   Introduction

Typical Windows programs use dialog boxes to open files, save files, print documents, select colors, and select fonts. These are known as *common* dialogs. For example, if you need to open a file, you have to provide the file and path information. You might also want to view file details, such as modification dates, before choosing the file. Windows provides a dynamic-link library named COMMDLG.DLL that contains the code required to implement dialog functionality for the common types just mentioned. Visual Basic contains the CommonDialog control. It provides an easy way to utilize the code in the dynamic-link library.

In our case, we are only interested in opening files. Later in this chapter we will also look at using the CommonDialog control to save files. (Use Visual Basic Help or other resources, such as Appendix D, for additional information on other types of common dialog boxes.)

8.2.2   A Few Technical Notes About the CommonDialog Control

In technical programmer parlance, we say that the CommonDialog control provides an *interface* between Visual Basic and the routines in the Microsoft Windows dynamic-link library COMMDLG.DLL. Note that COMMDLG.DLL must be in the Windows SYSTEM directory. To make sure that the control is available in the Toolbox, the file COMDLG16.OCX (for the 16-bit version) or COMDLG32.OCX (32-bit version) must be included in the project. It is likely that the file (and hence the control) is added automatically whenever you specify a new project. If it isn't available, you can add it directly to the project (or add it to project AUTOLD16 or AUTOLD32 for automatic inclusion in any project). To add or remove a control, select **Custom Controls** from the Tools menu, and then add or remove controls at will.

If you create an executable version of your program for a user, you must also install the .OCX file in the user's Microsoft Windows SYSTEM directory. The Visual Basic Application Setup Wizard can assist you with creating an installation program that automatically includes required files such as COMDLG16.OCX or COMDLG32.OCX.

8.2.3   The Open File Dialog

Figure 8.2 shows a typical Open File dialog used for the Simple Viewer program. The dialog permits the user to use the Look in: combo box to select the drive and directory path. The buttons to the right are, respectively, Up One Level, Create New Folder, List, and Details. They are fully functional, including the pop-up help balloons. The Files of type: combo box permits the user to select which types of files to view. In this case, files with extension .TXT are shown in the display box. If the user clicks the arrow, the dialog will display the Files of type as

```
Text (*.txt)
Pictures (*.bmp;*.ico)
Data (*.dat)
All Files (*.*)
```

Figure 8.2
A Common File Open Dialog Box

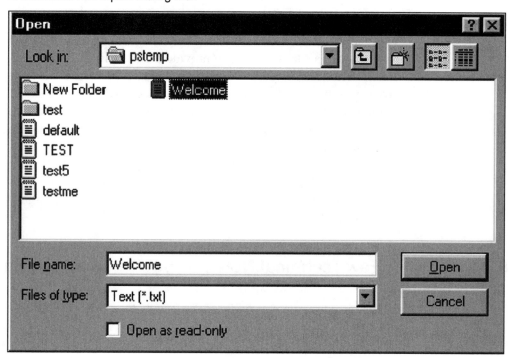

The other file types are used mainly for demonstration purposes. We could view files that are not text, but the result could look really strange, depending on the file type. For example, try to view a picture file. You will likely see strange characters, since this program can only interpret alphanumeric text. The Open and Cancel buttons perform their respective operations. Example 8.2 shows the code segment that handles this Open File dialog.

Example 8.2

```
' Code segment from Example 8.1 to handle the Open File dialog

' Specify File Dialog Filter format
' This is the list the user sees for combo box "Files of Type:"
' Filter syntax is: object.Filter [= description1 ¦filter1 ➥
¦description2 ¦filter2...]
' [description] describes the type of file
' [filter] specifies the filename extension
sFilter = "Text (*.txt)¦*.txt¦Pictures (*.bmp;*.ico)¦*.bmp;*.ico"
sFilter = sFilter & "¦Data (*.dat)¦*.dat¦All Files (*.*)¦*.*"

' Set some properties for the "File Open Dialog"
dlgFile.Flags = cdlOFNFileMustExist ' Only permit existing ➥
files to be opened
dlgFile.Filter = sFilter      ' Define "Files of Type:" list
dlgFile.DefaultExt = ".txt" ' Default file extension
dlgFile.FilterIndex = 1 ' By default, show only files with ➥
default extension
' In design mode, CancelError set True
```

```
' This is where the action starts.  Launch the File Open dialog now
dlgFile.ShowOpen    ' Display the File Open dialog
```

To use the CommonDialog control, modify its ***properties***. Then use one of the specific ***methods*** that it recognizes to specify the type of dialog. This control does not respond directly to events. Instead, we must use a menu control, which we will talk about later. Generally, we will explain the code segment from the bottom up. The CommonDialog Name property was set to `dlgFile` in the design mode. To indicate that we want to use the Open File dialog, use the `ShowOpen` method. Remember that a method is a function that operates on an object, but in the code we need to set up some properties that will govern some of the specifics in the dialog before we apply the method. For some reason, the Cancel button must be handled using error trapping. (It's not clear why Microsoft chose to consider a Cancel operation as an error.) To detect (trap) when the user clicks the Cancel button, it is necessary to set the CancelError property of the CommonDialog control to `True`.

The filter specifies the list displayed when the user clicks the arrow in the Files of type: combo box. The FilterIndex property specifies which filter item is displayed in the text box of the combo box. The DefaultExt property specifies which file type, as specified by the file extension, that the dialog shows if the user doesn't choose a specific type. The Filter property specifies the items displayed in the list portion of the Files of type: combo box. You must use a specific format to set the Filter property. A vertical bar separates the displayed descriptive text from the file extension specification that the dialog will use to choose files to display. The file extension specification is known as the ***filter***. Every alternate vertical bar separates the description and filter pairs. Study the filter format in Example 8.2.

8.3   MENU CONTROLS

8.3.1   About Menu Controls

A typical Windows program contains menu items below the window Title Bar (the Form Caption). Selecting a menu item will display other menu items (refer to Figure 8.1 and the code shown in Example 8.1). When the user selects the File menu, the program displays the Open, Save, and Exit menu items. This program has in fact five Menu controls named `mnuFile`, `mnuOpen`, `mnuSave`, `mnuSep1`, and `mnuExit`, respectively. (In the Hands-On Exercises later in this chapter we will see how to add and set up menu controls when in design mode using the Visual Basic Menu Editor). Menu controls only recognize (react to) a Click event.

There is no event procedure code for `mnuFile`. In design mode, the other menu controls were specified as submenu items, so selecting File automatically displays the submenu items. No extra code is required. One of the submenus is `mnuSep1`, which simply shows up as a separator bar between Save and Exit. Other than that, there is no functionality. Selecting Exit from the File menu will automatically launch the `mnuExit_Click` procedure. In this case, it calls `cdmExit_Click` to exit the program. (We will explain the purpose of the `Close` statement when we cover file operations.)

8.3.2   Some Menus as To-Be-Implemented Development Examples

Example 8.3 shows the code for the `mnuSave_Click` procedure:

Example 8.3

```
Private Sub mnuSave_Click()
    MsgBox "This feature not available yet", , MSGTITLE
End Sub
```

This code doesn't do much. It displays a message box informing the user that this feature is not available. The question is: Why bother to include it? When developing a program, it is useful to lay out the intended look and feel of the completed product. We want to eventually create a program for editing text files. This means that we need a means to save the file after modifications have been performed. During development, we may want to let some users test the program. Since development is in progress, some parts of the program may not be functional. It doesn't take too much coding to provide simple messages that inform the user about features that are currently lacking. It also serves to remind the programmer about outstanding work. The codes for procedures `mnuNew_Click` and `mnuSaveAs` are similar.

8.3.3   The Open Menu

When the user selects the Open menu, procedure `mnuOpen_Click` will run. We have already discussed how to code the segment that displays the Open dialog. The remaining part of the code handles opening the selected file if the user clicks the Open button in the dialog. It also handles the cancel operation if the user clicks the Cancel button. (We will describe how the code works after we have discussed how files are organized and handled.)

When the user clicks the Open button, the program sets the filename property of the CommonDialog control to the full file name selected or typed in by the user in the File name box. The filename property designates the full path, including the drive, directory, subdirectories if applicable, and the file name with the extension. Clicking Open also sets the FileTitle property. This is the name of the file without the drive and path information. Here is a code segment taken from Example 8.1 to show the use of these properties.

```
txtFileInfo.Text = dlgFile.filename ' Show selected file with ➡
full path information
txtFileInfo.Text = txtFileInfo.Text & sCRLF & dlgFile.FileTitle ➡
' Show file name portion only
```

Text box `txtFileInfo` is only used as an educational tool to illustrate the properties. The following code segment shows how we can use the FileTitle property to modify the Title Bar in the program. It is useful to show the file title first so that the file name (or portion of it) will be shown in the Windows Task Bar if the user chooses to switch to another task. Note that the Form Caption is modified only if there were no errors. We would not want to display misleading information in the Caption in case the file couldn't be accessed for some reason.

```
' Cue user that file has been loaded if no errors detected ➡
during loading
If Err.Number = 0 Then
        frmViewer1.Caption = dlgFile.FileTitle & " - Simple ➡
        Viewer V1"
End If
```

8.4   PROCESSING FILES

*A **file** is a group of bytes located on a disk.*

With Visual Basic we can access files in one of three ways:

- Sequential (see Figure 8.3)

- Random Access. (see Figure 8.4)

- Binary (see Figure 8.5)

8.4.1   Open and Close Operations

To read a book, you need to open the cover first. When you are finished, you close the cover. Accessing files is a similar operation. The computer reads from a file and writes to a file using special blocks of memory known as **buffers.** In order to set aside (or reserve) this block of memory as a buffer, it is necessary to open the file. To release the block of memory back to the operating system, it is necessary to perform a close operation. When reading and writing, the computer locates the buffer using a unique file number that identifies the buffer. Hence, before we can open a file, it is necessary to assign the file number that will be used. Since multiple files can be open at the same time, it is wise to let the operating system assign the file number. To obtain a file number from the operating system, use the FreeFile function. The computer also needs further instructions to know *how* to use the buffer, meaning it needs to know whether the file is sequential, random, or binary. To open a file, use the Open statement. For example, the program of Example 8.1 opens the file in the sequential mode, as shown in the following code segment:

```
nFileNum = FreeFile    ' Get next available file number
' Enable I/O to file for sequential input access
' Cue user that file opening in progress
lblFileContent.Caption = "Opening file ...."
DoEvents

Open dlgFile.filename For Input As #nFileNum
```

A file number is a handle for the program to use in order to work with a file.

The integer variable nFileNum is assigned the file number that is returned by calling function FreeFile. We use this file number in the Open statement. In this case we are opening the file for sequential access for input only since the program is only a viewer program.

The Close statement is necessary if we ever want to copy, rename, delete, or move the file. We should also close any open files used by the program when it exits. To close a specific file, specify the file number. To close all files used by the program, omit the file number. For example, to close the file opened in the previous example, use the following code:

```
' Close the file since it has been loaded
Close nFileNum
```

In procedure cmdExit_Click of Example 8.1, as a safety measure we close all files (if any are open) by using Close without any arguments. This ensures that no files are left open accidentally due to some unforeseen fault. In the following sections we will look at the variations of the Open statement that are required for the respective file access types.

8.4.2   Using Sequential Access Files

Note

The bytes in a sequential file are organized into lines. A *line* is a sequence of characters followed by the Carriage Return character and a Line Feed character.

Another term for a sequential file is *text file*. In other words, the file can be read by any text editor or be opened by a word processor using the text option. Data is stored as lines of text. An ASCII Carriage Return and Line Feed mark the end of a line. Each character of text is encoded as a byte using the ASCII code. Some characters represent format controls such as new line (carriage return and line feed) and tabbing. Figure 8.3 shows a typical layout. Note that the figure shows how the data is organized in a file. Figure 8.1 shows how this same data appears to a user when displayed on a screen (or printed onto paper).

Note that even numbers are stored as characters. Essentially, all data is of the String data type. When the file data is loaded in RAM, it will be converted into Unicode if you are using a system that uses Unicode. The use of a carriage return and line feed to end a line is similar to speech—unless you are listening to a professional auctioneer, you can tell when each sentence ends by detecting the pause between the sentences. There are three ways to open a file for sequential access: input, output, and append.

To input characters from a file, use a statement with the following format:

Open *PathAndFilename* **For Input As** *#FileNumber*

To output characters to a file, use a statement with the following format:

Open *PathAndFilename* **For Output As** *#FileNumber*

To append characters to a file, use a statement with the following format:

Open *PathAndFilename* **For Append As** *#FileNumber*

Input Using Sequential File Access

The file must already exist when you open it for Input. If the file doesn't exist, an error will occur. However, if you try to open a file that doesn't exist for Output or Append,

Figure 8.3

Example of a Sequential
File Structure

A sequential file is organized into lines, each ending with a
carriage return (#13) and a line feed (#10) character.
Each box represents a byte in the file containing an ASCII code.
See Figure 8.1 for the complete text.

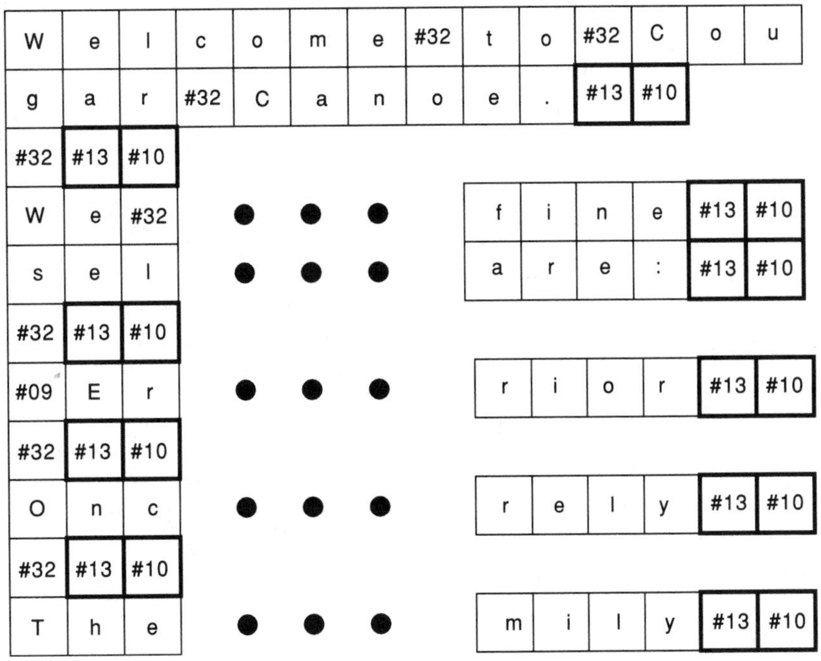

W	e	l	c	o	m	e	#32	t	o	#32	C	o	u
g	a	r	#32	C	a	n	o	e	.	#13	#10		

#32	#13	#10

| W | e | #32 | ● ● ● | f | i | n | e | #13 | #10 |
| s | e | l | ● ● ● | a | r | e | : | #13 | #10 |

#32	#13	#10

| #09 | E | r | ● ● ● | r | i | o | r | #13 | #10 |

#32	#13	#10

| O | n | c | ● ● ● | r | e | l | y | #13 | #10 |

#32	#13	#10

| T | h | e | ● ● ● | m | i | l | y | #13 | #10 |

#13 is ASCII code for Carriage Return
#10 is ASCII code for LineFeed
#09 is ASCII code for Horizontal Tab
#32 is ASCII code for Space Character

the file will be created. With sequential access, we can read or write a line at a time. Remember that a line is a sequence of bytes followed by Carriage Return and Line Feed characters to indicate the end of the line. Consider the following code segment from Example 8.1:

```
' Read in file data into buffer one line at a time
' until we reach the end of the file
Do While Not EOF(nFileNum) ' Loop until end of file
    Line Input #nFileNum, sNextLine   ' Get one line
    sBuffer = sBuffer & sNextLine & sCRLF  ' and add it to buffer
Loop

' Display contents of file using the buffer
txtFileContent.Text = sBuffer
```

The EOF (End Of File) function returns `True` when the end of the file is reached. Otherwise it returns `False`. The `Line Input` statement reads in the next line and stores the line in String variable `sNextLine`. However, it strips off the carriage return and line feed characters. The variable `sBuffer` is used to collect the lines. Since we want to use the variable to change the Text property of a Text Box (to display the information to the user), we need to append the Carriage Return and Line Feed characters (variable `sCRLF`).

Challenge

Why do you think this type of file access is called *sequential*?

Solution

If you want to read a line from the middle, you have to start at the beginning and read each line in sequence until you reach the target line. Again, think of speech: If you are listening in real time, the spoken words are uttered in a linear sequence.

Output Using Sequential File Access

Similarly, we can only write to the file in sequence. If the file is opened for Output, the lines are written in sequence starting from the beginning. If the file is opened for Append, lines are written starting from the last line in the file. If the file is opened for Input, we can't write to it! To write a line, use the Write statement. For example:

```
Write #nFileNum, "Welcome to Cougar Canoe"
```

The Write statement automatically appends the Carriage Return and Line Feed when writing the text into the file handled by the Integer file number value (nFileNum). (For more information about the Write statement, refer to Visual Basic Help.) In the editor program discussed later, we in fact use a different technique. All we have to do is use the Print statement to copy the contents of a text box (or String variable) into a file in one step:

```
Print #nFileNum, txtFileContent.Text
```

8.4.3   Using Random Access Files

The bytes in a random access file are organized into identical records. Each ***record*** *consists of data blocks known as* ***fields***.

Typically, a record contains information about some person or item. The fields classify the types of information stored for each record. Figure 8.4 illustrates a random access file being used to store customer information for Cougar Canoe. Each record represents a customer. There are fields for the customer's first name, last name, the Canoe model they purchased, the serial number of the purchased canoe, and their area code and local telephone number. Each record has the identical field structure. Each field is of a specific fixed size. The record organization looks like this:

First Name	String, which is 15 characters (bytes) long
Last Name	String, which is 15 character (bytes) long
Canoe Model	String, which is 8 characters (bytes) long
Serial Number	Long integer, which is 4 bytes long
Area Code	Integer, which is 2 bytes long
Local Telephone Number	Long integer, which is 4 bytes long

Hence, the record length is 48 bytes.

The term ***random*** refers to the fact that we can access any record in any order. To identify the record, state its position with respect to the beginning of the file. It is not necessary to start from the beginning to access any record for read-and-write purposes.

Figure 8.4
Example of a Random Access File Structure

A random access file is organized into records. Each record is organized identically into fields.

First Name as String * 15	Last Name as String * 15	Canoe Model as String * 8	Serial Number as Long	Area Code as Integer	Local Tel as Long
Sappho	Eresus	Erle	342123567	705	9329999
John	Barleycorn	Huron	342123568	606	5329009
Mary	February	Michigan	342123569	913	3456561
•					
•					
•					
Homer	Socrates	Ontario	344213567	403	6782349

However, we can only read or write one record at a time. For example, if we need to update the record for Mary, we can simply write a statement that puts data into record number 3. Also note that even String-data-type fields are of fixed width. For example, the first name field is 15 characters. If the information is shorter than 15 characters, the rest of the field will be filled with null characters. If you really want, you could roll your own variable length field structure using Binary access and some tricky coding. To open a file for random access, use the following syntax for the `Open` statement:

Open *PathAndFileName* **For Random As** *#FileNumber* **Len** = *RecordLength*

Keyword `Len` specifies the record length. Remember to use the `FreeFile` function to obtain a file number. For example, to open a file organized with the record structure shown in Figure 8.4:

```
m_sFileName = dlgFile.filename   ' Obtain file name from Open File ➥
dialog
m_nFileNum = FreeFile   ' Obtain a file number
Open m_sFileName For Random As #m_nFileNum Len = 48  ' Now open it
```

A random access file is automatically opened for both read and write operations. It will be necessary to use a new data type known as the ***User-defined type***. We will explain how to declare and use this type of variable in Section 8.6. For now, assume that we have already handled it. To read a record, use the `Get` statement:

Get *FileNumber, RecordPosition, User-definedTypeVariable*

Let's say that we want to read the information about John Barleycorn and store it in a variable named `ThisCustomer` of the User-defined type. Since this is record number 2 (see Figure 8.4), we could use the following statement:

```
Get m_nFileNum, 2, ThisCustomer
```

To write data to a record, use the `Put` statement:

Put *#FileNumber, RecordPosition, User-definedTypeVariable*

Let's say John changed his phone number. We could modify the contents of variable ThisCustomer to do this. (Section 8.6 will explain how to do this.) Again, we are accessing record number 2, so we could use the following statement:

```
Put #m_nFileNum, 2, ThisCustomer
```

We can also add records. To do this, set the value of the record position for the Put statement to one more than the number of records in the file. Let's say that the data for Homer Socrates is stored in record number 6359. If Fiona Ace purchased a canoe, we could add her information with something like the following:

```
Put #m_nFileNum, 6360, NewCustomer
```

It is not possible to directly delete records. However, there are ways (algorithms) to indirectly perform deletions. We will examine some of them in Chapter 9 when we cover data structures.

8.4.4   Using Binary Access Files

The bytes in a binary file are simply a sequence with no predefined organization. When we use binary access, there is no assumed structure. The file is simply treated as a sequence of bytes. Figure 8.5 shows the organization (or lack thereof).

Binary access would be useful to those who want to roll up their sleeves and get into the real nitty gritty of customizing their own file structure. For example, a file might contain a long list of Integer data that represents information obtained from a data logger for recording weather information. The first 5 bytes might contain a time stamp. To read each integer, we would have to start at the sixth byte and read every 2 bytes in sequence for each recorded measurement. Figure 8.5 shows the data in hexadecimal format. To open a file for binary access, use an Open statement with the following syntax:

Open *PathAndFileName* **For Binary As** *#FileNumber*

Let's say that the data logger records the data onto a floppy disk. Back at the laboratory, we could run a program containing something like the following statements to open the file.

```
nFileNum = FreeFile
Open A:\Weather\October.dat For Binary As #nFileNum
```

The Seek statement sets the position for the next read or write within a file opened using the Open statement. Then we can use the Get statement to read the data into the variable. For example, to read the integer at position 6, we can use

Figure 8.5
Example of a Binary
File Structure

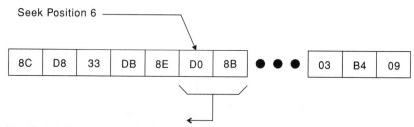

Use Get statement to read 2 bytes into an Integer variable.

Each box represents a byte containing a number shown in hexadecimal.

```
Seek nFileNum, 6
Get nFileNum, , nReading
```

or

```
Get nFileNum, 6, nReading
```

The Get statement knows to read in only 2 bytes because the last argument specifies the Integer data type. Similarly we could write data using the Put statement. (For more information about binary access and the Get, Put, and Seek statements, refer to Visual Basic Help.)

8.5   THE EDITOR PROGRAM

The Editor program is a simple text editor that adds functionality to the original viewer program shown in Figure 8.1 and Example 8.1. The program look and feel is the same as that shown in Figure 8.1. The difference is that all menu items are functional, and the window title displays the file name followed by "Edit Demo V1" instead of "Simple Viewer V1." Example 8.4 shows the code:

Example 8.4

```
' Simple Text Editor
' Program demonstrates Sequential File Access for both read and ➡
write operations
' User can select New, Open, Save and Save As menu items

    ' Note cmdExit_Click(), mnuExit_Click() same as Example 8.1

Option Explicit
Const MSGTITLE = "Edit File Demo"

Private Sub Form_Load()
    ' Set up file dialog properties and start as a new document

    ' Set up Filter format for file access dialogs,
    ' see comments in mnuOpen_Click in Example 8.1
    Dim sFilter As String

    sFilter = "Text¦ (*.txt)¦*.txt¦Pictures, ➡
    (*.bmp;*.ico)¦*.bmp;*.ico"
    sFilter = sFilter & "¦Data (*.dat)¦*.dat¦All Files (*.*)¦*.*"

    ' Save File Dialog
    dlgFile.Flags = cdlOFNFileMustExist ' Only permit existing ➡
    files to be opened
    dlgFile.Filter = sFilter    ' Define File Types list
    dlgFile.DefaultExt = ".txt" ' Default file extension
    dlgFile.FilterIndex = 1 ' Show default extension
    mnuNew_Click    ' To start as a new document
End Sub
```

```
Private Sub mnuNew_Click()
    ' Clear text box and remove previous file information
    txtFileContent.Text = ""
    frmEdit1.Caption = "Untitled - Edit Demo V1"
    dlgFile.filename = ""
    txtFileInfo.Text = ""
End Sub


Private Sub mnuSaveAs_Click()
    ' Displays the File Save As dialog and then saves it
    On Error Resume Next

    ' Common Dialog properties already set up in Form_Load
    dlgFile.ShowSave    ' Display the File Save dialog

    If Err.Number = cdlCancel Then  ' User clicked Cancel
        MsgBox "Operation cancelled", , MSGTITLE
        lblFileContent.Caption = "File Contents"
    Else
        Save
    End If

End Sub


Private Sub mnuSave_Click()
    ' Simply saves the current file.  If the user selects this ➡
    menu item
    ' "accidentally" without previously assigning a file name, we
    ' detect this and launch the Save As dialog
    If dlgFile.filename = "" Then
        mnuSaveAs_Click
    Else
        Save
    End If

End Sub


Sub Save()
    ' Save Current file.
    ' Procedure called from mnuSaveAs_Click or mnuSave_Click

    Dim sCRLF As String * 2 ' To generate new line in multiline ➡
    text boxes
    Dim nFileNum As Integer ' File number to handle file access

    On Error Resume Next

    sCRLF = Chr(13) & Chr(10)    ' CR and LF required for new lines

    txtFileInfo.Text = dlgFile.filename ' Show selected file ➡
    with full path information
```

```
        txtFileInfo.Text = txtFileInfo.Text & sCRLF & dlgFile.FileTitle ➥
        ' Show file name portion only
        ' Show Flag info.  See VB Help Topic Flags Property (File Dialog)
        txtFileInfo.Text = txtFileInfo.Text & sCRLF & "File Dialog ➥
        Flag = " & Hex(dlgFile.Flags)

        nFileNum = FreeFile     ' Get next available file number
        ' Enable I/O to file for sequential output access
        ' Cue user that file opening in progress
        lblFileContent.Caption = "Saving file ...."
        DoEvents

        Open dlgFile.filename For Output As #nFileNum

        ' Trap file open errors if they occur
        If Err.Number <> 0 Then
            MsgBox CStr(CVErr(Err.Number)) & " " & Err.Description, ➥
            , MSGTITLE
            lblFileContent.Caption = "File Contents"
            Exit Sub
        Else
            ' Contents of text box into file
            Print #nFileNum, txtFileContent.Text

            Close nFileNum
            ' Cue user that file has been saved
            lblFileContent.Caption = "File Contents"
            frmEdit1.Caption = dlgFile.FileTitle & " - Edit Demo V1"

        End If

        If Err.Number <> 0 Then      ' Error Handling if necessary
            MsgBox CStr(CVErr(Err.Number)) & " " & Err.Description, , ➥
            MSGTITLE
        End If

End Sub

Private Sub mnuOpen_Click()
    ' Displays File Open dialog.  Note that dialog properties are
    ' set up in Form_Load.

    Dim sCRLF As String * 2 ' To generate new line in multiline ➥
    text boxes
    Dim sNextLine As String ' Line read in from file
    Dim sBuffer As String   ' Buffer that stores contents of file
    Dim nFileNum As Integer ' File number to handle file access

    On Error Resume Next

    sCRLF = Chr(13) & Chr(10)
    dlgFile.ShowOpen    ' Display the File Open dialog

    If Err.Number = cdlCancel Then   ' User clicked Cancel
        MsgBox "Operation cancelled", , MSGTITLE
```

```
            lblFileContent.Caption = "File Contents"
            Exit Sub
    End If

    txtFileInfo.Text = dlgFile.filename ' Show selected file ➡
    with full path information
    txtFileInfo.Text = txtFileInfo.Text & sCRLF &
    dlgFile.FileTitle ' Show file name portion only
    ' Show Flag info.  See VB Help Topic Flags Property (File Dialog)
    txtFileInfo.Text = txtFileInfo.Text & sCRLF & "File Dialog ➡
    Flag = " & Hex(dlgFile.Flags)

    nFileNum = FreeFile    ' Get next available file number
    ' Enable I/O to file for sequential input access
    ' Cue user that file opening in progress
    lblFileContent.Caption = "Opening file ...."
    DoEvents

    Open dlgFile.filename For Input As #nFileNum

    ' Trap file open errors if they occur
    If Err.Number <> 0 Then
        MsgBox CStr(CVErr(Err.Number)) & " " & Err.Description, ➡
        , MSGTITLE
        lblFileContent.Caption = "File Contents"
        Exit Sub
    Else
        ' Read in file data into buffer one character at a time
        ' until we reach the end of the file.
        Do While Not EOF(nFileNum) ' Loop until end of file
            Line Input #nFileNum, sNextLine    ' Get one line
            sBuffer = sBuffer & sNextLine & sCRLF  ' and add it ➡
            to buffer
        Loop

        ' Display contents of file using the buffer
        txtFileContent.Text = sBuffer

        ' Close the file since it has been loaded
        Close nFileNum

        ' Cue user that file has been loaded if no errors ➡
        detected during loading
        If Err.Number = 0 Then
            frmEdit1.Caption = dlgFile.FileTitle & " - Edit Demo V1"
        End If
        lblFileContent.Caption = "File Contents"

    End If

    If Err.Number <> 0 Then      ' Error Handling if necessary
        MsgBox CStr(CVErr(Err.Number)) & " " & Err.Description, ➡
        , MSGTITLE
    End If
```

```
End Sub


Private Sub cmdExit_Click()
    Close    ' close all opened files
    End
End Sub


Private Sub mnuExit_Click()
    cmdExit_Click
End Sub
```

Example 8.4 shows the procedures in the order of a typical sequence of operations:

1. The form loads.

2. The user selects menu item New (perhaps after opening an existing file to simply view it).

3. The user types something in the text box (edit area) and selects menu item Save As.

4. The operation of procedures `Form_Load` and `mnuNew_Click` are to set up a clean slate for the editor. At this stage a user would typically type information in text box `txtFileContent`. This modifies the Text property setting. The user can save these changes by selecting Save As to save the information to a file. When the user selects menu item Save As, procedure `mnuSaveAs_Click` will execute. Note that the code to set up the common dialog will now be contained in `Form_Load` since the other file handling operations will use this common set of property settings.

Procedure `mnuSaveAs_Click` is similar to the early part of the `mnuOpen_Click` procedure. It applies the `ShowSave` method to the common dialog object to actually show the dialog to the user, as shown in the following statement:

```
dlgFile.ShowSave    ' Display the File Save dialog
```

If the user clicks OK, the program will call general procedure Save to do the main work of saving the text box information to the file, whatever its name is. The following shows the main part of this procedure:

```
nFileNum = FreeFile    ' Get next available file number
' Enable I/O to file for sequential output access
' Cue user that file opening in progress
lblFileContent.Caption = "Saving file ...."
DoEvents

Open dlgFile.filename For Output As #nFileNum

' Trap file open errors if they occur
If Err.Number <> 0 Then
    MsgBox CStr(CVErr(Err.Number)) & " " & Err.Description, , ➡
    MSGTITLE
    lblFileContent.Caption = "File Contents"
    Exit Sub
Else
    ' Write text box information into file
```

```
Print #nFileNum, txtFileContent.Text
Close nFileNum
' Cue user that file has been saved
lblFileContent.Caption = "File Contents"
frmEdit1.Caption = dlgFile.FileTitle & " - Edit Demo V1"
```

```
End If
```

We must first get a file number so that it can be opened. Note that when the user selects menu item Open, the file is actually closed after opening it. User changes to the text occur while the file is closed. In case the file is very lengthy, we modify a label to give the user some progress information. The statement to open the file is for sequential access to output characters. The file name is the one entered by the user the last time that the Save As dialog was used. Note that the actual operation to put the data into the file is a single statement.

```
Print #nFileNum, txtFileContent.Text
```

The Print statement will send the data that the file handled by the file number. After we have completed this operation, we close the file and provide status information via the label and the form Caption. During a typical editing session, the user will select Save from the File menu to save changes to the text document. This causes procedure mnuSave_Click to execute. Normally, it simply calls general procedure Save. However, the user might select the Save menu without assigning a file name earlier using the Save As menu. In this case, the procedure will trap the mistake and call procedure mnuSaveAs_Click to force the user to provide a name.

8.6   USER-DEFINED DATA TYPE AND MODULE FILES

When we discussed random access files, we mentioned that records are updated using the User-defined data type. In this section we will examine how to set up and use this type of variable. Records are similar to arrays, which we covered in Chapter 6. Remember that an array contains *multiple* elements, and each element of an array is of the *same* data type. The User-defined type also contains *multiple* elements. Each element can be of a *different* data type.

8.6.1   The Definition and Declaration

Before we can use this data type, we have to define it. To begin a definition for a User-defined type, use the keyword Type. To end the definition, use the keywords End Type. In the body of the definition, list the element names as variable declarations. Example 8.5 illustrates a sample definition. We will use this data type for the customer program that we will develop in the next section.

Example 8.5
```
' This code is in CUSTOM1.BAS
Option Explicit
```

```
' Set up a user-defined data type
' that can be used for records in a random access file
' The customer program will update records for each
' customer.  Figure 8.4 illustrates the record organization.

Type Customer
    sFirstName As String * 15    ' 15 characters ( or 30 bytes ➡
    if unicode )
    sLastName As String * 15     ' 15 characters ( or 30 bytes ➡
    if unicode )
    sCanoeModel As String * 8    ' 8 characters ( or 16 bytes ➡
    if unicode )
    lSerialNum As Long  ' 4 bytes
    nAreaCode As Integer    ' 2 bytes
    lLocalTel As Long     ' 4 bytes
End Type
```

Note that elements of the String data type are of fixed length. This is necessary in our case because we will be using the data type for updating records in a random access file. Now we can declare variables of our own User-defined data type. For example, we can declare a variable of type `Customer` as follows:

```
Dim m_ThisCustomer As Customer     ' A record variable
```

In this case, we are declaring it in the General Declarations area of the form for use by all procedures in the form. Our prefix convention will be that no prefix means that the variable is of a User-defined type. The prefix m_ means that its scope is module level instead of local.

8.6.2   The Dot Operator for Field Access

We will refer to *elements* as *fields* since they will eventually be used as the fields in a record for a random access file. To access an element to set its value or find out its value, use the dot operator. The dot operator is simply that, a dot (.). To access a field, indicate the name of the User-defined type variable followed by a dot, followed by the name of the field (or element). The following illustrates how we can set the Text property of some text box controls using these fields.

```
txtFirstName.Text = m_ThisCustomer.sFirstName
txtLastName.Text = m_ThisCustomer.sLastName
cboCanoeModel.Text = m_ThisCustomer.sCanoeModel
txtSerialNum.Text = CStr(m_ThisCustomer.lSerialNum)
txtAreaCode.Text = CStr(m_ThisCustomer.nAreaCode)
txtLocalTel.Text = CStr(m_ThisCustomer.lLocalTel)
```

The following shows how we can assign values to these fields. In this case, we decided to also show a syntax shortcut.

```
With m_ThisCustomer
    .sFirstName = ""
    .sLastName = ""
    .sCanoeModel = ""
    .lSerialNum = 0
```

```
        .nAreaCode = 0
        .lLocalTel = 0
End With
```

The `With` statement is useful for setting fields. It executes a series of statements on a Single object or a User-defined type. We do not need to state the name of the User-defined type (or object). The syntax is

```
With User-definedDataType-or-Object
    .FieldName-or-Property
    [.similar statements]
End With
```

As hinted, we can also use the `With` statement to access multiple properties of an object. For example, we can set some properties of text box `txtEdit` with the following statement:

```
With txtEdit
    .Text = "Hello"
    .Locked = False
    .TabIndex = 1
    .Visible = True
End With
```

8.6.3   Module Files

It seems that we know all that we need to know about User-defined types. But wait. It is not possible to define a User-defined data type in a Form. The definition must be placed in the declarations section of a *module*.

*A **module** is a set of declarations and procedures in a file named with the extension* `.BAS`.

Modules can be used in multiple projects. Let's say that we have a set of general procedures that we can use in several different programs. Each program is its own Visual Basic project with its own Form (or Forms). Instead of copying the procedures into each form, we can add the same module file to the project. In the Hands-On Exercises we will see how to create such files and subsequently add them to other projects. Actually, the Introduction Template used in the earlier chapters already includes module files. Refer to Figures 1.9a and 1.9b, which show two module files and one form file. In this case, you only wrote your code in the module `Runme.Bas`. The other files provided the framework to launch the programs you wrote. For our customer record situation, we will need to put the code of Example 8.5 in a module file. In this case we will name it `CUSTOM1.BAS`.

8.7   THE CUSTOMER PROGRAM, VERSION 1

Now we will create a program that Cougar Canoe can use to permanently keep track of their customers. Figure 8.6 shows the program in operation. Compare Figure 8.6 with Figure 8.4. Note that the bottom text box shows the record position. The other boxes, including the combo box, show the data corresponding to the fields in record number 2.

The data file is named COUGAR1.CUS, and the user is apparently a morning person. In Chapter 9, we will further develop the program to demonstrate data-handling techniques (algorithms) and organization (data structures), and to show off a few other features. All versions contain many lines of code. If we examined it all at once, it would be overwhelming. Instead, we will examine sections of the program to point out features relevant to the topic being discussed. (Section 9.5 will show the complete listing of the final version. The solution directories (SOLN) for Chapters 8 and 9 of the disk also contain the listings. Feel free to refer to any of these listings.) Figure 8.7 shows the general structure.

8.7.1   The Project Organization and General Declarations

The project file CUSTOM1.VBP defines the file components of the project, a Visual Basic program under development. It lists one form file, CUSTOM1.FRM, and one module file, CUSTOM1.BAS. The module file contains the User-defined data type declaration shown in Example 8.5 as well as one additional function declaration required for input validation. We will look at function TestInteger a bit later. Example 8.6 shows the General Declarations portion of the form CUSTOM1.FRM (Name frmCustomer1). The comments provide some information about the purpose of the variables. Note that there is more documentation work to be done.

Figure 8.6
The Customer Program, Version 1

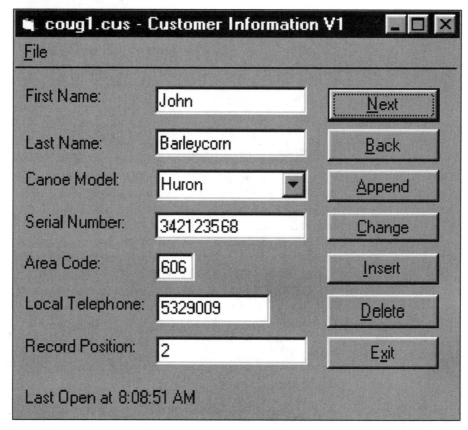

Figure 8.7
Structure Chart for Version 1
of the Customer Information
Program

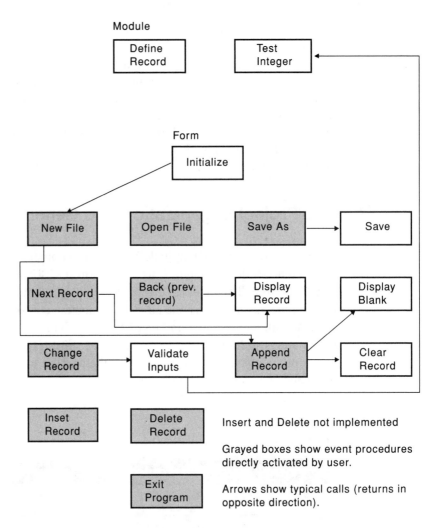

Insert and Delete not implemented

Grayed boxes show event procedures
directly activated by user.

Arrows show typical calls (returns in
opposite direction).

Example 8.6

```
' Customer Record Program - Version 1

Option Explicit

' To do, opening comments
' Also leave as exercise to improve documentation
' to add summary of procedures
' Constants for message boxes
Const MSGTITLE = "Customer Information"
' Some message boxes display Yes and No buttons with a question icon
Const DIALOGTYPE = vbYesNo + vbQuestion
' Form Title will display data file name and program VERSION
Const VERSION = " - Customer Information V1"
' Declare variables
Dim m_ThisCustomer As Customer     ' Contains information in the ➡
current record
Dim m_lPosition As Long    ' Tracks the current record
Dim m_lLastRecord As Long   ' Marks position of last record
Dim m_nRecordLength As Integer   ' Number of bytes in ➡
record stored on disk
```

```
Dim m_sFileName As String  ' Name of current file
Dim m_sNewFile As String   ' Name of new file
Dim m_nFileNum As Integer ' File Number for handling file
' Flag to indicate that user changed a field without ➡
saving it
Dim m_bChange As Boolean
```

In particular, note that we declare one module-level User-defined variable of type Customer.

```
Dim m_ThisCustomer As Customer    ' Contains information in the ➡
current record
```

Recall that data type Customer is defined in the module (see Example 8.5). We will talk about constant DIALOGTYPE a bit later.

8.7.2   Creating the Records

Version 1 does not support Insert and Delete features, hence clicking these buttons will display a message about the feature not being available. Here is an example.

Example 8.7

```
Private Sub cmdInsert_Click()
    ' We will add Insert functionality later
    MsgBox "Not implemented", , MSGTITLE
End Sub

Private Sub cmdDelete_Click()
    ' We will add Delete functionality later
    MsgBox "Not implemented", , MSGTITLE
End Sub
```

For Version 1, we can only append records to the end of a sequence of records. Several procedures are involved in this operation, as shown in Example 8.8.

Example 8.8

```
Private Sub cmdAppend_Click()
    ' Give user a chance to abort append
    ' if any changes had occurred without saving them.

    Dim sMessage As String, nResponse As Integer

    ' Message of warning query
    sMessage = " Something was modified.  "
    sMessage = sMessage & "Do you still want to append a ➡
record?"

     ' Display warning query if there had been a change
    If m_bChange Then
        nResponse = MsgBox(sMessage, DIALOGTYPE, MSGTITLE)
        ' ... and act depending on user response
        If nResponse = vbNo Then
            Exit Sub ' Abort exit if user changes mind
```

```
            Else
                ' User does not care about change
            End If
        End If

        ' Show user blank fields
        ' User will have to use Change button to save entries
        ' New intended record is blank until changed by user
        ClearThisCustomer

        ' Point to intended new record after last record
        m_lLastRecord = m_lLastRecord + 1
        m_lPosition = m_lLastRecord ' Show position to user
        DisplayBlank ' To cue user to enter information

        ' Disable another append until a record change committed by
        ' using Change button
        cmdAppend.Enabled = False
End Sub
```

When the user clicks Append, the program will set up a blank record by calling procedure `ClearThisCustomer`. It will also call `DisplayBlank` to present a new record to the user. At this point the user can enter the information in the text boxes and the combo box. The Append button is disabled so that the user cannot append another record until this one has been committed. We will come back later and examine the early part `cmdAppend_Click`. It warns the user if she or he clicked Append after typing changes to another record but did not save (commit) the modification.

Module variable `m_lLastRecord` maintains the count of records, so it is incremented. The procedure assigns the position indicator, `m_lPosition`, to the last record position since we want to show the new record to the user. General procedure `DisplayBlank` actually does the work of showing the record. Example 8.9 shows how general procedures `ClearThisCusotmer` and `DisplayBlank` operate.

Example 8.9

```
Sub ClearThisCustomer()

    ' Make the record blank
    With m_ThisCustomer
        .sFirstName = ""
        .sLastName = ""
        .sCanoeModel = ""
        .lSerialNum = 0
        .nAreaCode = 0
        .lLocalTel = 0
    End With
End Sub


Sub DisplayBlank()
    ' Show record as a blank
    ' More convenient to user if zeros do not show
    ' up in the serial number, area code and local tel inputs
    txtFirstName.Text = ""
```

```
        txtLastName.Text = ""
        cboCanoeModel.Text = ""
        txtSerialNum.Text = ""
        txtAreaCode.Text = ""
        txtLocalTel.Text = ""
        txtPosition.Text = CStr(m_lPosition)
End Sub
```

Note that module-level variable `m_lPosition` was incremented in `cmd-Append_Click`. At this stage, the user would normally type in the information and then click Change or press the express key combination ALT+C to put the new record into the file. The following shows the code for `cmdChange_Click`.

Example 8.10

```
Private Sub cmdChange_Click()
    ' Modify record that is currently displayed

    ' To do:  error trapping
    ' This version does not check if key (serial number) ➡
    already exists in the file

    If Not ValidInputs Then Exit Sub

    ' Get customer information from user inputs
    With m_ThisCustomer
        .sFirstName = txtFirstName.Text
        .sLastName = txtLastName.Text
        .sCanoeModel = cboCanoeModel.Text
        .lSerialNum = CLng(txtSerialNum.Text)
        .nAreaCode = CInt(txtAreaCode.Text)
        .lLocalTel = CLng(txtLocalTel.Text)
    End With

    ' Put the record into the file (if it exists)
    If m_sFileName = "" Then
        ' Prompt user to create file if necessary
        MsgBox "Use Save As from File menu to create a file ", ➡
        , MSGTITLE
    Else
        ' Modify record only if there is a file to modify
        Put #m_nFileNum, m_lPosition, m_ThisCustomer
        ' ... and reset flag to say change has been saved
        m_bChange = False
        ' Permit another append if record change was for last record
        If m_lPosition = m_lLastRecord Then
            cmdAppend.Enabled = True
        End If
    End If

End Sub
```

The first thing this procedure does is check and validate the inputs. Let's say that the user does not select a canoe model but clicks Change. According to Cougar Canoe's business rules, this would be invalid information. Function `ValidInputs` checks what the user typed in and returns `True` or `False`, depending on whether or not the inputs are valid. In this case, since the user did not select a model, the function returns `False` and `cmdChange_Click` exits. In fact, it is not possible to proceed beyond this point until all the inputs are valid. We will come back shortly and examine how function `ValidInputs` does this.

Once it has been established that the inputs are valid, the fields for variable `m_ThisCustomer` are modified according to the information placed in the text boxes by the user. Then the procedure checks if a file already exists. If not, it prompts the user to create one and then exits. The record information will not be put into a file until there is a file in which to put it. After the user has created a file by using Save As in the File menu, she or he would have to click Change again. Again note that it is not possible to append further records until the user commits this one by clicking Change. Assuming that a file already exists, the procedure uses the `Put` statement to finally write the changes physically to the file on disk.

```
Put #m_nFileNum, m_lPosition, m_ThisCustomer
```

After this statement is executed, some flags are cleared to permit the user to append additional records or move forward (next) and back to view records.

Review Challenge

Procedure `TestInteger` is declared in module file `CUSTOM1.BAS`. Can it access variable `m_lPosition`? Why?

Solution

No. Variable `m_lPosition` is module level in scope. Only procedures that are part of `CUSTOM1.FRM` can access this variable. To declare a variable as global for access by all procedures in the project, it is necessary to declare it in the General Declarations section of a module (not a form) using the keyword `Public`.

8.7.3   Navigation: Viewing the Records

Note that the user can change any existing record by clicking Next and Back as required to view the record, keying in the changes and then clicking Change to put the changes into the file. Procedures `cmdNext_Click` and `cmdBack_Click` implement moving to the next record or back to the previous record, respectively. After a considerable amount of overhead, and depending on various conditions, both procedures will call general procedure `DisplayInfo` to actually display the information. We will show the code for `DisplayInfo` now and show the code for `cmdNext_Click` and `cmdBack_Click` afterward.

Example 8.11

```
Sub DisplayInfo()

    ' Show current record information to user

    ' Blank information if last append not completed, unless ➥
    file just opened
```

```
    If cmdAppend.Enabled = False And m_lPosition = m_lLastRecord Then
        DisplayBlank        '
    Else       ' Otherwise show what the current record is
        txtFirstName.Text = m_ThisCustomer.sFirstName
        txtLastName.Text = m_ThisCustomer.sLastName
        cboCanoeModel.Text = m_ThisCustomer.sCanoeModel
        txtSerialNum.Text = CStr(m_ThisCustomer.lSerialNum)
        txtAreaCode.Text = CStr(m_ThisCustomer.nAreaCode)
        txtLocalTel.Text = CStr(m_ThisCustomer.lLocalTel)
    End If

    txtPosition.Text = CStr(m_lPosition)

End Sub
```

This procedure simply sets text properties to show what is in the current record. There is some overhead necessary to handle special circumstances, as explained in the comments. The procedures for the Next and Back buttons are similar. The portion for cmdNext_Click that handles showing the next record is

```
' Show next record
If m_lPosition < m_lLastRecord Then
    m_lPosition = m_lPosition + 1
    Get m_nFileNum, m_lPosition, m_ThisCustomer
    DisplayInfo
Else
    Beep
End If
```

It increments the position pointer m_lPosition unless the user is already viewing the last record. Then it gets the next record and calls DisplayInfo to present the information to the user. The portion for cmdBack_Click that handles showing the previous record is

```
' Show previous record
If m_lPosition > 1 Then
    m_lPosition = m_lPosition - 1
    Get m_nFileNum, m_lPosition, m_ThisCustomer
    DisplayInfo
Else
    Beep
End If
```

It works similarly except that pointer m_lPosition is decremented unless the user is already viewing the first record.

8.7.4   Warn the User About Record Changes

Soon we will show the complete code for cmdNext_Click and cmdBack_Click, but first let's look at additional code to handle record changes. It is possible that the user might key in some changes to a record and click Next and Back without clicking Change. Either the user changed his or her mind about the keyed-in modifications or simply forgot to commit the modifications by clicking Change (or pressing ALT+C). The algorithm to handle record change detection is shown in Example 8.12.

Example 8.12

```
In the event of attempted Append (as well as insert and delete)
    Disable further Append (as well as insert and delete)

In the event of any text change
    set Change flag

Next_Click or Back_Click or Append_Click
    If Change flag set then warn user
    If user ignores warning
        Then proceed and clear Change flag
        Else exit procedure (this permits user to commit Change)

Change_Click
    Clear Change flag
```

Note that there is a statement to disable button cmdAppend in procedure cmd-Append_Click (see Example 8.8):

```
' Disable another append until a record change committed by
' using Change button
cmdAppend.Enabled = False
```

To detect text changes, use the Change event.

Example 8.13

```
Private Sub txtFirstName_Change()
    ' Flag that change occurred
    m_bChange = True
End Sub


' ***************************************************************
'   Identical code for txtLastName_Click, cboCanoeModel_Change,
' txtSerialNum_Change, txtAreaCode_Change, and txtLocalTel_Change ***
' ***************************************************************
```

Note that in procedure cmdChange_Click (Example 8.10), there is a statement to clear the flag:

```
' ... and reset flag to say change has been saved
m_bChange = False
```

Now we will examine the part to warn the user and react according to the user response. Look back at procedure cmdAppend_Click (Example 8.8) and note the following code segment.

Example 8.14

```
' Give user a chance to abort append
' if any changes had occurred without saving them

Dim sMessage As String, nResponse As Integer

' Message of warning query
sMessage = " Something was modified.   "
sMessage = sMessage & "Do you still want to append a record?"
```

```
' Display warning query if there had been a change
If m_bChange Then
    nResponse = MsgBox(sMessage, DIALOGTYPE, MSGTITLE)
    ' ... and act depending on user response
    If nResponse = vbNo Then
        Exit Sub ' Abort exit if user changes mind
    Else
        ' User does not care about change
    End If
End If
```

Note that the If Then block executes only if there was a change, as indicated by flag m_bChange. To further understand this code segment, we need to look at customized message boxes.

8.7.5   Customized Message Boxes

Figure 8.8 shows a customized message box; Example 8.14 shows the use of the box. When a modification is detected (flag m_bChange is True), the program displays the message box. If the user clicks No, the procedure is exited. Otherwise, if the user clicks Yes, the program continues (the user chose to ignore the modification). We are using the MsgBox *function* instead of the MsgBox *statement*. The function returns a value to indicate the response to the message. The message box is an example of a ***modal window***.

*A window or dialog box that requires the user to take action before the focus can switch to another form or dialog box is called **modal**. **Modeless** describes a window or dialog box that does not require user action before the focus can be switched to another form or dialog box.*

The second argument specifies the characteristics of the message box and customizes it. If it is omitted, the default message box with no icon and an OK button is shown. In the General Declarations (see Example 8.6), there is a statement to define the constant DIALOGTYPE. Recall that the third argument specifies the title displayed in the message box.

```
' Constants for message boxes
Const MSGTITLE = "Customer Information"
' Some message boxes display Yes and No buttons with a question icon
Const DIALOGTYPE = vbYesNo + vbQuestion
```

Figure 8.8
A Customized Message Box to Query the User

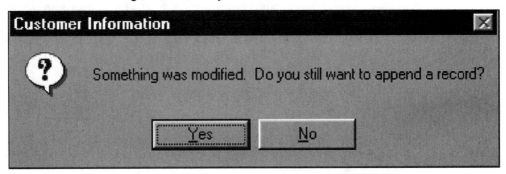

To define DIALOGTYPE, we add two Visual Basic constants, vbYesNo and vbQuestion. Generally, that is all there is to it. Behind the scenes, Visual Basic knows what type of dialog box to display by an integer code. With the use of Visual Basic Help, we would find that the value of these constants are

vbYesNo = 4 to display Yes and No buttons
vbQuestion = 32 to display the Warning Query icon (a question mark)

The function will return another integer code to indicate which button was pressed. Again, Visual Basic has predefined constants to indicate these codes:

vbYes = 6 meaning the user clicked Yes
vbNo = 7 meaning the user clicked No

To further emphasize that Visual Basic is using integer codes, note that the following code segment would do exactly the same thing as the corresponding segment shown in Example 8.14.

```
' Display warning query if there had been a change
If m_bChange Then
    nResponse = MsgBox(sMessage, 36, MSGTITLE)
    ' ... and act depending on user response
    If nResponse = 7 Then
        Exit Sub ' Abort exit if user changes mind
    Else
        ' User does not care about change
    End If
End If
```

The code for cmdNext_Click and cmdBack_Click performs similar operations. We show the complete code for both as Example 8.15.

Example 8.15

```
Private Sub cmdNext_Click()
    ' Give user a chance to abort the next move
    ' if any changes had occurred without saving them

    Dim sMessage As String, nResponse As Integer

    ' Message of warning query
    sMessage = " Something was modified.  "
    sMessage = sMessage & "Do you still want to go to the next ➡
    record?"

    ' Display warning query if there had been a change
    If m_bChange Then
        nResponse = MsgBox(sMessage, DIALOGTYPE, MSGTITLE)
        ' ... and act depending on user response
        If nResponse = vbNo Then
    Exit Sub ' Abort exit if user changes mind
        Else
            ' User does not care about change
        End If
    End If

    ' Show next record
```

```
        If m_lPosition < m_lLastRecord Then
            m_lPosition = m_lPosition + 1
            Get m_nFileNum, m_lPosition, m_ThisCustomer
            DisplayInfo
            'm_bChange = False    ' Reset Flag
        Else
            Beep
        End If


        ' Reset change flag since user ignored change warning
        m_bChange = False

End Sub


Private Sub cmdBack_Click()
        ' Give user a chance to abort the back move
        ' if any changes had occurred without saving them

        Dim sMessage As String, nResponse As Integer

        ' Message of warning query
        sMessage = " Something was modified.   "
        sMessage = sMessage & "Do you still want to go to the ➡
        previous record?"
        ' Display warning query if there had been a change
        If m_bChange Then
            nResponse = MsgBox(sMessage, DIALOGTYPE, MSGTITLE)
            ' ... and act depending on user response
            If nResponse = vbNo Then
                Exit Sub ' Abort exit if user changes mind
            Else
                ' User does not care about change
            End If
        End If

        ' Show previous record
        If m_lPosition > 1 Then
            m_lPosition = m_lPosition - 1
            Get m_nFileNum, m_lPosition, m_ThisCustomer
            DisplayInfo
        Else
            Beep
        End If
        ' Reset change flag since user ignored change warning
        m_bChange = False
End Sub
```

Next, we will look at the remaining parts of the Customer program.

8.7.6   Troubleshooting: Validate the Inputs

We need to ensure as much as possible that the records only contain data that match the real world and business rules of Cougar Canoe. The first and last names should not be null. Is it worthwhile to filter out possible nonsense names using a name dictionary? We use a combo box for canoe model selection—but this doesn't stop the user from typing something else in the text box portion. Serial numbers must be integers with nine digits. Area codes must have three digits, and the local telephone number must have seven digits. The telephone number rules are for North America—but what about the international market? Our input validation will not take care of all possible scenarios, but real-life design decisions often involve compromises to keep development costs in line.

The customer program uses two routines for input validation. `ValidInputs` is a programmer-defined function declared in the general procedures section of the form `frmCustomer1`. It returns `True` if the data entered by the user is valid. It uses a second function named `TestInteger` that returns `True` if the argument is an integer sequence (Long data type). Function `TestInteger` is declared in module `Custom1`. Both functions use the same basic algorithm. Clear a flag to be `False`, and apply various conditional tests. If all the tests are passed, then set the flag `True`.

Example 8.16

```
Function ValidInputs() As Boolean
    ' Force user to enter valid inputs before committing change ➥
    to record
    ' This function declared in the General Declarations ➥
    section of the form

    ' Initially assume false
    ValidInputs = False

    ' Trim all strings first
    txtFirstName.Text = Trim(txtFirstName.Text)
    txtLastName.Text = Trim(txtLastName.Text)
    cboCanoeModel.Text = Trim(cboCanoeModel.Text)
    txtSerialNum.Text = Trim(txtSerialNum.Text)
    txtAreaCode.Text = Trim(txtAreaCode.Text)
    txtLocalTel.Text = Trim(txtLocalTel.Text)

    ' Must have something in text fields
    If txtFirstName.Text = "" Then
        txtFirstName.SetFocus
    ElseIf txtLastName.Text = "" Then
        txtLastName.SetFocus
    ElseIf cboCanoeModel.Text = "" Then
        cboCanoeModel.SetFocus
    ' txtSerialNum.MaxLength = 9
    ElseIf Len(txtSerialNum.Text) <> 9 Then ' Must have 9 digits
        txtSerialNum.SetFocus
    ElseIf Not TestInteger(txtSerialNum.Text) Then
        txtSerialNum.SetFocus
    ' txtAreaCode.MaxLength = 3
    ElseIf Len(txtAreaCode.Text) <> 3 Then   ' Must have 3 digits
        txtAreaCode.SetFocus
    ElseIf Not TestInteger(txtAreaCode.Text) Then
        txtAreaCode.SetFocus
    ' txtLocalTel.MaxLength = 7
    ElseIf Len(txtLocalTel.Text) <> 7 Then
        txtLocalTel.SetFocus
```

```
    ElseIf Not TestInteger(txtLocalTel.Text) Then
        txtLocalTel.SetFocus
    Else
        ValidInputs = True   ' Otherwise okay
    End If


End Function

Function TestInteger(sTest As String) As Boolean
    ' This is an extension of IsNumeric to ensure that string
    ' data contains only digits.  Declared in the module
    ' Initially assume false

    TestInteger = False

    If IsNumeric(sTest) Then
        If InStr(sTest, ".") = 0 And InStr(sTest, "-") = 0 Then
            If InStr(sTest, ",") = 0 And InStr(sTest, "%") = 0 Then
                If InStr(sTest, "+") = 0 And InStr(sTest, "$") = 0 Then
                    TestInteger = True
                End If
            End If
        End If
    End If

End Function
```

Some comments state the MaxLength settings of some of the text boxes. In this case, we set the MaxLength properties during the visual development phase in design mode. It is possible to set properties in code instead of using design time settings. However, there is a minor performance penalty since the computer would have to execute these statements redundantly. The comments, on the other hand, make it clear (or remind us) about any relationships between the visual programming (design mode) settings and the coding.

Since the fields are of fixed length, we set the MaxLength properties to restrict the number of characters entered by the user. This is the case for txtSerialNum, txtAreaCode, and txtLocalTel. However, we left the MaxLength at its default setting for txtFirstName and txtLastName. The First Name and Last Name field in a record are declared as 15 characters each, so why didn't we set the MaxLength property of the corresponding text boxes to 15? It turns out that this has an undesirable side effect. (With Visual Basic, we can prototype sections of code to detect potential side effects.) Let's say we set the MaxLength property of txtFirstName and txtLastName to 15. When the program gets the record and assigns field values to the text boxes, it will pad the String values with extra spaces to make the length *exactly* 15 characters. Then it will be necessary for the user to delete the extra spaces in order to modify the text. We could fix this by using the Trim function to remove the extra spaces. We chose instead to leave the MaxLength properties of txtFirstName and txtLastName at their default values. With the MaxLength properties set at a default to 0 (0 means an unlimited number of characters), the user can type more than 15 characters in both the First Name and Last Name text boxes. However, the program will truncate the extra characters when the text is put in the record.

Note that `ValidInputs` uses the `SetFocus` method. Recall that *focus* means that the object can receive keyboard inputs. Furthermore, only one object at a time can have the *focus*. If a text box has the focus, the keyboard cursor is flashing inside the box waiting for input. The `SetFocus` method takes the focus away from any object that may have had it and gives it to the object to which the `SetFocus` method is being applied. If the user clicks Change, the Append button will not be enabled, and the cursor will flash in the first box with delinquent data.

The `InStr` function returns the first position of a string (specified by the second argument) within another string (specified by the first argument). For example, `InStr("Cougar Canoe ", "u ")` would return 3. The function would return 0 if the second string is not found. Visual Basic will accept certain strings that have numeric style formats as being numeric. For example, `"$4,300.00"` would be accepted as numeric (depending on system regional settings), but our requirements insist on digit sequences.

8.7.7   Facilitate Keyboard Use to Avoid the Mouse

The application is keyboard intensive because the user is entering or modifying data. With a typical Windows program, we can do several things to make the user's use of the keyboard easier. Pressing the TAB key can move the focus to the next object. Pressing SHIFT+TAB can move the focus back to the object that previously had the focus.

Refer to Figure 8.6. Wouldn't it be easier if the user could press the TAB key to move from one field to the next in the order of top to bottom? Wouldn't it be useful if pressing TAB did not force the user to move to each command button in order to edit the next record? The TabIndex property defines the order in which objects will receive the focus when the TAB key is pressed. The TabStop property determines whether the object is included in the tabbing sequence. If TabStop is set to `False`, the object can only receive the focus if the user clicks on it using the mouse or by pressing the corresponding express key combination. In this case, we will set the TabStop property to `False` for all command buttons. Thus, the only way to activate them by the keyboard is to use the corresponding access key combination, such as ALT+N for the Next button.

The Change button seems to be the one used most often. We can set its Default property to `True` so that pressing ENTER at any time will activate the button. Only one command button can have its Default property set to `True`. If the Cancel property of a command button is set to `True`, the user can activate it by pressing the ESC key. The Exit button seems to be a good candidate for having a Cancel property set `True` (only one button can have a Cancel property with a `True` setting.)

*Default set **True** means that the pressed button recognizes the Click event when the user presses ENTER (unless another button has the focus). Cancel set `True` means that the pressed button recognizes the Click event when the user presses ESC.*

Normally we could set these properties in the design mode by setting them in the Properties window. To make the purpose clear for setting these properties, we could code the property settings. The performance penalty isn't much of an issue since `Form_Load` is executed only once. Example 8.17 shows the `Form_Load` procedure used to set up these properties. It performs other required initialization, including the File dialog settings. (We will talk about the file dialog in the next section.)

Example 8.17

```
Private Sub Form_Load()
    ' Perform necessary initialization

    Dim sFilter As String    ' For common file dialog filter

    ' Determine record length
    m_nRecordLength = Len(m_ThisCustomer)

    ' Set up combo box
    cboCanoeModel.AddItem "Erie"
    cboCanoeModel.AddItem "Huron"
    cboCanoeModel.AddItem "Michigan"
    cboCanoeModel.AddItem "Ontario"
    cboCanoeModel.AddItem "Superior"
    cboCanoeModel.ListIndex = 0 ' Default Model

    mnuNew_Click    ' Set up brand new file

    ' set up filter for save dialog
    sFilter = "Customer (*.cus)¦*.cus¦Text (*.txt)¦*.txt¦All ➥
Files (*.*)¦*.*"

    ' Save File Dialog
    dlgFile.Filter = sFilter    ' Define File Types list

    dlgFile.DefaultExt = ".cus" ' Default file extension
    dlgFile.FilterIndex = 1 ' By default, show only files with ➥
default extension
    dlgFile.CancelError = True ' Enable handling if user clicks ➥
cancel in file dialog

    ' For curiosity, show record length in bytes (when stored ➥
on disk)
    MsgBox "Record size is " & CStr(Len(m_ThisCustomer)) & " ➥
file bytes."

    ' Set up tab index for convenience of user
    ' User can tab from one field to the next to minimize mouse use
    txtFirstName.TabIndex = 0
    txtLastName.TabIndex = 1
    cboCanoeModel.TabIndex = 2
    txtSerialNum.TabIndex = 3
    txtAreaCode.TabIndex = 4
    txtLocalTel.TabIndex = 5
    ' Disable tab action to other input controls
    ' User will have to use access key or mouse to use buttons
    cmdNext.TabStop = False
    cmdBack.TabStop = False
    cmdAppend.TabStop = False
    cmdChange.TabStop = False
    cmdInsert.TabStop = False
    cmdDelete.TabStop = False
```

```
        cmdExit.TabStop = False
        txtPosition.TabStop = False ' Show record position using ➥
        text box
        txtPosition.Locked = True   ' ... it is read only to user

        ' Make Change the Default button meaning that it receives ➥
        the ENTER key
        ' if no other button has the focus
        cmdChange.Default = True
        ' Make Exit the Cancel button meaning that it receives the ➥
        ESC key
        cmdExit.Cancel = True
        m_bChange = False ' No change detected until user does something
End Sub
```

From the code, note that the default extension for files being accessed is `.CUS`. (For a reminder about setting up the combo box, refer to Section 7.8.4.) This procedure also calls `mnuNew_Click` to set up a new file. The `Form_Load` procedure also executes the following `MsgBox` statement:

```
' For curiosity, show record length in bytes (when stored on disk)
MsgBox "Record size is " & CStr(Len(m_ThisCustomer)) & " file bytes."
```

This isn't necessary for the application itself. We included it for instructional purposes. It simply states how many bytes are used to store each record on disk.

8.7.8   File Menu Operations

The customer program has several menu items (menu objects). They are shown in Table 8.1.

The upper level menu item is `mnuFile`, and the others are submenus. Menu object `mnuSep1` is used to provide a separator bar, and its Caption is a single dash (-). As shown in Example 8.18, procedure `mnuNew_Click` is used to set up a new file.

Example 8.18

```
Private Sub mnuNew_Click()
        ' Set up title, filename, and record pointers for new file

        ' Give user a chance to abort the open
        ' if any changes have occurred and not been saved.
```

Table 8.1
Menu Objects for the Customer Program, Version 1

Name	Caption
mnuFile	&File
mnuNew	&New
mnuOpen	&Open...
mnuSaveAs	Save &As...
mnuSep1	-
mnuExit	E&xit

```
    Dim sMessage As String, nResponse As Integer

    ' Message of warning query
    sMessage = " Something was modified.   "
    sMessage = sMessage & "Do you still want to start new data?"

    ' Display warning query if there had been a change
    If m_bChange Then
        nResponse = MsgBox(sMessage, DIALOGTYPE, MSGTITLE)
        ' ... and act depending on user response
        If nResponse = vbNo Then
            Exit Sub ' Abort exit if user changes mind
        Else
            ' User does not care about change
        End If
    End If

    Close m_nFileNum ' Close previous file if applicable

    frmCustomer1.Caption = "Untitled" & VERSION
    ' m_sFileName = "Untitled.cus"
    m_sFileName = ""
    m_lPosition = 0     ' Current record is first one
    m_lLastRecord = 0    ' and it is the only one

    ' Show user that only no field exists until first one appended
    cmdAppend_Click
    ' Reset the flag
    m_bChange = False
End Sub
```

Note that this procedure calls cmdAppend_Click (see Example 8.8) so that the user sees the first record as a blank waiting for input. To open an existing file, the user can select the Open menu item, which will display the File Open dialog box (see Example 8.19).

Example 8.19

```
Private Sub mnuOpen_Click()
    On Error Resume Next
    ' Give user a chance to abort the open
    ' if any changes have occurred and not been saved
    Dim sMessage As String, nResponse As Integer

    ' Message of warning query
    sMessage = " Something was modified.   "
    sMessage = sMessage & "Do you still want to open another file?"
    ' Display warning query if there had been a change
    If m_bChange Then
        nResponse = MsgBox(sMessage, DIALOGTYPE, MSGTITLE)
        ' ... and act depending on user response
        If nResponse = vbNo Then
            Exit Sub ' Abort exit if user changes mind
        Else
            ' User does not care about change
        End If
    End If
```

```
            ' This is where the action starts.  Launch the File Open ➡
            dialog now!
            dlgFile.ShowOpen     ' Display the File Open dialog
            If Err.Number = cdlCancel Then  ' User clicked Cancel
                MsgBox "Operation canceled", , MSGTITLE
                Exit Sub
            End If
            Close m_nFileNum      ' Close existing file if applicable
            m_nFileNum = FreeFile    ' Get next available file number
            ' Cue user that file opening in progress
            lblMessage.Caption = "Opening file ...."
            DoEvents

            ' Open a different file for random access
            m_sFileName = dlgFile.filename
            Open m_sFileName For Random As #m_nFileNum Len = m_nRecordLength
            ' Trap file open errors if they occur
            If Err.Number <> 0 Then
                MsgBox CStr(CVErr(Err.Number)) & " " & Err.Description, ➡
                , MSGTITLE
                lblMessage.Caption = ""
                Exit Sub
            Else
                ' Cue user that file has been opened and show first record
                'if no errors occurred
                If Err.Number = 0 Then
                    lblMessage.Caption = "Last Open at " & CStr(Time)
                    frmCustomer1.Caption = dlgFile.FileTitle & VERSION
                    m_lPosition = 1 ' Point to first record
                    ' Get statement copies record(m_nPosition) into ➡
                    m_ThisCustomer
                    Get m_nFileNum, m_lPosition, m_ThisCustomer    ' ➡
                    Read the record

                    ' Show the first record to the user
                    txtFirstName.Text = m_ThisCustomer.sFirstName
                    txtLastName.Text = m_ThisCustomer.sLastName
                    cboCanoeModel.Text = m_ThisCustomer.sCanoeModel
                    txtSerialNum.Text = CStr(m_ThisCustomer.lSerialNum)
                    txtAreaCode.Text = CStr(m_ThisCustomer.nAreaCode)
                    txtLocalTel.Text = CStr(m_ThisCustomer.lLocalTel)

                    ' Find position of last record
                    m_lLastRecord = LOF(m_nFileNum) / m_nRecordLength
                    ' Enable Append button
                    cmdAppend.Enabled = True
                    ' Clear flag
                    m_bChange = False
                End If
            End If

            If Err.Number <> 0 Then      ' Error Handling if necessary
```

```
        MsgBox CStr(CVErr(Err.Number)) & " " & Err.Description, ➥
        , MSGTITLE
        lblMessage.Caption = "" ' Remove any message
    End If

End Sub
```

The main objective of this procedure is to open the selected file for random access:

```
' Open a different file for random access
m_sFileName = dlgFile.filename
Open m_sFileName For Random As #m_nFileNum Len = m_nRecordLength
```

Also, note how the code determines the position of the last record:

```
' Find position of last record
m_lLastRecord = LOF(m_nFileNum) / m_nRecordLength
```

The Length of File (LOF) function returns the number of bytes in the file. Divide this by the number of bytes in the record to obtain the number of records. The rest of the code is overhead to handle various scenarios and perform initialization. The customer program provides the ability to save a file under a new name. Example 8.20 shows the listing for the two procedures that do this.

Example 8.20

```
Private Sub mnuSaveAs_Click()
    ' Launch File Save Dialog and call general procedure Save ➥
    if applicable
    On Error Resume Next
    dlgFile.ShowSave   ' Display the File Save dialog
    m_sNewFile = dlgFile.filename
    If Err.Number = cdlCancel Then  ' User clicked Cancel
        MsgBox "Operation cancelled", , MSGTITLE
        lblMessage.Caption = ""
    Else
        Save    ' User must have clicked OK so go ahead and save
    End If
End Sub


Sub Save()
        ' Save Current file.
        On Error Resume Next
        Close m_nFileNum ' Close existing file if applicable
        ' Cue user that file saving in progress
        lblMessage.Caption = "Saving file ...."
        DoEvents
        ' Handle situation if this is the first time we are ➥
        saving this file
        If m_sFileName = "" Then
            m_nFileNum = FreeFile
            Open m_sNewFile For Random As #m_nFileNum Len = ➥
            m_nRecordLength
            m_sFileName = m_sNewFile ' Assign file name from dialog
        Else
```

```
            ' Otherwise copy existing file to new file
            FileCopy m_sFileName, m_sNewFile
            ' Open new file
            Open m_sNewFile For Random As #m_nFileNum Len = ➡
            m_nRecordLength
        End If

        ' Trap file copy errors if they occur
        If Err.Number = 70 Then
            ' User attempted to save using same file name
            MsgBox "File already exists", , MSGTITLE
            lblMessage.Caption = ""
            Exit Sub
        ElseIf Err.Number <> 0 Then
            MsgBox CStr(CVErr(Err.Number)) & " " & ➡
            Err.Description, , MSGTITLE
            lblMessage.Caption = "Last Save Unsuccessful"
            Exit Sub
        Else
            ' Update File Name
            m_sFileName = m_sNewFile
            frmCustomer1.Caption = m_sFileName & VERSION
            ' Cue user that file has been saved
            lblMessage.Caption = "Last Save at " & CStr(Time)
            frmCustomer1.Caption = dlgFile.FileTitle & VERSION
        End If

        If Err.Number <> 0 Then        ' Error Handling if necessary
            MsgBox CStr(CVErr(Err.Number)) & " " & ➡
            Err.Description, , MSGTITLE
        End If

End Sub
```

There is one more operation remaining. Example 8.21 shows the code to implement exiting the program.

Example 8.21

```
Private Sub mnuExit_Click()
    ' Exit the program
    cmdExit_Click
End Sub


Private Sub cmdExit_Click()
    ' Exit the program but give user a chance to abort the exit
    ' if any changes have occurred and not been saved
    Dim sMessage As String, nResponse As Integer

    ' Message of warning query
    sMessage = " Something was modified.  "
    sMessage = sMessage & "Do you still want to quit?"
    ' Display warning query if there had been a change
    If m_bChange Then
        nResponse = MsgBox(sMessage, DIALOGTYPE, MSGTITLE)
```

```
            ' ... and act depending on user response
        If nResponse = vbNo Then
            Exit Sub ' Abort exit if user changes mind
        Else
            Close   ' Close all files
            End ' Exit if user does not care about change
        End If
    Else ' Exit if no change occurred
        Close    ' Close all files
        End
    End If
End Sub
```

The Exit operation has safeguards that warn the user about changes before it closes files. However, the insistent user can bypass these by selecting Close from the Control menu box in the upper left corner of the window or by clicking the Close button in the upper right corner.

8.7.9   Looking Ahead

Notice how complex software development has become. Our customer program has plenty of functionality built into it and is quite robust. We can modify existing record files by changing existing records and appending new records. However, it does not yet implement the ability to insert new records in a record location of our choice. We cannot delete records. We will add this functionality in Chapter 9. We will also add additional features whose main purpose is to illustrate data structures.

SUMMARY

This chapter covered storage operations. The Simple Text Viewer program permits the user to view the contents of a file, although the format is assumed to be text. It introduces the use of the common dialog, menu controls, and file processing.

A dialog occurs when the program requires additional information from the user, or provides additional information to the user. The Visual Basic common dialog control permits one to easily implement such common Windows dialogs as

Open a file
Save a file
Select a font
Select a color
Print a file
Display and run a specified Help file

In this chapter, we covered dialogs to open and save files. To use the common dialog control, modify its properties. Then use one of the specific methods that it recognizes to specify the type of dialog. This control does not respond directly to events. To use a file open dialog, use the ShowOpen method. To use a file save dialog, use the ShowSave method.

To handle the situation of a user canceling a dialog when the user clicks Cancel, set up the control to trap a Cancel error in the code and trap the error. Section 8.2 describes other properties that need to be set up, or you can refer to Visual Basic Help.

To create the menu control objects, select the Menu Editor. The Hands-On Exercises explain how to use the Menu Editor. Selecting a menu item automatically displays sub-menu items, if there are any. Selecting one of these menus will cause the associated Click event procedure to execute.

Remember that a file is a group of bytes located on a disk. With Visual Basic we can access files in one of three ways:

- Sequential
- Random Access
- Binary

It is necessary to use a file number when accessing files. A file number is a handle for the program to use in order to work with a file. To obtain a file number, use the `FreeFile` function.

The bytes in a sequential file are organized into lines. A line is a sequence of characters followed by the Carriage Return character and a Line Feed character. There are three ways to open a file for sequential access:

```
To input characters from a file: Open PathAndFilename For Input ➥
As #FileNumber
To output characters to a file:  Open PathAndFilename For Output ➥
As #FileNumber
To append characters to a file:  Open PathAndFilename For Append ➥
As #FileNumber
```

The file must already exist when you open it for Input. If the file doesn't exist, an error will occur. However, if you try to open a file that doesn't exist for Output or Append, it will be created. With sequential access, we can read or write a line at a time. The EOF (End Of File) function returns `True` when the end of the file is reached; otherwise, it will return `False`. To write a line, use the `Write` statement.

To write the contents of entire text boxes to a file, we can enter something like: `Print #nFileNum, txtFileContent.Text`.

The bytes in a random access file are organized into identical records. Each record consists of data blocks known as fields. To open a file for random access, use the following syntax for the `Open` statement:

```
Open PathAndFileName For Random As #FileNumber Len = RecordLength
```

To read a record, use the `Get` statement:

```
Get FileNumber, RecordPosition, User-definedTypeVariable
```

To write data to a record, use the `Put` statement:

```
Put #FileNumber, RecordPosition, User-definedTypeVariable
```

The bytes in a binary file are simply a sequence with no predefined organization. To open a file for binary access, use an `Open` statement with the following syntax:

```
Open PathAndFileName For Binary As #FileNumber
```

Use the `Get` and `Put` statements to read and write data, respectively:

```
Get FileNumber, BytePosition, SomeVariable
Put FileNumber, BytePosition, SomeOtherVariable
```

The Editor program permits the user to view and modify the contents of a file, although the format is assumed to be text. It further develops the use of the common dialog, menu controls, and file processing.

A module is a set of declarations and procedures in a file with the extension .BAS. A module does not contain controls and does not appear as a form; it contains only code.

The User-defined data type also contains multiple elements. Each element can be of a different data type. Before we can use this data type, we have to define it. To begin a definition for a User-defined type, use the keyword Type. To end the definition, use the keywords End Type. In the body of the definition, list the element names (field names) as variable declarations. The definition must occur in the General Declarations section of a module, not a form. To declare a variable of the User-defined type, use the Dim statement. To access any element, use the variable name, followed by the dot operator, followed by the element name definition. To assign a value using the element, use something like:

```
picPicture.ForeColor = ThisPixel.lColor
```

Version 1 of the Customer Program demonstrates the use of random access files to implement a system for updating customer records and saving the updates to a file. It is possible to do the following with the program:

- Start a new set of records.

- Open an existing file of records.

- Append a record.

- Modify a record.

- Save records to a new file.

- Accept only modifications that follow certain defined input rules.

The program will not insert or delete records. In Chapter 9, we will enhance the program to include these features.

HANDS-ON EXERCISES

OVERVIEW

The activities will

- Enable you to process files for sequential and random access.

- Enable you to use the CommonDialog control.

- Enable you to use menu controls.

- Enable you to create customized message boxes.

- Familiarize you with developing larger programs.

To Get Started

1. Read the section "Read Me Before Attempting the Hands-On Exercises" if you have not already done so.

2. Run Windows.

3. Open the file CH08\EX08.TXT on your student disk and answer the questions. (The same questions are shown here so that you can still determine answers when you are not sitting in front of a computer.)

4. Run Visual Basic.

8.1   A SIMPLE TEXT VIEWER, PART 1

1. What is a viewer?

2. List some common viewers. Why would a vendor provide a viewer for free? Since this wasn't directly explained in the chapter, research the answer by studying the software marketplace.

Start Developing the Program

You will now begin developing the program. We will explain a bit later how to add the common dialog control and use the menu editor.

Select **New Project** from the File menu. Select **Save File/Form1 As** from the File menu. Save *file* FORM1 as **VIEWER1** in directory CH08. Select **Save Project As** from the File menu. Save *project* PROJECT1 as **VIEWER1** in directory CH08.

Modify the form so that it looks like Figure 8.1, but do not worry about adding the File menu item. Following are some property setting suggestions. Leave some space for the File menu when adding the other controls.

TextBox	Name	txtTime
Form	Name	frmViewer1
	BackColor	&H00E0E0E0&
	Caption	Simple Viewer = Version 1

For the upper text box shown in Figure 8.1:

TextBox	Name	txtFileInfo
	Locked	True
	MultiLine	True
	ScrollBars	0 - None

For the upper label above the previous text box:

| Label | Name | lblFileInfo |
| | Caption | File Information |

For the lower text box (with the scroll bars):

TextBox	Name	txtFileContent
	Locked	False
	MultiLine	True
	ScrollBars	3 - Both

For the label above the previous text box:

Label	Name	lblFileContent
	Caption	File Contents
CommandButton	Name	cmdExit
	Caption	E&xit

Save the project.

8.2 THE COMMON DIALOG

Refer to Figures 4.11a and 4.11b to find the common dialog (CommonDialog) button in the Toolbox, or simply point the mouse pointer over various Toolbox buttons until you see a pop-up balloon identifying the control. There is a possibility that the common dialog control is not in the Toolbox. If this is the case, add it as a custom control by following one of the following instructions, depending on your version of Visual Basic. (If it is already in the Toolbox, you can skip these instructions.)

If the Common Dialog Is Not in Toolbox With Visual Basic 4

Select **Custom Controls** from the Tools menu. Scroll through the list of the Custom Controls dialog to find Microsoft Common Dialog Control. Click on **it** to check it **on**. Then click **OK**. The CommonDialog button should appear in the Toolbox.

If the Common Dialog Is Not in Toolbox With Visual Basic 5

Select **Components** from the Project menu. Click the **Controls** tab in the Components dialog. Scroll through the list of the Components dialog to find Microsoft Common Dialog Control. Click on **it** to check it **on**. Then click **OK**. The CommonDialog button should appear in the Toolbox.

Double-click the CommonDialog Toolbox button. You should see the control placed on the form. You can move it anywhere you want since its position isn't important. The control will become invisible during runtime.

Name the control `dlgFile`. Set its CancelError property to `True`, and save the project. You will be setting up the rest of its properties in code. However, you might want to quickly check out an alternative. Make sure that `dlgFile` is selected. Click on the **(Custom)** property, and click on **its properties button** (has three dots). You should see a tabbed dialog that permits you to fill in information. Experiment with these settings.

8.3 MENU CONTROLS

In this section, you will learn how to use the Menu Editor. You can use it only if you are viewing the form instead of the code. Click **View Form** on the Project window, if necessary. Select Menu Editor from the Tools menu. You should see the Menu Editor dialog box. Alternatively, click the **Menu Editor** button on the Toolbar.

In the Caption box, type **&File**, and in the Name box, type **mnuFile** as the name of the first menu control. Click **Next**. Click the **right arrow button**. A series of three dashes should appear in the box below. The purpose of the right arrow button is to assign the following menu items as submenu items of menu control mnuFile. In the Caption box, type **&New** and in the Name box, type **mnuNew** as the name of this menu item. The menu editor should now look the same as that shown in Figure 8.9.

Click **Next** and use the same procedure to add the following menu controls. Once you have added all of them, click **OK** in the Menu Editor dialog.

Caption	Name
&Open...	mnuOpen
&Save	mnuSave
Save &As	mnuSaveAs
—	mnuSepBar1
E&xit	mnuExit

Figure 8.9
A Menu Editor Session in Progress

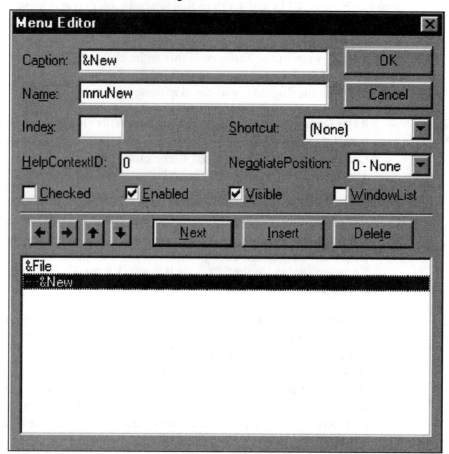

You should see menu item File on the form. Run the program, and select File. You should see menu items like those shown in Figure 8.1. Since you haven't written any code, no menu items are functional. Stop the program, and save the project.

Use the following procedure to add code to a menu control. In the design mode, select menu item File. You should see the submenu items. Select one of the items. You should see the Code window with the template Click event procedure for the menu control. For example, if you selected Open, you should see the template code (first and last lines) for procedure mnuOpen_Click. To find out more about the Menu Editor, view Menu Editor or the Menu Editor Dialog Box in Visual Basic Help. There is also additional information about using the Menu Editor, depending on which version of Visual Basic you are using.

Visual Basic 4

You can also select **Learning Microsoft Visual Basic** from the Help menu. Then select **Adding Menus**.

Visual Basic 5

Select **Visual Basic Books Online** from the Help menu, and click the **Contents** button. Then open the following books in sequence, if they are not already open:

   Start Here

   Programmer's Guide (All Editions)

File Handling   453

Part 2: What Can You Do With Visual Basic?
Creating a User Interface
Using Menus in Your Application

Then select the topic **Creating Menus With the Menu Editor.**

8.4 PROCESSING FILES AND COMPLETING THE SIMPLE VIEWER PROGRAM

3. What is a file?

4. What is the purpose of a file number?

5. Why is it necessary to open a file? To close a file?

6. Explain the organization of a sequential file. Describe the three ways to open a file for sequential access. Describe a way to read data from a sequential file. Describe a way to write data to it.

7. Explain the organization of a random access file. Describe how to open it, read data from it, and write data to it.

8. Explain the organization of a binary access file. Describe how to open it, read data from it, and write data to it.

If the **VIEWER1** project is not open, open it now using Visual Basic. **Write the code for it** as shown in Example 8.1. Save the project. If you do not have any text files available, create some using Notepad.

Run the program. Open one of the text files. You should see the contents in TextBox txtFileContent. You should see information about the file in TextBox txtFile-Info. If you are trying to open a large file, you may have to wait a while. If the file is extremely large, the attempt to open it may fail.

8.5 THE EDITOR PROGRAM

To run this program, open *project* VIEWER1 in directory CH08, if it is not already open. Save *file* VIEWER1 as **EDIT1** in directory CH08. Select **Save Project As** from the File menu. Save *project* VIEWER1 as **EDIT1** in directory CH08. Change the Name of the form to **frmEdit1,** and change the Caption to **Edit Demo - Version 1**. Save the project, and then enter and modify the **code** so that it is **the same as that shown in Example 8.4.** Save the project.

Run the program. Select **Open** from the File menu. Select a text file. Modify the text in TextBox txtFileContent. Select **Save As** from the File menu. Type in a **new name** for the file and click **OK**. Select **New** from the File menu. Type **some text**, and select **Save** from the File menu. This should launch the **Save As** dialog. Type in **another name** and click **OK**. Type in **more changes** and select **Save** from the File menu. The Save As dialog should not appear.

Select **Open** from the File menu and select **the file you edited earlier**. You should see this file with your modifications in TextBox txtFileContent. Open the **second file you edited.** You should see its contents with your modifications. Experiment with the program.

9. True or False? The Print menu was omitted because
   a. It is better to save trees.
   b. The author is too lazy.
   c. This feature is left as an exercise for the reader to add.

8.6   THE USER-DEFINED DATA TYPE AND MODULE FILES

Here you will begin to create the Customer Information Program, Version 1. In this section you will only add the module and enter its code. In the next section, you will complete the program. Select **New Project** from the File menu. Select **Save File/Form1 As** from the File menu. Save *file* FORM1 as **CUSTOM1** in directory CH08. Select **Save Project As** from the File menu. Save *project* PROJECT1 as **CUSTOM1** in directory CH08.

At this stage all you have is a bare-bones form. You will next add a module. To do this, select **Module** from the Visual Basic Insert menu. You should see the Code window for the module. Click on the **Project** window. You should see two items, the form and the module.

Click on the module item (**Module1**). Click on the **Properties** window. Note that it has only a Name property. Change its Name property to **Custom1**. Make sure the Module item is still highlighted in the Project window so that you can save the module. To save it, select **Save File As** from the File menu. Name the file **CUSTOM1** and click **Save**. Visual Basic will add the .BAS extension. Enter the **code shown in Example 8.5** in the General Declarations section of module Custom1, and save the project. There is an alternate way to add a module: Instead of using the Insert menu, click on the **Module** button in the Toolbar.

Tip

If you accidentally insert too many modules, click on *the name of the* module you want to remove in the Project window. Select *Remove File* from the Visual Basic File menu. An alternate way to remove a module (or form file) from a project is to right-click the item in the Project window. Select *Remove File* from the pop-up menu. A key point is that a project is a collection of forms and modules. Up to this point, we have been working with projects that contain only one form.

8.7   THE CUSTOMER PROGRAM, VERSION 1

Open project CUSTOM1 in directory CH08 if it is not already open. Select the **form** in the Project Window if necessary. View the form and create menu objects as described in Table 8.1 in Section 8.7.8. Add controls to the form and set their properties so that the form looks similar to that shown in Figure 8.6. You may find it necessary to set the Form Grid Settings to **Width 100** and **Height 100**. To do this, select **Options** from the Tools menu.

Visual Basic 4
Click the **Environment** tab.

Visual Basic 5
Click the **General** tab.

Type in the **Grid settings** and set the choice to **Align Controls to Grid**. Click **OK**.

Following are some property setting suggestions, with controls listed from top to bottom, left to right. Use Figure 8.6 to determine applicable Caption settings size (Height, Width) and position (Top, Left) properties.

Form	Name	frmCustomer1
	Caption	Customer Information - Version 1
Label	Name	lblFirstName
Label	Name	lblLastName
Label	Name	lblCanoeModel
Label	Name	lblSerialNum

Label	Name	lblAreaCode
Label	Name	lbl LocalTel
Label	Name	lblPosition
Label	Name	lblMessage
	Caption	*(Make it blank; i.e., null)*
TextBox	Name	txtFirstName
TextBox	Name	txtLastName
ComboBox	Name	cboCanoeModel
TextBox	Name	txtSerialNum
	MaxLength	9
TextBox	Name	txtAreaCode
	MaxLength	3
TextBox	Name	txtLocalTel
	MaxLength	7
TextBox	Name	txtPosition
	Locked	True
CommandButton	Name	cmdNext
CommandButton	Name	cmdBack
CommandButton	Name	cmdAppend
CommandButton	Name	cmdChange
CommandButton	Name	cmdInsert
CommandButton	Name	cmdDelete
CommandButton	Name	cmdExit
CommonDialog	Name	dlgFile
	CancelError	True

Note that label lblMessage will show the Last Open status (see Figure 8.6).

You already entered the code in the module as shown in Example 8.5. Now enter **the function** for TestInteger in the module (not the form), as shown in Example 8.16.

In the form (not the module), enter the **code shown in Examples 8.6, 8.7, 8.8, 8.9, 8.10, 8.11, 8.13, 8.15, 8.16, 8.17, 8.18, 8.19, 8.20, and 8.21**. Save the project periodically while you do this. This a lot of code.

When you have finished typing the code, save the project one more time. Cross your fingers and click the Run button in the Visual Basic Toolbar. You should see a dialog box that indicates how many bytes there are in the record. Click **OK,** and the form should appear. If you obtain errors (not surprising if you're typing a lot), check the code carefully and correct the typographic mistakes. Keep trying until you have success with the program displaying the form. Even then there may be a few subtle bugs lurking about, just waiting for the correct sequence of events to trigger them.

When the program successfully launches, you should see the flashing cursor in the First Name field. The Record Position should be 1. Type in **a name** and press **TAB**. The cursor should now be in the Last Name field. Type in **a last name**. **TAB** to the next field. Use the **up and down arrow keys** to select a model number. **TAB** to the next fields and enter **the numbers**.

When all the fields are filled in, press **ENTER**. One of two things will happen, depending on the data you keyed. If you didn't enter valid data, there will be a beep, and the cursor will flash in the first field that contains invalid data. Correct the data and press **ENTER** again. If all the data is valid, a message box will appear to inform you that you should specify a file using the Save As menu. Press **ENTER** to acknowledge the message. Press **ALT+F** followed by **A**. This should launch the Save dialog. Type in **a name** for the file and press **ENTER**. The form Caption should now state the name of the file. Note that the Append button is still not enabled; you have only saved a blank file. Press **ENTER** to put the new record into the file. The Append button should be enabled.

At this point you can press **ALT+A** to append the next record. Key in **the data for the fields** and press **ENTER** to put the record into the file. Continue doing this for a few more records. Then try the **Next** and **Back** buttons to view the records in the file. If you try to go beyond the last record using Next, there will be a beep. If you try to go before the first record using the Back button, there will also be a beep. To return the focus back to the fields, press **TAB**.

Key in **some changes** to any record in the middle, and press **Next** or **Back**. You should see a message warning you that a change has been made. Respond as you wish. Try the **New** menu item and save the file as **another name**. Append some records. Open the original file and check that the records are still there. Experiment with the program. Stop execution.

Open one of your record files using Notepad (record files have a default extension of .CUS). Since there are no carriage returns, you will have to scroll horizontally to see all of the records. You should be able to recognize the String data and the overall record structure, but some of the information will look very strange. This is because Notepad interprets data as text characters. Since some of the fields are of the Long or Integer data type, they will appear strange. It is possible that some of the fields may be unintentionally interpreted as ASCII control characters, thus making the appearance even stranger.

DOCUMENTATION EXERCISE

You may have noticed the comments in the General Declarations for the customer information program. It would be a good idea to summarize the procedures to let the programmer know what the different procedures do. Add comments to do this in the general declarations. For example, a summary for procedure ClearThisCustomer might look like this:

```
' General Procedure ClearThisCustomer
' Initializes fields of record m_ThisCustomer to be null for ➡
string fields and 0 for numeric fields
' Used to make a blank record
' Called by cmdAppend_Click to present a blank record to the user
```

ADDITIONAL PROBLEM SOLVING

In the Customer program, we can type in anything in the text portion of the combo box for the Canoe Model. Write a routine that sets the focus back to the ComboBox if the text typed does not match the ComboBox list items. **Hint:** Use Lost Focus to trigger the procedure.

Modify either the Area program in Chapter 6 or the Sum of Least Squares program in Chapter 7. When recording the points in the picture box, put the coordinates in a binary file. The program should also be able to get points from a binary file and display the points in the picture box.

CHAPTER 9

Data Structures

This chapter introduces the organization of data, which is often the key to manipulating data for a particular purpose.

Teamwork is important in sports such as field hockey, soccer, and tennis. Generally, players on the same team do not behave randomly and independently. They follow certain strategies that make their team perform more effectively. The players usually position themselves in certain patterns, depending on the game situation at the time. With a computer programming project, an effective programmer or programming team will organize data so that it can be used in an effective manner.

After completing this chapter, you should be able to

- Write programs that use the stack data structure.
- Write programs that use the queue data structure.
- Write programs that use linked lists.
- Write programs that can use object references.

In This Chapter

Cougar Canoe's customer information system permits an employee to modify customer information that is stored in files. It can insert and delete records as required.

ABOUT THIS CHAPTER

We will look at several common ways to structure (or organize) data. The first program will use a stack to add or remove points in the Sum of Least Squares program (Section 7.4). After this, we work solely on modifying the Customer Information program first introduced in Chapter 8. The first modification will be another demonstration of the stack to add menu items. The next variation will use a queue to implement dynamic menu items showing the most recently used files. The final variation will use a linked list to organize records. This will permit insertion and deletion of records. This is a nuts-and-bolts section that will provide insight into how commercial programs handle data; in Chapter 12 we will use off-the-shelf tools to handle the details of managing records.

9.1 ABOUT DATA STRUCTURES

This is an important topic that warrants some discussion. So far we have only looked at data as inherently structured by the language, Visual Basic. Step back a minute and take a look at what we know about data. We have

- Variables of Various Data Types
- Properties of Objects
- Arrays and Indices
- Control Arrays and Indices
- User-Defined Type and Records
- Files Organized for Sequential, Random, or Binary Access

There are ways to utilized these elemental structures into higher-level forms of organization (or structure). These structures are often useful in algorithms to perform useful work. *Objects* contain both data structures and procedures. In Visual Basic an object can have properties to define its data structure. Its methods define the procedures that act on it. Events trigger the execution of procedures that act on data structured as variables or properties. Often, a higher-level organization of data is needed. We have hinted earlier that we will examine stacks, queues, and linked lists, but we will omit other important structures that are best left to more advanced programming references. These include queue variations, binary trees, hash tables, and database design.

*A **data structure** is a method of organizing data.*

9.2 THE STACK

9.2.1 The Generic Stack

Back in Section 4.3.4 we mentioned the stack (see also Figure 4.4). It so happens that a computer uses a stack for its own internal operations to handle local variables and procedure calls. In this section, we are interested in building our own stack to directly handle an application requirement. Section 7.4 described the Method of Least Squares program used to fit the best straight line to a set of points (refer to Example 7.6 and Figure 7.3.) In that program the user clicks in the picture box to add points, but wouldn't it be useful to be able to remove points? One simple way would be use the left mouse button to add points; clicking the right mouse button would remove points in the reverse order. To make sure we understand this, consider the following sequence of left and right clicks.

Left (new point 1), Left (new point 2), Left (new point 3), Left (new point 4), Right (removes point 4), Right (removes point 3), Left (new point 3), Left (new point 4), Left (new point 5), Right (removes point 5), and so on.

Notice how points are added in sequence and how points are removed in reverse order.

*A **stack** is a list of items. Items are added at one end and removed from the same end. The last data put onto the list is the first data taken off the list.*

Sometimes we can refer to a stack as a **Last In First Out** (**LIFO**) queue. We can visualize a stack as a vertical pile of items, as shown in Figure 9.1. To add an item, you would use a push operation; to remove an item, you would use a pull operation. A deck of cards is a useful analogy. In a game such as Rummy, players place cards on a pile (push) and at times remove cards (pull) from the top of the pile (or deck). We can also refer to pull operations as *pop* operations.

Figure 9.1
A Stack With Push and Pull Operations

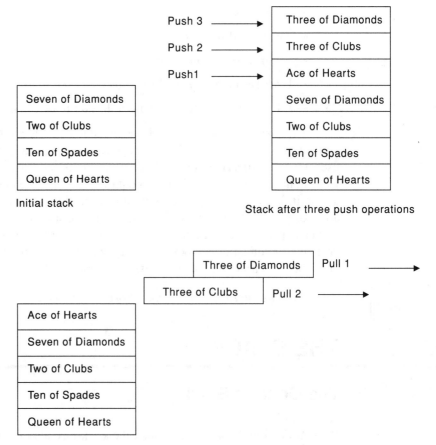

A stack also uses a special index known as the stack pointer. The stack pointer indicates the position of the last (top) item in the stack.

9.2.2   The Modified Method of Least Squares Program

To permit the user to remove recorded points, we modified the program of Example 7.6 to use a stack. Points recorded using the left mouse button are pushed onto the stack. When the user clicks with the right mouse button, the program pulls a point off the stack. Each point is defined by two values, which are the Y and X coordinates. Example 9.1 shows the listing for the revised picGraph_MouseDown procedure.

Example 9.1

```
Private Sub picGraph_MouseDown(Button As Integer, Shift As ➡
Integer, X As Single, Y As Single)
    ' Record and display points when user clicks with left ➡
    mouse button (vbMouseLButton)
    ' by "pushing" Y and X onto our "stack".
    ' Delete points in reverse order when user clicks with ➡
    right mouse button (vbMouseRButton)
    ' by "pulling" X and Y off our "stack".

    ' See VB Help Topic: KeyCode Constants
    On Error Resume Next    ' In case user goes hog-wild and ➡
    clicks forever
    If m_bStartFlag Then  ' Flag to permit point plotting only ➡
    when user clicked Start Plot

        If Button = vbKeyLButton Then    ' Add points when ➡
        clicked with left button
            ' PUSH operation when using LEFT button
            If m_nSP < 0 Then
                MsgBox "Error.  Negative count occurred", , MSGTITLE
                End ' Terminate program if this happens, ➡
                shouldn't have -ve count!
            Else
                ' Record point and draw point using X, Y

                Push (Y)    ' Record Y coordinate
                Push (X)    ' Record X coordinate
                picGraph.PSet (X, Y)    ' Plots the point
            End If ' End of left mouse button operation

        ' PULL operations with RIGHT button
            ' Prevent underflow of stack
            If m_nSP = 0 Then
                Beep
                Exit Sub
            End If
            ' Otherwise can pull data off the stack
            X = Pull(X)
            Y = Pull(Y)
```

```
                    ' Paint over the point in the picture box
                    picGraph.PSet (X, Y), picGraph.BackColor
            End If

      End If   ' End of m_bStartFlag check

      If Err.Number <> 0 Then ' Error handling if necessary
            MsgBox CStr(CVErr(Err.Number)) & " " & Err.Description, ➥
            , MSGTITLE
            txtLine.Text = ""    ' Clear line text since it is not valid
      End If

End Sub
```

Pulling data isn't hard, but we can't really remove a point once it has been painted on a picture box control using the PSet method. The second argument for the PSet method is optional. If used, it specifies the color of the point. To erase a point, we paint over it using the same background color as the picture box itself:

```
picGraph.PSet (X, Y), picGraph.BackColor
```

Example 9.2 shows the general declarations and procedures used for implementing the stack. Note that there is a stack pointer and that the only two operations are push and pull.

Example 9.2

```
' Least Squares Program to fit "best" straight line for a set ➥
of points
' It finds the slope (m) and offset (b) given experimental points
' The straight line equation is y = mx + b
' User clicks Start Plot to begin recording experimental points
' User clicks in graph area (picGraph) to record each point
' (Actually we use the MouseDown event, not the Click event)
' User clicks Fit Line, and the program launches ➥
cmdFitLine_Click
' to do the main work.  It determines m and b and plots the ➥
straight line
' User can subsequently click Clear to start again
Option Explicit
Const MSGTITLE = " Least Squares Line Fit"

' Modification to demo stack data structure
Dim m_fStack(400) As Single  ' The reserved space for stack ➥
data structure
Dim m_nSP    ' Stack pointer

Dim m_nCount As Integer ' Keeps track of number of points
Dim m_fY(200) As Single ' Y coordinate of all points
Dim m_fX(200) As Single ' X coordinate of all points
' Flag whether in mode to click in points on graph
Dim m_bStartFlag As Boolean
Const LF = 10   ' Line feed
Const CR = 13   ' Carriage Return
```

```
Sub Push(fItem As Single)
    ' Implements stack push operation
    ' Note this stack grows by "incrementing" the stack pointer
    ' " before" adding the item

    m_nSP = m_nSP + 1    ' Increment stack pointer to define new ➥
    top of stack

    ' Add item to top of stack
    m_fStack(m_nSP) = fItem
End Sub


Function Pull(fItem As Single) As Single
    ' Implements stack pull operation
    ' Note this stack shrinks by "decrementing" the stack pointer
     ' "after" removing the item

    '  Take item from top of stack
    Pull = m_fStack(m_nSP)
    m_nSP = m_nSP - 1    ' Decrement stack pointer to define new ➥
    top of stack
End Function
```

There is one other procedure that has been modified as a result of using a stack (see Figure 9.3).

Example 9.3

```
Private Sub cmdFitLine_Click()
    ' Procedure that does the main work to fit a straight line
    ' using the method of least squares
    ' Line equation is y = mx + b ; [fy = fm * fx + fb]
    ' Hence this procedure finds line paramters m and b given ➥
    set of x, y points
    ' and subsequently plots the line

    ' Line equation variables
    Dim fY As Single, fm As Single, fX As Single, fb As Single
    Dim fStartX As Single, fStartY As Single    ' Start point ➥
    for final line plot
    Dim fEndX As Single, fEndY As Single    ' End point for ➥
    final line plot

    ' Intermediate variables used in least squares technique
    '  m_nCount is the total number of points
    Dim nCount As Integer    ' Local counter used to calculate ➥
    the following
    Dim fSumXY As Single    ' Sum of all X * Y products for ➥
    each point
    Dim fSumY As Single ' Sum of all the Ys
    Dim fSumX As Single ' Sum of all the Xs
    Dim fSumX2 As Single    ' Sum of all the X^2s
    Dim fTemp As Single ' Temporary scratchpad for a bit of ➥
    optimization
```

```
Dim sCRLF As String ' Carriage return and line feed

On Error Resume Next

sCRLF = Chr(CR) & Chr(LF)    ' New line for text to display ➥
m, b line parameters

' Okay, let's get to work ...
' Find values of intermediate variables
    ' (local variable initial values are zero)
    ' Note stack storage in order of Y : X
    ' Hence Y referenced by nCount and X by nCount + 1
For nCount = 1 To m_nSP Step 2
    fSumXY = fSumXY + m_fStack(nCount + 1) * ➥
    m_fStack(nCount)
    fSumY = fSumY + m_fStack(nCount)
    fSumX = fSumX + m_fStack(nCount + 1)
    fSumX2 = fSumX2 + m_fStack(nCount + 1) ^ 2
Next nCount

' Find the slope m and the offset b
fTemp = m_nCount * fSumX2 - fSumX ^ 2    ' Divisor is same ➥
for both
fm = (m_nCount * fSumXY - fSumX * fSumY) / fTemp
fb = (fSumX2 * fSumY - fSumX * fSumXY) / fTemp

' Found the line parameters, now display it
txtLine.Text = "m = " & Format(fm, "##0.####") & sCRLF
txtLine.Text = txtLine.Text & "b = " & Format(fb, "##0.####")

' Determine start and end point of line in order to plot it
fStartX = 0
fStartY = fb
fEndX = 100
fEndY = fm * fEndX + fb
' Now plot the final line
picGraph.DrawWidth = 1  ' Can also set style if desired
picGraph.Line (fStartX, fStartY)-(fEndX, fEndY), QBColor(4)

' Prevent user from adding more points until Start Points clicked
m_bStartFlag = False    ' Prevent further points added

If Err.Number <> 0 Then ' Error handling if necessary
    MsgBox CStr(CVErr(Err.Number)) & " " & Err.Description, ➥
    , MSGTITLE
    txtLine.Text = ""    ' Clear result since it is not valid
End If

End Sub
```

This procedure differs from the one shown in Example 7.6 because the For Next loop iterates in steps of two to calculate intermediate values. The code for procedures Form_Load, cmdStartPoints_Click, and cmdClear_Clear is identical to that shown in Example 7.6.

9.2.3   A Stack Demo for the Customer Program

Version 2 of the Customer program begins the development of an enhancement that will be fully developed in Version 3. The prime purpose of Version 2 is to provide a visible means to see stack growth. Figure 9.2 shows that menu items have been added. The menu items for files PSTEST1.CUS and others are illustrating an upside-down stack. The most recently accessed file is pushed in at the bottom. If the user keeps opening new files, the list (stack) will continue to grow; it will even add items that are already in the stack. Other than showing that new menu items can be pushed in, the program adds no additional functionality to Version 1. Selecting one of the new menu items doesn't do anything.

We will show only the modifications to Version 1, not the entire program. However, you can find the entire listing named as project CUSTOM2 in directory CH09\SOLN on the program disk. Example 9.4 shows a new module-level variable in the general declarations.

Example 9.4

```
Option Explicit


' Version 2 of Customer program
' Modified from Version 1 to demonstrate stack
' data structure which dynamically adds recently used files
' to the file menu in a manner "similar" to typical Windows ➡
applications
' i.e., not exactly like a typical commercial program
' To do, opening comments
' Also leave as exercise to improve documentation
' to add summary of procedures


' Constants for message boxes
Const MSGTITLE = "Customer Information"
' Some message boxes display Yes and No buttons with a question icon
```

Figure 9.2
Version Two of the
Customer Program

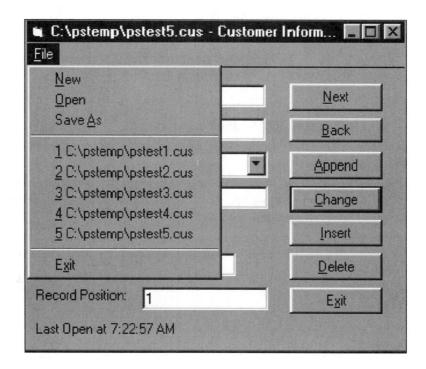

```
Const DIALOGTYPE = vbYesNo + vbQuestion
Const VERSION = " - Customer Information V2"     ' For Form Title Bar

' Version 2 addition, object reference that will be passed to
' procedures in the module
Dim mnuCustomer As Menu

' Rest of "Form" General Declarations the same as in Example 8.6
```

The variable is of the Menu object type. We will see shortly how we can use a Menu object data type. In order to add controls, we must create a control array at design time; then elements can be added or removed during runtime. The form has the menu objects shown in Table 9.1.

mnuQueueItem is a new Menu object. Note that it is the first element of a control array, since its Index property is set to zero. We named it mnuQueueItem instead of mnuStackItem so that we can use the same name in Versions 3 and 4 of the program. The only change in the Form_Load procedure of Example 8.17 is to initialize the stack pointer that is declared in the module Customer1 as a global (or public) variable.

Example 9.5

```
Private Sub Form_Load()
    Dim sFilter As String    ' For common file dialog filter

    ' VERSION 2 Modification, Initialize stack
    g_nSP = 0

    ' Rest is same as in Example 8.17
End Sub


' General Declarations Section of Module Customer2

Public g_nSP As Integer    ' Points to top of stack

' Rest is same as General Declarations section of Module ➡
Customer1 in Example 8.5


Private Sub mnuNew_Click()
    ' Same as in Example 8.18 up until ...
```

Table 9.1
Menu Objects for File
Menu Selections
(mnuFile)

Name	Caption	Index
mnuNew	&New	(none)
mnuOpen	&Open	(none)
mnuSaveAs	Save &As	(none)
mnuQueueItem	-	0
mnuSep1	-	(none)
mnuExit	E&xit	(none)

```
        Close m_nFileNum ' Close previous file if applicable

        ' This is the only VERSION 2 modification
        frmCustomer2.Caption = "Untitled" & VERSION

        m_sFileName = ""
        ' Rest is same as in Example 8.18

End Sub


Sub Save()

        ' Same as in Example 8.20 until ...
        Else
        ' Version 2 modification, refer to frmCustomer2
        ' Update File Name
        m_sFileName = m_sNewFile
        frmCustomer2.Caption = m_sFileName & VERSION

        lblMessage.Caption = "Last Save at " & CStr(Time)
        frmCustomer2.Caption = dlgFile.FileTitle & VERSION
        ' Version 2 modification end, rest of procedure same as ➡
        in Example 8.20

End Sub
```

We also showed the only change in procedure mnuNew_Click. Procedure Save
needs some modification because it refers to Form frmCustomer2 instead of frm-
Customer1. Procedure mnuOpen_Click shows how we can add menu items and
handle mnuCustomer, the variable of the Menu object data type.

Example 9.6

```
Private Sub mnuOpen_Click()
    ' Same as Example 8.19 up until ...

    ' Trap file open errors if they occur
    If Err.Number <> 0 Then
        MsgBox CStr(CVErr(Err.Number)) & " " & Err.Description, ➡
        , MSGTITLE
        lblMessage.Caption = ""
        Exit Sub
    Else
        ' Version 2 changes here ....
        ' Cue user that file has been opened and show first record
        ' if no errors occurred
        If Err.Number = 0 Then
            lblMessage.Caption = "Last Open at " & CStr(Time)
            frmCustomer2.Caption = m_sFileName & VERSION

            ' Push new menu item
            Set mnuCustomer = frmCustomer2.mnuQueueItem(g_nSP + 1)
            Push m_sFileName, mnuCustomer
            ' .... Version 2 changes end here.
```

```
' Rest is same as in Example 8.18
End Sub
```

One statement here is modified because the Form Name and Caption will be different. The other change concerns Menu object variables and the actual loading of additional Menu objects.

```
' Push new menu item
Set mnuCustomer = frmCustomer2.mnuQueueItem(g_nSP + 1)
Push m_sFileName, mnuCustomer
```

We could have avoided the use of Menu object variables by making procedure Push a part of the form instead of a module, but that would deny us the fun of investigating Object data types! In Visual Basic we must use the Set statement to assign an object reference to a variable. Hence we can use mnuCustomer to refer to the new element of the Menu control array. Example 9.7 shows the code for the Push procedure, which is declared in the Module.

Example 9.7

```
Public Sub Push(sItem As String, mnuMenu As Menu)
    ' This procedure declared inside a Module, not a Form
    ' Procedure to push an element of a menu control array ➡
    referenced
    ' by mnuMenu using the value of sItem to specify the menu ➡
    Caption

        ' Increment the stack pointer
        g_nSP = g_nSP + 1
        ' Push item onto stack by loading the control element
        Load mnuMenu
        ' This shows itself as a new menu item that
        ' shows the recently accessed file
        mnuMenu.Caption = "&" & CStr(g_nSP) & " " & sItem
End Sub
```

Note that procedure Push uses an argument whose data type is Menu. This means that we can pass a reference of an object (in this case, Menu) to the procedure in order to access the object's properties. We pass the Name (and Index) of the new menu item; then the procedure loads it and modifies its Caption. Now let's look at the queue data structure.

9.3   THE QUEUE DATA STRUCTURE

In Version 3 of the Customer program, we will show recently used files in the File menu in a more convenient format. This provides an opportunity to demonstrate another useful data structure: the queue.

9.3.1   The Generic Queue

*A **queue** is a list of items. The next item is added to the end, and items are removed from the beginning. Items are added and removed in a first-in, first-out order.*

To be explicit, and to distinguish a queue from a stack, we can refer to it as a *First In First Out (FIFO)* queue. One application for a queue is for buffering data during serial data input and output operations. The characters to be transmitted are added to a list of items in memory, the queue. When transmission occurs, the characters are removed from the queue to actually send to the transmit output line. A queue uses head and tail pointers to identify the beginning and end of the queue (see Figure 9.3).

9.3.2   A Queue Demo for the Customer Program

The File menu shows the four most recently used files, with the most recent shown first, as illustrated in Figure 9.4. If the user selects another file, this file will be shown as the most recent. The others will be shifted down, and the last one will be removed. Here, the queue length is four. The user can choose a recent file by selecting it from the menu instead of using the Open menu. The selected item then becomes the first item, and the others are shifted accordingly. If the user chooses a file with the Open menu that is already on the list, the item becomes the first element, and the others are shifted accordingly. (You will be able to see this in the Hands-On Exercises with program CUSTOM3. This is not a pure queue since elements can be reordered.)

It is easier to reference changes with Version 1. Example 9.8 shows the General Declarations in the Form and some other modifications of the Version 1 program that are required for Version 3.

Example 9.8

```
Option Explicit

' Version 3 of Customer program
' Modified from Version 2 to demonstrate queue data structure
' which dynamically adds recently used files to the file
' menu in a manner "similar" to typical Windows applications
' It is more like a typical commercial program, but
' the queue information is not saved when the program exits
```

Figure 9.3
A Queue Used in a Data
Transmission Application

Adding Items to a queue to prepare for transmission

Items in queue ready for transmission

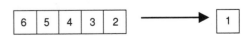

Removing items from a queue during transmission

Figure 9.4
Version Three of the
Customer Program

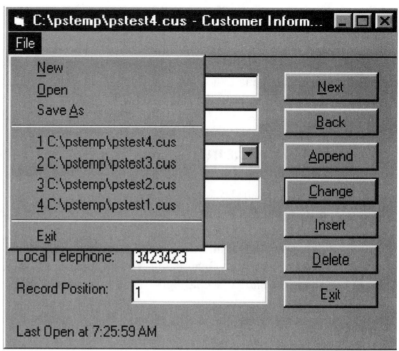

```
' Version 3 similar to Version 2, with Object variables refering ➡
to Form and Menu controls
Dim m_mnuCustomer As Menu ' Refer to Menu object for use by module
Dim m_frmForm As Form    ' Form object
Const VERSION = " - Customer Information V3"    ' For Form title

' Rest is same as Version 1 as shown in Example 8.6

Sub Save()
    ' Save Current file
    ' Version 3 same as Example 8.20 up until ... m_sFileName = ➡
    m_sNewFile

    Else
        ' Version 3 change, use Object variable to refer to Form
        ' Update File Name
        m_sFileName = m_sNewFile
        m_frmForm.Caption = m_sFileName & VERSION

        ' Cue user that file has been saved
        lblMessage.Caption = "Last Save at " & CStr(Time)
        m_frmForm.Caption = dlgFile.FileTitle & VERSION
        ' Rest is same as Example 8.20
    End If

    If Err.Number <> 0 Then     ' Error Handling if necessary
        MsgBox CStr(CVErr(Err.Number)) & " " & Err.Description, ➡
        , MSGTITLE
    End If
End Sub
```

```
Private Sub Form_Load()
    Dim sFilter As String    ' For common file dialog filter
    ' Version 3
    ' Initialize queue
    NewQueue
    ' Refer to Form object
    Set m_frmForm = frmCustomer3
    ' Refer to  Menu object
    Set m_mnuCustomer = m_frmForm.mnuQueueItem(0)
    m_nRecordLength = Len(m_ThisCustomer)
    ' Set up combo box, as in Example 8.17
    cboCanoeModel.AddItem "Erie"
    cboCanoeModel.AddItem "Huron"
    cboCanoeModel.AddItem "Michigan"
    cboCanoeModel.AddItem "Ontario"
    cboCanoeModel.AddItem "Superior"
    cboCanoeModel.ListIndex = 0 ' Default Model
    'mnuNew_Click     ' Remove this statement to set up ➥
    brand-new file
    ' Version 3 change
    m_mnuCustomer.Caption = "-"
    m_sFileName = ""
    m_lPosition = 0     ' Current record is first one
    m_lLastRecord = 0    ' and it is the only one

    ' Show user that no field exists until first one appended
    cmdAppend_Click
    ' Reset the flag
    m_bChange = False

    ' set up filter for save dialog
    sFilter = "Customer (*.cus)¦*.cus¦Text (*.txt)¦*.txt¦All ➥
    Files (*.*)¦*.*"
    ' Following previous statement, rest is same as in Example 8.17

End Sub


Private Sub mnuNew_Click()

    ' Same as Example 8.18 up until ... Close m_nFileNum

    Close m_nFileNum ' Close previous file if applicable
    ' Version 3 change
    m_frmCustomer.Caption = "Untitled" & VERSION
    m_sFileName = ""
    ' Rest is same as Example 8.18 following m_sFileName = ""

End Sub


Private Sub mnuOpen_Click()
```

```
                    ' Same as Example 8.19 up until ...
                    ' Open m_sFileName For Random As #m_nFileNum Len = ➥
                    m_nRecordLength

                    Open m_sFileName For Random As #m_nFileNum Len = ➥
                    m_nRecordLength

                    ' Version 3 change
                    ' Trap file open errors if they occur
                    If Err.Number <> 0 Then
                        MsgBox CStr(CVErr(Err.Number)) & " " & Err.Description, ➥
                        , MSGTITLE
                        lblMessage.Caption = ""
                        Exit Sub
                    Else
                        ' Cue user that file has been opened and show first record
                        ' if no errors occurred
                        If Err.Number = 0 Then
                            lblMessage.Caption = "Last Open at " & CStr(Time)
                            m_frmForm.Caption = m_sFileName & VERSION

                            Set m_mnuCustomer = frmCustomer3.mnuQueueItem ➥
                            (g_nTail + 1)

                            ' Add file reference to menu queue
                            AddToQueue m_sFileName, m_mnuCustomer

                            m_lPosition = 1 ' Point to first record
                            ' Get statement copies record(m_nPosition) into ➥
                            m_ThisCustomer
                            ' Read the record
                            Get m_nFileNum, m_lPosition, m_ThisCustomer

                            ' Show the first record to the user
                            txtFirstName.Text = m_ThisCustomer.sFirstName
                            ' Rest is same as Example 8.19 following ➥
                            txtFirstName ...

            End Sub


    Private Sub mnuSaveAs_Click()
        'Launch File Save Dialog and call general procedure Save ➥
        if applicable
        On Error Resume Next
        dlgFile.ShowSave    ' Display the File Save dialog
        m_sNewFile = dlgFile.filename

        If Err.Number = cdlCancel Then   ' User clicked Cancel
            MsgBox "Operation cancelled", , MSGTITLE
            lblMessage.Caption = ""
        Else
            Save
```

```
      ' In Version 3, add file reference to menu queue
      AddToQueue m_sNewFile, m_mnuCustomer
    End If
End Sub
```

The modifications either refer to differences in the Form Name and Caption or involve calling general procedures related to handling the queue. In Form_Load we initialize the queue using NewQueue. Procedure mnuOpen_Click calls procedure AddToQueue to add an item when opening a file:

```
' Add file reference to menu queue
AddToQueue m_sFileName, m_mnuCustomer
```

Procedure mnuSaveAs_Click also calls AddToQueue, since an existing file will be renamed and should be added to the queue of recently used files. We also need to include an additional event procedure to handle the menu controls that will be added. Example 9.9 shows the event procedure for mnuQueueItem_Click. It is similar to procedure mnuOpen_Click.

Example 9.9

```
Private Sub mnuQueueItem_Click(Index As Integer)
    ' New for Version 3
    ' Give user a chance to abort the open
    ' if any changes were not saved
    Dim sMessage As String, nResponse As Integer

    ' Message of warning query
    sMessage = " Something was modified.  "
    sMessage = sMessage & "Do you still want to open ➥
another file?"
    ' Display warning query if there had been a change
    If m_bChange Then
        nResponse = MsgBox(sMessage, DIALOGTYPE, MSGTITLE)
        ' ... and act depending on user response
        If nResponse = vbNo Then
            Exit Sub ' Abort exit if user changes mind
            ' User does not care about change
        End If
    End If

    Close m_nFileNum     ' Close existing file if applicable
    m_nFileNum = FreeFile    ' Get next available file number
    ' Cue user that file opening in progress
    lblMessage.Caption = "Opening file ...."
    DoEvents
    ' Get filename from caption of this menu control
    m_sFileName = GetFileName(Index, m_mnuCustomer)

    ' Following code almost same as last part of mnuOpen_Click
    ' — — — —
    ' Open a different file for random access
    Open m_sFileName For Random As #m_nFileNum Len = ➥
m_nRecordLength
    ' Trap file open errors if they occur
```

```
        If Err.Number <> 0 Then
            MsgBox CStr(CVErr(Err.Number)) & " " & Err.Description, ➡
            , MSGTITLE
            lblMessage.Caption = ""
            Exit Sub
        Else
            ' Cue user that file has been opened and show first record
            ' if no errors occurred
            If Err.Number = 0 Then
                lblMessage.Caption = "Last Open at " & CStr(Time)
                m_frmForm.Caption = m_sFileName & VERSION
                ModifyQueue Index, m_sFileName, m_mnuCustomer
                m_lPosition = 1 ' Point to first record
                ' Get statement copies record(m_nPosition) into ➡
                m_ThisCustomer
                ' Read the record
                Get m_nFileNum, m_lPosition, m_ThisCustomer

                ' Show the first record to the user
                txtFirstName.Text = m_ThisCustomer.sFirstName
                txtLastName.Text = m_ThisCustomer.sLastName
                cboCanoeModel.Text = m_ThisCustomer.sCanoeModel
                txtSerialNum.Text = CStr(m_ThisCustomer.lSerialNum)
                txtAreaCode.Text = CStr(m_ThisCustomer.nAreaCode)
                txtLocalTel.Text = CStr(m_ThisCustomer.lLocalTel)
                ' Find position of last record
                m_lLastRecord = LOF(m_nFileNum) / m_nRecordLength
                ' Enable Append button
                cmdAppend.Enabled = True
                ' Clear flag
                m_bChange = False
            End If
        End If

        If Err.Number <> 0 Then        ' Error Handling if necessary
            MsgBox CStr(CVErr(Err.Number)) & " " & Err.Description, ➡
            , MSGTITLE
            lblMessage.Caption = "" ' Remove any message
        End If
End Sub
```

The procedure calls another function that we have yet to declare, as shown by the following statement.

```
' Get filename from caption of this menu control
m_sFileName = GetFileName(Index, m_mnuCustomer)
```

The purpose is to reorder the elements in the queue when another new procedure is called in the following statement:

```
ModifyQueue Index, m_sFileName, m_mnuCustomer
```

The next code listing (Example 9.10) will show the code for module Customer3. It defines the procedures and variables required to implement the queue. The comments explain how the queue is handled.

Example 9.10

```
Option Explicit

' Module code for Record definition, Queue implementation and
' Utility function to test if a string represents an integer
' This module is not quite universal
' It assumes form contains control named mnuQueueItem

Type Customer
    sFirstName As String * 15    ' 15 characters or 30 bytes, ➡
    unicode ?
    sLastName As String * 15     ' 15 characters or 30 bytes
    sCanoeModel As String * 8    ' 8 characters or 16 bytes
    lSerialNum As Long  ' 4 bytes
    nAreaCode As Integer    ' 2 bytes
    lLocalTel As Long      ' 4 bytes
End Type

' Queue for list of recently used files
' Max of length of a finite number of elements
' Add new item to head of queue and push other down
' Delete from tail of queue when adding in excess of queue length
' If accessing item (file) already in queue then place
' item at head of queue and shift others down

' Define First In First Out (FIFO) Queue
Const MAXQUEUE = 4 ' Length of 4 in this case

' Pointers for First In First Out (FIFO) Queue
Public g_nHead As Integer  ' Insertion pointer for queue
Public g_nTail As Integer ' Deletion pointer for queue

Public Sub NewQueue()
    ' Create a new empty queue
    g_nHead = 0
    g_nTail = 0
End Sub

Public Sub AddToQueue(sItem As String, mnuMenu As Menu)
    ' Handle situation of using open
    ' menu to open file that is already in the queue
    Dim nCount As Integer
    Dim nLength As Integer  ' Length of caption string for ➡
    string manipulation
    Dim sCaption As String  ' Temporary string for string ➡
    manipulation
    Dim bItemExists As Boolean
    Dim nLast As Integer
    Dim sFile As String
    'Static mnuQueue(4) As Menu   ' Hold queue

    If g_nHead = 0 Then ' First time something added to empty queue
        g_nHead = 1
    End If
```

```
                ' Add menu element if queue not full
                If (g_nTail < MAXQUEUE) Then
                    g_nTail = g_nTail + 1
                    Load mnuMenu
                    Set m_mnuQueue(g_nTail) = mnuMenu
                End If


                ' Check if item already in queue
                For nCount = g_nHead To g_nTail Step 1
                    ' Find file name of queue element
                    Set mnuMenu = m_mnuQueue(nCount)
                    sFile = GetFileName(nCount, mnuMenu)
                    If sItem = sFile Then
                        bItemExists = True
                        nLast = nCount
                        ' Remove added menu control if still adding to ➥
                        queue
                        If mnuMenu.Caption = "-" Then
                            Unload mnuMenu
                            g_nTail = g_nTail - 1
                            Exit For     ' and exit loop
                        End If
                    End If
                Next nCount


                ' Signal to shift down entire queue if item not in queue
                If Not bItemExists Then
                    nLast = g_nTail
                End If
                ' Shift older items down
                    For nCount = nLast To 2 Step -1
                        ' Strip off index reference in previous caption
                        sCaption = m_mnuQueue(nCount - 1).Caption
                        nLength = Len(sCaption)
                        ' Gets filename portion
                        sCaption = Right(sCaption, nLength - 2)
                        ' Assign new captions
                        m_mnuQueue(nCount).Caption = "&" & CStr(nCount) & ➥
                        sCaption
                    Next nCount

                ' Then add the new item
                m_mnuQueue(g_nHead).Caption = "&" & CStr(g_nHead) & " " & sItem
            End Sub

Sub ModifyQueue(nIndex As Integer, sItem As String, mnuMenu As Menu)
        ' Rearrange items since one item selected from list
        Dim sCaption As String, nCount As Integer
        Dim nLength As Integer
        ' Shift older items down
            For nCount = nIndex To 2 Step -1
                ' Strip off index reference in previous caption
                sCaption = m_mnuQueue(nCount - 1).Caption
```

```
                    nLength = Len(sCaption)
                    sCaption = Right(sCaption, nLength - 2)   ' Gets ➡
                    filename portion
                    ' Assign new captions
                    m_mnuQueue(nCount).Caption = "&" & CStr(nCount) & ➡
                    sCaption
               Next nCount

         ' Then add the new item
         m_mnuQueue(g_nHead).Caption = "&" & CStr(g_nHead) & " " & sItem
    End Sub

    Function GetFileName(nIndex As Integer, mnuMenu As Menu) As String
         ' Returns file name from caption of selected recent files ➡
         menu item
         Dim sFileName As String, nLength As Integer

         sFileName = mnuMenu.Caption
         If sFileName = "-" Then Exit Function  ' Return Null in ➡
         case item is null
         nLength = Len(sFileName)
         sFileName = Right(sFileName, nLength - 3)
         GetFileName = sFileName
    End Function

    Function TestInteger(sTest As String) As Boolean
         ' Same as Example 8.16
    End Function
```

9.4   LINKED LISTS

9.4.1   The Generic Linked List

Lists can be used to organize a collection of records, such as customer information. They can also be sorted and ordered in any chosen manner. Consider operations in which list items need to be inserted or deleted. It is necessary to make room for a new inserted item; we have to shift all the items below the insertion position into the next position. To delete a file, it is necessary to shift items up a position in order to fill the missing portion. An alternative is to use linked lists.

*A **linked list** is a list of records in which one field contains the location of the next record.*

Figure 9.5 illustrates a simple linked list. The *logical* sequence is record 1, followed by record 3, followed by record 8, followed by record 4, followed by record 2. Records 5, 6, and 7 are not included in the sequence shown. The logical ordering does not correspond to the physical item location. Each record has a field that identifies where the next record is located. A value of zero in the next field indicates that it is the last record in the sequence.

Figure 9.5
A Linked List

Head

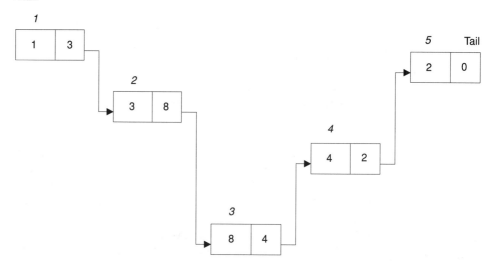

Normal type shows physical position; *italic* type shows logical position.

Using a linked list is similar to participating in a treasure hunt. When you find a clue, it tells you where to find the next clue. Eventually you will find the clue that tells where the treasure is. Computers use a linked list to determine where to find the physical sectors of a file on disk. After repeated editing and removal and addition of files on a disk, the sectors for a file may be scattered all over the disk.

Since we would like the be able to move forward and backward through the records, we need a double linked list. Like the single linked list shown in Figure 9.5, one field indicates the position of the next record. An extra field indicates the position of the preceding record. With the extra fields, it is necessary to modify the User-Defined data type used in Versions 1, 2, and 3 of the Customer program. In order to identify a record, it is also useful to have a key field to uniquely identify it. Example 9.11 shows the revised definition.

Example 9.11

```
Option Explicit

' This module is not quite universal
' It assumes form contains control named mnuQueueItem
' To implement a linked list, we need a link field
' Also include a key field although the Serial Number
' could be used as a unique key
' The changes to this structure mean that we cannot
' use the customer record files from the previous versions

Type Customer
    nRecNum As Integer ' 2 bytes, Holds record number the record
    sFirstName As String * 15    ' 15 characters or 30 bytes, ➡
    unicode?
    sLastName As String * 15     ' 15 characters or 30 bytes
    sCanoeModel As String * 8    ' 8 characters or 16 bytes
    lSerialNum As Long  ' 4 bytes
```

```
        nAreaCode As Integer      ' 2 bytes
        lLocalTel As Long      ' 4 bytes
        nBack As Integer       ' 2 bytes, Link field that points to ➡
        previous record
        nNext As Integer       ' 2 bytes, Link field that points to ➡
        next record
End Type


' Back = 0 indicates the first record.
' Next = 0 indicates the last record.


' The rest of the Module code is the same as that
' shown in Example 9.10 for Version 3
```

Note that there are three new fields to implement the double linked-list structure. Figure 9.6 illustrates how linking is accomplished after starting a new set of records by appending four records in sequence. In this case the logical order matches the physical order. The field identifying the record number is being used as the key field.

*A **key field** is the field normally used for identifying a record when sorting or searching a list of records.*

Note how a back field value of 0 means that the record is the first record. A next field value of 0 means that the record is the last one. Consider record number 3. Its back field value of 2 indicates that it follows record 2. The next field value of 4 means that record 4 is the next record. So far there is no apparent advantage to using a linked list, but the advantage should be apparent when we consider insertions and deletions.

*A **double linked list** is a list of records in which one field contains the location of the next record, and another field contains the location of the previous record.*

It is important to understand the difference between *logical* and *physical* ordering. The telephone numbers in a telephone book are logical listed by name in alphabetical order, but the (physical) numbers are normally not in a numerical order. Figure 9.7 illustrates the linked list after inserting a new record between logical records 2 and 3.

Figure 9.6
A Double Linked List
Initialized With Four
Contiguous Records

		Record position		Back	Next	
Head	*1*	1		0	2	
	2	2		1	3	
	3	3		2	4	
	4	4		3	0	Tail

Normal type shows physical position; *italic* type shows logical position.

Figure 9.7
A Double Linked List After Inserting a Record

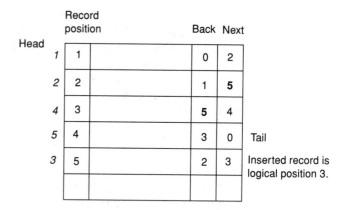

Normal type shows physical position; **bold** type shows modified fields; *italic* type shows logical position.

Start with the head of the list and follow the next fields in sequence. You should see that the ordering matches the logical positions. Start at the tail and follow the back fields in sequence. You should see that the sequence matches the logical ordering in reverse. In order to insert a record, you would append a physical record but modify the next and back fields of the new record and of the *logical* neighbor records. The pseudocode for inserting a record is shown as Example 9.12. We will also need two pointers to quickly locate the logical beginning and end. These are the head and tail pointers, respectively. In Figure 9.7, note that the tail is no longer pointing to the physical end. If we happen to insert a record before the first logical record, it will be necessary to update the head pointer.

Example 9.12

```
Insert
    ' Pseudocode for inserting between current record and ➡
    previous record
    ' Current record will be future next record
    ' For now, ignore situation if inserting before the first ➡
    logical record

    ' Assign key field of new record (known as ThisRecord)
    ThisRecord.RecordNumber = CurrentPosition
    ' New record should point back to previous record
    ' (which the current record does at this stage)
    ThisRecord.Back = NextRecord.Back
    ' New record should point forward to future next record
    ThisRecord.Next = NextRecord.RecordNumber
    ' Future next record should point back to new record
    Put ThisRecord.Next, NextRecord
    ' Update previous record (ignore case when inserting at ➡
    Head for now)
    ' Previous record should point forward to this record
    PreviousRecord.Next = ThisRecord.RecordNumber
    ' Write changes to records
    ' Now handle other fields for ThisRecord, etc.
    ' ...
End Insert
```

To delete a record, change the next field of the previous record so that it points forward to the next record, skipping the record to be deleted. Change the back field of the next record so that it points back to the previous record. The deleted record still physically exists, but it is no longer in the link chain Figure 9.8 illustrates the linked list after logical record 4 (physical record 3) of Figure 9.7 is deleted.

Start with the head of the list and follow the next fields in sequence. You should see that the ordering matches the logical positions, and that physical record 3 is skipped. Start at the tail and follow the back fields in sequence. You should see that the sequence matches the logical ordering in reverse, and that physical record 3 is also skipped. In order to delete a record, modify the next and back fields of the *logical* neighbor records so that they point to each other and skip the deleted record. The pseudocode for deleting a record is shown as Example 9.13. Remember that the deleted record physically remains but is taken out of the logical sequence chain.

Example 9.13

```
Delete
    ' Pseudocode for deleting record current known as ThisRecord
    ' which is between PreviousRecord and NextRecord
    ' Ignore special cases when ThisRecord at beginning or end

    ' Previous record should point to Next record
    PreviousRecord.Next = ThisRecord.Next
    ' Next record should point to Previous Record
    NextRecord.Back = ThisRecord.Back
    ' Write changes to records
    ' and handle other overhead, etc.
    ' ...
End Delete
```

Now let's take a look at moving forward and back in a linked list. The program should show the records in logical order, not physical order. To move forward, it will need to check the next field of the current record to find out where to physically find the next logical record. Similarly, it will need to check the back field of the current record to find out where to physically find the previous logical record. To detect the tail record

Figure 9.8
A Double Linked List
After Deleting a Record

Record Position		Back	Next	
Head *1*	1		0	2	
2	2		1	5	
	3		5	4	Deleted record
4	4		**5**	0	Tail
3	5		2	**4**	

Normal type shows physical position; **bold** type shows modified fields; *italic* type shows logical position.

(end of logical list), the program checks if the next field of the current record is zero. To detect the head record (beginning of logical list), the program checks if the back field of the current record is zero. Example 9.14 shows the pseudocode.

Example 9.14

```
Next
     ' Pseudocode for moving to the next record
     If ThisRecord.Next = 0
     Then
          Beep
     Else
          Position =  ThisCustomer.Next
     End If
     ' Other overhead as required
End Next


Back
     ' Pseudocode for moving to the previous record
     If ThisRecord.Back = 0
     Then
          Beep
     Else
          Position =  ThisCustomer.Back
     End If
End Back
```

We should also look at the algorithm for appending a record. To do this, we need to find the logical end. If the program continually updates the tail pointer, this should be easy. First, you must update the next field of the current end record (indicated by the tail) to contain the physical location of the new appended record. You then set the back field of the appended record to contain the physical location of the former end record, and set the next field of the appended record to zero. Example 9.15 shows the pseudocode. Figure 9.9 shows the list after appending a record.

Example 9.15

```
Append
      ' Pseudocode for appending record known as ThisCustomer to
      ' logically follow tail record known as LastRecord
```

Figure 9.9
A Double Linked List
Appending a Record

Record Position		Back	Next	
Head	1		0	2	
	2		1	5	
	3		5	4	Deleted record not in sequence chain.
	4		5	6	
	5		2	4	
	6		**4**	**0**	Tail

Normal type shows physical position; **bold** type shows modified fields; *italic* type shows logical position.

```
            ' Assign new record number
            ThisCustomer.RecordNumber = next available physical record
            ' Find record number of current last record
            Get Tail, LastRecord
            ' New record should point back to previous last record
            ThisCustomer.Back = LastRecord.RecordNumber
            ' and should be marked as last record
            ThisCustomer.Next = 0
            ' Previous last record should now point to new last record
            LastRecord.Next = ThisCustomer.RecordNumber
            ' Write changes to records
            ' and handle other overhead, etc.
End Append
```

Is there a disadvantage to using linked lists? If we delete many records, we could end up with plenty of wasted space. It is possible to modify the insert, delete, and append processes. The delete process could set the record number field of the deleted record to be some fixed value such as zero. This would *mark* the record as being deleted, thus indicating that the space can be reclaimed. An insert or append operation could first search for physical records containing a record number field of zero. If such a physical record space is found, it could be used for the new record. Our Customer program won't be quite that sophisticated, but don't be shy about modifying the program to operate this way.

9.4.2   Linked-List Demo for the Customer Program

Algorithms to Insert and Delete Records

As promised, this version will implement insertion and deletion. Primarily for demonstration purposes, we will use linked lists, as described earlier. It is possible to use physically sequential records, as shown in Example 9.16.

Example 9.16

```
' Pseudocode for inserting and deleting records with a ➡
sequential list of records

Insert New between Current and Previous
    Open new file (temporary)
    For record = head to Previous
    Put record in new file
    Next record
    Put New record in new file
    For record = Current to tail
        Put record in new file
    Next record
    Close old file
    Rename old file as new file
End Insert

Delete Current which is between Previous and Next
    Open new file (temporary)
    For record = head to Previous
        Put record in new file
    Next record
```

```
        ' skip Current
        For record = Next to tail
            Put record in new file
        Next record
        Close old file
        Rename old file as new file
End Insert
```

We can debate whether or not a linked list is preferable. If the records contain many fields, and we want to be able to reorder records by sorting based on different fields, we may prefer to maintain a separate list containing the link information. Then it would only be necessary to modify this list when sorting.

Introducing the Program

For now, we have made a commitment to using a double linked list for Version 4 of the Customer program. In this section, we show only portions of the code to explain specific highlights. Some of the code is the same as that of the earlier version, and some of it is different. The following section (Section 9.5) contains the complete code listing, which we can use as a reference. (In the Hands-On section, you can save Version 3 as Version 4; then refer to the complete listing to modify the code.)

The program looks the same as the previous versions shown in Figure 8.6. The title will indicate that we are working with Version 4. The data files from the earlier versions are incompatible with this version because of the extra fields. After you perform several insert, delete, and append operations, clicking Next and Back will show that the physical order shown in the Record Position box does not correspond to the logical position. For demonstration purposes, we show the *physical* record position instead of the *logical* record position. If you wish, modify the program to show both. Once the user has initiated an Append or Insert operation, he or she is committed to completing the operation because the program disables other controls that permit an Append or Insert operation to be abandoned. However, the user is free to delete the new record after completing the Append or Insert operation; this prevents the data file from being corrupted. Remember that a deleted file still physically exists, but it is not logically visible because links have been severed.

Inserting a Record

To insert a record, the user clicks Insert and types in the new field values and then clicks Change. Procedure cmdInsert_Click sets up the Insert operation (transaction). The procedure cmdChange_Click completes the operation by calling general procedure UpdateInsert. Remember that the record structure includes fields for linking, as shown in Example 9.11. (For a visual reminder about an insertion, refer to Figures 9.6 and 9.7 for a sample before and after views. Example 9.12 shows the pseudocode.) Example 9.17 shows the main part of cmdInsert_Click and the part of cmdChange_Click that is involved with inserting a record and procedure UpdateInsert.

Example 9.17

```
Private Sub cmdInsert_Click()
    ' Inserts a new record between this record and previous one
    ' At m_nThisCustomer when Insert clicked
    ' This is a partial listing.  See Section 9.5 for complete ➡
    listing
```

```
      ' Preserve information about the record we are at
      ' Current record before inserting will be future next record
      m_NextRecord = m_ThisCustomer

      ' Show user blank fields
      ' User will have to use Change button to save entries
      ' New intended record is blank (except for links) until ➡
      changed by user
      ClearThisCustomer   ' Clears m_ThisCustomer
      m_nRecCount = m_nRecCount + 1 ' Increment physical record count
      m_nPosition = m_nRecCount ' Inserted record will be ➡
      physically located at end
      ' Build new record links
      m_nOperation = opINSERT    ' Flag that Insert in progress
      DisplayBlank ' To cue user to enter information

      ' Disable another modification until a record change ➡
      committed by
      ' using Change button
      DisableOps
      ' Signal to cmdChange_Click that insert initiated.  ➡
      cmdChange will
      ' handle linked-list updating when committing changes to the
      file
      m_bChange = True

      ' For additional code, see Section 9.5
End Sub

Private Sub cmdChange_Click()
      ' Modify record that is currently displayed due to user ➡
      edit of existing
      ' record or when append or insert operation selected by user
      ' by calling UpdateAppend and UpdateInsert, respectively
      ' These three procedures are the only ones that use the Put
      ' statement to physically modify a data file
      ' This is a partial listing.  See Section 9.5 for complete ➡
      listing

      ' Update pointer links depending on operation
      If m_nOperation = opAPPEND Then UpdateAppend
      If m_nOperation = opINSERT Then UpdateInsert
      ' Modify other record fields
      Put #m_nFileNum, m_nPosition, m_ThisCustomer
      ' ... and reset flag to say change has been saved
      m_bChange = False
      m_nOperation = opDONE
      ' Permit other changes
      EnableOps
End Sub

Sub UpdateInsert()
      ' Commit changes to pointer fields for linked list handling
```

```
          ' when an insert operation initiated.
          ' Called by cmdChange_Click when user has entered data
          Dim ThisRecord As Customer
          Dim NextRecord As Customer
          Dim PreviousRecord As Customer

          ' Preserve information about the record we are at
          ' Current record before inserting will be next record
          ThisRecord = m_ThisCustomer
          ' Build new record links
          ThisRecord.nRecNum = m_nPosition
          ThisRecord.nBack = m_NextRecord.nBack
          ThisRecord.nNext = m_NextRecord.nRecNum
          ' Update Next Record
          m_NextRecord.nBack = ThisRecord.nRecNum
          Put m_nFileNum, ThisRecord.nNext, m_NextRecord
          ' Update Previous Record
          If ThisRecord.nBack > 0 Then    ' Inserting somwhere after ➡
          first record
              Get m_nFileNum, ThisRecord.nBack, PreviousRecord
              PreviousRecord.nNext = ThisRecord.nRecNum
              Put m_nFileNum, ThisRecord.nBack, PreviousRecord
          Else    ' If inserting at beginning
              ' there is no previous record!
              m_nHead = ThisRecord.nRecNum
          End If
          ' And finally write links to new intended record
          m_ThisCustomer = ThisRecord
End Sub
```

Module-level variable m_ThisCustomer always shows the current record that the user is viewing. An Insert operation will create a new record that is *logically* ahead of the viewed record (but *physically* added to the end). Hence, we assign it to record NextCustomer. We use module-level variable m_1RecCount to maintain a total count of *physical* records. This is necessary for assigning the physical position of any new records. Note that we use a module-level variable m_1Position to keep track of the physical record position, and note how the rest of the code updates the Next and Back fields of the neighboring records. Note that the head pointer is modified if the user is inserting at the beginning of the logical sequence. The only procedures in this sequence that write to the file using the Put statement are cmdChange_Click and UpdateInsert, which it calls. Later we will examine other procedures called by cmdChange_Click.

Deleting a Record

Remember that the record structure includes fields for linking, as shown in Example 9.11. (Refer to Figures 9.7 and 9.8 for a sample before-and-after view.) Example 9.13 shows the pseudocode. Example 9.18 shows the main part of cmdDelete_Click.

Example 9.18

```
Private Sub cmdDelete_Click()
    ' Deletes ThisRecord which is between PreviousRecord and ➡
    NextRecord
```

```
' This is a partial listing.  See Section 9.5 for complete ➥
listing

' Preserve information about the record we are at
ThisRecord = m_ThisCustomer
' — -> Mark record as erased
m_ThisCustomer.nRecNum = 0
Put m_nFileNum, ThisRecord.nRecNum, m_ThisCustomer

' Build new record links
If (ThisRecord.nBack > 0) And (ThisRecord.nNext > 0) Then
    ' Deleting somewhere between first record and last record
    Get m_nFileNum, ThisRecord.nBack, PreviousRecord
    PreviousRecord.nNext = ThisRecord.nNext
    Put m_nFileNum, ThisRecord.nBack, PreviousRecord
    Get m_nFileNum, ThisRecord.nNext, NextRecord
    NextRecord.nBack = ThisRecord.nBack
    Put m_nFileNum, ThisRecord.nNext, NextRecord
    ' Now NextRecord points to PreviousRecord and vice versa
    m_nPosition = NextRecord.nRecNum ' To show user next record

ElseIf ThisRecord.nBack = 0 And ThisRecord.nNext = 0 Then
    ' Deleting the one and only record
    ' Show user that no field exists until first one appended
    m_ThisCustomer = NextRecord ' Clear the record information
    cmdAppend_Click
    ' Reset the flag
    m_bChange = False
    Exit Sub
ElseIf ThisRecord.nBack = 0 Then
    ' Deleting first record
    Get m_nFileNum, ThisRecord.nNext, NextRecord
    NextRecord.nBack = 0
    Put m_nFileNum, ThisRecord.nNext, NextRecord
    m_nHead = NextRecord.nRecNum
    ' Now NextRecord is marked as first logical record
    m_nPosition = NextRecord.nRecNum ' To show user next record
ElseIf ThisRecord.nNext = 0 Then
    ' Deleting last record
    Get m_nFileNum, ThisRecord.nBack, PreviousRecord
    PreviousRecord.nNext = 0
    Put m_nFileNum, ThisRecord.nBack, PreviousRecord
    m_nTail = PreviousRecord.nRecNum
    m_nPosition = PreviousRecord.nRecNum  ' To show user ➥
    previous record
End If

' Access and display next (or previous) record
If m_nPosition <> 0 Then
    Get m_nFileNum, m_nPosition, m_ThisCustomer   ' Read ➥
    the record
    DisplayInfo
```

```
      End If

      ' Flag that Delete operation occurred
      m_bDelete = True

      ' For additional code, see Section 9.5
End Sub
```

Note that this procedure handles special cases when the record to be deleted is the only logical record, first logical record, or last logical record. Variable m_lPosition is updated so that the user is shown the record following the deleted record (if possible). The purpose of flag m_bDelete is to inform the cmdNext_Click and cmdBack_Click procedures that a record change is the result of a delete operation. When a delete operation occurs, it triggers a change in the Text properties, setting the flag m_bChange. As a reminder, note that these procedures check flag m_bChange to determine whether to warn the user about a record change in progress.

Moving to the Next Record or Back

Example 9.14 shows the pseudocode for moving to the next or previous record. Here is the main part of cmdNext_Click. The code for cmdBack_Click would be similar. Remember to refer to Section 9.5 to see the complete listing.

Example 9.19

```
Private Sub cmdNext_Click()
    ' Move to next "logical" record
    ' This is a partial listing.  See Section 9.5 for complete ➥
    listing
    ' Show next record if we are not at the end
    ' Get physical position of next logical record
    Get m_nFileNum, m_nPosition, m_ThisCustomer
    If m_ThisCustomer.nNext = 0 Then
        ' We are at last logical record
        Beep    ' and inform user
    Else    ' Otherwise go ahead an move to next logical record
        m_nPosition = m_ThisCustomer.nNext
        ' Then get the next logical record ...
        Get m_nFileNum, m_nPosition, m_ThisCustomer
        ' ... and display the information
        DisplayInfo
    End If
End Sub
```

Appending a Record

To append a record, the user clicks Append, types in the new field values, and clicks Change. Procedure cmdAppend_Click sets up the Append operation (transaction). The procedure cmdChange_Click completes the operation by calling general procedure UpdateAppend. Remember that the record structure includes fields for linking, as shown in Example 9.11. (Refer to Figures 9.8 and 9.9 for a sample before-and-after view.) Example 9.15 shows the pseudocode. Here is the main part of cmdAppend_Click, as well as the listing for UpdateAppend. To examine procedure cmdChange, refer back to

Example 9.17. Note that it checks if cmdAppend_Click set flag m_nOperation to the value of constant opAppend. Procedure cmdChange_Click subsequently uses this flag to call UpdateAppend (see Example 9.20).

Example 9.20

```
Private Sub cmdAppend_Click()
    ' Add (append) record to end of record list
    ' This is a partial listing.  See Section 9.5 for complete ➥
    listing

    ' Show user blank fields
    ' User will have to use Change button to save entries
    ' New intended record is written only when user clicks ➥
    Change to validate update
    ClearThisCustomer
    m_nRecCount = m_nRecCount + 1 ' Adding a new physical record
    ' This also assigns a new record number
    m_nPosition = m_nRecCount ' Show position to user
    ' Linked List handling
    DisplayBlank ' To cue user to enter information
    ' Disable another modification until a record change ➥
    committed by
    ' using Change button
    DisableOps
    ' Signal to cmdChange_Click that append initiated ➥
    and cmdChange will
    ' handle linked-list updating when committing changes to the file
    m_nOperation = opAPPEND

    ' For additional code, see Section 9.5
End Sub

Sub UpdateAppend()
    ' Commit changes to pointer fields for linked list handling
    ' when an append operation initiated
    ' Called by cmdChange_Click when user has entered data

    Dim LastRecord As Customer
    ' Handle first record
    If m_ThisCustomer.nRecNum = 0 Then
        m_ThisCustomer.nRecNum = m_nPosition  ' To set nRecNum ➥
        field to first position
        m_ThisCustomer.nNext = 0    ' Mark it as last record ➥
        for now
        m_ThisCustomer.nBack = 0   ' and also as first record
        m_nHead = m_nPosition ' Point to beginning record
        m_nTail = m_nPosition ' which is also its end record
    Else
        ' ... otherwise handle subsequent records
        ' Find record number of current last record
        Get m_nFileNum, m_nTail, LastRecord
```

```
            ' ... and assign it to back link of new record
            ' New record should point back to previous last record
            m_ThisCustomer.nBack = LastRecord.nRecNum
            ' Assign next link to zero since this is now the last ➡
            record
            m_ThisCustomer.nNext = 0
            ' Mark the Record Num (assigns new record number for ➡
            new record)
            m_ThisCustomer.nRecNum = m_nRecCount
            ' Update Next link of current last record
            LastRecord.nNext = m_nRecCount
            Put #m_nFileNum, m_nTail, LastRecord
            m_nTail = m_nRecCount    ' Now mark new record as the ➡
            last record
        End If
End Sub
```

Procedure UpdateAppend depends on using m_nTail to know where the current end (tail) record is located. The procedure is also responsible for updating m_nTail.

Detecting the Logical Beginning When Opening an Existing File

It is possible that the head (logical beginning) of a list of records is not the first physical record, so when we open a file, we need to search the physical list for the head record. Procedure mnuOpen_Click is similar to previous versions, but it uses the following statement to call general procedure OpenFile to handle these details:

```
' OpenFile procedure handles details to handle open file
OpenFile 0   ' 0 indicates that Open menu used
```

Example 9.21 shows the code segment for mnuOpen_Click that handles this:

Example 9.21

```
Sub OpenFile(nQueueItem As Integer)
    ' Open file, extract head and tail info, handle menu
    ' queue, and display first logical record.
    ' Parameter nQueueItem indicates how file is opened
    ' 0 means Open menu used, otherwise indicates file
    ' selected from recently used menu items (mnuQueueItem)
    ' Called from mnuOpen_Click, mnuQueueItem_Click

    ' This is a partial listing.  See Section 9.5 for complete ➡
    listing

        ' Find position of last physical record
        m_nRecCount = LOF(m_nFileNum) / m_nRecordLength
        ' Get m_nTail value (nonerased record with nNext = 0)
        nCount = 1
        m_nTail = 0
        Do
            Get m_nFileNum, nCount, m_ThisCustomer
            If m_ThisCustomer.nNext = 0 And ➡
            m_ThisCustomer.nRecNum <> 0 Then _
                m_nTail = m_ThisCustomer.nRecNum
```

```
        nCount = nCount + 1
    Loop Until m_nTail <> 0 Or nCount > m_nRecCount
    ' Get m_nHead value (nonerased record with nBack = 0)
    nCount = 1
    m_nHead = 0
    Do
        Get m_nFileNum, nCount, m_ThisCustomer
        If m_ThisCustomer.nBack = 0 And ➥
        m_ThisCustomer.nRecNum <> 0 Then _
            m_nHead = m_ThisCustomer.nRecNum
        nCount = nCount + 1
    Loop Until m_nHead <> 0 Or nCount > m_nRecCount

    m_nPosition = m_nHead ' Point to first logical record
    ' Get statement copies record(m_nPosition) into ➥
    m_ThisCustomer
    Get m_nFileNum, m_nPosition, m_ThisCustomer    ' Read ➥
    the record
    DisplayInfo ' User sees first logical record



    ' For additional code, see Section 9.5
End Sub
```

Handling Abandoned Modifications in Progress

As mentioned, the user could start a modification, such as inserting or appending. The operation isn't committed until the user activates cmdChange_Click by clicking the button or pressing ENTER (cmdChange.Default = True) when any field has the focus. Earlier we used the flag m_bChange to detect modifications, but an insert or delete operation also triggers the changes to cause the flag to set. No harm is done, but the user will see annoying and misleading messages. Previously we used text box Change event procedures to set the flag. In Example 9.22 we modify the practice by abandoning this approach, instead using other procedures to set the flag.

Example 9.22

```
Private Sub txtFirstName_KeyPress(KeyAscii As Integer)
    ' Flag that change occurred
    ' Same code used for other text boxes
    m_bChange = True
End Sub



Private Sub cboCanoeModel_GotFocus()
    ' Flag that change occurred
    m_bChange = True
End Sub
```

We have blocked out setting the flag due to inserting, deleting, and appending records. Only direct user interaction with the text boxes and combo box will set the flag. This solution isn't perfect for the combo box. The user may tab to the combo box and tab past it *without* modifying its contents, but the program believes a change occurred.

This is because the GotFocus event occurs when an object receives the focus. An object can receive the focus by user action, such as tabbing to or clicking the object. It is also possible to use the SetFocus method to change the focus using code.

9.5 THE COMPLETE SOURCE CODE FOR THE CUSTOMER INFORMATION PROGRAM, VERSION 4

Example 9.23 shows the code for the Form frmCustomer4.

Example 9.23

```
Option Explicit

' Version 4 of Customer program
' Modified from Version 3 to demonstrate linked-list
' data structure which facilitates insertion
' and deletion of records

' To do, opening comments
' Also leave as exercise to improve documentation
' to add summary of procedures

' Constants for message boxes
Const MSGTITLE = "Customer Information"
' Some message boxes display Yes and No buttons with a question icon
Const DIALOGTYPE = vbYesNo + vbQuestion
Const VERSION = " - Customer Information V4"
' Declare variables, some changes to handle linked list
Dim m_ThisCustomer As Customer     ' A record variable
Dim m_nPosition As Integer    ' Tracks the current record ➥
physical position
Dim m_nRecCount As Integer ' Tracks number of records
Dim m_nRecordLength As Integer
Dim m_sFileName As String
Dim m_sNewFile As String      ' Used for copying existing file ➥
when opening a new file
Dim m_nFileNum As Integer
' Flag to indicate that user changed a field without saving it
Dim m_bChange As Boolean      ' Flag to indicate that user ➥
modified something
Dim m_frmCustomer As Form ' Refer to form object for use by module
Dim m_bDelete   ' Flag that Delete button was pressed, used in ➥
Next and Back operations
                  ' to ignore text changes flagged by m_bChange
Dim m_nHead As Integer    ' Position of first logical record
Dim m_nTail As Integer    ' Position of last logical record
Dim m_NextRecord As Customer ' Temporary storage for insertion ➥
operation
Dim m_nOperation As Integer ' For communication between
' cmdChange and cmdAppend/Insert so linked
```

```vb
' records updated appropriately
Const opDONE = 0
list part of
Const opAPPEND = 1
Const opINSERT = 2


Sub ClearThisCustomer()
    ' Make the record blank
    With m_ThisCustomer
        .sFirstName = ""
        .sLastName = ""
        .sCanoeModel = ""
        .lSerialNum = 0
        .nAreaCode = 0
        .lLocalTel = 0
    End With
End Sub


Sub DisableOps()
    ' Disable user from corrupting insert and append in progress
    ' Clicking Change to commit change will enable changes by
    ' calling EnableOps.  Called from mnuNew_Click,
    ' cmdAppend_Click, cmdInsert_Click, OpenFile
    cmdDelete.Enabled = False
    cmdInsert.Enabled = False
    cmdAppend.Enabled = False
    cmdExit.Enabled = False
    cmdNext.Enabled = False
    cmdBack.Enabled = False
    mnuExit.Enabled = False
End Sub


Sub DisplayBlank()
    ' Show record as a blank
    ' More convenient to user if zeros do not show
    ' up in the serial number, area code, and local tel inputs
    txtFirstName.Text = ""
    txtLastName.Text = ""
    cboCanoeModel.Text = ""
    txtSerialNum.Text = ""
    txtAreaCode.Text = ""
    txtLocalTel.Text = ""
    txtPosition.Text = CStr(m_nPosition)
End Sub


Sub DisplayInfo()
    ' Show current record information to user
    txtFirstName.Text = m_ThisCustomer.sFirstName
    txtLastName.Text = m_ThisCustomer.sLastName
```

```
                    cboCanoeModel.Text = m_ThisCustomer.sCanoeModel
                    txtSerialNum.Text = CStr(m_ThisCustomer.lSerialNum)
                    txtAreaCode.Text = CStr(m_ThisCustomer.nAreaCode)
                    txtLocalTel.Text = CStr(m_ThisCustomer.lLocalTel)
                    txtPosition.Text = CStr(m_nPosition)
                End Sub


            Sub EnableOps()
                ' Enable user to perform append, insert, exit, and file ➥
                operations
                ' Undoes the effect of calling DisableOps
                ' Called from cmdChange_Click, OpenFile
                cmdDelete.Enabled = True
                cmdInsert.Enabled = True
                cmdAppend.Enabled = True
                cmdExit.Enabled = True
                cmdNext.Enabled = True
                cmdBack.Enabled = True
                mnuExit.Enabled = True
            End Sub


            Sub OpenFile(nQueueItem As Integer)
                ' Open file, extract head and tail info, handle menu
                ' queue, and display first logical record
                ' Parameter nQueueItem indicates how file is opened
                ' 0 means Open menu used, otherwise indicates file
                ' selected from recently used menu items (mnuQueueItem)
                ' Called from mnuOpen_Click, mnuQueueItem_Click

                On Error Resume Next
                Dim nCount As Integer    ' Counter for finding tail and head
                Open m_sFileName For Random As #m_nFileNum Len = ➥
                m_nRecordLength
                ' Trap file open errors if they occur
                If Err.Number <> 0 Then
                    MsgBox CStr(CVErr(Err.Number)) & " " & Err.Description, ➥
                    , MSGTITLE
                    lblMessage.Caption = ""
                    Exit Sub
                Else
                    ' Cue user that file has been opened and show first record
                    ' if no errors occurred
                    If Err.Number = 0 Then
                        lblMessage.Caption = "Last Open at " & CStr(Time)
                        m_frmCustomer.Caption = m_sFileName & VERSION
                        ' Handle recently used files queue in file menu
                        If nQueueItem = 0 Then
                            ' Add file reference to menu queue
                            AddToQueue m_sFileName, m_frmCustomer
                        Else
                            ' Re-order menu queue if chosen from existing list
                            ModifyQueue nQueueItem, m_sFileName, m_frmCustomer
                        End If
```

```
                    ' Find position of last physical record
                    m_nRecCount = LOF(m_nFileNum) / m_nRecordLength
                    ' Get m_nTail value (nonerased record with nNext = 0)
                    nCount = 1
                    m_nTail = 0
                    Do
                        Get m_nFileNum, nCount, m_ThisCustomer
                        If m_ThisCustomer.nNext = 0 And
                        m_ThisCustomer.nRecNum <> 0 Then _
                        m_nTail = m_ThisCustomer.nRecNum
                        nCount = nCount + 1
                    Loop Until m_nTail <> 0 Or nCount > m_nRecCount
                    ' Get m_nHead value (nonerased record with nBack = 0)
                    nCount = 1
                    m_nHead = 0
                    Do
                        Get m_nFileNum, nCount, m_ThisCustomer
                        If m_ThisCustomer.nBack = 0 And ➡
                        m_ThisCustomer.nRecNum <> 0 Then _
                        m_nHead = m_ThisCustomer.nRecNum
                        nCount = nCount + 1
                    Loop Until m_nHead <> 0 Or nCount > m_nRecCount

                    m_nPosition = m_nHead ' Point to first logical record
                    ' Get statement copies record(m_nPosition) into ➡
                    m_ThisCustomer
                    ' Read the record
                    Get m_nFileNum, m_nPosition, m_ThisCustomer    '
                    DisplayInfo ' User sees first logical record
                    ' Enable modification buttons if file is not empty
                    If m_nHead <> 0 And m_nTail <> 0 Then
                        EnableOps
                    Else
                        cmdAppend_Click ' ... or force user to append only
                        DisableOps
                    End If
                    ' Clear flag
                    m_bChange = False

            End If ' Error check
        End If

    ' If no valid records found, error message appears
        ' for example if opening a file in which all records
        ' were deleted but can still append
        If Err.Number <> 0 Then      ' Error Handling if necessary
            MsgBox CStr(CVErr(Err.Number)) & " " & ➡
            Err.Description, , MSGTITLE
            lblMessage.Caption = "" ' Remove any message
        End If
End Sub


Sub Save()
```

```
    ' Save Current file.
    On Error Resume Next
    Close m_nFileNum ' Close existing file if applicable
    'Cue user that file opening in progress
    lblMessage.Caption = "Saving file ...."
    DoEvents

    If m_sFileName = "" Then
        m_nFileNum = FreeFile
        Open m_sNewFile For Random As #m_nFileNum Len = ➡
        m_nRecordLength
        m_sFileName = m_sNewFile ' Assign file name from dialog
    Else
        ' Copy existing file to new file
        FileCopy m_sFileName, m_sNewFile
        ' Open new file
        Open m_sNewFile For Random As #m_nFileNum Len = ➡
        m_nRecordLength
    End If

    ' Trap file copy errors if they occur
    If Err.Number = 70 Then
        ' User attempted to save using same file name
        MsgBox "File already exists", , MSGTITLE
        lblMessage.Caption = ""
        Exit Sub
    ElseIf Err.Number <> 0 Then
        MsgBox CStr(CVErr(Err.Number)) & " " & ➡
        Err.Description, , MSGTITLE
        lblMessage.Caption = "Last Save Unsuccessful"
        Exit Sub
    Else
        ' Update File Name
        m_sFileName = m_sNewFile
        m_frmCustomer.Caption = m_sFileName & VERSION
        ' Cue user that file has been saved
        lblMessage.Caption = "Last Save at " & CStr(Time)
        m_frmCustomer.Caption = dlgFile.FileTitle & VERSION
    End If

    If Err.Number <> 0 Then      ' Error Handling if necessary
        MsgBox CStr(CVErr(Err.Number)) & " " & ➡
        Err.Description, , MSGTITLE
    End If
End Sub


Function ValidInputs() As Boolean
    ' Force user to enter valid inputs before committing ➡
    change to record
    ' Initially assume false
    ValidInputs = False
    ' Trim all strings first
```

```
        txtFirstName.Text = Trim(txtFirstName.Text)
        txtLastName.Text = Trim(txtLastName.Text)
        cboCanoeModel.Text = Trim(cboCanoeModel.Text)
        txtSerialNum.Text = Trim(txtSerialNum.Text)
        txtAreaCode.Text = Trim(txtAreaCode.Text)
        txtLocalTel.Text = Trim(txtLocalTel.Text)

        If txtFirstName.Text = "" Then
            txtFirstName.SetFocus
        ElseIf txtLastName.Text = "" Then
            txtLastName.SetFocus
        ElseIf cboCanoeModel.Text = "" Then
            cboCanoeModel.SetFocus
        ElseIf Len(txtSerialNum.Text) <> 9 Then ' Must have 9 ➥
        digits
            txtSerialNum.SetFocus
        ElseIf Not TestInteger(txtSerialNum.Text) Then
            txtSerialNum.SetFocus
        ElseIf Len(txtAreaCode.Text) <> 3 Then   ' Must have 3 ➥
        digits
            txtAreaCode.SetFocus
        ElseIf Not TestInteger(txtAreaCode.Text) Then
            txtAreaCode.SetFocus
        ElseIf Len(txtLocalTel.Text) <> 7 Then
            txtLocalTel.SetFocus
        ElseIf Not TestInteger(txtLocalTel.Text) Then
            txtLocalTel.SetFocus
        Else
            ValidInputs = True   ' Otherwise okay
        End If
End Function


Function TestInteger(sTest As String) As Boolean
    ' Return True if argument is an integer
    ' Sort of like IsNumeric for integers only
    ' Initially assume false
    TestInteger = False
    If IsNumeric(sTest) Then
        If InStr(sTest, ".") = 0 And InStr(sTest, "-") = 0
        Then
            If InStr(sTest, ",") = 0 And InStr(sTest, "%") ➥
            = 0 Then
                TestInteger = True
            End If
        End If
    End If
End Function


Sub UpdateAppend()
    ' Commit changes to pointer fields for linked-list handling
    ' when an append operation initiated
```

```
                ' Called by cmdChange_Click when user has entered data
                Dim LastRecord As Customer
                ' Handle first record
                If m_ThisCustomer.nRecNum = 0 Then
                    m_ThisCustomer.nRecNum = m_nPosition  ' To set ➥
                    nRecNum field to first position
                    m_ThisCustomer.nNext = 0     ' Mark it as last ➥
                    record for now
                    m_ThisCustomer.nBack = 0   ' and also as first record
                    m_nHead = m_nPosition ' Point to beginning record
                    m_nTail = m_nPosition ' which is also its end record
                Else
                    '  ... otherwise handle subsequent records
                    ' Find record number of current last record
                    Get m_nFileNum, m_nTail, LastRecord
                    ' ... and assign it to back link of new record
                    ' New record should point back to previous last record
                    m_ThisCustomer.nBack = LastRecord.nRecNum
                    ' Assign next link to zero since this is now the ➥
                    last record
                    m_ThisCustomer.nNext = 0
                    ' Mark the Record Num (assigns new record number ➥
                    for new record)
                    m_ThisCustomer.nRecNum = m_nRecCount
                    ' Update Next link of current last record
                    LastRecord.nNext = m_nRecCount
                    Put #m_nFileNum, m_nTail, LastRecord
                    m_nTail = m_nRecCount     ' Now mark new record as ➥
                    the last record
                End If
            End Sub


            Sub UpdateInsert()
                ' Commit changes to pointer fields for linked list handling
                ' when an insert operation initiated
                ' Called by cmdChange_Click when user has entered data
                Dim ThisRecord As Customer
                Dim NextRecord As Customer
                Dim PreviousRecord As Customer

                ' Preserve information about the record we are at
                ' Current record before inserting will be next record
                ThisRecord = m_ThisCustomer
                ' Build new record links
                ThisRecord.nRecNum = m_nPosition
                ThisRecord.nBack = m_NextRecord.nBack
                ThisRecord.nNext = m_NextRecord.nRecNum
                ' Update Next Record
                m_NextRecord.nBack = ThisRecord.nRecNum
                Put m_nFileNum, ThisRecord.nNext, m_NextRecord
                ' Update Previous Record
                If ThisRecord.nBack > 0 Then   ' Inserting somwhere ➥
                after first record
```

```
            Get m_nFileNum, ThisRecord.nBack, PreviousRecord
            PreviousRecord.nNext = ThisRecord.nRecNum
            Put m_nFileNum, ThisRecord.nBack, PreviousRecord
      Else    ' If inserting at beginning
            ' there is no previous record!
            m_nHead = ThisRecord.nRecNum
      End If
      ' And finally write links to new intended record
      m_ThisCustomer = ThisRecord
End Sub


Private Sub cboCanoeModel_GotFocus()
      ' Flag that change occurred
      m_bChange = True
End Sub


Private Sub cmdAppend_Click()
      ' Add (append) record to end of record list
      Dim nRecordNumber As Integer
      Dim nBackLink As Integer, nNextLink as Integer

      ' Give user a chance to abort append
      ' if any changes had occurred without saving them.
      Dim sMessage As String, nResponse As Integer
      ' Message of warning query
      sMessage = " Something was modified.  "
      sMessage = sMessage & "Do you still want to append a record?"
      ' Display warning query if there had been a change
      If m_bChange Then
            nResponse = MsgBox(sMessage, DIALOGTYPE, MSGTITLE)
            ' ... and act depending on user response
            If nResponse = vbNo Then
                Exit Sub ' Abort exit if user changes mind
            Else
                ' User does not care about change
            End If
      End If

      ' Show user blank fields
      ' User will have to use Change button to save entries
      ' New intended record is written only when user clicks ➡
      Change to validate update
      ClearThisCustomer
      m_nRecCount = m_nRecCount + 1 ' Adding a new physical record
      ' This also assigns a new record number
      m_nPosition = m_nRecCount ' Show position to user

      ' Linked List handling
      DisplayBlank ' To cue user to enter information
      ' Disable another modification until a record change
      ' committed by using Change button
```

```
        DisableOps
        ' Signal to cmdChange_Click that append initiated.
        ' cmdChange will handle linked-list updating when
        ' committing changes to the file
        m_nOperation = opAPPEND
    End Sub


    Private Sub cmdBack_Click()
        ' Give user a chance to abort the back move
        ' if any changes had occurred without saving them
        Dim sMessage As String, nResponse As Integer
        ' Message of warning query
        sMessage = " Something was modified.  "
        sMessage = sMessage & "Do you still want to go to the ➥
        previous record?"

        ' Display warning query if there had been a change
        If m_bChange And Not m_bDelete Then
            nResponse = MsgBox(sMessage, DIALOGTYPE, MSGTITLE)
            ' ... and act depending on user response
            If nResponse = vbNo Then
                Exit Sub ' Abort exit if user changes mind
            End If
        End If
        ' Clear Button flag since it has already been acknowledged
        m_bDelete = False
        ' Reset change flag since user ignored change warning
        m_bChange = False

        ' Show previous record if we are not at the beginning
        ' Get physical position of next logical record
        Get m_nFileNum, m_nPosition, m_ThisCustomer
        If m_ThisCustomer.nBack = 0 Then
            ' We are at first logical record
            Beep      ' and inform user
        Else      ' Otherwise go ahead and move to previous ➥
        logical record
            m_nPosition = m_ThisCustomer.nBack
            ' Then get the next logical record ...
            Get m_nFileNum, m_nPosition, m_ThisCustomer
            ' ... and display the information
            DisplayInfo
        End If
    End Sub


    Private Sub cmdChange_Click()
        ' Modify record that is currently displayed due to user ➥
        edit of existing
        ' record or when append or insert operation selected by user
        ' by calling UpdateAppend and UpdateInsert, respectively
        ' These three procedures are the only ones that use the Put
        ' statement to physically modify a data file
```

```
        On Error Resume Next

        ' This version does not check if key (serial number) ➡
        already exists in the file
        If Not ValidInputs Then Exit Sub
        ' Get customer information from user inputs
        With m_ThisCustomer
            .sFirstName = txtFirstName.Text
            .sLastName = txtLastName.Text
            .sCanoeModel = cboCanoeModel.Text
            .lSerialNum = CLng(txtSerialNum.Text)
            .nAreaCode = CInt(txtAreaCode.Text)
            .lLocalTel = CLng(txtLocalTel.Text)
        End With

        If m_sFileName = "" Then
            ' Prompt user to create file if necessary
            MsgBox "You will be prompted to create a new file", ➡
            , MSGTITLE
            mnuSaveAs_Click
        End If

        ' Update pointer links depending on operation
        If m_nOperation = opAPPEND Then UpdateAppend
        If m_nOperation = opINSERT Then UpdateInsert
        ' Modify other record fields
        Put #m_nFileNum, m_nPosition, m_ThisCustomer
        ' ... and reset flag to say change has been saved
        m_bChange = False
        m_nOperation = opDONE
        ' Permit other changes
        EnableOps

        If Err.Number <> 0 Then       ' Error Handling if necessary
            MsgBox CStr(CVErr(Err.Number)) & " " & ➡
            Err.Description, , MSGTITLE
            lblMessage.Caption = "" ' Remove any message
        End If
End Sub


Private Sub cmdDelete_Click()
        ' Deletes ThisRecord which is between PreviousRecord ➡
        and NextRecord

        On Error Resume Next
        Dim PreviousRecord As Customer
        Dim NextRecord As Customer
        Dim ThisRecord As Customer

        ' Give user a chance to abort delete
        ' if any changes had occurred without saving them
        Dim sMessage As String, nResponse As Integer
```

```
' Preserve information about the record we are at
ThisRecord = m_ThisCustomer
'---> Mark record as erased
m_ThisCustomer.nRecNum = 0
Put m_nFileNum, ThisRecord.nRecNum, m_ThisCustomer

' Build new record links
If (ThisRecord.nBack > 0) And (ThisRecord.nNext > 0) Then
    ' Deleting somewhere between first record and last ➡
    record
    Get m_nFileNum, ThisRecord.nBack, PreviousRecord
    PreviousRecord.nNext = ThisRecord.nNext
    Put m_nFileNum, ThisRecord.nBack, PreviousRecord
    Get m_nFileNum, ThisRecord.nNext, NextRecord
    NextRecord.nBack = ThisRecord.nBack
    Put m_nFileNum, ThisRecord.nNext, NextRecord
    ' Now NextRecord points to PreviousRecord and vice versa
    m_nPosition = NextRecord.nRecNum ' To show user ➡
    next record
ElseIf ThisRecord.nBack = 0 And ThisRecord.nNext = 0 Then
    ' Deleting the one and only record
    ' Show user that no field exists until first one ➡
    appended
    m_ThisCustomer = NextRecord ' Clear the record ➡
    information
    cmdAppend_Click
    ' Reset the flag
    m_bChange = False
    Exit Sub
ElseIf ThisRecord.nBack = 0 Then
    ' Deleting first record
    Get m_nFileNum, ThisRecord.nNext, NextRecord
    NextRecord.nBack = 0
    Put m_nFileNum, ThisRecord.nNext, NextRecord
    m_nHead = NextRecord.nRecNum
    ' Now NextRecord is marked as first logical record
    m_nPosition = NextRecord.nRecNum ' To show user ➡
    next record
ElseIf ThisRecord.nNext = 0 Then
    ' Deleting last record
    Get m_nFileNum, ThisRecord.nBack, PreviousRecord
    PreviousRecord.nNext = 0
    Put m_nFileNum, ThisRecord.nBack, PreviousRecord
    m_nTail = PreviousRecord.nRecNum
    m_nPosition = PreviousRecord.nRecNum   ' To show ➡
    user previous record
End If

' Access and display next (or previous) record
If m_nPosition <> 0 Then
    'Read the record
    Get m_nFileNum, m_nPosition, m_ThisCustomer
    DisplayInfo
End If
```

```
            ' Flag that Delete operation occurred
            m_bDelete = True

            If Err.Number <> 0 Then      ' Error Handling if necessary
                MsgBox CStr(CVErr(Err.Number)) & " " & ➡
                Err.Description, , MSGTITLE
                lblMessage.Caption = "" ' Remove any message
            End If
    End Sub


    Private Sub cmdExit_Click()
    ' Need to warn user if last change not saved, cmdAppend ➡
    disabled and LastRecord > 1

            ' Exit the program but give user a chance to abort the exit
            ' if any changes were not saved

            Dim sMessage As String, nResponse As Integer
            ' Message of warning query
            sMessage = " Something was modified.   "
            sMessage = sMessage & "Do you still want to quit?"
            ' Display warning query if there had been a change
            If m_bChange Then
                nResponse = MsgBox(sMessage, DIALOGTYPE, MSGTITLE)
                ' ... and act depending on user response
                If nResponse = vbNo Then
                    Exit Sub ' Abort exit if user changes mind
                End If
            End If
            ' Exit if no change occurred or user ignores changes
        Close
        End
    End Sub


    Private Sub cmdInsert_Click()
        ' Inserts a new record between this record and previous one
        ' At m_nThisCustomer when Insert clicked

        On Error Resume Next
        ' Give user a chance to abort append
        ' if any changes were not saved
        Dim sMessage As String, nResponse As Integer
        ' Message of warning query
        sMessage = " Something was modified.   "
        sMessage = sMessage & "Do you still want to insert a record?"

        ' Display warning query if there had been a change
        If m_bChange Then
            nResponse = MsgBox(sMessage, DIALOGTYPE, MSGTITLE)
            ' ... and act depending on user response
            If nResponse = vbNo Then
                Exit Sub ' Abort exit if user changes mind
```

```
            Else
                ' User does not care about change
            End If
        End If

        ' Preserve information about the record we are at
        ' Current record before inserting will be next record
        m_NextRecord = m_ThisCustomer
        ' Show user blank fields
        ' User will have to use Change button to save entries
        ' New intended record is blank (except for links) until ➡
        changed by user
        ClearThisCustomer    ' Clears m_ThisCustomer
        m_nRecCount = m_nRecCount + 1 ' Increment physical record count
        m_nPosition = m_nRecCount ' Inserted record will be ➡
        physically located at end
        ' Build new record links
        m_nOperation = opINSERT      ' Flag that Insert in progress
        DisplayBlank ' To cue user to enter information

        ' Disable another modification until a record change
        ' committed by using Change button
        DisableOps
        ' Signal to cmdChange_Click that insert initiated.  ➡
        cmdChange will
        ' handle linked-list updating when committing changes to the file
        m_bChange = True

        If Err.Number <> 0 Then      ' Error Handling if necessary
            MsgBox CStr(CVErr(Err.Number)) & " " & Err.Description, ➡
            , MSGTITLE
            lblMessage.Caption = "" ' Remove any message
        End If
End Sub


Private Sub cmdNext_Click()
    ' Move to next "logical" record
    ' Give user a chance to abort the next move
    ' if any changes were not saved

    Dim sMessage As String, nResponse As Integer
    ' Message of warning query
    sMessage = " Something was modified.  "
    sMessage = sMessage & "Do you still want to go to the next ➡
    record?"
    ' Display warning query if there had been a change
    If m_bChange And Not m_bDelete Then
        nResponse = MsgBox(sMessage, DIALOGTYPE, MSGTITLE)
        ' ... and act depending on user response
        If nResponse = vbNo Then
            Exit Sub ' Abort exit if user changes mind
        End If
    End If
```

```
    ' Clear Delete flag since it has already been acknowledged
    m_bDelete = False
    ' Reset change flag since user ignored change warning
    m_bChange = False

    ' Show next record if we are not at the end
    ' Get physical position of next logical record
    Get m_nFileNum, m_nPosition, m_ThisCustomer
    If m_ThisCustomer.nNext = 0 Then
        ' We are at last logical record
        Beep     ' and inform user
    Else    ' Otherwise go ahead and move to next logical record
        m_nPosition = m_ThisCustomer.nNext
        ' Then get the next logical record ...
        Get m_nFileNum, m_nPosition, m_ThisCustomer
        ' ... and display the information
        DisplayInfo
    End If
End Sub


Private Sub Form_Load()

    Dim sFilter As String    ' For common file dialog filter
    NewQueue       ' Initialize queue
    Set m_frmCustomer = frmCustomer4
    m_nRecordLength = Len(m_ThisCustomer)

    ' Set up combo box, maybe strings have to be 8 characters long?
    cboCanoeModel.AddItem "Erie"
    cboCanoeModel.AddItem "Huron"
    cboCanoeModel.AddItem "Michigan"
    cboCanoeModel.AddItem "Ontario"
    cboCanoeModel.AddItem "Superior"

    cboCanoeModel.ListIndex = 0 ' Default Model
    mnuNew_Click     ' Set up brand-new file

    ' set up filter for save dialog
    sFilter = "Customer (*.cus)¦*.cus¦Text (*.txt)¦*.txt¦All ➡
    Files (*.*)¦*.*"
    ' Save File Dialog
    dlgFile.Filter = sFilter     ' Define File Types list
    dlgFile.DefaultExt = ".cus" ' Default file extension
    dlgFile.FilterIndex = 1 ' By default, show only files with ➡
    default extension
    dlgFile.CancelError = True ' Enable handling if user clicks ➡
    cancel in File dialog

    ' For curiosity, show record length in bytes (when stored ➡
    on disk)
    MsgBox "Record size is " & CStr(Len(m_ThisCustomer)) & " ➡
    file bytes."
```

```
        ' Set up tab index for convenience of user
        ' User can tab from one field to the next to minimize mouse use
        txtFirstName.TabIndex = 0
        txtLastName.TabIndex = 1
        cboCanoeModel.TabIndex = 2
        txtSerialNum.TabIndex = 3
        txtAreaCode.TabIndex = 4
        txtLocalTel.TabIndex = 5
        ' Disable tab action to other input controls
        ' User will have to use access key or mouse to use buttons
        cmdNext.TabStop = False
        cmdBack.TabStop = False
        cmdAppend.TabStop = False
        cmdChange.TabStop = False
        cmdInsert.TabStop = False
        cmdDelete.TabStop = False
        cmdExit.TabStop = False

        txtPosition.TabStop = False ' Use text box to show record ➡
        position
        txtPosition.Locked = True    ' ... it is read only to user

        ' Make Change to the Default button meaning that it receives
        ' the ENTER key if no other button has the focus.
        cmdChange.Default = True
        ' Make Exit the Cancel button meaning that it receives the ➡
        ESC key
        cmdExit.Cancel = True
        cmdExit.Enabled = True   ' Enable exit operation
        mnuExit.Enabled = True
        m_bChange = False ' No change detected until user does something
End Sub


Private Sub mnuExit_Click()
        cmdExit_Click
End Sub


Private Sub mnuNew_Click()
        ' Set up title, filename, and record pointers for new file
        ' Give user a chance to abort the open record
        ' if any changes were not saved

        Dim sMessage As String, nResponse As Integer

        ' User must commit any changes before operation is allowed
        If m_bChange Then
            MsgBox "Commit changes first", , MSGTITLE
            Exit Sub
        End If
        Close m_nFileNum ' Close previous file if applicable
```

```
        m_frmCustomer.Caption = "Untitled" & VERSION
        m_sFileName = ""
        m_nPosition = 0     ' Current record is first one
        m_nRecCount = 0     ' and it is the only one
        ' Initialize linked list
        m_ThisCustomer.nBack = 0 ' ... and so far the only record
        m_ThisCustomer.nNext = 0
        m_nHead = 1
        m_nTail = 1

        ' Show user that no field exists until first one appended
        m_ThisCustomer.nRecNum = 0
        cmdAppend_Click
        ' Reset the flag
        m_bChange = False
        DisableOps  ' Initially, user may only enter data and click ➡
        Change
End Sub


Private Sub mnuOpen_Click()
        ' Open a data file
        Dim nResponse As Integer     ' For cancelling operation

        On Error Resume Next
        ' User must commit any changes before operation is allowed
        If m_bChange Then
            MsgBox "Commit changes first", , MSGTITLE
            Exit Sub
        End If

        ' This is where the action starts.  Launch the File Open ➡
        dialog now!
        dlgFile.ShowOpen     ' Display the File Open dialog
        If Err.Number = cdlCancel Then   ' User clicked Cancel
            MsgBox "Operation cancelled", , MSGTITLE
            Exit Sub
        End If
        Close m_nFileNum     ' Close existing file if applicable
        m_nFileNum = FreeFile     ' Get next available file number

        ' Cue user that file opening in progress
        lblMessage.Caption = "Opening file ...."
        DoEvents
        ' Open a different file for random access
        m_sFileName = dlgFile.filename
        ' OpenFile procedure handles details to handle open file
        OpenFile 0  ' 0 indicates that Open menu used
End Sub

Private Sub mnuQueueItem_Click(Index As Integer)

        On Error Resume Next
```

```
            ' User selected item from the queue - the most recently ➥
            used files as menu items
            Dim nCount As Integer    ' Counter for detecting head and ➥
            tail records
            ' User must commit any changes before operation is allowed
            If m_bChange Then
                MsgBox "Commit changes first", , MSGTITLE
                Exit Sub
            End If
            Close m_nFileNum    ' Close existing file if applicable
            m_nFileNum = FreeFile    ' Get next available file number
            ' Cue user that file opening in progress
            lblMessage.Caption = "Opening file ...."
            DoEvents

            ' Open a different file for random access
            ' Get filename from caption of this menu control
            m_sFileName = GetFileName(Index, m_frmCustomer)
            ' OpenFile procedure handles details to handle open file
            OpenFile Index   ' Nonzero Index means Queue item
        End Sub


        Private Sub mnuSaveAs_Click()
            ' Save a new file

            On Error Resume Next
            ' User must commit any changes before operation is allowed
            If m_bChange And m_nRecCount > 1 Then
                MsgBox "Commit changes first", , MSGTITLE
                Exit Sub
            End If

            ' Save File Dialog
            dlgFile.DefaultExt = ".cus" ' Default file extension, ➥
            normally used for Save dialog
            dlgFile.FilterIndex = 1 ' Show default extension
            dlgFile.ShowSave    ' Display the File Save dialog
            m_sNewFile = dlgFile.filename

            If Err.Number = cdlCancel Then   ' User clicked Cancel
                MsgBox "Operation cancelled", , MSGTITLE
                lblMessage.Caption = ""
                Err.Number = 0   ' Clear error
            Else
                Save
                ' Add file reference to menu queue
                AddToQueue m_sNewFile, m_frmCustomer
            End If

            If (Err.Number <> 0) And (Err.Number <> cdlCancel) Then    ➥
            ' Error Handling if necessary
                MsgBox CStr(CVErr(Err.Number)) & " " & Err.Description, ➥
                , MSGTITLE
```

```
        lblMessage.Caption = "" ' Remove any message
    End If
End Sub


Private Sub txtAreaCode_KeyPress(KeyAscii As Integer)
    ' Flag that change occurred
    m_bChange = True
End Sub

Private Sub txtFirstName_KeyPress(KeyAscii As Integer)
    ' Flag that change occurred
    m_bChange = True
End Sub


Private Sub txtLastName_KeyPress(KeyAscii As Integer)
    ' Flag that change occurred
    m_bChange = True
End Sub


Private Sub txtLocalTel_KeyPress(KeyAscii As Integer)
    ' Flag that change occurred
    m_bChange = True
End Sub


Private Sub txtSerialNum_KeyPress(KeyAscii As Integer)
    ' Flag that change occurred
    m_bChange = True
End Sub
```

Example 9.24 shows the code for Module Customer4.

Example 9.24

```
Option Explicit

' This module is not quite universal.
' It assumes form contains control named mnuQueueItem.

' To implement a linked list, we need a link field
' Also include a key field, although the Serial Number
' could be used as a unique key
' The changes to this structure mean that we cannot
' use the customer record files for the previous versions

Type Customer
        nRecNum As Integer ' 2 bytes, Holds record number the record
        sFirstName As String * 15    ' 15 characters or 30 ➥
        bytes, unicode?
        sLastName As String * 15     ' 15 characters or 30 bytes
        sCanoeModel As String * 8    ' 8 characters or 16 bytes
        lSerialNum As Long   ' 4 bytes
        nAreaCode As Integer     ' 2 bytes
```

```
        lLocalTel As Long      ' 4 bytes
        nBack As Integer       ' 2 bytes, Link field that points ➥
        to previous record
        nNext As Integer       ' 2 bytes, Link field that points ➥
        to next record
End Type


' Back = 0 indicates the first record
' Next = 0 indicates the last record

' The rest of the Module code is the same as that
' shown in Example 9.10 for Version 3

' Queue for list of recently used files
' Max of length of a finite number of elements
' Add new item to head of queue and push other down
' Delete from tail of queue when adding in excess of queue ➥
length
' If accessing item (file) already in queue then place
' item at head of queue and shift others down

' Define First In First Out (FIFO) Queue

Const MAXQUEUE = 4 ' Length of 4 in this case

' Pointers for First In First Out (FIFO) Queue
Public g_nHead As Integer  ' Insertion pointer for queue
Public g_nTail As Integer ' Deletion pointer for queue


Public Sub NewQueue()
    ' Create a new empty queue
    g_nHead = 0
    g_nTail = 0
End Sub

Public Sub AddToQueue(sItem As String, frmForm As Form)
    ' Add to list of recently used files menu items
    ' Add file if it is not already on list
    ' .. and if list already full, remove least recently ➥
    used item
    ' If file already on the list, make it the most ➥
    recently used
    ' ... it is possible that open menu operation specifies ➥
    file already in list

    Dim nCount As Integer    ' Counter for loop processing
    Dim nLength As Integer   ' Length of caption string for ➥
    string mainpulation
    Dim sCaption As String   ' Temporary string for string ➥
    manipulation
    Dim bItemExists As Boolean  ' Flag to indicate if item ➥
    already exists
    Dim nLast As Integer
```

```
        Dim sFile As String
        ' First time something added to empty queue
        If g_nHead = 0 Then
            g_nHead = 1
        End If

        ' Add menu element if queue not full
        If (g_nTail < MAXQUEUE) Then
            g_nTail = g_nTail + 1
            Load frmForm.mnuQueueItem(g_nTail)
        End If

    ' Check if item already in queue
    For nCount = g_nHead To g_nTail Step 1
        ' Find file name of queue element
        sFile = GetFileName(nCount, frmForm)
        If sItem = sFile Then
            bItemExists = True
            nLast = nCount
            ' Remove added menu control if still adding to ➥
            queue
            If frmForm.mnuQueueItem(g_nTail).Caption = "-" Then
                Unload frmForm.mnuQueueItem(g_nTail)
                g_nTail = g_nTail - 1
                Exit For    ' and exit loop
            End If
        End If
    Next nCount

    ' Signal to shift down entire queue if item not in queue
    If Not bItemExists Then
        nLast = g_nTail
    End If
    ' Shift older items down
    For nCount = nLast To 2 Step -1
        ' Strip off index reference in previous caption
        sCaption = frmForm.mnuQueueItem(nCount - 1).Caption
        nLength = Len(sCaption)
        sCaption = Right(sCaption, nLength - 2)    ' Gets ➥
        filename portion
        ' Assign new captions
        frmForm.mnuQueueItem(nCount).Caption = "&" & ➥
        CStr(nCount) & sCaption
    Next nCount

    ' Then add the new item
    frmForm.mnuQueueItem(g_nHead).Caption = "&" & CStr(g_nHead) ➥
    & " " & sItem
End Sub


Sub ModifyQueue(nIndex As Integer, sItem As String, frmForm As Form)
    ' Rearrange items since one item selected from list
    Dim sCaption As String, nCount As Integer
```

```
        Dim nLength As Integer

  ' Shift older items down
      For nCount = nIndex To 2 Step -1
      ' Strip off index reference in previous caption
      sCaption = frmForm.mnuQueueItem(nCount - 1).Caption
      nLength = Len(sCaption)
      sCaption = Right(sCaption, nLength - 2)    ' Gets ➡
      filename portion
      ' Assign new captions
      frmForm.mnuQueueItem(nCount).Caption = "&" & ➡
      CStr(nCount) & sCaption
      Next nCount
  ' Then add the new item
  frmForm.mnuQueueItem(g_nHead).Caption = "&" & CStr(g_nHead) ➡
  & " " & sItem
End Sub


Function GetFileName(nIndex As Integer, frmForm As Form) As String
  ' Returns file name from caption of selected recent files ➡
  menu item
  Dim sFileName As String, nLength As Integer
  sFileName = frmForm.mnuQueueItem(nIndex).Caption
  If sFileName = "-" Then Exit Function
  nLength = Len(sFileName)
  sFileName = Right(sFileName, nLength - 3)
  GetFileName = sFileName
End Function
```

9.6   ABOUT OBJECT-ORIENTED PROGRAMMING WITH CLASS

Visual Basic is an almost completely Object-Oriented Programming (OOP) language. A good understanding of data structures will lead smoothly into OOP programming. This section will give you a brief flavor of the topic to help you decide whether to pursue it further.

An *object* is a unit that contains both data and code. In programmer parlance, it contains *data members* and *member functions*. In terms of Visual Basic, an object's data is its *properties*, and the procedures (the code) that can act upon the object are its *methods*. The actions that are recognized by the object are its *events*. We can write event procedures to respond to events, and they can use properties and methods and trigger other events.

So far we have mentioned the Control, Form, Err, and Debug objects. It is possible to create objects using the Class object. In OOP, a *class* is the formal definition of an object. The class acts as the template from which objects can be created. The class defines the properties of the object and the methods used to control the object's behavior. For example, we can have a Canoe class, and some of its properties can be Length and Model. Some methods might be Paddle and Steer, and some events could be Buy and Sell. We can create objects (instances of the class) that belong to the Canoe class. For example, Her_Canoe and His_Canoe may be instances of the Canoe class. Possibly Her_Canoe is instantiated with Her_Canoe.Length = 16 and Her_Canoe.Model = "Erie". Possibly the Paddle method (e.g., Her_Canoe.Paddle X, Y) would reposition a graphical icon.

In Visual Basic 4 and Visual Basic 5, we can add a Class Module (ClassModule object) and any Forms or Modules to a project. A module contains the property and method definitions. The Class Module only recognizes the Initialize and Terminate events. (For more information, refer to Chapter 7 of the Visual Basic Programmer's Guide. Also refer to the Help topics about the ClassModule Object and related topics. In Chapter 11 we will work more with Object-Oriented Programming.)

CLOSING REMARKS

We've come a long way since writing that first program that displays "Welcome to Cougar Canoe." Now we can create programs that present a visually useful window, respond to events, handle files, and handle data structures.

You should now be able to create useful programs, but this is only the beginning. Consider it as the groundwork for finding out how to utilize other features of Visual Basic. For example, you should be able to use additional resources for finding further information; Appendix D lists some resources to get you started. The following chapters will also give you additional tools, such as Chapter 12 on the Data control. With the Data control we can build a front end to access commercial database files. Such a system permits a user to easily set up, access, update, and report on extensive record collections. The user could query the database for a list of customers who purchased canoes in a certain geographic region during a certain period of time. It is possible to create multimedia features to show graphic animations and play audio data for the user to hear (see Chapter 10). It is also possible to create programs for the Internet that will generate a customized page for the web browser, depending on previous user actions (see Chapter 11). We will be doing some of these things in the chapters that follow. Above all, enjoy programming and have fun.

SUMMARY

A data structure is a way of organizing data. Data structures include stacks, queues, and linked lists. A stack is a list of items. Items are added at one end and removed from the same end. The last data put onto the list is the first data taken off the list. Sometimes we refer to a stack as a Last In First Out (LIFO) queue. There are two fundamental operations: push and pull. To push, add elements in sequence. To pull, remove elements in reverse order. In the modified Method of Least Squares program, we used a stack to store the graph points. To record a new point, push the point coordinates onto the stack. To remove a recorded point, pull the point coordinates off the stack.

A queue is also a list of items. The next item is added to the end, and items are removed from the beginning. They are added and removed in a first-in and first-out order. To be explicit, and to distinguish a queue from a stack, we can refer to it as a

First In First Out (*FIFO*) queue. Add elements to the end of the queue; remove elements from the end of the queue. Version 3 of the Customer Information program did not use a pure queue. Instead, it implemented a modified queue that contained the list of most recently used files as menu controls. Elements are added to the end, but they can be accessed in any order with a subsequent reordering of elements.

A linked list is a list of records where one field contains the location of the next record. Version 4 of the customer information program implemented a double-linked list. A double-linked list is a list of records in which one field contains the location of the next record. Another field contains the location of the previous record. This means that records can be added or removed to rearrange the *logical* ordering of the records. The logical ordering is specified by the values of fields containing the next and previous record locations. It is not necessary to modify the *physical* ordering of the records. Figure 9.6 illustrates a sample double-linked list that has four records whose logical order corresponds to the physical order. A linked list should use a head and a tail to identify the physical location of the logical beginning and logical end. It is crucial to distinguish between physical record position and logical record position. Figure 9.7 and the pseudocode in Example 9.12 illustrate inserting a record; Figure 9.8 and the pseudocode in Example 9.13 illustrate deleting a record; the pseudocode in Example 9.14 illustrates moving forward and backward in logical sequence; and Figure 9.9 and the pseudocode in Example 9.15 illustrate appending a record.

The following code segments illustrate features related to handling linked lists: Example 9.17, insert a record; Example 9.18, delete a record; Example 9.19, move to Next record (Move to Back Record is similar); Example 9.20, append a record; and Example 9.21, find the first logical record (find the head). Section 9.5 shows the entire code listing. Section 9.6 briefly introduces object-oriented programming in terms of class definitions and manipulation of class instances.

HANDS-ON EXERCISES

OVERVIEW

The activities will

- Enable you to utilize the stack data structure.
- Enable you to use queue structure.
- Enable you to use the linked list data structure.

To Get Started

1. Read the section Read Me Before Attempting the Hands-On Exercises if you have not already done so.

2. Run Windows.

3. Open the file CH09\EX09.TXT on your student disk and answer the questions. (The same questions are shown here so that you can still determine answers when you are not sitting in front of a computer.)

4. Run Visual Basic.

9.1 ABOUT DATA STRUCTURES

1. Describe the ways that data is inherently organized by Visual Basic.

2. Describe the difference between a data structure and the types of data organization that Visual Basic inherently supports.

   The following questions assume you have read the entire chapter or have previous knowledge of the topic.

3. Describe an application for using a stack not mentioned in the chapter. Use this application to describe a stack.

4. Describe an application for using a queue not mentioned in the chapter. Use this application to describe a queue.

5. Describe an application for using a linked list not mentioned in the chapter. Use this application to describe a linked list.

9.2 THE STACK

The Method of Least Squares Program, Version 2

To run this program, open *project* LEASTSQ1 in directory CH07. Save *file* LEASTSQ1 as **LEASTSQ2** in directory CH09. Select **Save Project As** from the File menu. Save *project* LEASTSQ1 as **LEASTSQ2** in directory CH09. Change the Name of the form to **frmLeastSquares2** and change the version part of its Caption to state **Least Square Line Fitting - Version 2**. Save the project.

   Modify the code for picGraph_MouseDown to be the same as that shown in Example 9.1. Modify the general declarations as shown in Example 9.2, and save the project. Also write the code for sub procedure Push and function Pull as listed in Example 9.2, and save the project. Modify the code for procedure cmdFitLine_Click as listed in Example 9.3, and save the project.

   Run the program. Click **Start Points**, and click in the picture box with the left mouse button to add some graph points. Click with the right mouse button, and note how the points are removed in reverse order.

   Click the **Break** button. Set a breakpoint at the beginning of picGraph_Mouse-Down, and click the **Run** button. Click with the left mouse button. Single step the procedure and monitor the value of argument Button using instant watch. Step through the procedure to note how the coordinates are pushed onto the stack. Click **Run** to continue execution. Repeat the exercise for the right mouse button. Note how the coordinates are pulled off the stack. Experiment more with the program, and then stop execution.

The Customer Information Program, Version 2

To run this program, open *project* CUSTOM1 in directory CH08. Save *file* CUSTOM1 as **CUSTOM2** in directory CH09. Select **Save Project As** from the File menu. Save *project* CUSTOM1 as **CUSTOM2** in directory CH09. Change the Name of the form to **frmCustomer2** and change the version part of its Caption to state **Version 2**. Name the module **Customer2**, and save the project.

   Refer to Table 9.1 in Section 9.2.3. Use the menu editor to add a new menu object for mnuQueueItem. Save the project. Modify the code as explained in Section 9.2.3. If you get lost, refer to the solution listed in directory CH09\SOLN. Save the project.

Run the program. Open one of the files you created earlier with Version 1. If you don't have any files, you will have to append new records and save new files. Open different files. Note how the File menu shows an upside-down stack that shows each file you open being pushed onto the stack (at the bottom of the recently used menu items). After a while, when you select the File menu, you should see something similar to Figure 9.2. Stop execution.

9.3   THE QUEUE DATA STRUCTURE

It will probably be easier to modify Version 1 than Version 2: Open *project* CUSTOM1 in directory CH08. Save *file* CUSTOM1 as **CUSTOM3** in directory CH09. Select **Save Project As** from the File menu. Save *project* CUSTOM1 as **CUSTOM3** in directory CH09. Change the Name of the form to **frmCustomer3** and change the version part of its Caption to state **Version 2**. Name the module **Customer3**, and save the project.

Refer to Table 9.1 in Section 9.2.3. Use the menu editor to add a new menu object for mnuQueueItem. Save the project. Modify the code as explained in Section 9.3.2. If you get lost, refer to the solution listed in directory CH09\SOLN. Save the project.

Run the program. Open one of the files you created earlier with Versions 1 or 2. Open different files. Note that the File menu will only show the four most recently used files in order of most recently used to least recently used. Try to select a file that is already on the list using the Open menu. Note that the menu items have reordered themselves with the selected file now on top. Select one of the menu items in the list of recently used files. The file should be opened and the selected item should be on top of the list.

If you want, set a breakpoint and single step the code for mnuOpen_Click and the procedures in the Module. After you are done, stop execution.

9.4   LINKED LISTS

6. In your own words, write pseudocode to insert, delete, and append records.

9.5   THE CUSTOMER INFORMATION PROGRAM, VERSION 4

Open *project* CUSTOM3 in directory CH09, if it isn't already open. Save *file* CUSTOM3 as **CUSTOM4** in directory CH09. Select **Save Project As** from the File menu. Save *project* CUSTOM3 as **CUSTOM4** in directory CH09. Change the Name of the form to **frmCustomer4**, and change the version part of its Caption to state **Version 4**. Name the module **Customer4**, and save the project.

Modify the code so that it is the same as that shown in the complete source code listed in Section 9.5. If you prefer, delete the existing code and start from scratch. Save the project.

Run the program. You will have to start with a new record file, because the earlier record files will not be compatible. Append several records. Insert some records. Insert some files at the beginning of the list. Save the file with a new name. Delete some records and insert more records.

Open the original record file. It should show the first logical record (even if you inserted it ahead of the first physical record). Click **Next** several times. Note that the record position will change out of sequence since the logical order differs from the physical order (assuming you inserted records earlier). Delete some records. Click through the sequence using **Next** and **Back**. Note that the deleted records no longer appear. Open the file using

Notepad. Scroll horizontally. You should see that the deleted records still exist, but as described in Section 9.4, none of the other records will contain link references to them, so the Customer program will not show these records. Stop execution.

DOCUMENTATION EXERCISE

You may have noticed the comments in the General Declarations for the Customer Information program. It is a good idea to summarize the procedures to let the programmer know what they do. Add comments to the General Declarations to accomplish this.

ADDITIONAL PROBLEM SOLVING

Create a Version 5 of the Customer Information program. It will use the space taken up by deleted records for additional records. When the Insert button is clicked, the program will search the list for records that are deleted. If any are found, it will place the new record in that position.

CHAPTER 10

Graphics, Animation, and Multimedia

This chapter introduces moving pictures and sound to programs.

We create programs for others to use, and some users may enjoy a bit of flash and spice. Sometimes pictures and sound are the only way to present information; after all, not everyone can read sheet music and imagine sounds.

After completing this chapter, you should be able to

- Explain the different file formats used for graphics.

- Create programs that display graphics using the Picture property of the Form, PictureBox, or Image control.

- Create programs that use graphical controls (Line and Shape) and methods.

- Create programs that use the Picture property and graphical controls and methods to create animation.

- Describe key properties and events for the Multimedia control.

- Create programs that can play Wave audio, MIDI audio, AVI Video, and CD Audio using the multimedia control.

- Create programs that use more than one form.

In This Chapter

Cougar Canoe wants to include a program along with product information that introduces the company. This Welcome program will show animated images related to the theme of canoeing. When the program runs, the user will hear audio information and background music. The program will also permit the user to play video tracks. In this chapter, we will develop the Welcome program, as well as show a few other programs that illustrate the use of graphics, animation, and multimedia. At the end, we will develop a general-purpose program to play standard format multimedia files that are selected by the user.

10.1   THE REASON

A typical business or engineering application is usually to-the-point functional: It will perform to the specification asked for. An inventory program to order parts for manufacturing does not need a song and dance to entertain the production supervisor; in fact, this would normally be distractive. However, people usually enjoy entertainment and appreciate art. This can be appropriate for some kinds of programs such as interactive games, complex engineering simulations, and computer-based learning (CBL) programs.

Here we will create a simple Welcome program to demonstrate how to use the media. Ultimately, Cougar Canoe wishes to produce a CD-ROM that will provide product information and education about canoeing. It also wishes to place some of the same information on the World Wide Web. These kiosk, or educational, programs typically use graphics, animation, and multimedia:

- Graphics: A pictorial representation of an image

- Animation: Graphical images in motion

- Multimedia: Video and/or audio information

Graphics, animation, and multimedia exercise the visual and oral senses. What we see could be in motion. What we hear should be informative and include variety. An educational clip could include video that shows how to use a capsized canoe; the audio tracks could include background nature sounds as well as narration. Animated text could highlight important points.

The Story Board

In Chapter 2 we discussed the importance of *designing* the program prior to coding it. Similarly, one would determine the general sequences for an animation and/or multimedia presentation. The use of story boards was pioneered when producers such as Disney created their early cartoons. Cartoonists would write short descriptions about segments of a cartoon on sheets of paper. They would paste these on a wall. Later, they would view the wall, revise the sheets, and shift them around. Subsequently, they would refine this into a set of sheets formally describing cartoon segments. From this, the cartoonists could roll up their sleeves and actually generate the cartoon frames. Note that these cartoonists had to draw 30 images per second of animation, because human perception would interpret this as continuous motion.

With this many drawings to produce, we may appreciate why it would be crucial to have a guide, the story board, for a program that includes a video or audio presentation. We won't say much about story board development here because it is a specialization. However, it is important to recognize its importance in addition to using Visual Basic resources for animation and multimedia.

10.2   The Elements

The media elements are graphis, animation, audio, and video. Let's see what we can do with a programming language, and with Visual Basic in particular, to integrate media elements. Normally, one would use an authoring program such as PowerPoint or Toolbook to combine media elements. Alternatively, we can use a Visual Basic program to utilize and coordinate the various media. This is the approach we will cover here.

Specialized binary file formats encode the media information. Many of these are industry standards. It is necessary to have some understanding of the file formats in order to incorporate them in a program. In this subsection we briefly describe the file formats; in the rest of the chapter, we look at using appropriate Visual Basic controls that display or play the various file formats. The organizational system that any file uses to organize its data is known as its *file format*. Other applications understand how to interpret the format and use it to present the media information to the viewer. You may have already heard of some of these. Common formats include bitmap and wave. File extensions identify the format. The operating system and applications usually determine the format to use by the extension. For example, bitmap files may use the .BMP extension; wave files for audio use the .WAV extension. Opening a .BMP file in Windows will automatically launch the Paint accessory to display it (assuming a typical Windows setup).

Graphics

Graphics files are stored using either bitmapped or vector formats. A form, image control, or picture box control object may use the Picture property to show graphics.

Bitmap   Bitmaps are organized as a grid of picture elements known as *pixels*, as shown in Figure 10.1. A bitmap file contains information about the coordinate positions of the pixels. Each pixel contains information that specifies its color. (We will explain more about color later.)

> *A **pixel** represents a dot in an image, and it is the smallest graphic unit of measurement on a screen. The dimension of a pixel varies with the computer system and monitor hardware being used.*

Figure 10.1
Structure of a
Bitmap Image

Image as Normally Seen

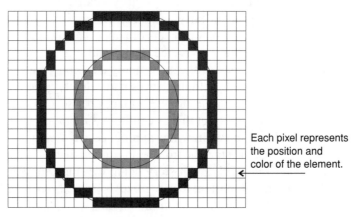

Each pixel represents
the position and
color of the element.

Image magnified as bitmap

Although more sophisticated drawing programs exist, you can use the Paint accessory that comes with Windows to edit or create bitmap image files. The normal file extension for bitmap files is .BMP. Visual Basic programs can use the form object, picture box, or image box controls to display images. Many programs recognize bitmap images. The file sizes become very large when larger images are used. Web browsers can display bitmaps that are stored in a compressed format known as .GIF. If you are using the Web as a source of images for your Visual Basic program, you will have to use another program to convert the .GIF file into .BMP format. For example, with Corel Draw, you can import a .GIF file and then export it as a .BMP file.

To See Pixels for Yourself   It is possible to edit pixels with the Paint accessory. To do so, run Paint and open any .BMP file. Select **Zoom** from the View menu. From the Zoom menu, select **Large** or **Custom**, as desired. At this point, the rectangular edges of the pixels will be visible.

Icons   An icon is a graphical representation to represent an object or concept in a Windows application. It is a specialized bitmap with a maximum size of 32×32 pixels. Icons have an .ICO filename extension. Visual Basic forms use a default icon that is placed on the upper left corner, but you can use a different icon by setting the form's Icon property to a different .ICO file.

Version 5 Graphics Formats   Visual Basic 5 supports additional graphic file formats. These are GIF and JPEG, both of which are standards for use on the World Wide Web.

Graphics Interchange Format (GIF)   CompuServe, an online service provider, created the GIF standard for online transfers of graphic information. Now it has been adopted by most online systems and is one of the standard graphic file formats, including for the World Wide Web. It is a bitmap format that uses lossy compression to minimize data transfer time over communication lines. Lossy compression loses some of the image details in the transfer.

Joint Photographic Experts Group (JPEG)   This is an international standard for image compression that offers compression with almost no losses at ratios up to 20:1. It is primarily used to compress photographic-quality (color and grayscale continuous tone) images. There is little loss of image quality.

Vectors and Metafiles

Files using a vector format describe an image by using mathematical equations to describe the lines, curves, and graphical elements (such as circles and rectangles) that make up the object. Sometimes it must also include bitmap information. Since a vector-format image uses a mathematical description, a program can more easily modify the image to resize it, change its orientation, or change its position. For Visual Basic programs, these are known as *metafiles*. The filename extension is .WMF for Windows Metafile or .EMF for Enhanced Metafile. Again, a Visual Basic program can display these images by setting the Picture property of a form, picture box, or image object (see Figure 10.2).

Visual Basic Graphic Controls and Methods

Visual Basic has several features to enhance the visual appearance of an application. It is possible to use simple schematic-like graphics without using external graphics files. We have already used some of these features in Chapters 6 and 7. (In a later section titled Graphic Methods, we will review them and introduce a few others.)

Figure 10.2
Structure of a Vector
(or Metafile) Image

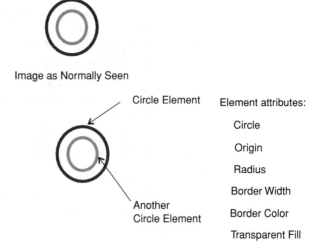

Image as Normally Seen

Circle Element

Element attributes:

Circle

Origin

Radius

Border Width

Border Color

Another
Circle Element

Transparent Fill

A vector file contains a description of the graphical elements.

Animation

Animation involves images that *appear* to change. A human can only detect differences in motion that are longer than $1/30$ of a second, so any image that changes at a rate greater than 30 times a second will appear to change continuously instead of using jerky motions. In Visual Basic, animation can be accomplished in several ways: We can show different images in a sequence or we can move images over time. We can also use the multimedia control to play video frames (AVI format).

Audio

Two file formats can be used to store audio information. We can then use a special control known as *the multimedia MCI control* to play the file. The multimedia MCI control manages the recording and playback of multimedia files on Media Control Interface (MCI) devices. For audio these are the wave (`.WAV`) and MIDI (`.MID`) file formats. Essentially, the wave format directly encodes sound information as the sound signal that would be sent to a speaker. The MIDI format describes sound in terms of commands to musical instruments. MIDI is an abbreviation for Musical Instrument Digital Interface. It is a standard for connecting electronic instruments to a computer. A MIDI sequencer executes the commands to convert them to speaker signals.

Video

The multimedia MCI control can play files stored in the animation file format (`.AVI`) that contains frames with both audio and video images. The frames are played over time. It is essentially the digital equivalent of a videotape.

10.3   GRAPHIC METHODS

In Section 6.6.4, which discussed the application to calculate the area under a curve, we used some graphics methods for a picture box control (see Figure 6.10 for an illustration). The picture box control can display a graphic from an external file, but it can also display graphic objects. Recall that a method acts on an object to modify it. The following describes the coordinate system, some properties, and some graphic methods that apply to the picture box control.

10.3.1   Using Coordinates

In order to use graphic controls and methods, it is necessary to understand the coordinate system used by Visual Basic. Normally, an object's position on a form or picture box is stated in terms of its upper left corner with respect to the upper left corner of the containing object (form or picture box). Hence the horizontal position (X-axis position) increases from left to right. However, unlike traditional graphing conventions, the vertical position (Y-axis position) increases in the downward direction starting at the top.

Various measurement units can be specified by setting the ScaleMode property of the form or picture box. The ScaleLeft and ScaleTop properties specify the left and top coordinates, respectively, and the ScaleHeight and ScaleWidth properties specify the vertical and horizontal size, respectively. Figure 10.3 illustrates a custom scale setup using the `Scale` method. It also illustrates the position and size of a circle drawn using the `Circle` method. Table 10.1 shows the possible ScaleMode settings.

The Scale Method

The Scale Method defines the coordinate system for a form, picturebox, or printer object. The syntax is

*NameOfObject.***Scale** *(fX1, fY1) - (fX2, fY2)*

The arguments are Single data types that have the following meanings.

Figure 10.3
A Coordinate System
Using a Custom Scale

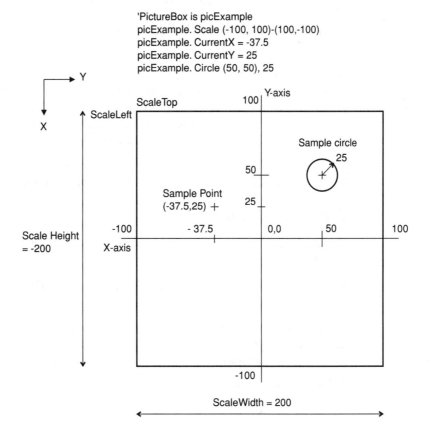

Table 10.1
ScaleMode Property Settings

Setting	Description
0	Custom coordinates
1	(Default) Twip (1,440 twips per logical inch; 567 twips per logical centimeter)
2	Point (72 points per logical inch)
3	Pixel (smallest unit of monitor or printer resolution)
4	Character (horizontal = 120 twips per unit; vertical = 240 twips per unit)
5	Inch
6	Millimeter
7	Centimeter

Top left corner:

fX1   Horizontal (X-axis) coordinate of left border
fY1   Vertical (Y-axis) coordinate of top border

Bottom right corner:

fX2   Horizontal (X-axis) coordinate of right border
fY2   Vertical (Y-axis) coordinate of bottom border

Figure 10.3 illustrates a use of this method.

CurrentX and CurrentY Properties

CurrentX and CurrentY are properties of a form, picture box, or printer object that specify position within the object. It returns or sets the horizontal (CurrentX) or vertical (CurrentY) coordinates for the next printing or drawing method. For example, consider Figure 10.3. Let's say we want to set the coordinate of the sample point. This happens to –37.5, 25 meaning –37.5 units horizontally (X-axis) and 25 units vertically (Y-axis). We could set the coordinates using the following statements:

```
picExample.CurrentX = -37.5  ' Horizontal Coordinate
picExample.CurrentY = 25  ' Vertical Coordinate
```

The Circle Method

This method draws a circle, ellipse, or arc on a form, picture box, or printer object. The syntax is

```
NameOfObject.Circle [Step] (fX, fY), fRadius, [lColor, fStart, ➡
fEnd, fAspect]
```

The keyword Step is optional. It specifies that the center (or origin) of the circle is relative to the position defined by the CurrentX and CurrentY properties of the containing object (such as a picture box). For example:

```
With picExample
    .CurrentX = -37.5
    .CurrentY = 25
```

```
     .Circle (50,50), 25  ' Draw circle at 50,50 with radius 25
     .Circle Step (50,50), 10  ' Draw circle at 12.5, 75 with ➡
     radius 10
     ' Note that 50 relative to -37.5 is 12.5 and 50 relative to ➡
     25 is 75
End With
```

The arguments are Single data types, with the exception of lColor, which is Long. Note that the ScaleMode property determines the units of measure used for coordinate or size information. These arguments have the following meanings:

- *(fX, fY)* are required values of type Single indicating the coordinates for the center point.

- *fRadius* is the radius.

- *lColor* is a Long integer value indicating the color code of the circle's outline. If omitted, the value of the ForeColor property is used. (Color is discussed in Section 10.3.2.)

The following are optional:

- *fStart* and *fEnd* specify the start and end positions of the arc in radians (not degrees). For an example, refer to Figure 10.4 and the code in Example 10.1 in the section about the Graphic Methods Sampler Program.

- *fAspect* is the *aspect ratio* of the circle/ellipse. This is the ratio of the vertical dimension with respect to the horizontal dimension. The default value is 1.0, meaning that the curve is a perfect circle. An aspect ratio greater than 1 shows an elliptical curve that stretches vertically (see Figure 10.4). An aspect ratio between 0 and 1 shows an elliptical curve that stretches horizontally.

The Cls Method

The Cls method clears graphics and text generated at runtime from a form or picture box. For example, the following statement would remove all graphical objects from the picture box (picExample) shown in Figure 10.4. Only the shape object (the rounded square) would remain.

```
picExample.Cls
```

The Line Method

The Line method draws lines or rectangles on a form, picture box, or printer object. Section 7.4 also introduced the Line method. The syntax is

*NameOfObject.***Line** [**Step**] *(fX1,fX2)* - [**Step**] *(fX2, fY2)*, [*lColor*], [***BF***]

The keyword Step is optional. It specifies that the line endpoint is relative to the position defined by the CurrentX and CurrentY properties of the containing object (such as a picture box).

- *(fX1, fY1)* are optional values of type Single indicating the coordinates for the starting point of the line. If omitted, the line begins at the position specified by the CurrentX and CurrentY property settings.

- *(fX2, fY2)* are required values indicating the coordinates for the end point of the line.

- *lColor* is a Long integer value indicating the color code of the line. If omitted, the value of the ForeColor property will be used.

- *B* is an optional argument. It causes a box to be drawn using the coordinates to specify opposite corners of the box.

- *F* is an optional argument. It specifies that the box is filled with the same color used to draw the box. You cannot use F without B. If B is used without F, the box will be filled with the current FillColor and FillStyle. The default value for Fill-Style is transparent.

For example, the following statement will draw a line from point 0,0 to -20,-30:

```
picExample.Line (0, 0)-(-20, -30)
```

The Move Method

The `Move` method changes the location of a control object or form object. The upper left corner of the object is used to specify its position. The syntax is

*NameOfObject.***Move** *fLeft, fTop, [fWidth, fHeight]*

- *fLeft* is a required value of type Single that indicates the new horizontal co-ordinate (X-axis) for the left edge of the object being moved.

- *fTop* is an optional value of type Single that indicates the new vertical coordi-nate (Y-axis) for the top edge of the object being moved.

- *fWidth* is an optional value that indicates the new width of the object.

- *fHeight* is an optional value that indicates the new height of the object.

For example, if we wanted to move a Shape object named `shpBox` to position 40.5,17.3, we could use the following statement:

```
ShpBox.Move 40.5, 17.3
```

The PSet Method

The `PSet` method sets a point to a specified color in addition to defining its position in a containing object. Section 7.4 also introduced the `PSet` method. The syntax is

*NameOfObject.***PSet** **[Step]** *(fX, fY), [lcolor]*

The keyword `Step` is optional. It specifies that the line endpoint is relative to the po-sition defined by the CurrentX and CurrentY properties of the containing object (such as a picture box).

- *(fX, fY)* are required values of type Single indicating the coordinates for the point being set.

- *lColor* is a Long integer value indicating the color code of the point. If omitted, the value of the ForeColor property will be used.

You can use the `RGB` function or `QBColor` function to specify the color. (Section 10.3.2 includes more information about color.)

Line and Shape Controls

Section 7.8 used the line control to draw a representation of an electronic circuit (see Fig-ures 7.7 and 7.8). With the shape control, it is possible to draw polygons such as rectangles, squares, ovals, circles, rounded rectangles, and rounded squares. By setting appropriate properties, we can define other aspects of their appearance such as size, position, color, and border style. We will be using the shape control in parts of this chapter.

10.3.2   Color Your World

In nature, objects absorb certain wavelengths, and the color we see is the combination of wavelengths reflected by the object. The primary colors are yellow, red, and blue, and all of the colors we see are the result of combinations of these primary colors. Computer monitors work with a different set of primary colors: red, green, and blue. Instead of absorbing colors with the result being those that are reflected, the monitor combines primary colors to create any possible color. For example, combining red and blue will create purple.

Visual Basic can use a 16-color system or 24-bit (2^{24} = 16,777,216 colors) system. A Long integer specifies the color. Three of the 8-bit fields (bytes) specify the relative intensity of the red, green, and blue components to make up the color. This is known as the *RGB format*. An RGB color value specifies the relative intensity of red, green, and blue to cause a specific color to be displayed. The RGB information is encoded as follows:

Byte 3	Byte 2	Byte 1	Byte 0
Not used for color	Blue code from 0 to255	Green code from 0 to 255	Red code from 0 to 255

When setting color properties in the design mode, we normally pick the color from a color palette. Visual Basic will set this selection to the appropriate color code. Let's say we selected a deep orange color for the BackColor property of a form. We may find that the Property window shows a BackColor property setting of

`&H000080FF&`

This is a hexadecimal number. The leading &H and trailing & mean that the number is shown using the hexadecimal code. This is a numbering system based on powers of 16, instead of the decimal system based on powers of 10. With the hexadecimal code, A represents decimal 10, B decimal 11, C 12, D 13, E 14, and F 15. It turns out that technical computer people will find hexadecimal to be a convenient shorthand for binary numbers, but don't worry, it is not necessary to understand hexadecimal in order to specify colors. It is useful to be aware of it when we see it being used as a color property, as the value of some constants, and for a few other things.

Every two digits of a hexadecimal number directly corresponds to 8 bits (a byte), so we can directly identify the RGB color components when the BackColor property is `&H000080FF&`. Starting from the right side, the Red component is hexadecimal FF, the Green component is 80 and the Blue component is 00.[1] In decimal format this translates to

Red = 255 (15×16 +15), Green = 128 (8×16 + 0), Blue = 0

---

[1] *The RGB format in hexadecimal reads Red Green Blue from right to left. This is because the Intel 80x86 and Pentium-type microprocessors use higher addresses for higher-order bytes when using multiple bytes to represent a number. This results in an appearance of reading the hexadecimal numbers from right to left.*

The RGB Function

An alternate way to make the background a deep orange would be to use the RGB function, as follows:

```
BackColor = RGB(255, 128, 0)
```

When calling the function, we can use arguments with decimal values to set the value of the red, green, and blue components. The RGB function returns the color code as a Long value. The color component arguments must be integers between 0 and 255, or any valid 8-bit number. To see for yourself, start a new project and type in the following code:

```
Private Sub Form_Click()
    BackColor = RGB(255, 128, 0)
    MsgBox CStr(Hex(BackColor))
End Sub
```

After you click on the form, it will turn deep orange and the message box will display the number 80FF. As you may guess, the Hex function converts the decimal value to hexadecimal. If hex-to-decimal conversion is something you enjoy, you could also use the following to set the color to deep orange.

```
BackColor = 33023        ' 128 * 256 + 255 = 33023
```

It works, but it is not obvious that red is full intensity (255), green is half intensity (128), and blue is absent (zero). For more information on the RGB function, refer to Visual Basic Help.

The QBColor Function

The QBColor function also returns the RGB color code corresponding to a color number. However, it uses only one integer argument (in the range of 0 to 15) and can only return codes for 16 colors, as shown in Table 10.2.

For example, to set the form background to green, you would use this statement:

```
BackColor = QBColor(2)
```

QB refers to the Quick Basic language used with earlier DOS computers. The QBColor function is useful when you need to work with only a limited set of colors.

Table 10.2
Color Codes Set Using the QBColor Function

Argument	Color	Argument	Color
0	Black	8	Gray
1	Blue	9	Light Blue
2	Green	10	Light Green
3	Cyan	11	Light Cyan
4	Red	12	Light Red
5	Magenta	13	Light Magenta
6	Yellow	14	Light Yellow
7	White	15	Bright White

Exercise

Use a graphical method to draw a yellow line diagonally from the upper left corner of a picture box to the lower right corner when the user clicks on a button.

Solution

```
Private Sub cmdLine_Click()
    With picExample
        picExample.Line (0, 0)-(.ScaleWidth, .ScaleHeight), ➥
        QBColor(6)
    End With
End Sub
```

10.3.3   The Graphic Methods Sampler Program

This program will illustrate the methods we have just described. Figure 10.4 illustrates the program during execution, and Example 10.1 shows the code. The name of the picture box is `picExample,` and the name of the shape object is `shpTarget`. Its Shape property is set to 5 to make it a rounded square.

Example 10.1

```
' Demonstration of Graphics Methods for picture box Control
Option Explicit
```

Figure 10.4
Graphic Methods Sampler Program

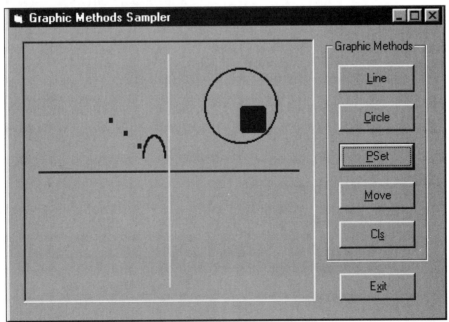

User clicked:
        Move twice
        Line once
        Circle once
        PSet three times

```
Private Sub cmdCircle_Click()
    ' Draw complete circle at position 30,30 with radius 5
    picExample.Circle (50, 50), 25
    ' Draw elliptical circle segment with center at
    ' -10, 10 with radius 15, color black, from
    ' 0 to 180 degrees with aspect ratio of 2
    picExample.Circle (-10, 10), 15, , 0, 3.14159, 2
    ' Comment out previous and remove comment from following
    ' picExample.Circle (-10, 10), 15, , 0, 3.14159, 0.5

End Sub

Private Sub cmdCls_Click()
    ' Clear objects that were drawn using Methods, Shape object ➡
    remains
    picExample.Cls
End Sub

Private Sub cmdExit_Click()
    End
End Sub

Private Sub cmdLine_Click()
    ' Draw vertical yellow line through center
    picExample.Line (-90, 0)-(90, 0), RGB(128, 0, 128)
    ' Draw horizontal purple line through center
    picExample.Line (0, 90)-(0, -90), RGB(255, 255, 0)
    ' Note that .CurrentX/Y properties now "approximately" 0, -90
    Debug.Print CStr(picExample.CurrentX), " ", ➡
    CStr(picExample.CurrentY)
End Sub

Private Sub cmdMove_Click()
    ' Move target shape diagonally.  If another method used ➡
    prior to using Move,
    ' the movement will be relative to updated CurrentX/Y properties
    ' If target moves outside picture box, next move will bring ➡
    it back in
    Static bMoveLeft As Boolean ' Flag to indicate direction

    With picExample
        If shpTarget.Left > .ScaleWidth + .ScaleLeft Or ➡
        shpTarget.Top > .ScaleTop Then
            bMoveLeft = True    ' Target crossed right or top border
        ElseIf shpTarget.Left < .ScaleLeft Or shpTarget.Top < ➡
        .ScaleHeight + .ScaleTop Then
            bMoveLeft = False   ' Shape crossed left or bottom border
        End If

        If bMoveLeft Then    ' Move diagonally in left downward ➡
        direction
            shpTarget.Move picExample.CurrentX - 20, ➡
            picExample.CurrentY - 20
            picExample.CurrentX = shpTarget.Left - ➡
            shpTarget.Width / 2
```

```
                            picExample.CurrentY = shpTarget.Top - ➡
                            shpTarget.Height / 2
                    Else      ' Move diagonally in right upward direction
                            shpTarget.Move picExample.CurrentX + 20, ➡
                            picExample.CurrentY + 20
                            picExample.CurrentX = shpTarget.Left + ➡
                            shpTarget.Width / 2
                            picExample.CurrentY = shpTarget.Top + ➡
                            shpTarget.Height / 2
                    End If
            End With
    End Sub


    Private Sub cmdPSet_Click()
        ' Draw point that is relative 10 left and 10 up from ➡
        CurrentX,Y
        picExample.DrawWidth = 4     ' Make dots more prominent
        picExample.PSet Step(-10, 10), RGB(128, 0, 0)
        picExample.DrawWidth = 2     ' Restore draw width
    End Sub

    Private Sub Form_Load()
        ' Use Scale Method to set up coordinate system that is
        ' -100 to 100 left to right and
        ' 100 to -100 top to bottom.
        ' Scale method arguments are (left, top)-(right, bottom)
        picExample.Scale (-100, 100)-(100, -100)
        picExample.CurrentX = 0
        picExample.CurrentY = 0
    End Sub
```

10.3.4   The Welcome Program, Version 1

Cougar Canoe is prototyping a program that promotes the company. In Version 1 of
this program, we use graphics to provide an informal introductory screen, as shown in
Figure 10.5. Eventually, we will further enhance the program to use animation and
multimedia, as well as to provide more content to describe the company. For now, all
that the user sees is what is shown on the form. (Since the drawings in this book are
black and white, you will have to actually run the program to see it in color. To do so
now, open project CH10\SOLN\COUGAR1 using Visual Basic.)

Behind the Scenes

Let's look at the visual layout used by the programmer. We obtain the canoe picture by
setting the Picture property of the form to refer to the extended Windows metafile of a
canoe (Canoe1.emf). An icon file (Sun.Ico) is used to set the Icon property of the
form. The label (lblMarquee) is a green color and is transparent so that only the text
(Caption property) is seen. Later we will make the label scroll horizontally, and thus it
will become a *marquee* (scrolling text). Note that the ForeColor and other color-related
properties are set using a sequence of digits and letters enclosed by ampersands (&). This
is the special code that defines the color in RGB format. Normally the programmer

Figure 10.5
The Welcome Program, Version 1*

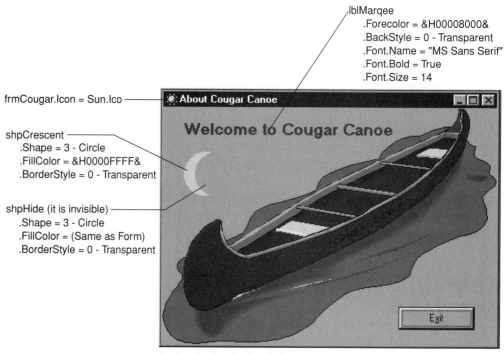

lblMarqee
.Forecolor = &H00008000&
.BackStyle = 0 - Transparent
.Font.Name = "MS Sans Serif"
.Font.Bold = True
.Font.Size = 14

frmCougar.Icon = Sun.Ico

shpCrescent
.Shape = 3 - Circle
.FillColor = &H0000FFFF&
.BorderStyle = 0 - Transparent

shpHide (it is invisible)
.Shape = 3 - Circle
.FillColor = (Same as Form)
.BorderStyle = 0 - Transparent

frmCougar.Picture = canoe1.emf

*Clipart courtesy of Corel Corporation. For viewing only. Not to be saved or copied.

would visually select a color from a palette when selecting the appropriate item in the Properties window. Visual Basic would then use this selection to set the appropriate color code (see Section 10.3.2).

Note

Icon files that are included with Visual Basic can be found in subdirectories of the Visual Basic ICONS subdirectory. For example, Sun.Ico is in Visual Basic subdirectory ICONS\ELEMENTS.

We have set the Font properties of the label to something other than the default settings. Actually, the Font property refers to a font object. The font object properties are font names, such as Times Roman, Arial, and so on. Other properties define the font size and whether it is boldface, italic, or in another style. For example the label uses MS Sans Serif, so control object lblMarquee has set its Font property to refer to the font object, the name property of which is set to MS Sans Serif (lblMarquee.Font.Name).

Two circular shapes create the crescent. One circle partially hides the other so that the user sees a crescent. The Visual Basic shape object is used to create both circles. Setting the Shape property to 3 defines the shape to be a circle. As with typical controls, the Top, Left and Height, Width properties define the position and size, respectively. The FillColor property of shpCrescent is the color code for Yellow. The FillColor of shpHide is set to whatever the BackColor property of the form is set. With the Border-Style property also set to 0, the shape is invisible. As you can see in Example 10.2, this program does not use a lot of code.

Example 10.2

```
' Graphical Welcome Program
' It demonstrates simple graphics
' using a metafile for the form
' frmCougar.Picture = (metafile)
' in this case, CANOE1.EMF
' Also uses Shape controls and sets some
' properties to enhance the Label control
Option Explicit

Private Sub cmdExit_Click()
    End
End Sub

Private Sub Form_Load()
    ' This circle partially hides another
    ' to create a crescent effect
    ' Hide circle by setting its color to
    ' be the same color as the form
    shpHide.FillColor = frmCougar.BackColor
End Sub
```

10.4 ANIMATION

10.4.1 The Butterfly Program

We can generate animation directly by moving a graphical control or an image. The Visual Basic development package contains sample programs that illustrate features of the language. One of these is known as *the first application*, and it turns out that it illustrates simple animation. We will show a variation of this program. Figure 10.6 shows two screen shots in succession. When the program runs, a butterfly appears to fly leftward and upward across the form. This repeats continuously, and when the butterfly moves off the right side it reappears on the left side.

Figure 10.6
The Butterfly Program – Simple Animation

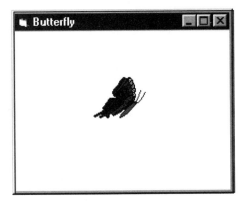

Display image with open wings:
User sees a butterfly in flight.

Display image with closed wings
further along the flight path

Figure 10.7 shows the program in design mode. The program uses three image controls, and this is the control that is normally used to display a graphic image. The image control uses fewer system resources than a picture box control, but there are fewer properties, events, and methods, so you can't do as much with it as with the picture box control. The advantage is that there will be less flicker because less work is required behind the scenes when Visual Basic does all the bit crunching that we programmers don't need to understand. Two image controls, `imgOpenWings` and `imgCloseWings`, have their Visible property set to `False`, so they are not visible when the program executes. During execution, the Timer event procedure uses the `Move` method to change the position of imgMain, so it appears to move continuously. The opening and closing of the wings is achieved by setting the Picture property of `imgMain` to that of `imgOpenWings` and `imgCloseWings` alternately. The sole purpose for using `imgOpenWings` and `imgCloseWings` is to provide a source of images to `imgMain`. Example 10.3 shows the code to accomplish this.

Example 10.3

```
' First Graphics Application
' This is a variation of the sample included in
' the VB directory samples\firstapp
' User launches program and sees a butterfly
' flying diagonally from left to right continuously
' on the form.
' This variation does not use a command button to exit
' and instead relies on the Form_Unload procedure
' to handle unloading the form.  Also it starts with the
' Window state at Normal instead of Maximized
' Some naming conventions also differ from the original

' Division by zero error occurs if user minimizes form
' Ironically solution to problem-solving exercise to force
```

Figure 10.7
The Butterfly Program in Design Mode

imgOpenWings
.Picture = Bfly1.Bmp
.Visible = False

imgCloseWings
.Picture = Bfly2.Bmp
.Visible = False

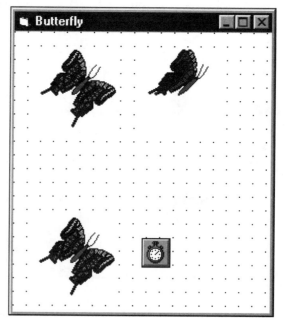

imgMain
.Picture = Bfly1.Bmp
.Visible = True

tmrTimer
.Interval = 200

```
' butterfly to stay within the form also eliminates the error

Option Explicit


Private Sub Form_Unload(Cancel As Integer)
    ' User clicks close button
    Unload frmButterfly
End Sub

Private Sub tmrTimer_Timer()
    Static bPickBmp As Boolean
    'Main.Move Main.Left + 20, Main.Top - 5
    ' The original used the previous line and suggested the
    ' following line as a variation
    imgMain.Move (imgMain.Left + 20) Mod ScaleWidth, _
    (imgMain.Top - 5 + ScaleHeight) Mod ScaleHeight
    ' The effect is to cause the butterfly to fly across the ➡
    form again
    ' after it has gone off the form.  In the original, the ➡
    butterfly
    ' flew off the form and stayed off
    If bPickBmp Then
        mgMain.Picture = imgOpenWings.Picture  ' Displays the ➡
        open butterfly picture
    Else
        imgMain.Picture = imgCloseWings.Picture ' Displays the ➡
        closed butterfly picture
    End If
    bPickBmp = Not bPickBmp      ' Toggle the value to choose ➡
    open or close

End Sub
```

In the Hands-On Exercises later in this chapter, you can modify the program so that the butterfly turns around and flies back when it reaches an edge of the form. Let's look at the highlights of this program.

1. Event procedure Form_Unload executes when the user clicks on the Close button in the upper right corner. The Unload statement causes the computer to remove the specified object from memory. In this case, we are removing the form itself (Name property of frmButterfly).

2. Event procedure tmrTimer_Timer executes every 200 milliseconds because its Interval property is set to 200. The flag variable bPickBmp is used to toggle the Picture property of imgMain between one for open wings and one for closed wings. The procedure uses the Move method to change the location of the image leftward and upward relative to its previous position (as set by its Left and Top properties). Recall that the Mod operator divides the first argument by the second and returns the remainder. When the image is within the boundaries of the form, the ScaleWidth setting is larger than that of imgMain.Left + 20. Hence the remainder is the setting of imgMain.Left + 20 and the image will move to that point. When the image passes the right boundary, the setting of ScaleWidth is smaller, so the Mod operation will return a remainder so that Left property will be assigned a smaller number. This will cause the program to

place the image close to the left border to repeat the process. The process is similar for the vertical direction. The user is free to resize the form except to minimize it. (In the Hands-On Exercises we will solve the minimization problem.)

You can try different settings for the Interval property if you wish. Since the rate is less than $1/30$ of a second, you will see discrete motions instead of continuous motion. If you attempt to use an Interval setting of 33, you may observe flicker, because Visual Basic cannot repaint the form fast enough.

10.4.2   The Alarm Clock Program, Version 2

Section 7.2 introduced an Alarm Clock program, which we will now enhance with some simple animation, including a moving pendulum. Later in this chapter we will add audio to use as an alarm sound. Figure 10.8 shows the program in action, as well as some of the code highlights. When the program runs, the pendulum will appear to swing left and right every second. In the Form_Load procedure we set up the scale of the picture box. In the timer event procedure, the Cls method clears out any graphics that were painted previously. Then it paints a new pendulum by drawing a circle and line using the Circle and Line methods, respectively. A half second later, the procedure executes again, except that the pendulum is drawn on the opposite side. Figure 10.8 shows the code for drawing the pendulum for the right swing. We will explain the method arguments and geometry that is required.

Figure 10.8
Alarm Clock Program
With Pendulum

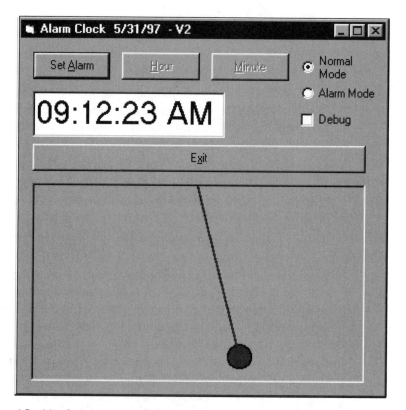

picPendulum.Scale (-100, 0)-(100, 110)
Const ANGLE = 3.141593 * 15 / 180 ' 15 degrees in radians

The code here is the same as that for Version 1 (see Section 7.2) except for the parts to handle the pendulum animation. The form is resized to accommodate the additional picture box. The Interval property of the timer control is changed to 500 to show a left and right swing for each second. Other code to handle the display update is modified to account for the fact that the Timer event now occurs twice per second, as shown in Example 10.4.

Example 10.4

```
' Alarm Clock Program, Version 2
' See Section 7.2.5 for additional code
' Opening comments and general declarations same as Version 1
' Version 2 includes pendulum motion
' to move pendulum left <— —> right

' Constant for pendulum graphics
Const ANGLE = 3.141593 * 15 / 180  ' 15 degrees in radians


' See Version 1 for following procedures
'   Sub CheckAlarm()
'   Private Sub cmdExit_Click()
'   Private Sub cmdHour_Click()
'   Private Sub cmdMinute_Click()
'   Private Sub cmdSetAlarm_Click()


'   Private Sub Form_Load()

    ' Set up initial conditions for Alarm Clock program

    Dim sToday As String     ' Used for displaying date in Title Bar
    tmrTime_Timer    ' Display initial time

    ' Set up Caption to display date
    ' (There is no mechanism -in this program -to roll over
    ' the date if the program runs from one day to the next)
    sToday = Date
    frmAlarmClock2.Caption = "Alarm Clock  " & sToday & "  - V2"

    m_dtAlarmSetting = "07:00:00 AM"  ' Set up default alarm ➥
    setting

    ' Set up initial settings for alarm mode control
    cmdSetAlarm.Caption = "Release &Alarm"  ' Need to be in on state
    cmdSetAlarm_Click   ' ... since this call will put it in ➥
    off state

    ' Additions for Pendulum, set scale, and create vertical ➥
    pendulum
    picPendulum.Scale (-100, 0)-(100, 110)
    ' Initial circle of pendulum
    picPendulum.Circle (0, 100), 7, 0
    ' Initial line of pendulum
    picPendulum.Line (0, 0)-(0, 100), &H8000&

End Sub
```

```
Private Sub tmrTime_Timer()

    ' Generates pendulum update every 1/2 second
    ' Generates the time display update every second
    ' (tmrTime.Interval = 500 for 500 ms)

    ' Static keyword means that this procedure will use the
    ' previous value from last call instead of re-initializing
    Static dtDebugTime As Date   ' For debugging and ➥
    development only
    ' See comments in version 1 about Debug feature

    ' Handle pendulum swing
    Static nCounter As Integer

    Select Case nCounter

    Case 0
        ' Go left
        picPendulum.Cls ' Initially clear picture
        picPendulum.Circle (-100 * Sin(ANGLE), 100 * ➥
        Cos(ANGLE)), 7, 0
        picPendulum.Line (0, 0)-(-100 * Sin(ANGLE), 100 * ➥
        Cos(ANGLE)), &H8000&
        nCounter = 1 ' Change state for pendulum
    Case 1
        ' Move Right
        picPendulum.Cls ' Initially clear picture
        picPendulum.Circle (100 * Sin(ANGLE), 100 * ➥
        Cos(ANGLE)), 7, 0
        picPendulum.Line (0, 0)-(100 * Sin(ANGLE), 100 * ➥
        Cos(ANGLE)), &H8000&

        ' Update time display only when pendulum at the right
        If chkDebug.Value = 0 Then   ' Using actual system time
            txtTime.Text = Format(Time$, "hh:mm:ss AM/PM")
        ElseIf chkDebug.Value = 1 Then   ' ... or using debug time
            dtDebugTime = dtDebugTime + "00:00:01"
            txtTime.Text = dtDebugTime
        Else     ' In theory, we should never see chkDebug with ➥
        value of 2
            MsgBox "We've got a problem"
            End
        End If

        ' If we are in alarm mode, generate alarm if
        ' the time is the same as the alarm setting
        If optAlarmMode.Value = True Then
            CheckAlarm
        ElseIf optNormalMode.Value = True Then
            ' No need to check alarm
        Else
            ' If neither is true something is seriously wrong
            MsgBox "We've got a problem here"
```

```
            End
        End If
        nCounter = 0 ' Change state for pendulum

    End Select

End Sub
```

The heart of the program to handle pendulum motion is the following segment in the Timer procedure that executes every half second.

```
' Handle pendulum swing
Static nCounter As Integer

Select Case nCounter

Case 0
    ' Go left
    picPendulum.Cls ' Initially clear picture
    picPendulum.Circle (-100 * Sin(ANGLE), 100 * Cos(ANGLE)), 7, 0
    picPendulum.Line (0, 0)-(-100 * Sin(ANGLE), 100 * ➡
    Cos(ANGLE)), &H8000&
    nCounter = 1 ' Change state for pendulum
Case 1
    ' Move Right
    picPendulum.Cls ' Initially clear picture
    picPendulum.Circle (100 * Sin(ANGLE), 100 * Cos(ANGLE)), 7, 0
    picPendulum.Line (0, 0)-(100 * Sin(ANGLE), 100 * ➡
    Cos(ANGLE)), &H8000&

    ' Update time display only when pendulum at the right
        ' See Example 10.4 for rest of code

    nCounter = 0 ' Change state for pendulum
End Select
```

Counter variable nCounter switches between 0 and 1 between each call. Note that the procedure updates the text time display only when nCounter is 1. To remove a previously drawn pendulum, the procedure uses a statement with the Cls method. Statements using the Circle method use a color argument of 0. This makes the outline black. Since the FillColor property of the picture box (picPendulum) is &H8000& and the FillStyle property is 0 (for Solid), the circle appears solid green. Statements using the Line method use a color argument of &H8000& to make the line the same green color. The origin of the line is 0,0. The circle and line endpoints are set using trigonometric formulas that keep the length of pendulum constant. (If you are interested in knowing about the formulas, refer to Figure 10.9 for an illustration of some trigonometry.)

10.4.3   The Welcome Program, Version 2

This program looks the same as that shown in Figure 10.5 for Version 1. The differences are

- The Welcome label (lblMarquee) scrolls across the screen from right to left and then repeats the scroll after it has disappeared off the form. Hence it acts like a marquee.

Figure 10.9
Determining X,Y Position
When Length Is Constant
and Angle Is Known

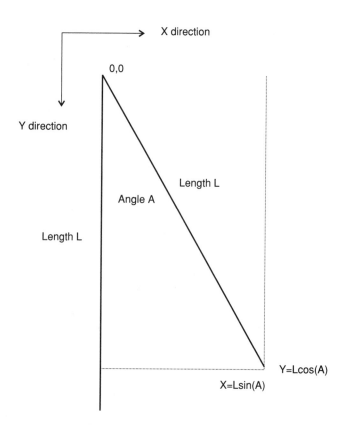

X direction

Y direction

0,0

Length L

Angle A

Length L

Y=Lcos(A)

X=Lsin(A)

- The phase of the moon changes continuously.

- The position of the Exit button remains at the same position relative to the lower right corner when the user changes the size of the form.

The animation isn't perfect, and the phase change of the moon isn't entirely realistic, but it does illustrate some animation using two shape objects. If the user makes the form much smaller, the moon animation begins to erase part of the canoe image during the lunar last quarter portion. The biggest problem is the noticeable flicker. This is because the *entire* form is redrawn every time a timer event occurs. Third-party animation controls are available to reduce the flicker problem. They may use sprites, a bitmap image in which some of the pixels are defined to be transparent in order to eliminate rectangular boundaries and permit overlapped graphics to be seen. The use of sprites eliminates the need to repaint an entire screen or window. Our animation techniques are limited to what is provided by Visual Basic without extra controls. Now let's look at how we accomplish this animation.

We add two timer controls, `tmrMarquee` and `tmrPhase`. In this case, we set `tmrMarquee.Interval` to `500` and `tmrPhase.Interval` to `1000`. Example 10.5 shows the code. Note that in both timer event procedures the moves are relative to the previous setting of the object's Left property. Also note that the Resize event occurs whenever the user modifies the size of the form. Procedure `Form_Resize` repositions the Exit button based on the new dimensions of the form.

Example 10.5

```
' Enhanced Welcome program that shows some simple animation
Option Explicit
```

```
Private Sub cmdExit_Click()
    End ' End the program
End Sub


Private Sub Form_Resize()
    ' Move the Exit button close to the bottom right when user
    ' changes the size of the form
    cmdExit.Left = frmCougar.ScaleWidth - cmdExit.Width - 10
    cmdExit.Top = frmCougar.ScaleHeight - cmdExit.Height - 10
End Sub

Private Sub tmrMarquee_Timer()
    ' Implement a simple marquee
    ' Label scrolls right to left until it is off the form
    ' Then it reappears at the right side and repeats scroll
    ' Demonstrates direct manipulation of position (Left)
    ' property instead of using the Move method
    With lblMarquee
        .Left = .Left - 60  ' Moves object left
        ' If label moved off the left side then place it on the ➡
        right
        If (.Left + .Width) <= frmCougar.ScaleLeft Then
            .Left = frmCougar.ScaleLeft + frmCougar.ScaleWidth
        End If
    End With
End Sub

Private Sub tmrPhase_Timer()
    ' Simple animation for moon phase change
    ' shpHide is same color as form background
    ' It moves across the moon (shpCrescent) to hide portions ➡
    of it
    With shpHide
        .Move .Left - 5 ' Moves object left
        ' If shpHide moves past shpCrescent then reposition it
        ' to the right of shpCrescent
        If (.Left + .Width) <= shpCrescent.Left Then
            .Move shpCrescent.Left + shpCrescent.Width
        End If
    End With
End Sub
```

In the Hands-On Exercises, you will modify the moon phase animation by using icons that are available in the Visual Basic ICONS\ELEMENTS directory.

10.5   THE MULTIMEDIA MCI CONTROL

A Visual Basic program can use the multimedia MCI control to play audio and video. The Media Control Interface (MCI) permits the computer to control audio boards, MIDI sequencers (used for electronic music), video files, audio CD players, videodisc players, and videotape recorders and players. The computer can control these devices by issuing special commands known as *MCI commands*. We can add a special control known as *the Multimedia MCI control* to send these commands. In this chapter we will play (no recording) the following:

- Audio using wave (.WAV) files

- Music audio using MIDI (.MID) files

- Video for Windows (.AVI) files

- Audio CD

For a particular MCI device to work in your system, you must have the device and appropriate driver software. Typical Windows computers already have a sound card, CD-ROM drive, and associated software drivers for the media we just listed. (If this isn't the case, you will only be able to do the Hands-On Exercises with the devices that are available in your system.)

Usually, the multimedia MCI control is not included in the Toolbox. If you are using the Professional or Enterprise edition of Visual Basic, you can add it to the Toolbox. If you are using the Standard edition, you may have to purchase a control that is equivalent. (In the Hands-On Exercises, we will show you how to add controls.) Once the multimedia MCI control is included in the Toolbox, you can place copies of this control on the form just as you would any other control. Figure 10.10 shows the control.

By default the media control buttons on the control are disabled. To enable them, we need to open an MCI device and set some properties. The heart of the multimedia control is its DeviceType property, FileName property, and Command property. The DeviceType property specifies the type of MCI device to use. The following lists some of the valid settings for the DeviceType property. Also refer to the Help topic for DeviceType Property, Multimedia MCI Control.

```
"AVIVideo"
"CDAudio"
"Sequencer"
"WaveAudio"
```

The FileName property specifies the media file to be used. We may need to set it to the name of the wave file if the DeviceType property is "WaveAudio". The Command property is used for issuing MCI commands. For example, it would be necessary to issue the MCI Open command before using a device. To make the control invisible at runtime, set the Visible property to False. Do this to create a program that plays media based on program logic instead of providing buttons for the user to play the media. We will cover some details of this control in the subsequent sections that use the control.

Figure 10.10
The Multimedia
MCI Control

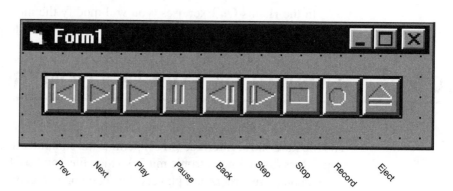

DirectX and the Future of the Media Control Interface

The Media Control Interface (MCI) provides a programming interface to control various media devices. Controls such as Visual Basic's multimedia MCI control are based on MCI. At the time of this writing, Microsoft stated they will continue to support MCI. However, they are introducing an advanced technology known as DirectX for multimedia and virtual reality applications. DirectX is still in the development stage. A component of DirectX is ActiveMovie, a new software architecture for handling audio and video. It will take advantage of advances in hardware to help programmers develop games and interactive presentations, including Internet applications. You can use an ActiveMovie control for this purpose. Internet Explorer (Microsoft's web browser), Version 3 and higher, already supports ActiveMovie. For more information about this technology, check out the website at `http://www.microsoft.com/directx/default.asp`

10.6   WAVE AUDIO

One of the ways to play audio is to use the multimedia MCI control to play a wave file. These files have a `.WAV` filename extension. Essentially a wave file is a recording of sound. The idea is similar to that of an audiocassette recording. An amplifier sends an electronic signal to a speaker, and the signal drives the speaker in and out to produce the sound waves we hear. A wave file also contains a recording, except that it is digitally encoded in binary. A sound card will convert this to an analog signal. Figure 10.11 shows a representation of the digital information, as well as the equivalent analog signal, that is eventually sent to the speaker(s).

10.6.1   The Alarm Clock Program, Version 3

This program will play the Microsoft Sound wave file when the alarm occurs. The earlier versions made beeps using the `Beep` statement. There are some changes to Version 2 in order to implement the change.

Figure 10.11
Wave File Representation
of an Analog Sound Signal

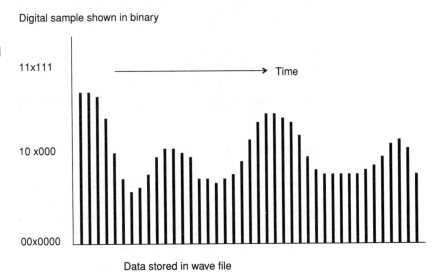

In the `Form_Load` procedure,

```
frmAlarmClock2.Caption = "Alarm Clock   " & sToday & "   - V2"
```

is changed to

```
frmAlarmClock3.Caption = "Alarm Clock   " & sToday & "   - V3"
```

Example 10.6's code has been added to the end of the procedure.

Example 10.6

```
' Addition to Version 2 of Form_Load to handle wave audio

    ' Initialization for Multimedia Control to play .WAV audio file
    mciAlarm.DeviceType = "WaveAudio"
    ' Set up to use the .WAV audio file 'the Microsoft Sound'
    ' which is included in a typical windows setup at
    ' the following path.  Modify if necessary
    mciAlarm.filename = "c:\windows\media\themic~1.wav"
    ' Note that mciAlarm.Visible = False
    ' and control moved into picture box area during design
```

In the design phase, we placed a multimedia MCI control onto the form. The position does not matter. The Name property has been set to `mciAlarm`. The DeviceType property is set to `"WaveAudio"` to tell the control that it will play wave audio. The filename property is set to `"c:\windows\media\themic~1.wav"` to specify the Microsoft Sound wave file. A typical Windows system will already contain this file. It is the same sound one hears when Windows starts up successfully. If your system has the `themic~1.wav` file (The `Microsoft Sound`) in a different directory, you will have to change the file path in the code. Example 10.7 shows the code for the revised subprocedure `CheckAlarm`.

Example 10.7

```
Sub CheckAlarm()

    ' Called by tmrTime_Timer every second if we
    ' are in the alarm mode
    ' Checks if actual hour: minute same as alarm setting
    ' Plays an audio file when alarm occurs - Version 3

    Dim bAlarm As Boolean    ' Flag to indicate alarm condition
    Dim sAlarmSetting As String ' Used for extracting hh: mm ➡
    portion of alarm setting
    Dim sTime As String ' Used for extracting hh: mm portion of ➡
    actual time

    On Error Resume Next

    ' Get time from text box which can be real or debug time
    ' Note that we only need time to nearest minute
    sAlarmSetting = Format(m_dtAlarmSetting, "hh:mm AM/PM")
    sTime = Format(txtTime.Text, "hh:mm AM/PM")
    ' Set alarm flag if actual hh:mm = setting hh:mm
    If sTime = sAlarmSetting Then bAlarm = True
```

```
        If bAlarm Then
            ' Open and play the audio .WAV file
            mciAlarm.Command = "Open"
            mciAlarm.Command = "Play"
        Else
            ' Close it so it can be played again later
            mciAlarm.Command = "Close"
        End If

        If Err.Number <> 0 Then ' Error handling if necessary
            MsgBox CStr(CVErr(Err.Number)) & " " & Err.Description, ➥
            , MSGTITLE
        End If
```

End Sub

The modification is the `If bAlarm Then ... End If` statement. When the Boolean flag bAlarm is `True` (meaning that an alarm condition occurred), some MCI commands are issued using the Command property of the multimedia MCI control. The `Open` command opens the MCI device as set by the DeviceType and filename properties. The `Play` command sends the wave file to the sound card for playing. Since the program does not use the `Prev` command to return to the beginning of the sound track, the sound is played only once. The flag bAlarm becomes false when the time advances to the next minute. This causes the program to issue the `Close` command to remove the wave file from memory. Another program can now use the wave device.

10.6.2   The Welcome Program, Version 3

Figure 10.12 shows the execution of this program. When the program first runs, it plays a welcome speech that a user can hear through the speakers. Subsequent clicking on the happy face will play the same welcome speech. You might also notice that the moon crescent and the marquee look different than that shown in Figure 10.5. This was the state of the animation at the time this screen image was captured. Three new images appear just above the center of the canoe. From left to right, these image controls are named imgWave (happy face), imgMidi (music notes), and imgAvi (water scene). Their Picture properties happen to correspond to icons that are part of the Visual Basic development system. They are in the `ICONS\MISC` subdirectory of the main Visual Basic directory. You may create more appropriate images using a graphic editor. The Picture properties are set to the following:

```
imgWave.Picture       Face03.Ico
imgMidi.Picture       Misc31.Ico
imgAvi.Picture        Misc41.Ico
```

We also added three multimedia MCI controls named mciWave, mciMidi, and mciAvi, all of which have their Visible properties set to `False`. For Version 3, the Midi and AVI controls are not functional. We will add functionality in subsequent versions of the program.

We made some additions to the Version 2 code in order to support playing the wave audio. Again, we need to set the DeviceType property to `"WaveAudio"` and the filename property to the file containing the wave information. The `Form_Load`

Figure 10.12
The Welcome Program,
Version 3

procedure also issues the MCI Open and Play commands so that the user will hear the sound when the program first runs. An event procedure for the Image control (imgWave_Click) will issue the MCI Prev command in order to *rewind* the audio and then issue the Play command. Example 10.8 shows the code.

Example 10.8

```
' Version 3 of the Welcome program builds on Version 2
' to include the playing of an audio wave message
Option Explicit


Private Sub cmdExit_Click()
    ' Version 3 includes MCI Close command
    mciWave.Command = "Close"
    End ' End the program
End Sub


Private Sub Form_Load()
    ' Initialization for Multimedia Control to play .WAV audio file
    mciWave.DeviceType = "WaveAudio"
    ' Set up to use the .WAV audio file
    ' Modify path if necessary
    mciWave.filename = "c:\introp\media\cougar1.wav"
    mciWave.Command = "Open"
    mciWave.Command = "Play"    ' Play welcome message when ➡
    program first runs
End Sub

Private Sub Form_Resize()
    ' Move the Exit button close to the bottom right when user
    ' changes the size of the form
    cmdExit.Left = frmCougar.ScaleWidth - cmdExit.Width - 10
```

```
        cmdExit.Top = frmCougar.ScaleHeight - cmdExit.Height - 10
End Sub

Private Sub Form_Unload(Cancel As Integer)
    ' Version 3 added procedure to make sure MCI devices closed
    cmdExit_Click
End Sub

Private Sub imgWave_Click()
    ' Permit user to replay the message by clicking on the image
    mciWave.Command = "Prev"    ' Rewind to beginning of audio track
    ' And play the wave welcome message
    mciWave.Command = "Play"
End Sub

Private Sub tmrMarquee_Timer()
    ' Implement a simple marquee
    ' Label scrolls right to left until it is off the form
    ' Then it reappears at the right side and repeats scroll
    ' Demonstrates direct manipulation of position (Left) property
    ' instead of using the Move method
    With lblMarquee
        .Left = .Left - 60  ' Moves object left
        ' If label moved off the left side then place it on the ➥
        right
        If (.Left + .Width) <= frmCougar.ScaleLeft Then
            .Left = frmCougar.ScaleLeft + frmCougar.ScaleWidth
        End If
    End With
End Sub

Private Sub tmrPhase_Timer()
    ' Simple animation for moon phase change
    ' shpHide is same color as form background
    ' It moves across the moon (shpCrescent) to hide portions of it
    With shpHide
        .Move .Left - 5 ' Moves object left
        ' If shpHide moves past shpCrescent, then repositions it
        ' to the right of shpCrescent
        If (.Left + .Width) <= shpCrescent.Left Then
            .Move shpCrescent.Left + shpCrescent.Width
        End If
    End With
End Sub
```

10.7   MIDI SOUND AND THE WELCOME PROGRAM, VERSION 4

About MIDI

Essentially a MIDI file stores *instructions* (or commands) for playing back various sounds. This is unlike a wave file, in which the sound signal is stored. The Musical Instrument Digital Interface (MIDI) is a digital communications language, and it is a hardware specification. The language could include actions such as playing a keyboard or varying the pitch of a musical note. The interface refers to the means of connecting musical instruments to a computer. (We won't be playing musical instruments, although feel free to do so.) MIDI data created by musicians can be stored using a special device known as a *sequencer*. They can also edit the data in the sequencer to modify the sounds. If you have a computer that includes a MIDI software driver and an appropriate sound card, you have, in effect, a MIDI sequencer device to output (play) the sounds. It is possible to use wave audio for playing music. However, MIDI files are more compact because they need not contain a description of the signal, only the instructions. This is similar to using sheet music to describe a song instead of providing a cassette recording of the song.

Using MIDI in the Welcome Program

In Version 4 of the Welcome program, we will use MIDI to play some background music. When the program first runs, it plays the MIDI sound sequence followed by the wave sound. Subsequent clicking on an image will play the associated media. In the code we will see that we must set the Notify property of mciMidi to True. This will tell Visual Basic to trigger the Done event when the next command (Play in this case) has completed. The Notify property, if True, causes the Done event to occur when the next MCI command is done. If the property is False, no Done event is generated. The procedure mciMidi_Done will issue the Play command for mciWave. When imgMidi_Click executes, it will set the Notify property of mciMidi to False. This will ensure that the Done event will not occur. Since we don't want the user to see the control, we reposition it off the form during the Form_Load procedure. There is also additional code to close the MCI devices when the user clicks Exit or the Close button on the form. Example 10.9 shows the code.

Example 10.9

```
' Version 4 of the Welcome Program builds on
' Version 3 to include playing MIDI music
' Only modifications to Version 3 are shown
Option Explicit

Private Sub cmdExit_Click()
    ' Version 3 includes MCI Close commands
    mciWave.Command = "Close"
    mciMidi.Command = "Close"
    End ' End the program
End Sub


Private Sub Form_Load()
    ' Play Midi sound followed by Wave audio as an
    ' introduction.  After that, media can be selectively
    ' replayed by clicking on associated icon

    ' Initialization for Multimedia Controls
    ' Note that .Visible  = False for mciWave and mciAvi
    ' except that mciMIDI is visible so that its Done event fires
    mciMidi.Left = ScaleLeft - 300   ' Move it off screen
```

```
                         ' so user can't see it
    mciWave.DeviceType = "WaveAudio"
    mciMidi.DeviceType = "Sequencer"
    ' Modify paths if necessary
    mciWave.filename = "c:\introp\media\cougar1.wav"
    mciMidi.filename = "c:\introp\media\cougar1.mid"
    mciWave.Command = "Open"
    mciMidi.Command = "Open"
    mciMidi.Notify = True    ' Enable Done event
    mciMidi.Command = "Play"
End Sub


Private Sub Form_Unload(Cancel As Integer)
    ' Version 3 added procedure to make sure MCI devices closed
    cmdExit_Click
End Sub

Private Sub imgMidi_Click()
    mciMidi.Command = "Next"    ' Return to beginning of track
    mciMidi.Notify = False
    mciMidi.Command = "Play"
End Sub


Private Sub mciMidi_Done(NotifyCode As Integer)
    ' Play wave message after MIDI sound played
    ' for first time in the introduction
    mciWave.Command = "Play"
End Sub
```

Note that procedure `imgMidi_Click` uses the `Next` command since the `Prev` command is not applicable. Procedures `tmrPhase_Timer`, `tmrMarquee_Timer`, `imgWave_Click`, and `Form_Resize` are identical to those in Versions 2 and 3.

10.8   AVI VIDEO AND THE WELCOME PROGRAM, VERSION 5

A conventional video is a sequence of frames containing still images that appear to move when the frames are displayed in sequence. An AVI file is also organized into frames. Typically, AVI files are created using a digital video camera. To play back the data, we can use the multimedia MCI control. To work with AVI, set the DeviceType property to `"AVIVideo"`. Then we can use AVI video in a way similar to using wave audio. In Version 5, the user clicks `imgAvi` to play the video. The multimedia control will display the video in its own window (unless we specify otherwise). The program requires additional code to initialize `mciAvi`, to close the AVI file when exiting, and to play the AVI file. Example 10.10 shows the code for portions of the program that differ from Version 4.

Example 10.10
```
' Version 5 of the Welcome Program builds on
' Version 4 to include playing AVI video
' Only modifications to Version 4 are shown

Option Explicit

Private Sub cmdExit_Click()
    ' Version 5 includes all MCI Close commands
    mciWave.Command = "Close"
    mciMidi.Command = "Close"
    mciAvi.Command = "Close"
    End ' End the program
End Sub


Private Sub Form_Load()

    ' Play Midi sound followed by Wave audio as an
    ' introduction.  After that, media can be selectively
    ' replayed by clicking on associated icon
    ' Initialization for Multimedia Controls including AVI
    ' Note that .Visible  = False for mciWave and mciAvi
    ' except that mciMIDI is visible so that its Done event fires
    mciMidi.Left = ScaleLeft - 300  ' Move it off screen
                         ' so user can't see it
    mciWave.DeviceType = "WaveAudio"
    mciMidi.DeviceType = "Sequencer"
    mciAvi.DeviceType = "AVIVideo"
    ' Modify paths if necessary.
    mciWave.filename = "c:\introp\media\cougar1.wav"
    mciMidi.filename = "c:\introp\media\cougar1.mid"
    mciAvi.filename = "c:\introp\media\cougar1.avi"
    mciWave.Command = "Open"
    mciMidi.Command = "Open"
    mciAvi.Command = "Open"
    mciMidi.Notify = True    ' Enable Done event
    mciMidi.Command = "Play"
End Sub

Private Sub imgAvi_Click()
    mciAvi.Command = "Prev"
    mciAvi.Command = "Play"
End Sub
```

10.9   THE MULTIMEDIA PLAYER, INCLUDING CD AUDIO

This is a general-purpose program that can open different media files and play them. It demonstrates more features of the multimedia MCI control, such as controlling playback by pausing or stopping. It also includes the ability to play CD audio. This program also happens to demonstrate the use of an additional form in a Visual Basic project. Figure 10.13 shows the initial user interface.

In Figure 10.13 the user has already started playing the Microsoft Sound wave file. The scroll bar shows how much of the selection has been played (approximately 15% in this case), and the caption shows which file is being played. A frame object contains the option button controls. The frame Caption indicates which media type is being used. The option button controls are being used in an unconventional sense: When selected, a file is opened, but the program resets the option button to `False` so that the user may use the same option to play a new file of the same media type. In more detail, the program works as follows:

1. If the user selects Wave Audio, MIDI Sequencer, or AVI Video, a File Open dialog box will appear that displays the corresponding file types. Figure 10.14 shows an example of the dialog when the user has selected MIDI Sequencer.

2. Once the file has been selected, the form caption indicates the filename. The appropriate multimedia MCI control buttons are enabled, and the user can click the Play button to begin playing the selection. At this point, the user may select other multimedia MCI buttons such as Pause or Stop. If the user selected CD Audio, the program shows a second Form, as shown in Figure 10.15.

The user can then play CD Audio, assuming that an audio CD has been placed in the CD-ROM drive. Interestingly enough, the user can still open and play other media types *while* the CD audio is playing. Now that we have seen how the program appears to the user, let's take a programmer's view.

10.9.1   Making Use of the Multimedia Control

The project (named PLAYMM) has two Forms:

File	Form Name
CDAUDIO.FRM	frmCDAudio
PLAYMM.FRM	frmPlayMM

Figure 10.13
The Multimedia
Player Program

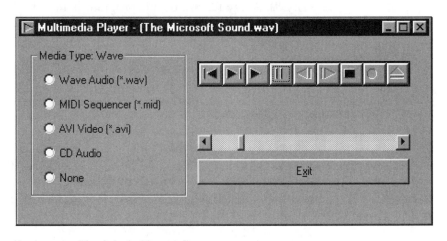

User has paused the playback of the wave file.

Figure 10.14
Open Dialog for
Media Type

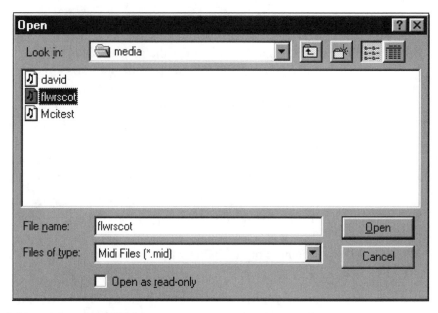

In this case, user selected MIDI Sequencer

Figure 10.15
A Separate Form for the
CD Audio Player

We must assign one of the forms to be the startup form, which is the form that Visual Basic will initially show when the program first runs. In this case, it will be frmPlayMM. A key feature of this program is that the Visible property of the multimedia controls is True. We will make use of the buttons provided by the control. Example 10.11 shows the part of the code that will perform initialization and handle user media selections.

Example 10.11

```
Option Explicit

' Multimedia Player Program
' CD still plays even when another device played
' Used separate mci and form for CD to avoid problems with
' not being able to access CD functionality once another
' multimedia device is used

Const FORMTITLE = "Multimedia Player "
```

```
Private Sub Form_Load()
    ' Initialization
    mciControl.UpdateInterval = 250 ' Status update every 250 ms
    optNone.Value = True    ' No media selected initially
    CMDialog1.FilterIndex = 1   ' Only one file type to list ➥
    once option selected
End Sub

Private Sub optWav_Click()
    ' User selects WAV audio
    fraMediaType.Caption = "Media Type: Wave"
    FileOpen    ' Automatically launch appropriate File Open Dialog
    optWav.Value = False    ' Enable user to select new file
End Sub


Private Sub optMIDI_Click()
    ' User selects MIDI
    fraMediaType.Caption = "Media Type: MIDI"
    FileOpen ' Automatically launch appropriate File Open Dialog
    optMIDI.Value = False   ' Enable user to select new file
End Sub

Private Sub optAvi_Click()
    ' User selects AVI type
    fraMediaType.Caption = "Media Type: AVI"
    FileOpen ' Automatically launch appropriate File Open Dialog
    optAvi.Value = False ' Enable user to select new file
End Sub

Private Sub optCD_Click()
    ' User selects CD Audio
    ' Launch a seperate window to handle CD Audio
    frmCDAudio.Show
    optCD.Value = False ' Be consistent with other option ➥
    button selections
                ' which may open a file
End Sub

Private Sub optNone_Click()
    ' User selects no media
    fraMediaType.Caption = "Media Type: None"
    mciControl.Command = "Close"
    mciControl.AutoEnable = True     ' Re-arm mci control for ➥
    next choice
    mciControl.Enabled = False
    optNone.Value = False   ' Be consistent with other option ➥
    button selections
                ' which may open a file
    frmPlayMM.Caption = FORMTITLE & "- (No file is loaded)"
    hsbPosition.Value = hsbPosition.Min
End Sub
```

The name of the multimedia control is `mciControl`. In the `Form_Load` procedure we set its Update property to 250. This causes the system to generate StatusUpdate events at 250 milliseconds (ms) intervals, which can be used to provide ongoing information while the media is being played. Thus, setting the Update property is like setting up a timer control where the StatusUpdate event is like the Timer event.

*The **Update** property of a multimedia MCI control specifies the number of milliseconds between successive StatusUpdate events. The **StatusUpdate** event for multimedia MCI control occurs automatically at intervals given by the UpdateInterval property.*

A frame object named `fraMediaType` is used to group the option buttons together. In general, a frame object is used to group related controls. In this case, we take advantage of its Caption property to cue the user as to what media type has been selected. Three of the option button Click event procedures call procedure `FileOpen` to open the media file. (We will look at this procedure shortly.) After the file is opened, the program sets the Value property of the chosen option button to `False`. This is certainly unconventional behavior for typical Windows programs. We made a decision to *break the rules* in this case. Setting the Value property `False` permits the user to select the same media type again.

In procedure `optCD_Click`, we use the `Show` method to reveal the form `frmCDAudio` to the user. Since this form was not the startup form, it was not initially made visible. (We will examine this form and its code shortly.)

Note

The `Show` method displays a form object.

Procedure `optNone_Click` manipulates some of the properties of the multimedia control. We have already seen how the Command property is used to send MCI commands to the multimedia device. In this case, we close the device (whichever one it happens to be). The AutoEnable property, if set to `True`, will enable buttons that are appropriate for the media type chosen and its operating mode. For example, the Eject button is not enabled for a wave device but is enabled for audio CD. If the property is set to `False`, it is up to the program code to control the multimedia buttons individually. Note that setting this property to `True` prepares the control. The buttons do not become functional until a media device is opened (in another procedure).

Note

The AutoEnable property determines if the multimedia MCI control can automatically enable or disable individual buttons in the control.

The procedure sets the Enabled property to `False` to ensure that the user cannot use the multimedia control when the None option was chosen.

Note

The Enabled property determines if the multimedia MCI control can respond to user-generated events, such as the KeyPress and mouse events.

The last statement in `optNone_Click` brings the box in the scroll bar status indicator to the left.

10.9.2   Setting Up the Media Type

Recall that three of the option button Click event procedures call `FileOpen`. This procedure handles opening the selected media file. The first thing it does is close any open devices; then it displays a dialog box that lists only the files of the selected media type. If the user cancels the Open operation, the procedure exits. Otherwise, it sets the DeviceType property of the multimedia control, depending on the choice made by the user. Then it opens the device and sets up the form caption and the status scroll bar. When the procedure ends, the program is ready to play the file. The user can now use the buttons on the multimedia control. Example 10.12 shows the code. We will look at some of the details following the listing.

Example 10.12

```
Private Sub FileOpen()
    ' Select a file (with the common dialog control)
    ' And set an error trap for Cancel, file access errors
    ' and if file is too long for scroll bar status
    On Error Resume Next

    With mciControl
        .Command = "Close"  ' Close any open devices if ➡
        applicable
        .Enabled = True ' Permit response to user
        ' Set up file open dialog for appropriate media type
        If optWav.Value = True Then
            dlgFileOpen.Filter = _
                "Wave Audio Files (*.wav)¦*.wav"
        ElseIf optMIDI.Value = True Then
            dlgFileOpen.Filter = _
                "Midi Files (*.mid)¦*.mid"
        ElseIf optAvi.Value = True Then
            dlgFileOpen.Filter = _
                "AVI Video (*.avi)¦*.avi"
        End If

    dlgFileOpen.ShowOpen   ' User sees dialog

    If Err.Number = cdlCancel Then   ' Abort if user cancels
        optNone_Click
        Exit Sub
    End If

    ' Open the selected file
        If optWav.Value = True Then
            .DeviceType = "WaveAudio"
            ' In the case for wave audio, we will use
            ' separate button enables in order to disable the ➡
            Record button
            ' This also demonstrates direct setting of ➡
            multimedia control buttons
            .AutoEnable = False
            .PrevEnabled = True
```

```
                    .NextEnabled = True
                    .PlayEnabled = True
                    .PauseEnabled = True
                    .BackEnabled = False
                    .StepEnabled = False
                    .StopEnabled = True
                    .RecordEnabled = False
                    .EjectEnabled = False
                ' Otherwise use automatic setup for other media types
                ElseIf optMIDI.Value = True Then
                    .DeviceType = "Sequencer"
                    .AutoEnable = True
                Else
                    .DeviceType = "AVIVideo"
                    .AutoEnable = True
                End If


                ' Open the media file
                .filename = dlgFileOpen.filename
                .Command = "Open"
                If .Error > 0 Then
                    frmPlayMM.Caption = _
                        FORMTITLE & "- (No file is loaded)"
                    MsgBox _
                        "Can't open " & dlgFileOpen.filename, _
                        vbCritical, "Error"
                Else
                    frmPlayMM.Caption = _
                        FORMTITLE & "- (" & dlgFileOpen.FileTitle & ")"
                    ' Set up time position information
                    hsbPosition.Min = 0
                    hsbPosition.Max = .Length
                    ' In case media is too long, do not use the scroll bar
                    If Err.Number = 0 Then
                        hsbPosition.Visible = True
                    Else
                        hsbPosition.Visible = False
                    End If
                    hsbPosition.Enabled = False ' Scroll bar as read only
                End If

        End With

End Sub
```

The playback of the MIDI Sequencer and AVI Video is simply a matter of setting the DeviceType and AutoEnable properties, as shown in the following code segment:

```
ElseIf optMIDI.Value = True Then
    .DeviceType = "Sequencer"
    .AutoEnable = True
Else
    .DeviceType = "AVIVideo"
    .AutoEnable = True
End If
```

Partially for demonstration purposes, we handle the wave media differently. If we set AutoEnable to `True` for this device, the Record button might also be enabled. We want to ensure that it is disabled, so we set the AutoEnable property to `False` and individually enable or disable the buttons, as shown in the following code segment:

```
If optWav.Value = True Then
    .DeviceType = "WaveAudio"
    ' In the case for wave audio, we will use
    ' separate button enables in order to disable the Record button
    ' This also demonstrates direct setting of multimedia ➡
    control buttons
    .AutoEnable = False
    .PrevEnabled = True
    .NextEnabled = True
    .PlayEnabled = True
    .PauseEnabled = True
    .BackEnabled = False
    .StepEnabled = False
    .StopEnabled = True
    .RecordEnabled = False
    .EjectEnabled = False
```

Note the following code segment to set up the scroll bar for status information:

```
' Set up time position information
hsbPosition.Min = 0
hsbPosition.Max = .Length
' In case media is too long, do not use the scroll bar
If Err.Number = 0 Then
    hsbPosition.Visible = True
Else
    hsbPosition.Visible = False
End If
hsbPosition.Enabled = False ' Scroll bar as read only
```

The Value, Min, and Max properties of a scroll bar are limited to the range of the Integer data type. An attempt to assign the Max property to the length of the media could result in an overflow error if the media length is beyond the range of the Integer data type. In fact, the data type of the Length property is of type Long, so the possibility for overflow exists.

Note

The Length property of the multimedia control specifies, in the current time format, the length of the media in an open MCI device.

10.9.3   Handling Media Playback

We make use of two events of the multimedia control, as shown in the code of Example 10.13. A Done event occurs when the control has finished playing the selection. In this case, the procedure issues commands that set up the media for subsequent replays.

Note

The Done event occurs when an MCI command for which the Notify property is True finishes.

Our code does not explicitly set up the Notify property. The Play command uses a default Notify setting of True. When the Play command completes (the selection has been played), the Done event fires.

Note

The Notify property determines if the next MCI command will generate a Done event, which occurs when the next MCI command is complete.

We also use the StatusUpdate event. This event occurs periodically at regular intervals, as mentioned in the previous section. In this case, we use it to set the position of the scroll bar based on the time duration position of the media.

Note

The Position property of the multimedia control specifies, in a time format, the current position of an open MCI device.

Example 10.13

```
Private Sub mciControl_Done(NotifyCode As Integer)
    ' When selection is played, return to its beginning
    If mciControl.Position = mciControl.Length Then
        mciControl.Notify = False    ' Prevent retriggering of event
        If mciControl.DeviceType = "Sequencer" Then
            mciControl.Command = "Next" '
        Else
            mciControl.Command = "Prev"
        End If
    End If
End Sub


Private Sub mciControl_StatusUpdate()
    ' Only use Position indicator if size of media within
    ' integer range - unless scaling used to increase range
    If hsbPosition.Visible = True Then
        hsbPosition.Value = mciControl.Position
    End If
    ' Note that Position is of type Long, and Value of type Integer
End Sub
```

10.9.4   Handling CD Audio

Recall that when the user selects CD Audio, procedure optCD_Click executes the statement

```
frmCDAudio.Show
```

This shows the form to the user. The form uses its own multimedia MCI control named mciCDAudio. As we can see in Example 10.14, the code is reasonably short.

Example 10.14

```
Option Explicit

' Handles CD Audio Playing
' User can control CD audio play

Private Sub Form_Load()
    With mciCDAudio
        .Command = "Close"  ' In case it was open before
        .DeviceType = "CDAudio" ' Set up for CD Audio
        .Command = "Open"   ' Permit user access
    End With
End Sub

Private Sub cmdDone_Click()
    ' Halt CD playing if applicable and close control
    Form_Unload (0)
    Unload Me    ' And remove this form from view
End Sub

Private Sub Form_Unload(Cancel As Integer)
    mciCDAudio.Command = "Stop" ' Halt CD playing
    mciCDAudio.Command = "Close" ' And close mci control
End Sub
```

In the Form_Load procedure, it is only necessary to set the DeviceType property and issue the Open command. Media files are not applicable for audio CDs. It is only necessary that an audio CD reside in the CD-ROM drive. Procedures cmdDone_Click and Form_Unload handle stopping playback. Procedure cmdDone_Click calls Form_Unload with an argument of zero. This is the Cancel argument. The Unload event uses the Cancel argument to determine whether the process of removing the form should continue. If the argument is 0, the form is removed. Normally an Unload event procedure can set the Cancel to something other than zero to abort the unloading process, if necessary. In this case, we don't use the argument, but we have to set it to zero when calling the Unload procedure.

Note

The Unload event can be caused by the Unload statement or by the user terminating the program without choosing Exit, such as by choosing the Close command on a form's Control menu.

The Form_Unload procedure stops playing the audio CD and closes the device. Otherwise, if the user has shut down the program, the audio CD may still be playing with no means to stop it except for restarting the program. Using the Unload event ensures that all means of exiting the program will stop the audio CD.

Procedure cmdDone_Click calls Form_Unload, but by itself this will not make the form disappear. Hence it is necessary to use the statement

```
Unload Me
```

The Unload statement removes a form or control from memory and from view. Its argument must be an object. Keyword Me is a reference to the object in which the statement using the word resides. We could have also used Unload frmCDAudio, but this statement would be dependent on the form Name.

10.9.5   Ending the Program

Now we return to the startup form, frmPlayMM. The procedure cmdExit_Click calls Form_Unload and ends the program. Procedure Form_Unload closes all multimedia controls, including CD Audio if it is on, and ensures that both forms are removed (see Example 10.15).

Example 10.15

```
Private Sub cmdExit_Click()
    ' Close multimedia controls and ensure CD Audio is off
    Form_Unload (0)
    End ' Stop program
End Sub

Private Sub Form_Unload(Cancel As Integer)
    ' Close multimedia controls and ensure CD Audio is off
    mciControl.Command = "Close"
    Unload frmCDAudio
End Sub
```

SUMMARY

Graphics, animation, and multimedia provide the user a richer way to interact with a program. Usually it is a good idea to make up a story board or equivalent. This will help plan how to incorporate the media in context to what the program will do for the user. However, the prime focus in this chapter is the technical programming required to implement the media. The elements that make up the media are

Graphics

- Bitmapped files (.BMP, .ICO)
- Vector (or meta) files (.WMF, .EMF)
- Graphical Controls, such as the Line and Shape controls
- Graphical Methods, such as Circle, Line, PSet

Animation

- Modify (including reposition) objects using graphical methods.
- Modify Picture property of objects.
- Use the multimedia control to play AVI Video files (.AVI).

Audio

- Use the multimedia control to play Wave files (.WAV).

- Use the multimedia control to play MIDI sequencer files (.MID).

Video

- Use the multimedia control to play AVI Video files (.AVI).

For graphics, we can use the form object, image control object, or picture box control object to contain the graphics. We do this by setting the Picture property of the object.

To use graphical methods and objects, we need to use coordinates and set colors. By default, the position of an object is relative to the upper left corner of its container. Use the Left property to set the horizontal position with respect to the ScaleLeft property of the containing object. Use the Top property to set the vertical position with respect to the ScaleHeight property of the containing object. To set the size of the object, set its Width and Height properties. We can create a customized scale by setting the ScaleMode property of the containing object, or by using the Scale method on the containing object. To set colors, use the RGB color code. We can set the code directly using a Long value, or we can use the RGB or QBColor function to return the required code.

THE MULTIMEDIA CONTROL

We can use the multimedia MCI (Media Control Interface) control to play various media as listed above. To use this control, we must add it to the Visual Basic project if it is not already included. When the compiled executable program is distributed to users, we must distribute it with the multimedia control. This is MCI16.OCX for the 16-bit version of Visual Basic 4, or MCI32.OCX for Visual Basic 5 and the 32-bit version of Visual Basic 4. We summarize key properties and events here. For complete information, see Help topic Multimedia MCI Control.

PROPERTIES

DeviceType

Determines the type of device with which the control can work. Examples are AVIVideo, CDAudio, Sequencer, or WaveAudio. The Sequencer device is used for MIDI. Data type is String.

FileName

Specifies the file to be opened by an Open command or saved by a Save command that is issued using the Command property. The DeviceType property should be initially set to specify the appropriate media type. Data type is String.

Command

Specifies a command that is recognized by an MCI device. Examples are Open, Close, Play, Prev, Back, Pause, and Stop. To set this property, it is first necessary to set the DeviceType and FileName properties. To issue commands, we must first issue the Open command. To use a new file, it is necessary to close the existing one and then open the new one, even if the DeviceType is the same. The data type is String.

AutoEnable

Determines if the multimedia MCI control can automatically enable (set True) or disable (set False) individual buttons in the control. When this property is True, the buttons for the multimedia control are automatically enabled or disabled to correspond to the playback mode. Data type is Boolean.

Enabled

The Enabled property determines if the multimedia MCI control can respond to user-generated events, such as the KeyPress and mouse events. Data type is Boolean.

Length

Specifies, in the current time format, the length of the media in an open MCI device. Data type is Long.

Notify

Determines if the next MCI command will generate a Done event, which occurs when the next MCI command is complete. Data type is Boolean.

Position

Specifies, in a time format, the current position of an open MCI device. Data type is Long.

UpdateInterval

Specifies the number of milliseconds between successive StatusUpdate events. Data type is Integer.

EVENTS

Done

Occurs when an MCI command for which the Notify property is True finishes. The Play command uses a default Notify setting of True, so when the Play command is complete (the selection has been played), the Done event fires, unless the Notify property had been previously set to False immediately prior to the command.

StatusUpdate

Occurs automatically at intervals given by the UpdateInterval property. Usually used to provide information to the user, such as how much of the media has been played.

ButtonClick

Occurs when the user presses and releases the mouse button over one of the buttons in the multimedia MCI control. By default, clicking a multimedia button will send the MCI command that corresponds to the button (see Figure 10.10). For example, clicking **Play** will send the Play command. In our programs, we did not override the default behavior, so we did not concern ourselves with the ButtonClick event.

HANDS-ON EXERCISES

OVERVIEW

The activities will enable you to

- Use bitmapped and vector (metafile) graphics in a program.
- Create animation using graphic files and/or graphic methods and controls.
- Add a custom control to a Visual Basic project.
- Add an extra form to a Visual Basic project.
- Use key properties and events of the Multimedia control.

To Get Started

1. Read the section Read Me Before Attempting the Hands-On Exercises if you have not already done so.
2. Run Windows.
3. Open the file CH10\EX10.TXT on your student disk and answer the questions. (The same questions are shown here so that you can still determine answers when you are not sitting in front of a computer.)
4. Run Visual Basic.

10.1   THE REASON

1. Why are graphics, animation, and multimedia sometimes included in programs?
2. What is a story board?
3. Why is it used?
4. Why do you think we did not say more about the story board in this chapter?

10.2   THE ELEMENTS

5. What is a file format? Identify some common formats, including file extensions.
6. Why is it important to be able to work with different file formats?
7. Is it easy to manipulate graphics stored in a bitmapped format? Explain.
8. Is it easy to manipulate graphics stored in a vector (or metafile) format? Explain.

10.3   GRAPHIC METHODS

9. Assuming the ScaleMode property of a form is set to 1, explain where the object is located if its Left and Top properties are both set to zero. Explain why, in terms of the coordinate system.
10. The Move method is applied to an object using the arguments 0,50. The original co-ordinates are 100,100. Does it move up or down the form? Assume that the Scale-Mode property of the containing object is 1.

11. A program executes the statement `picBox.Scale (400,-100)-(800,-500)`. Write a statement that will draw a circle with a radius of 75 such that it will touch the bottom and right border of the picture box object.

12. Write a statement that will set the BackColor of a form so that it is 25% red, 75% green, and 50% blue.

The Graphic Methods Sampler Program

To run this program, select **New Project** from the File menu. Then select **Save File/Form1 As** from the File menu. Save *file* FORM1 as **PICBOX1** in directory CH10. Select **Save Project As** from the File menu. Save *project* PROJECT1 as **PICBOX1** in directory CH10. Change the Name of the form to **frmPicBox**, and change the Caption to **Graphic Methods**. Save the project.

Refer to Figure 10.4 for placing all controls on the form. Draw **the frame control** on the form first, and position it on the form as shown in Figure 10.4. Name the frame **fraGraphicMethods**. Then place the **command buttons** on the frame, and place **one button** below the frame. Name the buttons (from top to bottom as shown in Figure 10.4) `cmdLine`, `cmdCircle`, `cmdPSet`, `cmdMove`, `cmdCls`. Name the button below the frame `cmdExit`.

Note

For any controls to be placed on a frame control, draw the frame first. Size it as required. Then *draw* the controls onto the frame. Do this by *single* clicking the **control on the Toolbox** (do not double-click). Move the mouse to the frame without pressing any buttons. Then press the **Left** button. While holding down the Left button, drag t**he mouse to draw the control** on the frame. If you place the control on the form and then drag it onto the frame, the control will not be part of the frame.

Draw the **picture box** on the form and name it **picExample**. Draw a **shape object** at the center of the picture box and name it **shpTarget**. Position it at the center of the picture box.

Note

For any controls to be contained by the picture box, draw the picture box first. Size it as required. Then *draw* the controls onto the picture box. Do this by *single* clicking the **control on the Toolbox** (do not double-click). Move the mouse to the picture box without pressing any buttons. Then press the **Left** button. While holding down the Left button, drag **the mouse to draw the control** on the picture box. If you place the control on the form and then drag it onto the picture box, the control will not be contained by the picture box.

Set the following properties of `shpTarget`:

FillColor	Choose a color such as `blue`
FillStyle	`0 - Solid`
Height	`405`
Shape	`5 - Rounded Square`
Width	`405`

Save the project. Enter **the code as shown in Example 10.1**, and save the project. Run the program and correct any syntax errors if necessary. Once the syntax errors are corrected (if this was necessary), run the program and try the different Command buttons. Note that the Move method will place the shape object relative to the CurrentX and CurrentY properties. Also note that PSet will place the dots relative to the CurrentX and CurrentY properties. The actual placement will depend on which buttons you clicked earlier to invoke other methods that modified the CurrentX and CurrentY properties. If you wish, set breakpoints and monitor the CurrentX and CurrentY properties using Debugging tools.

The Welcome Program, Version 1

Select New Project from the File menu.

Visual Basic 5

In the New Project dialog, select **Standard EXE** and click **OK.**

Select **Save File/Form1 As** from the File menu. Save *file* FORM1 as **COUGAR1** in directory CH10. Select **Save Project As** from the File menu. Save *project* PROJECT1 as **COUGAR1** in directory CH10. Change the Name of the form to **frmCougar**, and change the Caption to state **About Cougar Canoe**. Save the project.

Create **the form** as described in Section 10.3.4 and shown in Figure 10.5. The file CANOE1.EMF is already included in directory CH10. Save the project. Enter **the code as shown in Example 10.2**. Save the project.

Run the program. Resize the form. Note that the canoe image stretches with the form but the other controls stay in place. This program doesn't do much; we will build on it later. Stop execution of the program.

10.4 ANIMATION

The Butterfly Program

Select **New Project** from the File menu.

Visual Basic 5

In the New Project dialog, select **Standard EXE** and click **OK.**

Select **Save File/form1 As** from the File menu. Save *file* FORM1 as **BUTTERF** in directory CH10. Select **Save Project As** from the File menu. Save *project* PROJECT1 as **BUTTERF** in directory CH10. Change the Name of the form to **frmButterfly**, and change the Caption to state **Butterfly**. Save the project.

Create **the form** as described in Section 10.4.1 and shown in Figure 10.7. Files BFLY1.BMP and BFLY2.BMP are in subdirectory SAMPLES\FIRSTAPP of the Visual Basic main directory. Copy them to your own directory and save the project. Enter **the code as shown in Example 10.3.** Save the project.

Run the program. You should see a butterfly appear to fly repeatedly across the form. If the butterfly appears to include a visible square, stop the program and change the BackColor property of the form to white (setting is &H00FFFFFF&). Run the program. The butterfly should appear without the square. In case the square wasn't visible for your first attempt, experiment by temporarily setting the BackColor of the form to something else and run the program.

Set a breakpoint in procedure `trmTimer_Timer` and monitor execution of the procedure. Note the operation of the `Move` method and the alternating assignment of the Picture property. Stop execution of the program.

The Alarm Clock Program, Version 2

Open *project* ALARM1 in directory CH07. Save *file* ALARM1 as **ALARM2** in directory CH10. Select **Save Project As** from the File menu. Save *project* ALARM1 as **ALARM2** in directory CH10. Change the Name of the form to **frmAlarmClock2** and change the version part of its Caption to state **Alarm Clock - Version 2**. Save the project.

Refer to Figure 10.8 in Section 10.4.2. Resize the form to accommodate the additional picture box control. Draw the picture box on the form and name it **picPendulum**. Modify the code to include the modifications shown in Example 10.4. Save the project.

Run the program. Note the pendulum motion, and note that the pendulum graphics are created during runtime. No graphics were drawn on the picture box during design time. If you wish, set up breakpoints and monitor execution of the graphics methods using single stepping. Stop execution of the program. Later we will add an audio track for the alarm sound instead of using the `Beep` statement in procedure `CheckAlarm`.

The Welcome Program, Version 2

Open *project* COUGAR1 in directory CH10. Save *file* COUGAR1 as **COUGAR2** in directory CH10. Select **Save Project As** from the File menu. Save *project* COUGAR1 as **COUGAR2** in directory CH10. Save the project.

Add two timer controls, `tmrMarquee` and `tmrPhase`, as described in Section 10.4.3. Set `tmrMarquee.Interval` to **500** and `tmrPhase.Interval` to **1000**. Modify the code to include the modifications shown in Example 10.5. Save the project and run the program. You should see the scrolling effect of the marquee and the phase change of the moon. Resize the form and note that the Exit button remains in the lower right corner.

Some Problem Solving

Modify this program. Name the form and project files as **COUGAR2A**. The moon phase animation is not very good. Instead of using shape controls, we can use icons and image controls. Develop a program that shows an animation of lunar phase change by setting the Picture property of an image control to an icon file that shows a lunar phase. Develop the program and test it.

Hints   Refer to Figure 10.16. Subdirectory `ICONS\ELEMENTS` of the main Visual Basic directory contains icon files that show the different phases of the moon. Use a Timer event procedure to assign the Picture property of an image control by assigning it to the Picture property of a hidden image control array.

10.5   THE MULTIMEDIA MCI CONTROL

13. What is the purpose of the DeviceType property?

14. What is the purpose of the FileName property?

15. What is the purpose of the Command property?

Add A Custom Control

With Visual Basic, it is possible to add custom controls that are not already part of the Toolbox. Some of these may be controls purchased from other vendors or downloaded from the Internet. It is likely that the multimedia MCI control is not part of your

Figure 10.16
A Modified Welcome Program in Design Mode

Image Control

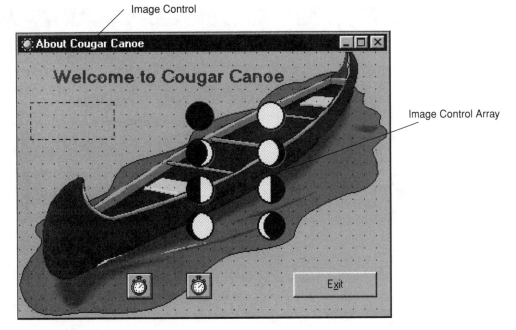

Image Control Array

Toolbox. If it isn't, you can use another control to practice this exercise. The following assumes that your setup does not already include the multimedia control (and that it is available, assuming the Professional or Enterprise Editions). Now, start a new project.

Visual Basic 4

Select **Custom Controls** from the Tools menu. You should see a Custom Controls dialog that is similar that shown in Figure 10.17a.

Visual Basic 5

Select **Components** from the Project Window. Click the **Controls** tab. You should see a Components dialog that is similar that shown in Figure 10.17b.

Note

Depending on your system, you may see a warning when attempting to add a custom control. It may state that the object server is not correctly registered. If you do see this message, click **OK** and ignore the warning. It probably refers to a different object server with which we are not concerned. We will talk about object servers in Chapter 11.

Click in the **check box** for Microsoft Multimedia Control to check it on, and click **OK**. You should see a new control button in the Toolbox. Double-click it. You should see the new control on the form. It should look the same as that shown in Figure 10.10.

10.6   WAVE AUDIO

For these exercises to work, you need a computer with a sound card connected to speakers or headphones.

Figure 10.17a
Adding a Custom Control in Visual Basic 4

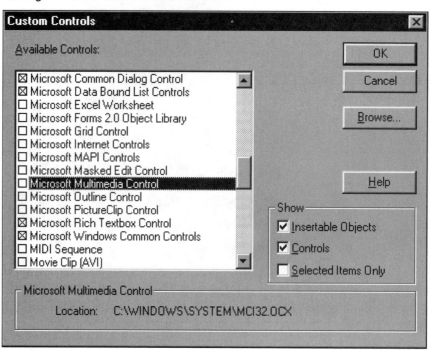

Figure 10.17b
Adding a Custom Control in Visual Basic 5

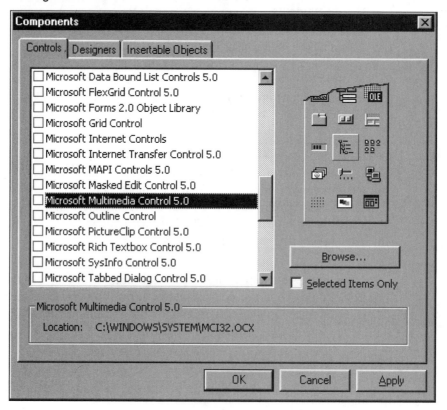

The Alarm Clock Program, Version 3

Open *project* ALARM2 in directory CH10. Save *file* ALARM2 as **ALARM3** in directory CH10. Select **Save Project As** from the File menu. Save *project* ALARM2 as **ALARM3** in directory CH10. Change the Name of the form to **frmAlarmClock3**, and change the version part of its Caption to state **Alarm Clock - Version 3**. Save the project.

Modify the code for procedure CheckAlarm as shown in Example 10.7. Note that if your system is set up differently, you may have to modify the path for the themic~1.wav file (The Microsoft Sound) to match that of your system. Save the project.

Run the program. Set the alarm to a few minutes past the actual time, and set the alarm mode. Wait for the alarm to occur. When the displayed time is the same as the alarm setting, you should hear the Microsoft Sound.

The Welcome Program, Version 3

Open *project* COUGAR2 in directory CH10. Save *file* COUGAR2 as **COUGAR3** in directory CH10. Select **Save Project As** from the File menu. Save *project* COUGAR2 as **COUGAR3** in directory CH10. Save the project.

Add the Microsoft Multimedia Control custom control, if necessary, and add three multimedia controls to the form. The location does not matter because you will be making them invisible. Add three image controls. Set the properties as follows. (For the Picture properties of the image controls, you can find the files in subdirectory ICONS\MISC of the main Visual Basic directory.)

MMControl

```
Name       mciWave
Left       52
Top        104
Visible    False
```

MMControl

```
Name       mciMidi
Left       52
Top        143
Visible    False
```

MMControl

```
Name       mciAvi
Left       52
Top        182
Visible    False
```

Image

```
Name       mciWave
Height     27
Left       143
Picture    Face03.Ico
Stretch    True
Top        52
Width      27
```

Image

```
Name       imgMidi
Height     27
```

```
Left        169
Picture     Misc31.Ico
Stretch     True
Top         52
Width       27
```

Image
```
Name        imgAvi
Height      27
Left        195
Picture     Misc41.Ico
Stretch     True
Top         52
Width       27
```

The media files will be on the program disk in directory CODE\MEDIA. Modify **the code so that it is the same as in Example 10.8**. Save the project. Run the program. You should hear audio when the program first starts. You should also hear the same audio when you click on the **happy face** image.

10.7   MIDI SOUND AND VERSION 4 OF THE WELCOME PROGRAM

Open *project* COUGAR3 in directory CH10. Save *file* COUGAR3 as **COUGAR4** in directory CH10. Select **Save Project As** from the File menu. Save *project* COUGAR3 as **COUGAR4** in directory CH10. Modify the code as shown in Example 10.9. Save the project.

Run the program. When the program first starts, you should hear the MIDI audio followed by the wave audio. Clicking on **the happy face** and **notes** images will play the wave and MIDI audio, respectively.

10.8   AVI VIDEO AND VERSION 5 OF THE WELCOME PROGRAM

Open *project* COUGAR4 in directory CH10. Save *file* COUGAR4 as **COUGAR5** in directory CH10. Select **Save Project As** from the File menu. Save *project* COUGAR4 as **COUGAR5** in directory CH10. Modify **the code as shown in Example 10.10**. Save the project.

Run the program. It works the same way as Version 4, except that clicking on the **sea** image will play a video in its own window. If you want to close this window, click on its **Close** button.

10.9   THE MULTIMEDIA PLAYER INCLUDING CD AUDIO

Start a new project. Select **Save File/Form1 As** from the File menu. Save *file* FORM1 as **PLAYMM** in directory CH10. Select **Save Project As** from the File menu. Save *project* PROJECT1 as **PLAYMM** in directory CH10. Change the Name of the form to **frmPlayMM**, and change the Caption to state **Multimedia Player**. Set the Icon property of the form to an icon available in the Visual Basic ICONS directory. You may wish to use the same one as shown in Figure 10.13. Save the project.

Note that this project will use two forms. We will start with the first one (and, so far, the only one).

Set Up the First Form

Refer to Figure 10.13 for placing all controls on the form. Draw **the frame control** on the form first, and position it on the form as shown in Figure 10.13. Name the frame **fraMediaType**. Then draw **the option button controls** on the frame. Remember to *draw* them on the frame. Do not double-click them onto the form. From top to bottom, name the option button controls **optWav**, **optMIDI**, **optAvi**, **optCD**, and **optNone**.

Set the Caption properties as shown in Figure 10.13. **Put the multimedia control, horizontal scroll bar**, and **command button** controls on the form. Name them mci-Control, hsbPosition, and cmdExit, respectively. Set **the Caption of cmdExit as shown in Figure 10.13**. Also put **a common dialog control** on the form. Figure 10.13 won't show it since it is not visible during the design mode. Place it anywhere and name it **dlgFileOpen**.

Add an Extra Form to a Visual Basic Project

You will add a second form to handle CD Audio. There are two ways to add an extra form with Visual Basic.

Visual Basic 4

Select **Form** from the Insert menu, or click the **Form** button on the Toolbar (see Figure 3.6a).

Visual Basic 5

Select **Add Form** from the Project menu, click the New tab in the Add Form dialog, select the **Form** icon, and click **Open**; or click the **Add Form** button on the Toolbar (see Figure 3.6b).

Either way, you will see an additional form with a default Name and Caption of Form2. Note that the Project window (or explorer) lists the two forms.

Note

When you work with the properties or code of a form and its controls, you must select it from the Project window.

About the Startup Form

In general, a Visual Basic program (project) may use many forms. A Visual Basic form may start with a specific form or a sub procedure named Main that is part of a Module. If a form is used, it is known as the *startup* form. By default, when you start a new project, Visual Basic will assign the first form as the startup form. For practice, let's check out defining the startup form (although we don't need to in this case).

Visual Basic 4

Select **Options** from the Tools menu. Click on the **Project** tab. You will see where the Startup Form is selected. The current startup form should be frmPlayMM. Click on the **Startup Form arrow**. You will see the choices, which are Sub Main and all the forms that currently belong to the project. Click **Cancel**.

Visual Basic 5

Select **Project1 Properties** from the Project menu. Click the **General** tab. In the Startup Object box, you will see where the Startup Form is selected. The current startup form should be frmPlayMM. Click on the **Startup Object arrow**. You will see the choices, which are Sub Main and all the forms that currently belong to the project. Click **Cancel**. Note that by default your project is named Project1. If you change this name, the Project menu will list the Properties item using the name of your project instead of Project1.

Set Up the Second Form

Remember that when you work with the properties or code of a form and its controls, you must select it from the Project window/explorer. Do this now. Select the **second form** in the Project window/explorer (it may already be highlighted). You will save the form. To do this, select **Save File/Form2 As** from the File menu. Do *not* select **Save Project As**. Save *file* FORM2 as **CDAUDIO** in directory CH10. Change the Name of the form to **frmCDAudio**, and change the Caption to state **CD Audio Player**. Save the project. Note that file PLAYMM.VBP will now include a reference to CDAUDIO.FRM. To see this for yourself, check the contents of PLAYMM.VBP using Windows Notepad. The Project window should now show two items.

```
CDAUDIO.FRM      frmCDAudio
PLAYMM.FRM       frmPlayMM
```

Refer to Figure 10.15. Size **the form** and place **a multimedia and command button control** on it. Name the controls **mciCDAudio** and **cmdDone**, respectively. Set **the Caption of cmdDone**. You can view both forms at the same time. Select **the first form** from the Project window and click **View Form**. You can select a form by clicking **the form** (if visible) or by selecting it from the Project window. You could position the forms so that they do not overlap. Save the project.

Visual Basic 5

The Form Layout window will show both forms. You can position them as desired.

Note

When you save a project, you update the .VBP project file and any files that belong to the project if they have been modified.

Note

When you save a file, you update the file that is currently selected in the project window. None of the other files in the project are updated.

Enter the Code

Remember to select **frmPlayMM** in the Project window/explorer. Click **View Code**. Enter **the code shown in Examples 10.11, 10.12, 10.13, and 10.15**.

For frmCDAudio, click **frmCDAudio** in the Project window/explorer. Then click **View Code**. Enter **the code shown in Example 10.14**.

Run the Program

Save the project. Place your favorite audio CD in the CD-ROM drive. Run the program. Select the media you wish to play. Try playing the audio and video files you worked with earlier. Play others if you have them. Then play the CD Audio. Note that this shows the second form as a second window. Use this window to play the audio CD.

ADDITIONAL PROBLEM SOLVING

Problem 1

Modify the Butterfly program so that the butterfly will turn around and fly back in the opposite direction whenever it reaches an edge of the form.

Hint You will need to create two additional bitmapped images. Actually, this is quite easy to do. Use the Windows Paint accessory to open one of the original bitmap files. Save a copy of it with a new name. Use the Image menu to flip and/or rotate the image as required. Repeat this for the second bitmap file.

Problem 2

Modify the Multimedia Player program so that it will show the numerical position when it plays wave audio, MIDI audio, or AVI Video.

CHAPTER 11

ActiveX: Object Linking and Embedding (OLE) and Automation

This chapter introduces the OLE Container Control and a method for using Automation to access code available in other applications.

If we were to build a dune buggy, we probably wouldn't build the engine from scratch in a machine shop; we might want to take an engine from an old car. Similarly, we can build programs from parts of existing programs if those parts are accessible. We can use the components of some programs without knowing the details of how the components worked. However, not all programs have accessible parts; some are sealed units, like watches. We wouldn't open a watch to use its components unless we knew it intimately and had the inclination to tinker. The same is true in programming.

After completing this chapter, you should be able to

- Explain Object Linking and Embedding (OLE), Automation, and ActiveX in terms of the Component Object Model (COM).

- Use properties and methods of the OLE Container Control.

- Create a program using the OLE Container Control.

- Use the properties and methods of external objects that are accessible via Automation.

- Create a program using objects accessible via Automation.

A SEMINAR INFORMATION APPLICATION

Cougar Canoe needs software that will permit customer representatives to view a word processed document and spreadsheet file that describes seminars. The company organizes these seminars for existing and potential customers. The document is an electronic copy of the promotional flyer that is sent out to invite participants. The file shows the seat bookings for the place where the seminar runs. It is possible to create a Visual Basic program that will directly display this information, but programs that perform these functions exist. Microsoft Word or WordPad can display a document in Word format. Microsoft Excel or the free Excel Viewer can display spreadsheets that are in Excel format. A Visual Basic program (or Windows programs in general) can provide an interface to access these programs. Thus the customer representative needs to use only one program to access the features he or she needs instead of using an assortment of separate applications.

AN HTML-BASED HELP SYSTEM APPLICATION

In another scenario, a Visual Basic program uses the functionality provided by the Internet Explorer web browser to implement an online help system. The user can navigate using Visual Basic. Internet Explorer responds to the Visual Basic program to display the web pages that are requested by the program. The pages are stored in the standard Hyper Text Markup Language (HTML) format used for the World Wide Web. In this case, we happen to use the same HTML files that are provided for the Help system on the program disk. Thus a Visual Basic program can be a front end for using other applications to conveniently access information required for an HTML-based help system. We can do this by using a Windows standard known as *Automation* (formerly known as *OLE Automation*).

11.1 A QUICK LOOK AT OLE IN ACTION

Before we look at some of the nuts and bolts of Automation, let's look at a simple use of Object Linking and Embedding (OLE) in action. This will give us a flavor of what this technology can do for the user—and why the programmer (us) should use it to serve the customer/user.

Let's say we run the WordPad accessory, a simple word processor that is included in all Windows systems. Create or open an existing document. If you perform the Insert Object operation, you will see a list of applications such as Bitmap image and WAV audio, some word processors, and perhaps some spreadsheet programs and other selections, depending on what is available in your system. There is a sample WordPad document on the program disk that we will use for demonstrating the OLE container control. It so happens that this document includes an *embedded* image that can be edited using the Paint accessory. Figure 11.1 shows the WordPad application. When the user double-clicks the image, the WordPad menus and controls change to those of Paint to permit editing of the image. Figure 11.2 shows this Paint mode. If the user clicks outside the image, the menus and controls revert back to those for WordPad document editing.

Figure 11.1
An Embedded Paint Object in a WordPad Document

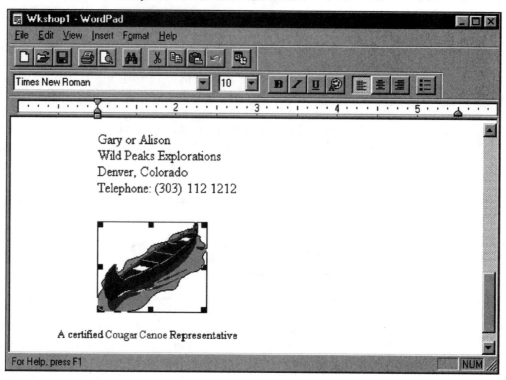

User has clicked on the image. Note that sizing handles permit resizing.

This particular example uses an ***embedded object*** instead of a ***linked object.*** An ***object*** is an entity with both data and code. For example, the Paint object is the image data as well as the ability to edit the image. In this case we are using the code available with the Paint accessory program. So what is the difference between *embedded* and *linked*?

*An **embedded** object is a new copy of the original data. It can be edited within a containing application without affecting the original data file.*

*A **linked** object is a reference (or pointer) to the original data. Modifying the original data will also affect the data in the containing application. Similarly, modifying the linked object will modify the original data. They are bound together.*

Examples include the following:

Embed a Paint image of a red canoe in WordPad. Modify the original Paint data file to make the canoe green. The WordPad document will still show a red canoe.

Link a Paint image of a red canoe in WordPad. Modify the original Paint data file to make the canoe green. The WordPad document will now show a green canoe.

Note that this use of OLE tends to be a more document-centered view of computing as opposed to an application-centered view. In document-centered computing, the user works with a document and the computer determines which application tools to use. Now, let's move on to the programmer view of tool reuse.

Figure 11.2
Editing the Embedded Paint Object in a WordPad Document

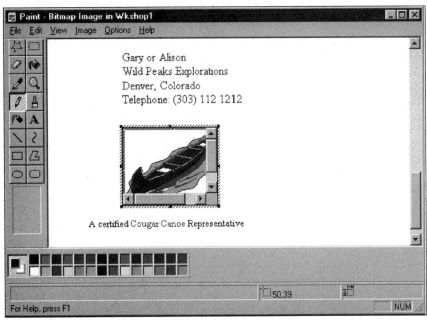

User has double-clicked image in Figure 11.1 to reveal the window shown here. The WordPad menus and tools have switched to those of Paint. If the user clicks in the text portion, the window menus and controls switch back to those of WordPad.

11.2   COMPONENT WARE— A DREAM COME TRUE?

Ancient alchemists dreamed about converting common materials to gold. Since software is typically complex, software designers have longed for sophisticated components that can be combined easily to create useful applications. For example, a program could create a word processed document that includes a manufacturing simulation. The programmer could create the program by using parts of both a word processor program and an engineering design program. If only it were so easy! A major hurdle to using components is *standardization*. Imagine if you had to assemble a bicycle and all the screws were different, and each required its own screwdriver. With standardization, we know that screws are available with specific lengths, diameters, and thread pitch. We can use a slotted, Phillips, or Robertson screwdriver to match the screw's head, and we can walk into any hardware store to buy these parts.

It is difficult to obtain universal agreement about software component standards. Since the Windows operating system is very popular, there has been some degree of component reuse. This is an evolving process. As new developments in software occur, there is a desire to incorporate them. At times the terminology changes during the span of a few months. Visual Basic 3 contained controls known as *Visual Basic Extensions (VBXs)* that permitted programmers to use them like standard controls. One example is the common dialog control. With Windows 3.1, Microsoft introduced a technology known as

Object Linking and Embedding (OLE) (pronounced "oh-lay"), which enabled some reuse of applications that supported this standard. For example, a word processed document could include a drawing. When the user needed to edit the drawing, a drawing program automatically took over. With Windows 95 and Visual Basic 4, a 32-bit environment, *Object Control Extensions (OCXs)*, replaced VBXs, and OLE was further developed. Shortly after the introduction of Visual Basic 4, Microsoft completely changed their strategy to embrace web technology for the Internet. OCXs were renamed *ActiveX controls*, but the files still use the .OCX extension. These controls were repackaged so that they could be used by a web browser connecting to a remote site (web server). Microsoft introduced a standard called the *Component Object Model (COM)*, which included ActiveX and OLE. When Visual Basic 5 was introduced, much of the terminology used in Visual Basic 4 was replaced by new terms. We will guide you through some of that component technology and terminology, but it is difficult to say whether more changes are in store since the introduction of Visual Basic 5.

Objects

Components are Objects. An object is a combination of code and data that is handled as a complete package. An object has methods (the code) and properties (the data). Methods are like verbs (actions) and properties are like adjectives (describe the object). An application can contain objects such as forms and controls, and an entire application can also be an object that contains other objects. The containing object can contain event procedures to handle external actions. With component ware, we can use the properties and methods of another object, and with standardization such as the Component Object Model (COM), we can even use the properties and methods of an object that is contained in another application.

Classes and Instances

A *class* is a template for an object. It describes the generic functionality of the object in terms of what the object can do (methods and events) and its attributes (properties). We used classes in an earlier chapter, but we avoided some of the terminology. The form object and various control objects, such as the command button and text box, are examples of classes. So far we have referred to objects using common names such as form, command button, and text box. When we create objects using statements, it is necessary to use formal class names, which are Form, CommandButton, and TextBox, respectively. The CommandButton class (for the command button control) defines the general appearance of a button and the fact that it is possible to set location, size, caption, and so on. It also defines that the button will react to the Click event and other events.

An *instance* of a class is the actual use of the class (object type). It is a physical realization (implementation) of the class. For example, we can create an instance of the CommandButton class by drawing it on the form, naming it as cmdExit, and then setting some properties and code to make it behave as an Exit button. Another instance of the CommandButton class could be one named cmdAdd that is used to add numbers typed in some text boxes. As we shall see later in the chapter, we will use a class named InternetExplorer, but to use it we will create an instance of the InternetExplorer class. The rules for naming a class and instances of a class are the same as for naming data types and variables.

The OLE Container Control and Automation

In the seminar information application mentioned earlier, we will use the OLE container control, which provides quick access to the applications that created the data. However, a Visual Basic program is not able utilize the code available in the applications. The OLE container can activate a document file using the application that created the document. In the Help system application, we use *Automation* to access some of the code that is available in another application.

11.2.1   ActiveX and the Component Object Model (COM)

Automation uses the Component Object Model (COM). A programmer can use some properties and methods of objects from other applications that support COM. COM is a Windows standard that defines how objects make their properties and methods available to other applications. These objects are known as *ActiveX objects* or controls. The *exposed* properties and methods are known as the object's *interface*. With Automation, we can:

- Create applications using ActiveX controls. The applications that use ActiveX controls (formerly OLE Controls) are known as *ActiveX clients* (formerly *OLE clients*). This chapter will cover the development of ActiveX clients for Automation.

- Create applications that can expose objects for other applications and programming tools to use. These applications are known as *ActiveX code components* (formerly known as *the OLE server* or *OLE Automation server*). This chapter will not cover the development of ActiveX code components, which is a topic for more advanced programming references.

Active X (code) components are physical files (such as .EXE *and* .DLL *files) that contain classes, which are definitions of objects.*

*An **ActiveX control** is an object whose interface can be used by (exposed to) other applications and programming tools.*

So far we have used terms like *exposed* and *interface*. What do they mean?

*An **interface** is the collection of properties and methods of an object.*

*The part of the object interface that is public, or available for other applications to use, is called **exposed** interface.*

Figure 11.3 illustrates ActiveX controls. Public methods and properties provide a means for external programs to use them. The implementation details are hidden as private methods and properties. Consider a car engine as an analogy: Its external mountings and fuel, air, and electrical connections are ***publicly*** available for use if we want to install the engine in another vehicle. However, the internal valves and chambers are considered to be ***private.*** They are not readily available (unless you are an expert in engine operations), yet they are necessary characteristics that determine how the engine performs.

Let's say that a program will use the wheel object as shown in Figure 11.3. To move the wheel, we can use its Move method. Let's say the interface specifies that we must use the keyword Move with a Single type argument specifying the horizontal position. That's all we need to know; we don't need to know how the code for Move works. It could be one of the following segments:

```
Public Sub Move(fPosition As Single)
    shpWheel.Move fPosition, VERTICAL
```

Figure 11.3
ActiveX Controls

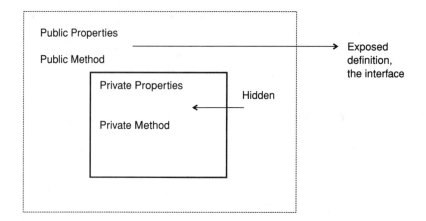

A generic ActiveX control (an object)

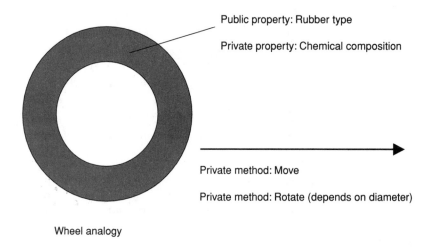

Wheel analogy

```
End Sub
```

or

```
Public Sub Move(fPosition As Single)
    shpWheel.Left = fPosition
End Sub
```

It does not matter which version is used. We can use it with something like the following:

```
MyWheel.Move(fNewPosition)
```

11.2.2   Interaction Between Clients and Components

Figure 11.4 illustrates the interaction between clients and objects within the COM. The client uses objects provided by the code components. The code components physically exist as binary files. How does the client know that a component exists? The operating

Figure 11.4
Interaction Between
ActiveX Clients and
ActiveX Objects

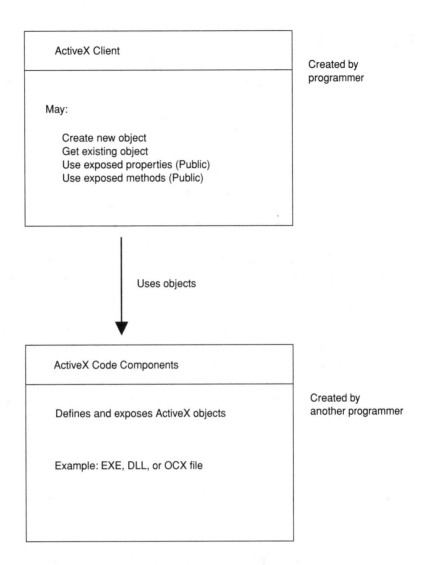

system handles this for us. The **Windows System Registry** defines how a specific Windows installation is set up. It is essentially a special database that is necessary for Windows to function properly. It includes information to state (register) what code components are available. When we install a new off-the-shelf program, it registers itself in the Registry, so other applications can use the components.

11.2.3   The Object Browser

How do we know which components exist? How do we know the interface definition of the object? This is where the **Visual Basic Object Browser** comes into play. First we add a reference to the component, if necessary. Then we can use the Object Browser to examine the interface of the component. (We will look at how to do this during the Hands-On Exercises at the end of this chapter.) Meanwhile, Figures 11.5 and 11.6 illustrate the kind of information that the Object Browser reveals. The look and feel differs slightly between Versions 4 and 5 of Visual Basic, but the information provided is essentially the same (except that Version 5 includes more information.)

Note

The listed libraries shown in Figure 11.5 may differ from those on your system because your system may be set up differently with different registered components. Both Figures 11.5 and 11.6 illustrate a system in which Microsoft Internet Explorer has been installed.

We use Internet Explorer to illustrate the Object Browser because later sections about Automation will use it. We chose Internet Explorer because there is a good chance that you already have it installed in your system. If you don't, you can download it for free from Microsoft's website at http://www.microsoft.com/ and follow their installation instructions. Both figures show that the components reside in a file named SHDocVw (actually SHDOCVW.DLL). Note that this component (library) has several classes, one of which is the InternetExplorer class. In Figure 11.5 the programmer has selected the Navigate method, but Visual Basic 4 only provides bare-bones information. We can surmise that Navigate is a method instead of a property because the bottom of the Object Browser shows what appears to be the syntax of a method. Only the URL argument is mandatory; the rest are optional, as indicated by the square bracket convention. The brief explanation states what the method does: Navigates to a URL or a file. If you are familiar with the Web, you know that URL stands for *Uniform Resource Locator*, the technical term for the address of a website. In Figure 11.6 we can see that the Visual Basic 5 Object Browser shows more information. Icons indicate whether the member is a property, event, or method, and the Classes pane shows constants in addition to the classes.

Note

It is best to have supplementary documentation to describe an ActiveX Code Component. However, with the Object Browser and some persistent experimentation, we can usually determine how to use the component in an application.

11.3   THE OLE CONTAINER CONTROL

The OLE Container Control offers a way of reusing code in another program without knowing anything about the properties, methods, and events that are made available by that other program. We briefly described OLE earlier: It is a Windows standard that permits an application to use parts of another application. This standard appeared before ActiveX and the COM. The introduction of ActiveX superseded OLE while maintaining compatibility with the older OLE standard.

OLE is a special case of ActiveX that enables you to create applications that contain components from various other applications. Visual Basic supplies a control known as the OLE container control. This is a quick way to incorporate the functionality already provided by other applications, provided that the application follows the OLE standard. Visual Basic is useful for building front-end applications that can incorporate elements of assorted applications, such as combining a word processor with a spreadsheet. Some products adhere more to the OLE standard than others. Since OLE is a Microsoft invention, it is not surprising that their Office Suite is often cited when describing OLE examples. A typical example is the use of an Excel spreadsheet in a Word document; both applications are Microsoft products.

Figure 11.5
Visual Basic 4 Object
Browser in Action

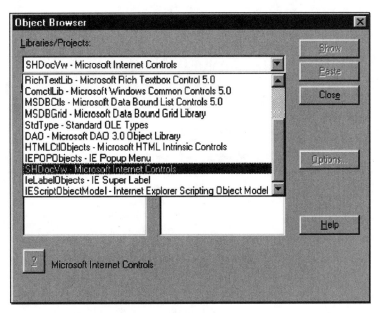

Showing some code components

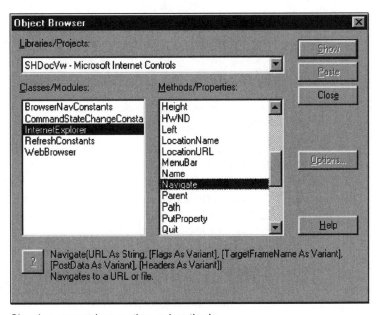

Showing exposed properties and methods

11.3.1   The Seminar Program

Earlier we mentioned an application that provides information for seminars hosted
by Cougar Canoe. For example, a seminar may be about wilderness survival, something that would be useful to canoeists, so it may attract more customers. A customer
representative will host and organize a seminar in his or her region. We will create a
program that representatives can use to show information about the seminar topic

Figure 11.6
Visual Basic 5 Object Browser in Action

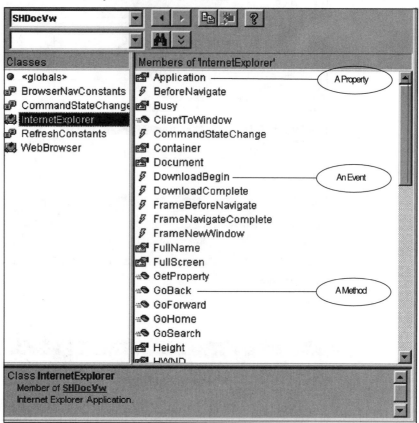

Showing some exposed properties and methods (as well as events)
after code component chosen

and information about who has reserved seats to attend the seminar. The topic information is a copy of the poster or flyer to advertise the seminar. The spreadsheet lists the names of those attending and displays how many seats are available for additional reservations. The program is a front-end application that uses a word processor to show the flyer and a spreadsheet program to display reservations information. A commercial word processor such as Word and a spreadsheet program such as Excel would be useful, but we will instead use packages that are available to any Windows user. WordPad, which is packaged on all Windows systems, and the Excel Viewer, which can be downloaded for free from Microsoft's website at http://www.microsoft.com. They include enough OLE functionality for our purposes. (If you wish, you may modify this example to use your favorite word processor and spreadsheet program, assuming they follow the OLE standard.) Figure 11.7 shows the front-end application prior to activating the WordPad and Excel Viewer components. Figure 11.8 shows the activation of both components.

Using the Program

The program is quite simple to use: The representative clicks on Flyer and WordPad launches to show the flyer information. Clicking Reservations launches the Excel Viewer to show the reservations information. Depending on how the WordPad and Excel Viewer windows are positioned and sized, the representative will see something

Figure 11.7
The Seminar Program as an OLE Container Application

OLE Container for WordPad

OLE Container for Excel Viewer

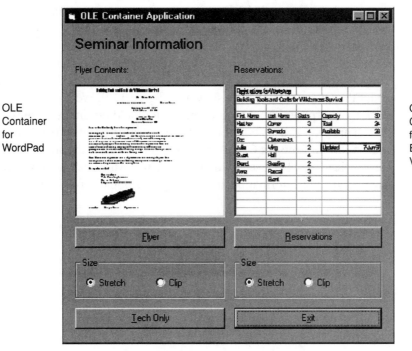

Figure 11.8
Activation of OLE Containers for WordPad and Excel Viewer

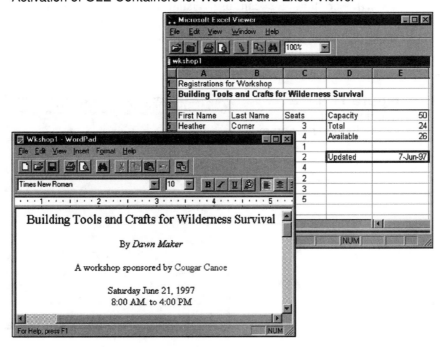

like Figure 11.8. The additional controls on the main form are included to demonstrate some uses of the OLE container properties. Clicking Clip will show the data in the associated container at full size. However, this is likely to be clipped because the container may not be large enough to show all of the data. Clicking Stretch will resize the data to fit within the container. When the user chooses Stretch, he or she can see an outline of the data, although it may not be legible, depending on the amount of data and the size of the container. For each OLE container, there is an associated frame object containing two option buttons. This permits the user to select one of each option button pair independently of the other. If we added the four option buttons on the form without using the frame controls, the user could select only one of the four options. Clicking the Tech Only button launches a new window (a new form) to display technical information about the OLE containers, as shown in Figure 11.9. We included this information for illustrative purposes about programming; it would not interest the typical user.

This project uses two forms. Form `frmContainer` (shown in Figure 11.7) is the startup form for project `CONTAIN1`. Form `frmTech` is the additional form for the project. Recall that we also used two forms in the Multimedia Player project described in Chapter 10. For information about using additional forms, refer to Section 10.9.

11.3.2   The Design

Table 11.1 shows the key control settings for `frmContainer`. For caption, size, and position settings, refer to Figure 11.7.

The Class property is the official name for the template describing an object that is part of an application. For WordPad, the official name is `WordPad.Document.1`, and for the Excel Viewer, it is `Excel.Sheet.5`. These names were chosen and registered by the developers who created the applications. The SourceDoc property refers to the data file that the external application will open. A data file opened by the application is known as the linked object (or embedded object). (In the Hands-On Exercises, we will see how we can use Visual Basic to automatically set the Class and SourceDoc properties at the same time without knowing the name of the Class.) Table 11.2 shows the key control properties for `frmTech`. For caption, size, and position settings, refer to Figure 11.9.

Figure 11.9
Supplemental Information
for the Seminar Program

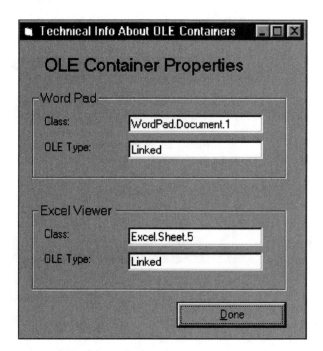

Table 11.1
Key Property Settings for frmContainer, the Startup Form for the Seminar Program

Object Class	Property	Setting
Label	Name	lblSeminar
	Font.Size	14
	Font.Bold	True
Label	Name	lblFlyer
Label	Name	lblReservations
OLE	Name	oleWordPad
	Class	WordPad.Document.1
	SizeMode	1-Stretch
	SourceDoc[a]	C:\INTROP\CODE\CH11\WKSHOP1.XLS
OLE	Name	oleExcelViewer
	Class	Excel.Sheet.5
	SizeMode	1-Stretch
	SourceDoc[a]	C:\INTROP\CODE\CH11\WKSHOP1.XLS
CommandButton	Name	cmdFlyer
CommandButton	Name	cmdReservations
CommandButton	Name	cmdTech
CommandButton	Name	cmdExit
Frame	Name	fraWPSize
Option Button[b]	Name	optWPStretch
	Value	True
OptionButton[b]	Name	optWPClip
	Value	False
Frame	Name	fraEVSize
OptionButton[c]	Name	optEVStretch
	Value	True
OptionButton[c]	Name	optEVClip
	Value	False

[a]File path may vary depending on setup. Files are included on the program disk.
[b]Contained by Frame fraWPSize, used for WordPad OLE container oleWordPad.
[c]Contained by Frame fraEVSize, used for Excel Viewer OLE container oleExcelViewer.

Table 11.2
Key Property Settings for `frmTech`, the Second Form for the Seminar Program

Object Class	Property	Setting
Label	Name	lblOLEStatus
	Font.Size	14
	Font.Bold	True
Frame	Name	fraWordPad
	Font.Size	10
Label[a]	Name	lblWPClass
Label[a]	Name	lblWPType
TextBox[a]	Name	txtWPClass
TextBox[a]	Name	txtWPType
Frame	Name	fraExcelView
	Font.Size	10
Label[b]	Name	lblEVClass
Label[b]	Name	lblEVType
TextBox[b]	Name	txtEVClass
TextBox[b]	Name	txtEVType
CommandButton	Name	cmdDone

[a]Contained by Frame `fraWordPad` used for WordPad OLE container `oleWordPad`.
[b]Contained by Frame `fraExcelView`, used for Excel Viewer OLE container `oleExcelViewer`.

Example 11.1 shows the code for the form `frmContainer`.

Example 11.1

```
Option Explicit

' Seminar Program
' Demonstrate using OLE container for objects from other ➥
applications
' In this case, use WordPad and Excel Viewer
' Class, SourceDoc properties set at design time by doing the ➥
following:
' Insert OLE container control and create from File using ➥
linked option
' (for WordPad may have to run it and open file before ➥
inserting the control)
' Use DoVerb Method to display or user can double-click icon

' Initial Size Mode is stretch
' In some cases WordPad becomes embedded after it is opened
' but Excel Viewer remains linked
```

```
' Edit/Open pop up in WordPad works only if WordPad app already running

Const PATH = "c:\introp\code\ch11\" ' Modify if necessary

Private Sub cmdExit_Click()
    End
End Sub


Private Sub cmdFlyer_Click()
    ' Show flyer information as a WordPad document
    ' Necessary to create link; otherwise unable to open object
    oleWordPad.CreateLink PATH & "wkshop1.doc"
    ' Open the application
    oleWordPad.DoVerb vbOLEOpen
End Sub

Private Sub cmdReservations_Click()
    ' Shows reservations as an Excel worksheet
    ' Not necessary to create link for Excel Viewer at runtime
    oleExcelViewer.DoVerb vbOLEOpen
End Sub

Private Sub cmdTech_Click()
    ' Show some technical information about OLE containers
    ' for demonstration purposes
    frmTech.Show
End Sub


Private Sub optEVClip_Click()
    ' Clip Excel Viewer data image in container
    oleExcelViewer.SizeMode = vbOLESizeClip
End Sub

Private Sub optEVStretch_Click()
    ' Stretch Excel Viewer data image in container
    oleExcelViewer.SizeMode = vbOLESizeStretch
End Sub

Private Sub optWPClip_Click()
    ' Clip WordPad data image in container
    oleWordPad.SizeMode = vbOLESizeClip
End Sub

Private Sub optWPStretch_Click()
    ' Stretch WordPad data image in container
    oleWordPad.SizeMode = vbOLESizeStretch
End Sub
```

Let's look at key features in the program. Procedure `cmdFlyer_Click` activates the WordPad document.

```
Private Sub cmdFlyer_Click()
    ' Show flyer information as a WordPad document
```

```
            ' Necessary to create link; otherwise unable to open object
            oleWordPad.CreateLink PATH & "wkshop1.doc"
            ' Open the application
            oleWordPad.DoVerb vbOLEOpen
End Sub
```

Note

In terms of OLE, both the WordPad and Excel Viewer documents are ***objects***.

The `CreateLink` method creates a linked object from the contents of a file. In this case, it creates a WordPad object for the file as specified in the argument and sets the SourceDoc property to indicate that the file is `wkshop1.doc`. This causes the OLE container control to display an image of the specified file. Once the object is created, we can use the `DoVerb` method to execute an action (verb) on the object. In general, the `DoVerb` method opens an OLE container control for an operation, such as editing. In this case, the procedure opens the document for editing (and viewing) in a separate WordPad window. The syntax is

OLEContainerObject.**DoVerb** *[verb]*

The verb argument is an Integer that we usually specify using a Visual Basic constant. If a `verb` value is not specified, the default value of zero is used to specify the default action for the object. The default will depend on the type of object. For example, a word processed document may behave differently than a multimedia clip. Table 11.3 shows the possible `verb` arguments.

In-place activation refers to the process of editing the object within the container instead of using a separate application window. It is not possible to use in-place activation for all objects. For information about the `DoVerb` method, refer to the Help topic in Visual Basic.

Procedure `cmdReservations_Click` operates similarly, except that the Excel Viewer application will not permit editing. It is a viewer only.

Table 11.3
DoVerb Method Arguments

Constant	Value	Meaning
vbOLEPrimary	0	Default action.
vbOLEShow	-1	Activate for editing, in-place activation if possible.
vbOLEOpen	-2	Open object in separate application window.
vbOLEHide	-3	For embedded objects, hides the application that created the object.
vbOLEUIActivate	-4	Like vbOLEShow, but show user interface tools.
vbOLEInPlaceActivate	-5	When OLE container gets the focus, prepare object for editing.
vbOLEDiscardUndoState	-6	When activated for editing, discard edit changes if possible.

Procedure `optEVClip_Click` modifies the SizeMode property of the OLE container control. In this case it causes the file contents to be full size, as they would be shown in an Excel Viewer application window. However, the document is likely to be clipped because the container is not large enough to show the entire document.

```
Private Sub optEVClip_Click()
    ' Clip Excel Viewer data image in container
    oleExcelViewer.SizeMode = vbOLESizeClip
End Sub
```

The SizeMode property returns or sets a value specifying how the OLE container control displays the image of the object it contains. The settings can be any of the following constants or corresponding integer values shown in Table 11.4.

The other option button Click procedures operate similarly. Procedure `cmdTech_Click` shows the other form that reveals some technical details to the user. Example 11.2 shows the code for the form `frmTech`.

Example 11.2

```
Option Explicit

' Show some technical details of OLE Container controls
' somewhat like a custom message box
Private Sub Form_Load()
    ' Assign new values for user to view every time user
    ' chooses to view this form
    ' Show Class and OLEType of objects (application data) ➡
    being contained

    With frmContainer

        txtWPClass.Text = CStr(.oleWordPad.Class)

        If .oleWordPad.OLEType = vbOLELinked Then
            txtWPType.Text = "Linked"
        ElseIf .oleWordPad.OLEType = vbOLEEmbedded Then
            txtWPType.Text = "Embedded"
        Else
            txtWPType.Text = "None"
        End If
```

Table 11.4
SizeMode Property Settings

Constant	Value	Meaning
vbOLESizeClip	0	Default, display actual size, and clip if image too large.
vbOLESizeStretch	1	Size (stretch) image to fill the container.
vbOLESizeAutoSize	2	Resize container to display entire object image.
vbOLESizeZoom	3	Resize object image to fill container as much as possible while maintaining proportions.

```
            txtEVClass.Text = CStr(.oleExcelViewer.Class)
            If .oleExcelViewer.OLEType = vbOLELinked Then
                txtEVType.Text = "Linked"
            ElseIf .oleExcelViewer.OLEType = vbOLEEmbedded Then
                txtWPType.Text = "Embedded"
            Else
                txtEVType.Text = "None"
            End If

    End With
End Sub

Private Sub cmdDone_Click()

    Hide          ' Remove form from view
    Unload Me     ' Permit new data to be displayed
              ' when form loaded again
End Sub
```

Let's look at what happens when the form is loaded (when the user clicks Tech Only on the main window); that is, when procedure `Form_Load` executes. The form reveals the Class property of the OLE containers. Recall that a class is a template describing an object (defines methods and properties). Some large Windows applications use several objects based on an object hierarchy (or object model). For example, Microsoft Excel 5.0 supports a number of objects, including worksheets and charts. Their class names are `Excel.Sheet.5` and `Excel.Chart.5`. WordPad uses an object known as *a document*. Its class name is `WordPad.Document.1`. In general, you can discover how the object hierarchy is organized by using the Object Browser.

The OLEType property returns the status of the object in an OLE container control. The status can be embedded or linked or none (no object). Recall that a linked object is one for which changes to the original data file (the object) change the contents of the OLE container. Similarly, modifying the contents of the OLE container changes the data file, because the container *is using* the data file. An embedded object is a copy of the original data. Table 11.5 shows the OLEType Property Settings.

When the user clicks the Done button, the `cmdDone_Click` procedure executes the `Hide` method to make the form disappear from view. Then it executes the `Unload` statement to remove the form from memory. The keyword `Me` refers to the form object in which the `Unload` statement is used. In other words, it tells the form to unload itself instead of another form. When the user clicks Tech Only on the main form, it is reloaded with fresh data. In fact, the properties for the WordPad container change after the user has activated WordPad. The Class becomes `Package` and the OLEType becomes `Embedded`. A Package is a Windows feature that permits OLE cut-and-paste operations. Activating the WordPad document automatically causes this modification. In contrast, activating the Excel Viewer does not modify its container properties.

Table 11.5
OLEType Property Settings

Constant	Value	Meaning
vbOLELinked	0	Container contains a linked object.
vbOLEEmbedded	1	Container contains an embedded object.
vbOLENone	3	Container does not contain an object.

11.3.3 A Seminar Program Using Runtime Property Settings, Including SourceItem

Figure 11.10 shows a variation of the Seminar program. The OLE container for the Excel Viewer only shows part of the spreadsheet data. This may be useful for a customer representative: She or he needs only to quickly check the number of reservations without worrying about reservation details. To show a portion of an object image, it is necessary to use the SourceItem property. In this case, we also illustrate how to set up properties during execution. During the design phase, the links to the containers were left blank. Example 11.3 shows the code.

Example 11.3

```
' OLE container application that uses runtime to set
' up properties of OLE container control

' It is possible to activate Excel Viewer but Excel Viewer
' suffers runtime error when closing the application while
' Client (Visual Basic) application is running
' This situation with Excel Viewer is outside our control

Option Explicit

Const PATH = "c:\introp\code\ch11\" ' Modify path if necessary


Private Sub cmdExit_Click()
    End
End Sub


Private Sub Form_Load()
    ' Initialize program settings
    ' Note it is possible to set at design time by
    ' Also clicking Class ellipsis in Properties window
    ' will show list of classes available in your system
```

Figure 11.10
OLE Container Program Using SourceItem Property and Runtime Settings

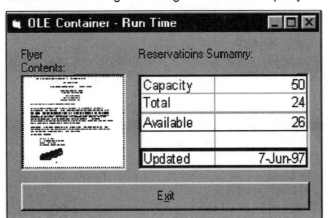

SourceItem property
specifies that only
part of the spreadsheet
data is shown.

```
' Set up OLE container for WordPad and open it
oleWordPad.Class = "Wordpad.Document.1"
oleWordPad.CreateLink PATH & "wkshop1.doc"
oleWordPad.DoVerb vbOLEOpen

' Set up OLE container for Excel Viewer to show only
' Row 4, Column 4 to Row 8, Column 5 of spreadsheet
oleExcelViewer.Class = "Excel.Sheet.5"
'Link to specified data using Excel Viewer
' CreateLink syntax is object.CreateLink sourcedoc, sourceitem
oleExcelViewer.CreateLink PATH & "wkshop1.xls", "R4C4:R8C5"
End Sub
```

To set up the OLE container, we set the Class property using an assignment statement. To determine the Class name, we can use the Properties window Class selection to view the available names. However, we choose not to select it but instead assign it using code. To set up SourceDoc and SourceItem properties, we use the `CreateLink` method, which creates a linked object from the contents of a file. The first argument for SourceDoc is necessary. The second argument for SourceItem is optional. The SourceItem property specifies to what portion of data to link. If it is not used, the entire data file is linked. The syntax for setting SourceItem varies with the application. To find the syntax, refer to Automation documentation about the application. For an Excel spreadsheet, we can use the row-column format to specify a rectangular area to which to link. Example 11.3 illustrates the format, specifying the row (R) and column (C) number for both the upper left corner and the lower right corner.

You can further explore the use of the OLE container using Help and/or the Programmer's Guide. Note that the Visual Basic Installation CD-ROM also contains the Programmer's Guide for online access. This may also be available, depending on how your system is set up. Now we will move on to using objects without using the OLE container.

11.4   CREATE AN ACTIVEX CLIENT FOR AUTOMATION

To use another applications object with more control, we need to use Automation. With Automation, we use objects (ActiveX controls) to access data without using the OLE container. Automation is a standard used by applications to provide objects for use by other applications. With Automation, we can borrow the functionality of another application for use in our own application. For example, a programmer could use the processing capabilities of a spreadsheet program to perform calculations.

11.4.1   The Internet Explorer Automation Program

We will create a program to control the operation of the Internet Explorer web browser. This will be the ActiveX control that our client program will use. If you don't have a copy of Internet Explorer, you can download it from http://www.microsoft.com. Since it is free, other applications may include copies of it. This will eliminate the need to use older Internet technology to download a browser when you do not already have a browser!

This section is based on using Version 3.02 of Internet Explorer. The program could be used to provide a help system based on the Internet HTML file format. Figure 11.11 shows the program in operation using the HTML files available on the program disk. The program provides another mechanism for selecting links. In this case, the hyper links on the pages themselves are redundant. You could create your own set of HTML pages without hyper links and use the program as the *only* mechanism for selecting links. If pages did not include links (very unconventional), it could be a useful way to restrict convenient access to a website. Only "authorized" visitors with the Automation program could navigate the site. Visitors without the program would have to guess the URLs.

Note

It is not necessary to have a live Internet connection to use a web browser, which can also load files stored locally on disk.

Users can use the Microsoft Internet Explorer (written as 2 words) as a web browser. We (as programmers) can use this browser as an object by referring to its formal class name of `InternetExplorer` (written as 1 word). When visually building the form, we include a *Reference* to the Microsoft Internet Controls so we can view methods and properties of the `InternetExplorer` class using the Object Browser explained in Section 11.2.3. Note that we are now talking about two different browsers! One is the Internet Explorer *web browser*. We will control this browser in the program. The other is the Visual Basic *Object Browser*. We use this Visual Basic tool to view properties and methods exposed by the InternetExplorer (web browser) class. If you wish, refer back to Figures 11.5 and 11.6; we will initially show the entire code as Example 11.4. Then we will highlight parts of it to illustrate the use of Automation. As a problem-solving exercise in the Hands-On Exercises, we will make the Forward and Back buttons functional.

Figure 11.11
Internet Explorer
Automation Program

Select an item on the list to cause the web browser to display the associated page.

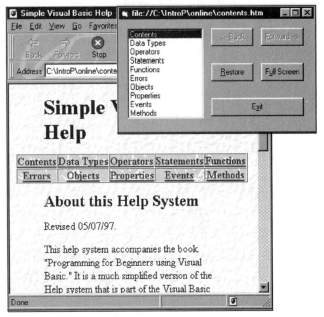

Example 11.4

```
Option Explicit

' Automation Demonstration
' Programs objects in the Microsoft Internet Explorer application
' Tested using MSIE v3.02
' Displays an extra window from which user can select pages
' from a list.  Also supports changing appearance of the browser
' Back and Forward through history not implemented
' Runtime error handling not implemented

Const PATH = "C:\IntroP\online\"     ' Modify if necessary

' Declare an object variable.  In order to declare it as
' type InternetExplorer, we must add a reference to
' Microsoft Internet Controls (SHDocVw.dll)
' Dim Browser As Object ' Try this instead of next line, see if ➥
load is slower?
Dim Browser As InternetExplorer

' If IE already running ...
' also may have runtime error on exit if previous IE running?

' Can exercise busy logic by quickly selecting second list item after
' clicking a first when first hasn't been cached yet

Sub BrowseTo(sFileName As String)
    ' Called by lstPages_Click
    ' It tells Internet Explorer to show the page
    ' indicated by the argument

    On Error Resume Next

    Browser.Navigate PATH & sFileName

    If Err.Number = 0 Then
        Browser.Visible = True
        Caption = Browser.LocationURL
        SetFocus     ' Set focus to Form to keep it on top
    End If
End Sub


Private Sub cmdExit_Click()

    Browser.Quit
    End
End Sub

Private Sub cmdFullScreen_Click()
    ' Full screen Explorer with no Toolbar, menu, or status bar
    Browser.FullScreen = True
    Browser.Toolbar = 0
```

```
      Browser.MenuBar = 0
      Browser.StatusBar = 0
End Sub


Private Sub cmdRestore_Click()
    ' Restored size Explorer including Toolbar, menu, and status bar
    Browser.FullScreen = False
    Browser.Toolbar = 1
    Browser.MenuBar = 1
    Browser.StatusBar = 1
End Sub


Private Sub Form_Click()
    ' test but error occurs unless navigation occurred?
    If Browser.Visible Then MsgBox Browser.Type
End Sub


Private Sub Form_Load()

    ' Reference IE object and set it up
    Set Browser = CreateObject("InternetExplorer.Application")
    cmdRestore_Click ' Set default browser viewing window
    ' Set up List Box
    lstPages.AddItem "Contents", 0
    lstPages.AddItem "Data Types", 1
    lstPages.AddItem "Operators", 2
    lstPages.AddItem "Statements", 3
    lstPages.AddItem "Functions", 4
    lstPages.AddItem "Errors", 5
    lstPages.AddItem "Objects", 6
    1stPages.AddItem "Properties", 7
    lstPages.AddItem "Events", 8
    lstPages.AddItem "Methods", 9

    ' Initially disable these buttons because no history yet
    cmdForward.Enabled = False
    cmdBack.Enabled = False


End Sub


Private Sub Form_Unload(Cancel As Integer)
    Browser.Quit
    End

End Sub
Private Sub lstPages_Click()
    ' Tell Internet Explorer to show page selected by user
    ' in list box.  Uses the BrowseTo procedure to show
    ' the page.
```

```
            If Browser.Busy Then
                ' Exercise browser busy message only by quickly
                ' selecting two non-cached pages in succession
                MsgBox "Browser busy"
            Else    ' Select page
                With lstPages
                    Select Case .ListIndex
                        Case 0  ' Contents
                            BrowseTo "contents.htm"
                        Case 1  ' Data Types
                            BrowseTo "datatype.htm"
                        Case 2  ' Operators
                            BrowseTo "operator.htm"
                        Case 3  ' Statements
                            BrowseTo "statemen.htm"
                        Case 4  ' Functions
                            BrowseTo "function.htm"
                        Case 5  ' Errors
                            BrowseTo "errors.htm"
                        Case 6  ' Objects
                            BrowseTo "objects.htm"
                        Case 7  ' Properties
                            BrowseTo "propert.htm"
                        Case 8  ' Events
                            BrowseTo "events.htm"
                        Case 9  ' Methods
                            BrowseTo "methods.htm"
                        Case Else
                            MsgBox "Invalid selection"
                    End Select

                End With
            End If
End Sub
```

11.4.2   Declaring and Setting Objects

If using Automation coding, we need to declare an insance of the class using

Dim *NameOfObject* **As** *ClassName*

if we are using early binding. For late binding we can use

Dim *NameOfObject* **As Object**

Before we can use the object, we need to create it. To create an object based on an external class, we need to set an instance of its class as follows:

Set *NameOfObject* = **CreateObject**(*RequiredClassName*)

The `CreateObject` function creates an Automation object. For example, if we are using the Microsoft Internet Controls, we could use the following statements.

```
Dim MyBrowser As InternetExplorer
Set MyBrowser = CreateObject("InternetExplorer.Application")
```

In this case, the `Application` class is part of the `InternetExplorer` class.

In Chapter 3 we saw that it is necessary to declare variables using their data type. Similarly, it is necessary to declare objects using their class. In Example 11.4, we declared the browser object as follows:

```
Dim Browser As InternetExplorer
```

We name the object `Browser`. We declare its type as the Class name for the object. We can use the object browser (see Figures 11.5 and 11.6) to determine that the Class name is `InternetExplorer`. We could declare it as type Object if we wish, which makes the declaration more generic. Using a Class name for the declaration type causes early binding, which results in quicker creation of the object later when we set the object. Using the more generic term Object results in late binding. **Binding** is the process of exposing an object's interface so that it may be used.

To create an instance of the object, we need to use the `Set` statement. This is equivalent to placing a specific control on a form, such as `cmdExit` and so on. We use the `Set` statement in the `Form_Load` procedure:

```
Set Browser = CreateObject("InternetExplorer.Application")
```

The `Set` statement assigns an object reference to a variable or property. The `CreateObject` function is a library function that creates an Automation object (formerly an OLE Automation object). Every application that supports Automation provides at least one type of object that we can use for accessing other properties and the methods. In this case we use the Application property of the `InternetExplorer` object. With the object browser we can determine that the Application property of an `InternetExplorer` object is of data type `Object`. It returns the object used for Automation.

To further illustrate the use of the `Set` statement, we can try the code shown in Example 11.5. For the code to work, we can place a button at the center of the form and name it `cmdButton`. If you run the program, you will see that the button appears at the top left corner with the caption Button.

Example 11.5

```
Option Explicit

Private Sub Form_Load()

    Dim Button As CommandButton
    Set Button = cmdButton
    Button.Left = 0
    Button.Top = 0
    Button.Caption = "Button"

End Sub
```

11.4.3   Using the Properties and Methods

Let's return our attention to the Automation program of Example 11.4. Procedure `cmdFullScreen_Click` causes Internet Explorer to display a page at full size in a window that has only a border. We can do this by setting the FullScreen, Toolbar, MenuBar, and StatusBar properties as shown.

```
Private Sub cmdFullScreen_Click()
    ' Full screen Explorer with no Toolbar, menu, or status bar
    Browser.FullScreen = True
    Browser.Toolbar = 0
    Browser.MenuBar = 0
    Browser.StatusBar = 0
End Sub
```

Procedure cmdRestore_Click causes Internet Explorer to display a restored window including the Toolbar, menu bar, and status bar (at bottom) that we normally see when running Internet Explorer as a stand-alone application (see Figure 11.11). The following shows how we can restore the settings in code.

```
Private Sub cmdRestore_Click()
    ' Restored size Explorer including Toolbar, menu, and status bar
    Browser.FullScreen = False
    Browser.Toolbar = 1
    Browser.MenuBar = 1
    Browser.StatusBar = 1
End Sub
```

Procedure lstPages_Click is used to select a page to view. If the Internet Explorer browser happens to be busy loading another page when the user makes a selection, it will inform the user about the busy status and continue loading the earlier page. If it is not busy, it will call another procedure to do the work of loading the specified HTML document. Here we are using the Busy property of the InternetExplorer object to determine whether it is available to load a page:

```
Private Sub lstPages_Click()
    ' Tell Internet Explorer to show page selected by user
    ' in list box.  Uses the BrowseTo procedure to show
    ' the page
    If Browser.Busy Then
        ' Exercise browser busy message only by quickly selecting
        ' two non-cached pages in succession
        MsgBox "Browser busy"
    Else    ' Select page
        With lstPages
            Select Case .ListIndex
                Case 0  ' Contents
                    BrowseTo "contents.htm"
                Case 1  ' Data Types
                    BrowseTo "datatype.htm"
                Case 2  ' Operators
                    BrowseTo "operator.htm"
                Case 3  ' Statements
                    BrowseTo "statemen.htm"
                Case 4  ' Functions
                    BrowseTo "function.htm"
                Case 5  ' Errors
                    BrowseTo "errors.htm"
                Case 6  ' Objects
                    BrowseTo "objects.htm"
                Case 7  ' Properties
                    BrowseTo "propert.htm"
```

```
                Case 8  ' Events
                    BrowseTo "events.htm"
                Case 9  ' Methods
                    BrowseTo "methods.htm"
                Case Else
                    MsgBox "Invalid selection"
            End Select

        End With
    End If
End Sub
```

Procedure `BrowseTo` does the actual work of loading a page for viewing. The `Navigate` method tells Internet Explorer which page to load. In this case, it is a local file, but it could be a remote Internet address. Assuming no error, the procedure sets the Visible property of the browser to `True` and uses the LocationURL property to set the Caption of the form for our Visual Basic program. This tells the user what page is being viewed.

```
Sub BrowseTo(sFileName As String)
    ' Called by lstPages_Click
    ' It tells Internet Explorer to show the page
    ' indicated by the argument

    On Error Resume Next

    Browser.Navigate PATH & sFileName

    If Err.Number = 0 Then
        Browser.Visible = True
        Caption = Browser.LocationURL
        SetFocus    ' Set focus to Form to keep it on top
    End If
End Sub
```

When the user has finished using the program, the `Quit` method terminates execution of Internet Explorer.

```
Private Sub cmdExit_Click()
    Browser.Quit
    End
End Sub
```

This is quite amazing: We are using our own program to control the operation of another application—without touching the code of the other application.

11.5   THE WEB BROWSER CONTROL

Even more amazing is how simple it is to create a web browser. In the previous section we used the Object Browser to reference classes and methods, and used code to declare and set an instance of the `InternetExplorer` class. In Chapter 10 we added a custom control for multimedia. As an alternative, we can insert the Microsoft Internet Controls as a custom control. It is an ActiveX control that can be used in the project. Now a web browser control (WebBrowser class) is included as part of the Toolbox. We can view its properties in the Properties window, and we can use the web browser control to draw an outline on a form. Figure 11.12 shows a program using this control; the web page is now shown on the form instead of in a separate window. Example 11.6 shows the code. Note that it is similar to the code for Example 11.4. During design mode, the programmer drew the web browser control on the form and named it Browser.

Example 11.6

```
Option Explicit

' Web Browser Control Demonstration
' Uses the web browser control
' Tested using MSIE v3.02
' Displays a HTML page inside the form within
' area defined by the drawn web browser control
' User can select pages from a list
' Back and Forward through history not implemented
' Runtime error handling not implemented

Const PATH = "C:\IntroP\online\"    ' Modify if necessary

' Internet Explorer can be already running
' Can exercise busy logic by selecting a list item and
' then immediately selecting another
' (before the former item is cached)

Sub BrowseTo(sFileName As String)
    ' Called by lstPages_Click
    ' It tells Web Browser to show the page
    ' indicated by the argument
```

Figure 11.12
A Simple Web Browser

```
    On Error Resume Next

    Browser.Navigate PATH & sFileName

    If Err.Number = 0 Then
        Browser.Visible = True
        Caption = Browser.LocationURL
    End If
End Sub


Private Sub cmdExit_Click()
    End
End Sub


Private Sub Form_Click()
    ' test but error occurs unless navigation occurred?
    If Browser.Visible Then MsgBox Browser.Type
End Sub

Private Sub Form_Load()

    ' Set up List Box
    lstPages.AddItem "Contents", 0
    lstPages.AddItem "Data Types", 1
    lstPages.AddItem "Operators", 2
    lstPages.AddItem "Statements", 3
    lstPages.AddItem "Functions", 4
    lstPages.AddItem "Errors", 5
    lstPages.AddItem "Objects", 6
    lstPages.AddItem "Properties", 7
    lstPages.AddItem "Events", 8
    lstPages.AddItem "Methods", 9

    ' Initially disable these buttons because no history yet
    cmdForward.Enabled = False
    cmdBack.Enabled = False

End Sub

Private Sub lstPages_Click()
    ' Tell Internet Explorer to show page selected by user
    ' in list box.  Uses the BrowseTo procedure to show
    ' the page.
    If Browser.Busy Then
        ' Exercise browser busy message only by quickly
        ' selecting two non-cached pages in succession
        MsgBox "Browser busy"
    Else    ' Select page
        With lstPages
            Select Case .ListIndex
```

```
            Case 0  ' Contents
                BrowseTo "contents.htm"
            Case 1  ' Data Types
                BrowseTo "datatype.htm" .
            Case 2  ' Operators
                BrowseTo "operator.htm"
            Case 3  ' Statements
                BrowseTo "statemen.htm"
            Case 4  ' Functions
                BrowseTo "function.htm"
            Case 5  ' Errors
                BrowseTo "errors.htm"
            Case 6  ' Objects
                BrowseTo "objects.htm"
            Case 7  ' Properties
                BrowseTo "propert.htm"
            Case 8  ' Events
                BrowseTo "events.htm"
            Case 9  ' Methods
                BrowseTo "methods.htm"
            Case Else
                MsgBox "Invalid selection"
        End Select

    End With
  End If
End Sub
```

SUMMARY

With Object Linking and Embedding (OLE) (pronounced "oh-lay"), the programmer can create applications that contain components from various other applications. It is a Windows standard that is now a special case of ActiveX. A typical use of OLE is when a data file (document, graphics, etc.) created using one application contains data that was created using another application. When the user works with the data, the program automatically switches its user interface to handle the type of data. For example, a word processor may reveal graphical editing controls when the user is working with a drawing that is part of a document.

An *object* is a combination of code and data that can be treated as a unit. For applications that support OLE, the data file is an object because it also includes information required to access the code of the application that originally created the data. For example, a Paint drawing is an object since a WordPad document can include it and include the *functionality* of the Paint accessory to work with the drawing.

Objects can be *embedded* or *linked*. An embedded object is a new copy of the original data. It can be edited within a containing application without affecting the original data file. A linked object is a reference to the original data. Modifying the original data will cause the containing application to show the modification as well. Similarly, modifying the linked object will modify the original data.

Programmers want to take off-the-shelf software parts and connect them together to make a needed application. The idea is to be able to build a program just as a child can build structures using interlocking plastic blocks. The components used in this type of programming are objects, self-contained units of code and data.

In Windows, the Component Object Model (COM) describes how objects make their properties (data) and methods (code) available to other applications. These objects are known as *ActiveX* objects or *controls*. An ActiveX control is an object whose interface can be used by (exposed to) other applications and programming tools. An *interface* is the collection of properties and methods of an object. The part of the object interface that is public, or available for other applications to use, is called *exposed*.

> *Automation (formerly called OLE Automation) is a technology that allows software packages to expose some of their functionality to other applications.*

The Object Browser is a Visual Basic tool that permits us to view some information about properties and methods of ActiveX controls. One pane lists the classes; the other pane lists the properties and methods associated with the selected class. A class is a template for an object that describes its general characteristics. The characteristics are its properties, methods, and events. To use an object, we need to create an instance of its class. For example, we may use cmdExit as an instance of the CommandButton class.

The OLE Container Control is a quick way to incorporate the functionality already provided by other applications, provided that the application follows the OLE standard. We can use this control to contain data from another application by linking or embedding that data into our program.

An OLE container can only contain one object at a time. We can implement linking or embedding at design time or at runtime. Some of its key properties and methods are shown in Tables 11.6 and 11.7.

A program that uses ActiveX controls is an ActiveX client. The ActiveX controls permit the program to use the functionality of other applications that are ActiveX code components. ActiveX controls are quite amazing since they enable a programmer to do a lot with somebody else's code. Essentially there are two ways to use an ActiveX control:

- **Automation Coding.** Set a reference to the Class Library. Declare and set object instances using code. Set all properties using code or defaults.

- **Custom Control.** Add it as a custom control to the Toolbox. Draw an instance of the control on a form. Set applicable properties using the Properties window.

In both cases, we can write code for event procedures and use the methods provided by the ActiveX control. When using Automation Coding or Custom Controls, we can set properties and use methods.

Table 11.6
Key Properties of the OLE Container

Property	Description
Class	The object category of the object being contained.
OLEType	Integer code specifying whether the object can be embedded, linked, or both. See Table 11.5.
SizeMode	Integer code specifying how data image is displayed in the container. See Table 11.4.
SourceDoc	Specifies the file to use for the source of data.
SourceItem	For linked objects, specifies the portion of the data file to use. Default is all data.

Table 11.7
Key Methods of the OLE Container

Method	Description
Close	For embedded objects, terminates the connection to the application that provided the object.
CreateEmbed	Creates an embedded object.
CreateLink	Creates a linked object.
DoVerb	Executes an action (verb) on the object. See Table 11.3.
InsertObjDlg	Display dialog box to permit user to select object at runtime.
Paste	Copies data from the system Clipboard to an OLE container control.
PasteSpecialDlg	Displays the Paste Special dialog to permit pasting a linked or embedded object.

HANDS-ON EXERCISES

OVERVIEW

The activities will enable you to

- Use the OLE container control to view data from other programs.
- Add a library reference in order to use an ActiveX control.
- Use the Object Browser to determine the interface of an ActiveX control.
- Control another application using Automation.
- Use the functionality of another application through Automation.

To Get Started

1. Read the section "Read Me Before Attempting the Hands-On Exercises" if you have not already done so.
2. Run Windows.
3. Open the file CH11\EX11.TXT on your student disk and answer the questions. (The same questions are shown here so that you can still determine answers when you are not sitting in front of a computer.)
4. Run Visual Basic.

11.1   A QUICK LOOK AT OLE IN ACTION

Run WordPad, a Windows accessory. Open the file CH11\WKSHOP1.DOC. You will see a document describing a seminar. Scroll down the document until you see an image of a canoe. Click on **the image** to select it. You should see sizing handles, and the window will look something like Figure 11.1. This image is an embedded object.

Make sure that the image is selected. Select **Bitmap Image Object** from the Edit menu. Select **Edit** from this menu item. Your window should change to show edit controls for the image, and the screen should look something like Figure 11.2. An alternate way to activate these controls would be to double-click on the image. Click outside the image onto a text area in WordPad. The program will replace the image (Paint) edit controls with the original controls associated with WordPad. Select the **Edit** menu and note that Edit menu item Bitmap Image Object is no longer available. Save two copies of the file, one as **WKSHOP2E.DOC** and one as **WKSHOP2L.DOC**.

An Embedded Object

Run the Paintbrush accessory, create **a simple picture**, and name it **WKSHOP2E.BMP**. Save a second copy as **WKSHOP2L.BMP** and close the file.

Run WordPad and open the file WKSHOP2E.DOC. Click **a place in the document** to insert a picture. From the Insert menu, select **Object**. Select the **Create from File** option. Click **Browse** and select **the file** WKSHOP2E.BMP. Do not select Link, but do click **OK**. You should see your picture in the document. Resize **the picture**, save the file, and close the document file. With Paintbrush, open and modify **the file WKSHOP2E.BMP**. Save the file and close the file.

With WordPad, open the document WKSHOP2E.DOC. Note that the original picture remains. An embedded object is a copy of the original data. Close the file.

A Linked Object

With WordPad, open the file WKSHOP2L.DOC. Click **a place in the document** to insert a picture. From the Insert menu, select **Object**. Select the **Create from File** option. Click **Browse** and select the file WKSHOP2L.BMP. Select **Link** and click **OK**. You should see your picture in the document. Resize the picture, save the file, and close the document file.

With Paintbrush, open and modify **the file WKSHOP2L.BMP**. Save the file and close the file.

With WordPad, open the document WKSHOP2L.DOC. Note that it now shows the modified picture. Close the file. A linked object maintains a reference to the original source of data, so modifying the original data will cause the containing application to show the modification as well. Save the file.

11.2   COMPONENT WARE—A DREAM COME TRUE?

1. What is an object?

2. Give an example of a class and an example of an instance.

3. Describe for what the OLE container control can be used.

4. Describe the difference between an embedded and a linked object.

5. What is an ActiveX control?

6. What is the interface of an ActiveX control? Explain how it is used in Automation.

Using the Object Browser

To do this exercise, you will need Microsoft Internet Explorer, including the file SHDOCVW.DLL. This file should be in your Systems directory. If you don't have Internet Explorer, download a copy from http://www.microsoft.com and install it.

We will start by creating a project that you will use later in this exercise. Start **a new project**. Select **Save File/Form1 As** from the File menu. Save *file* FORM1 as **IEAUTO1** in directory CH11. Select **Save Project As** from the File menu. Save *project* PROJECT1 as **IEAUTO1** in directory CH11. Change the Name of the form to **frmIEAuto** and change the Caption to state **IE Automation**. Save the project.

Visual Basic 4

From the Tools menu, select **References**. From the list of references, select **Microsoft Internet Controls**. Check **it on**, and click **OK**. Click the **Object Browser** button on the Toolbar (or select it from the View menu). View the list of Libraries/Projects. Your screen should look something like the top window in Figure 11.5. Select **ShdocVw - Microsoft Internet Controls**. You should see something like the bottom window in Figure 11.5. Select **InternetExplorer** and click **various Properties and Procedures**. Note the summarized information at the bottom of the window.

Visual Basic 5

From the Project menu, select **References**. From the list of references, select **Microsoft Internet Controls**. Check **it on**, and click **OK**. Click the **Object Browser** button on the Toolbar (or select it from the View menu). Click on **the top box** to view the list of Libraries/Projects. Select **SHDocVw**. Select **InternetExplorer** and click **various Properties and Procedures**. You should see something like the bottom window in Figure 11.6. Note the summarized information at the bottom of the window.

After adding the library reference, save the project. Experiment with the Object Browser. Select other Classes in SHDocVw and view their members. Add another reference that is available on your system. View this library with the Object Browser. Note the classes. Note the properties and methods available for the classes.

7. State the name for another library that is available on your system. State one of its classes. List its methods and properties.

11.3   THE OLE CONTAINER CONTROL

If you have Excel, you may use it instead of the Excel Viewer. If you don't have either, download the Excel Viewer from http://www.microsoft.com/ and install it.

The Seminar Program

Start **a new project**. Select **Save File/Form1 As** from the File menu. Save *file* FORM1 as **CONTAIN1** in directory CH11. Select **Save Project As** from the File menu. Save *project* PROJECT1 as **CONTAIN1** in directory CH11. Change the Name of the form to **frm-Container**, and change the Caption to state **OLE Container Application**. Save the project.

Setting Up the OLE Container Controls

Next, you will add the OLE controls in a manner that will automatically create links to WordPad and Excel Viewer files. In other words, it will automatically set the Class, SourceDoc, and SourceItem properties. The OLE container control is easy to find because it states OLE. If you do not have it, you may have to add it as a custom control. To make sure that the links are created without problem, run WordPad and the Excel Viewer and open files WKSHOP1.DOC and WKSHOP1.XLS, respectively.

Refer to Figure 11.7. Draw **the OLE control** for the WordPad object (the Flyer Contents). An Insert Object dialog box will appear. Select **Link** (to check on the check box). Select the **Create from File** option and click the **Browse** button. Select the file **WKSHOP1.DOC** in the CH11 directory and click **Insert**. Name the OLE control **oleWordPad** and set its SizeMode property to **1-Stretch**.

Draw **the OLE control** for the Excel Viewer object (Reservations). An Insert Object dialog box will appear. Select **Link** (to check on the check box). Select the **Create from File** option and click the **Browse** button. Select the file **WKSHOP1.XLS** in the CH11 directory and click **Insert**. Name the OLE control **oleExcelViewer**, and set its SizeMode property to **1-Stretch**.

Note the settings of the Class properties for both controls. At this stage, you can close the WordPad and Excel Viewer applications. Save the project.

Setting Up the Rest of the Controls

Using Figure 11.7 and Table 11.1, add and set up the **rest of the controls**. Note that you should add **the frame controls** and then draw **the option button controls** on the frame. Save the project.

Setting Up the Second Form

Add a new form. Name it **frmTech** and save it as **TECH**. Use Figure 11.9 and Table 11.2 to add and set up **the controls for this form**. Again, remember to draw **the frames** first and then draw **the applicable controls** on the frame. Save the project.

Type the Code

Add **the code for form frmContainer** as shown in Example 11.1. Don't forget to change the definition for the constant PATH to match that for your system. Add **the code for the Form frmTech** as shown in Example 11.2. Save the project.

Run the Program

Run the program. Click on the **Flyer** and **Reservations** buttons and note that their corresponding applications launch. Note the difference when the Stretch and Clip options are selected. Click **Tech Only** to view the technical information.

Also try right-clicking (the *secondary* mouse button) inside the container controls to activate the menus. Stop the program. Run the WordPad and Excel Viewer applications to view the data, and then run the program. Is there a difference in performance? One thing you may notice is that the Flyer object remains linked (instead of becoming embedded).

Problem Solving: The Embedded Version of the Seminar Program

Create **a new seminar program** (project) and name it **CONTAIN2**. Add **OLE container controls** to use embedded objects for the Flyer and Reservations information. Run the program. Note the differences. One thing you should note is that the WordPad and Excel Viewer windows will show that different files are used. They will be named differently than the original data files. They will likely be named something obscure, such as **Pkg42e6**. These embedded files are handled by the Object Packager. The Object Packager is the part of Windows you can use to install or remove such components as additional accessories.

A Seminar Program Using Runtime Property Settings, Including SourceItem

Start **a new project**. Select **Save File/Form1 As** from the File menu. Save *file* FORM1 as **CONTAIN3** in directory CH11. Select **Save Project As** from the File menu. Save *project* PROJECT1 as **CONTAIN3** in directory CH11. Change the Name of the form to **frmContainer**, and change the Caption to state **OLE Container - Run Time**. Save the project.

Refer to Figure 11.10. Draw **the OLE controls on the form**, except click **Cancel** when the Insert Object dialog appears. Set the SizeMode property of the OLE controls to **1-Stretch**. Refer to Figure 11.10 and Example 11.3 to set up the rest of the controls. Save the project.

Enter **the code shown in Example 11.3**. Save the project. Run the program. Note that on startup the program automatically shows a WordPad window to show the flyer information. It also uses the SourceItem property to link to only a portion of the spreadsheet data. Note that OLE properties were set at runtime. If you wish, set breakpoints and single step parts of the program to investigate its operation in more detail.

11.4   CREATE AN ACTIVEX CLIENT FOR AUTOMATION

For this exercise, you will need Microsoft Internet Explorer Version 3.02 or higher. If you don't already have it, download it from the http://www.microsoft.com/ website and install it.

The Internet Explorer Automation Program

While investigating the Object Browser, we already started working on the project. Now open *project* IEAUTO1 in directory CH11. Using Figure 11.11 and Example 11.4 as a guide, set up **the form and its controls**. Save the project. Enter **the code shown in Example 11.4**. While entering the code, check out the properties and methods using the Object Browser. Make sure that you have added a reference to the Microsoft Internet Controls library (as indicated earlier in these exercises). Also, modify **the PATH constant** to correspond to where the Help system files are stored on your system. Typically they will be in a directory named ONLINE that is part of the program disk directories. Save the project.

Run the program. If Internet Explorer was already open and there is no Internet connection at the time you start the program, you may see a warning message about the Microsoft home site not being located. Click **OK**. This is the usual Internet Explorer message that appears when there is no Internet connection. At this stage, select **an item** from the list. If you have not previously run the Explorer, you may have to wait some time for it to run. The browser should show the corresponding page. Select **a page you have not previously selected** and then quickly select another. If you are fast enough, you will see the Browser busy message. The reason for using a file you have not previously loaded is that a previously viewed file is cached by the web browser. A cached file is loaded very quickly, so you will not be able to interrupt the load.[1]

---

[1] *A cache is a special area in memory for storing external data for quick access. Instead of fetching the data from a physical place (such as disk or remote website), the computer can quickly load an image of the data from the cache. During a session, web browsers typically cache pages into local memory. This is why accessing a previously viewed page is usually quicker than loading a new page.*

Try the **Restore** and **Full Screen** buttons. When the browser is shown using full screen, note that there is no status bar, menu bar, or Toolbar. You may need to use the ALT+TAB key combination to switch to another task, since mouse controls for task switching may not be available. To use the ALT+TAB combination, hold down the ALT key and toggle TAB to select from the list of running tasks. Stop when you reach the task you want. For example, when you reach the Visual Basic program, stop toggling. Use the Visual Basic program to restore the window size by clicking the **Restore** button.

The Server Busy Message

Let's say you started the program and you selected the first page from the list. While it is busy loading Internet Explorer, you might try a command button. You may see the Server Busy message. Windows is telling you that the Automation process was still working when you tried to tell the ActiveX Code Components (formerly OLE server) to do something else. In most cases, you can simply select the default to permit the server (in this case, Internet Explorer) to continue with what it was doing.

11.5   THE WEB BROWSER CONTROL

Start **a new project**. Select **Save File/Form1 As** from the File menu. Save *file* FORM1 as **BROWSE1** in directory CH11. Select **Save Project As** from the File menu. Save *project* PROJECT1 as **BROWSE1** in directory CH11. Change the Name of the form to **frmBrowser**, and change the Caption to state **Browser**. Save the project.

Add a Custom Control

Add the Microsoft Internet Controls as a custom control.

Visual Basic 4

Note that you select **Custom Controls** instead of References to select the Microsoft Internet Controls. You should see a new button appear on the Toolbox. The control (class) will be called WebBrowser.

Visual Basic 5

Note that you select **Components** instead of References to select Microsoft Internet Controls. You should see a new button appear on the Toolbox. The control (class) will be called WebBrowser.

ADD CONTROLS AND THE CODE

Use Figure 11.12 and Example 11.6 as a guide to add the controls and code. Note that the WebBrowser control is named Browser. Run the program and select **pages from the list**. You should see the HTML page displayed within the WebBrowser control on the form. Stop the program to modify the size of the Form and WebBrowser control if you wish. Run the program again.

ADDITIONAL PROBLEM SOLVING

Problem 1

Modify program IEAUTO1 to implement the Forward and Back buttons. It is not necessary to handle situations when the user uses the Forward and Back buttons on the Explorer Toolbar.

Hint   Run the Internet Explorer by itself and view several pages. Note how its Forward and Back buttons operate. Then work on the program. With the Object Browser, note that there are methods for moving forward and back.

Problem 2

Modify the solution for Problem 1 to include error trapping. The error trapping code can display an error message and shut down the program.

CHAPTER 12

Database Programming

In this chapter we build a front-end program to a database engine so that the user can easily find, retrieve, and modify data records.

Imagine running a business (or maybe you already do). There are file folders, binders, filing cabinets, and shelves containing product information, marketing advertisements, correspondence, invoices for bills that need to be paid, customer billings, regulations, and other information. A program that can organize and track this information would be really useful.

After completing this chapter, you should be able to

- Describe the structure of a database and its application to the operation of an organization.

- Explain the different options for accessing data using the Jet database engine (used by Visual Basic).

- Create programs that use the data control and data-bound text box controls to navigate records in a database.

- Create programs that use Structured Query Language (SQL) to retrieve and display only the data that meets the specified criteria.

- Create programs that use other data-aware controls such as the database grid (DBGrid) control.

- Create programs that use data access objects (DAOs) to navigate and modify records in a database.

- Create programs that can access tables from non-Jet databases (possibly from remote database servers).

In This Chapter

Cougar Canoe needs to keep track of their customer, order, and product data in a front-end program and database. An employee or representative uses the front-end program to find a customer. The program shows the information necessary to contact the customer and shows information about the orders placed by the customer. The information about customers and orders is stored separately, yet the program links them together. It shows only the order data that matches the selected customer. Similarly, the program links the product information to the selected order. Figure 12.1 shows a prototype of the program.

12.1   THE WHY AND HOW OF DATABASES

*A **database** is a set of organized data related to a topic or organizational purpose.*

12.1.1   Overview

Mia is looking for accommodations in a new city. She checks out information on the World Wide Web (or a kiosk). One of the sites has a form to fill in. She types in such information as the following:

City Region
Shared (number of people)
Number of Bedrooms
Smoking or Nonsmoking
Basement, House, Low Rise, High Rise
Furnished or Not Furnished
And other ....

After sending her requirements, the system replies and sends her a list of all accommodations that satisfy her requirements. What has happened behind the scenes? Mia made a **query** to the database. In other words, she asked for information based on some **criteria.** The database, in this case, is a collection of information about all available accommodations in the city. The software (database engine) searches all of the accommodations in the database that satisfy the criteria. It returns a subset of the database for viewing. Later, when Mia starts her career representing Cougar Canoe, she will access the database to find information about people who have purchased canoes in the area.

It turns out that Visual Basic is a useful tool for creating ***front-end*** programs for a database. Figure 12.1 shows a program that displays information about customers. The type of information displayed resembles that handled by the Customer Information programs in Chapters 8 and 9, but there is a key difference. We do not get involved with the details of handling the file structure where the data is stored. Instead, a ***database engine*** does that work for us.

A front-end program provides user-friendly access to the database by using a database engine. A database engine, the software that handles the data in the database, retrieves and stores the data as required.

Figure 12.1
A Database Front End

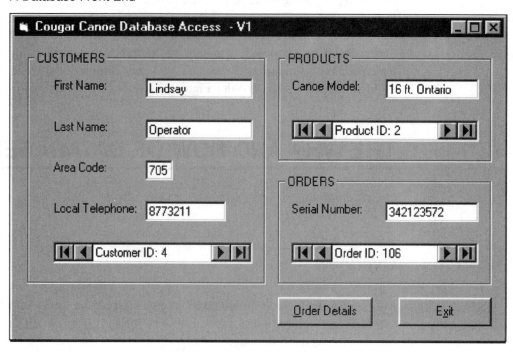

In Version 1, the PRODUCTS and ORDERS do not match
the CUSTOMERS. In subsequent versions, they will match.

Note that the database engine does the grunt work for storing data in the correct format, storing it in the correct place, searching data, making sure it is valid (performing validation checks), and so on. With Visual Basic we only need to access and use the database engine. There are a variety of options that we will discuss. In a nutshell, Visual Basic already contains a built-in database engine known as the *Jet Engine* (no kidding). The database itself is an external file stored in a standardized format. In this case, we will be working with files stored in the .MDB format that can be handled by the Microsoft Joint Engine Technology (Jet) Engine. This is the same format used by Microsoft Access, a program for creating databases (why is this not a surprise?). It is also possible to work with databases in some of the other standard formats, including those that are remote.

Visual Basic includes the Data Manager, a simplified tool for creating and modifying database files in the .MDB format.

12.1.2   The Cougar Canoe Database

Cougar Canoe needs to keep and maintain data that relates to customers, orders placed to purchase canoes, the product (the canoes themselves), shippers, representatives (including retailers), suppliers, inventory, accounts, and so on. Figure 12.2 shows a simplified model of the database. We simplified it in order to keep the programing examples simpler. You will probably notice that it is incomplete. Figure 12.2 illustrates the database COUGAR.MDB, which is included on the program disk. We will use it for the programming examples.

Figure 12.2
Simplified Model of the
Cougar Canoe Database

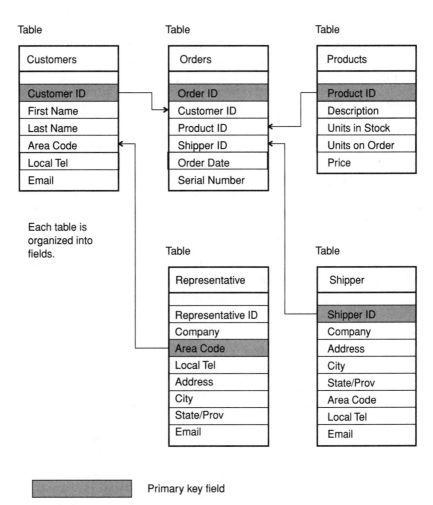

Each table is
organized into
fields.

Primary key field

Arrows show relationship between a table's key field and a matching field
in another table.

Generally note that a database is a collection of tables.[1] Each table is organized into records based on fixed-length fields. These are similar to random access files (see Figure 8.4). For information about records and fields, refer to Sections 8.4.3 and 8.6. Also note that there are relationships between the tables. A customer has some orders and each order has a product. Table 12.1 shows a portion of the Customers table in the database.

Notice that the table is organized into fields (rows) and records (columns). It turns out that field formats are similar to those used in the Customer program of Chapters 8 and 9 (see Figure 8.4).

Customer ID	Integer
First Name	String * 15 (Text)
Last Name	String * 15 (Text)
Area Code	Integer
Local Tel	Long
Email	String * 30 (Text)

---

[1]*Theoretically, it is possible to conceive of a database as a multidimensional structure instead of a collection of two-dimensional tables. In practice, a collection of tables is easier to manage.*

Table 12.1
A Portion of the Customer Table for the Cougar Canoe Database

Customer ID	1	2	3
First Name	Sappho	John	Mary
Last Name	Eresus	Barleycorn	February
Area Code	705	606	913
Local Tel	9329999	5329009	3456561
Email	seresus@cybernation.on.ca	NA	mfebrua@kansas.community.net

*A **field** is a category of information stored in a database. It is an element of a database table that categorizes (defines the format and type of) specific information, such as a last name. In Figure 12.2 and Table 12.1, a field corresponds to a row in a table. Note that Figures 8.4 and 9.6 to 9.9 show fields as columns.*

*A **record** is a set of related data about some item, person, or event. A table consists of records. Each record is composed of a set of related fields. In Figure 12.2 and Table 12.1, a record corresponds to a column in a table. Note that Figures 8.4 and 9.6 to 9.9 show records as rows.*

Each table has at least one **key** field. A key field is a means to index the table, and key fields permit easier retrieval of specific records. For example, we could list customers in order of last name instead of by customer identification (ID) number. Each table also must have one **primary key** field. The primary key uniquely identifies a record in the table. For example, there could be several customers with the same last name. An Employees table could use a Social Security number as the primary key. A table can contain fields that are **foreign keys**, which are keys that refer to a primary key in another (a foreign) table. For example, the Customer ID field in the Orders table is a foreign key. It refers to associated records in the Customers table. There is only one Customer ID for each customer, but that customer may have multiple orders. The database engine uses an index to cross-reference keys. As records are added, updated, or deleted, the software (database engine) updates the index.

So far we have discussed permanent tables stored in the database files. We can also have temporary tables that are generated as a result of making queries. For example, we could ask for all of the customer names that are represented by a particular representative. We could ask for all shippers who sent a canoe with a serial number in a specified range. This information is extractible and is also known as a **query result**. The database returns a dynamically created set of records (a dynamic table of sorts) that is the result of the query. In Visual Basic any set of records (permanent table or otherwise) is known as a **Recordset**. The result of a query is known as a **dynaset-type Recordset**. As we can see, we will have to become familiar with the terminology.

A database also contains table relationships and validation criteria (if used). For example, the Orders table is related to the Customers, Products, and Shipper tables. Remember that there is only one customer per Customer ID, but there may be multiple orders for that customer. The relationship between the Orders table and the Customers table is a one-to-many. Each customer may have many orders, but for each order there is only one customer. An example of validation could be that the Description in the Products table must be one of the canoe models manufactured by Cougar Canoe. Now we can give a more detailed definition of a database.

> *Visual Basic Help defines a **database** as a set of data related to a particular topic or purpose. A database contains tables and can also contain queries and indexes as well as table relationships, table and field validation criteria, and linkages to external data sources.*

Review Problem

In Chapter 2 we described problem-solving steps. What should a programmer do to ensure that he or she will create a database that will be useful for Cougar Canoe?

Solution

Talk with Cougar Canoe. Interview employees, supervisors, and customers. Job-shadow employees at work. Be a customer or role-play as a customer. Read business policy documents and so on.

Review Problem

Based on your experience, list some items that you believe are missing from the Cougar Canoe database.

Solution

For example, there is no mailing address for the customers. There can be only one representative per area code region. There is no easy way to handle shippers and representatives in other countries. Not all countries have three-digit area codes, provinces, or states. You may find other missing items.

12.1.3   Data Access Options for Visual Basic

Many databases are based on the ***Indexed Sequential Access Method (ISAM)***. We can use either the data control and/or data access objects (DAOs). We will show how to use both of them. There are other access options that involve other objects, application programming interfaces (APIs), and libraries that we will not cover. Figure 12.3 illustrates an overview of the use of both the data control and data access objects.

Essentially, we create a program (the front end) that uses data controls and/or data access objects. Both of these use the Microsoft Jet database engine to access databases. With the Jet databases engine, we can access three categories of databases:

Jet Databases: These are one type of ISAM database that can be created and manipulated *directly* by the Jet engine. Visual Basic and Microsoft Access (a database management tool) use the Jet engine.

Other Indexed Sequential Access Method (ISAM) Databases: These are databases created by other popular database tools such as dBase, Microsoft Visual FoxPro, and Paradox. We can specify this type of access when using Visual Basic.

Figure 12.3
Overview of Data Access
Using Visual Basic

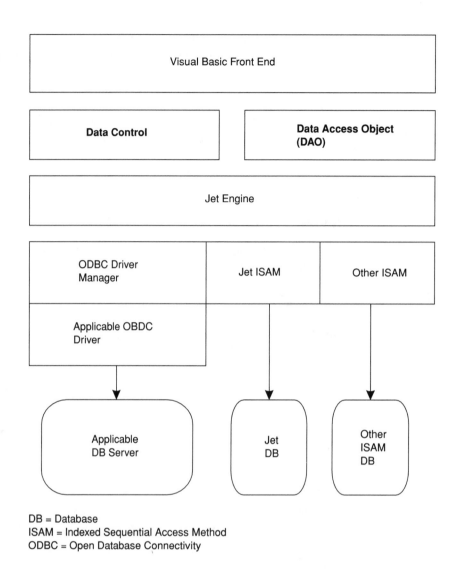

DB = Database
ISAM = Indexed Sequential Access Method
ODBC = Open Database Connectivity

Open Database Connectivity (ODBC)-Compatible Databases: Some databases are run on a remote computer known as a *database server*. Sometimes these are known as *client/server databases*. A front-end program run on another computer (the client) can access the remote database. This is useful for large organizations in which a common source of data needs to be accessed from remote locations on a network. Many database servers conform to a standard for remote access known as ODBC. These include the Microsoft SQL Server and the Oracle Database Server.

12.2   THE DATA CONTROL

Figure 12.1 shows the operation of a program that uses three data controls. Each data control accesses a corresponding table in the database. The controls appear with four buttons, as shown in Figure 12.4. This is a prototype for a front-end program that will be used by Cougar Canoe. The prototype serves as an introduction to the data control.

The data control permits us to access data using the Jet engine without writing code unless we want to use queries. There are two fundamental steps to using the data control:

1. For each table to access, add a data control to the form and set applicable properties to specify the database and table.

2. For each field to display to the user, add a data-bound control and set applicable properties to *bind* it to the data control.

Figure 12.4 shows the settings for the data control and associated *data-bound* text boxes for Customer information accessed by the program shown in Figure 12.1.

Let's examine the design of the CUSTOMERS portion of the program (see frame CUSTOMERS in Figure 12.1). We place a data control in frame fraCustomers (Caption CUSTOMERS) and name the data control as datCustomers. We then set some properties that are significant for data access.

The DatabaseName property determines to which database the control will connect. In this case we set the property to the path and filename for COUGAR.MDB. We set the RecordSet property to the (set of) records we wish to access. In this case, it is the Customers table. Since this table is named Customers, we set the property to Customers. We leave the RecordSetType property at its default value. Briefly, this property determines how the table data is accessed behind the scenes. We will elaborate later in the chapter.

Figure 12.4
Use of the Data Control

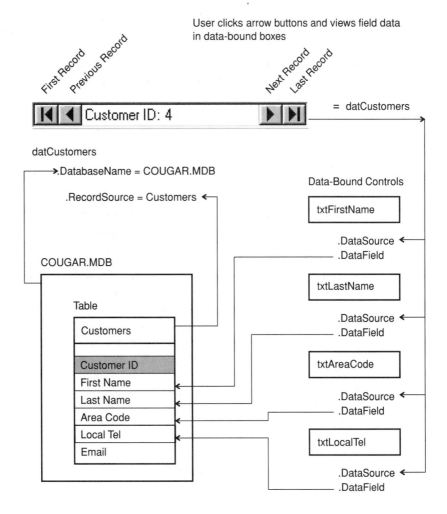

Data-Bound Controls

We cannot use the data control by itself to display the data. Instead, we need to use other controls that are capable of being **bound** to the data control. It is possible to bind several of the standard Visual Basic controls to a data control (or data access object). **To bind** means to specify the source of data for the control to another control or object. In this case we bind ordinary text box controls. You may or may not have noticed that a text box control can have a DataSource and DataField property; now we will use them. To bind, we will set the DataSource property to the name of the data control being used. This is `datCustomers`, a text box in the frame CUSTOMERS. Now the data control in effect controls the text boxes. To specify which field will be used as a source of the data, we set the DataField property. For example, we will set `txtFirstName.DataField` to `First Name`, the name of the field in the `Customers` table. Note that we must initially set up the data control, then the DataSource property, and then the DataField property, in that order.

The Database Access Program, Version 1

When the user runs the program, he or she clicks the arrow buttons on the data control. This causes the data control to access the applicable record in the table. Since the text boxes are data bound to the control (as specified by the DataSource property), they receive the associated field data as specified by the DataField property. We can think of the data control as something that grabs a table record and passes the field data to the associated (bound) text boxes. Table 12.2 shows the property settings that are related to data control.

In Table 12.2, note that all data access controls use the same database. The controls contained by a frame refer to the same set of records (a table in the database). The text boxes contained by a frame are bound to the data control contained by the frame. (For review, refer to Figures 12.1, 12.2, and 12.4, as well as Table 12.2, to see how the controls access the data in the database.) There is a lot of work involved in setting up data access, but it is worth the effort. The corresponding work to create the code is significantly minimized. Example 12.1 shows the code.

Example 12.1

```
Option Explicit

' Version 1 of Data Control Demonstration
' Display some fields from the Customers, Products,
' and Orders tables of the 'Cougar' database
' In Version 1, we view records from each table
' independently of the other tables
' That is, a record from the Orders or Products
' table does not necessarily correspond to the
' record in the Customers table

' Three hidden text boxes used to update Caption of Data control
' txtCustomerID, txtProductID and txtOrderID

Private Sub cmdExit_Click()
    End
End Sub

Private Sub cmdOrderDetails_Click()
    MsgBox "Not implemented"
End Sub
```

Table 12.2
Property Settings for Version 1 of the Cougar Canoe Database Access Program

Object Class	Property	Setting
Frame	Name	fraCustomers
DataControl	Name DatabaseName[a] RecordSource	datCustomers C:\IntroP\CODE\Cougar1.mdb Customers
TextBox	Name DataSource DataField	txtFirstName datCustomers First Name
TextBox	Name DataSource DataField	txtLastName datCustomers Last Name
TextBox	Name DataSource DataField	txt AreaCode datCustomers Area Code
TextBox	Name DataSource DataField	txtAreaCode datCustomers Area Code
TextBox	Name DataSource DataField	txtLocalTel datCustomers Local Tel
TextBox	Name (for hidden text box) DataSource DataField Visible	txtCustomerID datCustomers Customer ID False
DataControl	Name DatabaseName[a] RecordSource	datProducts C:\IntroP\CODE\Cougar1.mdb Products
TextBox	Name DataSource DataField	txtCanoeModel datProducts Description
TextBox	Name DataSource DataField Visible	txtProductID datProducts Product ID False
Frame	Name	fraOrders
DataControl	Name DatabaseName[a] RecordSource	datOrders C:\IntroP\CODE\Cougar1.mdb Orders
TextBox	Name DataSource DataField	txtSerialNum datOrders Serial Number
TextBox	DataSource DataField Visible	datOrders Order ID False

[a]File path may vary, depending on setup. Files are included on the program disk.

```
Private Sub datCustomers_Reposition()
    datCustomers.Caption = "Customer ID: " & txtCustomerID.Text
End Sub

Private Sub datOrders_Reposition()
    datOrders.Caption = "Order ID: " & txtOrderID.Text
End Sub

Private Sub datProducts_Reposition()
    datProducts.Caption = "Product ID: " & txtProductID.Text
End Sub
```

The user clicks an arrow on a data control to execute its corresponding Reposition event procedure. This procedure updates the caption of the data control. Note that the associated ID text box is data bound to the ID field of the corresponding table in the database.

The Reposition Event

A key feature in the code is the use of the *reposition event*. It occurs whenever the user clicks one of the arrow buttons on the data control. Let's look at the event in more detail. The record that is currently being viewed is known as the *current record*. For example (see Figure 12.1), records Customer ID 4, Product ID 2, and Order ID 106 are the current records for tables (Recordset objects) Customers, Products, and Orders, respectively. The event occurs *after* a record becomes the current record. Loading the form also causes the event because the first record in the Recordset object becomes the current record.

> *Note that in Visual Basic a table is a* ***Recordset*** *object, meaning an object that is a set of records. Later we will see how we can create sets of records based on portions of tables.*

Validate Event and Some Methods

The data control can also receive the Validate event. It occurs before a record becomes the current record. Table 12.3 summarizes some methods.

Briefly, a *copy buffer* is a temporary area of memory used as a scratchpad for modifying or adding records. Note that modifications or additions are not committed

Table 12.3
Method Summary for Data Control

Method	Description
AddNew	Creates a new record for a Recordset object.
Edit	Copies the current record from a Recordset object to the copy buffer for subsequent editing.
Update	Saves the contents of the copy buffer to a specified Recordset object.
Delete	Deletes the current record in an open Recordset object.
Seek	Locates a record that satisfies a specified criteria and makes that record the current record.

until the program executes the `Update` method. We will examine some of these methods later. Since a user might modify data when viewing a record, an event procedure for the Validate event might use the `Update` method to ensure that the changes are committed.

12.3   STRUCTURED QUERY LANGUAGE (SQL)

12.3.1   What Is SQL?

The next version of the Cougar Canoe program should show only the Order records associated with the selected customer record (current record in the Customers table). Also, it should show only the Product record associated with that Order. For example (see Figure 12.1), if the user is looking at customer 4, the user wants to see only the orders that were issued for customer 4, not all of them. Similarly, the user only wants to see information about the canoe for the order being viewed, not all canoes. To do this, we need to set criteria.

- Specify records from the Orders table based on the selected customer

- Specify a record from the Products table based on the Orders table (in turn based on the selected Customer).

In Visual Basic terminology, we can restate (refine) the criteria as:

- Set Orders Recordset object based on the current record in the Customers Recordset.

- Set Products Recordset object based on the current record in the Orders Recordset.

This may sound simple enough, but how do we word this in a way that Visual Basic understands? Actually, we don't! Remember that we are only using the program as a front end; the Jet database engine does the work, so we need to word the criteria in terms that Jet will understand. We set criteria by using the Structured Query Language (SQL), which the Jet database engine understands.

SQL, pronounced "sequel," is an industry-standard database language. Although it is a standard defined by the American National Standards Organization (ANSI), there are dialects that depend on the database being used. These dialects won't concern us here because we will only cover a small subset to illustrate SQL's use. However, the structure and functionality remain the same, so dialect differences can be worked out. SQL works with a relational model of a database, a collection of random access files related to one another through the use of common fields. In order to retrieve information based on relationships, we need to pose questions stating criteria; these questions are known as *queries*. For example, we want to see Order records that are *related* to a specific Customer record. As you may guess from SQL's full name—Structured Query Language—it is a formal means for making queries to get related information.

12.3.2   Stating a Query

*A **query** is a formal instruction to the database engine to tell it to return a set of records based on a specified criteria. We use SQL syntax to make up the query.*

So, how do we find Order records that are related to a specific Customer record? Refer to the Cougar database model shown in Figure 12.2. Note that the Orders table has a Customer ID field that relates to the Customer ID field in the Customers table. A customer (particularly, a retailer or resort operator) may purchase several canoes. Hence there may be several Order records with the same Customer ID. By using stepwise refinement, we could make up a pseudocode statement as follows:

```
Select records From Orders table
    Where Customer ID field = Customer ID of selected Customer ➡
    record
```

We can refine this further since we want to see only the serial number and ID fields:

```
Select Order ID and Serial Number from Orders table
    Where Customer ID = Customer ID of selected Customer record
```

This is still pseudocode. Let's look at an actual SQL statement to see the order information for customer 4. This is know as the *Select Query* or *SELECT statement*.

```
SELECT [Order ID], [Serial Number] FROM Orders WHERE [Customer ➡
ID] = 4
```

The syntax uses keywords such as SELECT, FROM, and WHERE. Square brackets [ ] enclose field names. Let's look at the keywords.

The SELECT statement instructs the database engine to return information from the database as a set of records. It stores the records in a new Recordset object. We can specify a *fieldlist* by enclosing field names in square brackets, and separate them using commas. To specify all fields in a record, we use the asterisk shortcut. For example, to select all fields in the Shipper table, we can use

```
SELECT * FROM Shipper
```

The FROM *clause* specifies the tables or queries that contain the fields listed in the SELECT statement. A SELECT statement must contain a FROM clause. The general (and simplified) syntax is

SELECT *fieldlist* **FROM** *tableexpression*

A *fieldlist* shows field names in square brackets separated by commas.
A *tableexpression* identifies one or more tables from which data is retrieved. (To use more tables, we need to perform *join* operations, which we will not go into in this book.)

The WHERE clause is optional. When used, it follows the FROM clause. It specifies the criteria for selecting records identified in the FROM clause. The database engine selects the records that meet the conditions listed in the WHERE clause. If the FROM clause is not used, the database engine returns all records. In our example, the equals sign (=) indicates an equality relationship, but other relationships are possible. For example, to find complete records for orders placed during the month of February 1997, we could use

```
SELECT * FROM Orders WHERE [Order Date] Between #2/1/97# ➡
AND #2/28/97#
```

Other criteria are possible. For example, other clauses such as GROUP, HAVING, and ORDER BY are possible. For more information, refer to Help topic SQL Queries and Chapter 6 in the Professional Features manual, *Writing SQL Queries*. This is getting complex for a typical user who is not a database expert. In fact, it can get much more complex when we want to find information such as "all customers who purchased Ontario canoes in the West Coast regions during the year 1996." The typical employee who needs to find this information shouldn't have to be a SQL expert and compose the statement. A programmer can create a front-end program that will make it easy for a user to find this type of information. The employee can select models, dates, and regions from list boxes and options, and/or can type in text boxes and then click a button. The program composes the SQL statement based on the employee selections. It then submits the query and returns the result for the employee to view.

Problem Solving

Compose a SQL statement to show the Product ID and Description for the Ontario and Erie models only. Use Table 6.1 to assign Product IDs ordered from left to right, top to bottom. For example, a 16-ft. Erie would have a Product ID of 5.

Solution

```
SELECT [Product ID], [Description] FROM Products WHERE [Product ➥
ID] Between 1 AND 6
```

12.3.3   The Database Access Program, Version 2

We can use a SQL statement (created as a string) to set the RecordSource property of a data control. This means that instead of a table, the Recordset object is the result of a query. When the user selects a customer, the program should show only the related Orders and Product information. The relationship is that the selected Product is related to Order. Selections of Orders is related to selected Customer. Hence:

Procedure datOrders_Reposition should assign the RecordSource for datProducts
Procedure datCustomers_Reposition should assign the RecordSource for datOrders

Refer to Figure 12.2: Field Product ID relates Products to Orders. The program will show the Product ID and Description fields. Procedure datOrders_Reposition could execute a SQL statement that looks like this:

```
SELECT [Product ID], [Description] FROM Products
    WHERE [Product ID] = |Product ID of Orders|
```

This syntax isn't quite correct. How do we specify |Product ID of Orders|? Recall that Version 1 of the program used hidden text boxes bound to the data controls. We can now use these text boxes. For instance, set the DataSource property of txtProductID to datOrders instead of datProducts, since both the Orders and Products tables use a related Product ID field. Hence we can obtain the Product ID of Orders by using the Text property of text box txtProductID. It happens to be invisible, so the user does not see it.

Similarly, field Customer ID relates Orders to Customers. The user only needs to see the Order ID and Serial Number. However, since we also need the Product ID for viewing Product information, the SQL statement for procedure datCustomers_Reposition would look like the following:

```
SELECT [Order ID], [Serial Number], [Product ID] FROM Orders
    WHERE [Customer ID] = |Customer ID of Customers|
```

Again, this is not the final syntax. To obtain the |Customer ID of Customers|, we can use the Text property of text box txtCustomerID, the DataSource property of which is datCustomers. Example 12.2 shows the code for Version 2.

Example 12.2

```
Option Explicit

' Version 2 of Data Control Demonstration

' Hidden and data-bound text boxes used to update
' caption of Data controls
' In Version 2, only show Order and Product
' information associated with selected Customer
' Demonstrates use of SQL queries

Private Sub cmdExit_Click()
    End
End Sub

Private Sub cmdOrderDetails_Click()
    MsgBox "Not Implemented"
End Sub

Private Sub datCustomers_Reposition()
    Dim sSQL As String
    datCustomers.Caption = "Customer ID: " & txtCustomerID.Text
    ' Retrieve Orders associated with Customer
    sSQL = "SELECT [Order ID], [Serial Number], [Product ID] ➥
    FROM Orders "
    sSQL = sSQL & "WHERE [Customer ID] = " & txtCustomerID.Text
    datOrders.RecordSource = sSQL
    datOrders.Refresh
End Sub

Private Sub datOrders_Reposition()
    Dim sSQL As String
    datOrders.Caption = "Order ID: " & txtOrderID.Text
    ' Retrieve Product associated with Order
    ' Note txtProductID.DataSource is datOrders, not datProducts
    sSQL = "SELECT [Product ID], [Description] FROM Products "
    sSQL = sSQL & "WHERE [Product ID] = " & txtProductID.Text
    datProducts.RecordSource = sSQL
    datProducts.Refresh
End Sub

Private Sub datProducts_Reposition()
    datProducts.Caption = "Product ID: " & txtProductID.Text
End Sub
```

Some key features to note are that the RecordSource property for datOrders and datProducts is assigned to a string that forms a SQL query. Again note the use of the hidden text boxes to complete the SQL query. We use the Refresh method to update the Data control because its RecordSource property has been modified.

12.4　OTHER DATA-AWARE CONTROLS

With the professional edition of Visual Basic, we can add data-aware controls for easier viewing of database information. These include the database list (DBList), database combo (DBCombo), and database grid (DBGrid) controls. In this chapter, we will illustrate the use of one of these controls, the database grid control. These controls permit the user to view more information in a convenient fashion without using separate text boxes. Version 3 of the Database Access program uses an additional form to show some Order details. Figure 12.5 shows the main form with an additional button that the user can click to view the details. Figure 12.6 shows a sample of the order details on the additional form. The user can use the scroll bar on the database grid control to view other fields as required. If there were more records, vertical scroll bars would also appear to permit viewing of other records.

Example 12.3 shows the code for the event procedure for command button `cmdOrderDetails`.

Example 12.3

```
Private Sub cmdOrderDetails_Click()
    ' Set the RecordSource property of the Data control on the
    ' Order Details form to an SQL statement that selects only the
    ' Order Details records for the current customer

    Dim sSQL As String
    sSQL = "Select * from [Orders] where " & _
```

Figure 12.5
The Main (Startup) Form for Version 3 of the Database Access Program

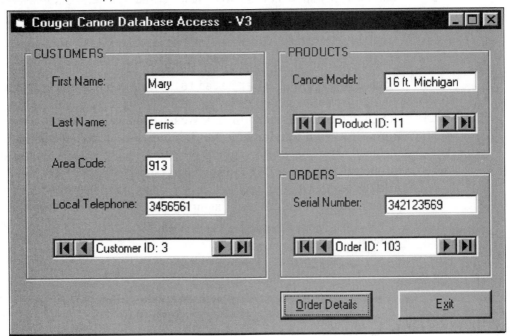

In Version 3, the user can click **Order Details** to view details
about the orders associated with the selected customer.

Figure 12.6
Order Details for the Selected Customer

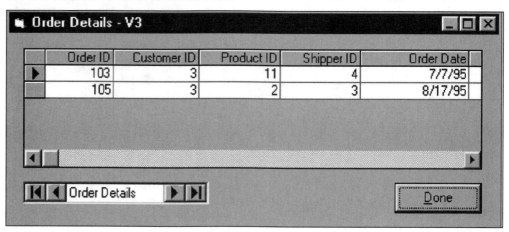

```
        "[Customer ID] = " & txtCustomerID.Text
    frmOrderDetails3.datOrderDetails.RecordSource = sSQL
    frmOrderDetails3.datOrderDetails.Refresh
    frmOrderDetails3.Show
End Sub
```

In the SQL query, the procedure selects all of the fields for the applicable Order records. The procedure also sets the RecordSource property of the data control (named `datOrderDetails`) that is on the details form (named `frmOrderDetails3`). Then it applies the `Refresh` method to update the data control because its RecordSource property has been modified. Finally, the procedure shows the form to the user. If we *want* to automatically show new details whenever the user selects a new customer, we can add the following statement at the end of procedure `datCustomers_Reposition`:

```
cmdOrderDetails_Click
```

In the design of form `frmOrderDetails3`, we have placed a data control and named it (here `datOrderDetails`). The RecordSource property of data control `datOrderDetails` has been left blank since the code will set the property based on a SQL query (see Example 12.3). We have then added the database grid control to the form. If it wasn't available in the Toolbox, we would have had to add it as a custom control. All we have to do with this control is place it and size it, and then set its name property (`dbgOrderDetails`) and set its DataSource property to a data control (`datOrderDetails`). We then added a command button (`cmdDone`, in this case) to remove the form from view. Example 12.4 shows the code for `frmOrderDetails3`. There isn't much code because the property settings handle the work of presenting data.

Example 12.4

```
Option Explicit
' The code for frmOrderDetails3
' Not much is there?
Private Sub cmdDone_Click()
    Me.Hide ' Remove form from view
End Sub
```

The DBGrid Control

This control displays a series of rows and columns representing the records and field from a Recordset object. In this case we used data control `datOrderDetails` to supply the Recordset object (a set of records based on the SQL query). The control automatically fills in header information about the field names. It automatically displays the number of required rows and provides scroll bars when the information does not fit in the display. It is also possible to manipulate the data in the control. (We won't go into more detail about this control. Refer to Help topic DBGrid Control for more information.)

12.5   USING DATA ACCESS OBJECTS (DAOS)

*A **data access object** (DAO) provides a programming interface to help simplify data access programming tasks. A DAO is an object defined by the Jet database engine. There are several object classes such as Database and Recordset that are used to organize and manipulate data by setting properties and applying methods.*

Recall that there are two fundamental ways to access data using the Jet database engine. Up to this point we have used the data control, which provides built-in access to a database and provides ready-made buttons to the user to permit the selection of records. While we can use the data control to quickly create a database front end, data access objects (DAOs) provide more flexibility and control over a database. For a review of how DAOs fit in with Visual Basic, refer back to Figure 12.3. It is possible to use both data controls and DAOs in the same program. This is in fact what we will do. We will also notice that more coding is required. With DAO we will modify the Database Access program so that a user can add, delete, and update records.

There are several types of data access objects. These include the Database and Recordset objects. We can use the object interface (methods and properties) to work with data in a database. The primary object we will use is the Recordset object. We can use it to view or change the data in a database. To use the data access object, it is necessary to set a reference to its library. With 32-bit versions of Visual Basic, this reference is DAO 3.0. For 16-bit versions, it is DAO 2.5. Normally this reference is set up automatically when Visual Basic is installed. However, we can explicitly set a reference to the library as we would with other Object libraries (as described in Chapter 11).

12.5.1   Navigating the Database Using DAO

In Version 4 of the Customer program, we replace the data control for the Customer records with two data access objects. Later, in Version 5, we will add some data editing capability to modify the Customer table. Version 4 also has an enhanced Order details form that shows product as a descriptive name (the canoe model). Figure 12.7 shows the main part of the program. Note that we now have to explicitly provide command buttons to permit the user to navigate through the records of the Customer table. Although there are buttons for editing the records, we will add code to implement this feature in Version 5.

Figure 12.7
Version 4 of the Database Access Program That Uses
Data Access Objects (DAO) and Data Controls

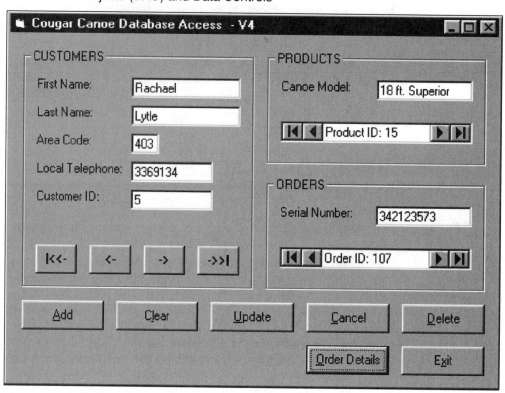

Data access objects are used to handle the records in the Customers table.

Example 12.5 shows part of the code. This is the portion that declares and sets up the data access objects. In this case we use objects of the Database and Recordset class. The code for procedure Display shows that we can no longer use data-bound text boxes but must instead explicitly set the Text properties in code.

Example 12.5

```
Option Explicit

' Version 4 of Data Control Demonstration
' Use data access objects (DAO) for Customer Table

' Use data-bound grid control to show details of
' orders based on selected customer

Const PATH = "C:\INTROP\CODE\"  ' Modify if necessary
' Declare the data access objects
Dim m_dbsCougar As Database, m_rstCustomers As Recordset

Private Sub Form_Load()
    ' Set the data access objects (create instances of them)
    Set m_dbsCougar = OpenDatabase(PATH & "COUGAR1.MDB")
    Set m_rstCustomers = m_dbsCougar.OpenRecordset("Customers", ➡
    dbOpenDynaset)
```

```
        Display ' Then display the fields for the first record
End Sub

Sub Display()
    ' Display the fields of the current record in the Customers
    ' table and update displays for Order and Product data

    ' Used for making query to match Orders and Products to ➡
    current Customer
    Dim sSQL As String

    ' Show Customer fields
    txtFirstName.Text = m_rstCustomers("First Name")
    txtLastName.Text = m_rstCustomers("Last Name")
    txtAreaCode.Text = m_rstCustomers("Area Code")
    txtLocalTel.Text = m_rstCustomers("Local Tel")
    txtCustomerID.Text = m_rstCustomers("Customer ID")

    ' Retrieve Orders associated with Customer
    sSQL = "SELECT [Order ID], [Serial Number], [Product ID] ➡
    FROM Orders "
    sSQL = sSQL & "WHERE [Customer ID] = " & txtCustomerID.Text
    datOrders.RecordSource = sSQL
    datOrders.Refresh

    ' Force data update on details form if it is visible
    If frmOrderDetails4.Visible = True Then
        frmOrderDetails4.cmdDone_Click  ' Note we made the ➡
        procedure Public
        cmdOrderDetails_Click
    End If
End Sub
```

In this segment of the program we declare the objects as follows:

```
Dim m_dbsCougar As Database, m_rstCustomers As Recordset
```

In the Form_Load procedure the program creates the actual objects. This is like setting the properties of a data control, as shown here:

```
Private Sub Form_Load()
    ' Set the data access objects (create instances of them)
    Set m_dbsCougar = OpenDatabase(PATH & "COUGAR1.MDB")
    Set m_rstCustomers = m_dbsCougar.OpenRecordset("Customers", ➡
    dbOpenDynaset)
    Display ' Then display the fields for the first record
End Sub
```

The OpenDatabase method opens a specified database and returns a reference to the Database object that represents it. The OpenRecordset method creates a new Recordset object. Didn't we mention that OpenDatabase is a method? Then why isn't it acting on an object? Actually, we have used a short form. It is acting on a default Workspace object.

Before the Form_Load procedure finishes execution, it calls Display, a general routine to display the Customer records and match Order and Product data to the currently selected Customer. To show a field, the program must set the Text property of a text box, as in the following statement:

```
txtFirstName.Text = m_rstCustomers("First Name")
```

This statement illustrates a syntax that we can use to access the named field in the Recordset object. Actually, each Recordset object contains a *collection* of Field objects. Field objects have Name, Type, Size, and Value properties, among others. This statement is a short form for the following statement:

```
txtFirstName.Text = m_rstCustomers.Fields("First Name").Value
```

This statement explicitly states that the Text is being assigned to the Value property of the "First Name" Field object, which is part of the m_rstCustomers Recordset object. The shortcut works because the Value property is the *default* property of the Field class. If no property is specified, the *default* property of an object is used. Each object may have only one default property. Hence the following statement would also work:

```
txtFirstName.Text = m_rstCustomers.Fields("First Name")
```

The Field collection is the default collection of a Recordset object, so we can use the following shortcut:

```
txtFirstName.Text = m_rstCustomers("First Name")
```

*A **collection** is a type of object that contains a set of related objects. For example, a Recordset object would contain a collection of Field objects known as a Field collection. A Form object contains a Controls collection. This is a set of objects the elements of which represent each control on a form.*

The second part of the Display procedure matches the Orders data control to retrieve only the Order records associated with the current Customer. Here we are still using a data control:

```
' Retrieve Orders associated with Customer
sSQL = "SELECT [Order ID], [Serial Number], [Product ID] FROM Orders "
sSQL = sSQL & "WHERE [Customer ID] = " & txtCustomerID.Text
datOrders.RecordSource = sSQL
datOrders.Refresh
```

The last part of the procedure handles updating the details form. The update is performed only if the form is already visible.

```
' Force data update on details form if it is visible
If frmOrderDetails4.Visible = True Then
    frmOrderDetails4.cmdDone_Click   ' Note we made the procedure ➡
    Public
    cmdOrderDetails_Click
End If
```

The code for cmdOrderDetails_Click is very similar to that for Version 3, as is shown in Example 12.6:

Example 12.6

```
Private Sub cmdCancel_Click()
    MsgBox "Not implemented"
```

```
End Sub

Private Sub cmdAdd_Click()
    MsgBox "Not implemented"
End Sub

Private Sub cmdPrevious_Click()
    m_rstCustomers.MovePrevious
    ' Do not move beyond first record
    If m_rstCustomers.BOF Then
        Beep
        m_rstCustomers.MoveFirst
    End If
    Display
End Sub

Private Sub cmdFirst_Click()
    ' Move to First record
    m_rstCustomers.MoveFirst
    Display
End Sub

Private Sub cmdClear_Click()
    MsgBox "Not implemented"
End Sub

Private Sub cmdDelete_Click()
    MsgBox "Not implemented"
End Sub

Private Sub cmdLast_Click()
    ' Move to Last record
    m_rstCustomers.MoveLast
    Display
End Sub

Private Sub cmdExit_Click()
    Unload frmOrderDetails4
    End
End Sub

Private Sub cmdNext_Click()
    m_rstCustomers.MoveNext
    ' Do not move beyond last record
    If m_rstCustomers.EOF Then
        Beep
        m_rstCustomers.MoveLast
    End If
    Display ' Show record to user
End Sub

Private Sub cmdOrderDetails_Click()
    'Set the RecordSource property of the Data control on the
    ' Order Details form to an SQL statement that selects only the
```

```
        Dim sSQL As String
        sSQL = "Select * from [Orders] where " & _
            "[Customer ID] = " & txtCustomerID.Text
        frmOrderDetails4.datOrderDetails.RecordSource = sSQL
        frmOrderDetails4.datOrderDetails.Refresh
        frmOrderDetails4.Show
End Sub

Private Sub cmdUpdate_Click()
        MsgBox "Not implemented"
End Sub

Private Sub datOrders_Reposition()
        Dim sSQL As String
        datOrders.Caption = "Order ID: " & txtOrderID.Text
        ' Retrieve Product associated with Order
        sSQL = "SELECT [Product ID], [Description] FROM Products "
        sSQL = sSQL & "WHERE [Product ID] = " & txtProductID.Text
        datProducts.RecordSource = sSQL
        datProducts.Refresh
End Sub

Private Sub datProducts_Reposition()
        datProducts.Caption = "Product ID: " & txtProductID.Text
End Sub
```

In particular, note the code for handling buttons cmdPrevious, cmdFirst, cmdLast, and cmdNext (the Captions of which are, respectively, <-, |<<-, ->>|, and ->). They use methods MovePrevious, MoveFirst, MoveLast, and MoveNext, respectively. These methods move to the previous, first, last, or next record in a specified Recordset object and make that record the current record. However, for the MovePrevious and MoveNext methods, it is necessary to trap attempts to move beyond the last or first record in the Recordset object. The BOF property of the Recordset object returns True if the current record position is before the first record; otherwise, it returns False. The EOF property returns True if the current record position is after the last record; otherwise, it returns False. Figure 12.8 shows the Order Details form.

Figure 12.8
Order Details for the Selected Customer for Version 4

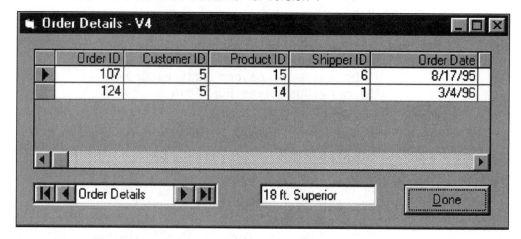

The form (named `frmOrderDetails4`) has an additional text box named `txtCanoeModel`. Its DataSource property is set to `datProducts`, a hidden data control placed on this form. The DataField property for txtCanoeModel is set to `Description`. The hidden data control is named `datProducts` with the following property settings:

datProducts

DatabaseName	`C:\IntroP\CODE\Cougar1.mdb`
RecordSource	`Products`
Visible	`False`

Note that the file and path may vary for different systems. There is an additional hidden text box named `txtProductID`. Its key properties are set as follows:

txtProductID

DataSource	`datOrderDetails`
DataField	[none, left blank]
Visible	`False`

Since we are showing the canoe model in the details form, we need to add code to handle this. We show this in Example 12.7. We use the two additional text boxes and the extra data control to do this. We use txtProduct to show the Product ID. Whenever we view a new record in the Recordset, `datOrderDetails_Reposition` calls `Display`. Procedure `Display` of this form uses a hidden data control to retrieve the Description of the product from the Products table. The procedure only does this if there is a Product ID. The text might be null in situations when new Customers are added. Since this program does not add Order records, there would be no Order, and hence no Product associated with any additional Customer.

Example 12.7

```
Option Explicit

' In Version 4, show canoe model as a descriptive name
' Hence we need access to Product records

Sub Display()
    Dim sSQL As String
    ' Update data display only if there is an associated order
    If txtProductID.Text <> "" Then
        ' Retrieve Product associated with Order
        sSQL = "SELECT [Product ID], [Description] FROM Products "
        sSQL = sSQL & "WHERE [Product ID] = " & txtProductID.Text
        datProducts.RecordSource = sSQL
        datProducts.Refresh
    End If
End Sub


Public Sub cmdDone_Click()
    ' Show that we can make procedure Public so it can be used ➡.
    by other form
    ' although it may be better to use frmOrderDetails.Hide in ➡
    other form
    Me.Hide
```

```
End Sub

Private Sub datOrderDetails_Reposition()
    Display
End Sub

Private Sub Form_Load()
    ' Set up Data Field during runtime since Data Source not
    ' defined at design time
    txtProductID.DataField = "Product ID"
End Sub
```

12.5.2   Modifying the Database Using DAO

In this program, the user can update, add, or delete Customer records. The main form looks identical to that shown in Figure 12.7 except that it states V5 instead of V4. The program uses the Save Details form as shown in Figure 12.8. To handle the fact that the user might add new records, we need to handle situations where there are no corresponding Order records. This not necessarily a bad thing; order information can be added later. To enter the field data, the user can type in the values, but the Customer ID field should be unique. For this reason, we should let the program generate this field. Example 12.8 shows the changes to the Form_Load and datOrders_Reposition procedures from Version 4.

Example 12.8

```
Private Sub Form_Load()
    ' Set the data access objects (create instances of them)
    txtCustomerID.Locked = True     ' Prevent user from ➡
    modifying
    Set m_dbsCougar = OpenDatabase(PATH & "COUGAR2.MDB")
    Set m_rstCustomers = m_dbsCougar.OpenRecordset("Customers", ➡
    dbOpenDynaset)
    Display ' Then display the fields for the first record
End Sub

Private Sub datOrders_Reposition()
    ' This procedure differs from that in earlier versions
    ' It is necessary to make other table data visible or
    ' invisible, depending if the current Customer record
    ' corresponds to a new record where no Order has been
    ' set up
    Dim sSQL As String
    If txtProductID.Text <> "" Then
        datOrders.Caption = "Order ID: " & txtOrderID.Text
        ' Retrieve Product associated with Order
        sSQL = "SELECT [Product ID], [Description] FROM ➡
        Products "
        sSQL = sSQL & "WHERE [Product ID] = " & ➡
        txtProductID.Text
        datProducts.RecordSource = sSQL
```

```
            datProducts.Refresh
            datOrders.Visible = True
            datProducts.Visible = True
            txtCanoeModel.Visible = True
            txtSerialNum.Visible = True
            cmdOrderDetails.Enabled = True
        Else    ' Situation when no Order exists
            datOrders.Visible = False
            datProducts.Visible = False
            txtCanoeModel.Visible = False
            txtSerialNum.Visible = False
            cmdOrderDetails.Enabled = False
        End If
End Sub
```

In the datOrders_Reposition procedure, we enable the capability to view Order and Product information only when there is a corresponding order (or more) for the customer. In the Form_Load, procedure the text box for Customer ID has been locked so the user cannot modify it. The next thing is to permit a user to modify a record whenever he or she clicks the Update button.

Example 12.9

```
Private Sub cmdUpdate_Click()
    If m_rstCustomers.EditMode = dbEditNone Then
        m_rstCustomers.Edit
    End If

        m_rstCustomers("First Name") = txtFirstName.Text
        m_rstCustomers("Last Name") = txtLastName.Text
        m_rstCustomers("Area Code") = txtAreaCode.Text
        m_rstCustomers("Local Tel") = txtLocalTel.Text
        m_rstCustomers("Customer ID") = txtCustomerID.Text
        m_rstCustomers.Update
    End Sub
```

In the code for the cmdUpdate_Click procedure, note that it sets the EditMode property. This property indicates where there is an edit operation in progress. There are three possibilities:

dbEditNone	No editing is occurring.
dbEditInProgress	The current record is in the copy buffer as a result of using the Edit method.
dbEditAdd	A new record is in the copy buffer as a result of using the AddNew method.

The database engine does not modify the records directly. Instead, it uses a copy buffer to hold a temporary copy of a modified (edited) or new record. The Update method saves the data from the copy buffer to the table. Either it replaces a record as a result of using the Edit method or it inserts a new record as a result of using the AddNew method. Figure 12.9 illustrates the operations.

The user modifies a record by typing changes in the text boxes and then clicking Update. Note that procedure cmdUpdate_Click applies the Edit method if it is not already being edited. This causes the database engine to write the record to the copy

Figure 12.9
Modifying or Adding
Records in a Table

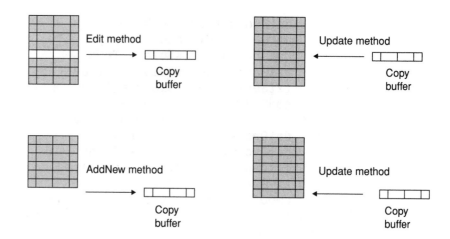

buffer. The assignment statements modify the fields in the copy buffer, not the actual record. Up to this point, it is still possible to undo the modifications since the data is not yet written to the actual database. When the Update method is used, the modifications are written to the database file. Once this has been done, the user has committed the change and there is no going back.

Example 12.10 shows the code for adding a record. Note that the user clicks Add, types in the new field data, and then clicks Update to commit the changes. It is also possible to click Cancel if the user changes her or his mind (more on that later).

Example 12.10

```
Private Sub cmdAdd_Click()
    Dim sEnd As String
    cmdLast_Click     ' Move to last record
    ' Preserve position of last record
    sEnd = CStr(CInt(txtCustomerID.Text) + 1)
    cmdClear_Click
    frmOrderDetails4.Hide
    ' Assign new ID
    txtCustomerID.Text = sEnd
    ' Force other data to be invisible since no
    ' Orders or Product information assigned to new customer - yet
    datOrders.Visible = False
    datProducts.Visible = False
    txtCanoeModel.Visible = False
    txtSerialNum.Visible = False
    cmdOrderDetails.Enabled = False
    m_rstCustomers.AddNew   ' Adds new record but not committed
            ' until user has updated it
End Sub
```

The procedure assigns a new Customer ID and forces the order and product information to disappear. Then it uses the AddNew method, which actually creates the "temporary" new record. Again, note that the record becomes part of the database when the Update method is used (by clicking the Update button).

It is possible to reverse a change in progress prior to clicking Update. The CancelUpdate method cancels any pending updates for the Recordset object. This is possible because the object has not yet been modified. The method clears the copy buffer. Example 12.11 shows the code for this operation.

Example 12.11

```
Private Sub cmdCancel_Click()
    ' Cancel a change made by the user
    If m_rstCustomers.EditMode = dbEditNone Then
        Exit Sub
    End If
    m_rstCustomers.CancelUpdate
    Display
End Sub
```

Example 12.12 shows the remaining code changes. In procedure cmd-Delete_Click, the Delete method removes the current record from the Recordset. It is up to the program to assign a new current record. We can use the MoveNext method for this. To handle the situation of deleting the last record, we use the MoveLast method to make the new last record the current record. The cmd-Clear_Click procedure provides a convenient means for the user to make all of the customer fields blank except for the Customer ID field.

Example 12.12

```
Private Sub cmdDelete_Click()
    m_rstCustomers.Delete
    m_rstCustomers.MoveNext
    If m_rstCustomers.EOF Then
        m_rstCustomers.MoveLast
    End If
    Display
End Sub

Private Sub cmdClear_Click()
    txtFirstName.Text = ""
    txtLastName.Text = ""
    txtAreaCode.Text = ""
    txtLocalTel.Text = ""
End Sub
```

There are other properties, methods, and events and other classes to complete the topic of data access objects (DAOs). In particular, we did not cover *transactions*. These are temporary changes that need to be explicitly committed in order to make a permanent modification to the database. Thus, if a transaction is initiated and several additions, modifications, and/or deletions have been made, it is possible to undo it (roll back the transaction) if the transaction has not been committed. Another feature of importance is to use data locking when multiple users access the same database. This is necessary in case two users try to modify the same record at the same time. Multiple-user situations could occur with external database access (as discussed next). For additional information about data access objects (and data controls), refer to the Help topic Data Access.

12.6   USING EXTERNAL DATABASES

Consider the situation of a company with offices and sites spread over a wide territory. The representatives for Cougar Canoe operate in different cities. It would be awkward for each to keep his or her own copy of the database. Maintenance of the database would be even more awkward. If a representative places a new order for a new customer, the databases for everyone else would also have to be updated to reflect the change. This can quickly turn into a data nightmare. Also, many businesses and organizations need to maintain databases with thousands of records. There are heavy-duty systems to handle such large databases. The locally installed database management system just won't do it. It would be like using a canoe to transport cargo across oceans. Many real-world applications of Visual Basic are front-end systems that provide convenient access to these large database systems.

In Section 12.1.3 we looked at data access options for Visual Basic (see Figure 12.3). A large remote computer runs the database to process query and update requests made by multiple users. The users connect to the remote computer either through a wide area network (WAN), local area network (LAN), or the Internet. Internet access is typically based on the Hypertext Transport Protocol (HTTP) used for the World Wide Web. This is like a *client server* model. In a client server system, the client (usually the user's computer) makes a request for service. The server is another computer that responds to carry out the request. Think of a customer in a restaurant. The customer (client) chooses from a menu and requests a meal. The waiter (server) takes the request and eventually returns to "serve" the meal. A database server is a computer that responds to requests to retrieve data and/or modify data that it maintains in a database. Common database servers include Sybase, Oracle, and Microsoft SQL Server. The client may be a Visual Basic program that accesses this external database using the database server. However, the connection between the client and the database server is not direct. The databases are sometimes known as *client/server databases*. Many systems are known as *three tier*, in which the client connects to a network or web server that then establishes a connection with the database server. Figure 12.10 shows the gereral idea of a three-tier system.

12.6.1   External Data Access Choices

Cougar Canoe works with partner companies that offer complementary products. One of their partners is the Blue Sky Tent Company, which, as the name suggests, makes tents. This partnership benefits all since each partner can refer potential customers to the other.

Figure 12.10
Three-Tier System for
Database Access

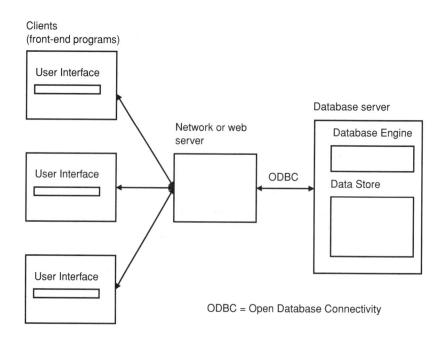

Cougar Canoe can provide information about tents by accessing the Blue Sky database. However, Blue Sky uses a Paradox™ database instead of one based on the Jet database engine, so a Cougar Canoe program would need to use another means to access the data.

Attach Versus Open

There are two fundamental ways to access external data:

- *Attach* the external data
- *Open* the external data

Attach a Table   Attaching a table creates a *reference* to the external table and saves the *reference* in the Jet database. This stored link keeps a record of the database table's *structure*. Note that the external data itself is not stored in the Jet database. This is like having a book that refers to another book located in another library. The first book specifies the second book and where to look in that second book. The next part of the analogy is strange but may help to distinguish *attach* from *open*: To view the information, you have to ask the other library to send a copy of it.

Open a Table   To open an external table, we need to *connect* to the external database. This means that the data control or data access object is directly accessing the external database. We can make a connection by setting the Connect property of a data control or the arguments of the `OpenDatabase` method for a data access object. The analogy is like having the second library send the other book so that we can access it directly and completely search its contents.

ISAM Databases

In some situations, an organization works with databases that cannot be handled directly by the Jet database engine. These include common indexed sequential access method (ISAM) databases such as dBase™, Paradox, Btrieve™, and FoxPro™. These databases are also external, even though they may reside on the same machine. A Visual Basic program must use a ***driver*** instead of using the Jet database engine. The Visual Basic development system includes drivers for these databases. The ***driver*** is the software that permits Visual Basic to work with this external database. To check out which ISAM drivers are available, add a data control and check settings available for the Connect property.

ODBC-Compliant Databases

Since there are several types of database servers, network servers, and clients, there is a standard for data access among these different components: Open Database Connectivity (ODBC). Many database servers use this standard, so a front-end client program would have to use ODBC. For Visual Basic, we need to install an ODBC driver for the specific type of server being used. The Visual Basic program still uses the Jet database engine. However, now the Jet database engine passes and receives data using the ODBC driver (see Figure 12.3). An ODBC-compliant database usually provides the ODBC driver. The purpose of the driver is to translate Jet operations to ODBC operations. Visual Basic provides ODBC drivers for Microsoft SQL Server and Oracle databases. (If drivers for both ISAM and ODBC databases are available in your system, they will be listed in the Windows registry of your system.)

12.6.2   Attaching External Tables to the Data Control

Recall that the Blue Sky Tent Company uses a Paradox database. Here we will show some simple prototype programs to illustrate how we can access this information. Version 1 of the Blue Sky program illustrates basic external access by using an external table attached to a database. We created a copy of the Cougar database and named it COUGAR2.MDB. Then we attached the table from the Blue Sky database using the Data Manager tool already included in Visual Basic. (The Hands-On Exercises later in this chapter explain how to attach the table.) The program disk includes a copy of this table (named BLUESKY1.DB). Figure 12.11 illustrates a demonstration program that views the records in the attached table. In this case, the tent is a four-person green tent, and the name of the model is Spruce.

There is very little code, and the data controls and data-bound text boxes have property settings that refer to records in the COUGAR2 database. It just so happens that the Blue Sky table is attached instead of an inherent part of the database. From the programming point of view, there is no difference. The handling of external references is done by the Jet database engine. Example 12.13 shows the code for the program, and Table 12.4 shows the main properties. The program permits the user only to view the records; it does not have any query capabilities.

Example 12.13
```
Option Explicit

' Version 1 of BlueSky program
' Access external table that is already
' attached to a Jet database
' COUGAR2.MDB is a working copy of COUGAR.MDB, which
' has an attached Paradox table named BlueSky
```

Figure 12.11
Accessing External Data

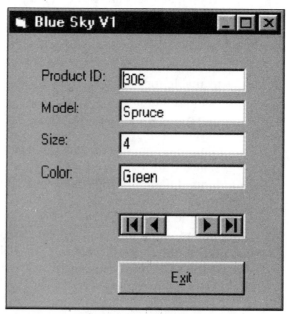

The data is from a table in a non-Jet database.

```
Private Sub cmdExit_Click()
    End
End Sub
```

12.6.3   Connecting External Tables to the Data Control

To connect to an external table, we need to set the Connect property to refer to the other database. For Version 1 of the Blue Sky program (see Table 12.4), note the Connect property for the Data control. It is `Access`. This means that we are still using the Jet database engine. Access is the database system part of Microsoft's Office Suite. Both Access and Visual Basic use the Jet engine for database operations. Hence the table being accessed must have been attached to the database. In Version 2 of the Blue Sky program, we will connect to the table. In order to connect, we set the Connect property of the data control to `Paradox 4.x` to specify that we need to access a Paradox database. The Connect property is used to pass additional information to ODBC and certain ISAM drivers as needed. It isn't used for Jet databases, except for those containing attached tables. In this case, we need to pass information to the Paradox ISAM driver. The DatabaseName property only contains the path to the database file(s).

Example 12.14 shows the program for Version 2, and Table 12.5 shows the property settings for the data control; everything else is the same as in Version 1. For Version 1, the RecordSource was named `BlueSky` since the attached table was given this name. ForVersion 2, the RecordSource is `BlueSky1`, which is the name of the Paradox file containing the table (set of records).

Table 12.4
Property Settings for the Blue Sky (External) Database Access Program

Object Class	Property	Setting
DataControl	Name	`datBlueSky`
	Connect	`Access`
	DatabaseName[a]	`C:\IntroP\CODE\Cougar2.mdb`
	RecordSource (external table is attached)	`BlueSky`
TextBox	Name	`txtProductID`
	DataSource	`datBlueSky`
	DataField	`Product ID`
TextBox	Name	`txtModel`
	DataSource	`datBlueSky`
	DataField	`Model`
TextBox	Name	`txtSize`
	DataSource	`datBlueSky`
	DataField	`Size`
TextBox	Name	`txtColor`
	DataSource	`datBlueSky`
	DataField	`Color`

[a]File path may vary, depending on setup. Files are included on the program disk.

Example 12.14
```
Option Explicit

' Version 2 of BlueSky program
' Open an external database table directly
' by setting Connect property of Data control
' to Paradox 4.x

Private Sub cmdExit_Click()
    End
End Sub
```

12.6.4   Attaching Tables to a Data Access Object

In Versions 1 and 2 of the Blue Sky program, we use a data control. In Versions 3 and 4, we use the data access object (DAO). Figure 12.12 shows Version 3.

In the previous programs using DAO, we used the Database object to represent an open database and the Recordset object to represent a set of records. Now we will also use the TableDef object. The TableDef object represents the stored ***definition*** of an attached table.

In order to access records in an external table, we need a table definition. The TableDef object provides the definition. We can also use the TableDef object to represent the definition of a Jet database table. This permits us to modify the structure of the table. To use an ISAM database (such as Paradox) with an attached table, we must create a new TableDef object. Then we will set the Connect and SourceTableName properties of the TableDef object. The SourceTableName property of a TableDef object returns or sets a value that specifies the name of an attached table. The following code segment shows how to access an external table:

```
Dim m_dbsCougar As Database, m_rstBlueSky As Recordset
' To attach table to existing Jet database, need TableDef ➥
object
Dim m_tdBlueSky As TableDef

    ' Set the data access objects (create instances of them)
    Set m_dbsCougar = OpenDatabase(PATH & "COUGAR2.MDB")
    ' COUGAR2.MDB has an attached table
    ' Create a TableDef object for the external table
```

Table 12.5
Property Settings for the Data Control Connected to an External Database

Property	Setting
DataControl	
Name	datBlueSky
Connect	Paradox 4.x;
DatabaseName	C:\IntroP\CODE\
RecordSource (external table is attached)	BlueSky1

```
Set m_tdBlueSky = m_dbsCougar.CreateTableDef("Attached ➥
Paradox Table")
' Set the TableDef object properties to refer to the ➥
attached table
m_tdBlueSky.Connect = "Paradox 4.X;DATABASE=" & PATH
m_tdBlueSky.SourceTableName = "BlueSky1"
```

The CreateTableDef method uses a string argument that uniquely names the TableDef object. The Connect property returns or sets a value that provides information about the source of an open database. In this case, we set the Connect property to state that we are using a Paradox ISAM database and the path (as defined by the constant PATH) to indicate where the data is stored. In general, the syntax for setting the Connect property is

object.**Connect** = [*databasetype;[parameters;]*]

The *object* can be a data control, Database object, QueryDef object, or a TableDef object. In other words, the object can be an instance of the Data class, Database class, QueryDef class, or TableDef class. The databasetype argument is a string representing a valid ISAM database format and driver that Visual Basic can use. The parameters provide additional information in order to use the ISAM driver. Usually, this is the path specifying where to find the database files. (For full information about settings, refer to Help topic Connect.) Once we have the attached table, we can open the table as follows.

```
Set m_rstBlueSky = m_dbsCougar.OpenRecordset("Attached Paradox ➥
Table")
```

The OpenRecordset method creates a new object of the Recordset class. The argument specifies the source of the records. In this case, it is the attached table. The rest of the code uses methods already described in Section 12.5. Example 12.15 shows the complete code for Version 3 of the Blue Sky program.

Figure 12.12
Accessing External Data
Using the Data Access
Object (DAO)

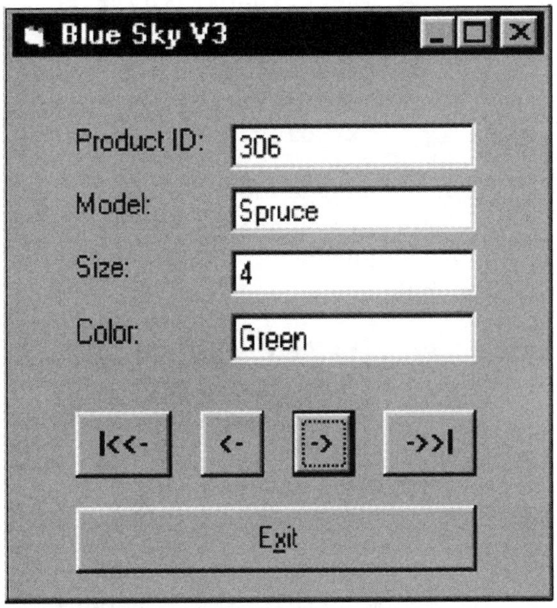

The data is from a table in a non-Jet database.

Example 12.15

```
Option Explicit

' Version 3 of BlueSky program using DAO to access a table
' that is already attached to a Jet database
' COUGAR2.MDB is a working copy of COUGAR.MDB that already
' has an attached Paradox 4.xtable

Const PATH = "C:\INTROP\CODE\"  ' Modify if necessary
' Declare the data access objects
Dim m_dbsCougar As Database, m_rstBlueSky As Recordset
' To attach table to existing Jet database, need TableDef object
Dim m_tdBlueSky As TableDef

Private Sub Form_Load()
    ' Set the data access objects (create instances of them)
    Set m_dbsCougar = OpenDatabase(PATH & "COUGAR2.MDB")
    ' COUGAR2.MDB has an attached table
    ' Create a TableDef object for the external table
    Set m_tdBlueSky = m_dbsCougar.CreateTableDef("Attached ➡
    Paradox Table")
    ' Set the TableDef object properties to refer to the ➡
    attached table
    m_tdBlueSky.Connect = "Paradox 4.X;DATABASE=" & PATH
    m_tdBlueSky.SourceTableName = "BlueSky1"
    ' Now TableDef object exists and since it is already ➡
    appended in
    ' COUGAR2.MDB, there is no need to append it in code
    Set m_rstBlueSky = m_dbsCougar.OpenRecordset("BlueSky")
    Display ' Then display the fields for the first record
End Sub

Sub Display()
    ' Display fields from recordset object
    txtProductID.Text = m_rstBlueSky("Product ID")
    txtModel.Text = m_rstBlueSky("Model")
    txtSize.Text = m_rstBlueSky("Size")
    txtColor.Text = m_rstBlueSky("Color")
End Sub

Private Sub cmdExit_Click()
    End
End Sub

Private Sub cmdFirst_Click()
    ' Move to First record
    m_rstBlueSky.MoveFirst
    Display
End Sub

Private Sub cmdLast_Click()
    ' Move to Last record
    m_rstBlueSky.MoveLast
    Display
```

```
End Sub

Private Sub cmdNext_Click()
    m_rstBlueSky.MoveNext
    ' Do not move beyond last record
    If m_rstBlueSky.EOF Then
        Beep
        m_rstBlueSky.MoveLast
    End If
    Display ' Show record to user
End Sub

Private Sub cmdPrevious_Click()
    m_rstBlueSky.MovePrevious
    ' Do not move beyond first record
    If m_rstBlueSky.BOF Then
        Beep
        m_rstBlueSky.MoveFirst
    End If
    Display
End Sub
```

12.6.5   Connecting Tables to a Data Access Object

It is possible to access an external ISAM table that is not already attached to a Jet database. Version 4 of the Blue Sky program does this. It is almost identical to Version 3, but it uses the Cougar database without a preattached table. Another difference is that it uses the Append method to attach the external table, as follows:

```
m_dbsCougar.TableDefs.Append m_tdBlueSky
```

The Append method adds a new data access object to a collection. Recall that a collection is an object that contains a set of related objects. In this case, the Database object contains Recordset and TableDef objects, among others. Hence it would have a Recordsets collection and a TableDefs collection. Since we want to append a TableDef object, we need to specify the TableDefs collection of the Database object (named m_dbsCougar here). (For more information about collections used for the Database object, refer to Help topic Database Object, Databases Collection.) Example 12.16 shows only the parts of the code where Version 4 differs from Version 3 (as shown in Example 12.15). It is also necessary to remove the TableDef object (named m_tdBlueSky) from the TableDefs collection. This is shown in procedure cmdExit_Click. If we did not remove it, the external table would become permanently attached to the database after the program executed.

Example 12.16

```
Option Explicit

' Version 4 of BlueSky program using DAO to attach and
' access a table that is external to a Jet database
' COUGAR1.MDB is a working copy of COUGAR.MDB and
' has no pre-attached external table
```

```
Const PATH = "C:\INTROP\CODE\"  ' Modify if necessary
' Declare the data access objects
Dim m_dbsCougar As Database, m_rstBlueSky As Recordset
' To attach table to existing Jet database, need TableDef object
Dim m_tdBlueSky As TableDef

Private Sub Form_Load()
    ' Set the data access objects (create instances of them)
    Set m_dbsCougar = OpenDatabase(PATH & "COUGAR1.MDB")
    ' COUGAR1.MDB does not have an attached table
    ' Create a TableDef object for the external table
    Set m_tdBlueSky = m_dbsCougar.CreateTableDef("Attached ➟
    Paradox Table")
    ' Set the TableDef object properties to refer to the ➟
    attached table
    m_tdBlueSky.Connect = "Paradox 4.X;DATABASE=" & PATH
    m_tdBlueSky.SourceTableName = "BlueSky1"
    ' Change to Version 3 is use of Append method
    ' Append the TableDef object to the TableDefs collection ➟
    with the Append
    ' method.  This step actually creates the object in the ➟
    database file
    m_dbsCougar.TableDefs.Append m_tdBlueSky
    Set m_rstBlueSky = m_dbsCougar.OpenRecordset("Attached ➟
    Paradox Table")
    Display ' Then display the fields for the first record
End Sub

Private Sub Form_Unload(Cancel As Integer)
    cmdExit_Click   ' Remove attached table
End Sub

Private Sub cmdExit_Click()
    ' Remove Attached table from database
    m_dbsCougar.TableDefs.Delete "Attached Paradox Table"
    End
End Sub
```

12.6.6   ODBC Access

With Open Database Connectivity (ODBC), we can access database information stored externally on a database server. This is useful for large corporations and organizations that need a single repository of data. However, it must also be one that can be accessed by multiple users at multiple locations. Refer back to Figure 12.10. Each client program would have to use the appropriate ODBC driver (see also Figure 12.3) to access the data served by the database server. A typical database server is the Oracle database server; another is the Microsoft SQL Server. In order to access a database server, we would need

- A network connection to the database server.

- An account on the database server.

To Set Up an ODBC Data Source

An *ODBC data source* is a term that refers to a remote source of data such as a database server. We can refer to it by a Data Source name. Before we can use Visual Basic with an ODBC-compliant database, we must install the appropriate ODBC drivers, and we must set up an ODBC data source. To install an ODBC driver and create a data source, use the Control panel in Windows. Select 32-bit ODBC or ODBC. Alternatively, use the appropriate setup program for the ODBC driver. When Visual Basic is installed, some drivers and data sources are already included.

Accessing a Table

Let's say that Cougar Canoe needs to access climate information maintained in an external database. This database happens to be run on an Oracle server. Cougar will use this data for a trip-planning database it will use to assist customers. The code for attaching an Oracle table may be something like that shown in Example 12.17. The server has a table named Rainfall. The data source name (DSN) is ClimateServe.

Example 12.17

```
Dim dbsPlanTrip As Database, rstRoute As Recordset
Dim tdRainfall As TableDef
Set dbsPlanTrip = OpenDatabase ("C:\PLANTRIP.MDB")
Set tdRainfall = dbsPlanTrip.CreateTableDef ("Attached Oracle ➡
Table")
tdRainfall.Connect =
"ODBC;DATABASE=ClimateDB;UID=Guest;PWD=xx;DSN=ClimateServe"
tdRainfall.SourceTableName = "Rainfall "
dbsPlanTrip.TableDefs.Append tdRainfall
Set rstRoute = dbsPlanTrip.OpenRecordset ("Attached Oracle ➡
Table")
```

For the Connect property, the *UID* refers to the user identification and *PWD* refers to the password. If this information is omitted, the login prompt is displayed. When the connect string states ODBC only, a dialog box listing all registered ODBC data source names is displayed by the ODBC driver. The user can then select a database.

12.7   NEW DATA ACCESS TOOLS

The traditional Visual Basic data access tools are the data control, data access objects (DAOs), and Open Database Connectivity (ODBC). The Enterprise edition of Visual Basic also includes remote data objects (RDOs). The Enterprise edition is used for developing client/server applications where several client programs interact with a program on a network server. To add to the mix, Microsoft is introducing newer tools:

- Object Linking and Embedding Database (OLE DB)
- Advanced Data Objects (ADO)
- Advanced Data Connector (ADC)
- Advanced Data Control (AdvDataCtrl)

This provides more choice, improvements, or confusion to the programmer, depending on your point of view. For more information, visit the websites at http://www.microsoft.com/oledb and http://www.microsoft.com/adc The July 1997 and November 1997 issues of *Visual Basic Programmer's Journal* (see Appendix D) contain a good overview article about these tools.

SUMMARY

A database is a set of organized data related to a topic or organizational purpose. It contains tables and can contain queries and indexes as well as table relationships, table and field validation criteria, and linkages to external data sources. Databases are collections of related tables (see Figure 12.1). Each table is a set of records (see Table 12.1). Each record is a structure consisting of (usually) fixed-size fields. A field is a category of information stored in a database. It is an element of a database table that categorizes (defines the format and type of) specific information, such as a last name. Tables are related to one another, which is why we use the term relational database when describing this type of database.

Both Visual Basic and Access (Microsoft's database system for their Office Suite) use the Jet database engine. It does the grunt work for storing data in the correct format and in the correct place; searches data, making sure it is valid (performs validation checks); and so on. A Visual Basic program can use Data controls and/or data access objects to work with the Jet engine to access a database stored in Jet format. It is also possible to access data in non-Jet databases by using the appropriate ISAM driver, if available, as shown in Figure 12.3.

The data control permits us to access data using the Jet engine without writing code, unless we want to use queries. There are two fundamental steps to using the data control:

1. For each table to access, add a data control to the form and set applicable properties to specify the database and table.

2. For each field to display to the user, add a data-bound control and set applicable properties to *bind* it to the data control.

The DatabaseName property returns or sets the name and location of the database (source of data) for a data control.

The RecordSource property is typically set to an existing table in the database. We can also set the RecordSource property to an SQL statement that returns records.

To permit the user to view the field data, it is necessary to use data-bound controls. The RecordSource property of a data control specifies the source of the records accessible through bound controls. To bind data, a data-bound control uses the DataSource property and DataField property. The DataSource property specifies the data control through which the current control is bound to a database. The DataField property returns or sets a value that binds a control to a field in the current record. Note that Figure 12.4 illustrates this relationship.

The two Data control events are

Reposition	Occurs after a record becomes the current record. The event procedure could perform calculations based on data in the current record.
Validate	Occurs before a different record becomes the current record. The event procedure could change values and update data.

The current record is the one that we can use to modify or examine data. For more information about events refer to Help topic Data Control, Link Events. For more information about Data control methods, see Table 12.3 or refer to Help topic Data Control, Link Methods.

The Structured Query Language (SQL) is an industry-standard database language that is used to obtain related information from a database. A query is a formal instruction to the database engine to tell it to return a set of records based on a specified criteria. We use SQL syntax to make up the query. The general (and simplified) syntax is

SELECT *fieldlist* **FROM** *tableexpression* **[WHERE]** *criteria*

A *fieldlist* shows field names in square brackets separated by commas. A *tableexpression* identifies one or more tables from which data is retrieved. *Criteria* specify the relationship for selecting records.

The FROM *clause* specifies the tables or queries that contain the fields listed in the SELECT statement. A SELECT statement must contain a FROM clause. The WHERE clause is optional and follows the FROM clause when used. The database engine selects the records that meet the conditions listed in the WHERE clause. If the FROM clause is not used, the database engine returns all records.

With the professional edition of Visual Basic, we can add data-aware controls for easier viewing of database information. These include the DBList, DBCombo, and DBGrid controls. These controls permit us to view more information in a convenient fashion without using separate text boxes. Figure 12.6 shows an example of using the DBGrid control. For additional information, refer to Help topics for DBList, DBCombo, and DBGrid controls.

A data access object (DAO) is an object defined by the Jet database engine. There are several object classes, such as Database, Recordset, and TableDef, which are used to organize and manipulate data by setting properties and applying methods.

Data access objects (DAOs) provide more flexibility and control over a database. These objects provide a programming interface to help simplify data-access programming tasks. We have examined three types of objects (or classes). This is only part of the many different types of DAOs. For more information, you can refer to Help topics such as Data Access Objects Overview or Data Access Objects Model. This can be quite overwhelming when first encountering the model. Figure 12.13 shows part of the model.

In general, each DAO object type (class) has a corresponding collection. A collection includes all of the existing objects of that type. For example, the Recordsets collection contains all open Recordset objects. Each collection is owned by another object at the next higher level in the hierarchy. A Database object owns a Recordsets collection.

In order to use data access objects, we need to declare them using Dim statements such as the following:

```
' Declare some data access objects
Dim dbsCougar As Database, rstCustomers As Recordset
Dim tdBlueSky As TableDef
```

Then we can use Set statements such as the following to create the objects:

```
' Set the data access objects (create instances of them)
Set m_dbsCougar = OpenDatabase(PATH & "COUGAR1.MDB")
Set m_rstCustomers = dbsCougar.OpenRecordset("Customers", ➡
dbOpenDynaset)
```

Figure 12.13
Part of Data Access
Object Model

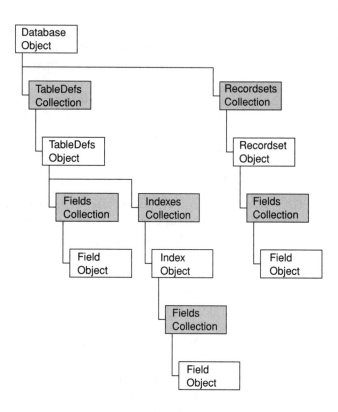

For a Database object, use the `OpenDatabase` method (applied to a default Work-space object) to open a specified database and return a reference to the Database object that represents it. For a Recordset object, use the `OpenRecordset` method to create a new Recordset object and append it to the Recordsets collection. To access a field, we can use a statement like the following:

```
txtFirstName.Text = rstCustomers("First Name")
```

Refer to Figure 12.13. A Field is part of the Fields collection, which in turn is part of a Recordset object. In this case, we are accessing the Value property of the First Name Field object. The Value property is the default property of a Field object. To explicitly refer to these relationships, we could use the statement

```
txtFirstName.Text = rstCustomers.Fields("First Name").Value
```

With objects, we can use methods and properties. For more information about properties and methods, refer to the Help topics about the various DAO classes.

It is possible to access database information provided by a database server on a network. Figure 12.10 illustrates how this is done. The information can be from a non-Jet database such as Paradox, an Oracle server, or even text and some spreadsheet formats.

One way to access this data is to attach an external table to a Jet database. Then we can access the table by setting the Recordsource property of a data control to refer to the table. To access an external table using DAO, we would have to use a TableDef object. A TableDef object represents the stored definition of a table.

Another way to access external data is to connect to an external database. For a data control, we can set the Connect property to the appropriate valid settings, such as `Paradox 4.x` or `ODBC`, which indicate the type of database access. The default setting is `Access` when working with a native Jet database. Also, we need to set the DatabaseName property to refer to the path of where the external database files reside. Then we can set the Record-source property to a table that belongs to the external (non-native/non-Jet) database. To connect using DAO, we can use the Append method to attach the external table.

The Append method adds a new data access object to a *collection*. (see Figure 12.13).

With Open Database Connectivity (ODBC), we can access database information stored externally on a database server. This is useful for large corporations and organizations that need a single repository of data. To use ODBC, it is necessary to have network access to a database server, including physical connections and a user account on the server (refer to Figure 12.10). The Client program needs to use an ODBC driver for the type of database server to which you're connecting. The connection on the client end is made by setting the Connect property of a data control. For DAO, it is possible to use a Connection object to access ODBC databases.

We have not covered all possible variations for accessing databases. It would not be surprising if you have to access a database; creating a front-end program is probably the most common use for Visual Basic. For specific information to suit your needs, refer to Help topics about data control, DAO, ODBC, and other database topics. This chapter provided a database programming foundation for further exploration. The exercises that follow will add to that foundation.

HANDS-ON EXERCISES

OVERVIEW

The activities will enable you to

- Use the (Visual) Data Manager to examine a database.
- Use the Data control to access a table in a database.
- Use the DataSource and DataField properties of a text box to data bind the control.
- Use SQL statements to retrieve data that meets a specified criteria.
- Use data access objects (DAOs) to access and modify a database.
- Create programs that can access data stored in both Jet and non-Jet database formats.

To Get Started

1. Read the section "Read Me Before Attempting the Hands-On Exercises" if you have not already done so.
2. Run Windows.
3. Open the file CH12\EX12.TXT on your student disk and answer the questions. (The same questions are shown here so that you can still determine answers when you are not sitting in front of a computer.)
4. Run Visual Basic.

12.1 THE WHY AND HOW OF DATABASES

1. What is a database? Explain in your own words using your own examples.
2. Why is a database used? Explain in your own words using your own examples.

3. How is a database used? Explain in your own words using your own examples.

4. Define *table, record*, and *field*.

5. Explain how Visual Basic uses the Jet database engine.

Exploring the Cougar Database

Determine where the database file COUGAR.MDB is located. It is probably in the parent directory of the various Chapter directories. Copy this file to a new one named COUGAR1.MDB. This will be your working copy for use with most of the programs.

You will use the Data Manager program to examine the database. This is an add-in to the Visual Basic development environment.

Visual Basic 4

Select **Data Manager** from the Add-Ins menu. You should see the Data Manager window. Select **Open Database** from the Files menu. Open the file COUGAR1.MDB. You should something like Figure 12.14. Click on a table in the Tables/QueryDefs window, and click **Open**. You can view the records in the table. Close the Table window. Select a **table** in the Tables/QueryDefs window, and click **Design**. You will see the Table Editor window. Examine how the fields are defined. Close the Table Editor window. Select a table in the Tables/QueryDefs window, and click Relations. You will see the Relations window. Note the Primary key field and the Table and field to which it is related. Close the Relations window.

Visual Basic 5

Select **Visual Data Manager** from the Add-Ins menu. When prompted for security, click **No**. You should see the VisData window. Select **Open Database** from the Files menu, and then select **Microsoft Access**. Open the file **COUGAR1.MDB**. You should see something like Figure 12.15. Click on a table in the Database window using the right mouse button. This pops up the Database Window menu. Select **Open**. You can view the records in the table. Close the Dynaset window, and select a table in the Database window. Right-click **the table** and select **Design**. You will see the Table Structure window. Note the upper part of the window to see how the fields are defined; note the bottom part to see the relations such as the Primary key field and the Table and field to which it is related. Close the Table Structure window.

If you accidentally corrupt or modify the database, close the Data Manager. Copy COUGAR.MDB to COUGAR1.MDB to overwrite the old copy and try again. Continue exploring the database and check that it is organized like the one shown in Figure 12.2. Answer question 6. Select **Exit** from the File menu to exit the (Visual) Data Manager.

6. Describe the design of the Shippers table.

12.2 THE DATA CONTROL

7. Describe the two fundamental steps for using the Data Control.

The Database Access Program, Version 1

Start a new project. Select **Save File/Form1 As** from the File menu. Save *file* FORM1 as **COUGDB1** in directory CH12. Select **Save Project As** from the File menu. Save *project* PROJECT1 as **COUGDB1** in directory CH12. Change the Name of the form to **frmCougarDB1**, and change the Caption to state **Cougar Database Access - V1**. Save the project.

Figure 12.14
Visual Basic 4 Data
Manager

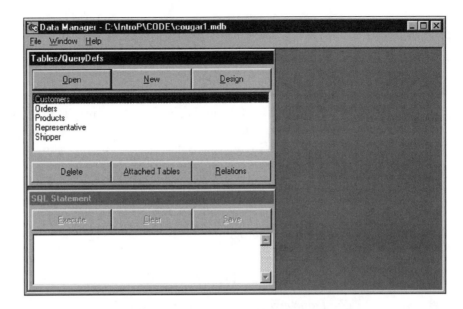

Figure 12.15
Visual Basic 5 (Visual)
Data Manager

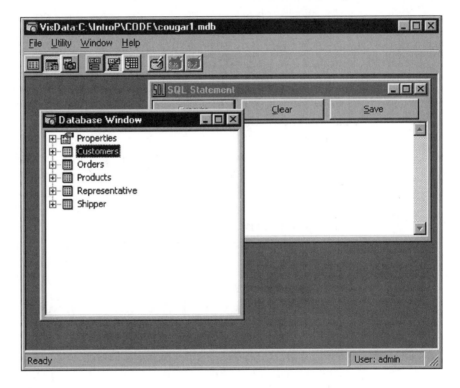

Refer to Figure 12.1 and Table 12.2. Place the frame controls first and set their properties. Then place the other controls in their respective frames and set their properties. Note that the text box controls txtCustomerID, txtOrderID, and txtProductID are hidden. You can place them anywhere, such as the space below the CUSTOMERS frame. Save the project. Type the code as shown in Example 12.1. Save the project.

Run the program. Note how it is possible to view records from the different tables independently of each other. The program does not set up any relationship between the tables. Stop execution of the program.

12.3 STRUCTURED QUERY LANGUAGE (SQL)

8. Use Help to give an example of an SQL statement. Indicate some of the reserved words.

The Database Access Program, Version 2

Open *project* COUGDB1 in directory CH12. Save *file* COUGDB1 as **COUGDB2** in directory CH12. Select **Save Project As** from the File menu. Save *project* COUGDB11 as **COUGDB2** in directory CH12. Change the Name of the form to **frmCougarDB2**, and change the version part of its Caption to state **Cougar Database Access - V2**. Save the project.

Use Example 12.2 to modify the code. Save the project. Run the program and note that the ORDERS control only shows records associated with the current CUSTOMER. The PRODUCTS control only shows records associated with the current ORDER. Stop execution of the program.

12.4 OTHER DATA-AWARE CONTROLS

The Database Access Program, Version 3

Open *project* COUGDB2 in directory CH12. Save *file* COUGDB2 as **COUGDB3** in directory CH12. Select **Save Project As** from the File menu. Save *project* COUGDB2 as **COUGDB3** in directory CH12. Change the Name of the form to **frmCougarDB3**, and change the version part of its Caption to state **Cougar Database Access - V3**. Save the project.

Add a new form to the project. Name it as **frmOrderDetails3**, and save this file as **ODETAIL3.FRM**. Refer to Figure 12.6. Add a data control. Set its Name property to **datOrderDetails**. Set its DatabaseName to the **COUGAR1** database. Leave its Record-Source property blank. Add a database grid control. If necessary, add the control (tool DBGrid) as a custom control. Set its Name property to **dbgOrderDetails**. Set its Data-Source property to **datOrderDetails**. Add a command button control, and name it **cmdDone**. Refer to Figure 12.6 and set other properties as required. Save the project.

Modify the code for form frmCougarDB3 as shown in Example 12.3. Type in the code for form frmOrderDetails3 as shown in Example 12.4. Save the project.

Run the program. Click **Order Details** to note that it is now possible to view some order details. For some customers there are multiple orders. Stop program execution.

12.5 USING DATA ACCESS OBJECTS (DAOS)

The Database Access Program, Version 4

Open *project* COUGDB3 in directory CH12. Save *file* COUGDB3 as **COUGDB4** in directory CH12. Select **Save Project As** from the File menu. Save *project* COUGDB3 as **COUGDB4** in directory CH12. Select form **frmCougarDB3.** Change the Name of the form to **frmCougarDB4**, and change the version part of its Caption to state **Cougar Database Access - V4**. Select form **frmOrderDetails3**. Save *file* ODETAIL3 as file **ODETAIL4** in directory CH12. Change the Name of the form to **frmOrderDetails4**. Save the project.

Remove data control datCustomers and any of its code from Form frmCougarDB4. Refer to Figure 12.7 and add the additional command button controls. Use Example 12.6 as a guide to naming the controls. Use Figure 12.7 as a guide to setting their Captions, size, and position. Save the project. Use Examples 12.5 and 12.6 to modify the code for form frmCougarDB4. Save the project.

Refer to Figure 12.8 as a guide for modifying form **frmOrderDetails4**. Add a text box named **txtCanoeModel**. Add two more controls that are invisible at runtime: a data control named datProducts and a text box named txtProductID. Set their Visible properties to **False**. For datProducts, set its DatabaseName to the **COUGAR1** database and set its RecordSource to **Products**. For txtProductID, set its DataSource to **datProducts**. Its DataField may remain blank. Type in the code for form frmOrder-Details4 as shown in Example 12.7. Save the project.

Run the program. You should be able to use the arrow buttons to show the customer records. Click **Order Details** and note that the order details include a descriptive name for the canoe model to match the Product ID in the Order record. Stop the program.

The Database Access Program, Version 5

Make a working copy of COUGAR1.MDB and name it **COUGAR2.MDB**. This will be a new working copy since you will be making modifications. Then open *project* COUGDB4 in directory CH12. Save *file* COUGDB4 as **COUGDB5** in directory CH12. Select **Save Project As** from the File menu. Save *project* COUGDB4 as **COUGDB5** in directory CH12. Select form **frmCougarDB4**. Change the Name of the form to **frm-CougarDB5**, and change the version part of its Caption to state **Cougar Database Access - V5**. We can use the same Order Details form (frmOrderDetails4) as before. Save the project.

Refer to Example 12.8 to change the code of the Form_Load and dat-Orders_Reposition procedures. Add the event procedure code shown in Examples 12.9 to 12.12, inclusive. Save the project.

Run the program. Try the various modification commands. You may encounter runtime errors in certain situations such as trying to update a record using an area code where there is no corresponding area code in the Representatives table. Stop the program.

9. List at least two types of data access objects.

10. Using one of the two types, describe how to declare and instantiate (create/set the instance of) the object.

11. Using one of the two types, list and describe some important properties and methods.

12.6 USING EXTERNAL DATABASES

12. What are the two ways for accessing data that are not part of a Jet database?

13. Explain the principle of a three-tier system for Database Access.

Determine where the database file BLUESKY1.DB is located. It is probably in the parent directory of the various Chapter directories. Since the program disk already contains the Paradox database file, you do not need Paradox itself. To experiment with other database formats, you can try other formats if you have the necessary programs to create the files.

Next, you will attach this table to a Jet database. If you wish, name your previous copy of COUGAR2.MDB **COUGAR3.MDB**. Create a working copy of COUGAR.MDB and name it **COUGAR2.MDB**.

Visual Basic 4
Run the Data Manager and open the COUGAR2 database. In the Tables/QueryDef dialog box, click **Attached Tables**.

Visual Basic 5

Run the Visual Data Manager and open the COUGAR2 database. Select **Attachments** from the Utility menu

The Attached Tables dialog box will appear. Click **New** and enter the following information.

Attachment Name:	**BlueSky**
Database Name:	**(Type in the path to file BLUESKY1.DB.)**
Connect String:	**(Select Paradox 4.X.)**
Table to Attach:	**(Select BlueSky1.)**

Once the information is entered, select **Attach**. Select **Close** and then exit the (Visual) Data Manager.

The Blue Sky Program, Version 1

In Visual Basic, start **a new project**. Select **Save File/Form1 As** from the File menu. Save *file* FORM1 as **BLUESKY1** in directory CH12. Select **Save Project As** from the File menu. Save *project* PROJECT1 as **BLUESKY1** in directory CH12. Change the Name of the form to **frmBlueSky**, and change the Caption to state **Blue Sky V1**. Save the project.

Refer to Figure 12.11 and Table 12.4. Place the controls on the form. Enter the code shown in Example 12.15. Save the project, and run the program. Note that you can view the records in this table. Stop execution of the program.

The Blue Sky Program, Version 2

Open *project* BLUESKY1 in directory CH12. Save *file* BLUESKY1 as **BLUESKY2** in directory CH12. Select **Save Project As** from the File menu. Save *project* BLUESKY1 as **BLUESKY2** in directory CH12. Change the version part of the Form Caption to state **Blue Sky V2**. Save the project.

Modify the property settings as shown in Table 12.5, and modify the code as shown in Example 12.14. Save the project and run the program. Note that you can view the records in this table. Stop execution of the program.

The Blue Sky Program, Version 3

Open *project* BLUESKY2 in directory CH12. Save *file* BLUESKY2 as **BLUESKY3** in directory CH12. Select **Save Project As** from the File menu. Save *project* BLUESKY2 as **BLUESKY3** in directory CH12. Change the version part of the Form Caption to state **Blue Sky V3**. Save the project.

Delete the Data control. Refer to Figure 12.12 and Example 12.15. Add the command button controls, and name them as shown in Example 12.15. Set their Captions as shown in Figure 12.12. Position and size the buttons as shown in Figure 12.12. Enter the code shown in Example 12.15. Save the project and run the program. Note that you can view the records in this table. Stop execution of the program.

The Blue Sky Program, Version 4

Open *project* BLUESKY3 in directory CH12. Save *file* BLUESKY3 as **BLUESKY4** in directory CH12. Select **Save Project As** from the File menu. Save *project* BLUESKY3 as **BLUESKY4** in directory CH12. Change the version part of the Form Caption to state **Blue Sky V4**. Save the project.

Figure 12.16
Customers Associated With a Representative

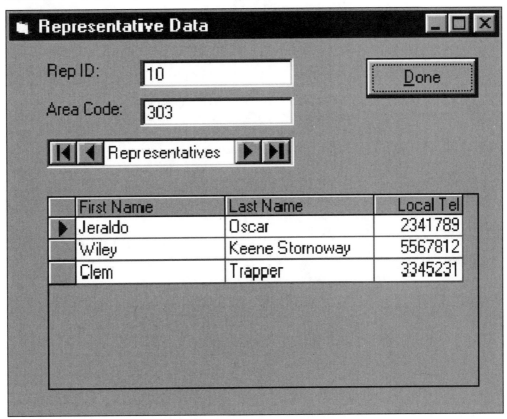

Modify the code as shown in Example 12.16. Save the project and run the program. Note that you can view the records in this table. Stop execution of the program.

ADDITIONAL PROBLEM SOLVING

Modify Version 5 to permit the user to view all customers associated with any representative. Figure 12.16 shows how an additional Form might look. Save the project as **COUGDB6**. Stop and rest before moving on. Good luck, and enjoy programming.

Conventions

Syntax Conventions

The following typographic conventions are used to illustrate syntax rules when explaining the format of a certain action.

Example (followed by specific example if applicable)

Description

Open project INTRO in directory CH01.

All capitals in MCPdigital font indicate a specific filename or directory.

End Use it to stop program execution. In this case no additional information is required.

Words in MCPdigital font **boldface** type with initial letter capitalized indicate words reserved for Visual Basic. You must use them exactly as shown in addition to information you may need to supply (shown in italics).

Public Sub *name***()**
The words **Public Sub** are reserved to start a block of program code. The name is additional information supplied by the programmer. The parentheses must follow programmer-supplied information.

In addition to reserved words (keywords), necessary nonalphabetic characters are shown in MCPdigital font **boldface** type (such as parentheses). Words in MCPdigital font *italic* type indicate generic information that you need to supply.

Public Sub ReadMe()
In this case the programmer chose to name the block of code ReadMe.

Specific example shown in MCPdigital font.

PrintMsg *message*
Use it to send a message to the output box when using the Introduction Template.

Words in MCPdigital font and initial letter capitalized indicate command words reserved for use in the Introduction Template. You must use them exactly as shown in addition to information you may need to supply (shown in italics).

667

```
PrintMsg "Please read"
```

In this case the programmer chose
the message "Please read."

Specific example shown in MCPdigital
font.

```
Dim fDo As Single, fRo As Single, ➡
fMo As Single
```
In this case the statement to declare
three variables is typed as one line in
the source code.

An arrow line continuation character
(➡) indicates that the code continued
from one line to the next in the book
is in fact one line in the code. This
occurs when it is not possible to
show a statement as one line because
the page isn't wide enough.

```
Dim variablename As data type
[, variablename As data type]...
```
Use the Dim statement to declare one
or more variables.

Items inside square brackets are
optional. The three dots, if shown,
indicate repetition of the option is
possible.

```
Dim fRadius As Single
    Dim fDo As Single, fRay As ➡
    Single, fMo As Single
```
Here one variable and then three
variables were declared.

Specific example shows one statement
without the option and another with
the option(s).

Introduction Template

We use a template Visual Basic Project to implement procedural coding without concerning ourselves with the graphical interface design or event-driven programming
that is typical for the Windows environment. Yet we can still take advantage of other
features that are typical in Windows programs.

The Introduction Template consists of three read-only files,

INTRO.VBP   The project file that specifies which files belong (like a packing list).
INTRO.FRM   The form file that specifies the graphical interface of the template.
INTRO.BAS   The module file that contains the code for the template commands.

and one modifiable file for the reader to use for his or her own code. It is

RUNME.BAS   The module file that will contain the main (reader's) program.

Generally, you should use the following methodology:

1. Select **Open Project** in the Toolbar (or select it in File menu).

2. Select **INTRO** (.VBP extension implied) in the appropriate directory and click **Open**.

3. Select **RUNME.BAS** in the project window.

4. Select **Save File As** to rename module file RUNME.BAS as your new name.

5. Select **Save Project As** to rename the project as your new name.

Hungarian Notation

Hungarian Notation Prefixes for Identifying the Data Types of Variables

Prefix	Data Type (or Intended Use)
a	Array (an intended use)
b	Boolean
c	Currency
d	Double
f	Single (single-precision floating point)
h	Handle (an intended use)
i	Index (an intended use)
l (lowercase letter l, not uppercase i or digit 1)	Long
n	Integer
s	String
u	Unsigned (not available in Visual Basic)
ul	Unsigned Long (not available in Visual Basic)
vnt	Variant
w	Word (not available in Visual Basic)

Note that some prefixes indicate the intended use of the variable, such as using the Index type when using an Integer or a Long variable to identify the subscript of an array or an item in a list.

Object Prefixes

Objects, Including Naming Prefixes

Prefix	Object Keyword	Purpose
cbo	ComboBox	User can enter information in text or select from a list.
chk	CheckBox	User can make *yes* or *no* type selection.
cmd	CommandButton	User can activate a process.
dir	DirListBox (Directory List)	Display directories and paths to permit user to select a file.

Prefix	Object Keyword	Purpose
drv	DriveListBox	Display disk drives to permit user to select a file.
fil	FileListBox	Display list of files to permit user to select a file or group of files.
fra	Frame	To group controls together. *See* OptionButton.
frm	Form	Window that is a container for controls
grd	Grid	Display data in a series of rows and columns.
hsb	HScrollBar (Horizontal Scroll Bar)	User can adjust a quantity (similar to sliding tuner of a radio).
img	Image	Displays a graphic.
lbl	Label	Display text information to user (can't modify it).
lin	Line	Displays a line.
lst	ListBox	Displays a list of items from which the user can select one or more.
mnu	Menu	User selects activity using a standard Windows-style menu.
opt	OptionButton (also known as a *radio button*)	User can make one selection from a group of selections. Other selections automatically turned off. Usually grouped within a frame. *See* Frame control.
pic	PictureBox	Display a graphic from a bitmap, icon, or metafile.
shp	Shape	Display rectangle, square, oval, circle, rounded rectangle, or rounded square.
txt	TextBox	User can enter text information.
tmr	Timer	Execute code at regular intervals.
vsb	VScrollBar (Vertical Scroll Bar)	User can adjust a quantity (similar to sliding volume control of an amplifier).

Language Summary

Introduction Template Command Summary

Note that these are not intrinsic Visual Basic commands. We have provided them as part of the Introduction Template to do some quick and easy programming in the early chapters.

Input Integer: `InputInt`

Prompts user and inputs a numerical value of data type Integer.

Syntax: `InputInt sPrompt, nNumber`

Displays a Program Input prompt as specified by string *sPrompt* and waits until the user enters data in the Program Input box. The command returns the data as an integer to assign it to variable *nNumber*. Note that if the user enters a number with a decimal fraction, the result will be rounded to the nearest integer.

Example
```
InputInt "Enter an integer", nMyNumber
```

This prompts the user with

```
Enter an integer
```

If the user enters

```
123.4567
```

(not an integer in this case), variable nMyNumber is assigned 123 (an integer).

Input Number: `InputNum`

Prompts user and inputs a numerical value. *See* Input Single.

Input Words: `InputWords`

Prompts user and inputs a word or words. *See* Input String.

Input Single: `InputSng`

Prompts user and inputs a numerical value of the Single data type.

Syntax: `InputSng sPrompt, fNumber`

Displays a Program Input prompt as specified by string *sPrompt* and waits until the user enters data in the Program Input box. The command returns the data as a number to assign it to variable *fNumber*.

Example

`InputSng "Enter a number", fMyNumber`

This prompts the user with

`Enter a number`

If the user enters

`123.4567`

variable `fMyNumber` is assigned 123.4567 (a Single data type).

Input String: `InputStr`

Prompts user and inputs data of the String data type.

Syntax: `InputStr sPrompt, sVariable`

Displays a Program Input prompt as specified by string *sPrompt*673and waits until the user enters data in the Program Input box. The command returns the data as a string to assign it to variable *sVariable*.

Example

`InputStr "Enter a string", sVariable`

This prompts the user with

`Enter a string`

If the user enters

`Use a canoe`

variable `sVariable` is assigned `"Use a canoe"` (a String data type).

Print Integer: `PrintInt`

Prints an explanation followed by an integer value.

Syntax: `PrintInt sMessage, nNumber`

Displays the string specified by *sMessage* in the Output Box followed by the value of integer variable *nNumber* on one line. Any following output will begin on the next line. The explanation is normally used to identify the value to the user.

Example

`PrintInt "The number of canoes is ", nNumberOfCanoes`

If variable `nNumberOfCanoes` has the value of 27, this displays the line

```
The number of canoes is 27
```

Print Message: PrintMsg

Prints a message.

Syntax: PrintMsg *sMessage*

Displays the string specified by *sMessage* in the Output Box on one line. Any following output will begin on the next line.

Example
```
PrintMsg "Use this canoe,"
PrintMsg "and enjoy the outdoors."
```

This displays the two lines

```
Use this canoe,
and enjoy the outdoors.
```

Note that *sMessage* could be a string variable instead of a constant string value.

Print Number: PrintNum

Prints a number. *See* Print Single.

Print Single: PrintSng

Prints an explanation followed by a single value.

Syntax: PrintSng *sMessage*, *fNumber*

Displays the string specified by *sMessage* in the Output Box followed by the value of single variable *fNumber* on one line. Any following output will begin on the next line. The explanation is normally used to identify the value to the user.

Example
```
PrintSng "The canoe capacity in kg is ", fCanoeCapacity
```

If variable `fCanoeCapacity` has the value of 515.5, this displays the line

```
The canoe capacity in kg is 515.5
```

Print String: PrintStr

Prints an explanation followed by a string value.

Syntax: PrintStr *sMessage*, *sVariable*

Displays the string specified by *sMessage* in the Output Box followed by the value of string variable *sVariable* on one line. Any following output will begin on the next line. The explanation is normally used to identify the value to the user.

Example
```
PrintStr "Your canoe model is  ", sCanoeModel
```

If variable `sCanoeName` has the value of `"Erie"`, this displays the line

```
Your canoe model is Erie
```

Operators

Arithmetic Operators

Table B.1 gives information pertaining to arithmetic operators.

Table B.1
Arithmetic Operators

Operator	Meaning	Example (f1 = 15.3 : f2 = 2.3)
^	Exponentiation	fAns = 2^-3 ' 0.125 is 1 divided by ' 2 multiplied by itself three times
-	Negation	fAns = -fAns ' -0.125 is negative of previous value
* /	Multiplication Floating Point Division	fAns = f1 * f2 '35.19 is 15.3 multiplied by 2.3 fAns = f1 / f2 ' 6.65217391304348 is 15.3 ➥ divided by 2.3
\	Integer Division	fAns = f1 \ f2 ' 7 since 15 divided by 2 is 7 ➥ with some remainder ' note 15.3 rounded to 15 and 2.3 ➥ rounded to 2
Mod	Modulus	fAns = f1 Mod f2 ' 1 is remainder of 15 \ 7
+	Addition	fAns = f1 + f2 ' 17.6 is 15.3 plus 2.3
-	Subtraction	fAns = f1 - f2 ' 13 is 15.3 subtract 2.3

String Operator

The only string operator is the concatenation operator (&):

```
sFullName = "Cody " & "Wizard" ' Variable is assigned "Cody Wizard"
```

Comparison Operators

Table B.2 gives information pertaing to comparison operators.

Table B.2
Comparison Operators

Symbol	Description	Expression examples that are	
		True	False
<	Less than	-7.8 < 4.5	4.5 < -7.8
<=	Less than or equal to	0.67 <= 0.68	0.68 <= 0.67
>	Greater than	"cougar" > "Cougar"	"Cougar" > "cougar"
>=	Greater than or equal to	"Dog" > "Cat"	"Cat" > "Dog"
<>	Not equal	1.00001 <> 1	1 / 2 <> 0.5
=	Equal	Sqr(2) * Sqr(2) = 2	Sqr(2) = 1.41421

Boolean (or Logic) Operators

Table B.3 shows the keywords used for Boolean operators.

```
' Sample assignments
nA = 10: nB = 8: nC = 6: nD = 4
```

Table B.3
Boolean (or Logic) Operators

Operator Keyword	Description	Examples that are True	False
And	Evaluates to True if, and only if, *both* expressions evaluate to True.	nA > nB And nC > nD nC < nD And nB > nC	nA < nB And nC > nD nD > nB And nD < nC
Or	Evaluates to True if *either* or both expressions evaluate to True.	nA < nB Or nC > nD nA > nB Or nC > nD	nA < nB Or nC < nD nD > nB Or nD > nC
Not	Evaluates to True if, and only if, the expression is False.	Not(nA < nB) Not(nC > nB)	Not(nA > nB) Not(nC < nB)
Xor	Evaluates to True if one, and *only one*, of the expressions evaluates to True	nA > nB Xor nD > nC nA < nB Xor nD < nC	nA < nB Xor nD > nC nA > nB Xor nC > nC

Operator Precedence

Table B.4 shows the order of precedence for operators.

Table B.4
Operator Precedure

Arithmetic	Comparison	Logical
Exponentiation (^)	Equality (=)	Not
Negation (–)'	Inequality (<>)	And
Multiplication and division (*, /)	Less than (<)	Or
Integer division (\)	Greater than (>)	Xor
Modulo arithmetic (Mod)	Less than or Equal to (<=)	Eqv
Addition and subtraction (+,–)	Greater than or Equal to (>=)	Imp
String concatenation (&)	Like	
	Is	

Highest to lowest precedence order shown as top to bottom from left to right with one exception: All comparison operators have equal precedence. The assignment operator (=) has the lowest precedence. For more information, refer to the Visual Help topic Operator Precedence.

Data Types

Common Visual Basic Data Types

Table B.5 illustrates the most commonly used data types.

Table B.5
Common Visual Basic Data Types

Data Type	Description	Examples
Integer	Whole number between −32,768 and 32,767	12, 0, -45, -4579, and 4679
Single	Number from ±3.403823 × 10^{38} to ±1.401298 × 10^{-45}	5.008, -0.00023, 7.567E24, and -9.00342E-12
String	Sequence (string) of characters, usually representing text information	"Charles Babbage", "R2D2", and "The world is round."

Other Language Topics

Visual Basic Help and its associated online books provide detailed information about the language and its integrated development environment. Figures B.1a and B.1b show the main contents of Visual basic Help for Versions 4 and 5, respectively.

A cruder but more beginner-friendly version of Help topics is available on the program disk. Open file ONLINE\CONTENTS.HTM using a web browser such as Netscape Navigator or Microsoft Internet Explorer to view the file.

Hexadecimal Numbers

Hexadecimal numbers are not really part of a language, but Visual Basic often defines some constants as hexadecimal numbers since the binary patterns are significant. For this reason we show hexadecimal digits to assist with interpreting them. Table B.6 shows hexadecimal digits and the way that they are represented in the decimal and binary number systems.

Figure B.1a
Visual Basic 4 Help
Contents (main part)

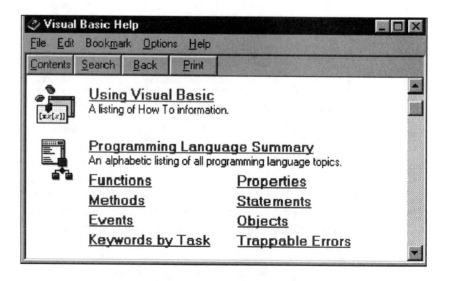

Figure B.1b
Visual Basic 5 Help
Contents (main part)

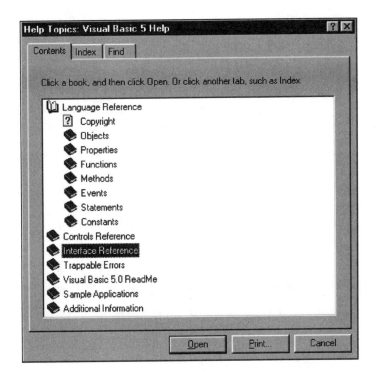

Table B.6
Hexadecimal Digits

Hexadecimal Digit	Decimal Equivalent	Four-Bit Binary
0	0	0000
1	1	0001
2	2	0010
3	3	0011
4	4	0100
5	5	0101
6	6	0110
7	7	0111
8	8	1000
9	9	1001
A	10	1010
B	11	1011
C	12	1100
D	13	1101
E	14	1110
F	15	1111

A hexadecimal number is shown as 0x followed by the hexadecimal digits. Also, each hexadecimal digit, represents four bits in binary. Hence a byte would have two hexadecimal digits, and a value of the Integer data type (two bytes) could be shown as four hexadecimal digits. For example, an Integer value of 0xC2 would be 194 in decimal, and in binary it would be 0000 0000 1100 0010.

Why would a Visual Basic programmer be interested in using hexadecimal? Consider the following common dialog constants as shown in Visual Basic Help.

cdlOFNHelpButton	0 × 10	Causes the dialog box to display the Help button.
cdlOFNNoValidate	0 × 100	Allows invalid characters in the returned filename.
cdlOFNAllowMultiselect	0 × 200	Allows the File Name list box to have multiple selections.

Let's say we wanted to exercise all three options. We could set the Flags property for a common dialog named dlgFile, as follows:

```
dlgFile.Flags = cdlOFNHelpButton + cdlOFNNoValidate + ➡
cdlOFNAllowMultiselect
```

In binary this addition becomes

$$0x0000\ 0000\ 0001\ 0000$$
$$0x0000\ 0001\ 0000\ 0000$$
$$+\ \underline{0x0000\ 0010\ 0000\ 0000}$$
$$0x0000\ 0011\ 0001\ 0000$$

Note that each constant has only one bit set. This means that under the hood, each bit position has significance in determining characteristics of the object. Other Visual Basic constants (but not all) can be interpreted similarly.

Glossary

16-bit Application An application created using the 16-bit version of Visual Basic 4. In other words, it can run in Windows 3.1 as well as newer versions of Windows. The application requires that the interpreter `VB40016.DLL` reside in the system (normally directory `WINDOWS\SYSTEM`). *See also* Bit Size.

32-bit Application An application created using Visual Basic 5 or the 32-bit version of Visual Basic 4. In other words, it can only run in Windows 95, NT, or newer systems. The application requires that the VB5 or VB4 interpreter (`MSVBVM50.DLL` or `VB40032.DLL`) reside in the system. *See also* Bit Size.

Access Key A key pressed while holding down the ALT key that allows the user to cause an action without having to use the mouse. For example, ALT+X may terminate program execution.

ActiveX Client An application that uses ActiveX controls.

ActiveX Code Component *See* ActiveX Control.

ActiveX Control A custom control (or self-contained application) that can be used by another application, such as a Visual Basic program or an interactive Web page. For example, the common dialog object is an ActiveX control. The controls are implemented as a file with an `.OCX` extension. It is an *object* whose *interface* can be used by other applications and programming tools.

Address A number that identifies the location of information in memory.

Algorithm A step-by-step sequence to solve a problem in a fixed period of time. It describes how a computation is to be performed.

Alpha Test An operational test of a program performed by programmers prior to using test users.

ANSI Stands for American National Standards Institute.

ANSI Character Set A character set used by Microsoft Windows that allows you to represent up to 256 characters using an 8-bit binary number. The first 128 characters (0 to 127) correspond to the ASCII character set. The second 128 characters (128 to 255) represent special characters, such as letters in international alphabets, accents, currency symbols, and fractions.

Argument A constant, variable, or expression passed to a procedure when the procedure is called.

Array A set of sequentially indexed elements having the same data type.

Array Index A number or set of numbers that identify an element in an array.

ASCII Stands for American Standard Code for Information Interchange.

ASCII Character Set A character set widely used to represent alphanumeric characters and symbols commonly found on a standard U.S. keyboard. Some characters represent control actions such as tab, carriage return, and bell. A 7-bit binary number, or more commonly an 8-bit number whose eighth bit is zero, represents each character.

Assignment Operator The equals symbol (=), used to assign a value to a variable, constant, property, or object reference.

Automation Infrastructure in Windows that permits applications to use components of other applications. It includes the OLE standard. *See also* COM.

AVI A format for encoding video information in a file.

Beta Testing An operational test of a program performed by test users after initial testing by programmers.

Binary Access File A file in which the bytes are simply accessed using a sequence with no predefined organization. It is up to the programmer to create his or her own system of identifying data components within the file.

Binding The process of running an object so that it may be used.

Bit Binary digit that is either 1 or 0. Eight bits make up a byte, the smallest unit of information that a computer can read from or write to memory.

Bit Size The number of bits that can be accessed by the computer at one time. Windows 95 and NT are 32-bit operating systems.

Bitmapped Graphic A graphical image encoded by using a grid of picture elements in digital format.

Boolean A data type, the value of which can be `True` or `False`. It is typically used for decision making during program execution.

Break Mode Temporary suspension of program execution while working with a program integrated development environment (IDE). The purpose of the break mode is to permit the programmer to examine expressions and monitor statement execution by single stepping.

Breakpoint A selected line in the code at which execution automatically enters the break mode. *See also* Break Mode.

Buffer A block of memory used for input and output operations.

Byte Eight-bit binary number that is the smallest unit of information that a computer can read from or write to memory. Decimal numbers from 0 to 255 can represent all of the possible bit combinations.

Call The action of executing another procedure.

Class A template from which objects can be created. It defines the properties and methods that can determine the behavior of the objects.

Close To disable file input/output operations by releasing the buffer for future operations. *See also* Buffer.

Collection An object that contains a set of related objects.

COM Stands for Component Object Model, a Windows standard that defines how objects make their properties and methods available to other applications.

Comment A statement that is not executed by the computer. Its purpose is to provide additional information to the programmer. In Visual Basic a comment begins with a single quote symbol (').

Comparison Operator An operator indicating a relationship between two expressions, such as greater than (>), equal to (=), or less than (<).

Compiler A program that translates the source code written by the programmer into machine code that can be executed by the computer.

Concatenation Combining (or appending) a string expression with another string expression. For example `"Wish"` concatenated with `"bone"` is `"Wishbone"`.

Constant A named item, the value of which does not change throughout the execution of a program. A program statement may use a constant in place of any fixed actual value. For example, the following statement uses the constant MACH: `fKmPerHour = MACH * fMachRate`

Context A condition of a variable during program execution that defines which procedures may access it. In other words, it is the same scope.

Context-Sensitive Help The ability for a Help system to present a topic appropriate to the user's current action based on pressing function key F1. For example, pressing F1 when an error is encountered will run Visual Basic Help to display information about the error.

Control Array A group of controls of the same type that share a common name but can be individually identified using an integer index number. For example, members of a command button array named `cmdCalculate` can be accessed as `cmdCalculate(0)`, `cmdCalculate(1)`, and so on.

Control Object An object, contained by a form, used to receive user input, display output, and trigger other activities (event procedures). Examples are the command button, text box, and others.

Criteria A set of conditions used to limit the set of records returned by a database query.

Current Statement The statement that is highlighted and is about to execute when viewing the code in the break mode.

Custom Control An ActiveX control that can be added to or removed from the Visual Basic Toolbox. It is a file with an `.OCX` extension.

DAO Stands for data access object, a type of object that provides a programming interface to help simplify data-access programming tasks. In Visual Basic there are several types, such as TableDef and Recordset.

Data Structure A way of organizing data that utilizes elemental data types (such as Integer and Single) to create higher-level forms of organization (or structure). Some examples are the stack, queue, and linked list.

Data Type It is the characteristics of the data (such as numerical or alphabetical) that determine what kind of data a variable can store. It is the organizational structure that determines how the "under the hood" binary information is interpreted and how many bytes are required to store the data. Examples are Integer, Single, and String.

Database An organized collection of information that permits one to pose questions (queries), such as "List all the cities whose yearly rainfall exceeded 50 cm." Usually it is a collection of related tables, forms, and reports. It can also contain queries and indexes as well as table relationships, table and field validation criteria, and linkages to external data sources.

Debugging The process of detecting and correcting program errors.

Declaration Code that names a constant, variable, or procedure and specifies applicable characteristics such as the data type for variables and arguments for procedures. A declaration is necessary to tell the computer how to handle the named items in terms of memory addressing and machine instructions, to processing the variable or argument data. One example is `Dim sCity as String`.

Definition A part of code that specifies the structure of a user-defined data type or a class.

Design Mode The state of the Visual Basic integrated development environment (IDE) in which the programmer can type code, add or delete controls and forms, and set values of some properties. The program is not executing and interacting with a user.

Dialog Box A window that is used to obtain more information from a user in order to continue with an operation, or that is used to provide additional information to the user. Examples are the File Open dialog used to obtain a filename and path information. Another example is to provide an error message.

DLL Stands for dynamic linked library, a set of routines that are loaded only if it is not already loaded and is required by the program to use procedures whose code are part of the library.

Double-Linked List A list of records where one field contains the location of the next record. Another field contains the location of the previous record.

Driver A special program used by application programs to work with devices and software services such as external databases.

Element A component of an array. Each element stores a value of a specified data type.

Embedded Object An object used in OLE that is a copy of the original data. *See* OLE.

Err Object A Visual Basic object that contains information about runtime errors.

Error *See* Syntax Error, Logical Error, and Runtime Error.

Error Trapping The process of handling an error.

Event An action recognized by an object, such as clicking the mouse or pressing a key, and for which the programmer can write code to respond. Events can occur as a result of a user action or program code, or they can be triggered by the system. Examples are Click, Load, and KeyPress.

Event-Driven Program A program that responds to the user. The user decides in what order the program will execute procedures.

Event Procedure A procedure that is automatically called when an associated event occurs.

.EXE The file extension for an executable program that can be given to the final user. The user can then run the program on his or her computer as a stand-alone without requiring any program development software. The file contents are in a format that can be directly executed by the computer, or as in the case for Visual Basic, are in the format of p-code, which can be interpreted by the appropriate Visual Basic runtime interpreter. Note that the appropriate interpreter would normally be distributed with the EXE file(s). It is the end result. The purpose of Visual Basic is to create an executable program (EXE file) that can be distributed to and run by the user.

Expression Any part of a statement that can be evaluated to a value.

Factorial A product of an integer and all lower integers.

False A Boolean value that is the opposite of `True`. Its numeric value is zero.

Field A data block in a record.

File A group of bytes located on a disk that can be accessed using the operating system.

File Number A handle for the program to use in order to work with a file. The number identifies a buffer used for file input and output operations. When using functions such as `Get` or `Put`, it is necessary to specify the file number as one of the arguments.

Flag A variable used to keep track of a condition during program execution. For example, a flag might indicate whether an item was found in a list of items.

Floating Point A numeric value encoded in a special format that represents a fractional component multiplied by two raised to an exponent.

Focus A property of a control object that means it can currently receive user input. Clicking an object gives it the focus (assuming it is enabled).

Form Object A window or dialog box. Forms contain controls, event procedures associated with the controls, and general procedures. A form file has a .FRM extension and contains the design-time property settings of the form and the controls it contains. It also contains the code for all procedures associated with the form.

Front-End Program A program that provides user access to an existing software system such as a database server.

Function A block of code that performs a specific task that always directly returns a value. For example:

```
fAnswer = Sqr(fNumber)  ' Return the square ➡
root of fNumber using function Sqr
```

Global Variable A variable that is accessible to all procedures in the program.

Hardware The physical components of an information system or computer.

Hexadecimal Numbering system that uses digits for numbers 0 to 15 to represent every possible combination of four bits. It is frequently used as a shorthand to represent binary information. Note that a byte (the smallest data unit that can be accessed by a program) can be represented using two hexadecimal digits. *See also* Hexadecimal Numbers in Appendix B.

IDE Stands for Integrated Development Environment, the collection of programming tools for developing and testing a program. This includes a source code editor, compiler or interpreter for translation, debugging tools, and, in the case of Visual Basic, a graphical user interface editor.

Information System A collection of computing resources, operating procedures, organizational practices, people, and other resources that help an organization perform its functions.

Input Validation The process of checking whether inputs meet specified conditions or limitations.

Instance An actual object instead of its generic class description. For example, we typically use cmdExit as an instance of the command button class.

Integer A fundamental data types that represents whole numbers in the range of -32,768 to 32,767 using 16 bits (2 bytes). Internally, they are stored in a signed (plus or minus) weighted binary format known as *2's complement*.

Interface The collection of properties and methods of an object.

Interpreter A program that translates each source code statement, immediately executes it, and then proceeds to do the same with the next statement. It does not make permanent machine code. For Visual Basic 4, it is the dynamic-link library (DLL) file VB40032.DLL for 32-bit applications or VB40016.DLL for 16-bit applications. For Visual Basic 5, it is MSVBVM50.DLL.

Jet Stands for Joint engine technology, the database engine used by Visual Basic and Microsoft Access. It handles the details for database access in Visual Basic. Also known as *the Jet Engine*.

Key Field The field normally used for identifying a record when sorting or searching a list of records. For example, a record of soil samples may need be to be ordered chronologically. Hence it uses a date field as the key field to specify the sort order.

Keyword A word or symbol that is reserved for use by the programming language and cannot be used to name something created by the programmer. For example, End cannot be used as a variable name. Visual Basic highlights keywords in blue (default setting) in the Code window.

Library Function An inherent function that has already been defined in Visual Basic. The programmer does not need to code the function declaration. Also known as *Visual Basic functions*.

Linked List A linked list is a list of records in which one field contains the location of the next record.

Linked Object An object used in OLE that contains a reference to the original data.

Local Variable A variable that is only accessible to statements in the procedure in which it is declared.

Logical Error A condition in the program that causes it to produce incorrect results. Logical errors are caused by the programmer making mistakes (as do all humans). For example, the programmer might code a statement to multiply when it should divide. Logical errors also often occur as a result of misunderstanding or not knowing what the program is supposed to do. This is the only type of error that the integrated development environment (IDE) does not directly catch, since it cannot read a programmer's mind.

Machine Code Program in a format that can be executed by the computer. It is a series of binary codes representing instructions that directly access the processor hardware. Note that Visual Basic source code is normally translated into p-code, not machine code. *See also* P-Code.

Make A term used by some integrated development environments (IDE) to translate the source code of all program components into an executable form that can be run stand-alone without the IDE.

Method A procedure that acts on an object to modify some aspect of its behavior and/or appearance. Some examples are `Line` and `Circle`.

MIDI Stands for Musical Instrument Digital Interface. It is a standard that describes how to play instruments using a computer. Also a file format that encodes the commands to play musical instruments.

Modal A window or dialog box that requires the user to take some action before the focus can switch to another form or dialog box.

Modeless A window or dialog box that does not require user action before the focus can be switched to another form or dialog box.

Module (1) In a generic context, a set of step-by-step statements that tell the computer how to do a specific task as part of a group of tasks that make up the entire program. For example, a business account program may need modules to calculate interest, schedule payments, and so on. (2) As a type of file used in Visual Basic, a set of declarations and procedures in a file with the extension .BAS that contains only code. It does not contain objects. Generally, the module is used for code that can be used in different programs (projects).

Multimedia Authoring Tool A software tool that permits one to create multimedia presentations without writing a program.

Native Code A program that will directly run in a computer without additional processing by other software components.

Null A value indicating that the variable has no defined data. For a string, it means that the string contains no characters.

Object A combination of code and data that can be treated as a unit. Typical examples in Visual Basic are the form object and various types of control objects.

.OCX The file extension used for ActiveX controls. Originally the abbreviation stood for Object Control eXtension, which superseded the earlier Visual Basic eXtension (VBX).

ODBC Shands for open database connectivity. A standard that permits different programs to access different database systems over a network.

OLE Stands for Object Linking and Embedding, a software technology used in Windows that permits applications to reuse components from other applications. Pronounced "Oh-lay."

Open To enable file input/output by assigning the file to a buffer. *See also* Buffer and File Number.

Operator A keyword (usually a symbol) that causes a change in an expression. For example, the assignment operator (=) causes a variable to be given (assigned) a new value, as in the following statement:

```
nCountUp = nCountUp + 1 ' Increment ➡
nCountUp by one
```

Order of Precedence The order in which the parts of an expression are evaluated. For example, multiplication and division are performed before addition and subtraction, as in the following statement:

```
nAnswer = 2 + 10 * 4 ' The answer is 42, not 48
```

Overflow The result of attempting to exceed a value specified by the range available. For example, the maximum possible value of the Integer data type is 32,767. An attempt to multiply an Integer value of 7,000 by itself would exceed the maximum, which causes an error. It is one of the runtime errors (Error Number 6) recognized by Visual Basic.

P-Code Abbreviation for *packed code*. It is the format of the binary information stored in an .EXE file that was made using Visual Basic. The information must be interpreted by a Visual Basic interpreter in order to execute. It is also known as *pseudo-code* (not to be confused with the more generic use of the term *pseudocode*).

Parameter Variable name by which an argument passed to a procedure is known within the procedure. This variable receives the argument passed into the procedure. Its scope ends when the procedure ends.

Parsing To scan and interpret information. For example, to find the surname when given a full name with title, the program would have to follow rules to handle such situations as Cody Wizard, Mr. Cody Wizard B.A., and other combinations.

Passing Refers to the process of transferring information from the calling procedure to the called procedure using arguments.

Pixel Picture element. It is the smallest item on a computer screen.

Private A variable that is only accessible within the procedure in which it is declared. This means that a procedure is accessible only to other procedures in the same module or form.

Procedure A named sequence of statements executed as a unit that can be scheduled (called) to completely execute a task or subtask.

Procedural Program A program with a preset sequence of processing steps.

Program A program is a set of step-by-step statements that tell the computer how to do a task.

Program Bug An error in the program code that causes the program to fail during execution (runtime error) or to produce incorrect results (logical error).

Programmer A person who develops and writes programs.

Programming Language The set of rules and reserved words that can be used to create a program.

Project A set of forms, modules, and controls that make up a program under development in the Visual Basic integrated development environment. A project file with a .VBP extension lists all the components and development options. To create an executable program, it is necessary to *make* an .EXE file using the project.

Property An attribute of an object. It can be considered as an element (or field) of a data type describing the object class. Examples are Height and Width.

Pseudocode (1) A set of nonambiguous step-by-step instructions that are similar to the instructions in a computer program. Written using a natural human language such as English, it is used to describe general program operation and algorithms without having to specify the detailed coding required to implement the program. (2) Can also refer to p-code.

Public A variable or procedure that is available to all procedures in the project (all forms and modules).

Query A question statement that returns data from a database based on specified criteria. An informal example is: "Show me the names of ships that have transported wheat in the Pacific Ocean during the month of July." *See also* SQL.

Queue A queue is a list of items in which the next item is added to the end and items are removed from the beginning. They are added and removed in a first-in, first-out order.

Random Access File A file where the bytes are organized into identical records.

Record Each record consists of data blocks known as *fields*. The structure of field ordering, data type, and size is the same for each record belonging to the same User-defined type. For example, each record for soil samples may be organized as follows:

```
fLatitude as Single, fLongitude as ➡
Single, dtSampleDate as Date, nMoisture ➡
as Integer
```

Recordset A set of records that may be created as a result of a database query. It may also be a type of data access object (DAO).

Register A place inside a computer where data can be modified or examined using machine code instructions. It is a component of the central processing unit and is not a part of memory.

Registry The Windows database that specifies how Windows is set up in a computer, such as what and where tasks are available in the Start Menu. It also states what ActiveX code components are available in the system, in addition to other user application and computer information.

RGB Red-Green-Blue color format. Refers to a combination of red, green, and blue colors to create any other color. Windows uses a binary code to define color using an RGB format.

Run Mode The time when the Visual Basic integrated development environment (IDE) is executing the program currently under development, and the programmer is testing the program by behaving as a user. It is only possible to set up breakpoints and watch expressions by putting the program in Break Mode or Design Mode.

Runtime The period of time when the processor is executing the program. This is when a user interacts with the program. This can be when the executable (.EXE file) is running and interacting with a user, or when the Visual Basic IDE is running the program in the Run Mode with the programmer acting like the user.

Runtime Error A situation that causes the processor to stop executing the program (unless error trapping is utilized). Typically, it is an attempt by the processor to do something invalid such as dividing by zero.

Scope Refers to when a variable may be accessed during execution of a program. A variable with local scope can only be used by statements in the procedure in which the variable was declared. A variable with global (or Public) scope can be accessed by any procedure in the program. A variable with module scope can be accessed only by procedures within the form or module in which the variable was declared.

Seed An initial value used to generate pseudorandom numbers.

Sequential Access File A file in which the bytes are organized into lines. A line is a sequence of characters followed by a carriage return and a line feed character. Also known as a *text file*.

Single One of the fundamental data types. It represents numbers with fractional components. They are stored as IEEE 32-bit (4-byte) *single-precision* floating-point numbers, ranging in value from –3.402823E38 to –1.401298E–45 for negative values and from 1.401298E–45 to 3.402823E38 for positive values.

Single Step The process of executing one statement at a time when the program is in the Break mode.

Software The nonhardware components of the computer, the programs (set of instructions) that tell the computer what to do. It may also refer to associated documentation that explains the programs. (We can also think of it as the stuff inside the shrinkwrapped box when purchasing a program.)

Sorting The process of ordering items in a specified order based on a key field. For example a record of soil samples may need to be ordered chronologically. Hence it uses a date field as the key field to specify the sort order.

Source Code The set of instructions in text format entered by the programmer using a high-level programming language such as Visual Basic. It must be translated (compiled or interpreted) before the computer can execute the instructions.

SQL Stands for Structured Query Language. A standard language for making database queries. *See also* Query.

Stack (1) A data structure that is a list of items in which items are added at one end and items are removed from the same end. Data access is in the following order: The last data put in is the first data taken out. (2) A part of computer memory used to store necessary overhead data required by the processor in order to execute properly. It grows and shrinks dynamically as required during program execution. Only a finite amount of memory space is available for use as a stack for each program. Examples of necessary overhead are local variables and arguments used during procedure calls.

Stack Overflow The condition caused when the computer runs out of stack space, typically due to a combination of using too many variables and nested procedure calls. It is one of the runtime errors (Error Number 28). *See also* Stack (2).

Stand-Alone A program that can execute without depending on other programs.

Standard Control Refers to a control that is always available in the Toolbox. Custom controls, on the other hand, can be added or removed. The standard controls are implemented directly within Visual Basic itself.

State A condition of a system that specifies how it will behave depending on the order in which certain inputs occur. The crucial point is that a state of a system is dependent on the previous inputs (or input history). A typical example is a button for on-and-off control. Click on it once to turn something on; click on the same button again to turn that something off. Hence it switches between the on and off states.

Statement A complete instruction that the computer can execute. It can express an action with operations, a declaration, or a definition. Typically, it is a single line of code, but multiple statements can occupy a line if each is separated by a colon (:). A statement can occupy multiple lines by using a line-continuation character (_) to continue the statement to the next line. For example:

```
Dim sAddress As String: sAddress = "539-A"
sAddress = sAddress & " Riverbank Edge"
sAddress = sAddress & Chr(10) & Chr(13)_
& "Global Village"
```

Static A local variable that retains its value (is not reinitialized) between procedure calls. Note that by default, local variables are reinitialized each time the procedure is called.

Step Into A debugging command to execute the current statement when Visual Basic is in Break Mode. If the current statement contains a call to a programmer-defined procedure, Step Into permits the programmer to single step the code inside the procedure being called. The Code window will display the first statement in the procedure as the next current statement.

Step Over Similar to Step Into except that if the current statement contains a call to a programmer-defined procedure, Step Over will skip single stepping the procedure being called. The Code window will display the statement immediately following the current statement. Visual Basic executes the procedure call in Run Mode and returns back to Break Mode when the called procedure has completed execution.

Stepwise Refinement The process of breaking down the general steps in a design into finer detail until it is possible to rewrite the steps in terms of program statements with correct syntax.

String One of the fundamental data types used to store alphanumeric information. Internally, it is stored as a sequence of characters (1 byte per character for ANSI strings, 2 bytes per character for Unicode strings). To assign a string value, enclose it in double quotes. For example:
```
Dim sAddress As String: sAddress = "539-A"
```

Sub Procedure A procedure (block of code) that performs an identifiable task when called during program execution. It directly returns a value upon returning to the procedure from which it was called. It may return values indirectly by passing an argument back to the calling procedure. A function, on the other hand, does directly return a value.

Subroutine *See* Sub Procedure.

Subscript Used to uniquely identify each element in an array. For example, `nPageNumber` is being used as a subscript for the array `sPage( )`, as follows: `sPage (nPageNumber) = sCurrentPage`

Syntax The rules for writing source code in a programming language. It specifies which symbols and keywords can be used and how to order them in statements. When the syntax is correct, the compiler or interpreter can translate the source code into machine code to execute it.

Syntax Error An error caused by mistakes in syntax. It prevents the program from being executed since the source code cannot be translated into machine code. We recommend that you do not use the Compile On Demand option in Visual Basic; otherwise, a syntax error in a procedure may go undetected for a long time if the procedure is never called.

Systems Analysis The process of identifying and defining problems in an information system.

Template Command General procedures written specifically for the Introduction Template used in this book.

True A Boolean value that is the opposite of `False`. Its numeric value is negative one (–1).

Unicode A system to represent the characters of every alphabet currently in use in the world. It uses 2 bytes for every character. If the high byte is zero, the code represents ANSI characters. The 32-bit version of Visual Basic handles strings in memory as Unicode, although file data may still be encoded using ANSI (1 byte per character). *See also* String.

User-Defined Data Type A data type that the programmer can create to contain multiple elements. Each element can be of different data types, unlike an array, in which each element must be of the same data type. This data type is often known as a *record*, and its elements may also be known as *fields*. The programmer can declare new variables using the new data type. Elements can be accessed using the dot operator. For example (here, `nMoisture` is an element of data type `SoilSample`):

```
' SoilSample data type was defined using ➡
the Type statement in a Module
' Declaring ThisSample
Dim ThisSample As SoilSample
ThisSample.nMoisture = 20  ' Scaled to ➡
represent 0.2%
```

Variable A unit of memory that can be altered during execution of a program. Each variable is assigned a unique name. Here is an example of using a variable named `sAddress`: `sAddress = "539-A"`

Variant A Visual Basic data type that permits the variable value to be any of the other fundamental data types. Behind the scenes, the variant uses some extra bytes to tell the computer whether to interpret its value as String, Integer, and so on. Variants use up extra memory and additional processing overhead and are simply not available in strongly typed languages such as Java. Even some die-hard Visual Basic professionals frown upon its use.

Vector Graphic A graphical image encoded by using mathematical equations to describe the image in digital format.

Watch Expression An expression in the code that is selected by the programmer for monitoring during program execution while in the Break Mode. The programmer can view the value of the watch expression in the Watch pane of the Debug window.

WAV A format for encoding audio information. Essentially, it is a digital recording of a sound signal.

Whitespace Character An ASCII character that represents one or more blank spaces. Examples include the space and tab characters.

Visual Basic Resources

Update Information for This Book

Check the file README.TXT in the enclosed program disk for any updates. Be sure to check for possible updates posted at the website for Prentice-Hall http://www.prenhall.com using your favorite web browser. It may contain additional resources and information that didn't make it into the book or the program disk in time for distribution. The author also has a personal website at http://fleming0.flemingc.on.ca/~pspasov/. From this page, check for any applicable links.

The software industry is very dynamic, and we are not responsible if the information here has changed. Some URLs may change. Products that were free may no longer be free. Corporate strategies change. Witness Microsoft's complete turnaround in strategy regarding the Internet during 1996.

Microsoft, Inc.

Naturally, the creators of Visual Basic would be a primary source (if not the ultimate authority) in matters concerning Visual Basic. Sources of information follows.

Visual Basic Help

This is the Help program that is supplied with Visual Basic itself. As described in this book, select Contents in the Help menu and explore what information is available. It can be a bit overwhelming to a beginner. However, once you have achieved some programming competency, it is a wonderful resource, even if some of it still doesn't make sense. The effort is part of the learning process.

Learning Visual Basic is a menu item that you can select from the Help menu when using Visual Basic 4. It contains some quick lessons on how to use the integrated development environment. It also gives a brief overview of the language itself. With Visual Basic 5, use Visual Basic Books Online and select the item **Visual Basic Basics.**

Visual Basic Books Online is another selection available in the Help menu. It is an electronic copy of the manuals, as well as a brief introduction and guide to using the samples. An advantage of the online format is that you can perform queries to search for topics of interest. Also, the contents include links to related material.

Visual Basic Samples are included in the commercial Visual Basic package. Usually they can be found in the SAMPLES subdirectory of the directory for Visual Basic itself. The samples illustrate features of the language.

The Visual Basic Programmer's Guide

This and other manuals are printed versions of what is available in Visual Basic Books Online.

Mastering Microsoft Visual Basic

This is a computer aided instruction CD that can be purchased from Microsoft Press. It covers enough material to prepare one to take the Visual Basic certification exam.

Microsoft Web Resources

The web resources are so extensive that we have placed them in a category of their own. The wonderful thing is that many of tutorials and software tools are even free (at least when I last looked).

Visual Basic Page

http://www.microsoft.com/vbasic/

The Contents section includes the latest news in the New User, Experienced User, Programmer, Web Developer, and other categories. Downloads include updates, beta software, and ActiveX controls. The Resources section includes an overview about the entire Visual Basic package, case studies, tips, lists of books, and courses. The rest of this subsection highlights a few resources.

Online Version of the Mastering Microsoft Visual Basic CD

http://www.microsoft.com/mastering/titles/demo/vb_title.htm

This course helps you prepare for the Microsoft Certified Professional exam for Programming in Microsoft Visual Basic. The site contains a comprehensive set of sample segments from the CD.

Knowledge Base

http://www.microsoft.com/kb/

Use the Knowledge Base to search for information concerning specific products. It also includes bug reports.

Microsoft Visual Basic for Applications (VBA)

http://www.microsoft.com/vba/

VBA is a subset of Visual Basic. It is the macro scripting language for the MS Office™ product family. Some third-party products have also adopted VBA as their macro language.

Microsoft VBScript

http://www.microsoft.com/vbscript/

VBScript is a subset of Visual Basic for Applications. It is a scripting language for HTML-based web pages that can be used instead of JavaScript (please note that

JavaScript is *not* Java). This permits programmers with Visual Basic expertise to rapidly develop interactive web applications. There are a few development tools such as Control Pad for inserting ActiveX controls and a Script Debugger that can be downloaded. They are actually quite good, and you can't beat the price; they're free.

Site Builder Workshop

http://www.microsoft.com/workshop/

The Site Builder Workshop is the place to get information about Microsoft's Internet technologies! It includes a section on Programming.

Microsoft Developer Network

http://www.microsoft.com/msdn/

This is a general site for information and tools concerning software development (using Microsoft technology, of course). There are sections explaining products, news related to the industry, software development kits (SDKs), a library of technical articles and samples, and other categories. However, to enjoy the complete benefits, you will have to join the network.

Visual Basic Programmer's Journal (VBPJ)

http://www.windx.com

This is an excellent source of techniques and tips as well as tutorials. The publication is monthly, and it costs a few dollars per month to subscribe. On average, it has about five feature articles plus columns for Intermediate and Expert programmers. Complete code described in the articles and columns is available online to subscribers. The section Visual Basic Heroes briefly describes applications used to solve real-world problems. Subscribers also receive special issues containing tips and tricks submitted by other readers. A CD-ROM subscription is also possible. The subscription address is

Visual Basic Programmer's Journal
P.O. Box 58872
Boulder, CO 80323-8872
USA

It is published by Fawcette Technical Publications, 209 Hamilton Avenue, Palo Alto, CA 94301. The telephone number is 650-833-7100 and the Fax number is 650-853-0230.
There is a sister publication, *Getting Started With Visual Basic*, that is oriented to beginners. Both are available on some newsstands.

Inside Visual Basic by the Cobb Group

http://www.cobb.com/ivb/index.htm

This is a monthly journal of tips and techniques for Visual Basic. The format is more concise and packed than VBPJ. The address is The Cobb Group, 9420 Bunsen Parkway, Louisville, KY 40220. The telephone number is 502-493-3300, and the fax number is 502-491-8050.

Carl and Gary's Visual Basic Page

http://www.apexsc.com/vb/

This might be the most popular site for Visual Basic programmers. As described in their opening, it is a gathering place for Visual Basic programmers to exchange ideas. This is an extract of their mission statement.

Carl & Gary's exists solely for the benefit of the Visual Basic Programming community. Our first loyalty is to the community. In that regard, we will continue to seek out and collect technical information that Visual Basic and other Windows developers can use on a regular basis.

There are articles, reviews of third-party software add-ons, information about seeking employment and hiring programmers, and much more. We really recommend that you check it out. Of particular interest might be their beginner's pages. Here is a sample of what is availabe.

Carl & Gary's Beginner's Pages

http://www.apexsc.com/vb/begin.html

This set of pages is a collection of items for the novice programmer. They periodically scan the net for articles targeted at the novice and put links to them here. It also includes their own articles, such as one page for complete beginners.

Visual Basic Downloads

http://www.apexsc.com/vb/files.html

A comprehensive source of free stuff, shareware, and other information.

Funnies

http://www.apexsc.com/vb/yuks.html

Need we say more? We all need to take that much-needed break.

Mailing Lists

Mailing lists (discussion lists) are forums for like-minded people to discuss issues and help each other. The following information is also available at Carl and Garry's Visual Basic Page. Generally, to use a mailing list, first send a subscription message to the list server address. Once subscribed, you will receive mail from everybody else who posts a message to the list. You can also send messages to all subscribers by mailing it to the list (not the list server).

VISBAS-BEGINNERS

This is a mailing list for beginners to help one another. For information, send e-mail to `LISTSERV@PEACH.EASE.LSOFT.COM` with the following in the message text:
INFO VISBAS-BEGINNERS

Microsoft Visual Basic Forum (VISBAS-L)

This list is for Visual Basic programming issues. To subscribe, send e-mail to LISTSERV@PEACH.EASE.LSOFT.COM with the following in the text:
SUB VISBAS-L *YourFirstName YourLastName*

You will be sent a confirmation e-mail message, to which you must simply reply with the word "ok" in your reply message. For example, Cody Wizard would use the following message when sending a subscription message:
SUB VISBAS-L Cody Wizard

VISUAL PROGRAMMING++

http://www.windx.com

This is a biweekly newsletter distributed using e-mail. It features reviews for Windows development products and Internet/intranet tools. VP++ is free to Visual Basic Programmer's Journal subscribers. Contact them at feedback@fawcette.com using e-mail.

Object Models

http://objects.windx.com

This site contains the object models for Word, Excel, and others.

Avatar The Online Magazine for Interactive Developers

http://www.avatarmag.com

This site is an online magazine for interactive programming that includes Visual Basic and other languages such as Visual C++ and Java.

Component Objects and Companion Products for Visual Basic

This catalog is usually included with Visual Basic. There are literally hundreds of products from third-party suppliers. Some of these products are for specialty applications such as real-time data acquisition, legacy mainframe interfacing, telecommunications, help authoring, and others.

INDEX